The
Complete Reader

SECOND EDITION

Edited by

Richard S. Beal

Boston University

Jacob Korg

University of Washington

PRENTICE-HALL, INC.

Englewood Cliffs, New Jersey

PRENTICE-HALL INTERNATIONAL, INC., *London*
PRENTICE-HALL OF AUSTRALIA, PTY. LTD., *Sydney*
PRENTICE-HALL OF CANADA, LTD., *Toronto*
PRENTICE-HALL OF INDIA (PRIVATE), LTD., *New Delhi*
PRENTICE-HALL OF JAPAN, INC., *Tokyo*

© 1961, 1967 by
PRENTICE-HALL, INC.
Englewood Cliffs, N.J.

Library of Congress Catalog Card No.: 67–12375

Current printing (*last digit*):

10   9   8   7   6   5   4   3   2   1

Printed in the United States of America
16233-C

Preface

Our purpose in this second edition of *The Complete Reader,* as in the first edition, has been to achieve a balance between range and variety of good writing in the various genres and reasonable brevity and compactness in the whole text. In this edition we have sought to replace those selections that experience proved the least successful, to include a cross section of more recent pieces, to increase the total representation in each genre, and to increase the number of poets for whom several poems are offered. We have tried throughout to make a collection wholly adequate for those courses that aim to introduce students to the college study of both literature and composition, but to avoid that inclusiveness and elaboration that discourages the use of additional individual books where appropriate. Within each section we have sought to bring the expressive resources of the form into relief by providing opportunities for effective comparison and contrast in both technique and form. Although we have consistently tried to keep the experience and abilities of students in mind in making our selections, we have not hesitated to represent a wide range of difficulty, as well as a variety of styles, within each genre.

The essay section offers narrative, descriptive, expository, and argumentative selections arranged generally in an ascending order of difficulty. Within the major type groupings, we have arranged these selections in related thematic groups, believing that the reader's sense of both intention and method are sharpened by noting the implicit contrasts of form and content in such groups. The section concludes with a group of essays which, while offering further examples of the methods and aims of nonfiction prose, serve also to introduce the student to some of the critical considerations relevant to the genres to which the later sections are devoted. The intention throughout this first section of the anthology has been to provide models and topics for student writing as well as examples of the various types of nonfiction as literary forms.

The story section is arranged in a way that will enable the instructor to provide a pocket course in the techniques of fiction. It first offers brief groups of stories, which the editors believe particularly useful for the study of four basic aspects of fiction, and follows these with a more loosely organized group of stories, which may be drawn from freely for further examples of these and other aspects of fiction. The drama section, necessarily modest in size, offers a classic tragedy, a modern comedy, a Shakespeare history play, which we believe to be particularly teachable and accessible to students, and a brief poetic drama of Yeats, which also serves to supplement the selection of his poems. The arrangement of poetry in roughly chronological order reflects the editors' belief that whereas most instructors wish to make an essentially critical approach to poetry, the historical arrangement is nonetheless meaningful in itself in this genre and leaves the instructor freest to make such selections for critical purposes as will best serve his own purposes. We have tried throughout the poetry section to illustrate generously the variety of poetic form, vocabulary, imagery, and tone; to emphasize more recent poetry; and to include enough selections of certain major poets to allow students to get some sense of the individuality of the poet both in theme and in technique.

Aside from brief suggestive introductions to each of the four major sections, we have stripped the anthology of apparatus, hoping thus to free the instructor to bring the material of the text most easily into the framework of his own approach. The editors' own notes, guides, and suggestions have been incorporated in a pamphlet edition of the *Editors' Notes* for the convenience of instructors.

The editors wish to thank those who have aided and abetted the preparation of this anthology with specific suggestions and general advice. Without their guidance the text would have been something less than it is. We should like particularly to acknowledge our indebtedness to the following, who were especially helpful in the preparation of either the first edition or this revision: Robert M. Gorrell, of the University of Nevada; David Novarr, of Cornell; John I. McCullum, Jr., of the University of Miami; Morris Freedman, of the University of New Mexico; Morton Berman, of Boston University; and Glenn Leggett, of Grinnell College.

R.S.B.
J.K.

Contents

The Range of Prose 1

The Short Story   146

ACTION

CHARACTER

SYMBOL

TONE

STORIES FOR FURTHER READING

Drama   313

Poetry   482

The Range of Prose

Prose writing other than fiction is as varied as its writers' intentions. It includes things as diverse as the scientific report, Howard Mumford Jones' argument for the "untrammeled right of the undergraduate to make his own mistakes," and the kind of literary narrative exemplified in James Thurber's "Here Lies Miss Groby." In spite of its diversity, it all differs from fiction, drama, or poetry. The latter forms, each in its own way, aim to communicate experience directly, to give the reader knowledge of the "thing as the thing it is—of the apple as apple." They attempt to make the abstract concrete through character, action, and image. Nonfiction is furthest from fiction when its intention is merely to inform—to communicate verifiable facts only, as in a set of directions or the description of a purely mechanical process. It is nearest to fiction when it aims to communicate the feel of an experience, as Kazin does in "A Brownsville Kitchen," or to recreate a character for the sake of the character, as Yeats does in "Grandfather Pollexfen," or to tell a story for the sake of the story, as Clarence Day does in "Father Interferes with the Twenty-third Psalm."

We read a good deal of informative prose from day to day in newspapers, magazines, and books simply to accumulate the factual information needed to live in our world. Some of the selections that follow have been included partly for the information they contain. The discussions of language by Sapir, Fromm, and Orwell, for example, and the discussions of literature and its forms, which make up the final group of explanatory pieces, provide information useful in the study of writing and literature. But much of the nonfiction collected here is intended to serve purposes other than the merely informative. It is the sort of nonfiction we can usefully read to sharpen our sense of our own experience and ideas by comparing them to those of others. We can also improve our own writing by noting the means that good writers have used to make their prose effective. Or finally, we can clarify our understanding of the unique function of literature by studying some of the ways in which nonfiction, on the one hand, and fiction, drama, and poetry, on the other, deal with similar ideas and feelings. Each of these aims is worth some further comment.

If we are to be liberally educated, we must understand ourselves, and to understand ourselves, we must examine our own feelings and ideas closely. Reading to acquire a knowledge of how others have felt and thought about the

recurrent experiences and ideas of men is almost indispensable to a clear understanding of ourselves. The places of our own childhood become clearer to us as
we measure them against the Delaware town in which Henry Canby grew up or
the Brownsville kitchen that Alfred Kazin describes. Our ideas of what we think
about the aims of education or the claims of morality become sharper as we try to
differentiate them from those of Housman and Jones, Mencken and Newman.
Such reading, particularly coupled with the reading of fiction, drama, and poetry,
does much to help us see how complex our own feelings and attitudes are and
how many-minded we are about most of the important intellectual, social, and
moral problems of men.

It is almost axiomatic that only those who read much learn to write well, for
writing, like the learning of all complex skills, is partly imitative. It is probably
safe to say that most good writers have at some time more or less consciously
studied the methods followed by writers they admire. To this end, any of us may
usefully study the ways in which other writers expand and develop their ideas, the
kinds of language they use, how they handle such major units of writing as the
paragraph and the sentence, and the patterns of organization into which their
writing falls. Specifically, for example, we can note the essentially spatial pattern
of Canby's description of his home town, the use of comparison and contrast in
Drucker's "Myth of American Uniformity," or the tactics of definition in
Leonard Woolf's "Chronicle and History" and in Erich Fromm's discussion of
symbolic language. We can study the ways in which such writers as Jones and
Mencken use the lively and vivid example to give texture to their ideas or the
ways in which Housman and Cardinal Newman use more tightly reasoned
logical argument. Or we may observe the ways in which writers as different as
Edmund Wilson and Joseph Wood Krutch choose words. To the extent that we
are able and willing to analyze such matters, we make ourselves not only better
readers but also better writers.

Finally, if we put a straightforward description or an essay or article beside
a short story or poem and look at them closely, we can learn a good deal about
the intention and structure of both. Description, for example, is an integral part
of most fiction. It is particularly crucial to such short stories as Jack London's
"To Build a Fire" and Stephen Crane's "An Episode of War," in the second part
of this anthology. Nonetheless, in these stories description is not an end in itself,
as it is in the selection by Mark Twain, which opens the first section. To
understand how the short-story writer uses description to serve his larger intention is to understand something more about the nature of fiction. We may make
the same kind of enlightening comparison by placing such articles as those of
Drucker and Russell, which comment analytically upon the problem of conformity in our time, beside such poems as Eliot's "The Love Song of J. Alfred
Prufrock" and Auden's "The Unknown Citizen," which comment quite differently upon much the same kind of issue.

Whichever of these several purposes we are concerned with in our study of
nonfiction, one basic concept will be useful to us, the concept of intention. The
first step toward understanding an author is to understand his intention in the

piece we are reading, just as the first step toward clear writing is to understand wholly one's own intention. If we think that Mark Twain is trying to give us information about farms or that Edward Sapir is arguing for a particular view, we are bound to miss the point.

Leaving aside the special intentions of fiction, drama, and poetry, the basic intentions of prose are four, which have dictated its division into the four classical types of discourse represented in the selections in the first section of this anthology: *narration, description, exposition,* and *argument. Narration* aims to present an event or series of events to the reader, to tell what happened and how it happened, and to convey some impression of the event. *Description* aims to make the reader see or feel something as clearly and vividly as the writer himself has seen or felt it, to give the reader as far as possible the quality of the experience. *Exposition* aims to give information, to explain something, to make clear an idea, define a term, or to analyze a situation or character. *Argument* aims to make its audience change its mind or point of view or feelings about something.

It is true that we seldom meet these types in their pure form. Most extended pieces of writing provide within themselves examples of several types. Gwen Raverat, for example, in her autobiographical narrative "Religion in Childhood," uses description; Howard Mumford Jones, in his argument against prescriptive college curricula, does much explaining. But in both these instances, the controlling intention is clear: Miss Raverat's, to give us as vivid a sense of her experience as possible; and Jones', to persuade us that our substitution of general education programs for the older free elective system may be something less than wholly good. As readers we understand Miss Raverat and Professor Jones in proportion as we understand their controlling intentions. As students of writing we can learn much from them precisely by seeing how they have used responsibly various types of discourse to further their controlling purposes.

NARRATION AND DESCRIPTION

Mark Twain

The Farm

I can see the farm yet, with perfect clearness. I can see all its belongings, all its details; the family room of the house, with a "trundle" bed in one corner and a spinning-wheel in another—a wheel whose rising and falling wail, heard from a distance, was the mournfullest of all sounds to me, and made me homesick and low-spirited, and filled my atmosphere with the wandering spirits of the dead; the vast fireplace, piled high, on winter nights, with flaming hickory logs from whose ends a sugary sap bubbled out, but did not go to waste, for we scraped it off and ate it; the lazy cat spread out on the rough hearthstones; the drowsy dogs braced against the jambs and blinking; my aunt in one chimney corner, knitting; my uncle in the other, smoking his corn-cob pipe; the slick and carpetless oak floor faintly mirroring the dancing flame tongues and freckled with black indentations where fire coals had popped out and died a leisurely death; half a dozen children romping in the background twilight; "split"-bottomed chairs here and there, some with rockers; a cradle—out of service, but waiting, with confidence; in the early cold mornings a snuggle of children, in shirts and chemises, occupying the hearthstone and procrastinating—they could not bear to leave that comfortable place and go out on the wind-swept floor space between the house and kitchen where the general tin basin stood, and wash. . . .

As I have said, I spent some part of every year at the farm until I was twelve or thirteen years old. The life which I led there with my cousins was full of charm, and so is the memory of it yet. I can call back the solemn twilight and mystery of the deep woods, the earthy smells, the faint odors of the wild flowers, the sheen of rain-washed foliage, the rattling clatter of drops when the wind shook the trees, the far-off hammering of woodpeckers and the muffled drumming of wood pheasants in the remoteness of the forest, the snapshot glimpses of disturbed wild creatures scurrying through the grass—I can call it all back and make it as real as it ever was, and as blessed. I can call back the prairie, and its loneliness and peace, and a vast hawk hanging motionless in the sky, with his wings spread wide and the blue of the vault showing through the fringe of their end feathers. I can see the woods in their autumn dress, the oaks purple, the hickories washed with gold, the maples and the sumachs luminous with crimson fires, and I can hear the rustle made by the fallen leaves as we plowed through them. I can see the blue clusters of wild grapes hanging among the foliage of the saplings, and I remember the taste of them and the smell. I know how the wild blackberries looked, and how they tasted, and the same with the pawpaws, the hazelnuts, and the persimmons; and I can feel the thumping rain, upon my head, of hickory nuts and walnuts when we were out in the frosty dawn to scramble for them with the pigs, and the gusts of wind loosed them and sent them down. I know the stain of blackberries, and how pretty it is, and I know the stain of walnut hulls, and how little it minds soap and water, also what grudged experience it had of either of them. I know the taste of maple sap, and when to gather it, and how to arrange the troughs and the delivery tubes, and how to boil down the juice, and how to hook the sugar after it is made, also how much better hooked sugar tastes than any that is honestly come by, let bigots say what they will. I know how a prize watermelon looks when it is sunning its fat rotundity among pumpkin vines and "simblins"; I know how to tell when it is ripe without "plugging" it; I know how inviting it looks when it is cooling itself in a tub of water under the bed, waiting; I know how it looks when it lies on the table in the sheltered great floor space between house and kitchen, and the children gathered for the sacrifice and their mouths watering; I know the crackling sound it makes when the carving knife enters its end, and I can see the split fly along in front of the blade as the knife cleaves its way to the other end; I can see its halves fall apart and display the rich red meat and the black seeds, and the heart standing up, a luxury fit for the elect; I know how a boy looks behind a yard-long slice of that melon, and I know how he feels; for I have been there. I know the taste of the watermelon which has been honestly come by, and I know the taste of the watermelon which has been acquired by art. Both taste good, but the experienced know which tastes best. I know the look of green apples and peaches and pears on the trees, and I know how entertaining they are when they are inside of a person. I know how ripe ones look when they are piled in pyramids under the trees, and how pretty they are and how vivid their colors. I know how a frozen apple looks, in a barrel down cellar in the wintertime, and how hard it is to bite, and how the frost makes the teeth ache, and yet how good it is, notwithstanding. I know the disposition of elderly people to select the speckled apples for the children, and I once knew ways to beat the game. I know the look of an apple that is roasting and sizzling on a hearth on a winter's evening, and I know the comfort that comes of eating it hot, along with some sugar and drenched in cream. I know the delicate art and mystery of so cracking hickory nuts and walnuts on a flatiron with a hammer that the kernels will be delivered whole, and I know how the nuts, taken in conjunction with winter apples, cider, and dough-nuts, make old people's old tales and old jokes sound fresh and crisp and enchanting, and juggle an evening away before you know what went with the time. I know the look of Uncle Dan'l's kitchen as it was on the privileged nights, when I was a child, and I can see the white and black children grouped on the hearth, with the firelight playing on their faces and the shadows flickering upon the walls, clear back toward the cavernous gloom of the rear, and I can hear Uncle Dan'l telling the immortal tales which Uncle Remus Harris was to gather into his book and charm the world with, by and by; and I can feel again the creepy joy which quivered through me when the time for the ghost story was reached—and the sense of regret, too, which came over me, for it was always the last story of the evening and there was nothing between it and the unwelcome bed.

I can remember the bare wooden stairway in my uncle's house, and the turn to the left above the landing, and the rafters and the slanting roof over my bed, and the squares of moonlight on the floor, and the white cold world of snow outside, seen through the curtainless window. I can remember the howling of the wind and the quaking of the house on stormy nights, and how snug and cozy one felt, under the blankets, listening; and how the powdery snow used to sift in, around the sashes, and lie in little ridges on the floor and make the place look chilly in the morning and curb the wild desire to get up—in case there was any. I can remember how very dark that room was, in the dark of the moon, and how packed it was with ghostly stillness when one woke up by accident away in the night, and forgotten sins came flocking out of the secret chambers of the memory and wanted a hearing; and how ill chosen the time seemed for this kind of business; and how dismal was the hoo-hooing of the owl and the wailing of the wolf, sent mourning by on the night wind.

I remember the raging of the rain on that roof, summer nights, and how pleasant it was to lie and listen to it, and enjoy the white splendor of the lightning and the majestic booming and crashing of the thunder. It was a very satisfactory room, and there was a lightning rod which was reachable from the window, an adorable and skittish thing to climb up and down, summer nights, when there were duties on hand of a sort to make privacy desirable.

I remember the 'coon and 'possum hunts, nights, with the Negroes, and the long marches through the black gloom of the woods, and the excitement which fired everybody when the distant bay of an experienced dog announced that the game was treed; then the wild scramblings and stumblings through briers and bushes and over roots to get to the spot; then the lighting of a fire and the felling of the tree, the joyful frenzy of the dogs and the Negroes, and the weird picture it all made in the red glare—I remember it all well, and the delight that everyone got out of it, except the 'coon.

I remember the pigeon seasons, when the birds would come in millions and cover the trees and by their weight break down the branches. They were clubbed to death with sticks; guns were not necessary and were not used. I remember the squirrel hunts, and prairie chicken hunts, and wild-turkey hunts, and all that; and how we turned out, mornings, while it was still dark, to go on these expeditions, and how chilly and dismal it was, and how often I regretted that I was well enough to go. A toot on a tin horn brought twice as many dogs as were needed, and in their happiness they raced and scampered about, and knocked small people down, and made no end of unnecessary noise. At the word, they vanished away toward the woods, and we drifted silently after them in the melancholy gloom. But presently the gray dawn stole over the world, the birds piped up, then the sun rose and poured light and comfort all around, everything was fresh and dewy and fragrant, and life was a boon again. After three hours of tramping we arrived back wholesomely tired, overladen with game, very hungry, and just in time for breakfast.

Alfred Kazin

A Brownsville Kitchen

In Brownsville tenements the kitchen is always the largest room and the center of the household. As a child I felt that we lived in a kitchen to which four other rooms were annexed. My mother, a "home" dressmaker, had her workshop in the kitchen. She told me once that she had begun dressmaking in Poland at thirteen; as far back as I can remember, she was always making dresses for the local women. She had an innate sense of design, a quick eye for all the subtleties in the latest fashions, even when she despised them, and great boldness. For three or four dollars she would study the fashion magazines with a customer, go with the customer to the remnants store on Belmont Avenue to pick out the material, argue the owner down—all remnants stores, for some reason, were supposed to be shady, as if the owners dealt in stolen goods—and then for days would patiently fit and baste and sew and fit again. Our apartment was always full of women in their housedresses sitting around the kitchen table waiting for a fitting. My little bedroom next to the kitchen was the fitting room. The sewing machine, an old nut-brown Singer with golden scrolls painted along the black arm and engraved along the two tiers of little drawers massed with needles and thread on each side of the treadle, stood next to the window and the great coal-black stove which up to my last year in college was our main source of heat. By December the two outer bedrooms were closed off, and used to chill bottles of milk and cream, cold borscht and jellied calves' feet.

The kitchen held our lives together. My mother worked in it all day long, we ate in it almost all meals except the Passover *seder*, I did my homework and first writing at the kitchen table, and in winter I often had a bed made up for me on three kitchen chairs near the stove. On the wall just over the table hung a long horizontal mirror that sloped to a ship's prow at each end and was lined in cherry wood. It took up the whole wall, and drew every object in the kitchen to itself. The walls were a fiercely stippled whitewash, so often rewhitened by my father in slack seasons that the paint looked as if it had been squeezed and cracked into the walls. A large electric bulb hung down the center of the kitchen at the end of a chain that had been hooked into the ceiling; the old gas ring and key still jutted out of the wall like antlers. In the corner next to the toilet was the sink at which we washed, and the square tub in which my mother did our clothes. Above it, tacked to the shelf on which were pleasantly ranged square, blue-bordered white sugar and spice jars, hung calendars from the Public National Bank on Pitkin Avenue and the Minsker Progressive Branch of the Workman's Circle; receipts for the payment of insurance premiums, and household bills on a spindle; two little boxes engraved with Hebrew letters. One of these was for the poor, the other to buy back the Land of Israel. Each spring a bearded little man would suddenly appear in our kitchen, salute us with a hurried Hebrew blessing, empty the boxes (sometimes with a sidelong look of disdain if they were not full), hurriedly bless us again for remembering our less fortunate Jewish brothers and sisters, and so take his departure until the next spring, after vainly trying to persuade my mother to take still another box. We did occasionally remember to drop coins in the boxes, but this was usually only on the dreaded morning of "mid-terms" and final examinations, because my mother thought it would bring me luck. She was extremely superstitious, but embarrassed about it, and always laughed at herself whenever, on the morning of an examination, she counseled me to leave the house on my right foot. "I know it's silly," her smile seemed to say, "but what harm can it do? It may calm God down."

The kitchen gave a special character to our lives; my mother's character. All my memories of that kitchen are dominated by the nearness of my mother sitting all day long at her sewing machine, by the clacking of the treadle against the linoleum floor, by the patient twist of her right shoulder as she automatically pushed at the wheel with one hand or lifted the foot to free the needle where it had got stuck in a thick piece of material. The kitchen was her life. Year by year, as I began to take in her fantastic capacity for labor and her anxious zeal, I realized it was ourselves she kept stitched together. I can never remember a time when she was not working. She worked because the law of her life was work, work and anxiety; she worked because she would have found life meaningless without work. She read almost no English; she could read the Yiddish paper, but never felt she had time to. We were always talking of a time when I would teach her how to read, but somehow there was never time. When I awoke in the morning she was already at her machine, or in the great morning crowd of housewives at the grocery getting fresh rolls for breakfast. When I returned from school she was at her machine, or conferring over *McCall's* with some neighborhood woman who had come in pointing hopefully to an illustration—"Mrs. Kazin! Mrs. Kazin! Make me a dress like it shows here in the picture!" When my father came home from work she had somehow mysteriously interrupted herself to make supper for us, and the dishes cleared and washed, was back at her machine. When I went to bed at night, often she was still there, pounding away at the treadle, hunched over the wheel, her hands steering a piece of gauze under the needle with a finesse that always contrasted sharply with her swollen hands and broken nails. Her left hand had been pierced through when as a girl she had worked in the infamous Triangle Shirtwaist Factory on the East Side. A needle had gone straight through the palm, severing a large vein. They had sewn it up for her so clumsily that a tuft of flesh always lay folded over the palm.

The kitchen was the great machine that set our lives running: it whirred down a little only on Saturdays and holy days. From my mother's kitchen I gained my first picture of life as a white, overheated, starkly lit workshop redolent with Jewish cooking, crowded with women in housedresses, strewn with fashion magazines, patterns, dress material, spools of thread—and at whose center, so lashed to her machine that bolts of energy seemed to dance out of her hands and feet as she worked, my mother stamped the treadle hard against the floor, hard, hard, and silently, grimly at war, beat out the first rhythm of the world for me.

Every sound from the street roared and trembled at our windows—a mother feeding her child on the doorstep, the screech of the trolley cars on Rockaway Avenue, the eternal smash of a handball against the wall of our house, the clatter of *"der Italyéner"* 's cart packed with watermelons, the sing-song of the old-clothes men walking Chester Street, the cries *"Arbes! Arbes! Kinder! Kinder! Heyse gute árbes!"* All day long people streamed into our apartment as a matter of course—"customers," upstairs neighbors, downstairs neighbors, women who would stop in for a half-hour's talk, salesmen, relatives, insurance agents. Usually they came in without ringing the bell—everyone knew my mother was always at home. I would hear the front door opening, the wind whistling through our front hall, and then some familiar face would appear in our kitchen with the same bland, matter-of-fact inquiring look: no need to stand on ceremony: my mother and her kitchen were available to everyone all day long.

At night the kitchen contracted around the blaze of light on the cloth, the patterns, the ironing board where the iron had burned a black border around the tear in the muslin cover; the finished dresses looked so frilly as they jostled on their wire hangers after all the work my mother had put into them. And then I would get that strangely ominous smell of tension from the dress fabrics and the burn in the cover of the ironing board—as if each piece of cloth and paper crushed with light under the naked bulb might suddenly go up in flames. Whenever I pass some small tailoring shop still lit up at night and see the owner hunched over his steam press; whenever in some poorer neighborhood of the city I see through a window some small crowded kitchen naked under the harsh light glittering in the ceiling, I still smell that fiery breath, that warning of imminent fire. I was always holding my breath. What I must have felt most about ourselves, I see now, was that we ourselves were like kindling—that all the hard-pressed pieces of ourselves and all the hard-used objects in that kitchen were like so many slivers of wood that might go up in flames if we came too near the white-blazing filaments in that naked bulb. Our tension itself was fire, we ourselves were forever burning—to live, to get down the foreboding in our souls, to make good.

Twice a year, on the anniversaries of her parents' deaths, my mother placed on top of the ice-box an ordinary kitchen glass packed with wax, the *yortsayt,* and lit the candle in it. Sitting at the kitchen table over my homework, I would look across the threshold to that mourning-glass, and sense that for my mother the distance from our kitchen to *der heym,* from life to death, was only a flame's length away. Poor as we were, it was not poverty that drove my mother so hard; it was loneliness—some endless bitter brooding over all those left behind, dead or dying or soon to die; a loneliness locked up in her kitchen that dwelt every day on the hazardousness of life and the nearness of death, but still kept struggling in the lock, trying to get us through by endless labor.

With us, life started up again only on the last shore. There seemed to be no middle ground between despair and the fury of our ambition. Whenever my mother spoke of her hopes for us, it was with such unbelievingness that the likes of us would ever come to anything, such abashed hope and readiness for pain, that I finally came to see in the flame burning on top of the ice-box death itself burning away the bones of poor Jews, burning out in us everything but courage, the blind resolution to live. In the light of that mourning-candle, there were ranged around me how many dead and dying—how many eras of pain, of exile, of dispersion, of cringing before the powers of this world!

It was always at dusk that my mother's loneliness came home most to me. Painfully alert to every shift in the light at her window, she would suddenly confess her fatigue by removing her pince-nez, and then wearily pushing aside the great mound of fabrics on her machine, would stare at the street as if to warm herself in the last of the sun. "How sad it is!" I once heard her say. "It grips me! It grips me!" Twilight was the bottommost part of the day, the chillest and loneliest time for her. Always so near to her moods, I knew she was fighting some deep inner dread, struggling against the returning tide of darkness along the streets that invariably assailed her heart with the same foreboding—Where? Where now? Where is the day taking us now?

Yet one good look at the street would revive her. I see her now, perched against the windowsill, with her face against the glass, her eyes almost asleep in enjoyment, just as she starts up with the guilty cry—"What foolishness is this in me!"—and goes to the stove to prepare supper for us: a moment, only a moment, watching the evening crowd of women gathering at the grocery for fresh bread and milk. But between my mother's pent-up face at the window and the winter sun dying in the fabrics—"Alfred, see how beautiful!"—she has drawn for me one single line of sentience.

Gwen Raverat

Religion in Childhood

The first religious experience that I can remember is getting under the nursery table to pray that the dancing mistress might be dead before we got to the Dancing Class. I was about half-way through the exasperating business which dancing class entailed: being changed right down to my skin, and washed and brushed, and having the comfortable dirt taken out of my fingernails. Margaret was sitting on the table, while Nana made her hair into long sausage-curls, with a wet brush round her finger. We thought the sausages very ugly, but Nana admired them, and we all loved Nana so much that we would do anything she liked. So Margaret bore it as well as she could, and only gave a little snarl when a drop of cold water fell on her bare neck. Charles was carefully washing his hands without any soap, the usual expression of philosophic calm on his round face. I think that he sometimes washed without any water either, for I well remember the smooth and permanent pale grey texture of his fingers.

When I was about half dressed, as I said, in my white flannel petticoat to be exact, I considered my costume suitable, and I got under the table for religious seclusion, and took up an attitude modelled on Sir Joshua Reynolds' "Infant Samuel kneeling in Prayer," as the correct position for divine transactions. We knew the Infant Samuel very well, from the picture-card game of National Gallery, which we often played.

It was not that I had any grudge against that particular dancing mistress, who was called, I think, Miss Ratcliffe. Of course, all dancing mistresses were affected jades. Hamlet's words perfectly described them, when I read them later on: *"You jig, you amble, you lisp and nickname God's creatures and make your wantonness your ignorance."* But that would not have mattered to me if only they had kept their jigging and ambling to themselves and left me in peace. But as it was, we were forced to go, and I really could think of no other weapon of self-defense except prayer. Not that I believed in that much; still, perhaps it was worth trying.

But, of course, prayer did not succeed. Prayers, at least *my* prayers, never did. So far as I can remember, none of the dancing mistresses from whom I suffered ever had so much as a cold in the head in all the time I knew them. There they always were, that scourge of the human race; and we always had to go through the whole degrading ritual, from the first March Past with its elegant bows to Miss Ratcliffe, right down to the bitter end of the waltz or the lancers.

I have sometimes wondered what would have been my reaction if the dancing mistress had fallen down dead, as I came into the classroom. I suppose I should have felt rather guilty; but after all it would have been God's doing, not mine; and that He should have done such a thing at my request would have destroyed my respect for Him, once and for all.

For the only virtue God had, to my mind, was that of impartiality; and so prayer itself seemed to me to be an immoral proceeding. It was as if you were trying to bribe the Judge. My idea of prayer was: "Please God, if you will let there be Chocolate Pudding for lunch, I will be very good to-day." I am now told that this is not the right idea of prayer, but it was mine then. Well, now: could it be right that God should suddenly put Chocolate Pudding into the head of the cook, when she had intended to make Marmalade Pudding, which I hated, but which other people liked? No, it would be exceedingly unjust. In fact, it would be a shabby thing for me to try to do a deal for myself in that way; and most unfair of God to agree to my terms. But, anyhow, He never did; God simply never did what I asked Him; so that on the whole I thought Him incorruptible, which was just as well. There remained the possibility that prayer might work as magic. But even as magic it never succeeded. It was altogether a bad idea. After that, prayer became synonymous for me with giving up hope; if ever I prayed again, it was only in a final frenzy of despair, and was the first step toward resignation at not getting what I wanted.

God had a smooth oval face, with no hair and no beard and no ears. I imagine that He was not descended, as most Gods are, from Father Christmas, but rather from the Sun Insurance Office sign. Even now this hairless, earless, egg-shaped face gives me a sort of holy feeling in my stomach. He sat up in the night sky like that, sending out Good Things with one hand, and Bad Things with the other hand. This was somehow connected with not letting your right hand know what your left hand was doing. There were probably an equal number of Good Things and Bad Things, and they were probably sent out with fair impartiality; at least, I was willing to give God the benefit of the doubt about it—though certainly it did seem as if the Bad Things had a strong tendency to go to the Good people; and vice versa. For from my earliest childhood I knew very well that Being Good did not pay. It was just a thing that you might—or might not—like for its own sake; and the verse about the wicked flourishing like the green bay tree was one of the few texts that went home to me with a click. God was not good and kind; at best, He was indifferent and the world was beautiful but quite pitiless.

Prayer was not the only idea of the grown-ups which seemed to me wrong in itself. They had a complete set of values for Badness and Goodness, which I will call System A; and this only partly coincided with my own private set of values: System B. I was always troubled by the confusion of trying to reconcile the two incompatible codes. System A and System B overlapped and agreed in disapproving of dishonesty, cruelty and cowardliness; but otherwise they had little in common; and there might often be very different points of view about what constituted dishonesty or cowardliness. For instance, when I had been obliged to steal some sugar, I felt that it made it perfectly honest if I put my head through the drawing-room door and shouted: "I've taken three lumps of sugar out of the pantry," and then ran away. My conscience was quite clear after that, and it did not prevent me from doing it again. This is the principle of Confession. I should have minded very much if I had felt myself to be dishonest; but I did not mind if they scolded me for disobedience. Obedience, though important in System A, had no place at all in System B.

Of course all kinds of goodness, in both systems, were hampered by being, by definition, something which you did not want to do. If you did want to do it, then it wasn't goodness. Thus being kind to a person you liked didn't count at all, because you wanted to do it; and being kind to a person you didn't like was no use either; because—as I thought then—the person always knew perfectly well that you disliked them, and so of course the kindness could not please them. So kindness was no use anyway. Nor were other efforts at Goodness more successful. For one thing Goodness never made me feel nice afterwards; I must be abnormal, for the reputed after-glow of virtue simply did not occur. Goodness-against-the-grain simply made me feel mean, hypocritical and servile; so that Goodness only resulted in a weight on my conscience; a weight often heavier than if I had been Bad on purpose; and nearly as heavy as if I had been Bad by accident.

For the most muddling thing of all was that the Badnesses you did *by accident* were what made you feel most guilty. Of course, this was all wrong by System A. The grown-ups pretended that it was what you did *on purpose* that mattered. This was, and is, quite untrue. No one ever really regrets doing a Badness on purpose. For instance, if you were rude or disobedient to Miss X, a governess you rightly despised, you felt rather pleased with yourself afterwards; or if you paddled without asking leave, anyhow you had had the paddling, and no one could ever take it away from you again.

But if you were unkind or rude by mistake to someone you loved—Ah, then you just wished you were dead. Once when Nana was ill in hospital, and my mother wanted to take me to see her, I refused to go, in all innocence. I could not bear the idea of seeing her changed, and sick, and surrounded by strangers. What could I say to her in public? We could only look at each other from far off, so what was the use of going? If I could possibly have believed that she would have liked to see me, I would willingly have gone; but that never occurred to me at all. This is the sort of thing one is sorry for afterwards, just because one did not do it on purpose.

My own code of virtue, System B, took this strange fact into account, but the grown-ups' System A was not realistic enough to do so. Yet if they could only be honest, even old people would admit that when they forget an appointment or are cross on purpose, they don't feel sorry at all; whereas, if they did the same things by accident, they would feel thoroughly guilty. Can it be called anything but Remorse, the anguish which pierces your breast when you discover that you have thrown away your return ticket, or lost your latchkey, by your own carelessness?

Anyhow, whether by accident or on purpose, by being Good or by being Bad, System A or System B, I always had a weight on my conscience of many pounds —if conscience weight is measured in pounds? Guiltiness was a permanent condition, like rheumatism; and one just had to learn to disregard it, and to carry on under it, as best one could. Huckleberry Finn has the last word on conscience—and I was as conscience-ridden as poor Huck himself.

"It don't make no difference whether you do right or wrong, a person's conscience ain't got no sense, and just goes for him anyway. If I had a yaller dog that didn't know more than a person's conscience, I would pison him. It takes up more room than all the rest of a person's insides, and yet ain't no good, nohow."

This is most terribly TRUE.

Clarence Day

Father Interferes with the Twenty-third Psalm

When we boys were little, we used to go to Mother's room Sunday evenings, on our way upstairs to bed, and sit in a circle around her, while she told us a story from the Bible or talked to us about how good we ought to be and how much we ought to love God. She loved God herself as much as she dared to,

From *Life with Father,* by Clarence Day. Copyright 1935 by Clarence Day. Reprinted by permission of Alfred A. Knopf, Inc.

and she deeply loved us, and she was especially tender and dear on those Sunday evenings. One of my brothers told me years afterward how much they had meant to him in those days, and how he had cherished the memory of them all his life.

I was a little older than my brothers, though, and my feelings were mixed. I loved Mother and hated to disappoint her, but I couldn't respond as easily as the other boys to her gentle appeals. I never seemed to have the emotions that she waited for me to show. I wish now that I could have listened uncritically and have thought only of the look in her eyes. What difference need it have made to me whether we had the same ideas about God, or whether the stories Mother thought lovely seemed less so to me? But there I sat, staring uncomfortably at the carpet and trying to avoid answering questions.

One night she repeated the Twenty-third Psalm to us and asked us to learn it by heart. "The Lord is my shepherd," she whispered softly. "He maketh me to lie down in green pastures: he leadeth me beside the still waters." She raised her eyes and went on bravely, although with a quiver of fear: "Thy rod and thy staff they comfort me." She had often felt the Lord's rod.

I heard Father going by in the hall. He looked in at the doorway and smiled affectionately at us and at Mother. Then he went off, and I heard his firm step as he walked on toward his room.

He hadn't meant to interfere with Mother's teachings. He hadn't spoken one word. But I found myself speculating all of a sudden on what his opinion would be of the Twenty-third Psalm.

I couldn't imagine Father being comforted by the Lord's rod and staff, or allowing anybody whatever to lead him to a pasture and get him to lie down somewhere in it. I could see him in my mind's eye, in his tailed coat and top hat, refusing point-blank even to enter a pasture. He would as soon have thought of wearing overalls. In spite of my admiring him for this attitude, it seemed wicked of him. I felt resentful about it. It would have been so much easier for me to be properly reverent if he had not been around. My idea was that if Mother was too religious, Father wasn't religous enough.

"Good night, Clarence," I heard Mother saying. "You won't forget, darling?"

I kissed her and went out, wondering what I was not to forget. Oh, yes—she had asked us to learn that psalm by heart.

Up in my bedroom, I got out my Bible. It was full of paper bookmarks, to help me find texts that I'd had to memorize, and these bookmarks in turn were full of pictures I had drawn of Biblical scenes. A picture of Adam looking doubtfully at the Tree of Knowledge in Eden, with a complete set of school books dangling heavily down from its boughs. A picture of Sarah "dealing hardly with Hagar," driving her out with a broomstick. A picture of the sun, moon, and stars bowing politely to Joseph.

I sat down and added to the collection a picture of Job in pajamas, weeping copiously as he endeavored, on top of all his other trials, to learn the Twenty-third Psalm. I also drew his three unsatisfactory friends, sitting in a row staring at Job. Each friend wore a sardonic expression and had a large mustache and imperial like Napoleon the Third.

I got out another Bible that Mother had lent me. This one was in French, and it sometimes shocked me deeply to read it. As my belief was that when God had created the world He had said, "Let there be light," it seemed to me highly irreverent to put French words in His mouth and have Him exclaim, *"Que la lumière soit!"* Imagine the Lord talking French! Aside from a few odd words in Hebrew, I took it completely for granted that God had never spoken anything but the most dignified English.

The French were notoriously godless, however. It made me laugh, though it frightened me, too, to see what liberties they had taken. In my English Bible, David was a fine Anglo-Saxon type, "a youth, ruddy and of a fair countenance." In the French, he was a revolting little snip from the boulevards, *"un enfant, blond, et d'une belle figure."* Where my Bible spoke of "leviathan," the French said *"le crocodile,"* which ruined the grandeur and mystery of that famous beast. And where mine said, "Behold now behemoth," they said, *"Voici l'hippopotame!"*

Instead of the children of Israel fearing lest the Lord should be wroth, the French said *"Les enfants d'Israel"* were afraid lest *"le Seigneur"* should be *"irrité."* This word *"irrité"* appeared everywhere in the French version. It wasn't only the Lord. Cain was *"très irrité."* Moise (which seemed to me a very jaunty way of referring to Moses) was *"irrité"* again and again. Everybody was *"irrité."* When my regular Bible, the real one, impressively described men as "wroth," their anger seemed to have something stately and solemn about it. If they were full of mere irritation all the time, they were more like the Day family.

I turned at last to the Twenty-third Psalm. They had spoiled that, too. They had twisted it around until it read as though the scene were in Paris. "Green pastures" were changed into *"parcs herbeux,"* and "thy rod and thy staff" had become *"ton bâton,"* as though the Lord were leading David up and down the Bois de Boulogne like a drum major.

I decided to go to bed and let that psalm wait for a day or two. But before putting the books back on my shelf, I hunted up the one place in the French Bible that I really liked. "Blessed are the meek," my English Bible said, "for they shall inherit the earth." I had always hated that verse. It made all religion so difficult. Uriah Heep typified the meek, to my mind. The meek were a snivelling, despicable, and uncomfortable lot. But in poring over the French Bible one evening, I had found to my delight that some daring Frenchman had altered this passage, and had changed the Sermon on the Mount into something that a fellow could stand. *"Heureux les débonnaires,"* he had represented Jesus as saying, *"car ils hériteront de la terre."*

The debonair! That was more like it! I cheerfully jumped into bed.

James Thurber

Here Lies Miss Groby

Miss Groby taught me English composition thirty years ago. It wasn't what prose said that interested Miss Groby; it was the way prose said it. The shape of a sentence crucified on a blackboard (parsed, she called it) brought a light to her eye. She hunted for Topic Sentences and Transitional Sentences the way little girls hunt for white violets in springtime. What she loved most of all were Figures of Speech. You remember her. You must have had her, too. Her influence will never die out of the land. A small schoolgirl asked me the other day if I could give her an example of metonymy. (There are several kinds of metonymies, you may recall, but the one that will come to mind most easily, I think, is Container for the Thing Contained.) The vision of Miss Groby came clearly before me when the little girl mentioned the old, familiar word. I saw her sitting at her desk, taking the rubber band off the roll-call cards, running it back upon the fingers of her right hand, and surveying us all separately with quick little henlike turns of her head.

Here lies Miss Groby, not dead, I think, but put away on a shelf with the other T squares and rulers whose edges had lost their certainty. The fierce light that Miss Groby brought to English literature was the light of Identification. Perhaps, at the end, she could no longer retain the dates of the birth and death of one of the Lake poets. That would have sent her to the principal of the school with her resignation. Or perhaps she could not remember, finally, exactly how many Cornishmen there were who had sworn that Trelawny should not die, or precisely how many springs were left to Housman's lad in which to go about the woodlands to see the cherry hung with snow.

Verse was one of Miss Groby's delights because there was so much in both its form and content that could be counted. I believe she would have got an enormous thrill out of Wordsworth's famous lines about Lucy if they had been written this way:

> A violet by a mossy stone
> Half hidden from the eye,
> Fair as a star when ninety-eight
> Are shining in the sky.

It is hard for me to believe that Miss Groby ever saw any famous work of literature from far enough away to know what it meant. She was forever climbing up the margins of books and crawling between their lines, hunting for the little gold of phrase, making marks with a pencil. As Palamides hunted the Questing Beast, she hunted the Figure of Speech. She hunted it through the clangorous halls of Shakespeare and through the green forests of Scott.

Night after night, for homework, Miss Groby set us to searching in "Ivanhoe" and "Julius Caesar" for metaphors, similes, metonymies, apostrophes, personifications, and all the rest. It got so that figures of speech jumped out of the pages at you, obscuring the sense and pattern of the novel or play you were trying to read. "Friends, Romans, countrymen, lend me your ears." Take that, for instance. There is an unusual but perfect example of Container for the Thing Contained. If you read the funeral oration unwarily—that is to say, for its meaning—you might easily miss the C.F.T.T.C. Antony is, of course, not asking for their ears in the sense that he wants them cut off and handed over; he is asking for the function of those ears, for their power to hear, for, in a word, the thing they contain.

At first I began to fear that all the characters in Shakespeare and Scott were crazy. They confused cause with effect, the sign for the thing signified, the thing held for the thing holding it. But after a while I began to suspect that it was I myself who was crazy. I would find myself lying awake at night saying over and over, "The thinger for the thing contained." In a great but probably misguided attempt to keep my mind on its hinges, I would stare at the ceiling and try to think of an example of the Thing Contained for the Container. It struck me as odd that Miss Groby had never thought of that inversion. I finally hit on one, which I still remember. If a woman were to grab up a bottle of Grade A and say to her husband, "Get away from me or I'll hit you with the milk," that would be a Thing Contained for the Container. The next day in class I raised my hand and brought my curious discovery straight out before Miss Groby and my astonished schoolmates. I was eager and serious about it and it never occurred to me that the other children would laugh. They laughed loudly and long. When Miss Groby had quieted them she said to me rather coldly, "That was not really amusing, James." That's the mixed-up kind of thing that happened to me in my teens.

In later years I came across another excellent example of this figure of speech in a joke long since familiar to people who know vaudeville or burlesque (or radio, for that matter). It goes something like this:

A: What's your head all bandaged up for?
B: I got hit with some tomatoes.
A: How could that bruise you up so bad?
B: These tomatoes were in a can.

I wonder what Miss Groby would have thought of that one.

I dream of my old English teacher occasionally. It seems that we are always in Sherwood Forest and that from far away I can hear Robin Hood winding his silver horn.

"Drat that man for making such a racket on his cornet!" cries Miss Groby. "He scared away a perfectly darling Container for the Thing Contained, a great, big, beautiful one. It leaped right back into its context when that man blew that cornet. It was the most wonderful Container for the Thing Contained I ever saw here in the Forest of Arden."

"This is Sherwood Forest," I say to her.

"That doesn't make any difference at all that I can see," she says to me.

Then I wake up, tossing and moaning.

William Butler Yeats

Grandfather Pollexfen

Some of my misery was loneliness and some of it fear of old
William Pollexfen my grandfather. He was never unkind, and I cannot remember that he ever spoke harshly to me, but it was the custom to fear and admire
him. He had won the freedom of some Spanish city, for saving life perhaps, but
was so silent that his wife never knew it till he was near eighty, and then from
the chance visit of some old sailor. She asked him if it was true and he said it was
true, but she knew him too well to question and his old shipmate had left the
town. She too had the habit of fear. We knew that he had been in many parts of
the world, for there was a great scar on his hand made by a whaling-hook, and in
the dining-room was a cabinet with bits of coral in it and a jar of water from the
Jordan for the baptizing of his children and Chinese pictures upon rice-paper and
an ivory walking-stick from India that came to me after his death. He had great
physical strength and had the reputation of never ordering a man to do anything
he would not do himself. He owned many sailing ships and once, when a captain
just come to anchor at Rosses Point reported something wrong with the rudder,
had sent a messenger to say "Send a man down to find out what's wrong." "The
crew all refuse" was the answer, and to that my grandfather answered, "Go
down yourself," and not being obeyed, he dived from the main deck, all the
neighbourhood lined along the pebbles of the shore. He came up with his skin
torn but well informed about the rudder. He had a violent temper and kept a
hatchet at his bedside for burglars and would knock a man down instead of
going to law, and I once saw him hunt a party of men with a horsewhip. He had
no relation for he was an only child and, being solitary and silent, he had few
friends. He corresponded with Campbell of Islay who had befriended him and
his crew after a shipwreck, and Captain Webb, the first man who had swum the
Channel and who was drowned swimming the Niagara Rapids, had been a mate
in his employ and a close friend. That is all the friends I can remember and yet
he was so looked up to and admired that when he returned from taking the
waters at Bath his men would light bonfires along the railway line for miles;
while his partner William Middleton whose father after the great famine had
attended the sick for weeks, and taken cholera from a man he carried in his arms
into his own house and died of it, and was himself civil to everybody and a
cleverer man than my grandfather, came and went without notice. I think I
confused my grandfather with God, for I remember in one of my attacks of
melancholy praying that he might punish me for my sins, and I was shocked and
astonished when a daring little girl—a cousin I think—having waited under a
group of trees in the avenue, where she knew he would pass near four o'clock on
the way to his dinner, said to him, "If I were you and you were a little girl, I
would give you a doll."

Yet for all my admiration and alarm, neither I nor any one else thought it wrong to outwit his violence or his rigour; and his lack of suspicion and something helpless about him made that easy while it stirred our affection. When I must have been still a very little boy, seven or eight years old perhaps, an uncle called me out of bed one night, to ride the five or six miles to Rosses Point to borrow a railway-pass from a cousin. My grandfather had one, but thought it dishonest to let another use it, but the cousin was not so particular. I was let out through a gate that opened upon a little lane beside the garden away from earshot of the house, and rode delighted through the moonlight, and awoke my cousin in the small hours by tapping on his window with a whip. I was home again by two or three in the morning and found the coachman waiting in the little lane. My grandfather would not have thought such an adventure possible, for every night at eight he believed that the stable-yard was locked, and he knew that he was brought the key. Some servant had once got into trouble at night and so he had arranged that they should all be locked in. He never knew, what everybody else in the house knew, that for all the ceremonious bringing of the key the gate was never locked.

Even to-day when I read *King Lear* his image is always before me and I often wonder if the delight in passionate men in my plays and in my poetry is more than his memory. He must have been ignorant, though I could not judge him in my childhood, for he had run away to sea when a boy, "gone to sea through the hawsehole" as he phrased it, and I can but remember him with two books—his Bible and Falconer's *Shipwreck,* a little green-covered book that lay always upon his table; he belonged to some younger branch of an old Cornish family. His father had been in the Army, had retired to become an owner of sailing ships, and an engraving of some old family place my grandfather thought should have been his hung next a painted coat of arms in the little back parlour. His mother had been a Wexford woman, and there was a tradition that his family had been linked with Ireland for generations and once had their share in the old Spanish trade with Galway. He had a good deal of pride and disliked his neighbours, whereas his wife, a Middleton, was gentle and patient and did many charities in the little back parlour among frieze coats and shawled heads, and every night when she saw him asleep went the round of the house alone with a candle to make certain there was no burglar in danger of the hatchet. She was a true lover of her garden, and before the care of her house had grown upon her, would choose some favourite among her flowers and copy it upon rice-paper. I saw some of her handiwork the other day and I wondered at the delicacy of form and colour and at a handling that may have needed a magnifying glass it was so minute. I can remember no other pictures but the Chinese paintings, and some coloured prints of battles in the Crimea upon the wall of a passage, and the painting of a ship at the passage end darkened by time.

Bruce Catton

Grant and Lee: A Study in Contrasts

When Ulysses S. Grant and Robert E. Lee met in the parlor of a modest house at Appomattox Court House, Virginia, on April 9, 1865, to work out the terms for the surrender of Lee's Army of Northern Virginia, a great chapter in American life came to a close, and a great new chapter began.

These men were bringing the Civil War to its virtual finish. To be sure, other armies had yet to surrender, and for a few days the fugitive Confederate government would struggle desperately and vainly, trying to find some way to go on living now that its chief support was gone. But in effect it was all over when Grant and Lee signed the papers. And the little room where they wrote out the terms was the scene of one of the poignant, dramatic contrasts in American history.

They were two strong men, these oddly different generals, and they represented the strengths of two conflicting currents that, through them, had come into final collision.

Back of Robert E. Lee was the notion that the old aristocratic concept might somehow survive and be dominant in American life.

Lee was tidewater Virginia, and in his background were family, culture, and tradition . . . the age of chivalry transplanted to a New World which was making its own legends and its own myths. He embodied a way of life that had come down through the age of knighthood and the English country squire. America was a land that was beginning all over again, dedicated to nothing much more complicated than the rather hazy belief that all men had equal rights and should have an equal chance in the world. In such a land Lee stood for the feeling that it was somehow of advantage to human society to have a pronounced inequality in the social structure. There should be a leisure class, backed by ownership of land; in turn, society itself should be keyed to the land as the chief source of wealth and influence. It would bring forth (according to this ideal) a class of men with a strong sense of obligation to the community; men who lived not to gain advantage for themselves, but to meet the solemn obligations which had been laid on them by the very fact that they were privileged. From them the country would get its leadership; to them it could look for the higher values—of thought, of conduct, of personal deportment—to give it strength and virtue.

Lee embodied the noblest elements of this aristocratic ideal. Through him, the landed nobility justified itself. For four years, the Southern states had fought a desperate war to uphold the ideals for which Lee stood. In the end, it almost seemed as if the Confederacy fought for Lee; as if he himself was the Confederacy . . . the best thing that the way of life for which the Confederacy stood could ever have to offer. He had passed into legend before Appomattox. Thousands of tired, underfed, poorly clothed Confederate soldiers, long since past the simple enthusiasm of the early days of the struggle, somehow considered Lee the symbol of everything for which they had been willing to die. But they could not quite put this feeling into words. If the Lost Cause, sanctified by so much heroism and so many deaths, had a living justification, its justification was General Lee.

Grant, the son of a tanner on the Western frontier, was everything Lee was not. He had come up the hard way and embodied nothing in particular except the eternal toughness and sinewy fiber of the men who grew up beyond the mountains. He was one of a body of men who owed reverence and obeisance to no one, who were self-reliant to a fault, who cared hardly anything for the past but who had a sharp eye for the future.

These frontier men were the precise opposites of the tidewater aristocrats. Back of them, in the great surge that had taken people over the Alleghenies and into the opening Western country, there was a deep, implicit dissatisfaction with a past that had settled into grooves. They stood for democracy, not from any reasoned conclusion about the proper ordering of human society, but simply because they had grown up in the middle of democracy and knew how it worked. Their society might have privileges, but they would be privileges each man had won for himself. Forms and patterns meant nothing. No man was born to anything, except perhaps to a chance to show how far he could rise. Life was competition.

Yet along with this feeling had come a deep sense of belonging to a national community. The Westerner who developed a farm, opened a shop, or set up in business as a trader, could hope to prosper only as his own community prospered—and his community ran from the Atlantic to the Pacific and from Canada down to Mexico. If the land was settled, with towns and highways and accessible markets, he could better himself. He saw his fate in terms of the nation's own destiny. As its horizons expanded, so did his. He had, in other words, an acute dollars-and-cents stake in the continued growth and development of his country.

And that, perhaps, is where the contrast between Grant and Lee becomes most striking. The Virginia aristocrat, inevitably, saw himself in relation to his own region. He lived in a static society which could endure almost anything except change. Instinctively, his first loyalty would go to the locality in which that society existed. He would fight to the limit of endurance to defend it, because in defending it he was defending everything that gave his own life its deepest meaning.

The Westerner, on the other hand, would fight with an equal tenacity for the broader concept of society. He fought so because everything he lived by was tied to growth, expansion, and a constantly widening horizon. What he lived by would survive or fall with the nation itself. He could not possibly stand by unmoved in the face of an attempt to destroy the Union. He would combat it with everything he had, because he could only see it as an effort to cut the ground out from under his feet.

So Grant and Lee were in complete contrast, representing two diametrically opposed elements in American life. Grant was the modern man emerging; beyond him, ready to come on the stage, was the great age of steel and machinery, of crowded cities and a restless, burgeoning vitality. Lee might have ridden down from the old age of chivalry, lance in hand, silken banner fluttering over his head. Each man was the perfect champion of his cause, drawing both his strengths and his weaknesses from the people he led.

Yet it was not all contrast, after all. Different as they were—in background, in personality, in underlying aspiration—these two great soldiers had much in common. Under everything else, they were marvelous fighters. Furthermore, their fighting qualities were really very much alike.

Each man had, to begin with, the great virtue of utter tenacity and fidelity. Grant fought his way down the Mississippi Valley in spite of acute personal discouragement and profound military handicaps. Lee hung on in the trenches at Petersburg after hope itself had died. In each man there was an indomitable quality . . . the born fighter's refusal to give up as long as he can still remain on his feet and lift his two fists.

Daring and resourcefulness they had, too; the ability to think faster and move faster than the enemy. These were the qualities which gave Lee the dazzling campaigns of Second Manassas and Chancellorsville and won Vicksburg for Grant.

Lastly, and perhaps greatest of all, there was the ability, at the end, to turn quickly from war to peace once the fighting was over. Out of the way these two men behaved at Appomattox came the possibility of a peace of reconciliation. It was a possibility not wholly realized, in the years to come, but which did, in the end, help the two sections to become one nation again . . . after a war whose bitterness might have seemed to make such a reunion wholly impossible. No part of either man's life became him more than the part he played in their brief meeting in the McLean house at Appomattox. Their behavior there put all succeeding generations of Americans in their debt. Two great Americans, Grant and Lee—very different, yet under everything very much alike. Their encounter at Appomattox was one of the great moments of American history.

Virginia Woolf

Beau Brummell

He [Beau Brummell] had no advantage of birth, and but little of fortune. His grandfather had let rooms in St. James's Street. He had only a moderate capital of thirty thousand pounds to begin with, and his beauty, of figure rather than of face, was marred by a broken nose. Yet without a single noble, important, or valuable action to his credit he cuts a figure; he stands for a symbol; his ghost walks among us still. The reason for this eminence is now a little difficult to determine. Skill of hand and nicety of judgment were his, of course, otherwise he would not have brought the art of tying neck-cloths to perfection. The story is, perhaps, too well known—how he drew his head far back and sunk his chin slowly down so that the cloth wrinkled in perfect symmetry, or if one wrinkle were too deep or too shallow, the cloth was thrown into a basket and the attempt renewed, while the Prince of Wales sat, hour after hour, watching. Yet skill of hand and nicety of judgment were not enough. Brummell owed his ascendancy to some curious combination of wit, of taste, of insolence, of independence—for he was never a toady—which it were too heavy handed to call a philosophy of life, but served the purpose. At any rate, ever since he was the most popular boy at Eton coolly jesting when they were for throwing a bargee into the river, "My good fellows, don't send him into the river; the man is evidently in a high state of perspiration, and it almost amounts to a certainty that he will catch cold," he floated buoyantly and gaily and without apparent effort to the top of whatever society he found himself among. Even when he was a captain in the Tenth Hussars and so scandalously inattentive to duty that he only knew his troop by "the very large blue nose" of one of the men, he was liked and tolerated. When he resigned his commission, for the regiment was to be sent to Manchester—and "I really could not go—think, your Royal Highness, Manchester!"—he had only to set up house in Chesterfield Street to become the head of the most jealous and exclusive society of his time. For example, he was at Almack's one night talking to Lord ———. The Duchess of ——— was there, escorting her young daughter, Lady Louisa. The Duchess caught sight of Mr. Brummell, and at once warned her daughter that if that gentleman near the door came and spoke to them she was to be careful to impress him favourably, "for," and she sank her voice to a whisper, "he is the celebrated Mr. Brummell." Lady Louisa might well have wondered why a Mr. Brummell was celebrated, and why a Duke's daughter need take care to impress a Mr. Brummell. And then directly he began to move towards them the reason of her mother's warning became apparent. The grace of his carriage was so astonishing; his bows were so exquisite. Everybody looked overdressed or badly dressed—some, indeed, looked positively dirty beside him. His clothes seemed to melt into each other with the perfection of their cut and the quiet harmony of their colour. Without a single point of emphasis everything was distinguished—from his bow to the way he opened his snuff-box, with his left hand invariably. He was the personification of freshness and cleanliness and order. One could well believe that he had his chair brought into his dressing-room and was deposited at Almack's without letting a puff of wind disturb his curls or a spot of mud stain his shoes. When he actually spoke to her, Lady Louisa would be at first enchanted—no one was more agreeable, more amusing, had a manner that was more flattering and enticing—and then she would be puzzled. It was quite possible that before the evening was out he would ask her to marry him, and yet his manner of doing it was such that the most ingenuous débutante could not believe that he meant it seriously. His odd grey eyes seemed to contradict his lips; they had a look in them which made the sincerity of his compliments very doubtful. And then he said very cutting things about other people. They were not exactly witty; they were certainly not profound; but they were so skilful, so adroit—they had a twist in them which made them slip into the mind and stay there when more important phrases were forgotten. He had downed the Regent himself with his dexterous "Who's your fat friend?" and his method was the same with humbler people who snubbed him or bored him. "Why, what could I do, my good fellow, but cut the connection? I discovered that Lady Mary actually ate cabbage!"—so he explained to a friend his failure to marry a lady. And, again, when some dull citizen pestered him about his tour to the North, "Which of the lakes do I admire?" he asked his valet. "Windermere, sir." "Ah, yes—Windermere, so it is—Windermere." That was his style, flickering, sneering, hovering on the verge of insolence, skimming the edge of nonsense, but always keeping within some curious mean, so that one knew the false Brummell story from the true by its exaggeration. Brummell could never have said, "Wales, ring the bell," any more than he could have worn a brightly coloured waistcoat or a glaring necktie. That "certain exquisite propriety" which Lord Byron remarked in his dress, stamped his whole being, and made him appear cool, refined, and debonair among the gentlemen who talked only of sport, which Brummell detested, and smelt of the stable, which Brummell never visited. Lady Louisa might well be on tenter-hooks to impress Mr. Brummell favourably. Mr. Brummell's good opinion was of the utmost importance in the world of Lady Louisa.

And unless that world fell into ruins his rule seemed assured. Handsome, heartless, and cynical, the Beau seemed invulnerable. His taste was impeccable, his health admirable; and his figure as fine as ever. His rule had lasted many years and survived many vicissitudes. The French Révolution had passed over his head without disordering a single hair. Empires had risen and fallen while he experimented with the crease of a neck-cloth and criticised the cut of a coat. Now the battle of Waterloo had been fought and peace had come. The battle left him untouched; it was the peace that undid him. For some time past he had been winning and losing at the gaming-tables. Harriette Wilson had heard that he was ruined, and then, not without disappointment, that he was safe again. Now, with the armies disbanded, there was let loose upon London a horde of rough, ill-mannered men who had been fighting all those years and were determined to enjoy themselves. They flooded the gaming-houses. They played very high. Brummell was forced into competition. He lost and won and vowed never to play again, and then he did play again. At last his remaining ten thousand pounds was gone. He borrowed until he could borrow no more. And finally, to crown the loss of so many thousands, he lost the six-penny-bit with a hole in it which had always brought him good luck. He gave it by mistake to a hackney coachman: that rascal Rothschild got hold of it, he said, and that was the end of his luck. Such was his own account of the affair—other people put a less innocent interpretation on the matter. At any rate there came a day, 16th May 1816, to be precise—it was a day upon which everything was precise—when he dined alone off a cold fowl and a bottle of claret at Watier's, attended the opera, and then took coach for Dover. He drove rapidly all through the night and reached Calais the day after. He never set foot in England again.

Henry Seidel Canby
The Town

Our town was founded where two creeks ran together and made a channel which led to the broad stretches of the lower Delaware. The Swedish pioneers of 1638, who were timid navigators, sailed from the ocean on up the river until the creek mouth tempted them, and entering found a point of rocks on which they could land dryshod. The rocks were the last outpost of a range of hills, and up these hills our town was built.

In my youth Wilmington was still a red-brick town with streets of cobble, through which horsecars bumped and rattled. Along one creek shore railroads and factories covered the old marshes and meadows, with here and there a fine gable of a settler's house unnoticed in the dirt and smoke. As the town grew, it climbed. Walking uphill on Market Street was a progress through the history of American architecture, past dilapidated colonial houses and really lovely banks and markets of the beginning of the nineteenth century, to the Second Empire of the Grand Opera House, and the shapeless severity of the library and the one big hotel.

From the ballroom at the top of the opera house where we went for dancing school there was a view of the whole town at once; and it always surprised me to see how deeply its crisscross of streets was buried in foliage. The factory districts below were grimy and bare, but to the north and the west the roofs were hid in a forest with only a "mansion" here and there or a church steeple projecting.

Beyond the business and shopping section, and toward the hilltops, were tight little streets, heavily shaded and walled with red-brick fronts built cheek-to-cheek, with decent chins of white marble steps, and alley archways for ears. Here the well-to-do had lived when the city was still a little town, and had been content to hide their arbored side porches and deep if narrow gardens from the street.

The industrial prosperity of the eighties had ended this Quaker restraint. In my day those who could afford it lived farther westward in houses that sprawled in ample yards, thickset with trees and shrubbery behind iron or wooden fences. Here was a God's plenty of architecture. Brick boxes of the seventies, with cupolas or mansard roofs, and porches screened with graceful scrolls of ironwork were set in old-fashioned contrast beside new contraptions, some of green serpentine, but the latest of brick pseudo-Gothic, with turrets, pointed towers, and Egyptian ornaments of wood. And a little off line with the right-angle streets were still to be seen a few old farmhouses of weathered Brandywine granite as colorful as a slice of plum cake, so severe and pure in line that they made the neighboring mansions seem opulent and vulgar, as indeed many of them were.

The main streets were cobble, too rough for our hard-tired bicycles which had to keep to the brick sidewalks, rutty with the roots of the many trees. Side streets were bedded with yellow clay, morasses in the spring and most of the winter and impassable then except on stepping-stones. Two-wheeled carts dragged through them and sometimes stuck fast. Every house of any pretensions had its iron hitching-post and marble landing-block on which fastidious feet could step from the carriages. There were iron stags on the lawns, but our specialty was iron dogs, especially greyhounds, which crouched on either side of the steps. It was a comfortable region of homes, never quite beautiful, nor ugly, certainly not monotonous, and entirely innocent of those period houses out of magazines, with their shrubbery by the local dealer, which are the current ideal of the American home.

To the southward of the hilltops lived the "plain people" by thousands in rows of brick houses with identical windows and doors, no more differentiation in homes than in their lives; and below them again, reaching down into the factories, were the slums, where congestion was painful, dirty water ran over broken pavements, and the yards behind were reduced to a dump heap. Here the decent order of our town broke into shrill voices, fighting, smells, and drunkenness.

Each street had its character for us, at least in those neighborhoods where we felt at home. There were subtle social distinctions which by no means ran with size or elegance of dwelling. The town indeed was divided into neighborhoods, so that the division by streets was as artificial as the division of the Union into states. Nothing of this, however, showed geographically. There was only a progression from older to newer as the prosperous American felt for elbow room. Zoning, of course, was rudimentary. Each neighborhood outside the slums was a little town in itself, with a store or two, a livery stable, wooden houses tucked in behind for the darkies, vacant lots held for speculation, solid dwellings of the quality, raw-built mansions of the new rich, and rows of little houses for the "plain people."

It all began to seem very ugly when the change of taste came in the early nineteen-hundreds, yet, looking back now, it has a quiet beauty of its own. There were so many trees, so much variety, such individualism manifest. Homes then did represent some quality of the inhabitant, for the architects, having no style of their own, gave the buyer what he wanted: the *nouveaux riches* got exactly the parapets and ornamental porches and zig-zag skyline they longed for; simple people had simple houses; solid folk solid brick with plate-glass windows and heavy metal roofs; and transients, who stayed a year or so and then moved on, precisely the thrown-together houses they deserved. As the Scotch or English farmer was known by the name of his farm, so when I think of many of our citizens I see their homes before I can recall their faces.

And in every neighborhood were houses of mystery—withdrawn in dense trees or shrubbery, little lighted, always shuttered, where misers, old maids, or eccentrics that did not like their fellow humans, found homes that exactly suited them. Where do such people find congenial surroundings now? For you cannot take cover in an apartment house!

On the very top of our hill was a stone house, of perhaps 1750, above a spring sheltered by an oak that certainly was old when the Swedes sailed up the Delaware. A recluse lived there in a confusion of family portraits, letters, documents from the makers of the Republic, and furniture of that excellent beauty which Philadelphia craftsmen of the seventeen-seventies and eighties had mastered. Each year or so he sold a lot from his estate, and each year a red-brick house stepped nearer to the old gray place, which shrank as the town intruded, and closed every door and shutter. It was the one property which boys respected, even though both walnuts and cherry trees grew by the house. When the first new home was built on the very edge of the noble lawn which had once stretched down in a long green curve toward the river, old Caesar Rodney shot himself. Thus, part old in dignity, part plain and simple, part new and pretentious, part dirty and vicious, our town told its story to whoever could read.

James Morris

New York

Through the drab flatlands of New Jersey sweeps the turnpike, eight lanes wide and fearfully busy: past oil refineries spouting smoke and flame, ships in dock and aircraft on the tarmac, railway lines and incinerators and dismal urban marshes, until it plunges into the tunnel under the Hudson River. All is ordered and regimented. Your speed is regulated, and your route, and the traffic moves nose to tail through the tunnel in a glare of harsh lights, a rumble of engines and a stink of impatient exhausts. You feel like a machine yourself, urged in jerks along a conveyor belt, and behind you the mass of America seems to extend in a wasteland of automation, tranquillizers and winking lights.

The moment you emerge from that tunnel, though, and drive blinking into Manhattan on the other side, all the old dream of America comes to life again. Instantly, as the skyscrapers greet you with a sheen of glass, a miracle occurs—a sort of daily renaissance, a flowering of the commuter's spirit. The cars and trucks and buses, no longer confined to their lanes, suddenly spring away in all directions like animals off a leash. At once, instead of conformity, all is profusion. Policemen irritably chivvy you on. Men push racks of summer frocks along the sidewalk. Trains rumble through blackened cuttings. Great liners tower above the street. There are shops with unpronounceable Central European names, and racks of strange newspapers, and black-eyed dowdy-haired women with shopping bags, and drivers hurling imprecations out of taxi windows, and bright colours everywhere, and spiced smells, skinny cats on window sills, bus-drivers with weary, patient faces, and always above you, shiny of flank and sharp of outline, the tremendous meditative shapes of the skyscrapers. You are in New York, the noblest of the American symbols, the most exciting of the cities of the earth, and in some ways the nastiest.

New York is the richest of mixtures—rich in sheer wealth, rich figuratively. A fusion of races contributes to this cornucopia, and a restless disregard for things past or permanent, and a spirit of hope and open-heartedness that still survives, if only just, from the days of free immigration, when America was the haven of the earth. The Statue of Liberty, graphically described in one reference book as "a substantial figure of a lady," is dwarfed by the magnificence of the harbour skyline, and from the deck of a ship it is easy to miss it: but in New York, more than anywhere else in the United States, there is still dignity to the lines carved upon its plinth, and reproduced a century later at the airport of Idlewild:

> Give me your tired, your poor,
> Your huddled masses yearning to breathe free,
> The wretched refuse of your teeming shore.

Even today New York is not the all-American city, and perhaps reflects the state of the nation less faithfully than Chicago, say, or even Boston: but here the idea of America is still at its bold best, enlivening every situation, ennobling every squalor. To comprehend the magic of New York, and her very real glory, bear in mind that London had been in existence for fifteen centuries before the first settler built his shack on Manhattan.

Everyone has read of the magical glitter of this place, but until you have set foot in New York it is difficult to conceive of a city so sparkling that at any moment Mr. Fred Astaire might quite reasonably come dancing his urbane way down Fifth Avenue. It is a marvellously exuberant place, even when the bitter winds of the fall howl through its canyons. The taxi-drivers talk long and fluently—sometimes with a tiresome affectation of home-spun philosophy, often in pungent recollection of Russia, old Naples, wartime England or derelict Ireland. The waiters are sometimes brusque but often jolly. ("Ask for anything in the world," one dear old boy at the Waldorf likes to tell the wondering provincial, "and if we ain't got it, we'll get it.") Down at the Rockefeller Center skating rink, one of the very nicest places in America, there is always something pleasant to see—pretty girls showing off, children doubled up in hilarity, brave old ladies determined to succeed or wild-eyed eccentrics of diabolical skill.

For boundless vivacity and verve are the inspiration of Manhattan. The thrill of America is fading a little, as the haven matures into the greatest of Powers, but in the downtown streets of this city, away from the slums and dingy suburbs, you are still in a world of ever-spirited astonishment. The best of the new buildings are glass eyries, gay and delicate. The stores breathe a most cultivated kind of opulence—not the seductive allure of the French shops, nor the masculine distinction of London's, but something more homely without being less sophisticated. Clouds of steam from the central heating systems periodically issue from the streets, like small urban geysers, and sometimes if you look through a grille in the sidewalk you may see the gleaming metal of a great express on the underground tracks beneath. Wander up to Central Park, and you will find a row of hansom cabs, heated in the winter with little charcoal stoves, tended by elderly gentlemen in top hats, and much in demand by susceptible romantics for bumpy dalliances in the park. Potter down to the water-front, and you may stand in the shadows of the Atlantic liners, the ultimate ships, or watch a tall Yankee tug steam insolently beneath the girders of Brooklyn Bridge, her captain chewing his gum with splendid nonchalance on his high curved bridge.

This is a beautiful city—beautiful of silhouette, of colour, of dramatic impact. Nor is it a vulgar one, as long-outdated European slander has it. There are palaces of great pictures in New York, and millions go each year to see them. Each week a whole page of the *New York Times* is filled with concert announcements. There are incomparable museums, scores of theatres, famous publishing houses, a great university, private art galleries beyond number, every conceivable variety of antique dealer, bookseller, bric-a-brac merchant, jade carver, chinoiserie expert, clock-dealer, specialist in mediaeval mosaics or esoteric philately. Two or three of the New York restaurants are, by common consent of the most demanding gourmets, among the best in the world. New York is no longer the gauche *nouvelle-riche* of her lingering reputation; she has achieved a civilization if not as mellow, at least as close-knit and complete as the cultures of the old European capitals.

But somewhere behind the glitter, I sometimes feel, there is embedded a kernel of disappointment, as though all this wealth and celebrity is not quite what the city originally intended for itself. New York is an entertaining city indeed, but she is often sour to the taste: a spinster sourness, unfulfilled. Power weighs heavily upon her shoulders nowadays, and makes her sometimes a rather terrifying place. This is the seat of the United Nations, where the grandees stride and the mediocrities bicker, and it is also the prime bastion of the capitalist system, the Moscow of the West. The newest buildings of Manhattan are dreadful in their size and grandeur, and there is something eerie to the pace and frequency with which the New Yorkers tear their city down and build it up again—ever bigger, ever grander, ever more domineering. It is an almost Pharaonic zeal that inspires these mighty structures: and though it sometimes seems the result of some unbearable frustration, some unrevealed disappointment, nevertheless, as a sensitive New Yorker recently observed (himself a little frightened, I think, by the scale and savagery of the process), only a great people could erect such buildings—or demolish them with such an absolute lack of ritual or superstition.

So New York, though always stimulating, is not always happy. Beggars abound in these streets of endless promise, litter flaps depressingly through the side streets, and all around the fiery-coloured centre stretch drab sandstone suburbs, pallid housing estates, slums or sordid tenements. The inner perimeters of New York are frayed, down-at-heel and testy, full of squabbling racial conglomerations, Negroes, Puerto Ricans, Poles or Italians. The Jewish genius of the city, at its best witty and imaginative to a degree, curdles at its worst into a cruel grumpiness. The crime rate is appalling. The greed and endless rivalry of the place become depressing after a day or two. The pervasive suggestion of sham and false intention sometimes becomes so overpowering that no face value seems acceptable, and even your dearest friend appears to have an ulterior motive, as he grips you by the arm and leads you off to a martini. This is a selfish city, in some ways a vicious one, where it is exceedingly foolish to walk across the park after dusk, and where even the nursing recruitment authorities can think of no more altruistic slogan than "Learn to take care of others, and you will know how to take care of yourself."

But what can you expect? New York is, *par excellence,* the city acquisitive, and though marvellous incidentals have sprung from the aspiration, nevertheless most of her citizens came here in the first place to get rich—to be free too, of course, but preferably rich as well. Whatever her discontents complain about, they do not often reject the system that raised these skyscrapers with such lovely arrogance into the clouds. Even the poorest layabout likes to boast of the wealth of New York, and even the laziest striking longshoreman seldom seems to reject the proposition that if ya don't wanta get on, move over, and make way for a guy who does.

New York is a hard city perhaps, but always extraordinary, like the Jews who have made her what she is, and leaving her is like retreating from a snow summit. When you drive back along that turnpike the very air seems to relax about you, as you re-acclimatize yourself to a lower plane. The electric atmosphere softens, the noise stills, the colours blur and fade, the pressure eases, the traffic reluctantly thins. Soon you are out of the city's spell, only pausing to look behind, over the tenements and marshes, to see the lights of the skyscrapers riding the night.

Edmund Wilson

Miami

Cotton Blossom Express: I went to sleep in the winter darkness, and wake up to a dazzle of golden light on green palms and low-growing pines that drip with Florida moss. An extraordinary pageant of bird-life presents itself outside the window: snowy egrets, several kinds of heron—some bluish, some beige—and other darker long-winged birds that I take to be buzzards—all looking as if they had flown straight out of Audubon: how excited he must have been when he came here. There are also some smaller birds that fly in flocks with quick twinkling wingbeats, and one experiences a pleasure that has something in common with the pleasure derived from music in following the contrasts of tempo between these and the slower rhythms of the larger birds that hover. They all fly quite close to the train and not far from the endless pale swamps and plains. It is wonderful to watch an egret alighting and folding its wings, deliberately, with dignity and grace.

Miami: I have never been here before and am astounded and appalled by this place. It is not that it is particularly different from other American seaside resorts, from Asbury Park to Coronado Beach, but that here both the cheap and the expensive aspects have been developed on a scale that I have never elsewhere seen equaled. You have acres of nougat-like shops, mountain ranges of vanilla ice-cream hotels. Miami Beach goes on for miles, with its monotonous lines of palms, its thousands of hotels and houses which seem to have had imposed on them, by the exigency of a city-planning board, a blanched and insipid uniformity. It even makes one feel more kindly toward Southern California, with its elements of lunatic fantasy. What draws people down to this vacuum? How do they amuse themselves here?

These vacationists look soft and vapid. You rarely see a really pretty girl, and the men do not give the impression of doing much fishing or swimming. You find them at the movies in the evening. The American ideal of luxury is in Miami carried to lengths that I have never encountered before. At my hotel, I had the annoyance of removing encasements of cellophane from the toilet seat and the drinking tumbler. In the movie-house, the seats are the kind that swing noiselessly back and forth to let people get in and out, and their cushions melt beneath one like a featherbed. A subdued indirect lighting, like the sweet creamy liquid of an ice-cream soda, bathes a dove-gray and shrimp-pink interior, the walls of which are ornamented with large cameo-like white seashells framing naked mythological figures that seem to have been badly imitated from the bas-reliefs of Paul Manship in Rockefeller Center, and with branching white plaster exfoliations that remind one of the legs and defensive antennae of the crawfish in the Miami aquarium. The film—*Oh, You Beautiful Doll*—was a technicolor that covered the whole surface of a high and overpowering screen with a routine sentimental romance, trumped up to manufacture glamor from the career of an

From *Red, Black, Blond and Olive,* by Edmund Wilson (Oxford Press, 1956). Reprinted by permission of Edmund Wilson.

31

American song-writer whose songs were widely sung in my college days. They were commonplace enough then, and today they are simply sickly. These attempts on the part of Hollywood to exploit the immediate past—in which the fashions of the eighties and nineties are sometimes confused with those of the twenties—show the precipitous decline of the movies as purveyors of entertainment, since the producers, after wrecking such contemporary talent as their salaries have tempted to Hollywood, have now been obliged to fall back on the favorites, first, second or third rate, of the day before yesterday and yesterday, when it was possible for a producer or an actor, a composer or a dancer, to perfect an art of his own and create for himself a reputation. Yet this product has its steady customers: one finds oneself among them here. Comfortably padded in the muffled atmosphere that seems to smell of scented face-powder—one cannot tell whether the theater has been perfumed or the women are all using the same cosmetics—this inert and featureless drove that have been drifting through the bleached sunny streets now sit watching stereotyped characters that are made to appear impressive by being photographed in very bright colors and gigantically magnified. The three shorts that follow the first showing of the film all happen to deal with animals: a hunting number, an animated cartoon that gets some not ill-deserved laughs, and a picture about racing whippets. The commentator seems slightly embarrassed at the spectacle of the uniformed attendants who have a full-time job grooming the whippets. "You may think they work as hard as the dogs," he propounds, with his microphone emphasis that gropes through time and space and can never drive any nails. "Well, they work a lot *harder!*" The truth is that so many Americans, specialized in operating machines or in transacting long-distance business, have deteriorated as animal organisms, that we now have a special pleasure in watching almost any agile animal. What the audience gets out of these animal shorts is the same thing that I have been getting out of looking out the window at the birds and contrasting them with the Miami vacationers.

This is all the kind of thing, I realize, that strikes foreigners who visit this country, but that I have long ago arranged my life in such a way as to avoid or ignore, so that I am likely to be shocked by and to discount the uncomplimentary reports of visitors. Miami is a rude revelation: I had not really known this was going on. I read uneasily of President Truman's recent arrival in Florida for one of a long series of sunlit holidays. This is the place where he seems most at home. It is only when I get to the airfield that my national self-respect picks up. It is a feat to have conceived, to have built and to navigate these passenger planes. We humans have contrived our wings by deliberate calculations, out of inorganic materials, instead of growing them out of our bodies, and this does leave us less hardy than the buzzard, less graceful than the white egret; but we have, after all, by our planes, in other ways surpassed the birds, and there had been moments in Miami when I was doubtful of that before I took off for Haiti. And those disparate rhythms of flight that I found so delightful to watch, Walt Disney, in his film *Snow White,* where deer and rabbits and other animals are shown running together at different speeds and gaits, has rendered them for the first time in plastic art. The multiplied drawings of the studio that turns out the Disney cartoons are as anonymous as the hundreds of parts that go to make up a plane. I couldn't myself have invented the simplest of these mechanisms or processes; but the current prestige of the United States is partly derived from these, and I cannot help feeling a pride in them.

Miguel de Unamuno

Large and Small Towns

I regret that I have not by me a certain essay dealing with this subject by Guglielmo Ferrero. I read it in some review the name of which I have forgotten, but I preserve a clear recollection of it, for it interested me greatly. Ferrero treated the subject from the historical and sociological point of view, and I, who am neither an historian nor a sociologist, intend to treat it, as is my custom, from the point of view of purely personal opinion and individual impression. (This is my custom, and yet in spite of the fact I cannot prevent people from insisting on calling me a savant and talking about my theories. I have no theories. I have only impressions and sensations.)

But, since I am unable to put some quotation from Ferrero at the head of this essay—this habit of basing our assertions upon authority is the conventional way of giving them a deceptive air of objectivity—I will head it by a sentence from George Meredith, that extremely subtle English novelist. In *The Egoist* it is stated that Willoughby "abandoned London as the burial-place of the individual man."

I, to-day, am one with Willoughby in believing that great cities de-individualize, or rather de-personalize, us. This may perhaps be due to the fact that, though not an egoist like the hero of Meredith's novel, I still remain, according to Ramiro de Maeztu, an incorrigible egotist.

Great cities are levelling; they lift up the low and depress the high; they exalt mediocrity and abase superlativeness—the result of the action of the mass, as powerful in social life as in chemistry.

Soon after I came to this ancient city of Salamanca which has now become so dear to me, a city of some thirty thousand souls, I wrote to a friend and told him that if after two years' residence here he should be informed that I spent my time playing cards, taking siestas and strolling round the square for a couple of hours every day, he might give me up for lost; but if at the end of that time I should

From *Essays and Soliloquies,* by Miguel de Unamuno, translated and with an Introductory Essay by J. E. Crawford Flitch. Copyright 1924 by Alfred A. Knopf, Inc. Reprinted by permission of Alfred A. Knopf, Inc.

still be studying, meditating, writing, battling for culture in the public arena, he might take it that I was better off here than in Madrid. And so it has proved to be.

I remember that Guglielmo Ferrero's conclusion, based upon a review of ancient Greece, of the Italy of the Renaissance and of the Germany of a century ago, is that for the life of the spirit, small cities of a population like that of Salamanca are the best—better than very small towns or large ones of over a hundred thousand inhabitants.

This depends, of course, upon the quality of the spirit in question. I am convinced that the monastic cloister, which so often atrophies the soul and reduces the average intelligence to a lamentable slavery to routine, has in certain exceptional cases exalted the spirit by its arduous discipline.

Great cities are essentially democratic, and I must confess that I feel an invincible platonic mistrust of democracies. In great cities culture is diffused but vulgarized. People abandon the quiet reading of books to go to the theatre, that school of vulgarity; they feel the need of being together; the gregarious instinct enslaves them; they must be seeing one another.

I think it was Taine who observed that the majority of French geniuses were either themselves country-born or the sons of country-born parents. And I assure you that I should find it difficult to believe in the genius of a Parisian born of Parisians.

Guerra Junqueiro said to me: "You are fortunate in living in a city in which you can walk along the streets dreaming, without fear of people disturbing your dream!" And certainly in Madrid it is impossible to walk along the streets dreaming, not so much for fear of motors, trams and carriages as because of the continual stream of unknown faces. The distraction of a great city, so agreeable to those who must have something, no matter what, to occupy their imagination, is necessarily vexatious to those whose chief concern is not to have their imagination diverted. Personally I find nothing more monotonous than a Paris boulevard. The people seem to me like shadows. I cannot endure a crowd of unknown faces.

I am afraid of Madrid. That is to say, I am afraid of myself when I go there. It is easy to say that in great cities everyone can live the life that suits him best, but it is easier to say it than to do it. When I am in the capital, I return home every night regretting having gone to the party or to the meeting that I went to and resolving never to go again, but only to break my vow the very next day. I am surrounded, hemmed in and invaded by a lethal atmosphere of compliance, an atmosphere that is generated by this so-called life of society.

I have always felt an aversion from this so-called life of society, which has for its object the cultivation of social relationships. Is there anything more terrible than a "call"? It affords an occasion for the exchange of the most threadbare commonplaces. Calls and the theatre are the two great centres for the propagation of platitudes.

A man of society, a drawing-room man who can make himself agreeable to women when he pays a call, is always a man whose principal concern is to suppress any arresting spontaneity, not to let his own personality show through. For it is a man's own personality that people find irritating. People like to meet the average man, the normal man, the man who has nothing exceptional about him. The exception is always irritating. How many times I have heard the terrible phrase: "This man irritates me." Yes, it is "the man" that irritates, and the hardest fight for the man who feels that he is a man is the fight to win respect for his own individuality.

And in a small town? Its stage is very restricted; the players soon tire of playing the parts allotted to them and the real men begin to appear underneath, with all their weaknesses—that is to say, with precisely that which makes them men. I have a great liking for provincial life, for there it is easiest to discern tragedy lurking beneath an appearance of calm. And just as much as I abhor comedy, I love tragedy. And, above all, tragi-comedy.

I have heard it said that there are no such seething intestine rancours and dissensions as in a merchant vessel or a monastery; that whenever men are obliged to live together, cut off from the rest of the world, their personalities, their most real and intimate selves, immediately clash against one another. And I dare say that this is the only way of attaining that knowledge of ourselves which ought to be our chief aim. It seems to me scarcely possible that a man should get to know himself by shutting himself up in the wilderness, contemplating—what? The best way of knowing one's self is to clash, heart against heart, that is to say, rock against rock, with one's fellow.

I know that I shall be told that I am indulging my love of paradox, but nevertheless I maintain that if it is true that the most ardent admirations are those which are disguised in the form of envy, very often the strongest attractions are those which take the appearance of hate. In one of these tragi-comic, or rather comi-tragic, small towns I know two men who, though obliged to see one another constantly in the way of business, never greet one another in the street and profess a mutual detestation. Nevertheless at bottom they feel themselves reciprocally attracted to one another and each one is continually preoccupied by the other.

These irreconcilable feuds into which small towns are so often divided are much more favourable to the development of strong personalities than the bland comedy of a great metropolis, where those who fight a duel to the death on the public stage embrace one another behind the scenes. Do you suppose that the tragedy of Romeo and Juliet is possible in a city that counts its inhabitants by the million?

And I ask you, do you suppose that anyone who sees a multitude of people in the course of the day, listens to this man to-day, to another man to-morrow and to another man the day after, and attends twenty or thirty conferences—do you think that such a one can preserve his spiritual integrity without any leakage? In such a life a hedgehog would end by becoming a lamb, its quills would turn into softest fleece, and for my part I would rather be a hedgehog than a lamb.

I understand why Willoughby fled from London as from the burial-place of the individual man. Is it not a terrible thing to walk through two or three miles of city streets and pass two or three thousand people without meeting a single known face to set a spark to a train of human thought? A glance of hate from a known enemy is sweeter than a glance of indifference, if not of disdain, from an unknown stranger. For man has acquired the habit of disdaining those whom he does not know, and seems to suppose that every stranger must be presumed to be an imbecile until he proves himself otherwise.

And those who say that they are bored in a small town? The reason is because they have not dug down to its tragic roots, to the august severity of the depths of its monotony.

It is my belief that in great cities proud natures become vain, that is to say, the quills become fleece.

And for the man who is engaged in any kind of work in which he can exercise his influence from a distance, for the writer or the painter, the small town offers the inestimable advantage of enabling him to live far from his public and of its being possible that the effects which his work produces either do not reach him or reach him only after a searching process of filtration. He can live more or less independently of his public, without allowing himself to be influenced by it, and this is the only way of making a public for oneself instead of adapting oneself to it.

If this be the case, it may be urged that a village would be better than a small town, a hamlet or perhaps even a remote farmhouse. But no, for then there would be lacking that minimum of organic society without which our personality runs as much risk as it runs in the heart of a metropolis.

Essentially, in the sphere of psychologico-sociological relations—this is for the benefit of those who insist on labelling me savant—it is a question of what is perhaps the most fundamental of all problems, the problem of maxima and minima. This is the problem that is the nerve of physical mechanics and the nerve also of social mechanics or economics. The problem always is how to obtain the maximum result or profit with the minimum effort or expense, the largest return with the least expenditure. It is also the fundamental problem of aesthetics; it is at the root of all the problems of life.

And with regard to the subject I am now considering, it is a question of obtaining the maximum of our own personality with the minimum of others' society. Less society, or a society less complex, would diminish our personality, and so also would more society, or a society apparently more complex. And I say apparently, for I am not aware that an elephant is more complex than a fox.

Very well then—he who has no sense of his own personality and is willing to sacrifice it on the altar of sociability, let him go and lose himself among the millions of a metropolis. For the man who has a longing for Nirvana the metropolis is better than the desert. If you want to submerge your own "I," better the streets of a great city than the solitudes of the wilderness.

It is not a bad thing now and again to visit the great city and plunge into the sea of its crowds, but in order to emerge again upon terra firma and feel the solid ground under one's feet. For my part, since I am interested in individuals—in John and Peter and Richard, in you who are reading this book—but not in the masses which they form when banded together, I remain in the small town, seeing every day at the same hour the same men, men whose souls have clashed, and sometimes painfully, with my soul; and I flee from the great metropolis where my soul is whipped with the icy whips of the disdainful glances of those who know me not and who are unknown to me. People whom I cannot name . . . horrible!

EXPOSITION AND ARGUMENT

John Stuart Mill

The Principle of Contradiction

There is a class of persons (happily not quite so numerous as formerly) who think it enough if a person assents undoubtingly to what they think true, though he has no knowledge whatever of the grounds of the opinion, and could not make a tenable defence of it against the most superficial objections. Such persons, if they can once get their creed taught from authority, naturally think that no good, and some harm, comes of its being allowed to be questioned. Where their influence prevails, they make it nearly impossible for the received opinion to be rejected wisely and considerately, though it may still be rejected rashly and ignorantly; for to shut out discussion entirely is seldom possible, and when it once gets in, beliefs not grounded on conviction are apt to give way before the slightest semblance of an argument. Waiving, however, this possibility—assuming that the true opinion abides in the mind, but abides as a prejudice, a belief independent of, and proof against, argument—this is not the way in which truth ought to be held by a rational being. This is not knowing the truth. Truth, thus held, is but one superstition the more, accidentally clinging to the words which enunciate a truth.

If the intellect and judgment of mankind ought to be cultivated . . . on what can these faculties be more appropriately exercised by any one, than on the things which concern him so much that it is considered necessary for him to hold opinions on them? If the cultivation of the understanding consists in one thing more than in another, it is surely in learning the grounds of one's own opinions. Whatever people believe, on subjects on which it is of the first importance to believe rightly, they ought to be able to defend against at least the common objections. But, some one may say, "Let them be *taught* the grounds of their

From *On Liberty* by John Stuart Mill.

opinions. It does not follow that opinions must be merely parroted because they are never heard controverted. Persons who learn geometry do not simply commit the theorems to memory, but understand and learn likewise the demonstrations; and it would be absurd to say that they remain ignorant of the grounds of geometrical truths, because they never hear any one deny, and attempt to disprove them." Undoubtedly: and such teaching suffices on a subject like mathematics, where there is nothing at all to be said on the wrong side of the question. The peculiarity of the evidence of mathematical truths is, that all the argument is on one side. There are no objections, and no answers to objections. But on every subject on which difference of opinion is possible, the truth depends on a balance to be struck between two sets of conflicting reasons. Even in natural philosophy, there is always some other explanation possible of the same facts; some geocentric theory instead of heliocentric, some phlogiston instead of oxygen; and it has to be shown why that other theory cannot be the true one: and until this is shown and until we know how it is shown, we do not understand the grounds of our opinion. But when we turn to subjects infinitely more complicated, to morals, religion, politics, social relations, and the business of life, three-fourths of the arguments for every disputed opinion consist in dispelling the appearances which favor some opinion different from it. The greatest orator, save one, of antiquity, has left it on record that he always studied his adversary's case with as great, if not with still greater, intensity than even his own. What Cicero practised as the means of forensic success, requires to be imitated by all who study any subject in order to arrive at the truth. He who knows only his own side of the case, knows little of that. His reasons may be good, and no one may have been able to refute them. But if he is equally unable to refute the reasons on the opposite side; if he does not so much as know what they are, he has no ground for preferring either opinion. The rational position for him would be suspension of judgment, and unless he contents himself with that, he is either led by authority, or adopts, like the generality of the world, the side to which he feels most inclination. Nor is it enough that he should hear the arguments of adversaries from his own teachers, presented, as they state them, and accompanied by what they offer as refutations. This is not the way to do justice to the arguments, or bring them into real contact with his own mind. He must be able to hear them from persons who actually believe them; who defend them in earnest, and do their very utmost for them. He must know them in their most plausible and persuasive form; he must feel the whole force of the difficulty which the true view of the subject has to encounter and dispose of, else he will never really possess himself of the portion of truth which meets and removes that difficulty. Ninety-nine in a hundred of what are called educated men are in this condition, even of those who can argue fluently for their opinions. Their conclusion may be true, but it might be false for anything they know: they have never thrown themselves into the mental position of those who think differently from them, and considered what such persons may have to say; and consequently they do not, in any proper sense of the word, know the doctrine which they themselves profess. They do not know those parts of it which explain and justify the remainder; the considerations which show that a fact which seemingly conflicts with another is reconcilable with it, or that, of two apparently strong reasons, one and not the other ought to be preferred. All that part of the truth which turns the scale, and decides the judgment of a completely informed mind, they are strangers to; nor is it ever really known, but to those who have attended equally and impartially to both sides, and endeavored to see the reasons of both in the strongest light. So essential is this discipline to a real understanding of moral and human subjects, that if opponents of all important truths do not exist, it is indispensable to imagine them and supply them with the strongest arguments which the most skilful devil's advocate can conjure up.

To abate the force of these considerations, an enemy of free discussion may be supposed to say, that there is no necessity for mankind in general to know and understand all that can be said against or for their opinions by philosophers and theologians. That it is not needful for common men to be able to expose all the mistatements or fallacies of an ingenious opponent. That it is enough if there is always somebody capable of answering them, so that nothing likely to mislead uninstructed persons remains unrefuted. That simple minds, having been taught the obvious grounds of the truths inculcated on them, may trust to authority for the rest, and being aware that they have neither knowledge nor talent to resolve every difficulty which can be raised, may repose in the assurance that all those which have been raised have been or can be answered, by those who are specially trained to the task.

Conceding to this view of the subject the utmost that can be claimed for it by those most easily satisfied with the amount of understanding of truth which ought to accompany the belief of it; even so, the argument for free discussion is no way weakened. For even this doctrine acknowledges that mankind ought to have a rational assurance that all objections have been satisfactorily answered; and how are they to be answered if that which requires to be answered is not spoken? Or how can the answer be known to be satisfactory, if the objectors have no opportunity of showing that it is unsatisfactory? If not the public, at least the philosophers and theologians who are to resolve the difficulties, must make themselves familiar with those difficulties in their most puzzling form; and this cannot be accomplished unless they are freely stated, and placed in the most advantageous light which they admit of. . . .

If, however, the mischievous operation of the absence of free discussion, when the received opinions are true, were confined to leaving men ignorant of the grounds of those opinions, it might be thought that this, if an intellectual, is no moral evil, and does not affect the worth of the opinions, regarded in their influence on the character. The fact, however, is, that not only the grounds of the opinion are forgotten in the absence of discussion, but too often the meaning of the opinion itself. The words which convey it, cease to suggest ideas, or suggest only a small portion of those they were originally employed to communicate. Instead of a vivid conception and a living belief, there remain only a few phrases retained by rote; or, if any part, the shell and husk only of the meaning is retained, the finer essence being lost. The great chapter in human history which this fact occupies and fills, cannot be too earnestly studied and meditated on.

It is illustrated in the experience of almost all ethical doctrines and religious creeds. They are all full of meaning and vitality to those who originate them, and to the direct disciples of the originators. Their meaning continues to be felt in undiminished strength, and is perhaps brought out into even fuller consciousness, so long as the struggle lasts to give the doctrine or creed an ascendancy over other creeds. At last it either prevails, and becomes the general opinion, or its progress stops; it keeps possession of the ground it has gained, but ceases to spread further. When either of these results has become apparent, controversy on the subject flags, and gradually dies away. The doctrine has taken its place, if not as a received opinion, as one of the admitted sects or divisions of opinion: those who hold it have generally inherited, not adopted it; and conversion from one of these doctrines to another, being now an exceptional fact, occupies little place in the thoughts of their professors. Instead of being, as at first, constantly on the alert either to defend themselves against the world, or to bring the world over to them, they have subsided into acquiescence, and neither listen, when they can help it, to arguments against their creed, nor trouble dissentients (if there be such) with arguments in its favor. From this time may usually be dated the decline in the living power of the doctrine. . . .

[This] holds true, generally speaking, of all traditional doctrines—those of prudence and knowledge of life, as well as of morals or religion. All languages and literatures are full of general observations on life, both as to what it is, and how to conduct oneself in it; observations which everybody knows, which everybody repeats, or hears with acquiescence, which are received as truisms, yet of which most people first truly learn the meaning, when experience, generally of a painful kind, has made it a reality to them. How often, when smarting under some unforeseen misfortune or disappointment, does a person call to mind some proverb or common saying familiar to him all his life, the meaning of which, if he had ever before felt it as he does now, would have saved him from the calamity. There are indeed reasons for this, other than the absence of discussion; there are many truths of which the full meaning *cannot* be realized, until personal experience has brought it home. But much more of the meaning even of these would have been understood, and what was understood would have been far more deeply impressed on the mind, if the man had been accustomed to hear it argued *pro* and *con* by people who did understand it. The fatal tendency of mankind to leave off thinking about a thing when it is no longer doubtful is the cause of half their errors. A contemporary author has well spoken of "the deep slumber of a decided opinion."

But what! (it may be asked) Is the absence of unanimity an indispensable condition of true knowledge? Is it necessary that some part of mankind should persist in error, to enable any to realize the truth? Does a belief cease to be real and vital as soon as it is generally received—and is a proposition never thoroughly understood and felt unless some doubt of it remains? As soon as mankind have unanimously accepted a truth, does the truth perish within them? The highest aim and best result of improved intelligence, it has hitherto been thought, is to unite mankind more and more in the acknowledgment of all important truths: and does the intelligence only last as long as it has not achieved its object? Do the fruits of conquest perish by the very completeness of the victory?

I affirm no such thing. As mankind improve, the number of doctrines which are no longer disputed or doubted will be constantly on the increase: and the well-being of mankind may almost be measured by the number and gravity of the truths which have reached the point of being uncontested. The cessation, on one question after another, of serious controversy, is one of the necessary incidents of the consolidation of opinion; a consolidation as salutary in the case of true opinions, as it is dangerous and noxious when the opinions are erroneous. But though this gradual narrowing of the bounds of diversity of opinion is necessary in both senses of the term, being at once inevitable and indispensable, we are not therefore obliged to conclude that all its consequences must be beneficial. The loss of so important an aid to the intelligent and living apprehension of a truth, as is afforded by the necessity of explaining it to, or defending it against, opponents, though not sufficient to outweigh, is no trifling drawback from, the benefit of its universal recognition. Where this advantage can no longer be had, I confess I should like to see the teachers of mankind endeavoring to provide a substitute for it; some contrivance for making the difficulties of the question as present to the learner's consciousness, as if they were pressed upon him by a dissentient champion, eager for his conversion.

But instead of seeking contrivances for this purpose, they have lost those they formerly had. The Socratic dialectics, so magnificently exemplified in the dialogues of Plato, were a contrivance of this description. They were essentially a negative discussion of the great questions of philosophy and life, directed with consummate skill to the purpose of convincing any one who had merely adopted the commonplaces of received opinion, that he did not understand the subject— that he as yet attached no definite meaning to the doctrines he professed; in order that, becoming aware of his ignorance, he might be put in the way to attain a stable belief, resting on a clear apprehension both of the meaning of doctrines and of their evidence. The school disputations of the Middle Ages had a somewhat similar object. They were intended to make sure that the pupil understood his own opinion, and (by necessary correlation) the opinion opposed to it, and could enforce the grounds of the one and confute those of the other. These last-mentioned contests had indeed the incurable defect, that the premises appealed to were taken from authority, not from reason; and, as a discipline to the mind, they were in every respect inferior to the powerful dialectics which formed the intellects of the "Socratici viri": but the modern mind owes far more to both than it is generally willing to admit, and the present modes of education contain nothing which in the smallest degree supplies the place either of the one or of the other. A person who derives all his instruction from teachers or books, even if he escape the besetting temptation of contenting himself with cram, is under no compulsion to hear both sides; accordingly it is far from a frequent accomplishment, even among thinkers, to know both sides; and the weakest part of what everybody says in defence of his opinion, is what he intends as a reply to antagonists. It is the fashion of the present time to disparage negative logic—that which points out weaknesses in theory or errors in practise, without establishing positive truths. Such negative criticism would indeed be poor enough as an ultimate result; but as a means to attaining any positive knowledge or conviction worthy the name, it cannot be valued too highly; and until people are again systematically trained to it, there will be few great thinkers, and a low general average of intellect, in any but the mathematical and physical departments of speculation.

On any other subject no one's opinions deserve the name of knowledge, except so far as he has either had forced upon him by others, or gone through of himself, the same mental process which would have been required of him in carrying on an active controversy with opponents. That, therefore, which when absent, it is so indispensable, but so difficult, to create, how worse than absurd is it to forego, when spontaneously offering itself! If there are any persons who contest a received opinion, or who will do so if law or opinion will let them, let us thank them for it, open our minds to listen to them, and rejoice that there is some one to do for us what we otherwise ought, if we have any regard for either the certainty or the vitality of our convictions, to do with much greater labor for ourselves.

A. E. Housman

Knowledge

The acquisition of knowledge needs no [formal] justification: its true sanction is a much simpler affair, and inherent in itself. People are too prone to torment themselves with devising far-fetched reasons: they cannot be content with the simple truth asserted by Aristotle: "all men possess by nature a craving for knowledge." πάντες ἄνθρωποι τοῦ εἰδέναι ὀρέγονται ϕύσει. This is no rare endowment scattered sparingly from heaven that falls on a few heads and passes others by: curiosity, the desire to know things as they are, is a craving no less native to the being of man, no less universal through mankind, than the craving for food and drink. And do you suppose that such a desire means nothing? The very definition of the good, says Aristotle again, is that which all desire. Whatever is pleasant is good, unless it can be shewn that in the long run it is harmful, or, in other words, not pleasant but unpleasant. [Herbert] Spencer himself on another subject speaks thus: "So profound an ignorance is there of the laws of life, that men do not even know that their sensations are their natural guides, and (when not rendered morbid by long continued disobedience) their trustworthy guides." The desire of knowledge does not need,

From *Introductory Lecture*, by A. E. Housman. Published, 1937, by Cambridge University Press and reprinted by their permission.

nor could it possibly possess, any higher or more authentic sanction than the happiness which attends its gratification.

Perhaps it will be objected that we see, every day of our lives, plenty of people who exhibit no pleasure in learning and experience no desire to know; people, as Plato agreeably puts it, who wallow in ignorance with the complacency of a brutal hog. We do; and here is the reason. If the cravings of hunger and thirst are denied satisfaction, if a man is kept from food and drink, the man starves to death, and there is an end of him. This is a result which arrests the attention of even the least observant mind; so it is generally recognised that hunger and thirst cannot be neglected with impunity, that a man ought to eat and drink. But if the craving for knowledge is denied satisfaction, the result which follows is not so striking to the eye. The man, worse luck, does not starve to death. He still preserves the aspect and motions of a living human being; so people think that the hunger and thirst for knowledge can be neglected with impunity. And yet, though the man does not die altogether, part of him dies, part of him starves to death: as Plato says, he never attains completeness and health, but walks lame to the end of his life and returns imperfect and good for nothing to the world below.

But the desire of knowledge, stifle it though you may, is none the less originally born with every man; and nature does not implant desires in us for nothing, nor endow us with faculties in vain. "Sure," says Hamlet,

> Sure, He that made us with such large discourse,
> Looking before and after, gave us not
> That capability and godlike reason
> To fust in us unused.

The faculty of learning is ours that we may find in its exercise that delight which arises from the unimpeded activity of any energy in the groove nature meant it to run in. Let a man acquire knowledge not for this or that external and incidental good which may chance to result from it, but for itself; not because it is useful or ornamental, but because it is knowledge, and therefore good for man to acquire. "Brothers," says Ulysses in Dante, when with his old and tardy companions he had left Seville on the right hand and Ceuta on the other, and was come to that narrow pass where Hercules assigned his landmarks to hinder man from venturing farther: "Brothers, who through a hundred thousand dangers have reached the West, deny not, to this brief vigil of your senses that remains, experience of the unpeopled world behind the sunset. Consider of what seed ye are sprung: ye were not formed to live like brutes, but to follow virtue and knowledge." For knowledge resembles virtue in this, and differs from other possessions, that it is not merely a means of procuring good, but is good in itself simply: it is not a coin which we pay down to purchase happiness, but has happiness indissolubly bound up with it. Fortitude and continence and honesty are not commended to us on the ground that they conduce, as on the whole they do conduce, to material success, nor yet on the ground that they will be rewarded hereafter: those whose office it is to exhort mankind to virtue are ashamed to degrade the cause they plead by proffering such lures as these. And let us too disdain to take lower ground in commending knowledge: let us insist that the pursuit of knowledge, like the pursuit of righteousness, is part of a man's duty to himself; and remember the Scripture where it is written: "He that refuseth instruction despiseth his own soul."

I will not say, as Professor Tyndall has somewhere said, that all happiness belongs to him who can say from his heart "I covet truth." Entire happiness is not attainable either by this or by any other method. Nay it may be urged on the contrary that the pursuit of truth in some directions is even injurious to happiness, because it compels us to take leave of delusions which were pleasant while they lasted. It may be urged that the light shed on the origin and destiny of man by the pursuit of truth in some directions is not altogether a cheerful light. It may be urged that man stands to-day in the position of one who has been reared from his cradle as the child of a noble race and the heir to great possessions, and who finds at his coming of age that he has been deceived alike as to his origin and his expectations; that he neither springs from the high lineage he fancied, nor will inherit the vast estate he looked for, but must put off his towering pride, and contract his boundless hopes, and begin the world anew from a lower level: and this, it may be urged, comes of pursuing knowledge. But even conceding this, I suppose the answer to be that knowledge, and especially disagreeable knowledge, cannot by any art be totally excluded even from those who do not seek it. Wisdom, said Aeschylus long ago, comes to men whether they will or no. The house of delusions is cheap to build, but draughty to live in, and ready at any instant to fall; and it is surely truer prudence to move our furniture betimes into the open air than to stay indoors until our tenement tumbles about our ears. It is and it must in the long run be better for a man to see things as they are than to be ignorant of them; just as there is less fear of stumbling or of striking against corners in the daylight than in the dark.

Nor again will I pretend that, as Bacon asserts, "the pleasure and delight of knowledge and learning far surpasseth all other in nature." This is too much the language of a salesman crying his own wares. The pleasures of the intellect are notoriously less vivid than either the pleasures of sense or the pleasures of the affections; and therefore, especially in the season of youth, the pursuit of knowledge is likely enough to be neglected and lightly esteemed in comparison with other pursuits offering much stronger immediate attractions. But the pleasure of learning and knowing, though not the keenest, is yet the least perishable of pleasures; the least subject to external things, and the play of chance, and the wear of time. And as a prudent man puts money by to serve as a provision for the material wants of his old age, so too he needs to lay up against the end of his days provision for the intellect. As the years go by, comparative values are found to alter: Time, says Sophocles, takes many things which once were pleasures and brings them nearer to pain. In the day when the strong men shall bow themselves, and desire shall fail, it will be a matter of yet more concern than now, whether one can say "my mind to me a kingdom is"; and whether the windows of the soul look out upon a broad and delightful landscape, or face nothing but a brick wall.

Well then, once we have recognised that knowledge in itself is good for man, we shall need to invent no pretexts for studying this subject or that; we shall import no extraneous considerations of use or ornament to justify us in learning one thing rather than another. If a certain department of knowledge specially attracts a man, let him study that, and study it because it attracts him; and let him not fabricate excuses for that which requires no excuse, but rest assured that the reason why it most attracts him is that it is best for him. The majority of mankind, as is only natural, will be most attracted by those sciences which most nearly concern human life; those sciences which, in Bacon's phrase, are drenched in flesh and blood, or, in the more elegant language of the Daily Telegraph, palpitate with actuality. The men who are attracted to the drier and the less palpitating sciences, say logic or pure mathematics or textual criticism, are likely to be fewer in number; but they are not to suppose that the comparative unpopularity of such learning renders it any the less worthy of pursuit. Nay they may if they like console themselves with Bacon's observation that "this same *lumen siccum*[1] doth parch and offend most men's watery and soft natures," and infer, if it pleases them, that their natures are less soft and watery than other men's. But be that as it may, we can all dwell together in unity without crying up our own pursuits or depreciating the pursuits of others on factitious grounds. We are not like the Ottoman sultans of old time, who thought they could never enjoy a moment's security till they had murdered all their brothers. There is no rivalry between the studies of Arts and Laws and Science but the rivalry of fellow-soldiers in striving which can most victoriously achieve the common end of all, to set back the frontier of darkness.

It is the glory of God, says Solomon, to conceal a thing: but the honour of kings is to search out a matter. Kings have long abdicated that province; and we students are come into their inheritance: it is our honour to search out the things which God has concealed. In Germany at Easter time they hide coloured eggs about the house and the garden that the children may amuse themselves in hunting after them and finding them. It is to some such game of hide-and-seek that we are invited by that power which planted in us the desire to find out what is concealed, and stored the universe with hidden things that we might delight ourselves in discovering them. And the pleasure of discovery differs from other pleasures in this, that it is shadowed by no fear of satiety on the one hand or of frustration on the other. Other desires perish in their gratification, but the desire of knowledge never: the eye is not satisfied with seeing nor the ear filled with hearing. Other desires become the occasion of pain through dearth of the material to gratify them, but not the desire of knowledge: the sum of things to be known is inexhaustible, and however long we read we shall never come to the end

[1] *Lumen siccum:* dry light.

of our story-book. So long as the mind of man is what it is, it will continue to exult in advancing on the unknown throughout the infinite field of the universe; and the tree of knowledge will remain for ever, as it was in the beginning, a tree to be desired to make one wise.

Howard Mumford Jones

Undergraduates on Apron Strings

I wish to argue an unpopular cause: the cause of the old, free elective system in the academic world, or the untrammeled right of the undergraduate to make his own mistakes. Doubtless my case is one-sided and prejudiced, though it seems to me the case for controlled education is equally one-sided; nor does the fact that controlled education is just now in the ascendant make the present system eternal. Doubtless also there was a vast deal of waste in the old system. But as I have seen no study of waste under the present controlled system, I am prepared to hazard the guess that the present philosophy, though it produces bright, interchangeable students in quantity with almost no pain, is not inevitably the philosophy of education that will preserve this republic unto the latest generation.

I take it everybody knows what is meant by the old, free elective system. It was common in American colleges and universities in the last decades of the nineteenth century, and it lasted into the twentieth. In its time it was heralded as a tremendous advance over an older form of educational control. Theoretically everything was wrong with it, if you are to believe the twentieth-century diagnosticians. It was, they pontificate, the quintessence of laissez faire. It encouraged individualism—rugged or otherwise. It let the student choose his courses and his instructors, something that he had come to college to do. It permitted the lazy man to be lazy and it permitted the student who had found, or thought he had found, his vocation, to concentrate on that vocation—that is, in the jargon of the present hour, to "narrow" his education by electing courses that seemed to him to fit his own particular case. The theory of the old, free elective system was a function of an obsolescent notion of the college and of the university, a notion advanced by Ezra Cornell, who wanted to found a university in which anybody could study anything. Nobody has ever made it clear to me why this idea is a product of the Old Nick himself.

Manifold objections were raised to the old, free elective system as practiced, for example, at Harvard under President Charles W. Eliot. It was argued that

Reprinted from *The Atlantic Monthly,* October, 1955. Copyright 1955 by Howard Mumford Jones and The Atlantic Monthly Company, Boston 16, Massachusetts. By permission.

when an undergraduate could choose chemistry for fourteen out of his sixteen courses required for the bachelor's degree, he was not receiving a proper education. Whether the youth in question was merely eccentric I do not know—he may have been a genius, though I do not see how the authorities could tell; and all I can say is that, if you put college credits aside and look at the thing in terms of self-development, he was following the path originally trodden by persons like Thomas A. Edison, Henry Ford, John Stuart Mill, and Napoleon. The last was so bored by ordinary courses he showed no ability at Brienne except in matters that had to do with his genius for war. I have sometimes speculated what another Napoleon or Edison would do in our carefully calculated courses in general education. Is it at all conceivable that in setting up these required patterns of instruction we are either postponing or obliterating the expression of talent? This is, of course, the century of the common man. But I wonder what Leonardo da Vinci would do in the century of the common man.

It is also argued that the old, free elective system was, as I have indicated, a godsend to the lazy. I do not dispute it. I only want to know what the lazy are doing in the present well-regulated systems of general education. Have they disappeared from the college campus? Are these courses—overviews of the history of Western Man, for the most part—so exciting that the lazy now automatically catch fire and kindle to intellectual challenge?

Am I to infer that pedagogical skill has so vastly increased, the lazy have ceased to be? I have lately been rereading Vincent Sheean's *Personal History,* including the wonderful passage in which he narrates how and why the University of Chicago taught him nothing in particular and taught it very well. But nobody later than Mr. Sheean seems to have confessed. All I know has to do with the complaints of English teachers about the indifference of students to ordinary requirements in prose.

Another customary charge against the old, free elective system is that it overcompensated the "popular" teacher and ignored the specialist who really knew. Perhaps it did. But has the situation altered under the present controlled system? As I watch the ebb and flow of enrollment in various courses nowadays, I wonder whether the world of the campus has changed. I seem to see, cynical fellow that I am, the same fashions at work—a surge into psychology or social anthropology, a surge into Russian, a surge into modern poetry. I see, or dream I see, the idols of the campus drawing their usual full houses while the classrooms of essential scholars have their modest quotas where the real work of the university is done. I venture to doubt that the "popular" teacher has somehow miraculously dissolved into the smooth, impersonal fabric of required courses in general education.

Products of the free elective system, graduating any year between 1895 and 1915 (my dates are approximate, or, as the New Critics would say, symbolical only), came into social or economic or cultural or political power in this republic some ten or twenty years after being graduated. They fought World War I. They carried forward the technological revolution that accompanied or followed that catastrophe. They were in the saddle during the administrations of Wilson, Harding, and Coolidge, and you can, if you like, say they are responsible for the twenties, for the stockmarket crash of 1929, and for a variety of other sins. Perhaps I have no defense. All I can murmur is that American literature, American art, American music, American science, and American technology came of age during this quarter-century; and though I am as ready as the next historian to admit that 1929 was a catastrophic year, I am not persuaded that the world-wide depression setting in at the end of the twenties was the direct result of the old, free elective system.

It is also argued that the free elective system did not produce an informed citizenry, aware of the glorious history of the United States, alert to the significance of Western culture, and alive to the philosophic values of democracy. I dare say some part of the charge is true. But as I think of the careers of Robert M. La Follette, Frederick Jackson Turner, Robert Morss Lovett, Edward A. Ross, Charles E. Merriam, Frank Norris, Albert Bushnell Hart, and a variety of other persons associated with education in those years, I wonder where these characters and others like them picked up their singular dedication to civic virtue, and I speculate also on the immaculate morality of American public life when, some twenty or twenty-five years from now, graduates of the present controlled theories of education shall have completed their labors in the way of loyalty oaths and filled all the key posts of the republic with pure and righteous men. I seem to recall that teachers such as Royce with his doctrine of loyalty to the Great Community, James with his philosophy of the average man trying it on, and Dewey with his notion that if you want democracy you begin with the young—I seem to recall, I say, that these gentlemen had a particular knowledge of the democratic process. It would be vulgar of me to say that a crisp version of this philosophy may be found on the postcard which said: "Live every day so that you can look any man in the face and tell him to go to hell." On this assumption Mr. Lincoln Steffens seemed to think that there was something to be said even for the corrupt political boss, and Reverend Walter Rauschenbusch seemed to believe there might be something that Christian ethics had to offer society. Nowadays we have the disciples of Freud and the neo-Calvinists.

II

Well, it may be asked, what have we substituted for the old, free elective system? The substitution is not altogether bad. We have many, many more undergraduates in our colleges than we had in 1880 or 1900, and we have to do something with them; otherwise they will be disappointed of a degree, and the consequences may be disastrous for college financing. And inasmuch as ours is an excessively mobile population, we have invented for education what we invented for industry—a beautiful system of interchangeable parts. You may start your education in California and finish it in North Carolina, but it will not be much of a jar as you move, say, from Stanford to Duke. If Harvard has courses in general education, so do several hundred other colleges. If Wisconsin has a student radio, so do scores of other universities. If Iowa has a student theater, so do Michigan, Yale, Texas, and, for all I know, The Greater Southwest Teachers College State University. The philosophy of rugged individualism, which in its time gave a unique flavor to the new Johns Hopkins University, has now so far passed from favor that when they instituted Brandeis University in Waltham, Massachusetts, they ignored the opportunity to make an institution dedicated to intellectual excitement and created a school as much like the other schools around it as they could.

Putting intellectual matters aside, I submit that the motto of our present prevailing system of interchangeable parts is "adjustment." The freshman "adjusts" to his college. The sophomore "adjusts" to his professors, and by and by the senior is supposed to "adjust" to the outside world, nobody asks why. I doubt that "adjustment" would have made much sense to Emerson or Thorstein Veblen or Edgar Allan Poe or John Sloan or Jonathan Edwards or Frank Lloyd Wright or Carlson of Chicago or Einstein of Princeton. In my observation the world adjusts to the genius, not the genius to the world; and if Woodrow Wilson was right in saying that the principal purpose of a liberal education is to enable you to know a good man when you see him, I doubt that psychological testing is a proper telescope. Of course it can be argued that the thousands who annually pass through the American college are not geniuses, and this is true. But what about the genius who would like to be trained in his calling? Are we keeping paths open for the lonely talents who really shape culture and who are not content to imitate culture in others? Or are we so universally bent on "adjustment," all in the interests of a smoothly running society, we propose to break or smother the John Reeds and the Thorstein Veblens before they develop into dangerous reds?

Adjustment operates, in the jargon of the day, on two levels: the intellectual and the personal. Intellectual adjustment begins as required courses for freshmen (and sometime sophomores) who have commonly just escaped from a good many required courses in the secondary school. And these required courses are the products of the kindest thoughts and a considerable administrative skill. Their instructors are hand-picked and, being selected, brood conscientiously over Great Books, The Development of Western Man, Humanism, and other well-meant exercises supposed to replace the old, pernicious survey course in English literature or the history of Europe. Commonly, however, inspection shows that the new required courses are simply the old courses blown up out of all manageable size. I may call them processing courses; and like all processing, they are directed at the average, the medium, the median, or the mean, whatever one's statistical philosophy devises. The difficulty is that in these enormous surveys instruction, like the radius vector of the planets, sweeps over equal areas in equal times. Meanwhile those who are not average are bored.

But the precious ointment in our sight is not intellectual adjustment but personal adjustment, and this is a sacred cause—so sacred that we have invented a weird and unique hierarchy of secular priests to see that the student forever "adjusts." There is on the face of the civilized globe no other group like it. We have deans, tutors, counselors, vocational guides, counselors on marriage, alumni advisers, medical men, and psychiatrists. We have orientation week, campus week, the reading period, religious retreats, and summer camps. I am not prepared to argue down the validity of any one of these inventions taken singly; all I am prepared to say is that, taken as a whole, they befog the idea that higher education is an intellectual exercise. Higher education becomes adjustment. And what these well-meant therapeutic devices do is to postpone decision-making. The symbol of this refusal to face the fact that in life as in war there are final occasions is the make-up examination.

Under the old, free elective system, when a youth went off to college, he went off to a mysterious place where he had to learn the rules by himself or suffer the consequences of not knowing them. This situation, however naïve in terms of "adjustment," had one big advantage: he was at last Away From Home. Going to college was like Bar Mitzvah in Hebrew tradition: once past it, you not only entered upon man's estate, but, moreover, there was no return. You had cut the leading strings; and the fiction of the nineties that pictures the Yale undergraduate with his bulldog and his pipe was true to the facts. Today we do not cut the leading strings, we merely lengthen them. It is not true that an American lad cannot make a significant mistake as a young collegian, but it is true to say that an entire battery of adjusters is happily at work to see that his mistakes shall never, never harm him. Mistakes should not be harmless. Experience, said Oscar Wilde, is the name we give to our mistakes. Take away the mistakes, and what good is the experience?

American college life is, or has become, a wan attempt to prolong adolescence as far as it can be stretched. If this seems excessive, look at any alumni reunion. To the intent of keeping the young idea in "adjustment" this regiment of supervisors dedicates a zealous professional activity. And their intent could not be more laudable. The intent is to promote the unalienable right to happiness. The intent is to do away with waste. The intent is, in the name of democracy, to see that the son or daughter of any or every taxpayer shall not fail. In order not to fail, the offspring must "get something" out of a college education. This, of course, puts an excessive strain upon the advisory staff, which forever demands more recruits, just as it puts an excessive strain upon the intellectual staff, and partly as a means of reducing this strain it has proved easier to channel young America into true and tried educational courses, usually set forth as required work in general education.

General education proves in fact to be a reduction in the classroom for average consumption of a certain average quantum of information about the behavior of Western Man. Why does this sort of thing represent an advance on my zealous scientific undergraduate who, inspired with enthusiasm for chemistry, took seven-eighths of his work in what he came to college to find out? I cheerfully grant that, however superior as a chemist, he may have been a poor citizen, but are we turning out better citizens? The hope of the republic rests upon an informed citizenry. All the investigations into the book-reading habits of Americans, college graduates included, reveal that the reading of books drops sharply at the school-leaving age, and that we read fewer books in proportion to our population than does any other nation of the West.

The ancient fable of Mark Hopkins on a log is only a fable, and I do not favor the log. But I do favor Mark Hopkins. That is to say, I think there is a good deal to be said for the lopsided zealot, on fire with fanatical enthusiasm for the first crusade, aerodynamics, quaternions, the Federal Reserve system, or the superiority of William Butler Yeats to all other recent poets. I do not expect him to transmit this enthusiasm to the sad average, but I should like to give him the opportunity to collogue with his younger kind. In Blake's words, the way to the palace of wisdom leads through excess. I suggest that our well-meant hope that waste may be reduced may mean that excellence is reduced also. I suggest that the purpose of an academic institution is, or ought to be, to produce men of singular and exceptional talent, not merely conformable citizens. I am not quite clear, and never have been, why everybody has to be exposed to equal parts of Euripides and Beethoven, the Middle Ages and modern times, biology and mathematics. Like Mr. James Thurber, all I could ever see in the microscope they gave me in botany was a reflection of my own eye.

But of course this is merely an exercise in dissent.

Robert Benchley

What College Did to Me

My College Education was no haphazard affair. My courses were all selected with a very definite aim in view, with a serious purpose in mind—no classes before eleven in the morning or after two-thirty in the afternoon, and nothing on Saturday at all. That was my slogan. On that rock was my education built.

As what is known as the Classical Course involved practically no afternoon laboratory work, whereas in the Scientific Course a man's time was never his own until four P.M. anyway, I went in for the classics. But only such classics as allowed for a good sleep in the morning. A man has his health to think of. There is such a thing as being a studying fool.

In my days (I was a classmate of the founder of the college) a student could elect to take any courses in the catalogue, provided no two of his choices came at the same hour. The only things he was not supposed to mix were Scotch and gin. This was known as the Elective System. Now I understand that the boys have to have, during the four years, at least three courses beginning with the same letter. This probably makes it very awkward for those who like to get away of a Friday afternoon for the weekend.

From *The Early Worm,* reprinted in *Inside Benchley,* by Robert Benchley. Copyright 1927 by Harper & Brothers. Reprinted by permission of Harper & Brothers.

Under the Elective System my schedule was somewhat as follows:

Mondays, Wednesdays and Fridays at 11:00:
  Botany 2a (The History of Flowers and Their Meaning)
Tuesdays and Thursdays at 11:00
  English 26 (The Social Life of the Minor Sixteenth-Century Poets)
Mondays, Wednesdays and Fridays at 12:00:
  Music 9 (History and Appreciation of the Clavichord)
Tuesdays and Thursdays at 12:00:
  German 12b (Early Minnesingers—Walter von Vogelweider, Ulric
  Glannsdorf and Freimann von Stremhofen. Their Songs and Times)
Mondays, Wednesdays and Fridays at 1:30:
  Fine Arts 6 (Doric Columns: Their Uses, History and Various
  Heights)
Tuesdays and Thursdays at 1:30:
  French 1c (Exceptions to the verb *être*)

This was, of course, just one year's work. The next year I followed these courses up with supplementary courses in the history of lace-making, Russian taxation systems before Catharine the Great, North American glacial deposits and Early Renaissance etchers.

This gave me a general idea of the progress of civilization and a certain practical knowledge which has stood me in good stead in thousands of ways since my graduation.

My system of studying was no less strict. In lecture courses I had my notebooks so arranged that one-half of the page could be devoted to drawings of five-pointed stars (exquisitely shaded), girls' heads, and tick-tack-toe. Some of the drawings in my economics notebook in the course on Early English Trade Winds were the finest things I have ever done. One of them was a whole tree (an oak) with every leaf in perfect detail. Several instructors commented on my work in this field.

These notes I would take home after the lecture, together with whatever supplementary reading the course called for. Notes and textbooks would then be placed on a table under a strong lamplight. Next came the sharpening of pencils, which would take perhaps fifteen minutes. I had some of the best sharpened pencils in college. These I placed on the table beside the notes and books.

At this point it was necessary to light a pipe, which involved going to the table where the tobacco was. As it so happened, on the same table was a poker hand, all dealt, lying in front of a vacant chair. Four other chairs were oddly enough occupied by students, also preparing to study. It therefore resolved itself into something of a seminar, or group conference, on the courses under discussion. For example, the first student would say:

"I can't open."

The second student would perhaps say the same thing.

The third student would say: "I'll open for fifty cents."

And the seminar would be on.

At the end of the seminar, I would go back to my desk, pile the notes and books on top of each other, put the light out, and go to bed, tired but happy in the realization that I had not only spent the evening busily but had helped put four of my friends through college.

An inventory of stock acquired at college discloses the following bits of culture and erudition which have nestled in my mind after all these years.

Things I Learned Freshman year

1. Charlemagne either died or was born or did something with the Holy Roman Empire in 800.

2. By placing one paper bag inside another paper bag you can carry home a milk shake in it.

3. There is a double l in the middle of "parallel."

4. Powder rubbed on the chin will take the place of a shave if the room isn't very light.

5. French nouns ending in "aison" are feminine.

6. Almost everything you need to know about a subject is in the encyclopedia.

7. A tasty sandwich can be made by spreading peanut butter on raisin bread.

8. A floating body displaces its own weight in the liquid in which it floats.

9. A sock with a hole in the toe can be worn inside out with comparative comfort.

10. The chances are against filling an inside straight.

11. There is a law in economics called *The Law of Diminishing Returns,* which means that after a certain margin is reached returns begin to diminish. This may not be correctly stated, but there *is* a law by that name.

12. You begin tuning a mandolin with A and tune the other strings from that.

Sophomore Year

1. A good imitation of measles rash can be effected by stabbing the forearm with a stiff whisk-broom.

2. Queen Elizabeth was not above suspicion.

3. In Spanish you pronounce z like *th*.

4. Nine-tenths of the girls in a girls' college are not pretty.

5. You can sleep undetected in a lecture course by resting the head on the hand as if shading the eyes.

6. Weakness in drawing technique can be hidden by using a wash instead of black and white line.

7. Quite a respectable bun can be acquired by smoking three or four pipefuls of strong tobacco when you have no food in your stomach.

8. The ancient Phoenicians were really Jews, and got as far north as England where they operated tin mines.

9. You can get dressed much quicker in the morning if the night before when you are going to bed you take off your trousers and underdrawers at once, leaving the latter inside the former.

Junior Year

1. Emerson left his pastorate because he had some argument about communion.

2. All women are untrustworthy.

3. Pushing your arms back as far as they will go fifty times each day increases your chest measurement.

4. Marcus Aurelius had a son who turned out to be a bad boy.

5. Eight hours of sleep are not necessary.

6. Heraclitus believed that fire was the basis of all life.

7. A good way to keep your trousers pressed is to hang them from the bureau drawer.

8. The chances are that you will never fill an inside straight.

9. The Republicans believe in a centralized government, the Democrats in a de-centralized one.

10. It is not necessarily effeminate to drink tea.

Senior Year

1. A dinner coat looks better than full dress.

2. There is as yet no law determining what constitutes trespass in an airplane.

3. Six hours of sleep are not necessary.

4. Bicarbonate of soda taken before retiring makes you feel better the next day.

5. You needn't be fully dressed if you wear a cap and gown to a nine-o'clock recitation.

6. Theater tickets may be charged.

7. Flowers may be charged.

8. May is the shortest month in the year.

The foregoing outline of my education is true enough in its way, and is what people like to think about a college course. It has become quite the cynical thing to admit laughingly that college did one no good. It is part of the American Credo that all that the college student learns is to catch punts and dance. I had to write something like that to satisfy the editors. As a matter of fact, I learned a great deal in college and have those four years to thank for whatever I know today.

(The above note was written to satisfy those of my instructors and financial backers who may read this. As a matter of fact, the original outline is true, and I had to look up the date about Charlemagne at that.)

R. M. MacIver

Civilization and Culture

Society has an inner environment which it makes, besides the outer which it only molds. The former consists in the whole apparatus of custom and institution, the complex and multiform mechanism of order, the devices and instruments by which nature is controlled, the modes of expression and communication, the comforts, refinements, and luxuries which determine standards of living, and the economic system through which they are produced and distributed. It includes all that human intelligence and art have wrought to make the world a home for the human spirit. It includes alike the technological and the institutional equipment, parliaments and telephone exchanges, corporation charters and railroads, insurance agencies and automobiles. This whole apparatus of life we shall here call civilization. It is obvious that the political system belongs to this region and constitutes one great division of it.

From civilization we must distinguish culture as its animating and creating spirit. Civilization is the instrument, the body, even the garment of culture. Civilization expresses itself in politics, in economics, in technology, while culture expresses itself in art, in literature, in religion, in morals. Our culture is what we are, our civilization is what we use. There is a technique of culture, but the culture itself is not technique. Culture is the fulfilment of life, revealed in the things we want in themselves, and not in their results. No one wants banking systems and factories and ballot-boxes for any intrinsic significance they possess. If we could attain the products without the process we would gladly dispense with the latter. But the objects of culture have a direct significance. It is the difference between the mode of achieving and the thing achieved, between the way of living and the life led. The interest in technique is derivative, though like any other it may come to engross the mind, but the interest in culture is primary.

There is a great difference between an object of civilization and a work of culture. An institutional or technical achievement raises, so to speak, the level of civilization. It is an improvement on the past. Once the spinning-machine or the railway-locomotive or the typewriter is discovered, men go on developing it. Civilization is cumulative. The new model betters the old, and renders it obsolete. The achievement perpetuates itself and is the basis for further achievement. Civilization is rightly described as a "march," for each step leads to another and is always forward. Great historical catastrophes can interrupt this cumulation, but nothing seems able to break it altogether. It is a poor age indeed that does not add some stones to this rising edifice of civilization. But culture is not cumulative. It has to be won afresh by each new generation. It is not a simple inheritance like civilization. It is true that here too past attainment is the basis of present achievement, but there is no surety that the present will equal, still less that it will improve on, the past. The heights reached by Greek art and Greek drama are not held by succeeding ages. The achievement of Dante or of Shakespeare is not

From *The Modern State*, by R. M. MacIver. Published, 1926, by the Clarendon Press, Oxford. Used by permission of the publisher.

equalled by those who follow them. What Archimedes or Galileo or Newton discovered is the basis of further discovery that exceeds any of theirs, but what Sophocles or Michaelangelo or Milton expressed is not expressed better or more fully by others who have their works before them. We do not deny that there is advance in culture also, but it is no steady advance. It is variable and seems capricious, subject to retreats and setbacks.

The reason thereof suggests another difference between civilization and culture. Culture must always be won afresh, because it is a direct expression of the human spirit. In a very real sense a musician composes only for musicians and an artist paints only for artists. A poet can write only for those who have themselves the poetic quality. Every work of art implies at least two artists, he who creates and he who understands, and so with all the achievements of culture. Cultural expression is communication between likes and is possible only by reason of their likeness. The work of the artist is only for other artists, but the work of the engineer is not for other engineers. The bridge-builder does not construct for other bridge-builders, but for those who themselves may appreciate nothing of his skill. Millions may use a technical invention without the least understanding of it. Devices for use are in fact the more perfect the less understanding they require, and the aim of the inventor is to make his invention, in the American phrase, "fool-proof." We would get an entirely false conception of the intelligence and capacity of our age, and an entirely false standard of comparison between it and other ages, if we judged it by its institutions and its technical equipment. Our estimate would be much more just if we judged it by the books men read and write, by the ideals they cherish, by the pleasures they pursue, by the religions which they practise, by all the things they really care about and think about.

It follows that one people can borrow civilization from another people in a way in which culture cannot be borrowed. Technical devices can be transplanted without change. Institutional devices, being more nearly related to the form of culture which they serve, undergo some change when they are borrowed. The barbarian can learn more easily to use the rifle than the ballot-box. The institutions of Western democracy do not accommodate themselves without strain to the social life of the Orient or even of South America. Nevertheless they are transferable to a degree, and have in fact been adopted in many countries to which they were not native. But a culture cannot be adopted. A culture may be assimilated gradually, by peoples who are ready for it and who are brought into constant contact with it, but even so they inevitably change it in making it their own. When extraneous considerations lead to the nominal acceptance of an alien culture it becomes a travesty or an empty form. The extraordinary transmogrifications of Christianity in the course of two thousand years, involving not merely the restatement but often the rejection of its original principles, offer a splendid illustration of the truth that a culture cannot be "adopted." The culture of a people expresses their character and can express nothing else. Hence civilization is far more pervasive than culture. Japan can speedily adopt the civilization of the West, but it neither can nor cares to adopt its culture. Of course we must not imply that the two factors are entirely separate. Civilization, whether native or adopted, is a kind of social environment, and human beings respond in similar ways to similar conditions. Civilization and culture necessarily react on one another. Nevertheless it seems clear that cultures can remain distinctive within the form of a common civilization. Given the means of communication, it is inevitable that civilization should become, in its larger aspects, one and universal. But under this seeming uniformity of life great cultural differences remain, both within and between the peoples of the earth.

One further distinction can now be made. We have pointed out that civilization, in contrast to culture, is cumulative. This is true in another sense also. Means can be massed into great engines of power. Systems can be extended into vaster systems. But culture resists the mechanics of addition and multiplication. I have elsewhere expressed this truth as follows: "We can add the wealth of a group or a nation and get some kind of a total. We can add its man-power and get a total. But we cannot make a sum of its health or its habits or its culture. A thousand weak purposes cannot be rolled into one strong purpose as a thousand weak units of force are joined into one strong force. We cannot add wisdom as we can add wealth. A thousand mediocrities do not sum up into one genius."

William Golding

The Glass Door

I don't know how far the Alleghenies stretch. They are the small patch of brown, half-way up the map of America on the right-hand side. They consist of parallel ranges, and cover, I suppose, more area than the British Isles. They are not very distinguished as mountains go. They are relatively low, and tree-clad. They have no violence, but abundant charm. How should they not? They pass through Virginia, where charm is laid on so thick you could saw it off in chunks and export it.

Here, in Virginia, is none of the restless energy, the determined modernity, the revolutionary fervour, which in retrospect I see to have characterized my own country. I crossed the Atlantic from the passionate antagonisms of Salisbury traffic on a market day, to the controlled silence of New York in a rush hour. New York traffic flows in a tide too full for sound or foam, and is peaceful by comparison. I thought then that the allegedly horrifying pace of American life was a European invention; and when I got to Virginia I was certain of it. Shout at Virginia, shake it, slap its face, jump on it—Virginia will open one eye, smile vaguely, and go to sleep again.

Our base of operations is Hollins, a rich girls' college, lapped about by fields,

From *The Hot Gates and Other Occasional Pieces,* © 1965, by William Golding. Reprinted by permission of Harcourt, Brace & World, Inc.

and set down in a fold of the Alleghenies. It is ineffably peaceful. Wherever you look, there are hills looped along the skyline. Every circumstance pleases, woos, soothes and makes comprehension difficult. We arrived during the Indian summer, when every blade of grass, every leaf, was loaded down with cicadas, each of which seemed to be operating a small dentist's drill. Eagles and buzzards floated a thousand feet up in the hot air. Blue jays played in the fields and a delicately built mocking-bird balanced on the white fence by our window like a lady with a parasol on a tightrope. On the day of our arrival, a mountain bear—probably walking in his sleep—wandered into the nearby town, saw himself in the glass door of the library, panicked, woke up the neighbourhood, was anaesthetized and taken home again.

Hollins sits among its mountains and fields, remembering the eighteenth century. There is a sulphur spring in the grounds, surrounded by a sort of bandstand. In the old days, mammas would take pallid or spotty daughters here to have them cleared up; and the place became a spa. Judging by the pictures of strolling ladies and young bloods driving curricles, it must have been a thriving marriage market—an activity which it has never wholly lost. But in the 1840's the mammas left, social rooms and dormitories were built, and the place became a college.

Hollins, set in its estate of several hundred acres, grew to be an enclave of colonial architecture, all white pillars and porches, grouped round a quadrangle of grass and splendid trees. Lately, a most expensive chapel has taken the place of the old one. A magnificent library building has been added, modern to the last air-conditioned, glass-fronted detail, where the bookstacks have a most generous expanse of working space round them. It is typical of the almost parody southernism of the place that the laboratories are still inadequate. But I have to admit that this choice of what things come first seems splendidly liberal to me, who have suffered from the contrary conception.

Here, then, we work gently, with cushions under us, and plate glass between us and the rest of the world. It is pleasant to contemplate the clock on the administration buildings, by which we regulate our affairs. For the clock is a Virginian clock. The minute hand toils up, lifting the heavy weight of the hour until it totters upright. Then, as if that effort had exhausted the mechanism, the hand falls down to half past three and stays there, collapsed. Long may it continue so to make a mock of the arbitrary, enslaving time-stream! It is as useless and decorative as the carillon which tinkles out Mozart minuets, or hymns, or snatches of old song, from the chapel spire.

Under the trees, along the cemented paths, go the drifts of girls, sympathetic and charming, giggling or absorbed, shy of the bearded foreigner behind his plate glass, but courteous to the helplessness of old age. Some of them are northerners, but the most part southern, and some are from the deep South. Like all women students, they are inveterate, comically obsessive note-takers, who hope by this method to avoid the sheer agony of having to think for themselves. Often they have an earnestness before the shrine of this unknown god Education, which seems at odds with their careful make-up and predatory scent. They will propose a scheme of studies which leaves them no time to eat in the middle of the day; but 40 per cent of them leave to get married before they reach the end of their studies. They are intimidating, ingenuous, and delightful; and about the realities of life in the world at large they know absolutely nothing at all.

Yet how should they? Problems are smoothed over, and have the sharp edges blunted for them by space, prosperity, and the American capacity for presenting any situation in a series of ready-made phrases. Even that problem in the South, which has made such a stir in the world does not occur here so acutely, since the coloured population in this neighbourhood is only about 10 per cent of the whole. Certainly it exists; and an Englishman, who sees everything at one remove, understands not only the discourtesy of meddling with it, but the difficulty of dealing with the problem precisely because it is *not* acute. Hollins is an enclave, an educated and liberal one. It has preserved almost as an archaeological relic what was inoffensive in the white/black pattern, without perhaps noticing what was going on.

Across the field outside our window is a wood, under Tinker Mountain. In the wood, and partly visible, is a hamlet, a red church with a white, clapboard spire. This is a Negro village. In the old days, when girls came to Hollins, they brought their body slaves with them, and sometimes these slaves stayed on. They settled in the hamlet, and now provide the servants for the college. I see them every afternoon, making their dignified way across the field, large, comfortable women in bright clothes, young men who go whistling and with a dancing step. As your eyes grow accustomed to the light of this ancient country, you begin to see that the man who empties your ashcan is coloured, so are the men who sweep your road or work in the power house, so are the girls who clean or wash or sew, or serve in the canteen. Yet at Hollins, because of its isolation, the relationship is a historical relic. What keeps a girl out of Hollins is not a colour bar but an economic one. It costs more than £1,000 a year to keep a girl there.

For the problem is smoothed over, is down out of sight. The servants, like college servants everywhere, have a long tradition of service. They seem proud of the college and the college is proud of them. Here, embalmed, is a tiny section, a left-over bit of history, which loyalty, education and kindliness have minimized until it has a sort of willow-pattern charm. Yet north of us is an area where the public schools have shut down to avoid integration. South of us, the railway has segregated waiting rooms.

The problem is at once too foreign, too vast, and too muted for my comprehension. At least there is a fund of human goodwill here, which makes the cheap jibes flung from outside seem blunted weapons. Let me do no more, therefore, than record a scene, before the adjustments, the manoeuvres, the shrugs of history have taken it away for ever. I emerged the other day from a book-lined room to the shock of autumn's air on the campus. A dozen coloured men stood by leaf-piles, with brooms and rakes in their hands. Some of them talked, and pushed the leaves about. Others stood motionless, leaning on rakes. They wore bright blue and red, rich brown. They worked, when they worked, with inspired slowness, under the Virginian clock. Silhouetted against the white columns, among thick trunks and clattering leaves, standing among drifts of girls who tinkled here and there with laughter, the dark men seemed a still life. They seemed happy to do this, as the girls seemed happy to do that. Passing among them in the brisker air, some obscure compulsion made me speak to the oldest man of all. He was small and gnarled, dressed in bright blue, his black face startling under a stubble of white hair. I made some inane remark about the weather, which woke him up. He laughed and crowed, and his body jerked. "Yas-suh!" he said; and we both knew, with one of those psychic flashes that are so often wrong, that we were taking part in some ripe old comedy of the South—"Yas-suh!"

I reeled on, conscious at last of my solid presence in this mild, foreign land, and struck myself a shattering blow on the invisible glass door of the library. I tottered inside as the carillon tinkled out a minuet by Mozart; and sank into a seat among the girls who were studying the mythological sources of Oedipus and Hamlet, or surveying Spanish Literature, or reading *The Rights of Man*.

For the problem has not yet come consciously to Hollins. Perhaps it never will, but be by-passed. Yet the enclave is not secure. As the town expands, the value of the Hollins land goes up and presently there will be pressure to sell. Moreover, now that America has inherited an ancient mantle, exotic students are coming to Hollins; Indian and Korean, like the business interests pressing south into Virginia, they are a sign of things to come. They are a colourful sight, in the national costume which is their only defence against the ancient intolerance of the countryside. Moreover, an inter-State highway is advancing across the land, majestically shouldering hills out of its way; and like it or not, that road will divide the estate not half a mile from the campus.

Yet for today, preserved, there stands the pattern; the friendly faculty, the girls, the tall, colonial columns, the dark servants and the quiet sun.

Peter F. Drucker

The Myth of American Uniformity

"How can you Americans stand all this uniformity?" Every one of the dozens of visitors from all over Europe who, during these past few years, have discussed their American impressions with me, has asked this question in one form or another. Yet what makes every single one—businessman, clergyman, or scientist; teacher, lawyer, or journalist; labor leader or civil servant—come to me for information is bewilderment, if not shock, at the incomprehensible and boundless diversity of this country.

"But *somebody* must lay out the standard curriculum for the liberal arts colleges. If the federal or the state governments do not do it, who does?"

From "The Myth of American Uniformity," *Harper's Magazine* (May, 1952). Reprinted by permission of Peter F. Drucker.

"In what grade does the American high school student start Latin? How many hours a week are given to it? And what works of Shakespeare are normally read in the American high schools?"

"It can't really be true that there is no one labor union policy on industrial engineering. I am told that some unions actually insist on a time and motion study of each job, some unions acquiesce in it, and others refuse to allow any industrial engineers. But surely no union movement could possibly operate pulling in opposite directions on a matter as important as this?"

"Please explain to us what American managements mean when they talk of 'decentralization.' Wouldn't this mean that different units of a company would do things differently, adopt different policies, follow different ideas? And how could any management allow that and still keep its authority and control?"

The going gets really rough when the talk turns to political institutions or to the churches. That it makes all the difference in the world what congressional committee a pending bill is assigned to, will upset even the urbane visitor—if indeed he believes it. And among the most frustrating hours of my life was an evening spent with a Belgian Jesuit who insisted that there must be one simple principle that decides when and where agencies of the Catholic Church in this country work together with other faiths, and when not. The only comfort was that he obviously had got no more satisfaction from his American brethren in the order than from me.

Yet it is quite clearly not in diversity that the visitors see the essence of America. They are baffled by it, shocked by it, sometimes frightened by it. But they don't really believe in it. Their real convictions about this country come out in the inevitable question: "But don't you find it trying to live in so uniform a country?"

It is not only the casual visitor, spending a few weeks here, who believes in "American uniformity" despite all he sees and hears. The belief survives extended exposure to the realities of American life.

A few months ago a well-known English anthropologist, reviewing an exhibition of American paintings for a most respectable London Sunday paper, explained the "mediocrity of American painting" by a reference to "the uniformity of the American landscape—all prairie and desert." One might remind the reviewer that nothing is more startling to the immigrant who comes to America to live than the tremendous variety of the landscape and the violence of the contrasts in the American climate, soils, geology, fauna, and flora. Or one might reduce the argument to its full absurdity by asking which of these sons of Kansas, for example, is the typically uniform prairie product—William Allen White, Earl Browder, or General Eisenhower? But the essential fact is not that the argument is nonsense. It is that Geoffrey Gorer, the anthropologist, knows this country well, and that the newspaper that printed his nonsense is unusually knowledgeable about things American on the whole. Yet though they know all about New England or Virginia or Minnesota or Oregon, though they probably also know about the artists who paint in the desert of Cape Cod—or is it a prairie?—they immediately think of "uniformity" when something American needs explanation.

I am not discussing here the *quality* of American culture, whether it be crude, shallow, vulgar, commercialized, materialist, or, as Marxists maintain, full of "bourgeois idealism." My concern here is solely with the prevailing European conviction of American uniformity. And that conviction is an obvious absurdity. Nor could it be anything else considering the pragmatic bent of the American people and their deeply engrained habit of voluntary and local community action and community organization.

Indeed any serious student of America has to raise the question whether there is not *too much* diversity in this country. There is the danger that diversity will degenerate into aimless multiplicity—difference for difference's sake. Jefferson, de Tocqueville, and Henry Adams, as well as recent critics of American education such as Robert Hutchins, have seen in this the major danger facing American society and culture.

There is actually more uniformity in European countries, both materially and culturally, than in the United States. It may no longer be true that the French Minister of Education knows at every hour exactly what line of what page of what book is being read in every French school. But still, in education, in religious life, in political life, in business as well as in its cultural ideals, European countries tend to have at most a few "types," a few molds in which everything is formed. What then can the European possibly mean when he talks of the "uniformity of America"?

He himself, as a visitor, unconsciously furnishes the answer in the way he sorts out his American experiences, in the questions he asks, in the answers he understands and those he doesn't. When he thinks of "diversity" he tends to think of the contrast between the ways in which social and economic classes live. He is used to seeing a definite and clear-cut upper-class civilization and culture dominating. And that indeed he does not find in this country. Therefore the bewildering differences in American life appear to him meaningless—mere oddities.

I still remember how the sage of our neighborhood in suburban Vienna, the wife of the market gardener across the street, explained the "Great War," the war of 1914–18, when I was a small boy of ten or eleven: "The war had to come because you couldn't tell maids from their ladies by their dress any more." Frau Kiner's explanation of history differed from that offered during the nineteen twenties by Europe's learned sociologists, whether of the Right or of the Marxist persuasion, mainly by being brief and simple. They all assumed that there must be a distinct upper-class way of life, an upper-class architecture, upper-class dress, upper-class goods in an upper-class market—and contrasted with it the "folk culture" of the peasantry or the equally distinct ways of life of the middle class and working class. Indeed the eminently sane, that notoriously Americophile magazine, the London *Economist*, echoed Frau Kiner only a few months ago when it reported with apparent amazement that "to the best of their ability—and their ability is great—the [American] manufacturers make clothes for the lower income groups that look just as smart as those they make for the more fortunate"

—and explained this perverse attempt to make the maids look like their ladies as the result of the "egalitarian obsession" of this country.

The class-given differentiation in Europe is even more pronounced in the nonmaterial, the cultural spheres. One example is the tremendous importance of the "right speech" in practically every European country; for the "right speech" is upper-class speech. Another example is the extent to which European educational systems are based on the education of a ruling class. The Renaissance Courtier, the Educated Man of the Humanists, the Christian Gentleman of nineteenth-century England—the ideal types which embody the three basic educational concepts of modern Europe—were all in origin and intent ruling-class types. The rising middle class not only did not overthrow the class concept of education, it emphasized it as a symbol of its own emergence into the ruling group. Similarly, in Occupied Germany the working-class leaders—to the chagrin as well as the complete bewilderment of American educational advisers—have shown no enthusiasm for the plan to convert the traditional *"Gymnasium"* into an American high school. To deprive these schools of their ruling-class character would actually deprive them of social meaning for the working-class children.

Europe has even succeeded in turning diversities and differences that were not social in their origin into class distinctions. One of the best examples of this is the way in which the "gentry" and its retainers became identified with the Church of England while the "tradesman" went to "Chapel"—a distinction that held till very recent times and is not quite gone yet.

Thus the European myth of American uniformity tells us less about America than about Europe. For it is based, in the last analysis, on Frau Kiner's belief that a class structure of society is the only genuine moral order.

That today the theme of "American uniformity" is played on above all by Communist propaganda is thus no accident. For the "proletariat" of communist ideology is indeed a "master class." It is a reaffirmation of the European ruling-class concept and of its ruling-class way of life in an extreme form—only turned upside down. On this rests to a considerable extent the attraction of Communism for European intellectuals. There is an old Slav proverb: "There will always be barons for there must always be peasants." All Vishinsky would have to do to change it into an orthodox Soviet proverb would be to change "barons" to "proletarian commissars." And Frau Kiner's philosophy of history he would not have to change at all.

But Frau Kiner's statement could never have been made in this country, not even by a sociology professor in a three-volume tome. Whether the United States really has no ruling class at all—or whether, as the Marxists assert, the classes are only camouflaged in this country, one thing is certain: this country knows no distinct upper-class or lower-class "way of life." It knows only different ways of making a living.

Indeed there has been only one genuine ruling-class way of life in this country since its beginning: that of the plantation aristocracy in the Old South between 1760 and 1860. When the *nouveaux riches* in that period between the Civil War and the first world war made the attempt to set themselves up as "Society" they failed miserably. They could not even develop an upper-class American architecture—and of all the arts architecture is the mirror of the way of life. The tycoons had to be content with imitation French châteaux, Italian Renaissance palaces, and Tudor manors—the white elephants which their servantless grandchildren are now frantically turning over to monasteries, hospitals, or schools. (It is not entirely an accident, perhaps, that the people most eager to live today in the baronial halls of yesterday's capitalists seem to be the Soviet delegates.) To find an upper-class way of life the tycoons had to gate-crash the Scottish grouse moors, the Cowes Regatta, or the Kaiser's maneuvers in Kiel. In this country it was difficult indeed to lead a ruling-class life.

The closest we come today in this country to anything that might be called an "upper-class way of life" is to be found in the top hierarchy of the big business corporations. The way people in some of these companies talk about the "twelfth floor" or the "front office" faintly echoes Frau Kiner's concept of the "ladies." At work the big business executive has indeed some of the trappings of a distinct style of living in the ceremonial of receptionist, secretary, and big office, in his expense account, in the autographed picture of the "big boss" on the wall, the unlisted telephone, and so forth. But only at work. As soon as he leaves the office the "big shot" becomes simply another businessman, anonymous and indistinguishable from millions of others. And he is quite likely to live, like the president of our largest corporation, in an eight-room house in a pleasant and comfortable but not particularly swank suburb.

In fact, it does not even make too much sense to talk of this country as a "middle-class" society. A middle class has to have a class on either side to be in the middle. There is more than a grain of truth in the remark made jokingly by one of my European visitors, an Italian student of American literature: "If there were such a thing as a working-class literature, *Babbitt* and *Arrowsmith* would be its models."

Bertrand Russell

Modern Homogeneity

The European traveller in America—at least if I may judge by myself—is struck by two peculiarities: first the extreme similarity of outlook in all parts of the United States (except the old South), and secondly the passionate desire of each locality to prove that it is peculiar and different from every other. The second of these is, of course, caused by the first. Every place wishes to have a reason for local pride, and therefore cherishes whatever is distinctive in the way of

From *In Praise of Idleness* by Bertrand Russell. Used by permission of George Allen & Unwin Ltd.

geography or history or tradition. The greater the uniformity that in fact exists, the more eager becomes the search for differences that may mitigate it. The old South is in fact quite unlike the rest of America, so unlike that one feels as if one had arrived in a different country. It is agricultural, aristocratic, and retrospective, whereas the rest of America is industrial, democratic, and prospective. When I say that America outside the old South is industrial, I am thinking even of those parts that are devoted almost wholly to agriculture, for the mentality of the American agriculturist is industrial. He uses much modern machinery; he is very conscious of the distant markets to which his products are sent; he is in fact a capitalist who might just as well be in some other business. A peasant, as he exists in Europe and Asia, is practically unknown in the United States. This is an immense boon to America, and perhaps its most important superiority as compared to the Old World, for the peasant everywhere is cruel, avaricious, conservative, and inefficient. I have seen orange groves in Sicily and orange groves in California; the contrast represents a period of about two thousand years. Orange groves in Sicily are remote from trains and ships; the trees are old and gnarled and beautiful; the methods are those of classical antiquity. The men are ignorant and semi-savage, mongrel descendants of Roman slaves and Arab invaders; what they lack in intelligence towards trees they make up for by cruelty to animals. With moral degradation and economic incompetence goes an instinctive sense of beauty which is perpetually reminding one of Theocritus and the myth about the Garden of the Hesperides. In a California orange grove the Garden of the Hesperides seems very remote. The trees are all exactly alike, carefully tended and at the right distance apart. The oranges, it is true, are not all exactly of the same size, but careful machinery sorts them so that automatically all those in one box are exactly similar. They travel along with suitable things being done to them by suitable machines at suitable points until they enter a suitable refrigerator car in which they travel to a suitable market. The machine stamps the word "Sunkist" upon them, but otherwise there is nothing to suggest that nature has any part in their production. Even the climate is artificial, for when there would otherwise be frost, the orange grove is kept artificially warm by a pall of smoke. The men engaged in agriculture of this kind do not feel themselves, like the agriculturists of former times, the patient servants of natural forces; on the contrary, they feel themselves the masters, and able to bend natural forces to their will. There is therefore not the same difference in America as in the Old World between the outlook of industrialists and that of agriculturists. The important part of the environment in America is the human part; by comparison the non-human part sinks into insignificance. I was constantly assured in Southern California that the climate turned people into lotus eaters, but I confess I saw no evidence of this. They seemed to me exactly like the people in Minneapolis or Winnipeg, although climate, scenery, and natural conditions were as different as possible in the two regions. When one considers the difference between a Norwegian and a Sicilian, and compares it with the lack of difference between a man from (say) North Dakota and a man from Southern California, one realizes the immense revolution in human affairs which has been brought about by man's becoming the master instead of the slave of his physical environment. Norway and Sicily both have ancient traditions; they had pre-Christian religions embodying men's reactions to the climate, and when Christianity came it inevitably took very different forms in the two countries. The Norwegian feared ice and snow; the Sicilian feared lava and earthquakes. Hell was invented in a southern climate; if it had been invented in Norway, it would have been cold. But neither in North Dakota nor in Southern California is Hell a climatic condition: in both it is a stringency on the money market. This illustrates the unimportance of climate in modern life.

America is a man-made world; moreover it is a world which man has made by means of machinery. I am thinking not only of the physical environment, but also and quite as much of thoughts and emotions. Consider a really stirring murder: the murderer, it is true, may be primitive in his methods, but those who spread the knowledge of his deed do so by means of all the latest resources of science. Not only in the great cities, but in lonely farms on the prairie and in mining camps in the Rockies, the radio disseminates all the latest information, so that half the topics of conversation on a given day are the same in every household throughout the country. As I was crossing the plains in the train, endeavouring not to hear a loud-speaker bellowing advertisements of soap, an old farmer came up to me with a beaming face and said, "Wherever you go nowadays you can't get away from civilization." Alas! How true! I was endeavouring to read Virginia Woolf, but the advertisements won the day.

Uniformity in the physical apparatus of life would be no grave matter, but uniformity in matters of thought and opinion is much more dangerous. It is, however, a quite inevitable result of modern inventions. Production is cheaper when it is unified and on a large scale than when it is divided into a number of small units. This applies quite as much to the production of opinions as to the production of pins. The principal sources of opinion in the present day are the schools, the Churches, the Press, the cinema, and the radio. The teaching in the elementary schools must inevitably become more and more standardized as more use is made of apparatus. It may, I think, be assumed that both the cinema and the radio will play a rapidly increasing part in school education in the near future. This will mean that the lessons will be produced at a centre and will be precisely the same wherever the material prepared at this centre is used. Some Churches, I am told, send out every week a model sermon to all the less educated of their clergy, who, if they are governed by the ordinary laws of human nature, are no doubt grateful for being saved the trouble of composing a sermon of their own. This model sermon, of course, deals with some burning topic of the moment, and aims at arousing a given mass emotion throughout the length and breadth of the land. The same thing applies in a higher degree to the Press, which receives everywhere the same telegraphic news and is syndicated on a large scale. Reviews of my books, I find, are, except in the best newspapers, verbally the same from New York to San Francisco, and from Maine to Texas, except that they become shorter as one travels from the north-east to the south-west.

Perhaps the greatest of all forces for uniformity in the modern world is the cinema, since its influence is not confined to America but penetrates to all parts of the world, except the Soviet Union, which, however, has its own different uniformity. The cinema embodies, broadly speaking, Hollywood's opinion of what is liked in the Middle West. Our emotions in regard to love and marriage, birth and death, are becoming standardized according to this recipe. To the young of all lands Hollywood represents the last word in modernity, displaying both the pleasures of the rich and the methods to be adopted for acquiring riches. I suppose the talkies will lead before long to the adoption of a universal language, which will be that of Hollywood.

It is not only among the comparatively ignorant that there is uniformity in America. The same thing applies, though in a slightly less degree, to culture. I visited book shops in every part of the country, and found everywhere the same best-sellers prominently displayed. So far as I could judge, the cultured ladies of America buy every year about a dozen books, the same dozen everywhere. To an author this is a very satisfactory state of affairs, provided he is one of the dozen. But it certainly does mark a difference from Europe, where there are many books with small sales rather than a few with large sales.

It must not be supposed that the tendency towards uniformity is either wholly good or wholly bad. It has great advantages and also great disadvantages: its chief advantage is, of course, that it produces a population capable of peaceable co-operation; its great disadvantage is that it produces a population prone to persecution of minorities. This latter defect is probably temporary, since it may be assumed that before long there will be no minorities. A great deal depends, of course, on how the uniformity is achieved. Take, for example, what the schools do to southern Italians. Southern Italians have been distinguished throughout history for murder, graft, and aesthetic sensibility. The Public Schools effectively cure them of the last of these three, and to that extent assimilate them to the native American population, but in regard to the other two distinctive qualities, I gather that the success of the schools is less marked. This illustrates one of the dangers of uniformity as an aim: good qualities are easier to destroy than bad ones, and therefore uniformity is most easily achieved by lowering all standards. It is, of course, clear that a country with a large foreign population must endeavour, through its schools, to assimilate the children of immigrants, and therefore a certain degree of Americanization is inevitable. It is, however, unfortunate that such a large part of this process should be effected by means of a somewhat blatant nationalism. America is already the strongest country in the world, and its preponderance is continually increasing. This fact naturally inspires fear in Europe, and the fear is increased by everything suggesting militant nationalism. It may be the destiny of America to teach political good sense to Europe, but I am afraid that the pupil is sure to prove refractory.

With the tendency towards uniformity in America there goes, as it seems to me, a mistaken conception of democracy. It seems to be generally held in the United States that democracy requires all men to be alike, and that, if a man is in any way different from another, he is "setting himself up" as superior to that other. France is quite as democratic as America, and yet this idea does not exist in France. The doctor, the lawyer, the priest, the public official are all different types in France; each profession has its own traditions and its own standards, although it does not set up to be superior to other professions. In America all professional men are assimilated in type to the business man. It is as though one should decree that an orchestra should consist only of violins. There does not seem to be an adequate understanding of the fact that society should be a pattern or an organism, in which different organs play different parts. Imagine the eye and the ear quarrelling as to whether it is better to see or to hear, and deciding that each would do neither since neither could do both. This, it seems to me, would be democracy as understood in America. There is a strange envy of any kind of excellence which cannot be universal except, of course, in the sphere of athletics and sport, where aristocracy is enthusiastically acclaimed. It seems that the average American is more capable of humility in regard to his muscles than in regard to his brains; perhaps this is because his admiration for muscle is more profound and genuine than his admiration of brains. The flood of popular scientific books in America is inspired partly, though of course not wholly, by the unwillingness to admit that there is anything in science which only experts can understand. The idea that a special training may be necessary to understand, say, the theory of relativity, causes a sort of irritation, although nobody is irritated by the fact that a special training is necessary in order to be a first-rate football player.

Achieved eminence is perhaps more admired in America than in any other country, and yet the road to certain kinds of eminence is made very difficult for the young, because people are intolerant of any eccentricity or anything that could be called "setting one's self up," provided the person concerned is not already labelled "eminent." Consequently many of the finished types that are most admired are difficult to produce at home and have to be imported from Europe. This fact is bound up with standardization and uniformity. Exceptional merit, especially in artistic directions, is bound to meet with great obstacles in youth so long as everybody is expected to conform outwardly to a pattern set by the successful executive.

Standardization, though it may have disadvantages for the exceptional individual, probably increases the happiness of the average man, since he can utter his thoughts with a certainty that they will be like the thoughts of his hearer. Moreover it promotes national cohesion, and makes politics less bitter and violent than where more marked differences exist. I do not think it is possible to strike a balance of gains and losses, but I think the standardization which now exists in America is likely to exist throughout Europe as the world becomes more mechanized. Europeans, therefore, who find fault with America on this account should realize that they are finding fault with the future of their own countries, and are setting themselves against an inevitable and universal trend in civilization. Undoubtedly internationalism will become easier as the differences between nations diminish, and if once internationalism were established, social cohesion would become of enormous importance for preserving internal peace. There is a certain risk, which cannot be denied, of an immobility analogous to that of the late Roman Empire. But as against this, we may set the revolutionary forces of modern science and modern technique. Short of a universal intellectual decay, these forces, which are a new feature in the modern world, will make immobility impossible, and prevent that kind of stagnation which has overtaken great empires in the past. Arguments from history are dangerous to apply to the present and the future, because of the complete change that science has introduced. I see therefore no reason for undue pessimism, however standardization may offend the tastes of those who are unaccustomed to it.

E. B. White

The Family Which Dwelt Apart

On a small, remote island in the lower reaches of Barnetuck Bay there lived a family of fisherfolk by the name of Pruitt. There were seven of them, and they were the sole inhabitants of the place. They subsisted on canned corn, canned tomatoes, pressed duck, wholewheat bread, terrapin, Rice Krispies, crabs, cheese, queen olives, and homemade wild-grape preserve. Once in a while Pa Pruitt made some whiskey and they all had a drink.

They liked the island and lived there from choice. In winter, when there wasn't much doing, they slept the clock around, like so many bears. In summer they dug clams and set off a few pinwheels and salutes on July 4th. No case of acute appendicitis had ever been known in the Pruitt household, and when a Pruitt had a pain in his side he never even noticed whether it was the right side or the left side, but just hoped it would go away, and it did.

One very severe winter Barnetuck Bay froze over and the Pruitt family was marooned. They couldn't get to the mainland by boat because the ice was too thick, and they couldn't walk ashore because the ice was too treacherous. But inasmuch as no Pruitt had anything to go ashore for, except mail (which was entirely second class), the freeze-up didn't make any difference. They stayed indoors, kept warm, and ate well, and when there was nothing better to do, they played crokinole. The winter would have passed quietly enough had not someone on the mainland remembered that the Pruitts were out there in the frozen bay. The word got passed around the county and finally reached the Superintendent of State Police, who immediately notified Pathé News and the United States Army. The Army got there first with three bombing planes from Langley Field, which flew low over the island and dropped packages of dried apricots and bouillon cubes, which the Pruitts didn't like much. The newsreel plane, smaller than the bombers and equipped with skis, arrived next and landed on a snow-covered field on the north end of the island. Meanwhile, Major Bulk, head of the state troopers, acting on a tip that one of the Pruitt children had appendicitis, arranged for a dog team to be sent by plane from Laconia, New Hampshire, and also dispatched a squad of troopers to attempt a crossing of the bay. Snow began falling at sundown, and during the night three of the rescuers lost their lives about half a mile from shore, trying to jump from one ice cake to another.

The plane carrying the sled dogs was over southern New England when ice began forming on its wings. As the pilot circled for a forced landing, a large meat bone which one of the dogs had brought along got wedged in the socket of the main control stick, and the plane went into a steep dive and crashed against the side of a powerhouse, instantly killing the pilot and all the dogs, and fatally injuring Walter Ringstead, 7, of 3452 Garden View Avenue, Stamford, Conn.

Shortly before midnight, the news of the appendicitis reached the Pruitt house itself, when a chartered autogiro from Hearst's International News Service made a landing in the storm and reporters informed Mr. Pruitt that his oldest boy, Charles, was ill and would have to be taken to Baltimore for an emergency operation. Mrs. Pruitt remonstrated, but Charles said his side did hurt a little, and it ended by his leaving in the giro. Twenty minutes later another plane came in, bearing a surgeon, two trained nurses, and a man from the National Broadcasting Company, and the second Pruitt boy, Chester, underwent an exclusive appendectomy in the kitchen of the Pruitt home, over the Blue Network. This lad died, later, from eating dried apricots too soon after his illness, but Charles, the other boy, recovered after a long convalescence and returned to the island in the first warm days of spring.

He found things much changed. The house was gone, having caught fire on the third and last night of the rescue when a flare dropped by one of the departing planes lodged in a bucket of trash on the piazza. After the fire, Mr. Pruitt had apparently moved his family into the emergency shed which the radio announcers had thrown up, and there they had dwelt under rather difficult conditions until the night the entire family was wiped out by drinking a ten-percent solution of carbolic acid which the surgeon had left behind and which Pa Pruitt had mistaken for grain alcohol.

Barnetuck Bay seemed a different place to Charles. After giving his kin decent burial, he left the island of his nativity and went to dwell on the mainland.

Arthur Koestler

The Challenge of Our Time

I would like to start with a story—it is a story which you all know, but it will lead us straight to the heart of our problem.

On the 18th of January, 1912, Captain Scott and his four companions reached

Opening talk of a BBC broadcast series, Spring, 1947. Reprinted by permission of the author.

the South Pole, after a march of sixty-nine days. On the return journey Petty Officer Evans fell ill, and became a burden to the party. Captain Scott had to make a decision. Either he carried the sick man along, slowed down the march and risked perdition for all; or he let Evans die alone in the wilderness and tried to save the rest. Scott took the first course; they dragged Evans along until he died. The delay proved fatal. The blizzards overtook them; Oates, too, fell ill and sacrificed himself; their rations were exhausted; and the frozen bodies of the four men were found six months later only ten miles, or one day's march, from the next depot which they had been unable to reach. Had they sacrificed Evans, they would probably have been saved.

This dilemma, which faced Scott under eighty degrees of latitude, symbolises the eternal predicament of man, the tragic conflict inherent in his nature. It is the conflict between expediency and morality. I shall try to show that this conflict is at the root of our political and social crisis, that it contains in a nutshell the challenge of our time.

Scott had the choice between two roads. Let us follow each of them into their logical extensions. First, the road of expediency, where the traveller is guided by the principle that the End justifies the Means. He starts with throwing Evans to the wolves, as the sacrifice of one comrade is justified by the hope of saving four. As the road extends into the field of politics, the dilemma of Captain Scott becomes the dilemma of Mr. Chamberlain. Evans is Czechoslovakia; the sacrifice of this small nation will buy the safety of bigger ones—or so it is hoped. We continue on the straight, logical mental road which now leads us from Munich No. 1 to Munich No. 2: the Ribbentrop-Molotov Pact of 1939, where the Poles go the way the Czechs have gone. By that time the number of individual Evanses is counted by the million: in the name of expediency the German Government decides to kill all incurables and mentally deficients. They are a drag on the nation's sledge and rations are running short. After the incurables come those with bad heredity—Gypsies and Jews: six millions of them. Finally, in the name of expediency, the Western democracies let loose the first atomic bombs on the crowded towns of Hiroshima and Nagasaki, and thus implicitly accept the principle of total and indiscriminate warfare which they hitherto condemned. We continue on our logical road, which has now become a steep slope, into the field of party politics. If you are convinced that a political opponent will lead your country into ruin and plunge the world into a new war—is it not preferable that you should forget your scruples and try to discredit him by revelations about his private life, frame him, blacken him, purge him, censor him, deport him, liquidate him? Unfortunately, your opponent will be equally convinced that you are harmful, and use the same methods against you. Thus, the logic of expediency leads to the atomic disintegration of morality, a kind of radioactive decay of all values.

And now let us turn to the second alternative before Scott. This road leads into the opposite direction; its guiding principles are: respect for the individual, the rejection of violence, and the belief that the Means determine the End. We have seen what happened to Scott's expedition because he did *not* sacrifice Evans. And we can imagine what would have happened to the people of India had Mr. Gandhi been allowed to have his saintly way of non-resistance to the Japanese invader; or what would have been the fate of this country had it embraced pacifism, and with it the Gestapo with headquarters in Whitehall.

The fact that both roads lead to disaster creates a dilemma which is inseparable from man's condition; it is not an invention of the philosophers, but a conflict which we face at each step in our daily affairs. Each of us has sacrificed his Evans at one point or another of his past. And it is a fallacy to think that the conflict can always be healed by that admirable British household ointment called "the reasonable compromise." Compromise is a useful thing in minor dilemmas of daily routine; but each time we face major decisions, the remedy lets us down. Neither Captain Scott nor Mr. Chamberlain could fall back on a reasonable compromise. The more responsible the position you hold, the sharper you feel the horns of the dilemma. When a decision involves the fate of a great number of people, the conflict grows proportionately. The technical progress of our age has enormously increased the range and consequence of man's actions, and has thus amplified his inherent dilemma to gigantic proportions. This is the reason for our awareness of a crisis. We resemble the patient who hears for the first time, magnified by a loudspeaker, the erratic thundering of his heart.

The dilemma admits no final solution. But each period has to attempt a temporary solution adapted to its own condition. That attempt has to proceed in two steps. The first is to realise that a certain admixture of ruthlessness is inseparable from human progress. Without the rebellion of the Barons, there would be no Magna Carta; without the storming of the Bastille, no proclamation of the Rights of Man. The more we have moral values at heart, the more we should beware of crankiness. The trouble with some well-meaning ethical movements is that they have so many sectarians and quietists and cranks in their midst.

But the second and more important step is to realise that the End only justifies the Means within very narrow limits. A surgeon is justified in inflicting pain because the results of the operation are reasonably predictable; but drastic large-scale operations on the social body involve many unknown factors, lead to unpredictable results, and one never knows at what point the surgeon's lancet turns into the butcher's hatchet. Or, to change the metaphor: ruthlessness is like arsenic; injected in very small doses it is a stimulant to the social body, in large quantities it is deadly poison. And to-day we are all suffering from moral arsenic poisoning.

The symptoms of this disease are obvious in the political and social field; they are less obvious but no less dangerous in the field of science and philosophy. Let me quote as an example the opinions of one of our leading physicists, Professor J. D. Bernal. In an article called "Belief and Action" recently published by the *Modern Quarterly*, he says that "the new social relations" require "a radical change in morality," and that the virtues "based on excessive concern with individual rectitude" need readjustment by a "change from individual to collective morality." "Because collective action is the only effective action, it is the only virtuous action," says Professor Bernal. Now let us see what this rather abstract statement really means. The only practical way for Tom, Dick or Harry to take "effective collective action" is to become a member of an army, political party or movement. His choice will be determined (a) by his nationality, and (b) by his political opinions or prejudices. Once he has joined the collective of his choice, he has to subordinate his "individual rectitude" to the interests of the group or party. This is precisely what, for instance, the accused in the Belsen Trial did. Their excuse was that they had to service the gas chamber and push the victims into it out of loyalty to their party, because their individual responsibility was subordinated to collective responsibility. Counsel for the Defence of Irma Grese could have quoted verbatim Professor Bernal's reflections on ethics—though politically Bernal is a staunch opponent of Nazism and supports, to quote his own words, "the theories of Marx and the practice of Lenin and Stalin." His article actually contains some reservations to the effect that there should be no question of "blind and obedient carrying out of orders," which, he says, leads to the *Führerprinzip*. He does not seem to have noticed that blind obedience plus the *Führerprinzip* are nowhere more in evidence to-day than in the Party to which Professor Bernal's sympathies belong. In short, I believe that much confusion could be avoided if some scientists would stick to their electrons and realise that human beings do not fit into mathematical equations. And it should be realised that this is not an abstract philosophical quarrel, but a burning and very concrete issue on which it depends whether our civilisation shall live or die.

Let me return to my starting-point, the dilemma between expediency and morality. In the course of our discussion, the symbolic sledge of Scott's small party has grown into the express train of mankind's progress. On this train expediency is the engine, morality the brake. The action of the two is always antagonistic. We cannot make an abstract decision in favour of one or the other. But we can make temporary adjustments according to the train's progress. Two hundred years ago, during the train's laborious ascent from the stagnant marshes of feudal France towards the era of the Rights of Man, the decision would have been in favour of the engine and against the brake. Since about the second half of the nineteenth century our ethical brakes have been more and more neglected until totalitarian dynamism made the engine run amok. We must apply the brake or we shall crash.

I am not sure whether what the philosophers call ethical absolutes exist, but I am sure that we have to act as if they existed. Ethics must be freed from its utilitarian chains; words and deeds must again be judged on their own merits and not as mere makeshifts to serve distant and nebulous aims. These worm-eaten ladders lead to no paradise.

H. L. Mencken

The Origin of Morality

Children come into the world without any visible understanding of the difference between good and bad, right and wrong, but some sense of it is forced upon them almost as soon as they learn the difference between light and dark, hot and cold, sweet and sour. It is a kind of knowledge that seems to be natural and essential to all creatures living in societies, and it shows itself in many of the lower animals quite as well as in human beings. To be sure, they do not appear to formulate a concept of evil per se, and certainly they know nothing about the highly metaphysical abstraction that mankind calls sin, but many species are well acquainted with concrete acts of wickedness, and punish them severely. Theft and adultery are familiar examples. A dog will pursue and, if it can, castigate another dog which steals its bone, and an ape will try to kill any bachelor intruder which makes too free with its wives. This sharp and often bloody discrimination between *meum* and *tuum* is to be observed not only in mammals, but also in animals of lower orders, including birds, insects and even fishes. Much of the uproar that goes on among sparrows and starlings is caused by conflicts over property rights, and everyone has seen two goldfishes in a globe fighting over a speck of food, with one claiming it and trying to gobble it and the other seeking to make off with it.

A German popular naturalist, Dr. Theodor Zell, has gone to the length of writing a treatise called "Moral in der Tierwelt" (Morality in the Animal World), in which he argues that many species, especially among the social insects, entertain not only the somewhat negative idea of vice but also the positive idea of virtue. The ants, he says, are better citizens than the members of any known human society, for they never go on strike. If the workers of a given colony should quit work their queen would starve, and each of them would enjoy thereby the democratic privilege of aspiring to her power and circumstance, but they never cease to feed her so long as any food is obtainable. Thus they are true patriots, and show a luxuriant development of that loyalty to the established order which is put so high among the virtues of human beings.

Here it may be argued that such acts and attitudes in the lower animals are purely instinctive, and that it would be irrational to dignify them by calling them moral. But to that it may be answered that the motives and impulses lying behind many of the moral concepts of human beings seem to be instinctive in exactly the same sense, and almost to the same extent. No teaching is required to induce a baby to recognize a given rattle as its own; all the power of pedagogy must be devoted to inducing it to surrender its property on demand. Nor is there any reason to believe that the various manifestations of sexual rivalry among men are any nobler in origin than those observed among apes or dogs; the whole tendency of an advancing culture is to obliterate them, not to nourish them. In the days when anthropology was a pseudo-science chiefly cultivated by missionaries there was a belief that the lower races of men had no morals at all—that they yielded to their impulses in a naïve and irrational manner, and had no conception whatever of property rights, whether in goods or in women, or of duties, whether to their gods or to their fellow men. But it is now known that savages are really rather more moral, if anything, than civilized men. Their ethical systems, in some ways, differ from ours, just as their grammatical systems differ, and their theological and governmental systems, but even the most primitive of them submit unquestioningly to complicated and onerous duties and taboos, and not only suffer punishment willingly when the Old Adam lures them into false steps, but also appear to be tortured by what, on higher levels, is called conscience—to the extent, at times, of falling into such vapors of remorse that they languish and die.

Primitive man, in this respect as in others, seems to have been much like the savages of today. At the time when we get our first vague glimpse of him, lurking in the dark of his spooky caves, he was already a family man, and hence had certain duties, rights and responsibilities. We know, of course, very little about him, but we are at least reasonably sure that he did not habitually share his wife with all comers, or kill and eat his children, or fail in what he conceived to be his duty to the gods. To that extent, at least, he was a moral agent, and as completely so as any Christian. Later on in human history, when men discovered the art of writing and began to record their thoughts and doings for posterity, they devoted almost as much time and energy to setting down their notions of right and wrong as they gave to recording their prodigies and glories. In the very first chapter of the collection of hoary documents which we call the Bible there are confident moral mandates, and similar ones are to be found in the ancient books of every other people. The earliest conquerors and despots of whom we have any news seem to have regarded themselves, precisely like their colleagues of today, as the heralds of an ethical enlightenment, and every one of them was apparently just as eager as the celebrated Hammurabi to be known as "the king of righteousness."

In the world that we now live in the moral sense seems to be universally dispersed, at all events among normal persons beyond infancy. No traveler has ever discovered a tribe which failed to show it. There are peoples so primitive that their religion is hard to distinguish from a mere fear of the dark, but there is none so low that it lacks a moral system, elaborate and unyielding. Nor is that system often challenged, at least on the lower cultural levels, by those who lie under it. The rebellious individual may evade it on occasion, but he seldom denies its general validity. To find any such denial on a serious scale one must return to Christendom, where a bold and impatient re-examination of the traditional ethical dogma has followed the collapse of the old belief in revelation. But even in Christendom the most formidable critics of the orthodox system are still, as a rule, profoundly moral men, and the reform they propose is not at all an abandonment of moral imperatives, but simply a substitution of what they believe to be good ones for what they believe to be bad ones. This has been true of every important iconoclast from Hobbes to Lenin, and it was pre-eminently true of the arch-iconoclast Nietzsche. His furious attack upon the Christian ideal of humility and abnegation has caused Christian critics to denounce him as an advocate of the most brutal egoism, but in point of fact he proposed only the introduction of a new and more heroic form of renunciation, based upon abounding strength rather than upon hopeless weakness; and in his maxim "Be hard!" there was just as much sacrifice of immediate gratification to ultimate good as you will find in any of the *principia* of Jesus.

The difference between moral systems is thus very slight, and if it were not for the constant pressure from proponents of virtues that have no roots in ordinary human needs, and hence appeal only to narrow and abnormal classes of men, it would be slighter still. All of the really basic varieties of moral good have been esteemed as such since the memory of mankind runneth not to the contrary, and all of the basic wickednesses have been reprehended. The Second Commandment preached by Jesus (Mark XII, 31) was preached by the Gautama Buddha six centuries before Him, and it must have been hoary with age when the Gautama Buddha made it the center of his system. Similarly, the Ten Commandments of Exodus and Deuteronomy were probably thousands of years old when the Jewish scribes first reduced them to writing. Finally, and in the same way, the Greeks lifted their concept of wisdom as the supreme good out of the stream of time, and if we think of them today as its inventors, it is only because we are more familiar with their ethical speculations than we are with those of more ancient peoples.

The five fundamental prohibitions of the Decalogue—those leveled at murder, theft, trespass, adultery and false witness—are to be found in every moral system ever heard of, and seem to be almost universally supported by human opinion. This support, of course, does not mean that they are observed with anything properly describable as pedantic strictness; on the contrary, they are evaded on occasion, both by savages and by civilized men, and some of them are evaded very often. In the United States, for example, the situations in which killing a fellow human being is held to be innocent are considerably more numerous than those in which it is held to be criminal, and even in England, the most moral of great nations, there are probably almost as many. So with adultery. So, again, with theft, trespass and false witness. Theft and trespass shade by imperceptible gradations into transactions that could not be incommoded without imperiling the whole fabric of society, and bearing false witness is so easy to condone that bishops are sometimes among its most zealous practitioners. But despite this vagueness of moral outline and this tolerance of the erring the fact remains that all normal and well-disposed men, whether civilized or uncivilized, hold it to be axiomatic that murder, theft, trespass, adultery and false witness, in their cruder and plainer forms, are anti-social and immoral enterprises, and no one argues seriously, save maybe in time of war, when all the customary moral sanctions are abandoned, that they should be countenanced. When they are perpetrated in a naked manner, without any concession of the ancient and ineradicable feeling against them, they are viewed with abhorrence, and the guilty are severely punished.

John Henry Newman

Secular Knowledge

People say to me, that it is but a dream to suppose that Christianity should regain the organic power in human society which once it possessed. I cannot help that; I never said it could. I am not a politician; I am proposing no measures, but exposing a fallacy, and resisting a pretence. Let Benthamism reign, if men have no aspirations; but do not tell them to be romantic, and then solace them with glory; do not attempt by philosophy what once was done by religion. The ascendency of Faith may be impracticable, but the reign of Knowledge is incomprehensible. The problem for statesmen of this age is how to educate the masses, and literature and science cannot give the solution.

Not so deems Sir Robert Peel; his firm belief and hope is, "that an increased sagacity will administer to an exalted faith; that it will make men not merely believe in the cold doctrines of Natural Religion, but that it will so prepare and temper the spirit and understanding, that they will be better qualified to comprehend the great scheme of human redemption." He certainly thinks that scientific pursuits have some considerable power of impressing religion upon the mind of the multitude. I think not, and will now say why.

Science gives us the grounds or premises from which religious truths are to be inferred; but it does not set about inferring them, much less does it reach the inference;—that is not its province. It brings before us phenomena, and it leaves us, if we will, to call them works of design, wisdom, or benevolence; and further still, if we will, to proceed to confess an Intelligent Creator. We have to take its facts, and to give them a meaning, and to draw our own conclusions from them. First comes Knowledge, then a view, then reasoning, and then belief. This is why Science has so little of a religious tendency; deductions have no power of persuasion. The heart is commonly reached, not through the reason, but through the imagination, by means of direct impressions, by the testimony of facts and events, by history, by description. Persons influence us, voices melt us, looks subdue us, deeds inflame us. Many a man will live and die upon a dogma: no man will be a martyr for a conclusion. A conclusion is but an opinion; it is not a thing which *is,* but which *we are "certain about";* and it has often been observed, that we never say we are certain without implying that we doubt. To say that a thing *must* be, is to admit that it *may not* be. No one, I say, will die for his own calculations; he dies for realities. This is why a literary religion is so little to be depended upon; it looks well in fair weather, but its doctrines are opinions, and, when called to suffer for them, it slips them between its folios, or burns them at its hearth. And this again is the secret of the distrust and raillery with which moralists have been so commonly visited. They say and do not. Why? Because they are contemplating the fitness of things, and they live by the square, when they should be realizing their high maxims in the concrete. Now Sir Robert thinks better of natural history, chemistry, and astronomy, than of such ethics;

From *The Tamworth Reading Room,* by John Henry Newman.

but they too, what are they more than divinity *in posse*?[1] He protests against "controversial divinity": is *inferential* much better?

I have no confidence, then, in philosophers who cannot help being religious, and are Christians by implication. They sit at home, and reach forward to distances which astonish us; but they hit without grasping, and are sometimes as confident about shadows as about realities. They have worked out by a calculation the lie of a country which they never saw, and mapped it by means of a gazetteer; and like blind men, though they can put a stranger on his way, they cannot walk straight themselves, and do not feel it quite their business to walk at all.

Logic makes but a sorry rhetoric with the multitude; first shoot round corners, and you may not despair of converting by a syllogism. Tell men to gain notions of a Creator from His works, and, if they were to set about it (which nobody does), they would be jaded and wearied by the labyrinth they were tracing. Their minds would be gorged and surfeited by the logical operation. Logicians are more set upon concluding rightly, than on right conclusions. They cannot see the end for the process. Few men have that power of mind which may hold fast and firmly a variety of thoughts. We ridicule "men of one idea"; but a great many of us are born to be such, and we should be happier if we knew it. To most men argument makes the point in hand only more doubtful, and considerably less impressive. After all man is *not* a reasoning animal; he is a seeing, feeling, contemplating, acting animal. He is influenced by what is direct and precise. It is very well to freshen our impressions and convictions from physics, but to create them we must go elsewhere. Sir Robert Peel "never can think it possible that a mind can be so constituted, that, after being familiarized with the wonderful discoveries which have been made in every part of experimental science, it can retire from such contemplations without more enlarged conceptions of God's providence, and a higher reverence for His name." If he speaks of religious minds, he perpetrates a truism; if of irreligious, he insinuates a paradox.

Life is not long enough for a religion of inferences; we shall never have done beginning, if we determine to begin with proof. We shall ever be laying out foundations; we shall turn theology into evidences, and divines into textuaries. We shall never get at our first principles. Resolve to believe nothing, and you must prove your proofs and analyse your elements, sinking further and further, and finding "in the lowest depth a lower deep," till you come to the broad bosom of scepticism. I would rather be bound to defend the reasonableness of assuming that Christianity is true, than to demonstrate a moral governance from the physical world. Life is for action. If we insist on proofs for everything, we shall never come to action: to act you must assume, and that assumption is faith.

Let no one suppose that in saying this I am maintaining that all proofs are equally difficult, and all propositions equally debatable. Some assumptions are greater than others, and some doctrines involve postulates larger than others, and more numerous. I only say that impressions lead to action, and that reasonings lead from it. Knowledge of premises, and inferences upon them,—this is not to

---

[1] *In posse:* potentially.

live. It is very well as a matter of liberal curiosity and of philosophy to analyse our modes of thought; but let this come second, and when there is leisure for it, and then our examinations will in many ways even be subservient to action. But if we commence with scientific knowledge and argumentative proof, or lay any great stress upon it as the basis of personal Christianity, or attempt to make man moral and religious by Libraries and Museums, let us in consistency take chemists for our cooks, and mineralogists for our masons.

Now I wish to state all this as matter of fact, to be judged by the candid testimony of any persons whatever. Why we are so constituted that Faith, not Knowledge or Argument, is our principle of action, is a question with which I have nothing to do; but I think it is a fact, and if it be such, we must resign ourselves to it as best we may, unless we take refuge in the intolerable paradox, that the mass of men are created for nothing, and are meant to leave life as they entered it. So well has this practically been understood in all ages of the world, that no Religion has yet been a Religion of physics or of philosophy. It has ever been synonymous with Revelation. It never has been a deduction from what we know: it has ever been an assertion of what we are to believe. It has never lived in a conclusion; it has ever been a message, or a history, or a vision. No legislator or priest ever dreamed of educating our moral nature by science or by argument. There is no difference here between true Religions and pretended. Moses was instructed, not to reason from the creation, but to work miracles. Christianity is a history supernatural, and almost scenic; it tells us what its Author is, by telling us what He has done. I have no wish at all to speak otherwise than respectfully of conscientious Dissenters, but I have heard it said by those who were not their enemies, and who had known much of their preaching, that they had often heard narrow-minded and bigoted clergymen, and often Dissenting ministers of a far more intellectual cast; but that Dissenting teaching came to nothing,—that it was dissipated in thoughts which had no point, and inquiries which converged to no centre, that it ended as it began, and sent away its hearers as it found them;— whereas the instruction in the Church, with all its defects and mistakes, comes to some end, for it started from some beginning. Such is the difference between the dogmatism of faith and the speculations of logic.

Lord Brougham himself, as we have already seen, has recognized the force of this principle. He has not left his philosophical religion to argument; he has committed it to the keeping of the imagination. Why should he depict a great republic of letters, and an intellectual Pantheon, but that he feels that instances and patterns, not logical reasonings, are the living conclusions which alone have a hold over the affections, or can form the character?

George Santayana

Leaving Church

Protestant faith does not vanish into the sunlight as Catholic faith does, but leaves a shadowy ghost haunting the night of the soul. Faith, in the two cases, was not faith in the same sense; for the Catholic it was belief in a report or an argument: for the Protestant it was confidence in an allegiance. When Catholics leave the church they do so by the south door, into the glare of the market-place, where their eye is at once attracted by the wares displayed in the booths, by the flower-stalls with their bright awnings, by the fountain with its baroque Tritons blowing the spray into the air, and the children laughing and playing round it, by the concourse of townspeople and strangers, and by the soldiers, perhaps, marching past; and if they cast a look back at the church at all, it is only to admire its antique architecture, that crumbling filigree of stone so poetically surviving in its incongruous setting. It is astonishing sometimes with what contempt, with what a complete absence of understanding, unbelievers in Catholic countries look back on their religion. For one cultivated mind that sees in that religion a monument to his racial genius, a heritage of poetry and art almost as precious as the classical heritage, which indeed it incorporated in a hybrid form, there are twenty ignorant radicals who pass it by apologetically, as they might the broken toys or dusty schoolbooks of childhood. Their political animosity, legitimate in itself, blinds their imagination, and renders them even politically foolish; because in their injustice to human nature and to their national history they discredit their own cause, and provoke reaction.

Protestants, on the contrary, leave the church by the north door, into the damp solitude of a green churchyard, amid yews and weeping willows and overgrown mounds and fallen illegible gravestones. They feel a terrible chill; the few weedy flowers that may struggle through that long grass do not console them; it was far brighter and warmer and more decent inside. The church—boring as the platitudes and insincerities were which you listened to there for hours—was an edifice, something protective, social, and human; whereas here, in this vague unhomely wilderness, nothing seems to await you but discouragement and melancholy. Better the church than the mad-house. And yet the Protestant can hardly go back, as the Catholic does easily on occasion, out of habit, or fatigue, or disappointment in life, or metaphysical delusion, or the emotional weakness of the death-bed. No, the Protestant is more in earnest, he carries his problem and his religion within him. In his very desolation he will find God. This has often been a cause of wonder to me: the Protestant pious economy is so repressive and morose and the Catholic so charitable and pagan, that I should have expected the Catholic sometimes to sigh a little for his Virgin and his saints, and the Protestant to shout for joy at having got rid of his God. But the trouble is that the poor Protestant can't get rid of his God; for his idea of God is a vague symbol that

"Leaving Church" is reprinted with the permission of Charles Scribner's Sons from *Soliloquies in England and Later Soliloquies,* pages 88–90, by George Santayana (1922).

stands not essentially, as with the Catholic, for a particular legendary or theological personage, but rather for that unfathomable influence which, if it does not make for righteousness, at least has so far made for existence and has imposed it upon us; so that go through what doors you will and discard what dogmas you choose, God will confront you still whichever way you may turn. In this sense the enlightened Catholic, too, in leaving the church, has merely rediscovered God, finding him now not in the church alone, but in the church only as an expression of human fancy, and in human life itself only as in one out of a myriad forms of natural existence. But the Protestant is less clear in his gropings, the atmosphere of his inner man is more charged with vapours, and it takes longer for the light dubiously to break through; and often in his wintry day the sun sets without shining.

Joseph Wood Krutch

The Mystique of the Desert

Of the official mystical writers I am no great reader. The clarity of their visions, the overwhelming certainty of their conviction that ultimate truth has been revealed to them, is foreign to my own experience. At most I have "intimations," not assurances, and I doubt that I could ever go further in recommendation of the complete mystics than William James goes when he bids the ordinary mortal recognize the reality, in some realm, of the phenomena to which the mystics testify, no matter what interpretation we ordinary mortals put upon them. Yet I, and many whose temperaments are no more mystical than mine, do know moments when we draw courage and joy from experiences which lie outside the getting and spending of everyday life.

The occasions of such experiences are many. The commonest and perhaps the least obviously related are these: reading a poem and contemplating a child—human or animal. But the experiences come to different men in many different ways. Some are most likely to be aware of them in solitude, others in crowds; some while looking at the stars, some while watching the waves roll in upon a beach. And whether you call the experience infrarational or superrational, it involves the momentary acceptance of values not definable in terms of that common sense to which we ordinarily accord our first loyalty. And to all such experiences one thing is common. There is a sense of satisfaction which is not personal but impersonal. One no longer asks, "What's in it for me?" because one is no longer a separate selfish individual but part of the welfare and joy of the whole.

Those to whom such mystical experiences are habitual and hence more ordinary than what most people call ordinary life, can often call upon them at will as the religious mystics do by the repetition of a prayer. But to the majority there is no certain formula or ritual—not even a private, much less a communicable one. At most we can only, for example, plunge into the crowd or retire into a solitude, knowing that sometimes in the one situation or the other we will glimpse out of the corner of our eyes what, if one may believe the true mystics, is usually at the very center of the true mystic's vision.

I happen to be one of those, and we are not a few, to whom the acute awareness of a natural phenomenon, especially of a phenomenon of the living world, is the thing most likely to open the door to that joy we cannot analyze. I have experienced it sometimes when a rabbit appeared suddenly from a bush to dash away to the safety which he values so much, or when, at night, a rustle in the leaves reminds me how many busy lives surround my own. It has also come almost as vividly when I suddenly saw a flower opening or a stem pushing out of the ground.

But what is the content of the experience? What is it that at such moments I seem to realize? Of what is my happiness compounded?

First of all, perhaps, there is the vivid assurance that these things, that the universe itself, really do exist, that life is not a dream; second, that the reality is pervasive and, it seems, unconquerable. The future of mankind is dubious. Perhaps the future of the whole earth is only somewhat less dubious. But one knows that all does not depend upon man, that possibly, even, it does not depend upon this earth. Should man disappear, rabbits may well still run and flowers may still open. If this globe itself should perish, then it seems not unreasonable to suppose that what inspires the stem and the flower may exist somewhere else. And I, it seems, am at least part of all this.

God looked upon the world and found that it was good. How great is the happiness of being able, even for a moment, to agree with Him! And how much easier that is if one is not committed to considering only some one section of the world or of the universe.

Long before I ever saw the desert I was aware of the mystical overtones which the observation of nature made audible to me. But I have never been more frequently or more vividly aware of them than in connection with the desert phenomena. And I have often wondered why.

Were I to believe what certain psychologists have been trying to tell me, the thing which I call a "mystique" and especially what I call "the mystique of the desert" is only the vague aura left behind by certain experiences of infancy and childhood. Should I search my memory of the latter I should certainly find there what nearly every other American or European would: a Christmas card showing Wise Men crossing the desert and also, in some school geography, another picture of rolling dunes, a camel and the caption, "Sahara Desert." Both seemed then to be things I should never see; both were remote from the scene of my sorrows—whatever at the moment I found my sorrows to be. "Poof!" say those psychologists. The "mystique" is mysterious no longer. To adjust yourself to your environment would have been a simple matter. Had you been so adjusted you would never have gone to live in the American Southwest. And you would not give a damn whether Dipodomys drinks or not.

If those psychologists are right, then I am glad that I, at least, was not "adjusted" to everything and hence incapable of giving a damn about anything whatsoever. But I am not sure that they *are* right. Curiosity is not always the result of conditioning and there are words at which most imaginations kindle. Among them are all those words which suggest the untamed extravagances or the ultimate limits of nature in any one of her moods. We may prefer to live amid hills and meadows, fields and woodlots, or even, for that matter, surrounded by steel and concrete. But "wilderness," "jungle," and "desert" are still stirring words, as even movie-makers know. And it is just possible that they will continue to be such after the last Christmas card having anything to do with Christmas has disappeared from the shops and after school geographies have consented to confine themselves exclusively to "things relevant to the child's daily life." Perhaps the mind is not merely a blank slate upon which anything may be written. Perhaps it reaches out spontaneously toward what can nourish either intelligence or imagination. Perhaps it is part of nature and, without being taught, shares nature's intentions.

Most of the phrases we use glibly to exorcise or explain away the realities of our intimate experience are of quite recent origin—phrases like "emotional conditioning," "complex," "fixation," and even "reflex." But one of the most inclusive, and the most relevant here, is older. It was Ruskin, of all people, who invented the term "pathetic fallacy" to stigmatize as in some sense unjustified our tendency to perceive a smiling landscape as "happy," a somber one as "sad." But is it really a fallacy? Are we so separate from nature that our states are actually discontinuous with it? Is there nothing outside ourselves which is somehow glad or sad? Is it really a fallacy when we attribute to nature feelings analogous to our own?

Out of the very heart of the romantic feeling for nature the question arose. And it was Coleridge, again of all people, who gave the answer upon which the post-romantic "scientific" attitude rests: "Only in ourselves does nature live." But Wordsworth, who recorded Coleridge's dictum, was not himself always sure. When he was most himself it seemed to him that, on the contrary, the joy of nature was older than the joy of man and that what was transitory in the individual was permanent somewhere else. When the moment of happiness passed, it was not because the glory had faded but only because his own sight had grown dim.

> There was a time when meadow, grove, and stream,
> The earth, and every common sight,
>   To me did seem
> Apparelled in celestial light,
> The glory and the freshness of a dream.
>
> .   .   .   .

Oh joy! that in our embers
Is something that doth live,
That nature yet remembers
What was so fugitive!

Something like this is what, in clumsy prose, I am trying to suggest. "Wilderness," "jungle," "desert," are not magic words because we have been "conditioned" to find them such but because they stand for things which only conditioning can make seem indifferent or alien. How could the part be greater than the whole? How can nature's meaning come wholly from man when he is only part of that meaning? "Only in ourselves does nature live" is less true than its opposite: "Only in nature do *we* have a being."

The most materialistic of historians do not deny the influence upon a people of the land on which they live. When they say, for instance, that the existence of a frontier was a dominant factor in shaping the character of the American people, they are not thinking only of a physical fact. They mean also that the idea of a frontier, the realization that space to be occupied lay beyond it, took its place in the American imagination and sparked the sense that there was "somewhere else to go" rather than that the solution of every problem, practical or spiritual, had to be found within the limits to which the man who faced them was confined.

In the history of many other peoples the character of their land, even the very look of the landscape itself, has powerfully influenced how they felt and what they thought about. They were woodsmen or plainsmen or mountaineers not only economically but spiritually also. And nothing, not even the sea, has seemed to affect men more profoundly than the desert, or seemed to incline them so powerfully toward great thoughts, perhaps because the desert itself seems to brood and to encourage brooding. To the Hebrews the desert spoke of God, and one of the most powerful of all religions was born. To the Arabs it spoke of the stars, and astronomy came into being.

Perhaps no fact about the American people is more important than the fact that the continent upon which they live is large enough and varied enough to speak with many different voices—of the mountains, of the plains, of the valleys and of the seashore—all clear voices that are distinct and strong. Because Americans listened to all these voices, the national character has had many aspects and developed in many different directions. But the voice of the desert is the one which has been least often heard. We came to it last, and when we did come, we came principally to exploit rather than to listen.

To those who do listen, the desert speaks of things with an emphasis quite different from that of the shore, the mountains, the valleys or the plains. Whereas they invite action and suggest limitless opportunity, exhaustless resources, the implications and the mood of the desert are something different. For one thing the desert is conservative, not radical. It is more likely to provoke awe than to invite conquest. It does not, like the plains, say, "Only turn the sod and uncountable riches will spring up." The heroism which it encourages is the heroism of endurance, not that of conquest.

Precisely what other things it says depends in part upon the person listening. To the biologist it speaks first of the remarkable flexibility of living things, of the processes of adaptation which are nowhere more remarkable than in the strange devices by which plants and animals have learned to conquer heat and dryness. To the practical-minded conservationist it speaks sternly of other things, because in the desert the problems created by erosion and overexploitation are plainer and more acute than anywhere else. But to the merely contemplative it speaks of courage and endurance of a special kind.

Here the thought of the contemplative crosses the thought of the conservationist, because the contemplative realizes that the desert is "the last frontier" in more senses than one. It is the last because it was the latest reached, but it is the last also because it is, in many ways, a frontier which *cannot* be crossed. It brings man up against his limitations, turns him in upon himself and suggests values which more indulgent regions minimize. Sometimes it inclines to contemplation men who have never contemplated before. And of all answers to the question "What is a desert good for?" "Contemplation" is perhaps the best.

The eighteenth century invented a useful distinction which we have almost lost, the distinction between the beautiful and the sublime. The first, even when it escapes being merely the pretty, is easy and reassuring. The sublime, on the other hand, is touched with something which inspires awe. It is large and powerful; it carries with it the suggestion that it might overwhelm us if it would. By these definitions there is no doubt which is the right word for the desert. In intimate details, as when its floor is covered after a spring rain with the delicate little ephemeral plants, it is pretty. But such embodiments of prettiness seem to be only tolerated with affectionate contempt by the region as a whole. As a whole the desert is, in the original sense of the word, "awful." Perhaps one feels a certain boldness in undertaking to live with it and a certain pride when one discovers that one can.

I am not suggesting that everyone should listen to the voice of the desert and listen to no other. For a nation which believes, perhaps rightly enough, that it has many more conquests yet to make, that voice preaches a doctrine too close to quietism. But I am suggesting that the voice of the desert might well be heard occasionally among the others. To go "up to the mountain" or "into the desert" has become part of the symbolical language. If it is good to make occasionally what the religious call a "retreat," there is no better place than the desert to make it. Here if anywhere the most familiar realities recede and others come into the foreground of the mind.

A world traveler once said that every man owed it to himself to see the tropics at least once in his life. Only there can he possibly realize how completely nature can fulfill certain potentialities and moods which the temperate regions only suggest. I have no doubt that he was right. Though I have never got beyond the outer fringe of the tropical lands, I hope that some day I shall get into their heart. But I am sure that they are no more necessary than the desert to an adequate imaginative grasp of the world we live in. Those who have never known it are to be pitied, like a man who has never read *Hamlet* or heard the

Jupiter Symphony. He has missed something which is unique. And there is nothing else which can give him more than a hint of what he has missed. To have experienced it is to be prepared to see other landscapes with new eyes and to participate with a fresh understanding in the life of other natural communities.

Leonard Sidney Woolf

Chronicle and History

Mankind in the mass has often been compared, cynically or otherwise, to insects. To the historian proper the image of an ant-heap is almost inevitable. When he looks back into the past, he sees no great men or famous names, but myriads of minute and nameless human insects, hurrying this way and that, making wars and laws, building and destroying cities and civilizations. The swarm ebbs and flows over the earth and through the centuries, the groups converging and coalescing or breaking up and scattering. The story of this ant-heap, of its impersonal groups and communities and of their ebb and flow upon the earth, is history.

History may be a bare record of mankind in groups or communities. The historian takes a section of the ant-heap at a certain time or period, examines its records and documents, and tells us what was happening at the moment inside it. "They" were wearing togas or trousers, building Nineveh or burning Rome, making a king into a god or cutting his head off. The works of these recorders are often called chronicles, and it is frequently said that early historians should rightly be called chroniclers. But the point of view of the chronicler still exists, even when history has become highly developed and sophisticated. He is impersonal and undiscriminating in the sense that he rarely has a theory or is concerned with cause and effect. The scope of his vision into the past is limited to a particular moment of time, for he is the natural historian of the human insect, and what interests him is the bare fact that the insect was doing a particular thing at a particular time. In consequence the resemblance between the activities of the human race and those of an ant-heap is nowhere more striking than in the pages of chroniclers. There is the same hurrying and scurrying of hordes of little creatures, each terribly intent upon its own particular piece of business, which at the same time in some mysterious way is obviously part of the communal business. And that business in the unanalyzed and isolated narrative of the chronicle seems to be made up of a number of blind, irrational, and inexplicable impulses. Read, for instance, in such a book as the *History of Persia* by Sir Percy Sykes, which is essentially a chronicle, the narrative of what is known about those "early

From *After the Deluge* by Leonard Woolf. Reprinted by permission of Harcourt, Brace and World, Inc., and Leonard Woolf.

civilizations" of Assyrians, Elamites, Babylonians, who built and burned their cities and slaughtered one another for many centuries in and around Mesopotamia. If we were not hypnotized by the tradition and dogma that there is some meaning and purpose in human history, it would be impossible to read that bare story without the same kind of shrinking or disgust as is caused by the spectacle of a mass of flies and other insects swarming over a dead body. Or take a long leap forward with the imagination, from this chronicle of what we are pleased to call primitive civilizations or uncivilized peoples, to our own times: imagine the history of the years 1914 to 1918 told in the style of a chronicle. The chronicler, with little or no comment or explanation, without searching for causes or troubling about effects, would relate the bald story of what the human race, divided into the groups called European nations, was doing between September 1914 and November 1918. Such a narrative might be extremely interesting and illuminating, but, if it were read by anyone who did not know that European man was highly civilized and rational, with a divine spark in his breast or brain (sometimes called a soul), with his eyes turned heavenwards and his feet steadily mounting the ladder of evolution, he would only see a strange spectacle of millions of little creatures engaged in destroying one another (when not burrowing in the earth) ; of other swarms frantically beating their ploughshares into shells; of lesser swarms, in the safe background and over the heads of the fighters, perpetually screaming abuse and noble words of defiance at one another; while here and there some little creatures, raised somewhat above their fellows, shake their fists at one another and explain in unintelligible language the causes of the commotion and their determination never to allow it to end.

It is possible that the chronicler is the only really scientific and philosophical historian, that there is no more to be said about the human insect than such facts as these: that in the year 2218 B.C. upon a plain in the land of Shinar it was trying to build out of bricks and slime a tower which might reach to heaven; that 1700 or 1800 years later around the Aegean Sea it was fighting, producing the plays of Sophocles and Aeschylus, and at nights upon Greek mountains by the light of torches, clothed in deer-skins and carrying ivy-wreathed wands, it tore in pieces goats and other animals and danced wildly to the sound of flutes and cymbals; that in A.D. 33 it crucified the Son of God; that 1500 years later it slaughtered in Germany and Holland 100,000 persons because they not only demanded the right to fish and hunt, but believed that adults and not infants should be baptized; and that in 1914 it slaughtered millions of persons in an effort to decide whether the world should be ruled by the German Emperor or by democracy. It may indeed be that there is nothing more to be recorded of the human race than bare facts such as these, and that history, unperverted by human arrogance, should be an almost infinite series of such facts. If so, the chronicler is a far profounder historian than philosophers like Signor Croce would ever be capable of imagining.

The philosophy of history which underlies the chronicle is so pessimistic and so humiliating that in this age of science and proud idealism we cannot accept it without a struggle. The historian introduces two theories, which are alien to the chronicler and his outlook, in order at least to make the story of human communities compatible with human dignity. These are the theories of progress and regression and of cause and effect. As I propose to accept them as a working hypothesis in this book, it is necessary to explain in what sense they are to be accepted.

History differs from chronicle, when besides recording a mere series of facts or events, it traces or implies in its record of them a movement and direction. And the movement is that of the life of the human animal as it is lived in communities, while the direction is conceived as either up or down, forward or backward. History is, in fact, either consciously or implicitly directed and inspired by the idea of "civilization." It no longer conceives the communal past of the human race as consisting of an infinite number of isolated events, acts, and activities, all of them equally significant and important, but as a continuous "life" in whose procession a series of events only acquires historical significance in so far as it indicates progress or regression. To the chronicler the fact that slime was used instead of mortar to build the tower of Babel is just as important, and therefore as worthy of record, as the object of the architecture; the historian may be able to read in the slime some evidence as to the level which material civilization had reached in the land of Shinar, but the fact which he will seize upon as infinitely more relevant is the communal object of the builders, for it is that which really throws light upon their "cultural development," their civilization.

John Nef

Art, Science, and Life

As a historian I would suggest that the inner experiences of individual persons can be of compelling importance to the future of the human race. Simone Weil was right in saying that: "Personal feelings play a role in the great events of this world that is never perceived to its full extent. The fact that friendship exists or does not exist between two men, or between two groups of human beings, in some cases can prove decisive for the destiny of the human race."

If this was true in the past, it is even truer now, when an economy of abundance has for the first time in history replaced an economy of scarcity in many parts of the world. The need for a change in the aspirations of human beings away from force in the direction of friendship and love has been accentuated by the growing futility of force now that, without it, there is the possibility of distributing sufficient material commodities to satisfy the legitimate wants of the many. The need for this change has been made still more compelling by the

Reprinted with permission from the February 1959 issue of the *Bulletin of the Atomic Scientists*. Copyright 1959 by the Educational Foundation for Nuclear Science.

overwhelming increase in the powers of destruction. Whatever may have been the justification for treating force as the final arbiter of earthly destiny in the past, there is none now that force is less likely to rule than to destroy the world.

The experiences of friendship and love which should now mean to us more than ever before in history (and alas, of course, the experiences of enmity and hate) cannot in the fullest sense be communicated through art. They can only be lived. They cannot be repeated or preserved, though the glow they produce in the participants is indestructible and is capable of being at least partially transmitted to many others, who share in the pleasure and warmth which great happiness and great beauty alone can diffuse. But these experiences, these moments of perfection, can be photographed or televised or reproduced even less adequately than a work of art, for that, once finished and released by its creator, stays put.

Such moments in life as I speak of are never forced or premeditated. They spring up within us, sometimes without preparation, though almost always out of materials, and with the help of motives, that have been much in our minds and hearts. In any event the particular form which they take is unpredictable. It derives its overwhelming strength partly from this mysterious element of surprise. This comes from the recognition of a truth that always existed but has never before been so clearly grasped, and whose relevance to one's personal experience is recognized for the first time.

In these respects the deepest experiences of life partly differ from and partly resemble works of art. They differ because they are the result of a relationship between at least two persons, whereas a work of art can hardly come successfully except from a single mind and imagination. But they also resemble works of art because the artist, in the process of creation, is carried forward in his greatest flights of genius by intuitive inner experiences which are as little premeditated as are the greatest moments between two lovers. If we try to reproduce, to define, or to explain these moments with brush strokes, or notes or even with words, we fail as artists. Yet, though this appears to be contradictory, unless the artist has lived such moments and is able to transfuse their essence into the stories he tells, the poems he writes, the symphonies he composes, he can hardly achieve the highest levels of art. I think it was Goethe who said that the universal is the unique. It is a Goethe, a Shakespeare or a Dante who is able, as the result of a kind of inner dialogue, to snatch out of eternity something of the permanence, the richness, and the freshness which come to some few human beings without words in the supreme moments of living.

I have suggested that a work of art stays put once the artist has finished with it, but in another sense the greatest works of art are continually in movement. That is what makes them living works. How is it that in these works the artist has managed to escape from the prison to which all craftsmen are condemned because of the formal rules of their craft and because of the necessity they are under to finish one composition and start another? In trying to answer this question we are helped by a distinction that needs to be drawn between art and natural science. If artistic statement, even at its greatest, lacks something of the freshness of the greatest moments of life, scientific statement, while often fascinating to the intelligence, leaves aside all the crucial questions of man's inner life. As Schrödinger has said: "The scientific picture of the real world around us ... knows nothing of beautiful and ugly, good or bad, God and eternity."[1]

Another scientist remarked to me recently that the great success of modern scientific methods has resulted from the simplicity of the problems raised for solution. But, he went on to say, the problems that stand in vital need of solution in the atomic age are in another realm; they are not simple but immensely complicated problems. They are problems which, as Schrödinger says in the same passage, relate to the human personality; so they involve the soul. Here, Schrödinger suggests, science has "used the greatly simplifying device of cutting our own personality out, removing it."[2] If this is essentially true, then the enormous interest of governments and private enterprise in subsidizing science and technology, while desirable and valuable, leaves untouched those issues on which the future happiness of the human race depends, save insofar as a higher standard of living might provide men leisure to concern themselves with those issues. What are they? Are they not the conditions that will make possible a sufficient growth of international understanding to diminish the danger of total war?

Now the artist never can set out to solve practical problems, or to preach sermons, or to engage in any kind of propaganda; I mean he cannot do these things and remain an artist. But if he is concerned with truth, virtue, and beauty, he is far nearer to the issues that are vital to the future of mankind than is the scientist. For the artist is concerned with those matters on which science is ghastly silent—God and eternity, good and bad, beautiful and ugly, love and hatred—all that is close to the heart. In dealing with his subject, the artist must also seek to simplify. He aims to achieve as great an economy, as great an inevitability as possible in his lines and colors, his notes, or his words, but this is never done by rendering the human problems that he chooses for his subject less complex than they are. The essentials that he seeks are those which help us to understand the complexities of the universal, and so help to provide a guiding light for men and women of all classes, all races, all generations.

The artist's purpose in simplifying is different from the natural scientist's; in some ways it is the antithesis of the natural scientist's. Human motives, human passions, human faith and hope are not ruled out insofar as possible, as in scientific statements; they are given a central position in a true work of art. It is the complexities embodied in what is made to seem simple, even to verge on the banal, that can make such a work permanently enriching. While a consciousness of its beauty is likely to well up in a sensitive person at the first meeting, the sense of its many-sided significance grows with familiarity; for it is somewhat as with love: the test of the authenticity of a work of art is hidden in its capacity to withstand and to triumph over familiarity.

Why do these distinctions exist between art (and life) and science? It is

[1] Erwin Schrödinger, *Nature and the Greeks,* Cambridge, 1954, p. 93.
[2] *Ibid.,* p. 94.

because cutting out the human personality is as fatal to art as it has been apparently necessary to modern science. Unlike a scientific statement, a great work of art depends for its power more on a richness than on a precision of meaning. This isn't the same as saying that the words, the sounds, the lines or the colors are unclear; they have indeed a perfect clarity that is hardly possible in a scientific statement because the truths they express are so much more varied and weighty, so much more human and divine than those contained in scientific statements.

This essential character of a work of art can perhaps be best exemplified with reference to music. One may almost say that the more wonderful a musical composition is, the more it is likely to strike the listener differently each time he hears it. It says new things whenever it is performed, and these varied resources of meaning are inexhaustible. That is what gives it, of course, its extraordinary fascination for the performer of genius. The late Artur Schnabel played the piano with a perfect naturalness and a love which made him, for me at least, the most moving musical interpreter of his times. I never heard him play any compositions other than those of Bach, Mozart, Beethoven, Schubert, Schumann, and Brahms. And in fact in his maturity those were the only works he played. He once explained to me that as a young man he had memorized for performance many pieces of other composers, but he discovered that when he played them once in public he was able to play them as well as it seemed to him they could be played. Whereas no matter how many times he tried, he was never able to play the works of Mozart, Beethoven, and Schubert in particular as well as they could be played. Each performance of these was, in consequence, a new experience, and this enabled him to fall in love with the work each time, which is the condition of doing anything human supremely well. That was how he achieved such freshness, without a trace of the mechanical, how he achieved the humility and self-efface-ment that is possible only in submission to what is divinely inspired.

I had heard him play several of the same pieces a number of times, and so was able to recognize the validity of his explanation. But I must not be understood to be saying that the greatest music or the greatest works of art can be interpreted any way anyone pleases. There is a limit to the freedom of interpretation.

With every work of art there is this problem of interpretation. If the work is not performed—like a musical composition or a drama—or read aloud like a poem, the person who reads or contemplates it interprets it directly instead of through the medium of performers. Whatever the medium between the author who creates and the individual who receives his creation, it is not any interpreta-tion that will do. The poet, the novelist, the painter can no more be held responsible for a failure of interpretation on the part of the reader or spectator than a composer could be held responsible for the failure of one of his more perfect compositions when performed without skill or understanding.

It is not that the artist has no responsibility for his works once they are given to the public. His responsibility is of a different kind from that of the scientist. The meaning of a scientist's results for those who understand them can hardly be equivocal. But the consequences of these results, when they are utilized for practical ends, can be dangerous to the whole future of the human race. Scientists

have known of this danger at least since the times of Archimedes, but the danger
has assumed overwhelming proportions only in the twentieth century, after the
scientists had been caught off guard because of the reassuring opinion, held
widely during the eighteenth and nineteenth centuries, that mankind was under-
going a kind of moral perfection which was making total war impossible. In
view of the nature of scientific problems, and the evolution of scientific methods,
scientific statements have no direct effects on the moral condition and ethical
conduct of human beings. But works of art can have a most profound influence
on the human personality and on conduct. And the very variety and richness of
the results which the great artist manages to achieve make the influence of a work
of art up to a point equivocal in the highly complex realm of experience which it
is the glory of the artist to explore. That a work of art has, unlike a scientific
result, a direct moral effect is certain, but the nature of that moral effect is, alas,
much less certain than the intellectual effect of a scientific statement. So much
depends not on the work but on the individual who experiences the work of art.
It is possible for a work whose ethical *intentions* are above reproach to be used by
a weak man as a justification for doing evil; it is possible for a publication whose
ethical intentions are vicious, for example, a piece of pornographic writing, to
fortify the virtue of a strong man.

The risks have to be taken. Beauty is an explosive compound. But the dangers
in the explosions from art are small in comparison with those in the explosions
from science. And the complex problems that confront the human race today, for
which science is partly responsible, but which modern science cannot answer, are
problems much more closely related to art.

What folly, then, it would be to suggest that the search for beauty be absorbed
by science. That would be a way of abandoning beauty, on the ground that the
greatest works of art have sometimes corrupted men or women who were already
on the slope leading to the abyss. Yet these references to the Christian Gospel
remind us of the artist's true responsibility. It is to be better than he is, both as an
artist and a man, for if art and life gain by being drawn to each other, the split
between art and the good is always at the expense of both. My historical work is
leading me to believe that both "civilization," in the original eighteenth-century
sense of the word, and the industrialism which grew out of this "civilization,"
were at long last an outcome of the Christian Gospel, in the sense that without
the Christian experience the world would have had neither civilization nor industrialism. If there is anything in this view, there will be few perhaps who
would suggest that we would have been better off without Christianity, fewer still
who would suggest that the moral dangers in the Gospel outweigh the hopes of
redemption which it has nourished.

A fundamental component of beauty then is virtue. The two are one and both
are one with truth. If the artists now become aware of these truths, and strive to
fashion their lives and their art in the light of them, the world that is so
perilously near to destruction might be saved by art and by the love which is
inseparable from it. In all humility I can only say that I can conceive of no other
way to save it.

Allan Nevins

The Struggle to Make the Past Alive

Clio, the Muse of History, does not dwell (as most people think) in cozy libraries and shaded archives. She presides over a dangerous battlefield, where angry groups charge and grapple, and one cohort no sooner gains a height than an enfilading fire is opened from both flanks. Among skirmishers and guerrillas two great central combats never cease. One is fought between Hegelians, who believe that the facts of the past should be pushed and locked into a philosophic system, and the followers of Gibbon and Von Ranke, who believe in an open-minded and relativist approach to the data of history. The other unceasing, clangorous battle rages between those who hold that the best approach to historical truth is that of the artist with his power of divination and those who fight for the scientific approach, with its calipers and micrometer.

These two main battles about the writing of history will never end; for history has to be interpretive, and ideas upon the proper method of interpretation must always differ. Nor will minor skirmishes and engagements ever end, for history constantly has to be lifted out of conventional ruts. This is what lends history its deepest interest. To the true student it is never dead; it is always aggressively, challengingly alive. It is never written once and for all, but has incessantly to be rewritten.

The history texts state that Sherman's March to the Sea was one of the great pivotal events of the Civil War. But a writer arises who points out that Lieutenant General John M. Schofield believed that the war would have ended just as quickly had Sherman never made that march; that other notable military authorities believed that Thomas' destruction of Hood's army was the really crucial event in the West; and that Sherman himself wrote that his march northward from Savannah was ten times more important than the swath to the sea. Where then stands the old view?

The conventional texts give great emphasis to the Forty-niners, the other gold rushes, and the Comstock and other mining camps. But a historian rises to point out that all the gold and silver produced throughout the world since 1492 has been worth only about sixteen billions of dollars, a sum probably less than the cost of finding and extracting it; that the petroleum pumped in the United States alone between 1859 and 1947 had an estimated field value of more than sixty billions; and that the American petroleum output of the past four years was very likely worth more than the gold output of the globe since Columbus. How then can we justify the heavy space given to gold rushes, and the very limited space to oil, in most texts of American history?

"In vain the sage, with retrospective eye," wrote Pope, "would from the apparent *what* conclude the *why.*" Of the two main battles over historical interpretation mentioned above, that between the school of Ranke and the school of Hegel seems especially far from a termination.

The true historical attitude, argues one side, is a search for all the facts about a

Reprinted by permission of *The New York Times* and Allan Nevins.

given situation, force, or event—the Puritan regime, the Abolitionist Movement, Pearl Harbor—which slowly, painfully, accurately dredges up an interpretation *not* mapped out in advance. That is, history should operate by the inductive, not the deductive, use of evidence. An Olympian historian like Gibbon says in effect: "Let us collect and collate all the relevant facts, and find what conclusions emerge from their impartial analysis." Not so, says the other side; the true way to the truth about the past is to use a theory which will grope deep into the confusing array of facts and occurrences. Such a deductive historian as Charles A. Beard remarks, in effect: "Let us take this provocative theory of what happened at a given time, say in making the Constitution, and see if we can collect an array of evidence which offers overwhelming proof." Enemies of this school cry, "Tendentious history!" And in rebuttal, enemies of the open-minded school shout: "Plodding history! History without ideas!"

But, by contrast, the battle between the literary and the scientific schools of historical interpretation, so stubborn and protracted, does show a definite contemporaneous tendency toward the victory of the artist over the micrometrist. For evidence we need only point to the publishing lists of the last quarter-century, and particularly of the last decade. A century ago, when Prescott and Motley were at the height of their powers, when Irving was still alive and Parkman just well launched in his race, the literary historian was dominant in this country, as he was in the England of Macaulay, Carlyle, and Froude. Francis Parkman, by common consent the greatest of our historians, enunciated in two sentences the creed of his illustrious group: "Faithfulness to history involves far more than a research, however patient and scrupulous, into special facts. Such facts may be detailed with the most scrupulous minuteness, and yet the narrative, taken as a whole, may be unmeaning or untrue."

This was a great truth. The Dryasdusts whom Carlyle so often denounced, with all their dedication to precise fact, often did more to falsify the picture of the past than the most careless artist. Unhappily, for a long generation after Parkman's climactic "Montcalm and Wolfe" (1884) this truth was obscured. A school of Teutonic tradition and training, which exalted monographic thoroughness, declared that nothing mattered but endless research, laborious sifting of facts, and rigorous analysis of evidence. The scientific element was all-important; the literary element was subsidiary and unessential if not positively harmful. For that long generation Americans, offered a fare represented by Von Holst, Justin Winsor, Osgood, and Channing (able men of their type, and true scholars), either ceased to read history for pleasure or read John Fiske and Edward Eggleston in spite of sneers.

Yet Theodore Roosevelt was entirely correct when, revolting against the arid precisians, he wrote that history is not good unless it is "a vivid and powerful presentation of scientific matter in *literary form*." For, as Roosevelt himself helped prove in "The Winning of the West" (G. P. Putnam), form and substance are not separable entities; and certain virtues of literary form are as vital to a complete presentation of historical truth as are certain virtues of scientific method. The historian can no more ascertain the truth about the past and convey it to his reader without literary power than without scientific discipline. The over-dull writer falsifies the past just as damagingly as did the over-romantic William Wirt or the over-imaginative Emil Ludwig.

Imagination is an artistic quality. Now imagination does not disable a conscientious writer from presenting facts in accurate form; it enormously assists him in doing so. Any researcher can collect overwhelming masses of facts and yet leave them utterly lifeless, drab and unmeaning. Was the past lifeless? On the contrary, it was as much alive as is the world of the present—but only imagination sees this. Lord Macaulay in one of his most famous passages protested that the want of imagination in most of the historians preceding him had caused them to miss the full truth.

"A truly great historian," he wrote, "would reclaim those materials which the novelist has appropriated. We should not then have to look for the wars and votes of the Puritans in Clarendon, and for their phraseology in 'Old Mortality,' for one half of King James in Hume and the other half in 'The Fortunes of Nigel.' . . . Society would be shown from the highest to the lowest, from the throne of the legate to the chimney corner where the begging friar regaled himself. Palmers, minstrels, crusaders, the stately monastery with the good cheer in its refectory, and the tournament with the herald and ladies, the trumpets and the cloth of gold, would give truth and life to the presentation."

Without life, there is no truth to history, and without imagination there is no life. Imagination joined with research in the wonderful narratives which both Motley and Froude wrote of the destruction of the Great Armada. It was because he possessed the kind of imagination which could convert a handful of prosaic facts into an arresting picture that Macaulay penned so vivid an account of the starvation of Londonderry ("There was scarcely a cellar in which some corpse was not decaying") and the entry of the rescuing army. It was by use of the imagination that Parkman made so real Wolfe's battle-array on the Plains of Abraham, and that capitulation of Vaudreuil at Montreal which he summed up in one unforgettable sentence—"Half the continent had changed hands at the scratch of a pen."

Human warmth and sympathy are allied qualities which, belonging to the artist and not the scientific researcher, are indispensable to a faithful reconstruction of the past. The power of understanding character is primarily a literary gift; it has little to do with erudite grubbing (though that is not to be despised, but honored) in tons of manuscripts. Human sympathy is a gift which brings novelist, poet and historian near together. We need not wonder that Walter Scott and Victor Hugo wrote history, or that Parkman, Prescott, and Froude all wrote novels. Sympathy extends to places, to things and to atmosphere, but it is most valuable to the historian when used to penetrate human nature. Without a profound sympathy with the people of the North, Carl Sandburg could never have written his chapter on the Deep Shadows of early 1863 in the third volume of his "Abraham Lincoln: The War Years"; without sympathy, Douglas Freeman could never have written his chapter on The Sword of Lee.

For literary and artistic virtues have flowed back, full tide, into the best historical writing of the present generation. Narrative history—a good story, racily told—has regained its old and proper ascendency over analytical discussion. The panoramic theme, as distinguished from the monograph, is no longer neglected. For a time a chasm seemed opening in America between the academic and non-academic writers of history; but now the best academic historians write with as much dash as their outside brethren, and the best non-academic historians with a scholarship unexcelled in ivied walls.

With imagination, with sympathy, and with stylistic eloquence, there has come into historical writing a deepened moral sense much needed in this troubled age. The greatest of all living historians has set on the title page of his greatest series of works, the motto: "In War, Resolution. In Defeat, Defiance. In Victory, Magnanimity. In Peace, Good Will." That furnishes readers of Mr. Churchill's noble chronicle something of what Thomas Carlyle called "the divine idea"; and not a little historical writing of the time is pervaded with the sense that human life has to be given moral dignity, or it is worth nothing.

Edward Sapir

The Social Functions of Language

It is difficult to see adequately the functions of language, because it is so deeply rooted in the whole of human behavior that it may be suspected that there is little in the functional side of our conscious behavior in which language does not play its part. The primary function of language is generally said to be communication. There can be no quarrel with this so long as it is distinctly understood that there may be effective communication without overt speech and that language is highly relevant to situations which are not obviously of a communicative sort. To say that thought, which is hardly possible in any sustained sense without the symbolic organization brought by language, is that form of communication in which the speaker and the person addressed are identified in one person is not far from begging the question. The autistic speech of children seems to show that the purely communicative aspect of language has been exaggerated. It is best to admit that language is primarily a vocal actualization of the tendency to see realities symbolically, that it is precisely this quality which renders it a fit instrument for communication and that it is in the actual give and take of social intercourse that it has been complicated and refined into the form in which it is known today. Besides the very general function which language fulfills in the spheres of thought, communication, and expression which are implicit in its very

From *Encyclopedia of the Social Sciences*, by Edward Sapir. Copyright 1939 by The Macmillan Company and used with their permission.

nature, there may be pointed out a number of special derivatives of these which are of particular interest to students of society.

Language is a great force of socialization, probably the greatest that exists. By this is meant not merely the obvious fact that significant social intercourse is hardly possible without language but that the mere fact of a common speech serves as a peculiarly potent symbol of the social solidarity of those who speak the language. The psychological significance of this goes far beyond the association of particular languages with nationalities, political entities, or smaller local groups. In between the recognized dialect or language as a whole and the individualized speech of a given individual lies a kind of linguistic unit which is not often discussed by the linguist but which is of the greatest importance to social psychology. This is the subform of a language which is current among a group of people who are held together by ties of common interest. Such a group may be a family, the undergraduates of a college, a labor union, the underworld in a large city, the members of a club, a group of four or five friends who hold together through life in spite of differences of professional interest, and untold thousands of other kinds of groups. Each of these tends to develop peculiarities of speech which have the symbolic function of somehow distinguishing the group from the larger group into which its members might be too completely absorbed. The complete absence of linguistic indices of such small groups is obscurely felt as a defect or sign of emotional poverty. Within the confines of a particular family, for instance, the name "Georgy," having once been mispronounced "Doody" in childhood, may take on the latter form forever after; and this unofficial pronunciation of a familiar name as applied to a particular person becomes a very important symbol indeed of the solidarity of a particular family and of the continuance of the sentiment that keeps its members together. A stranger cannot lightly take on the privilege of saying "Doody" if the members of the family feel that he is not entitled to go beyond the degree of familiarity symbolized by the use of "Georgy" or "George." Again, no one is entitled to say "trig" or "math" who has not gone through such familiar and painful experience as a high school or undergraduate student. The use of such words at once declares the speaker a member of an unorganized but psychologically real group. A self-made mathematician has hardly the right to use the word "math" in referring to his own interests because the student overtones of the word do not properly apply to him. The extraordinary importance of minute linguistic differences for the symbolization of psychologically real as contrasted with politically or sociologically official groups is intuitively felt by most people. "He talks like us" is equivalent to saying "He is one of us."

There is another important sense in which language is a socializer beyond its literal use as a means of communication. This is in the establishment of rapport between the members of a physical group, such as a house party. It is not what is said that matters so much as that something is said. Particularly where cultural understandings of an intimate sort are somewhat lacking among the members of a physical group it is felt to be important that the lack be made good by a constant supply of small talk. This caressing or reassuring quality of speech in general, even where no one has anything of moment to communicate, reminds us how much more language is than a mere technique of communication. Nothing better shows how completely the life of man as an animal made over by culture is dominated by the verbal substitutes for the physical world.

The use of language in cultural accumulation and historical transmission is obvious and important. This applies not only to sophisticated levels but to primitive ones as well. A great deal of the cultural stock in trade of a primitive society is presented in a more or less well defined linguistic form. Proverbs, medicine formulae, standardized prayers, folk tales, standardized speeches, song texts, genealogies are some of the more overt forms which language takes as a culture-preserving instrument. The pragmatic ideal of education, which aims to reduce the influence of standardized lore to a minimum and to get the individual to educate himself through as direct a contact as possible with the realities of his environment, is certainly not realized among the primitives, who are often as word-bound as the humanistic tradition itself. Few cultures perhaps have gone to the length of the classical Chinese culture or of the rabbinical Jewish culture in making the word do duty for the thing or the personal experience as the ultimate unit of reality. Modern civilization as a whole, with its schools, its libraries, and its endless stores of knowledge, opinion, and sentiment stored up in verbalized form, would be unthinkable without language made eternal as document. On the whole, we probably tend to exaggerate the differences between "high" and "low" cultures or saturated and emergent cultures in the matter of traditionally conserved verbal authority. The enormous differences that seem to exist are rather differences in the outward form and content of the cultures themselves than in the psychological relation which obtains between the individual and his culture.

In spite of the fact that language acts as a socializing and uniformizing force, it is at the same time the most potent single known factor for the growth of individuality. The fundamental quality of one's voice, the phonetic patterns of speech, the speed and relative smoothness of articulation, the length and build of the sentences, the character and range of the vocabulary, the scholastic consistency of the words used, the readiness with which words respond to the requirements of the social environment, in particular the suitability of one's language to the language habits of the persons addressed—all these are so many complex indicators of the personality. "Actions speak louder than words" may be an excellent maxim from the pragmatic point of view but betrays little insight into the nature of speech. The language habits of people are by no means irrelevant as unconscious indicators of the more important traits of their personalities, and the folk is psychologically wiser than the adage in paying a great deal of attention, willingly or not, to the psychological significance of a man's language. The normal person is never convinced by the mere content of speech but is very sensitive to many of the implications of language behavior, however feebly (if at all) these may have been consciously analyzed. All in all, it is not too much to say that one of the really important functions of language is to be constantly declaring to society the psychological place held by all of its members.

Besides this more general type of personality expression or fulfillment there is to be kept in mind the important role which language plays as a substitutive means of expression for those individuals who have a greater than normal difficulty in adjusting to the environment in terms of primary action patterns. Even in the most primitive cultures the strategic word is likely to be more powerful than the direct blow. It is unwise to speak too blithely of "mere" words, for to do so may be to imperil the value and perhaps the very existence of civilization and personality.

Erich Fromm

The Nature of Symbolic Language

Let us assume you want to tell someone the difference between the taste of white wine and red wine. This may seem quite simple to you. *You* know the difference very well; why should it not be easy to explain it to someone else? Yet you find the greatest difficulty putting this taste difference into words. And probably you will end up by saying, "Now look here, I can't explain it to you. Just drink red wine and then white wine, and you will know what the difference is." You have no difficulty in finding words to explain the most complicated machine, and yet words seem to be futile to describe a simple taste experience.

Are we not confronted with the same difficulty when we try to explain a feeling experience? Let us take a mood in which you feel lost, deserted, where the world looks gray, a little frightening though not really dangerous. You want to describe this mood to a friend, but again you find yourself groping for words and eventually feel that nothing you have said is an adequate explanation of the many nuances of the mood. The following night you have a dream. You see yourself in the outskirts of a city just before dawn, the streets are empty except for a milk wagon, the houses look poor, the surroundings are unfamiliar, you have no means of accustomed transportation to places familiar to you and where you feel you belong. When you wake up and remember the dream, it occurs to you that the feeling you had in that dream was exactly the feeling of lostness and grayness you tried to describe to your friend the day before. It is just one picture, whose visualization took less than a second. And yet this picture is a more vivid and precise description than you could have given by talking *about* it at length. The picture you see in the dream is a *symbol* of something you felt.

What is a symbol? A symbol is often defined as "something that stands for something else." This definition seems rather disappointing. It becomes more interesting, however, if we concern ourselves with those symbols which are sensory expressions of seeing, hearing, smelling, touching, standing for a "some-

thing else" which is an inner experience, a feeling or thought. A symbol of this
kind is something outside ourselves; that which it symbolizes is something inside
ourselves. Symbolic language is language in which we express inner experience as
if it were a sensory experience, as if it were something we were doing or
something that was done to us in the world of things. Symbolic language is
language in which the world outside is a symbol of the world inside, a symbol
for our souls and our minds.

If we define a symbol as "something which stands for something else," the
crucial question is: *What is the specific connection between the symbol and that
which it symbolizes?*

In answer to this question we can differentiate between three kinds of symbols:
the *conventional,* the *accidental* and the *universal* symbol. As will become apparent presently, only the latter two kinds of symbols express inner experiences as if
they were sensory experiences, and only they have the elements of symbolic
language.

The *conventional* symbol is the best known of the three, since we employ it in
everyday language. If we see the word "table" or hear the sound "table," the
letters T-A-B-L-E stand for something else. They stand for the thing table that
we see, touch and use. What is the connection between the *word* "table" and the
thing "table"? Is there any inherent relationship between them? Obviously not.
The thing table has nothing to do with the sound table, and the only reason the
word symbolizes the thing is the convention of calling this particular thing by a
particular name. We learn this connection as children by the repeated experience
of hearing the word in reference to the thing until a lasting association is formed
so that we don't have to think to find the right word.

There are some words, however, where the association is not only conventional.
When we say "phooey," for instance, we make with our lips a movement of
dispelling the air quickly. It is an expression of disgust in which our mouths
participate. By this quick expulsion of air we imitate and thus express our
intention to expel something, to get it out of our system. In this case, as in some
others, the symbol has an inherent connection with the feeling it symbolizes. But
even if we assume that originally many or even all words had their origins in
some such inherent connection between symbol and the symbolized, most words
no longer have this meaning for us when we learn a language.

Words are not the only illustration for conventional symbols, although they
are the most frequent and best-known ones. Pictures also can be conventional
symbols. A flag, for instance, may stand for a specific country, and yet there is no
connection between the specific colors and the country for which they stand. They
have been accepted as denoting that particular country, and we translate the visual
impression of the flag into the concept of that country, again on conventional
grounds. Some pictorial symbols are not entirely conventional; for example, the
cross. The cross can be merely a conventional symbol of the Christian church and
in that respect no different from a flag. But the specific content of the cross
referring to Jesus' death or, beyond that, to the interpenetration of the material

and spiritual planes, puts the connection between the symbol and what it symbolizes beyond the level of mere conventional symbols.

The very opposite to the conventional symbol is the *accidental* symbol, although they have one thing in common: there is no intrinsic relationship between the symbol and that which it symbolizes. Let us assume that someone has had a saddening experience in a certain city; when he hears the name of that city, he will easily connect the name with a mood of sadness, just as he would connect it with a mood of joy had his experience been a happy one. Quite obviously there is nothing in the nature of the city that is either sad or joyful. It is the individual experience connected with the city that makes it a symbol of a mood.

The same reaction could occur in connection with a house, a street, a certain dress, certain scenery, or anything once connected with a specific mood. We might find ourselves dreaming that we are in a certain city. In fact, there may be no particular mood connected with it in the dream; all we see is a street or even simply the name of the city. We ask ourselves why we happened to think of that city in our sleep and may discover that we had fallen asleep in a mood similar to the one symbolized by the city. The picture in the dream represents this mood, the city "stands for" the mood once experienced in it. Here the connection between the symbol and the experience symbolized is entirely accidental.

In contrast to the conventional symbol, the accidental symbol cannot be shared by anyone else except as we relate the events connected with the symbol. For this reason accidental symbols are rarely used in myths, fairy tales, or works of art written in symbolic language because they are not communicable unless the writer adds a lengthy comment to each symbol he uses. In dreams, however, accidental symbols are frequent, and later in this book I shall explain the method of understanding them.

The *universal* symbol is one in which there is an intrinsic relationship between the symbol and that which it represents. We have already given one example, that of the outskirts of the city. The sensory experience of a deserted, strange, poor environment has indeed a significant relationship to a mood of lostness and anxiety. True enough, if we have never been in the outskirts of a city we could not use that symbol, just as the word "table" would be meaningless had we never seen a table. This symbol is meaningful only to city dwellers and would be meaningless to people living in cultures that have no big cities. Many other universal symbols, however, are rooted in the experience of every human being. Take, for instance, the symbol of fire. We are fascinated by certain qualities of fire in a fireplace. First of all, by its aliveness. It changes continuously, it moves all the time, and yet there is constancy in it. It remains the same without being the same. It gives the impression of power, of energy, of grace and lightness. It is as if it were dancing and had an inexhaustible source of energy. When we use fire as a symbol, we describe the inner experience characterized by the same elements which we notice in the sensory experience of fire; the mood of energy, lightness, movement, grace, gaiety—sometimes one, sometimes another of these elements being predominant in the feeling.

Similar in some ways and different in others is the symbol of water—of the ocean or of the stream. Here, too, we find the blending of change and permanence, of constant movement and yet of permanence. We also feel the quality of aliveness, continuity and energy. But there is a difference; where fire is adventurous, quick, exciting, water is quiet, slow and steady. Fire has an element of surprise; water an element of predictability. Water symbolizes the mood of aliveness, too, but one which is "heavier," "slower," and more comforting than exciting.

That a phenomenon of the physical world can be the adequate expression of an inner experience, that the world of things can be a symbol of the world of the mind, is not surprising. We all know that our bodies express our minds. Blood rushes to our heads when we are furious, it rushes away from them when we are afraid; our hearts beat more quickly when we are angry, and the whole body has a different tonus if we are happy from the one it has when we are sad. We express our moods by our facial expressions and our attitudes and feelings by movements and gestures so precise that others recognize them more accurately from our gestures than from our words. Indeed, the body is a symbol—and not an allegory—of the mind. Deeply and genuinely felt emotion, and even any genuinely felt thought, is expressed in our whole organism. In the case of the universal symbol, we find the same connection between mental and physical experience. Certain physical phenomena suggest by their very nature certain emotional and mental experiences, and we express emotional experiences in the language of physical experiences, that is to say, symbolically.

The universal symbol is the only one in which the relationship between the symbol and that which is symbolized is not coincidental but intrinsic. It is rooted in the experience of the affinity between an emotion or thought, on the one hand, and a sensory experience, on the other. It can be called universal because it is shared by all men, in contrast not only to the accidental symbol, which is by its very nature entirely personal, but also to the conventional symbol, which is restricted to a group of people sharing the same convention. The universal symbol is rooted in the properties of our body, our senses, and our mind, which are common to all men and, therefore, not restricted to individuals or to specific groups. Indeed, the language of the universal symbol is the one common tongue developed by the human race, a language which it forgot before it succeeded in developing a universal conventional language.

There is no need to speak of a racial inheritance in order to explain the universal character of symbols. Every human being who shares the essential features of bodily and mental equipment with the rest of mankind is capable of speaking and understanding the symbolic language that is based upon these common properties. Just as we do not need to learn to cry when we are sad or to get red in the face when we are angry, and just as these reactions are not restricted to any particular race or group of people, symbolic language does not have to be learned and is not restricted to any segment of the human race. Evidence for this is to be found in the fact that symbolic language as it is employed in myths and dreams is found in all cultures in so-called primitive as well as such highly developed cultures as Egypt and Greece. Furthermore, the symbols used in these various cultures are strikingly similar since they all go back to the basic sensory as well as emotional experiences shared by men of all cultures. Added evidence is to be found in recent experiments in which people who had no knowledge of the theory of dream interpretation were able, under hypnosis, to interpret the symbolism of their dreams without any difficulty. After emerging from the hypnotic state and being asked to interpret the same dreams, they were puzzled and said, "Well, there is no meaning to them—it is just nonsense."

The foregoing statement needs qualification, however. Some symbols differ in meaning according to the difference in their realistic significance in various cultures. For instance, the function and consequently the meaning of the sun is different in northern countries and in tropical countries. In northern countries, where water is plentiful, all growth depends on sufficient sunshine. The sun is the warm, life-giving, protecting, loving power. In the Near East, where the heat of the sun is much more powerful, the sun is a dangerous and even threatening power from which man must protect himself, while water is felt to be the source of all life and the main condition for growth. We may speak of dialects of universal symbolic language, which are determined by those differences in natural conditions which cause certain symbols to have a different meaning in different regions of the earth.

Quite different from these "symbolic dialects" is the fact that many symbols have more than one meaning in accordance with different kinds of experiences which can be connected with one and the same natural phenomenon. Let us take up the symbol of fire again. If we watch fire in the fireplace, which is a source of pleasure and comfort, it is expressive of a mood of aliveness, warmth, and pleasure. But if we see a building or forest on fire, it conveys to us an experience of threat or terror, of the powerlessness of man against the elements of nature. Fire, then, can be the symbolic representation of inner aliveness and happiness as well as of fear, powerlessness, or of one's own destructive tendencies. The same holds true of the symbol water. Water can be a most destructive force when it is whipped up by a storm or when a swollen river floods its banks. Therefore, it can be the symbolic expression of horror and chaos as well as of comfort and peace.

Another illustration of the same principle is a symbol of a valley. The valley enclosed between mountains can arouse in us the feeling of security and comfort, of protection against all dangers from the outside. But the protecting mountains can also mean isolating walls which do not permit us to get out of the valley and thus the valley can become a symbol of imprisonment. The particular meaning of the symbol in any given place can only be determined from the whole context in which the symbol appears, and in terms of the predominant experiences of the person using the symbol. We shall return to this question in our discussion of dream symbolism.

A good illustration of the function of the universal symbol is a story, written in symbolic language, which is known to almost everyone in Western culture: the Book of Jonah. Jonah has heard God's voice telling him to go to Nineveh and preach to its inhabitants to give up their evil ways lest they be destroyed. Jonah cannot help hearing God's' voice and that is why he is a prophet. But he is an unwilling prophet, who, though knowing what he should do, tries to run away from the command of God (or, as we may say, the voice of his conscience). He is a man who does not care for other human beings. He is a man with a strong sense of law and order, but without love.[1]

How does the story express the inner processes in Jonah?

We are told that Jonah went down to Joppa and found a ship which should bring him to Tarshish. In mid-ocean a storm rises and, while everyone else is excited and afraid, Jonah goes into the ship's belly and falls into a deep sleep. The sailors, believing that God must have sent the storm because someone on the ship is to be punished, wake Jonah, who had told them he was trying to flee from God's command. He tells them to take him and cast him forth into the sea and that the sea would then become calm. The sailors (betraying a remarkable sense of humanity by first trying everything else before following his advice) eventually take Jonah and cast him into the sea, which immediately stops raging. Jonah is swallowed by a big fish and stays in the fish's belly three days and three nights. He prays to God to free him from this prison. God makes the fish vomit out Jonah unto the dry land and Jonah goes to Nineveh, fulfills God's command, and thus saves the inhabitants of the city.

The story is told as if these events had actually happened. However, it is written in symbolic language and all the realistic events described are symbols for the inner experiences of the hero. We find a sequence of symbols which follow one another: going into the ship, going into the ship's belly, falling asleep, being in the ocean, and being in the fish's belly. All these symbols stand for the same inner experience: for a condition of being protected and isolated, of safe withdrawal from communication with other human beings. They represent what could be represented in another symbol, the fetus in the mother's womb. Different as the ship's belly, deep sleep, the ocean, and a fish's belly are realistically, they are expressive of the same inner experience, of the blending between protection and isolation.

In the manifest story events happen in space and time: *first,* going into the ship's belly; *then,* falling asleep; *then,* being thrown into the ocean; *then,* being swallowed by the fish. One thing happens after the other and, although some events are obviously unrealistic, the story has its own logical consistency in terms of time and space. But if we understand that the writer did not intend to tell us the story of external events, but of the inner experience of a man torn between his conscience and his wish to escape from his inner voice, it becomes clear that his various actions following one after the other express the same mood in him; and that *sequence in time* is expressive of a *growing intensity* of the same feeling. In his attempt to escape from his obligation to his fellow men Jonah isolates himself more and more until, in the belly of the fish, the protective element has so given

---

[1] Cf. the discussion of Jonah in E. Fromm's *Man for Himself* (New York, Rinehart & Co., 1947), where the story is discussed from the point of view of the meaning of love.

way to the imprisoning element that he can stand it no longer and is forced to pray to God to be released from where he had put himself. (This is a mechanism which we find so characteristic of neurosis. An attitude is assumed as a defense against a danger, but then it grows far beyond its original defense function and becomes a neurotic symptom from which the person tries to be relieved.) Thus Jonah's escape into protective isolation ends in the terror of being imprisoned, and he takes up his life at the point where he had tried to escape.

There is another difference between the logic of the manifest and of the latent story. In the manifest story the logical connection is one of causality of external events. Jonah wants to go overseas *because* he wants to flee from God, he falls asleep *because* he is tired, he is thrown overboard *because* he is supposed to be the reason for the storm, and he is swallowed by the fish *because* there are man-eating fish in the ocean. One event occurs because of a previous event. (The last part of the story is unrealistic but not illogical.) But in the latent story the logic is different. The various events are related to each other by their association with the same inner experience. What appears to be a causal sequence of external events stands for a connection of experiences linked with each other by their association in terms of inner events. This is as logical as the manifest story—but it is a logic of a different kind. If we turn now to an examination of the nature of the dream, the logic governing symbolic language will become more transparent.

George Orwell
Politics and the English Language

Most people who bother with the matter at all would admit that the English language is in a bad way, but it is generally assumed that we cannot by conscious action do anything about it. Our civilization is decadent, and our language—so the argument runs—must inevitably share in the general collapse. It follows that any struggle against the abuse of language is a sentimental archaism, like preferring candles to electric light or hansom cabs to aeroplanes. Underneath this lies the half-conscious belief that language is a natural growth and not an instrument which we shape for our own purposes.

Now, it is clear that the decline of a language must ultimately have political and economic causes: it is not due simply to the bad influence of this or that individual writer. But an effect can become a cause, reinforcing the original cause and producing the same effect in an intensified form, and so on indefinitely. A man may take to drink because he feels himself to be a failure, and then fail all the more completely because he drinks. It is rather the same thing that is happening to the English language. It becomes ugly and inaccurate because our thoughts are foolish, but the slovenliness of our language makes it easier for us to have foolish thoughts. The point is that the process is reversible. Modern English, especially written English, is full of bad habits which spread by imitation and which can be avoided if one is willing to take the necessary trouble. If one gets rid of these habits one can think more clearly, and to think clearly is a necessary first step towards political regeneration: so that the fight against bad English is not frivolous and is not the exclusive concern of professional writers. I will come back to this presently, and I hope that by that time the meaning of what I have said here will have become clearer. Meanwhile, here are five specimens of the English language as it is now habitually written.

These five passages have not been picked out because they are especially bad—I could have quoted far worse if I had chosen—but because they illustrate various of the mental vices from which we now suffer. They are a little below the average, but are fairly representative samples. I number them so that I can refer back to them when necessary:

(1) I am not, indeed, sure whether it is not true to say that the Milton who once seemed not unlike a seventeenth-century Shelley had not become, out of an experience ever more bitter in each year, more alien (*sic*) to the founder of that Jesuit sect which nothing could induce him to tolerate.

Professor Harold Laski (Essay in *Freedom of Expression*)

(2) Above all, we cannot play ducks and drakes with a native battery of idioms which prescribes such egregious collocations of vocables as the Basic *put up with* for *tolerate* or *put at a loss* for *bewilder.*

Professor Lancelot Hogben (*Interglossa*)

(3) On the one side we have the free personality; by definition it is not neurotic, for it has neither conflict nor dream. Its desires, such as they are, are transparent, for they are just what institutional approval keeps in the forefront of consciousness; another institutional pattern would alter their number and intensity; there is little in them that is natural, irreducible, or culturally dangerous. But *on the other side,* the social bond itself is nothing but the mutual reflection of these self-secure integrities. Recall the definition of love. Is not this the very picture of a small academic? Where is there a place in this hall of mirrors for either personality or fraternity?

Essay on psychology in *Politics* (*New York*)

(4) All the "best people" from the gentlemen's clubs, and all the frantic fascist captains, united in common hatred of Socialism and bestial horror of the rising tide of the mass revolutionary movement, have turned to acts of provocation, to foul incendiarism, to medieval legends of poisoned wells, to legalize their own destruction of proletarian organizations, and rouse the agitated petty-bourgeoisie to chauvinistic fervor on behalf of the fight against the revolutionary way out of the crisis.

Communist pamphlet

(5) If a new spirit *is* to be infused into this old country, there is one thorny and contentious reform which must be tackled, and that is the humanization and galvanization of the B.B.C. Timidity here will bespeak canker and atrophy of the soul. The heart of Britain may be sound and of strong beat, for instance, but the British lion's roar at present is like that of Bottom in Shakespeare's *Midsummer Night's Dream*—as gentle as any sucking dove. A virile new Britain cannot continue indefinitely to be traduced in the eyes, or rather ears, of the world by the effete languors of Langham Place, brazenly masquerading as "standard English." When the Voice of Britain is heard at nine o'clock, better far and infinitely less ludicrous to hear aitches honestly dropped than the present priggish, inflated, inhibited, school-ma'amish arch braying of blameless bashful mewing maidens.

Letter in Tribune

Each of these passages has faults of its own, but quite apart from avoidable ugliness, two qualities are common to all of them. The first is staleness of imagery; the other is lack of precision. The writer either has a meaning and cannot express it, or he inadvertently says something else, or he is almost indifferent as to whether his words mean anything or not. This mixture of vagueness and sheer incompetence is the most marked characteristic of modern English prose, and especially of any kind of political writing. As soon as certain topics are raised, the concrete melts into the abstract and no one seems able to think of turns of speech that are not hackneyed: prose consists less and less of *words* chosen for the sake of their meaning, and more and more of *phrases* tacked together like the sections of a prefabricated hen-house. I list below, with notes and examples, various of the tricks by means of which the work of prose-construction is habitually dodged:

Dying metaphors. A newly invented metaphor assists thought by evoking a visual image, while on the other hand a metaphor which is technically "dead" (e.g., *iron resolution*) has in effect reverted to being an ordinary word and can generally be used without loss of vividness. But in between these two classes there is a huge dump of worn-out metaphors which have lost all evocative power and are merely used because they save people the trouble of inventing phrases for themselves. Examples are: *Ring the changes on, take up the cudgels for, toe the line, ride roughshod over, stand shoulder to shoulder with, play into the hands of, an axe to grind, grist to the mill, fishing in troubled waters, on the order of the day, Achilles' heel, swan song, hotbed.* Many of these are used without knowledge of their meaning (what is a "rift" for instance?), and incompatible metaphors are frequently mixed, a sure sign that the writer is not interested in what he is saying. Some metaphors now current have been twisted out of their original meaning without those who use them even being aware of the fact. For example, *toe the line* is sometimes written *tow the line.* Another example is *the hammer and the anvil,* now always used with the implication that the anvil gets the worst of it. In real life it is always the anvil that breaks the hammer, never the other way about: a writer who stopped to think what he was saying would be aware of this, and would avoid perverting the original phrase.

Operators, or *verbal false limbs.* These save the trouble of picking

out appropriate verbs and nouns, and at the same time pad each
sentence with extra syllables which give it an appearance of symmetry.
Characteristic phrases are: *render inoperative, militate against, prove
unacceptable, make contact with, be subjected to, give rise to, give
grounds for, have the effect of, play a leading part* (role) *in, make
itself felt, take effect, exhibit a tendency to, serve the purpose of, etc.,
etc.* The keynote is the elimination of simple verbs. Instead of being a
single word, such as *break, stop, spoil, mend, kill,* a verb becomes a
phrase, made up of a noun or adjective tacked on to some general-
purposes verb such as *prove, serve, form, play, render.* In addition, the
passive voice is wherever possible used in preference to the active, and
noun constructions are used instead of gerunds (*by examination of*
instead of *by examining*). The range of verbs is further cut down by
means of the *-ize* and *de-* formations, and banal statements are given
an appearance of profundity by means of the *not un-* formation.
Simple conjunctions and prepositions are replaced by such phrases as
*with respect to, having regard to, the fact that, by dint of, in view of,
in the interests of, on the hypothesis that;* and the ends of sentences
are saved from anti-climax by such resounding commonplaces as
*greatly to be desired, cannot be left out of account, a development to
be expected in the near future, deserving of serious consideration,
brought to a satisfactory conclusion,* and so on and so forth.

Pretentious diction. Words like *phenomenon, element, individual*
(as noun), *objective, categorical, effective, virtual, basis, primary,
promote, constitute, exhibit, exploit, utilize, eliminate, liquidate,* are
used to dress up simple statements and give an air of scientific impartiality to biased judgments. Adjectives like *epoch-making, epic,
historic, unforgettable, triumphant, age-old, inevitable, inexorable,
veritable,* are used to dignify the sordid processes of international
politics, while writing that aims at glorifying war usually takes on an
archaic color, its characteristic words being: *realm, throne, chariot,
mailed fist, trident, sword, shield, buckler, banner, jackboot, clarion.*
Foreign words and expressions such as *cul de sac, ancien régime, deus
ex machina, mutatis mutandis, status quo, gleichschaltung, weltan-
schauung,* are used to give an air of culture and elegance. Except for
the useful abbreviations *i.e., e.g.,* and *etc.,* there is no real need for any
of the hundreds of foreign phrases now current in English. Bad writers,
and especially scientific, political and sociological writers, are nearly
always haunted by the notion that Latin or Greek words are grander
than Saxon ones, and unnecessary words like *expedite, ameliorate,
predict, extraneous, deracinated, clandestine, subaqueous* and hundreds
of others constantly gain ground from their Anglo-Saxon opposite
numbers.[1] The jargon peculiar to Marxist writing (*hyena, hangman,
cannibal, petty bourgeois, these gentry, lackey, flunkey, mad dog,
White Guard, etc.*) consists largely of words and phrases translated
from Russian, German or French; but the normal way of coining a
new word is to use a Latin or Greek root with the appropriate affix
and, where necessary, the *-ize* formation. It is often easier to make up

---

[1] An interesting illustration of this is the way in which the English flower names which
were in use till very recently are being ousted by Greek ones, *snap-dragon* becoming
antirrhinum, forget-me-not becoming *myosotis,* etc. It is hard to see any practical reason
for this change of fashion: it is probably due to an instinctive turning-away from the
more homely word and a vague feeling that the Greek word is scientific.

words of this kind (*deregionalize, impermissible, extramarital, non-fragmentary* and so forth) than to think up the English words that will cover one's meaning. The result, in general, is an increase in slovenliness and vagueness.

Meaningless words. In certain kinds of writing, particularly in art criticism and literary criticism, it is normal to come across long passages which are almost completely lacking in meaning.[2] Words like *romantic, plastic, values, human, dead, sentimental, natural, vitality,* as used in art criticism, are strictly meaningless, in the sense that they not only do not point to any discoverable object, but are hardly even expected to do so by the reader. When one critic writes, "The outstanding feature of Mr. X's work is its living quality," while another writes, "The immediately striking thing about Mr. X's work is its peculiar deadness," the reader accepts this as a simple difference of opinion. If words like *black* and *white* were involved, instead of the jargon words *dead* and *living,* he would see at once that language was being used in an improper way. Many political words are similarly abused. The word *Fascism* has now no meaning except in so far as it signifies "something not desirable." The words *democracy, socialism, freedom, patriotic, realistic, justice,* have each of them several different meanings which cannot be reconciled with one another. In the case of a word like *democracy,* not only is there no agreed definition, but the attempt to make one is resisted from all sides. It is almost universally felt that when we call a country democratic we are praising it: consequently the defenders of every kind of régime claim that it is a democracy, and fear that they might have to stop using the word if it were tied down to any one meaning. Words of this kind are often used in a consciously dishonest way. That is, the person who uses them has his own private definition, but allows his hearer to think he means something quite different. Statements like *Marshal Pétain was a true patriot, The Soviet Press is the freest in the world, The Catholic Church is opposed to persecution,* are almost always made with intent to deceive. Other words used in variable meanings, in most cases more or less dishonestly, are: *class, totalitarian, science, progressive, reactionary, bourgeois, equality.*

Now that I have made this catalogue of swindles and perversions, let me give another example of the kind of writing that they lead to. This time it must of its nature be an imaginary one. I am going to translate a passage of good English into modern English of the worst sort. Here is a well-known verse from *Ecclesiastes:*

> I returned, and saw under the sun, that the race is not to the swift, nor the battle to the strong, neither bread to the wise, nor yet riches to men of understanding, nor yet favor to men of skill; but time and chance happeneth to them all.

[2] Example "Comfort's catholicity of perception and image, strangely Whitmanesque in range, almost the exact opposite in aesthetic compulsion, continues to evoke that trembling atmospheric accumulative hinting at a cruel, an inexorably serene timelessness . . . Wrey Gardiner scores by aiming at simple bullseyes with precision. Only they are not so simple, and through this contented sadness runs more than the surface bittersweet of resignation." (*Poetry Quarterly.*)

Here it is in modern English:

> Objective consideration of contemporary phenomena compels the
> conclusion that success or failure in competitive activities exhibits no
> tendency to be commensurate with innate capacity, but that a consider-
> able element of the unpredictable must invariably be taken into account.

This is a parody, but not a very gross one, Exhibit (3), above, for instance,
contains several patches of the same kind of English. It will be seen that I have
not made a full translation. The beginning and ending of the sentence follow the
original meaning fairly closely, but in the middle the concrete illustrations—race,
battle, bread—dissolve into the vague phrase "success or failure in competitive
activities." This had to be so, because no modern writer of the kind I am
discussing—no one capable of using phrases like "objective consideration of
contemporary phenomena"—would ever tabulate his thoughts in that precise and
detailed way. The whole tendency of modern prose is away from concreteness.
Now analyze these two sentences a little more closely. The first contains 49 words
but only 60 syllables, and all its words are those of everyday life. The second
contains 38 words of 90 syllables: 18 of its words are from Latin roots, and one
from Greek. The first sentence contains six vivid images, and only one phrase
("time and chance") that could be called vague. The second contains not a single
fresh, arresting phrase, and in spite of its 90 syllables it gives only a shortened
version of the meaning contained in the first. Yet without a doubt it is the second
kind of sentence that is gaining ground in modern English. I do not want to
exaggerate. This kind of writing is not yet universal, and outcrops of simplicity
will occur here and there in the worst-written page. Still, if you or I were told to
write a few lines on the uncertainty of human fortunes, we should probably come
much nearer to my imaginary sentence than to the one from *Ecclesiastes*.

As I have tried to show, modern writing at its worst does not consist in
picking out words for the sake of their meaning and inventing images in order to
make the meaning clearer. It consists in gumming together long strips of words
which have already been set in order by someone else, and making the results
presentable by sheer humbug. The attraction of this way of writing is that it is
easy. It is easier—even quicker, once you have the habit—to say *In my opinion it
is a not unjustifiable assumption that* than to say *I think*. If you use ready-made
phrases, you not only don't have to hunt about for words; you also don't have to
bother with the rhythms of your sentences, since these phrases are generally so
arranged as to be more or less euphonious. When you are composing in a
hurry—when you are dictating to a stenographer, for instance, or making a
public speech—it is natural to fall into a pretentious, Latinized style. Tags like *a
consideration which we should do well to bear in mind* or *a conclusion to which
all of us would readily assent* will save many a sentence from coming down with
a bump. By using stale metaphors, similes and idioms, you save much mental
effort at the cost of leaving your meaning vague, not only for your reader but for
yourself. This is the significance of mixed metaphors. The sole aim of a metaphor
is to call up a visual image. When these images clash—as in *The Fascist octopus*

has sung its swan song, the jackboot is thrown into the melting pot—it can be taken as certain that the writer is not seeing a mental image of the objects he is naming; in other words he is not really thinking. Look again at the examples I gave at the beginning of this essay. Professor Laski (1) uses five negatives in 53 words. One of these is superfluous, making nonsense of the whole passage, and in addition there is the slip *alien* for akin, making further nonsense, and several avoidable pieces of clumsiness which increase the general vagueness. Professor Hogben (2) plays ducks and drakes with a battery which is able to write prescriptions, and, while disapproving of the everyday phrase *put up with,* is unwilling to look *egregious* up in the dictionary and see what it means. (3), if one takes an uncharitable attitude towards it, is simply meaningless: probably one could work out its intended meaning by reading the whole of the article in which it occurs. In (4), the writer knows more or less what he wants to say, but an accumulation of stale phrases chokes him like tea leaves blocking a sink. In (5), words and meaning have almost parted company. People who write in this manner usually have a general emotional meaning—they dislike one thing and want to express solidarity with another—but they are not interested in the detail of what they are saying. A scrupulous writer, in every sentence that he writes, will ask himself at least four questions, thus: What am I trying to say? What words will express it? What image or idiom will make it clearer? Is this image fresh enough to have an effect? And he will probably ask himself two more: Could I put it more shortly? Have I said anything that is avoidably ugly? But you are not obliged to go to all this trouble. You can shirk it by simply throwing your mind open and letting the ready-made phrases come crowding in. They will construct your sentences for you—even think your thoughts for you, to a certain extent—and at need they will perform the important service of partially concealing your meaning even from yourself. It is at this point that the special connection between politics and the debasement of language becomes clear.

In our time it is broadly true that political writing is bad writing. Where it is not true, it will generally be found that the writer is some kind of rebel, expressing his private opinions and not a "party line." Orthodoxy, of whatever color, seems to demand a lifeless, imitative style. The political dialects to be found in pamphlets, leading articles, manifestoes, White Papers and the speeches of under-secretaries do, of course, vary from party to party, but they are all alike in that one almost never finds in them a fresh, vivid, home-made turn of speech. When one watches some tired hack on the platform mechanically repeating the familiar phrases—*bestial atrocities, iron heel, bloodstained tyranny, free peoples of the world, stand shoulder to shoulder*—one often has a curious feeling that one is not watching a live human being but some kind of dummy: a feeling which suddenly becomes stronger at moments when the light catches the speaker's spectacles and turns them into blank discs which seem to have no eyes behind them. And this is not altogether fanciful. A speaker who uses that kind of phraseology has gone some distance towards turning himself into a machine. The appropriate noises are coming out of his larynx, but his brain is not involved as it would be if he were choosing his words for himself. If the speech he is making is

one that he is accustomed to make over and over again, he may be almost
unconscious of what he is saying, as one is when one utters the responses in
church. And this reduced state of consciousness, if not indispensable, is at any
rate favorable to political conformity.

In our time, political speech and writing are largely the defense of the inde-
fensible. Things like the continuance of British rule in India, the Russian purges
and deportations, the dropping of the atom bombs on Japan, can indeed be
defended, but only by arguments which are too brutal for most people to face,
and which do not square with the professed aims of political parties. Thus
political language has to consist largely of euphemism, question-begging and
sheer cloudy vagueness. Defenseless villages are bombarded from the air, the
inhabitants driven out into the countryside, the cattle machine-gunned, the huts
set on fire with incendiary bullets: this is called *pacification*. Millions of peasants
are robbed of their farms and sent trudging along the roads with no more than
they can carry: this is called *transfer of population* or *rectification of frontiers*.
People are imprisoned for years without trial, or shot in the back of the neck or
sent to die of scurvy in Arctic lumber camps: this is called *elimination of
unreliable elements*. Such phraseology is needed if one wants to name things
without calling up mental pictures of them. Consider for instance some comfortable English professor defending Russian totalitarianism. He cannot say out-
right, "I believe in killing off your opponents when you can get good results by
doing so." Probably, therefore, he will say something like this:

> While freely conceding that the Soviet régime exhibits certain features
> which the humanitarian may be inclined to deplore, we must, I
> think, agree that a certain curtailment of the right to political opposition
> is an unavoidable concomitant of transitional periods, and that the
> rigors which the Russian people have been called upon to undergo have
> been amply justified in the sphere of concrete achievement.

The inflated style is itself a kind of euphemism. A mass of Latin words falls
upon the facts like soft snow, blurring the outlines and covering up all the
details. The great enemy of clear language is insincerity. When there is a gap
between one's real and one's declared aims, one turns, as it were instinctively, to
long words and exhausted idioms, like a cuttlefish squirting out ink. In our age
there is no such thing as "keeping out of politics." All issues are political issues,
and politics itself is a mass of lies, evasions, folly, hatred and schizophrenia.
When the general atmosphere is bad, language must suffer. I should expect to
find—this is a guess which I have not sufficient knowledge to verify—that the
German, Russian and Italian languages have all deteriorated in the last ten or
fifteen years as a result of dictatorship.

But if thought corrupts language, language can also corrupt thought. A bad
usage can spread by tradition and imitation, even among people who should and
do know better. The debased language that I have been discussing is in some
ways very convenient. Phrases like *a not unjustifiable assumption, leaves much to
be desired, would serve no good purpose, a consideration which we should do*

well to bear in mind, are a continuous temptation, a packet of aspirins always at one's elbow. Look back through this essay, and for certain you will find that I have again and again committed the very faults I am protesting against. By this morning's post I have received a pamphlet dealing with conditions in Germany. The author tells me that he "felt impelled" to write it. I open it at random, and here is almost the first sentence that I see: "[The Allies] have an opportunity not only of achieving a radical transformation of Germany's social and political structure in such a way as to avoid a nationalistic reaction in Germany itself, but at the same time of laying the foundations of a cooperative and unified Europe." You see, he "feels impelled" to write—feels, presumably, that he has something new to say—and yet his words, like cavalry horses answering the bugle, group themselves automatically into the familiar dreary pattern. This invasion of one's mind by ready-made phrases *(lay the foundations, achieve a radical transformation)* can only be prevented if one is constantly on guard against them, and every such phrase anesthetizes a portion of one's brain.

I said earlier that the decadence of our language is probably curable. Those who deny this would argue, if they produced an argument at all, that language merely reflects existing social conditions, and that we cannot influence its development by any direct tinkering with words and constructions. So far as the general tone or spirit of a language goes, this may be true, but it is not true in detail. Silly words and expressions have often disappeared, not through any evolutionary process but owing to the conscious action of a minority. Two recent examples were *explore every avenue* and *leave no stone unturned,* which were killed by the jeers of a few journalists. There is a long list of fly-blown metaphors which could similarly be got rid of if enough people would interest themselves in the job; and it should also be possible to laugh the *not un-* formation out of existence,[3] to reduce the amount of Latin and Greek in the average sentence, to drive out foreign phrases and strayed scientific words, and, in general, to make pretentiousness unfashionable. But all these are minor points. The defense of the English language implies more than this, and perhaps it is best to start by saying what it does *not* imply.

To begin with, it has nothing to do with archaism, with the salvaging of obsolete words and turns of speech, or with the setting-up of a "standard English" which must never be departed from. On the contrary, it is especially concerned with the scrapping of every word or idiom which has outworn its usefulness. It has nothing to do with correct grammar and syntax, which are of no importance so long as one makes one's meaning clear, or with the avoidance of Americanisms, or with having what is called a "good prose style." On the other hand it is not concerned with fake simplicity and the attempt to make written English colloquial. Nor does it even imply in every case preferring the Saxon word to the Latin one, though it does imply using the fewest and shortest

[3] One can cure oneself of the *not un-* formation by memorizing this sentence: *A not un-black dog was chasing a not unsmall rabbit across a not ungreen field.*

words that will cover one's meaning. What is above all needed is to let the meaning choose the word, and not the other way about. In prose, the worst thing one can do with words is to surrender them. When you think of a concrete object, you think wordlessly, and then, if you want to describe the thing you have been visualizing, you probably hunt about till you find the exact words that seem to fit it. When you think of something abstract you are more inclined to use words from the start, and unless you make a conscious effort to prevent it, the existing dialect will come rushing in and do the job for you, at the expense of blurring or even changing your meaning. Probably it is better to put off using words as long as possible and get one's meaning as clear as one can through pictures or sensations. Afterwards one can choose—not simply *accept*—the phrases that will best cover the meaning, and then switch round and decide what impressions one's words are likely to make on another person. This last effort of the mind cuts out all stale or mixed images, all prefabricated phrases, needless repetitions, and humbug and vagueness generally. But one can often be in doubt about the effect of a word or a phrase, and one needs rules that one can rely on when instinct fails. I think the following rules will cover most cases:

(i) Never use a metaphor, simile or other figure of speech which you are used to seeing in print.

(ii) Never use a long word where a short one will do.

(iii) If it is possible to cut a word out, always cut it out.

(iv) Never use the passive where you can use the active.

(v) Never use a foreign phrase, a scientific word or a jargon word if you can think of an everyday English equivalent.

(vi) Break any of these rules sooner than say anything barbarous.

These rules sound elementary, and so they are, but they demand a deep change of attitude in anyone who has grown used to writing in the style now fashionable. One could keep all of them and still write bad English, but one could not write the kind of stuff that I quoted in these five specimens at the beginning of this article.

I have not here been considering the literary use of language, but merely language as an instrument for expressing and not for concealing or preventing thought. Stuart Chase and others have come near to claiming that all abstract words are meaningless, and have used this as a pretext for advocating a kind of political quietism. Since you don't know what Fascism is, how can you struggle against Fascism? One need not swallow such absurdities as this, but one ought to recognize that the present political chaos is connected with the decay of language, and that one can probably bring about some improvement by starting at the verbal end. If you simplify your English, you are freed from the worst follies of orthodoxy. You cannot speak any of the necessary dialects, and when you make a stupid remark its stupidity will be obvious, even to yourself. Political language—and with variations this is true of all political parties, from Conservatives to Anarchists—is designed to make lies sound truthful and murder respectable, and to give an appearance of solidity to pure wind. One cannot change this all in a moment, but one can at least change one's own habits, and from time to time one can even, if one jeers loudly enough, send some worn-out and useless phrase—some *jackboot, Achilles' heel, hotbed, melting pot, acid test, veritable inferno* or other lump of verbal refuse—into the dustbin where it belongs.

James Baldwin

The Creative Dilemma

Perhaps the primary distinction of the artist is that he must actively cultivate that state which most men, necessarily, must avoid: the state of being alone. That all men *are,* when the chips are down, alone, is a banality—a banality because it is very frequently stated, but very rarely, on the evidence, believed. Most of us are not compelled to linger with the knowledge of our aloneness, for it is a knowledge that can paralyze all action in this world. There are, forever, swamps to be drained, cities to be created, mines to be exploited, children to be fed. None of these things can be done alone. But the conquest of the physical world is not man's only duty. He is also enjoined to conquer the great wilderness of himself. The precise role of the artist, then, is to illuminate that darkness, blaze roads through that vast forest, so that we will not, in all our doing, lose sight of its purpose, which is, after all, to make the world a more human dwelling place.

The state of being alone is not meant to bring to mind merely a rustic musing beside some silver lake. The aloneness of which I speak is much more like the aloneness of birth or death. It is like the fearful aloneness that one sees in the eyes of someone who is suffering, whom we cannot help. Or it is like the aloneness of love, the force and mystery that so many have extolled and so many have cursed, but which no one has ever understood or ever really been able to control. I put the matter this way, not out of any desire to create pity for the artist—God forbid!—but to suggest how nearly, after all, is his state the state of everyone, and in an attempt to make vivid his endeavor. The states of birth, suffering, love, and death are extreme states—extreme, universal, and inescapable. We all know this, but we would rather not know it. The artist is present to correct the delusions to which we fall prey in our attempts to avoid this knowledge.

It is for this reason that all societies have battled with that incorrigible disturber of the peace—the artist. I doubt that future societies will get on with him any better. The entire purpose of society is to create a bulwark against the inner and the outer chaos, in order to make life bearable and to keep the human race alive. And it is absolutely inevitable that when a tradition has been evolved,

"The Creative Process" by James Baldwin from *Creative America,* Ridge Press.

whatever the tradition is, the people, in general, will suppose it to have existed from before the beginning of time and will be most unwilling and indeed unable to conceive of any changes in it. They do not know how they will live without those traditions that have given them their identity. Their reaction, when it is suggested that they can or that they must, is panic. And we see this panic, I think, everywhere in the world today, from the streets of New Orleans to the grisly battleground of Algeria. And a higher level of consciousness among the people is the only hope we have, now or in the future, of minimizing human damage.

The artist is distinguished from all other responsible actors in society—the politicians, legislators, educators, and scientists by the fact that he is his own test tube, his own laboratory, working according to very rigorous rules, however unstated these may be, and cannot allow any consideration to supersede his responsibility to reveal all that he can possibly discover concerning the mystery of the human being. Society must accept some things as real; but he must always know that visible reality hides a deeper one, and that all our action and achievement rests on things unseen. A society must assume that it is stable, but the artist must know, and he must let us know, that there is nothing stable under heaven. One cannot possibly build a school, teach a child, or drive a car without taking some things for granted. The artist cannot and must not take anything for granted, but must drive to the heart of every answer and expose the question the answer hides.

I seem to be making extremely grandiloquent claims for a breed of men and women historically despised while living and acclaimed when safely dead. But, in a way, the belated honor that all societies tender their artists proves the reality of the point I am trying to make. I am really trying to make clear the nature of the artist's responsibility to his society. The peculiar nature of this responsibility is that he must never cease warring with it, for its sake and for his own. For the truth, in spite of appearances and all our hopes, is that everything is always changing and the measure of our maturity as nations and as men is how well prepared we are to meet these changes and, further, to use them for our health.

Now, anyone who has ever been compelled to think about it—anyone, for example, who has ever been in love—knows that the one face that one can never see is one's own face. One's lover—or one's brother, or one's enemy—sees the face you wear, and this face can elicit the most extraordinary reactions. We do the things we do and feel what we feel essentially because we must—we are responsible for our actions, but we rarely understand them. It goes without saying, I believe, that if we understood ourselves better, we would damage ourselves less. But the barrier between oneself and one's knowledge of oneself is high indeed. There are so many things one would rather not know! We become social creatures because we cannot live any other way. But in order to become social, there are a great many other things that we must not become, and we are frightened, all of us, of those forces within us that perpetually menace our precarious security. Yet the forces are there; we cannot will them away. All we can do is learn to live with them. And we cannot learn this unless we are willing to tell the truth about ourselves, and the truth about us is always at variance with what we wish to be. The human effort is to bring these two realities into a relationship resembling reconciliation. The human beings whom we respect the most, after all—and sometimes fear the most—are those who are most deeply involved in this delicate and strenuous effort, for they have the unshakable authority that comes only from having looked on and endured and survived the worst. That nation is healthiest which has the least necessity to distrust or ostracize or victimize these people—whom, as I say, we honor, once they are gone, because somewhere in our hearts we know that we cannot live without them.

The dangers of being an American artist are not greater than those of being an artist anywhere else in the world, but they are very particular. These dangers are produced by our history. They rest on the fact that in order to conquer this continent, the particular aloneness of which I speak—the aloneness in which one discovers that life is tragic, and therefore unutterably beautiful—could not be permitted. And that this prohibition is typical of all emergent nations will be proved, I have no doubt, in many ways during the next fifty years. This continent now is conquered, but our habits and our fears remain. And, in the same way that to become a social human being one modifies and suppresses and, ultimately, without great courage, lies to oneself about all one's interior, uncharted chaos, so have we, as a nation, modified and suppressed and lied about all the darker forces in our history. We know, in the case of the person, that whoever cannot tell himself the truth about his past is trapped in it, is immobilized in the prison of his undiscovered self. This is also true of nations. We know how a person, in such a paralysis, is unable to assess either his weaknesses or his strengths, and how frequently indeed he mistakes the one for the other. And this, I think, we do. We are the strongest nation in the Western world, but this is not for the reasons that we think. It is because we have an opportunity that no other nation has of moving beyond the Old World concepts of race and class and caste, to create, finally, what we must have had in mind when we first began speaking of the New World. But the price of this is a long look backward whence we came and an unflinching assessment of the record. For an artist, the record of that journey is most clearly revealed in the personalities of the people the journey produced. Societies never know it, but the war of an artist with his society is a lover's war, and he does, at his best, what lovers do, which is to reveal the beloved to himself and, with that revelation, to make freedom real.

Henry Miller

To Read or Not to Read

After writing a work (*The Books in My Life*) which the critics find too long and too disorderly, I find it somewhat difficult to say in a few words what I was unable to say in a single volume. Perhaps the best would be to restate a few salient observations which apparently failed to hit the mark.

First of all, I tried to make it clear that, as a result of indiscriminate reading over a period of sixty years, my desire now is to read less and less. (A difficult thing to accomplish!) With every mail there comes an unsolicited batch of books, most of which I never look at. If I had been wise enough to follow the example set me by the friend of my youth, Robert Hamilton Challacombe, I would today probably have better eyesight, better physique, and a keener intellect. I believe it was in the *Tropic of Capricorn* that I explained how this friend instructed me, all unwittingly, in the art of reading. Up until the age of thirty he himself had not read more than three or four books. (Whitman, Thoreau, Emerson.) I have never again met anyone who could get so much from a book, or one who had so little need to refer to books. To squeeze every drop of juice out of a book is an art, almost as great an art as writing itself. When one learns it, one book does the work of a hundred.

It is not the so-called bad books whose influence I deplore as much as the mediocre ones. A bad book may often exert as stimulating an effect upon the reader as a so-called good book. I say "so-called" because I honestly believe that no man can tell another what may be a good or bad book—*for him*. The mediocre work, on the other hand, which is the daily fare for most of us, I regard as harmful because it is produced by automatons for automatons. And it is the automatons among us who are more of a hazard to society than the evil ones. If it is our fate to be destroyed by a bomb, it is the sleepwalker who is most apt to do the trick.

In my book I stressed a point which seems to have been completely ignored or overlooked. I said that one ought to begin (his reading) with his own time, with his contemporaries. Our educational system the world over is built on the fallacy that the young should first know everything that has led up to the present, and then begin. I can think of nothing more absurd, more futile, or more reprehensible. Small wonder that adults, so called, have little originality, even less imagination, and virtually no flexibility. The wonder is that we are not all lunatics by the time we come of age.

When I think of what it means merely to know the literature of one's own country I am flabbergasted. To say nothing about acquiring a smattering of art, science, religion and philosophy. How well I remember the day I quit college! (I was there only three months when I walked out.) It was Spenser's *Faerie Queene* which decided the issue for me. To think that this huge epic is still considered indispensable reading in any college curriculum! Only the other day I dipped into it again, to reassure myself that I had not made a grave error of judgment. Let me confess that today it seems even more insane to me than when I was a lad of eighteen. I am talking, be it understood, of "the poets' poet," as the English call him. What a poor second to Pindar!

No, I am not ashamed to repeat that from my comrades of the gutter I learned more, gained a greater appreciation of literature, than ever I did from the pedagogues who clutter our halls of learning. School never provided us with an open forum where we could discuss passionately and freely the books and authors we found to our liking. It all serves to remind me of our so-called democratic system of voting. We vote only for the figures who are nominated—men who, need I say, are scarcely the sort an intelligent person would like to see in office.

But perhaps the point which was supremely overlooked by the critics is the nonliterary character of my escapades in the realm of books. All the jumble and confusion which so irritates the critics is really the heart of my tale. Of what use books if they lead us not back to life, if they fail to make us drink more avidly of life? The very search for a book, as some of us know, is sometimes more rewarding than the reading of the book.

What I wish to say, briefly, is that a book, like anything else, often serves as a pretext for that which we really seek. Books recommended to us by our mentors may, if they happen to reach us at the right moment, produce the desired result, but how on earth can such happy coincidences be predicated? On the other hand, if these books—and I am referring to the treasures of literature, not the trash!— happen to fall into our hands before we are ready for them, or when we are sated or jaded, or if they are thrust upon us against the grain, the results can be disastrous. If "the open road" is the way to take in journeying through life, surely the same applies to reading. Let it be an adventure! Let it *happen!* Enough buttons are being pushed every day to make this world increasingly unfit to live in!

What we all hope, in reaching for a book, is to meet a man after our own heart, to experience tragedies and delights which we ourselves lack the courage to invite, to dream dreams which will render life more hallucinating, perhaps also to discover a philosophy of life which will make us more adequate in meeting the trials and ordeals which beset us. To merely add to our store of knowledge or improve our culture—whatever that may mean—seems worthless to me. I would rather see a man moved to crime, if he cannot be otherwise moved, than to see him grow more and more bookish.

But perhaps the greatest thing to be gained from the reading of books is the desire to truly communicate with one's fellow man. To read a book properly is to wake up and live, to acquire a renewed interest in one's neighbors, more especially those who are alien to us in every way. Never has there been such a plethora of books and never has there been such an abysmal indifference to the plight of our fellow man. Or such little ability to think and act for oneself.

On the whole, I must say, I have found better men—better in every sense of the word—among the uncultured than among the cultured ones of this world. The most monstrous crimes against humanity are being committed every day by those who have had all the advantages of learning. By making people more literate, more book conscious, we can hardly say that we are thereby making better citizens of them.

A book is no better than, and usually not as good as, a rock, a tree, a creature of the wild, a wisp of cloud, a wave, or a shadow on the wall. We who make books are indebted not to books but to the things which impel men to write books: earth, air, fire and water. If there were not a common source from which author and reader alike draw, there would be no books. Would it be such a calamity, a world without books? Could we not still communicate our joys, our discoveries, by word of mouth? Falling back on the tongue there would be no need to destroy whole forests, mar the landscape, befoul the air, or dull the minds and bodies of those who toil to provide us with mental and spiritual fodder in the form of books.

Thomas De Quincey

The Literature of Knowledge and the Literature of Power

What is it that we mean by *literature?* Popularly, and amongst the thoughtless, it is held to include everything that is printed in a book. Little logic is required to disturb *that* definition; the most thoughtless person is easily made aware, that in the idea of *literature,* one essential element is—some relation to a general and common interest of man, so that, what applies only to a local, or professional, or merely personal interest, even though presenting itself in the shape of a book, will not belong to literature. So far the definition is easily narrowed; and it is as easily expanded. For not only is much that takes a station in books not literature; but inversely, much that really *is* literature never reaches a station in books. The weekly sermons of Christendom, that vast pulpit literature which acts so extensively upon the popular mind—to warn, to uphold, to renew, to comfort, to alarm, does not attain the sanctuary of libraries in the ten-thousandth part of its extent. The drama again, as for instance, the finest of Shakespeare's plays in England, and all leading Athenian plays in the noontide of the Attic stage, operated as a literature on the public mind, and were (according to the strictest letter of that term) *published* through the audiences that witnessed[1] their representation some time before they were published as things to be

---

This is a section of De Quincey's review of "The Works of Alexander Pope, Esquire. By W. Roscoe, Esq.," which first appeared in *The North British Review,* August 1848.

[1] Charles I, for example, when Prince of Wales, and many others in his father's court, gained their known familiarity with Shakespeare—not through the original quartos, so slenderly diffused, nor through the first folio of 1623, but through the court representations of his chief dramas at Whitehall.

read; and they were published in this scenical mode of publication with much more effect than they could have had as books, during ages of costly copying, or of costly printing.

Books, therefore, do not suggest an idea coextensive and interchangeable with the idea of literature; since much literature, scenic, forensic, or didactic (as from lecturers and public orators), may never come into books; and much that *does* come into books, may connect itself with no literary interest.[2] But a far more important correction, applicable to the common vague idea of literature, is to be sought—not so much in a better definition of literature, as in a sharper distinction of the two functions which it fulfils. In that great social organ, which, collectively, we call literature, there may be distinguished two separate offices that may blend and often *do* so, but capable, severally, of a severe insulation, and naturally fitted for reciprocal repulsion. There is, first, the literature of *knowledge;* and, secondly, the literature of *power.* The function of the first is—to *teach;* the function of the second is—to *move:* the first is a rudder; the second, an oar or a sail. The first speaks to the *mere* discursive understanding; the second speaks ultimately, it may happen, to the higher understanding or reason, but always *through* affections of pleasure and sympathy. Remotely, it may travel towards an object seated in what Lord Bacon calls *dry* light; but, proximately, it does and must operate, else it ceases to be a literature of *power,* on and through that *humid* light which clothes itself in the mists and glittering *iris* of human passions, desires, and genial emotions. Men have so little reflected on the higher functions of literature, as to find it a paradox if one should describe it as a mean or subordinate purpose of books to give information. But this is a paradox only in the sense which makes it honorable to be paradoxical. Whenever we talk in ordinary language of seeking information or gaining knowledge, we understand the words as connected with something of absolute novelty. But it is the grandeur of all truth, which *can* occupy a very high place in human interests, that it is never absolutely novel to the meanest of minds: it exists eternally by way of germ or latent principle in the lowest as in the highest, needing to be developed, but never to be planted. To be capable of transplantation is the immediate criterion of a truth that ranges on a lower scale. Besides which, there is a rarer thing than truth, namely, *power,* or deep sympathy with truth. What is the effect, for instance, upon society, of children? By the pity, by the tenderness, and by the peculiar modes of admiration, which connect themselves with the helplessness, with the innocence, and with the simplicity of children, not only are the primal affections strengthened and continually renewed, but the qualities which are dearest in the sight of heaven—the frailty, for instance, which appeals to forbearance; the innocence which symbolizes the heavenly, and the simplicity which

2 What are called the *Blue Books,* by which title are understood the folio Reports issued every session of Parliament by committees of the two Houses, and stitched into blue covers,—though often sneered at by the ignorant as so much waste paper, will be acknowledged gratefully by those who have used them diligently, as the main well-heads of all accurate information as to the Great Britain of this day. As an immense depository of faithful (*and not superannuated*) statistics, they are indispensable to the honest student. But no man would therefore class the *Blue Books* as literature.

is most alien from the worldly, are kept up in perpetual remembrance, and their ideals are continually refreshed. A purpose of the same nature is answered by the higher literature, viz., the literature of power. What do you learn from *Paradise Lost?* Nothing at all. What do you learn from a cookery-book? Something new—something that you did not know before, in every paragraph. But would you therefore put the wretched cookery-book on a higher level of estimation than the divine poem? What you owe to Milton is not any knowledge, of which a million separate items are still but a million of advancing steps on the same earthly level; what you owe, is *power,* that is, exercise and expansion to your own latent capacity of sympathy with the infinite, where every pulse and each separate influx is a step upwards—a step ascending as upon a Jacob's ladder from earth to mysterious altitudes above the earth. *All* the steps of knowledge, from first to last, carry you further on the same plane, but could never raise you one foot above your ancient level of earth: whereas, the very *first* step in power is a flight—is an ascending movement into another element where earth is forgotten.

Were it not that human sensibilities are ventilated and continually called out into exercise by the great phenomena of infancy, or of real life as it moves through chance and change, or of literature as it recombines these elements in the mimicries of poetry, romance, &c., it is certain that, like any animal power or muscular energy falling into disuse, all such sensibilities would gradually droop and dwindle. It is in relation to these great *moral* capacities of man that the literature of power, as contradistinguished from that of knowledge, lives and has its field of action. It is concerned with what is highest in man; for the Scriptures themselves never condescended to deal by suggestion or co-operation, with the mere discursive understanding: when speaking of man in his intellectual capacity, the Scriptures speak not of the understanding, but of *"the understanding heart,"*— making the heart, i.e., the great *intuitive* (or nondiscursive) organ, to be the interchangeable formula for man in his highest state of capacity for the infinite. Tragedy, romance, fairy tale, or epopee, all alike restore to man's mind the ideals of justice, of hope, of truth, of mercy, of retribution, which else (left to the support of daily life in its realities) would languish for want of sufficient illustration. What is meant, for instance, by *poetic justice?*—It does not mean a justice that differs by its object from the ordinary justice of human jurisprudence; for then it must be confessedly a very bad kind of justice; but it means a justice that differs from common forensic justice by the degree in which it *attains* its object, a justice that is more omnipotent over its own ends, as dealing—not with the refractory elements of earthly life—but with the elements of its own creation, and with materials flexible to its own purest preconceptions. It is certain that, were it not for the literature of power, these ideals would often remain amongst us as mere arid notional forms; whereas, by the creative forces of man put forth in literature, they gain a vernal life of restoration, and germinate into vital activities.

The commonest novel, by moving in alliance with human fears and hopes, with human instincts of wrong and right, sustains and quickens those affections. Calling them into action, it rescues them from torpor. And hence the pre-eminency over all authors that merely *teach,* of the meanest that *moves;* or that teaches, if at all, indirectly *by* moving. The very highest work that has ever existed in the literature of knowledge, is but a *provisional* work: a book upon trial and sufferance, and *quamdiu bene se gesserit.* Let its teaching be even partially revised, let it be but expanded, nay, even let its teaching be but placed in a better order, and instantly it is superseded. Whereas the feeblest works in the literature of power, surviving at all, survive as finished and unalterable amongst men. For instance, the *Principia* of Sir Isaac Newton was a book *militant* on earth from the first. In all stages of its progress it would have to fight for its existence: first, as regards absolute truth; secondly, when that combat was over, as regards its form or mode of presenting the truth. And as soon as a La Place, or anybody else, builds higher upon the foundations laid by this book, effectually he throws it out of the sunshine into decay and darkness; by weapons won from this book he superannuates and destroys this book, so that soon the name of Newton remains, as a mere *nominis umbra,* but his book, as a living power, has transmigrated into other forms. Now, on the contrary, the *Iliad,* the *Prometheus* of Æschylus,—the *Othello* or *King Lear,*—the *Hamlet* or *Macbeth,*—and the *Paradise Lost,* are not militant but triumphant for ever as long as the languages exist in which they speak or can be taught to speak. They never *can* transmigrate into new incarnations. To reproduce *these* in new forms, or variations, even if in some things they should be improved, would be to plagiarize. A good steam-engine is properly superseded by a better. But one lovely pastoral valley is not superseded by another, nor a statue of Praxiteles by a statue of Michael Angelo. These things are separated not by imparity, but by disparity. They are not thought of as unequal under the same standard, but as different in *kind,* and if otherwise equal, as equal under a different standard. Human works of immortal beauty and works of nature in one respect stand on the same footing; they never absolutely repeat each other; never approach so near as not to differ; and they differ not as better and worse, or simply by more and less: they differ by undecipherable and incommunicable differences, that cannot be caught by mimicries, that cannot be reflected in the mirror or copies, that cannot become ponderable in the scales of vulgar comparison.

Applying these principles to Pope, as a representative of fine literature in general, we would wish to remark the claim which he has, or which an equal writer has, to the attention and jealous winnowing of those critics, in particular, who watch over public morals. Clergymen, and all the organs of public criticism put in motion by clergymen, are more especially concerned in the just appreciation of such writers, if the two canons are remembered, which we have endeavored to illustrate, viz., that all works in this class, as opposed to those in the literature of knowledge, first, work by far deeper agencies; and, secondly, are more permanent; in the strictest sense they are κτήματα ἐς ἀεί:[3] and what evil they do, or what good they do, is commensurate with the national language, sometimes long after the nation has departed. At this hour, five hundred years

---

[3] "Possessions for eternity."

since their creation, the tales of Chaucer, never equalled on this earth for their tenderness, and for life of picturesqueness, are read familiarly by many in the charming language of their natal day, and by others in the modernizations of Dryden, of Pope, and Wordsworth. At this hour, one thousand eight hundred years since their creation, the Pagan tales of Ovid, never equalled on this earth for the gaiety of their movement and the capricious graces of their narrative, are read by all Christendom. This man's people and their monuments are dust; but *he* is alive: he has survived them, as he told us that he had it in his commission to do, by a thousand years; "and *shall* a thousand more."

All the literature of knowledge builds only ground-nests, that are swept away by floods, or confounded by the plough; but the literature of power builds nests in aërial altitudes of temples sacred from violation, or of forests inaccessible to fraud. *This* is a great prerogative of the *power* literature; and it is a greater which lies in the mode of its influence. The *knowledge* literature, like the fashion of this world, passeth away. An Encyclopædia is its abstract; and, in this respect, it may be taken for its speaking symbol—that, before one generation has passed, an Encyclopædia is superannuated; for it speaks through the dead memory and unimpassioned understanding, which have not the repose of higher faculties, but are continually enlarging and varying their phylacteries. But all literature, properly so called—literature κατ' ἐξοχήν,[4] for the very reason that it is so much more durable than the literature of knowledge, is (and by the very same proportion it is) more intense and electrically searching in its impressions. The directions in which the tragedy of this planet has trained our human feelings to play, and the combinations into which the poetry of this planet has thrown our human passions of love and hatred, of admiration and contempt, exercise a power bad or good over human life, that cannot be contemplated, when stretching through many generations, without a sentiment allied to awe.[5] And of this let every one be assured—that he owes to the impassioned books which he has read, many a thousand more of emotions than he can consciously trace back to them. Dim by their origination, these emotions yet arise in him, and mould him through life like forgotten incidents of his childhood.

[4] "par excellence."

[5] The reason why the broad distinctions between the two literatures of power and knowledge so little fix the attention, lies in the fact, that a vast proportion of books—history, biography, travels, miscellaneous essays, &c., lying in a middle zone, confound these distinctions by interblending them. All that we call "amusement" or "entertainment," is a diluted form of the power belonging to passion, and also a mixed form; and where threads of direct *instruction* intermingle in the texture with these threads of *power*, this absorption of the duality into one representative *nuance* neutralizes the separate perception of either. Fused into a *tertium quid*, or neutral state, they disappear to the popular eye as the repelling forces, which, in fact, they are.

Hugh MacLennan

The Shadow of Captain Bligh

Not long ago, in the same evening, I listened to my gramophone recording of Haydn's *Mass for St. Cecilia* and then went upstairs and began rereading the account of the mutiny on H.M.S. *Bounty* as written by Nordhoff and Hall. The grand cadences of the Mass kept sounding through my mind, and every now and then I stopped reading to let them swell and subside. I was rereading the book for a purpose and I didn't feel I could put it down. But the counterpoint made me realize with a sensation of shock that Joseph Haydn and Captain Bligh were contemporaries, that the society that had produced and honored the one was the same society that had employed and respected the other.

Haydn's *Mass for St. Cecilia,* which was partially lost until Dr. Brand recovered it little more than a decade ago, and which hardly anyone had heard performed until it appeared recently in a recording of the Haydn Society, is certainly one of the most sublime works the human spirit has ever created. It seems to me worth all the music composed since the death of Beethoven. Beethoven himself was never able to sustain the power that is manifest here, for his struggle with himself and his medium was too great. Haydn's Mass, like the greatest work of Shakespeare, is at once majestic and intimate. Above all it seems effortless, and its joy and triumph are so breath-taking that no one who is moved by music can easily listen to it without reflecting that our modern world has produced no creative genius with his originality, his joyousness, or his power.

Yet Haydn was not unique in his time. His career overlapped those of Bach, Handel, Mozart, and Beethoven. Though his age acclaimed him a master, it occurred to nobody in the eighteenth century to think it miraculous that he was able to compose those immensely complex works, some of great length, in so short a time. The best of his contemporaries were equally prolific and worked with equal speed. Handel composed *The Messiah* in a few weeks and Mozart wrote one of his most famous symphonies in a few days. Compared to these eighteenth-century masters, a modern creative artist moves at a snail's pace. Our most famous poets will die leaving behind only a slim body of published verse. The average modern novelist takes from two to three years to write a single good novel. Our musicians—men like Sibelius, Stravinsky, and Vaughan Williams— have together, in their long lives equalled only a fraction of Haydn's output.

How lucky Haydn was to have lived before the radio and the telephone, before civic societies which would have made exorbitant and unavoidable demands on his time and energy, before publicity and interviewers and income tax and traffic horns and metropolitan dailies—to have lived, in short, before the age of distraction.

But *Mutiny on the Bounty* reminded me of the other side of the eighteenth century. The very fact of Captain Bligh implies that the forces which have made

From *Thirty and Three* by Hugh MacLennan, by permission of Russell & Volkening, Inc. Copyright 1955 by Hugh MacLennan.

ours an age of distraction are far subtler and less avoidable than technical innovations like the telephone and the radio. *Mutiny on the Bounty* should be required reading for anyone who is apt, like myself, to be romantic about past ages and to decry his own. For Captain Bligh was just as typical of the eighteenth century as Haydn was. When I bow before Haydn I must remember that Haydn accepted without question and apparently without remorse the fact that he lived in a world that contained Captain Bligh.

Nothing Mickey Spillane has ever written can be compared in horror to some of the factual scenes in *Mutiny on the Bounty*. Few passages in literature describe more revolting episodes than those of the *Bounty* sailors being seized in the gangway and flogged until the flesh hung in strips from their backs. With our modern knowledge of neurology, we know that the agonies of these poor creatures did not end when the boatswain's mate ceased swinging the cat. Such beatings damaged the nerve roots along the spine and condemned the victims to permanent suffering. What makes those scenes of torture so unbearable to think about is the added realization that they were not sporadic, were not the offshoots of a psychopathic movement like Naziism, but were standard practice in one of the most stable and reflective societies that ever existed. Captain Bligh's cruelty had the weight and approval of his entire society behind it. When the mutineers were later court martialed, the court had no interest in determining whether Bligh had been cruel or not. It was interested solely in whether the accused had obeyed to the letter the harsh laws of the British Navy.

Haydn, Bach, Handel, and Mozart, sublime spirits full of mercy, with sensibilities exquisitely delicate, knew that men like Bligh were the mainstays of the societies they inhabited. Yet this knowledge which to us would be a shame, felt personally, seldom if ever troubled their dreams or ruffled their serenity. The humanitarianism that disturbed Beethoven a generation later had not dawned when Haydn wrote the *Mass for St. Cecilia*.

Haydn reached his prime in the last moments when it was possible for a creative artist to mind his own business in the sense that his conscience could remain untroubled by the sufferings of the unfortunate. If sailors were flogged to death and peasants had no rights, if a neighboring country was ruined by famine or pestilence, if laws were unjust or princes cruel, none was Haydn's affair. He was compelled to no empathy in the suffering of others as modern artists are.

It is this awareness of personal responsibility for the welfare of strangers that makes uneasy all men of imagination today, that troubles their work and makes much of it seem tortured, that frustrates it too, for seldom can a modern man of creative imagination do anything concrete to change the world he lives in.

Responsible only to himself, to his family, and to his God, Haydn enjoyed a freedom few artists have known since. The result was as glorious as it is inimitable. It is on most of his successors that the shadow of Captain Bligh has fallen and remained.

As Haydn represents the spiritual grandeur of the eighteenth-century imagination, Bligh represents its irresponsibility. In Bligh's own words, it was only through fear and cruelty that the stupid, the weak, the incompetent, the ignorant, and the unfortunate could be ruled and compelled to do what their masters considered to be their duty. Unless they were so compelled, the supporters of the system argued, there could be no fineness, no spiritual grandeur, no great literature or beautiful buildings, no masses for St. Cecilia. Civilization, as men of Haydn's day conceived it, could not exist if it yielded to the promptings of a social conscience.

When we realize this it becomes easier to reconcile ourselves to the fact that the world we live in is producing no more Haydns or Mozarts. In the nineteenth century men of imagination turned their attention to the miseries of the world they saw about them, accepted responsibility for it, and forever lost the peace and concentration of spirit which enabled the Haydns and Mozarts to devote the full force of their genius to the realization of the gifts God had given them.

Could a modern artist witness a public flogging and then go home and compose exquisite music? Could he even live quietly under a régime that permitted such atrocities and retain his own respect and that of others?

Merely to ask such questions is to answer them. Musicians who took no more active part in the Hitler régime than perform for a Nazi audience have had to spend years as outcasts before western society would accept them again. The social conscience of today demands the service of every artist alive, and does not forgive him if he refuses it.

On the other hand western society did not make outcasts of the physicists, chemists, and engineers who served Hitler. Until very recently science reserved for itself the same mental freedom that art enjoyed in Haydn's day. If politicians or monsters used the work of science for evil purposes, the scientists felt no personal responsibility. Enjoying such peace of mind, physicists and chemists have been able to devote the full force of their intellects to their work, and so their work has been more impressive than that of the artists who were their contemporaries. No wonder our age, when it looks for a genius to match Bach or Haydn, does not even stop to search among the ranks of the artists. It picks Einstein.

But when the atomic bomb fell on Hiroshima any number of scientists succumbed to a social conscience as the artists had done long ago. Einstein, Oppenheimer, and hundreds of others were overcome with a Hamlet-like self-questioning. If our world lasts long enough it will be interesting to see whether science in the next generation will be as original and productive as it has been in the last three. For a conscience, as Shakespeare knew when he created Hamlet, inhibits action and beclouds genius. Our collective conscience may not have made the modern artist a coward, but it has certainly made him a prisoner.

Consider in contrast to Haydn the life of Albert Schweitzer. Schweitzer began as a musician, and had he lived in the eighteenth century there is no knowing what masterpieces he might have composed. But his conscience would not permit him to devote his entire life to music, so he studied theology and became a minister of the Gospel. Then his conscience told him that preaching was not enough, so he studied medicine and became a doctor. His conscience then informed him that it was self-indulgent to practice medicine in a comfortable European city while there were millions in the world without medical care of any kind. So Schweitzer took his gifts to one of the most primitive parts of Africa. There he has lived and worked ever since, among men so elemental that they can know nothing of Bach or Haydn and cannot even guess at the greatness of the strange healer who came to help them.

Albert Schweitzer will die leaving behind him no tangible or audible monument, no record of objective achievement beyond a few books which are mere by-products of his life and interests. His enormous powers have been spread so widely in the service of others that neither as a musician, nor as a theologian, nor as a doctor-scientist, has his work, in itself, been such as to ensure his immortality. An earlier age would have said that Schweitzer had squandered his gifts on savages. But our age, rightly or wrongly, acclaims him as one of its noblest representatives because his life has translated into action, as hardly any other life has done, the highest aspirations of our social conscience.

No other modern artist I know of has made the total sacrifice of his talents that Schweitzer made; yet no modern artist (musician or poet or even the great individualist Picasso) has been undisturbed by the social conscience of our day.

Critics who argue that the subject-matter of modern art is proof of the decadence of modern society don't really understand what they are talking about. Art has always been a reflection of the aspirations and obsessions of its time and the art of today is no exception. If it is haunted and distracted, if it is often ugly and even horrifying, it does not mean that the artists themselves are worse men than Haydn was. It means only that they have not refused, as Haydn did, to accept responsibility for Captain Bligh. For all its horrors, the twentieth century is better than the eighteenth; no politician or dictator who has tried to defy its conscience has been able, in the end, to succeed.

Some time in the future art may reflect the tranquillity that Haydn knew. If it does so, it will not be because those artists of the future are likely to be abler men than artists of today. It will happen because, after this age of transition, the shadow of Captain Bligh has been removed from the whole world.

Joyce Cary

On the Function of the Novelist

It has been said of Trollope that you can walk about in his books with your hat on. The notion is that his world is more real than that of Dickens. He thought so himself, and so misled a great many innocents, who concluded that a writer's job was to copy life, and got nowhere. For to copy life would be to produce nonsense.

Trollope found in life what we all find, a mass of detail without meaning, of useless cruelty, stupid evil, blind fate, fools doing accidental good and well-meaning saints doing immense evil; what he did was what every writer does, even those modest writers who frankly work for the pay: he created a work of art to give a certain kind of experience.

He said in effect: "This is the shape of things under the confusion of appearance; these are the forces which really move people to action." His whole story, however complex, was designed to illustrate and develop a theme. His essential task was the same as that of Dickens; he used only a different method.

As it is a philosopher's job to make sense of life to the mind, to present it as a rational unity, so it is a novelist's job to make sense of it to the feelings. And this means that we must have a consistent point of view. For it is only from one point of view that experience, like landscape, can be ranged in any kind of order.

It is dangerous perhaps to say that a book must have a moral, so let us call it a meaning. What, then, does "Tristram Shandy" mean? To read it is an event, like the first hearing of Stravinsky's "Petrouchka," and it remains a memory, as of a single experience, like a meeting of which one says, "That meant a lot to me." We can't define the effect in words, but we know that it was definite and lasting.

The objection, in fact, even to books that convey morals is not really to a form of art, but to bad art. Critics who find fault with Zola in his "Nana" for moralizing and driving his moral home with crude means should have protested against a crude moral. If Zola's forte was in brass, he had every right to compose for brass, but not, after he had stunned his audience into attention, to offer them a platitude or a fraud.

When at the end of the fable Nana dies of what Zola calls the small, but was, I fancy, originally the great pox, just as the French mob of the Second Empire is shouting in the streets "à Berlin," we are revolted by the cheapness of a device which suggests that there is anything in common between the dissolution of a harlot and the crisis of an empire. We see behind it the vulgar illusions, or suspect, what is worse, the claptrap, of a mind fed on party politics.

Zola was not a time-server. He fought for justice in the Dreyfus case at the risk of his life. But he was not a profound writer. He made a world rich in characters, but they moved on a surface. He was blind to all the large dimensions of history or morality. He could add intensity to old impressions, but he did not give a new intuition, much less a great one, if we mean by great rich in scope.

A great writer in this sense, whether poet, historian or novelist, is one whose world of organized experience harmonizes into one coherent impression the largest area of actual confusion. Tolstoy's "War and Peace" is a deliberate attempt to make sense, both to mind and feeling, of the whole realm of human action and inhuman fate. He did not succeed. For various reasons, both technical and real, no one is likely to succeed. But "War and Peace" is still one of the great achievements of art. And men live by art, greatly in great arts or cheaply in small arts.

Yet writers who, like Zola, give intensity to a common and superficial idea of the world are doing a useful work. The reason is that a very large number of people cease when quite young to add anything to a limited stock of judgments. After a certain age, say 25, they consider that their education is finished.

It is perhaps natural that having passed through that painful and boring process, called expressly education, they should suppose it over, and that they are equipped for life to label every event as it occurs and drop it into its given pigeonhole. But one who has a label ready for everything does not bother to observe any more, even such ordinary happenings as he has observed for himself, with attention, before he went to school. He merely acts and reacts.

For people who have stopped noticing, the only possible new or renewed experience, and, therefore, new knowledge, is from a work of art. Because that is the only kind of experience which they are prepared to receive on its own terms, they will come out from their shells and expose themselves to music, to a play, to a book, because it is the accepted method of enjoying such things. True, even to plays and books they may bring artistic prejudices which prevent them from seeing *that* play or comprehending *that* book. Their artistic sensibilities may be as crusted over as their minds.

But it is part of an artist's job to break crusts, or let us say rather that artists who work for the public and not merely for themselves are interested in breaking crusts because they want to communicate their intuitions.

Painters, for instance, had used impressionism in their sketches, made only for their private record and pleasure, during hundreds of years before Turner and Constable in England, Monet and his school in France, seized upon the sketch technique as a means to convey their new intuition, or vision, of nature as a play of light.

Of course, since they were born into a world which was accustomed to see nature as classical landscape, poetical objects composed in formal recession, they were not understood. They were labeled ignorant daubers or mountebanks, because these were the only pigeonholes then available for them. There was as yet no impressionist pigeonhole into which new and often original painting could be thrown and forgotten.

But the new school was resolved to be understood. It insisted on exhibiting its work. And since it had a brilliant technique and bold invention, since, too, it early attracted young and independent minds as well as smart dealers, it did finally break through the crust and give to the world a new and rich experience of permanent value, a new realm of ideal appreciation.

Great writers have done this over and over again. Richardson astonished Europe with his new world of sentiment; Rousseau followed hard upon him with his Emile and the Savoyard Vicar, and the crust which they broke was the crust of the feudal society. Its foundations were washed away—chiefly by sentimental tears.

Rousseau and Tolstoy have had direct revolutionary effect on history. But I am not proposing them as great artists only on that account. All art makes history but most of it by indirect and obscure means. Jane Austen was a great artist, and she is more read now than any writer of her time.

Her influence on minds has been enormous but subtle. It springs not from the novelty but the comprehension and balance of her idea of life and the technical power with which she conveys it. Her world is limited in surface but deep in content and, as far as it goes, more self-consistent than either Rousseau's or Tolstoy's. And she breaks the crust of a dry imagination not by a violent assault but by a series of light taps.

It is her style, her humor, that penetrate. And this, of course, is the means appropriate to her purpose. She was not going to open a tea party with a maroon or a blast of trumpets. She had too much of what Henry James called taste, meaning sense of proportion, both esthetic and moral. Much of her greatness as a novelist is precisely in her clear understanding of her job, which was to make a complete thing and have it felt. The function of the novel, in short, is to make the world contemplate and understand itself, not only as rational being but as experience of value, as a complete thing.

Maxwell Anderson
The Essence of Tragedy

Anybody who dares to discuss the making of tragedy lays himself open to critical assault and general barrage, for the theorists have been hunting for the essence of tragedy since Aristotle without entire success. There is no doubt that playwrights have occasionally written tragedy successfully, from Aeschylus on, and there is no doubt that Aristotle came very close to a definition of what tragedy is in his famous passage on catharsis. But why the performance of tragedy should have a cleansing effect on the audience, why an audience is willing to listen to tragedy, why tragedy has a place in the education of men, has never, to my knowledge, been convincingly stated. I must begin by saying that I have not solved the Sphinx's riddle which fifty generations of skillful brains have left in shadow. But I have one suggestion which I think might lead to a solution if it were put to laboratory tests by those who know something about philosophical analysis and dialectic.

There seems no way to get at this suggestion except through a reference to my own adventures in playwriting, so I ask your tolerance while I use myself as an instance. A man who has written successful plays is usually supposed to know something about the theory of playwriting, and perhaps he usually does. In my own case, however, I must confess that I came into the theater unexpectedly,

From *Off Broadway: Essays About the Theater,* by Maxwell Anderson. Reprinted by permission of William Sloane Associates. Copyright 1947 by Maxwell Anderson.

without preparation, and stayed in it because I had a certain amount of rather accidental success. It was not until after I had fumbled my way through a good many successes and an appalling number of failures that I began to doubt the sufficiency of dramatic instinct and to wonder whether or not there were general laws governing dramatic structure which so poor a head for theory as my own might grasp and use. I had read the *Poetics* long before I tried playwriting, and I had looked doubtfully into a few well-known handbooks on dramatic structure, but the maxims and theories propounded always drifted by me in a luminous haze—brilliant, true, profound in context, yet quite without meaning for me when I considered the plan for a play or tried to clarify an emotion in dialogue. So far as I could make out every play was a new problem, and the old rules were inapplicable. There were so many rules, so many landmarks, so many pitfalls, so many essential reckonings, that it seemed impossible to find your way through the jungle except by plunging ahead, trusting to your sense of direction and keeping your wits about you as you went.

I shan't trouble you with the details of my search for a criterion, partly because I can't remember it in detail. But I reread Aristotle's *Poetics* in the light of some bitter experience, and one of his observations led me to a comparison of ancient and modern playwriting methods. In discussing construction he made a point of the recognition scene as essential to tragedy. The recognition scene, as Aristotle isolated it in the tragedies of the Greeks, was generally an artificial device, a central scene in which the leading character saw through a disguise, recognized as a friend or as an enemy, perhaps as a lover or a member of his own family, some person whose identity had been hidden. Iphigeneia, for example, acting as priestess in an alien country, receives a victim for sacrifice and then recognizes her own brother in this victim. There is an instant and profound emotional reaction, instantly her direction in the play is altered. But occasionally, in the greatest of the plays, the recognition turned on a situation far more convincing though no less contrived. Oedipus, hunting savagely for the criminal who has brought the plague upon Thebes, discovers that he is himself that criminal—and since this is a discovery that affects not only the physical well-being and happiness of the hero, but the whole structure of his life, the effect on him and on the direction of the story is incalculably greater than could result from the more superficial revelation made to Iphigeneia.

Now scenes of exactly this sort are rare in the modern drama except in detective stories adapted for the stage. But when I probed a little more deeply into the memorable pieces of Shakespeare's theater and our own I began to see that though modern recognition scenes are subtler and harder to find, they are none the less present in the plays we choose to remember. They seldom have to do with anything so naïve as disguise or the unveiling of a personal identity. But the element of discovery is just as important as ever. For the mainspring in the mechanism of a modern play is almost invariably a discovery by the hero of some element in his environment or in his own soul of which he has not been aware— or which he has not taken sufficiently into account. Moreover, nearly every teacher of playwriting has had some inkling of this, though it was not until after I had worked out my own theory that what they said on this point took on accurate meaning for me. I still think that the rule which I formulated for my own guidance is more concise than any other, and so I give it here: A play should lead up to and away from a central crisis, and this crisis should consist in a discovery by the leading character which has an indelible effect on his thought and emotion and completely alters his course of action. The leading character, let me say again, must make the discovery; it must affect him emotionally; and it must alter his direction in the play.

Try that formula on any play you think worthy of study, and you will find that, with few exceptions, it follows this pattern or some variation of this pattern. The turning point of *The Green Pastures,* for example, is the discovery by God, who is the leading character, that a God who is to endure must conform to the laws of change. The turning point of *Hamlet* is Hamlet's discovery, in the play scene, that his uncle was unquestionably the murderer of his father. In *Abe Lincoln in Illinois* Lincoln's discovery is that he has been a coward, that he has stayed out of the fight for the Union because he was afraid. In each case, you will note, the discovery has a profound emotional effect on the hero, and gives an entirely new direction to his action in the play. . . .

Now this prime rule has a corollary which is just as important as the rule itself. The hero who is to make the central discovery in a play must not be a perfect man. He must have some variation of what Aristotle calls a tragic fault; and the reason he must have it is that when he makes his discovery he must change both in himself and in his action—and he must change for the better. The fault can be a very simple one—a mere unawareness, for example—but if he has no fault he cannot change for the better, but only for the worse, and for a reason which I shall discuss later, it is necessary that he must become more admirable, and not less so, at the end of the play. In other words, a hero must pass through an experience which opens his eyes to an error of his own. He must learn through suffering. In a tragedy he suffers death itself as a consequence of his fault or his attempt to correct it, but before he dies he has become a nobler person because of his recognition of his fault and the consequent alteration of his course of action. In a serious play which does not end in death he suffers a lesser punishment, but the pattern remains the same. In both forms he has a fault to begin with, he discovers that fault during the course of the action, and he does what he can to rectify it at the end. In *The Green Pastures* God's fault was that he believed himself perfect. He discovered that he was not perfect, that he had been in error and must make amends. Hamlet's fault was that he could not make up his mind to act. He offers many excuses for his indecision until he discovers that there is no real reason for hesitation and that he has delayed out of cowardice. Lincoln, in *Abe Lincoln in Illinois,* has exactly the same difficulty. In the climactic scene it is revealed to him that he had hesitated to take sides through fear of the consequences to himself, and he then chooses to go ahead without regard for what may be in store for him. From the point of view of the playwright, then, the essence of a tragedy, or even of a serious play, is the spiritual awakening, or regeneration, of his hero.

When a playwright attempts to reverse the formula, when his hero makes a discovery which has an evil effect, or one which the audience interprets as evil, on his character, the play is inevitably a failure on the stage. In *Troilus and Cressida* Troilus discovers that Cressida is a light woman. He draws from her defection the inference that all women are faithless—that faith in woman is the possession of fools. As a consequence he turns away from life and seeks death in a cause as empty as the love he has given up, the cause of the strumpet Helen. All the glory of Shakespeare's verse cannot rescue the play for an audience, and save in *Macbeth* Shakespeare nowhere wrote so richly, so wisely, or with such a flow of brilliant metaphor.

For the audience will always insist that the alteration in the hero be for the better—or for what it believes to be the better. As audiences change the standards of good and evil change, though slowly and unpredictably, and the meanings of plays change with the centuries. One thing only is certain: that an audience watching a play will go along with it only when the leading character responds in the end to what it considers a higher moral impulse than moved him at the beginning of the story, though the audience will of course define morality as it pleases and in the terms of its own day. It may be that there is no absolute up or down in this world, but the race believes that there is, and will not hear of any denial.

And now at last I come to the point toward which I've been struggling so laboriously. Why does the audience come to the theater to look on while an imaginary hero is put to an imaginary trial and comes out of it with credit to the race and to himself? . . . The theater originated in two complementary religious ceremonies, one celebrating the animal in man and one celebrating the god. Old Greek Comedy was dedicated to the spirits of lust and riot and earth, spirits which are certainly necessary to the health and continuance of the race. Greek tragedy was dedicated to man's aspiration, to his kinship with the gods, to his unending, blind attempt to lift himself above his lusts and his pure animalism into a world where there are other values than pleasure and survival. However unaware of it we may be, our theater has followed the Greek patterns with no change in essence, from Aristophanes and Euripides to our own day. Our more ribald musical comedies are simply our approximation of the Bacchic rites of Old Comedy. In the rest of our theater we sometimes follow Sophocles, whose tragedy is always an exaltation of the human spirit, sometimes Euripides, whose tragicomedy follows the same pattern of an excellence achieved through suffering. . . .

Our comedy is largely the Greek New Comedy, which grew out of Euripides' tragicomedy, and is separated from tragedy only in that it presents a happier scene and puts its protagonist through an ordeal which is less than lethal.

And since our plays, aside from those which are basically Old Comedy, are exaltations of the human spirit, since that is what an audience expects when it comes to the theater, the playwright gradually discovers, as he puts plays before audiences, that he must follow the ancient Aristotelian rule: he must build his plot around a scene wherein his hero discovers some mortal frailty or stupidity in himself and faces life armed with a new wisdom. He must so arrange his story that it will prove to the audience that men pass through suffering purified, that, animal though we are, despicable though we are in many ways, there is in us all some divine, incalculable fire that urges us to be better than we are.

It could be argued that what the audience demands of a hero is only conformity to race morality, to the code which seems to the spectators most likely to make for race survival. In many cases, especially in comedy, and obviously in the comedy of Molière, this is true. But in the majority of ancient and modern plays it seems to me that what the audience wants to believe is that men have a desire to break the molds of earth which encase them and claim a kinship with a higher morality than that which hems them in. The rebellion of Antigone, who breaks the laws of men through adherence to a higher law of affection, the rebellion of Prometheus, who breaks the law of the gods to bring fire to men, the rebellion of God in *The Green Pastures* against the rigid doctrine of the Old Testament, the rebellion of Tony in *They Knew What They Wanted* against the convention that called on him to repudiate his cuckold child, the rebellion of Liliom against the heavenly law which asked him to betray his own integrity and make a hypocrisy of his affection, even the repudiation of the old forms and the affirmation of new by the heroes of Ibsen and Shaw, these are all instances to me of the groping of men toward an excellence dimly apprehended, seldom possible of definition. They are evidence to me that the theater at its best is a religious affirmation, an age-old rite restating and reassuring man's belief in his own destiny and his ultimate hope. The theater is much older than the doctrine of evolution, but its one faith, asseverated again and again for every age and every year, is a faith in evolution, in the reaching and the climb of men toward distant goals, glimpsed but never seen, perhaps never achieved, or achieved only to be passed impatiently on the way to a more distant horizon.

Louis Kronenberger

Some Notes on Comedy

Comedy is not just a happy as opposed to an unhappy ending, but a way of surveying life so that happy endings must prevail. But it is not to be confused, on that account, with optimism, any more than a happy ending is to be confused with happiness. Comedy is much more reasonably associated with pessimism—with at any rate a belief in the smallness that survives as against the greatness that is scarred or destroyed. In mortal affairs it is tragedy, like forgiveness, that seems divine; and comedy, like error, that is human. . . .

From *The Republic of Letters*, by Louis Kronenberger. Copyright 1952, 1955 by Louis Kronenberger. Reprinted by permission of Alfred A. Knopf, Inc.

Comedy appeals to the laughter, which is in part at least the malice, in us; for comedy is concerned with human imperfection, with people's failure to measure up either to the world's or to their own conception of excellence. All tragedy is idealistic and says in effect, "The pity of it"—that owing to this fault of circumstance or that flaw of character, a man who is essentially good does evil, a man who is essentially great is toppled from the heights. But all comedy tends to be skeptical and says in effect, "The absurdity of it"—that in spite of his fine talk or noble resolutions, a man is the mere creature of pettiness and vanity and folly. Tragedy is always lamenting the Achilles tendon, the destructive flaw in man; but comedy, in a sense, is always looking for it. Not cheaply, out of malevolence or cynicism; but rather because even at his greatest, man offers some touch of the fatuous and small, just as a murderer, even at his cleverest, usually makes some fatal slip. In tragedy men aspire to more than they can achieve; in comedy, they pretend to more.

The difference, again, between the two is the very question of difference. A great tragic hero—an Oedipus or Lear—strikes us as tremendously far removed from common humanity. But comedy, stripping off the war-paint and the feathers, the college degrees or the military medals, shows how very like at bottom the hero is to everybody else. Tragedy cannot flourish without giving its characters a kind of aura of poetry, or idealism, or doom; comedy scarcely functions till the aura has been dispelled. And as it thrives on a revelation of the true rather than the trumped-up motive, as it is in one way sustained by imposture, so in another it is sustained by incongruity. Here is the celebrated philosopher cursing the universe because he has mislaid a book. Here are all those who, like King Canute, would bid the clock go backward or the waves stand still. Here is not only the cheat, but the victim who but for his own dishonest desires could never be cheated.

Comedy, in brief, is criticism. If through laughing at others we purge ourselves of certain spiteful and ungenerous instincts—as through tragedy we achieve a higher and more publicized catharsis—that is not quite the whole of it. Comedy need not be hostile to idealism; it need only show how far human beings fall short of the ideal. The higher comedy mounts, the airier and more brilliant its forms, the more are we aware of man's capacity for being foolish or self-deluded or complacent; in the very highest comedy, such as the finale of Mozart's *Marriage of Figaro,* we are in a very paradise of self-deceptions and misunderstandings and cross-purposes. At the heart of high comedy there is always a strain of melancholy, as round the edges there is all gaiety and ebullience and glitter; and Schiller was perhaps right in regarding high comedy as the greatest of all literary forms.

Comedy is criticism, then, because it exposes human beings for what they are in contrast to what they profess to be. How much idealism, it asks, shall we find entirely free from self-love? How much beneficence is born of guilt, how much affection is produced by flattery? At its most severe, doubtless, comedy is not just skeptical but cynical; and asks many of the same questions, returning many of the same answers, as that prince—or at any rate duke—of cynics, La Rochefoucauld.

"Pride," La Rochefoucauld remarked, "does not wish to owe, and vanity does not wish to pay." Or again: "To establish oneself in the world, one does all one can to seem established there." Of these and many similar maxims, a play or story might easily be written; from each much cold and worldly comedy, or harsh and worldly farce, might be contrived. But comedy need not be so harsh, and seldom is: though it can be harsher still, can be—as in Ben Jonson—gloating and sardonic. But always it is the enemy, not of virtue or idealism, but of hypocrisy and pretense; and what it does in literature is very much, I suppose, what experience does for most of us in life: it knocks the bloom off the peach, the gilt off the gingerbread.

But though the comic spirit is, in Meredith's phrase, "humanely malign," it is also kindly and even companionable, in the sense that it brings men together as fellow-fools and sinners, and is not only criticism but understanding. Comedy is always jarring us with the evidence that we are no better than other people, and always comforting us with the knowledge that most other people are no better than we are. It makes us more critical but it leaves us more tolerant; and to that extent it performs a very notable social function. Its whole character, indeed— quite aside from that point—is rather social than individual.

The social basis rests in the very subject-matter of comedy—in all that has to do with one's life as part of a group; with one's wish to charm or persuade or deceive or dazzle others. Thus no exhibitionist can exist in solitude, no hypocrite or poseur can work without an audience. There are indeed so many social situations that engender comedy that many of them are notably hackneyed. There are all kinds of classic family jokes—the mother-in-law joke preëminently; but equally the rich-uncle theme, or the country cousin, or the visiting relative who forgets to leave, or the one that proffers advice, or the one that prophesies disaster. Right in the home there is the precocious brat or the moping adolescent; there are countless varieties of comic servants; and there is finally the question, though it perhaps belongs in a different category, of who heads the family—the husband or the wife.

The idea of husband and wife more likely belongs with the social aspects of sex, with the War Between the Sexes as it is fought out in the drawing room. As a purely sexual conflict, this war would not be social; but by the same token it would not be comedy. The question whether man really makes the decisions— including the decision to marry—or is merely permitted to think he does, is, whatever the answer, thoroughly social in nature. Or there is the business of how men and women perform in society for one another's benefit: being the fearless protector or the clinging vine, the woman who always understands or the man who is never understood. We have social comedy again when we pit one na- tionality as well as one sex against another, when the American puritan is ensnared by a continental siren, or when the suitor is German and humorless, and the besought one is French and amused. There is still another social aspect when we add a third person to the situation, a mistress as well as a wife, or a lover as well as a husband; or—for the situation need not be illicit, it need only be triangular—when the wife's old beau or the husband's old flame, reappears on the scene. Or there is the man who does not know which of two sisters, or two heiresses, or two widows to marry; or the girl which of a half dozen suitors.

Comedy, indeed, must gain admittance into any part of the world—including prisons and sickrooms and funerals—where people are thrown together. Any institution involving hierarchies and rivalries—for example, a university—is a perfect hotbed of it. There will be everybody's relation to the President or the President's wife; or the President's relation to the President's wife; or to his trustees; all the struggles for precedence and the problems of protocol; the progressives on the faculty and the die-hards; the wives who can't help looking dowdy, the wives who suppose they look chic. For obviously any institution, whether a college or a department store, an artist colony or a country club, provides a cross-section of social types and traits, and brings us face to face with a hundred things out of which comedy is distilled: ambition and pride, arrogance and obsequiousness; a too-slavish following or a too-emphatic flouting of convention; all the stratagems men use in order to outwit or get their way.

And of course comedy becomes purely social in that best known and perhaps best liked of all its higher forms—the comedy of manners. Here we have hardly less than a picture of society itself; here the men and women are but parts of a general whole, and what survives—if we have it from the past—is likely to be known as the Restoration Scene, or Regency London, or Victorian Family Life. Here the drawing room is not merely the setting of the play or novel, but the subject and even the hero; here enter all the prejudices, the traditions, the taboos, the aspirations, the absurdities, the snobberies, of a group. The group, to constitute itself one, must partake of a common background and accept a similar view of life: though there will usually exist some outsider, some rebel, some nonconformist who, as the case may be, is ringing the doorbell or shattering the window panes; trying desperately to get in or desperately to get out; bending the knee or thumbing his nose. Or the comedy of manners will contrast one social milieu with another—the urban and the rustic, the capital and the provinces, Philistia and Bohemia, America and Europe. And in the comedy of manners, ignorance of good form has much the same value that, in straight drama, ignorance of some vital fact has.

And with ignorance of one kind or another we begin coming close to the very mainspring of comedy, or at any rate of comedy in action. For most comedy is born of ignorance or false knowledge; is based on misunderstanding. (Obviously not knowing the truth—though here one might add "until it is too late"— applies to much tragedy also.) At the level of ordinary farce or romantic comedy, the lovers are estranged until a quarter of eleven because the young man misunderstood why the young lady was walking with Sir Robert in the garden. At a higher level, it will not be mere circumstance or coincidence, but qualities of character that block the way. Envy proves an obstruction, or arrogance; or a too-great tendency to be suspicious or to take offense. . . . Comedy at its greatest is criticism indeed; is nothing less, in fact, than a form of moral enlightenment. . . .

And this brings up the point that though Comedy has its permanent subject-matter and even its body of laws, it is liable, like everything else, to changes in fashion and taste, to differences of sensibility. One generation's pleasure is the next generation's embarrassment; much that the Victorians shuddered at merely makes us laugh, much that they laughed at might well make us shudder. One always reacts—and quite fortunately—from the vantage-point of one's own age; and it is probably a mistake, and certainly a waste of breath, to be arrogant or snobbish or moral about what amuses or does not amuse one: we may fancy we are less callous than our grandfathers and only be less callous about different things. The cuckold was clearly, in Restoration comedy, a figure to hoot at. Simply for being cuckolded we do not today find a man so comic, or even comic at all; though the moment we add an extra element to his role, such as his elation over cuckolding others, he becomes a comic figure for us. To what extent sex itself is a comic theme must naturally vary with the morality of a particular age; there are times when it seems shocking for a man ever to have a mistress; there are times when it seems even more shocking for a man never to have one. Right in the same age, what is considered virtue by the parson may be termed repression by the psychiatrist; and in such an age, which is usually one of moral transition, we may well find conflicting comedy values. The pendulum-swing of taste always makes it hard for people to know what they really like: if they are in revolt against gentility, they are likely to confuse what is funny with what is merely bold or obscene; if they are converts to gentility, they will be too much outraged by the indecent to inquire whether it is funny. There is nothing at which the Comic Spirit must smile more than our fickle and inconstant notions as to what constitutes comedy. We need not always look back to Shakespeare's drearier clowns as an instance of how tastes change: sometimes we need only attend a revival of what convulsed us ten years before.

W. H. Auden and J. Garrett

Memorable Speech

Of the many definitions of poetry, the simplest is still the best: "memorable speech." That is to say, it must move our emotions, or excite our intellect, for only that which is moving or exciting is memorable, and the stimulus is the audible spoken word and cadence, to which in all its power of suggestion and incantation we must surrender, as we do when talking to an intimate friend. We must, in fact, make exactly the opposite kind of mental effort to that we make in grasping other verbal uses, for in the case of the latter the aura of suggestion around every word through which, like the atom radiating

From the introduction to *The Poet's Tongue*, edited by W. H. Auden and J. Garrett. Reprinted by permission of G. Bell & Sons, Ltd.

lines of force through the whole of space and time, it becomes ultimately a sign for the sum of all possible meanings, must be rigorously suppressed and its meaning confined to a single dictionary one. For this reason the exposition of a scientific theory is easier to read than to hear. No poetry, on the other hand, which when mastered is not better heard than read is good poetry.

All speech has rhythm, which is the result of the combination of the alternating periods of effort and rest necessary to all living things, and the laying of emphasis on what we consider important; and in all poetry there is a tension between the rhythm due to the poet's personal values, and those due to the experiences of generations crystallised into habits of language such as the English tendency to alternate weak and accented syllables, and conventional verse forms like the hexameter, the heroic pentameter, or the French Alexandrine. Similes, metaphors of image or idea, and auditory metaphors such as rhyme, assonance, and alliteration help further to clarify and strengthen the pattern and internal relations of the experience described.

Poetry, in fact, bears the same kind of relation to Prose, using prose simply in the sense of all those uses of words that are not poetry, that algebra bears to arithmetic. The poet writes of personal or fictitious experiences, but these are not important in themselves until the reader has realised them in his own consciousness.

> Soldier from the war returning,
> Spoiler of the taken town.

It is quite unimportant, though it is the kind of question not infrequently asked, who the soldier is, what regiment he belongs to, what war he had been fighting in, etc. The soldier is you or me, or the man next door. Only when it throws light on our own experience, when these lines occur to us as we see, say, the unhappy face of a stockbroker in the suburban train, does poetry convince us of its significance. The test of a poet is the frequency and diversity of the occasions on which we remember his poetry.

Memorable speech then. About what? Birth, death, the Beatific Vision, the abysses of hatred and fear, the awards and miseries of desire, the unjust walking the earth and the just scratching miserably for food like hens, triumphs, earthquakes, deserts of boredom and featureless anxiety, the Golden Age promised or irrevocably past, the gratifications and terrors of childhood, the impact of nature on the adolescent, the despairs and wisdoms of the mature, the sacrificial victim, the descent into Hell, the devouring and the benign mother? Yes, all of these, but not these only. Everything that we remember no matter how trivial: the mark on the wall, the joke at luncheon, word games, these, like the dance of a stoat or the raven's gamble, are equally the subject of poetry. . . .

A great many people dislike the idea of poetry as they dislike over-earnest people, because they imagine it is always worrying about the eternal verities.

Those, in Mr. Spender's words, who try to put poetry on a pedestal only succeed in putting it on the shelf. Poetry is no better and no worse than human nature; it is profound and shallow, sophisticated and naïve, dull and witty, bawdy and chaste in turn.

In spite of the spread of education and the accessibility of printed matter, there is a gap between what is commonly called "highbrow" and "lowbrow" taste, wider perhaps than it has ever been.

The industrial revolution broke up the agricultural communities, with their local conservative cultures, and divided the growing population into two classes: those whether employers or employees who worked and had little leisure, and a small class of shareholders who did no work, had leisure but no responsibilities or roots, and were therefore preoccupied with themselves. Literature has tended therefore to divide into two streams, one providing the first with a compensation and escape, the other the second with a religion and a drug. The Art for Art's sake of the London drawing-rooms of the '90's, and towns like Burnley and Rochdale, are complementary.

Nor has the situation been much improved by the increased leisure and educational opportunities which the population to-day as a whole possess. Were leisure all, the unemployed would have created a second Athens.

Artistic creations may be produced by individuals, and because their work is only appreciated by a few it does not necessarily follow that it is not good; but a universal art can only be the product of a community united in sympathy, sense of worth, and aspiration; and it is improbable that the artist can do his best except in such a society.

Something of this lies behind the suspicion of and attack upon the intellectual which is becoming more and more vocal. It is hardly possible to open a number of *Punch* without seeing him spectacled, round-shouldered, rabbit-toothed, a foil to a landscape of beautifully unconscious cows, or a whipping-boy for a drawing-room of dashing young sahibs and elegant daughters of the chase. Cross the channel and this dislike, in more countries than one, has taken a practical form, to which the occasional ducking of an Oxford aesthete seems a nursery tiff.

If we are still of the opinion that poetry is worth writing and reading, we must be able to answer such objections satisfactorily at least to ourselves.

The "average" man says: "When I get home I want to spend my time with my wife or in the nursery; I want to get out on to the links or go for a spin in the car, not to read poetry. Why should I? I'm quite happy without it." We must be able to point out to him that whenever, for example, he makes a good joke he is creating poetry, that one of the motives behind poetry is curiosity, the wish to know what we feel and think, and how, as E. M. Forster says, can I know what I think till I see what I say, and that curiosity is the only human passion that can be indulged in for twenty-four hours a day without satiety.

The psychologist maintains that poetry is a neurotic symptom, an attempt to compensate by phantasy for a failure to meet reality. We must tell him that phantasy is only the beginning of writing; that, on the contrary, like psychology, poetry is a struggle to reconcile the unwilling subject and object; in fact, that since psychological truth depends so largely on context, poetry, the parabolic approach, is the only adequate medium for psychology.

The propagandist, whether moral or political, complains that the writer should use his powers over words to persuade people to a particular course of action, instead of fiddling while Rome burns. But Poetry is not concerned with telling people what to do, but with extending our knowledge of good and evil, perhaps making the necessity for action more urgent and its nature more clear, but only leading us to the point where it is possible for us to make a rational and moral choice.

Elizabeth Drew

Poetry and Meaning

There are readers who are quite content with what they can get from poetry without "understanding." They find enough in the communication of sound, fleeting association, mood, suggestion, color, overtones and atmosphere, without any kind of logical or intellectual content. Empson has defined the opposite position in *Seven Types of Ambiguity*. Arguing against the belief that it is enough for the appreciation of poetry to understand the meanings of the words in isolation, he goes on:

> It has been deduced from this belief that you are liable to destroy the poem if its meaning is discovered, that it is important to preserve one's innocence about the meaning of verses, that one must use sensibility, and as little intelligence as possible. This is often true, but I take a moral line here, and say it is true only of bad poetry.

It is difficult indeed not to believe that the value of an overtone is its relation to a full tone, and the value of an association is its relation to a central theme. And to say that because the reality of poetry is something very much larger than its rational content, it can therefore dispense with a rational content altogether, is unconvincing. The final use of the works of a watch, however delicate and exquisite in design and craftsmanship, is that when assembled they tell the time. If the dial be omitted, the function of the watch is gravely impaired.

And yet that image is inadequate. The poem should, we may believe, "tell the time," but not as a watch-dial does. A dial suggests a statement of scientific precision and accuracy, which is the last thing aimed at or required by the method of poetry. If we want language which is scientifically accurate the proper medium is prose of the kind used for traffic regulation or notices in railway trains. Poetry reveals its truths in language which is supple, pliant and yielding; it works by suggestion, ambiguity and obliquity. There are no rigid confines to its boundaries of "meaning." The potentialities of language are its whole width of compass, not only its intellectual aspect, its content of ideas. This intellectual aspect, its common logical basis, is recognized by everyone and is easily communicable to everyone, but what distinguishes poetry from prose is precisely that the poet explores and exploits all the elements beyond that, the elements lurking in the emotional and sensuous values of words. This means all the qualities of beauty, strangeness and power in rhythm and music, texture, color, oddness and subtle collisions. The arguments around obscurity are really arguments as to how far these particular uses of language can *replace* the simple logical values of statement to which we are accustomed.

Eliot, discussing the extreme complexity of the problems of synthesis which face the modern poet in his effort to unify the different planes of his experience, declared that inevitably the poet has to be "more comprehensive, more allusive, more indirect, in order to force, to dislocate, if necessary, language to his meaning." He realized that by doing this his "meaning" would no longer be the expected and familiar one:

> The chief use of the "meaning" of a poem, in the ordinary sense, may be . . . to satisfy one habit of the reader, to keep his mind diverted and quiet, while the poem does its work upon him: much as the imaginary burglar is always provided with a bit of nice meat for the house-dog. This is a normal situation of which I approve. But the minds of all poets do not work that way: some of them, assuming that there are other minds like their own, become impatient of this "meaning" which seems superfluous, and perceive possibilities of intensity through its elimination. I am not asserting that this situation is ideal; only that we must write our poetry as we can, and take it as we find it.

Hart Crane pleaded in the same way for this elimination of "meaning" expressed in logical statement:

> If the poet is to be held completely to the already evolved and exploited sequences of imagery and logic, what field of added consciousness and increased perception . . . can be expected when one has to relatively return to the alphabet every breath or so? In the minds of people who have sensitively read, seen and experienced a great deal, isn't there a terminology something like shorthand as compared to usual description and dialectics, which the artist ought to be right in trusting as a reasonable connective agent toward fresh concepts, more inclusive valuations?

Both the strength and the weakness of the position is shown in *The Waste Land*. The fragmentary, "dislocated," formal arrangement reflected very strikingly the sense of disintegration, both personal and social, behind the poem; and the intensity created by the character of the imagery and the rhythm of the verse drove its way into the consciousness of the reader even where the "meaning" eluded him. He felt that here was a projection of some poignant personal conflict, a drama of inner and outer spiritual disorder which was the work of a deliberate artist, attempting to evoke and present a contemporary consciousness in words, symbols and associations which should communicate its reality without further elucidation (in much the way that modern painters such as Matisse and Picasso and masters such as El Greco and Cézanne have distorted the conventional, representational mode to fit their personal feelings for formal relationships). At the same time the necessity for consulting works of reference to clarify the symbolism, the unfamiliarity of many of the poet's literary associations, the private springs of certain images, and the lack of connectives between the various sets of symbols, all acted as barricades against the storming of the imagination and continue to do so after twenty years of commentary.

"We have so built into our nervous systems a demand for intellectual coherence, even in poetry, that we find a difficulty in doing without it," says I. A. Richards. This is very true. Our early responses to poetry are usually educated on the romantic poets, who seldom transgress logical coherence, and on Shakespeare, who appeals at so many different levels that it is quite easy to ignore those on which he communicates poetic effects in very obscure and difficult language. It is well to remind ourselves again that the problem of the right sort of poetry includes the problem of the right sort of reader.

> If all the good people were clever
> And all clever people were good,
> The world would be better than ever
> We thought that it possibly could;
> But somehow 'tis seldom or never
> The two hit it off as they should,
> The good are so harsh to the clever
> The clever so rude to the good.

In the slight note of exasperation which can be heard in Hart Crane's statement of his position, the voice of the clever is heard addressing the good, and the attitude of the good is hinted at by Coleridge when he declares: "In all perplexity there is a portion of fear which predisposes the mind to anger." But it is not only anger which the old-fashioned reader feels towards the obscurity of modern verse. He feels that wide implications towards the whole of life are entangled with these problems of literary practice. He complains of the obscurity on moral and human grounds: he feels that the spiritual and emotional function of poetry in his life has been denied him by the new cult.

Nobody will deny that he has a case. To stress only the supernormal vision of the poet, to reduce poetry to the effects which can be won from language when its direct qualities of common communication are eliminated, to put all the emphasis on the significance of its obscure and ambiguous elements, is to isolate the poetic activity from all common experience. This is undoubtedly a solution of the poet's dilemma, but it is a negative and partial solution and tends to restrict the poet's audience to the supersensitive "poet's party."

The desire for unification and harmony is the ruling spirit of human aspiration in both life and art. Psychoanalysis has given us a picture of the human organism as the battleground of two conflicts: a conflict between conscious and unconscious elements in man's own being, and a conflict between himself and the world in which he lives. The urge which the poet shares with all men to harmonize these conflicts may express itself purely in terms of his art. The poet, particularly in times of social disintegration such as the present, may withdraw from any attempt to contemplate the reality of the external world, and concentrate upon giving formal verbal outline to his personal *response* to the problem of living. The discipline of creation is itself a rigid exercise in the achievement of psychic equilibrium. If he achieves it by poetic means which satisfy himself it will be a matter of no importance to him whether he communicates freely with his fellows. But the poet who feels also the compulsion to relate himself organically with the external world, who includes both the reality of that world and the reality of his own consciousness in the material he aims to synthesize, must inevitably find some method of communication which appeals not only to a partial and limited activity of the human potential, but to the whole of it. Since the poet is an artist in language, he will inevitably use language in its intuitive and symbolic and ambiguous aspects as well as in its direct and intellectual ones, but he will—indeed, he must—use language through which he can appeal to the common human nature of his audience. It will be the whole being of the poet which participates in his act of creation, and the whole being of the reader which responds.

The Short Story

The analysis of short stories is a source of unlimited pleasure, and there are unlimited ways of going about it. Close examination of plot, character, setting, point of view, style, tone, and the other elements of fiction is essential to the full understanding and enjoyment of good short stories. But for the student who proposes to devote serious thought to the short story for the first time, two concepts are particularly useful; these are *theme* and *conflict*.

The concept of *theme* is best described by a comparison. If you were to make a diary record of all the events that occurred to you in a given period of time, such as an ordinary day, the result would not be a story but a string of more or less unrelated episodes. The main difference between such a record and a well-told piece of fiction is that the events in the diary relate to different issues and interests, whereas all the content of the piece of fiction, particularly if it is a short story, relates, directly or indirectly, to a single issue or interest. The short-story writer's aim is to project a point of view about a subject, and the more strictly he can limit the elements of his story to material that is relevant to this point of view, the more effective will his story be. This controlling idea, the point of view about a particular subject which the writer is expressing through the elements of the story, is the real subject of the story and is called the theme.

Of course, the short story is, in effect, nearly always a retelling of an actual experience, either the author's or someone else's, so that it might be said that, at its origin, the material of the story is the same as the material of the diary entry. But the writer has chosen to write about these experiences because they seem especially meaningful to him. This significance is a clue to the theme that is in his mind, often without his being fully aware of it himself. When he works the actual experiences into a story, he will find himself omitting details that are irrelevant to the theme and rearranging the episodes so that they project the theme better than did the actual events. The result of this process of shaping and organization is what we mean by the form of a story. It means that the events in a story are narrated in a coherent and orderly manner, that the reader is given sufficient information about the people, places, and episodes, and that whatever is started in the story is finished before the story is over.

The reader of the serious short story will enjoy it more and understand it better if he analyzes it to identify its theme and determine the ways in which its elements support the theme. Of course, not every detail in a story is related directly to the theme itself. Some details are related to elements that directly support the theme, some to elements that support these secondary elements, and so on. In William Carlos Williams' "The Use of Force," for example, the theme is concerned with the idea that it is evil to compel a person to do something against his will. The sick girl in the story refuses to let the doctor see her throat. When he violently forces her to submit to an examination, he finds that she is dangerously ill. The girl illustrates the theme directly. Her illness, however, has no direct connection with it; it is a feature of the character, not an illustration of the idea. But the sickness is essential to the point of the story, for if the girl turned out not to be sick, the story would suggest that it is evil to use force for a mistaken purpose, whereas the theme of the story as it stands, which is no doubt the one intended by the author, is that force is *always* evil, even when it is used for a purpose that is laudable.

The real subject, or theme, of a good story is nearly always some general idea of vital importance to human beings, and it is rarely obvious. For example, it would not be very meaningful to say that the subject of John Steinbeck's "The Promise" is the birth of a colt or the death of a mare. These episodes are obviously central events in the story, but they are important for their contributions to a broader and deeper theme—the idea that the fulfillment of our desires involves not only willing sacrifices, like the chores Jody performs, but also unexpected and involuntary ones. This, one would say, is what the story is *really* about. The interest of the story, however, does not lie in the subject alone, important as it may be, nor in the actions and events, vivid and exciting as they may be, but in the relationship between them. The final effect of a good reading of a good story is a strong impression of how intimately the general is involved in the specific, of how the simple actions of ordinary people can be so presented as to make us feel again the force of familiar and forgotten truths.

"The Promise" also provides a useful illustration of how the theme of a story operates to control its content. One might ask why Steinbeck does not go on to describe the growth of the colt and perhaps the boy's attachment to him. But Steinbeck obviously wants to emphasize sacrifice and suffering, not fulfillment. He does not want to suggest that sacrifice may be worthwhile (though there is no reason to think that he does not believe it is), but only that it is unavoidable. An account of the colt's life and the boy's love for him would only contradict the knowledge of suffering the boy sees in Billy Buck's eyes at the end of the story. Thus, we see that the author's theme controls his selection of content and that conversely, we, as readers, come to understand his theme by noting carefully what he has included and excluded in his telling of the story.

A second concept useful in analyzing short stories is that of *conflict*. It is perhaps not very illuminating to say that every event in fiction, as in life, is an aspect of some conflict, but the process of identifying the conflicting forces in a story is usually very helpful in enabling the reader to grasp its significance. Conflicts in fiction may occur on the physical or on the psychological level. They may lie between two people, between a person and some abstract force, such as prejudice or ignorance, or between the contradictory impulses or desires of a single person. In Katherine Mansfield's "Revelations" we have an example of a

conflict between a character and her environment: The woman is constantly
trying to impose her own views and preferences upon a world they do not fit. "A
Domestic Dilemma" contains an example of an inner conflict: The husband hates
his wife because her alcoholism is destroying the family, but he realizes, at the
end of the story, that he also loves her.

Like the theme, the conflict of a story may lie far below the surface and may
be difficult to isolate. Once firmly understood, however, it helps to make the
reading of a story an illuminating and satisfying experience.

ACTION

Jack London

To Build a Fire

Day had broken cold and gray, exceedingly cold and gray, when the
man turned aside from the main Yukon trail and climbed the high earth-bank,
where a dim and little-traveled trail led eastward through the fat spruce timber-
land. It was a steep bank, and he paused for breath at the top, excusing the act to
himself by looking at his watch. It was nine o'clock. There was no sun nor hint
of sun, though there was not a cloud in the sky. It was a clear day, and yet there
seemed an intangible pall over the face of things, a subtle gloom that made the
day dark, and that was due to the absence of sun. This fact did not worry the
man. He was used to the lack of sun. It had been days since he had seen the sun,
and he knew that a few more days must pass before that cheerful orb, due south,
would just peep above the sky-line and dip immediately from view.

The man flung a look back along the way he had come. The Yukon lay a mile
wide and hidden under three feet of ice. On top of this ice were as many feet of
snow. It was all pure white, rolling in gentle undulations where the ice-jams of
the freeze-up had formed. North and south, as far as his eye could see, it was
unbroken white, save for a dark hair-line that curved and twisted from around the
spruce-covered island to the south, and that curved and twisted away into the
north, where it disappeared behind another spruce-covered island. This dark hair-
line was the trail—the main trail—that led south five hundred miles to the
Chilcoot Pass, Dyea, and salt water; and that led north seventy miles to Dawson,
and still on to the north a thousand miles to Nulato, and finally to St.
Michael on Bering Sea, a thousand miles and half a thousand more.

But all this—the mysterious, far-reaching hair-line trail, the absence of sun

Printed by permission of Irving Shepard, copyright owner.

from the sky, the tremendous cold, and the strangeness and weirdness of it all—made no impression on the man. It was not because he was long used to it. He was a newcomer in the land, a *chechaquo,* and this was his first winter. The trouble with him was that he was without imagination. He was quick and alert in the things of life, but only in the things, and not in the significances. Fifty degrees below zero meant eighty-odd degrees of frost. Such fact impressed him as being cold and uncomfortable, and that was all. It did not lead him to meditate upon his frailty as a creature of temperature, and upon man's frailty in general, able only to live within certain narrow limits of heat and cold; and from there on it did not lead him to the conjectural field of immortality and man's place in the universe. Fifty degrees below zero stood for a bite of frost that hurt and that must be guarded against by the use of mittens, earflaps, warm moccasins and thick socks. Fifty degrees below zero was to him just precisely fifty degrees below zero. That there should be anything more to it than that was a thought that never entered his head.

As he turned to go on, he spat speculatively. There was a sharp, explosive crackle that startled him. He spat again. And again, in the air, before it could fall to the snow, the spittle crackled. He knew that at fifty below spittle crackled on the snow, but this spittle had crackled in the air. Undoubtedly it was colder than fifty below—how much colder he did not know. But the temperature did not matter. He was bound for the old claim on the left fork of Henderson Creek, where the boys already were. They had come over across the divide from the Indian Creek country, while he had come the roundabout way to take a look at the possibilities of getting out logs in the spring from the islands in the Yukon. He would be in to camp by six o'clock; a bit after dark, it was true, but the boys would be there, a fire would be going, and a hot supper would be ready. As for lunch, he pressed his hand against the protruding bundle under his jacket. It was also under his shirt, wrapped up in a handkerchief and lying against the naked skin. It was the only way to keep the biscuits from freezing. He smiled agreeably to himself as he thought of those biscuits, each cut open and sopped in bacon grease, and each enclosing a generous slice of fried bacon.

He plunged in among the big spruce trees. The trail was faint. A foot of snow had fallen since the last sled had passed over, and he was glad he was without a sled, traveling light. In fact, he carried nothing but the lunch wrapped in the handkerchief. He was surprised, however, at the cold. It certainly was cold, he concluded, as he rubbed his numb nose and cheek-bones with his mittened hand. He was a warm-whiskered man, but the hair on his face did not protect the high cheek-bones and the eager nose that thrust itself aggressively into the frosty air.

At the man's heels trotted a dog, a big native husky, the proper wolf-dog, gray-coated and without any visible or temperamental difference from its brother, the wild wolf. The animal was depressed by the tremendous cold. It knew that it was no time for traveling. Its instinct told it a truer tale than was told to the man by the man's judgment. In reality, it was not merely colder than fifty below zero; it was colder than sixty below, than seventy below. It was seventy-five below zero. Since the freezing-point is thirty-two above zero, it meant that one hundred and seven degrees of frost obtained. The dog did not know anything about thermometers. Possibly in its brain there was no sharp consciousness of a condition of very cold such as was in the man's brain. But the brute had its instinct. It experienced a vague but menacing apprehension that subdued it and made it slink along at the man's heels, and that made it question eagerly every unwonted movement of the man as if expecting him to go into camp or to seek shelter somewhere and build a fire. The dog had learned fire, and it wanted fire, or else to burrow under the snow and cuddle its warmth away from the air.

The frozen moisture of it breathing had settled on its fur in a fine powder of frost, and especially were its jowls, muzzle, and eyelashes whitened by its crystaled breath. The man's red beard and mustache were likewise frosted, but more solidly, the deposit taking the form of ice and increasing with every warm, moist breath he exhaled. Also, the man was chewing tobacco, and the muzzle of ice held his lips so rigidly that he was unable to clear his chin when he expelled the juice. The result was that a crystal beard of the color and solidity of amber was increasing its length on his chin. If he fell down it would shatter itself, like glass, into brittle fragments. But he did not mind the appendage. It was the penalty all tobacco-chewers paid in that country, and he had been out before in two cold snaps. They had not been so cold as this, he knew, but by the spirit thermometer at Sixty Mile he knew they had been registered at fifty below and at fifty-five.

He held on through the level stretch of woods for several miles, crossed a wide flat of niggerheads, and dropped down a bank to the frozen bed of a small stream. This was Henderson Creek, and he knew he was ten miles from the forks. He looked at his watch. It was ten o'clock. He was making four miles an hour, and he calculated that he would arrive at the forks at half-past twelve. He decided to celebrate that event by eating his lunch there.

The dog dropped in again at his heels, with a tail drooping discouragement, as the man swung along the creek-bed. The furrow of the old sled-trail was plainly visible, but a dozen inches of snow covered the marks of the last runners. In a month no man had come up or down that silent creek. The man held steadily on. He was not much given to thinking, and just then particularly he had nothing to think about save that he would eat lunch at the forks and that at six o'clock he would be in camp with the boys. There was nobody to talk to; and, had there been, speech would have been impossible because of the ice-muzzle on his mouth. So he continued monotonously to chew tobacco and to increase the length of his amber beard.

Once in a while the thought reiterated itself that it was very cold and that he had never experienced such cold. As he walked along he rubbed his cheek-bones and nose with the back of his mittened hand. He did this automatically, now and again changing hands. But rub as he would, the instant he stopped his cheek-bones went numb, and the following instant the end of his nose went numb. He was sure to frost his cheeks; he knew that, and experienced a pang of regret that he had not devised a nose-strap of the sort Bud wore in cold snaps. Such a strap passed across the cheeks, as well, and saved them. But it didn't matter much, after all. What were frosted cheeks? A bit painful, that was all; they were never serious.

Empty as the man's mind was of thoughts, he was keenly observant, and he noticed the changes in the creek, and curves and bends and timber-jams, and always he sharply noted where he placed his feet. Once, coming around a bend, he shied abruptly, like a startled horse, curved away from the place where he had been walking, and retreated several paces back along the trail. The creek he knew was frozen clear to the bottom—no creek could contain water in that arctic winter—but he knew also that there were springs that bubbled out from the hillsides and ran along under the snow and on top of the ice of the creek. He knew that the coldest snaps never froze these springs, and he knew likewise their danger. They were traps. They hid pools of water under the snow that might be three inches deep, or three feet. Sometimes a skin of ice half an inch thick covered them, and in turn was covered by the snow. Sometimes there were alternate layers of water and ice-skin, so that when one broke through he kept on breaking through for awhile, sometimes wetting himself almost to the waist.

That was why he had shied in such panic. He had felt the give under his feet and heard the crackle of a snow-hidden ice-skin. And to get his feet wet in such a temperature meant trouble and danger. At the very least it meant delay, for he would be forced to stop and build a fire, and under its protection to bare his feet while he dried his socks and moccasins. He stood and studied the creek-bed and its banks, and decided that the flow of water came from the right. He reflected awhile, rubbing his nose and cheeks, then skirted to the left, stepping gingerly and testing the footing for each step. Once clear of the danger, he took a fresh chew of tobacco and swung along at his four-mile gait.

In the course of the next two hours he came upon several similar traps. Usually the snow above the hidden pools had a sunken, candied appearance that advertised the danger. Once again, however, he had a close call; and once, suspecting danger, he compelled the dog to go on in front. The dog did not want to go. It hung back until the man shoved it forward, and then it went quickly across the white, unbroken surface. Suddenly it broke through, floundered to one side, and got away to firmer footing. It had wet its forefeet and legs, and almost immediately the water that clung to it turned to ice. It made quick efforts to lick the ice off its legs, then dropped down in the snow and began to bite out the ice that had formed between the toes. This was a matter of instinct. To permit the ice to remain would mean sore feet. It did not know this. It merely obeyed the mysterious prompting that arose from the deep crypts of its being. But the man knew, having achieved a judgment on the subject, and he removed the mitten from his right hand and helped tear out the ice-particles. He did not expose his fingers more than a minute, and was astonished at the swift numbness that smote them. It certainly was cold. He pulled on the mitten hastily, and beat the hand savagely across his chest.

At twelve o'clock the day was at its brightest. Yet the sun was too far south on its winter journey to clear the horizon. The bulge of the earth intervened between it and Henderson Creek, where the man walked under a clear sky at noon and cast no shadow. At half-past twelve, to the minute, he arrived at the forks of the creek. He was pleased at the speed he had made. If he kept it up, he would certainly be with the boys at six. He unbuttoned his jacket and shirt and drew forth his lunch. The action consumed no more than a quarter of a minute, yet in that brief moment the numbness laid hold of the exposed fingers. He did not put the mitten on, but, instead, struck the fingers a dozen sharp smashes against his leg. Then he sat down on a snow-covered log to eat. The sting that followed upon the striking of his fingers against his leg ceased so quickly that he was startled. He had had no chance to take a bite of biscuit. He struck the fingers repeatedly and returned them to the mitten, baring the other hand for the purpose of eating. He tried to take a mouthful, but the ice-muzzle prevented. He had forgotten to build a fire and thaw out. He chuckled at his foolishness, and as he chuckled he noted the numbness creeping into the exposed fingers. Also, he noted that the stinging which had first come to his toes when he sat down was already passing away. He wondered whether his toes were warm or numb. He moved them inside the moccasins and decided that they were numb.

He pulled the mitten on hurriedly and stood up. He was a bit frightened. He stamped up and down until the stinging returned into the feet. It certainly was cold, was his thought. That man from Sulphur Creek had spoken the truth when telling how cold it sometimes got in the country. And he had laughed at him at the time! That showed one must not be too sure of things. There was no mistake about it, it *was* cold. He strode up and down, stamping his feet and threshing his arms until reassured by the returning warmth. Then he got out matches and proceeded to make a fire. From the undergrowth, where high water of the previous spring had lodged a supply of seasoned twigs, he got his firewood. Working carefully from a small beginning, he soon had a roaring fire, over which he thawed the ice from his face and in the protection of which he ate his biscuits. For the moment the cold of space was outwitted. The dog took satisfaction in the fire, stretching out close enough for warmth and far enough away to escape being singed.

When the man had finished, he filled his pipe and took his comfortable time over a smoke. Then he pulled on his mittens, settled the earflaps of his cap firmly about his ears, and took the creek trail up the left fork. The dog was disappointed and yearned back toward the fire. This man did not know cold. Possibly all the generations of his ancestry had been ignorant of cold, or real cold, of cold one hundred and seven degrees below freezing-point. But the dog knew; all its ancestry knew, and it had inherited the knowledge. And it knew that it was not good to walk abroad in such fearful cold. It was the time to lie snug in a hole in the snow and wait for a curtain of cloud to be drawn across the face of outer space whence this cold came. On the other hand, there was no keen intimacy between the dog and the man. The one was the toil-slave of the other, and the only caresses it had ever received were the caresses of the whip-lash and of harsh and menacing throat-sounds that threatened the whip-lash. So the dog made no effort to communicate its apprehension to the man. It was not concerned in the welfare of the man; it was for its own sake that it yearned back toward the fire. But the man whistled, and spoke to it with the sound of whip-lashes, and the dog swung in at the man's heels and followed after.

The man took a chew of tobacco and proceeded to start a new amber beard. Also, his moist breath quickly powdered with white his mustache, eyebrows, and lashes. There did not seem to be so many springs on the left fork of the Henderson, and for half an hour the man saw no signs of any. And then it happened. At a place where there were no signs, where the soft, unbroken snow seemed to advertise solidity beneath, the man broke through. It was not deep. He wet himself half way to the knees before he floundered out to the firm crust.

He was angry, and cursed his luck aloud. He had hoped to get into camp with the boys at six o'clock, and this would delay him an hour, for he would have to build a fire and dry out his foot-gear. This was imperative at that low temperature—he knew that much; and he turned aside to the bank, which he climbed. On top, tangled in the underbrush about the trunks of several small spruce trees, was a high-water deposit of dry fire-wood—sticks and twigs, principally, but also larger portions of seasoned branches and fine, dry, last year's grasses. He threw down several large pieces on top of the snow. This served for a foundation and prevented the young flame from drowning itself in the snow it otherwise would melt. The flame he got by touching a match to a small shred of birch-bark that he took from his pocket. This burned even more readily than paper. Placing it on the foundation, he fed the young flame with wisps of dry grass and with the tiniest dry twigs.

He worked slowly and carefully, keenly aware of his danger. Gradually, as the flame drew stronger, he increased the size of the twigs with which he fed it. He squatted in the snow, pulling the twigs out from their entanglement in the brush and feeding directly to the flame. He knew there must be no failure. When it is seventy-five below zero, a man must not fail in his first attempt to build a fire—that is, if his feet are wet. If his feet are dry, and he fails, he can run along the trail for half a mile and restore his circulation. But the circulation of wet and freezing feet cannot be restored by running when it is seventy-five below. No matter how fast he runs, the wet feet will freeze the harder.

All this the man knew. The oldtimer on Sulphur Creek had told him about it the previous fall, and now he was appreciating the advice. Already all sensation had gone out of his feet. To build the fire he had been forced to remove his mittens, and the fingers had quickly gone numb. His pace of four miles an hour had kept his heart pumping blood to the surface of his body and to all the extremities. But the instant he stopped, the action of the pump eased down. The cold of space smote the unprotected tip of the planet, and he, being on that unprotected tip, received the full force of the blow. The blood of his body recoiled before it. The blood was alive, like the dog, and like the dog it wanted to hide away and cover itself up from the fearful cold. So long as he walked four miles an hour, he pumped that blood, willy-nilly, to the surface; but now it ebbed away and sank down into the recesses of his body. The extremities were the first to feel its absence. His wet feet froze the faster, and his exposed fingers numbed the faster, though they had not yet begun to freeze. Nose and cheeks were already freezing, while the skin of all his body chilled as it lost its blood.

But he was safe. Toes and nose and cheeks would be only touched by the frost, for the fire was beginning to burn with strength. He was feeding it with twigs the size of his finger. In another minute he would be able to feed it with branches the size of his wrist, and then he could remove his wet foot-gear, and, while it dried, he could keep his naked feet warm by the fire, rubbing them at first, of course, with snow. The fire was a success. He was safe. He remembered the advice of the oldtimer on Sulphur Creek, and smiled. The oldtimer had been very serious in laying down the law that no man must travel alone in the Klondike after fifty below. Well, here he was; he had had the accident; he was alone; and he had saved himself. Those oldtimers were rather womanish, some of them, he thought. All a man had to do was to keep his head, and he was all right. Any man who was a man could travel alone. But it was surprising, the rapidity with which his cheeks and nose were freezing. And he had not thought his fingers could go lifeless in so short a time. Lifeless they were, for he could scarcely make them move together to grip a twig, and they seemed remote from his body and from him. When he touched a twig, he had to look and see whether or not he had hold of it. The wires were pretty well down between him and his finger-ends.

All of which counted for little. There was the fire, snapping and crackling and promising life with every dancing flame. He started to untie his moccasins. They were coated with ice; the thick German socks were like sheaths of iron halfway to the knees; and the moccasin strings were like rods of steel all twisted and knotted as by some conflagration. For a moment he tugged with his numb fingers, then, realizing the folly of trying to work with that lifeless flesh, he drew his sheath-knife.

But before he could cut the strings, it happened. It was his own fault or, rather, his mistake. He should not have built the fire under the spruce tree. He should have built it in the open. But it had been easier to pull the twigs from the brush and drop them directly on the fire. Now the tree under which he had done this carried a weight of snow on its boughs. No wind had blown for weeks, and each bough was fully freighted. Each time he had pulled a twig he had communicated a slight agitation to the tree—an imperceptible agitation, so far as he was concerned, but an agitation sufficient to bring about the disaster. High up in the tree one bough capsized its load of snow. This fell on the boughs beneath, capsizing them. This process continued, spreading out and involving the whole tree. It grew like an avalanche, and it descended without warning upon the man and the fire, and the fire was blotted out! Where it had burned there was now spread a mantle of fresh and disordered snow.

The man was shocked. It was as though he had just heard his own sentence of death. For a moment he sat and stared at the spot where the fire had been. Then he grew very calm. Perhaps the oldtimer on Sulphur Creek was right. If he had only had a trailmate he would have been in no danger now. The trail-mate could have built the fire. Well, it was up to him to build the fire over again, and this second time there must be no failure. Even if he succeeded, he would most likely lose some toes. His feet must be badly frozen by now, and there would be some time before the second fire was ready.

Such were his thoughts, but he did not sit and think them. He was busy all the time they were passing through his mind. He made a new foundation for a fire, this time in the open, where no treacherous tree could blot it out. Next, he gathered dry grasses and tiny twigs from the high-water flotsam. He could not bring his fingers together to pull them out, but he was able to gather them by the handful. In this way he got many rotten twigs and bits of green moss that were undesirable, but it was the best he could do. He worked methodically, even collecting an armful of the larger branches to be used later when the fire gathered strength. And all the while the dog sat and watched him, a certain yearning wistfulness in its eyes, for it looked upon him as the fire-provider, and the fire was slow in coming.

When all was ready, the man reached in his pocket for a second piece of birchbark. He knew the bark was there, and though he could not feel it with his fingers, he could hear its crisp rustling as he fumbled for it. Try as he would, he could not clutch hold of it. And all the time, in his consciousness, was the knowledge that each instant his feet were freezing. This thought tended to put him in a panic, but he fought against it and kept calm. He pulled up his mittens with his teeth, and threshed his arms back and forth, beating his hands with all his might against his sides. He did this sitting down, and he stood up to do it, and all the while the dog sat in the snow, its wolf-brush of a tail curled around warmly over its forefeet, its sharp wolf-ears pricked forward intently as it watched the man. And the man, as he beat and threshed with his arms and hands, felt a great surge of envy as he regarded the creature that was warm and secure in its natural covering.

After a time he was aware of the first far-away signals of sensation in his beaten fingers. The faint tingling grew stronger till it evolved into a stinging ache that was excruciating, but which the man hailed with satisfaction. He stripped the mitten from his right hand and fetched forth the birch-bark. The exposed fingers were quickly going numb again. Next he brought out his bunch of sulphur matches. But the tremendous cold had already driven the life out of his fingers. In his effort to separate one match from the others, the whole bunch fell in the snow. He tried to pick it out of the snow, but failed. The dead fingers could neither touch nor clutch. He was very careful. He drove the thought of his freezing feet, and nose, and cheeks, out of his mind, devoting his whole soul to the matches. He watched, using the sense of vision in place of that of touch, and when he saw his fingers on each side of the bunch, he closed them—that is, he willed to close them, for the wires were down, and the fingers did not obey. He pulled the mitten on the right hand, and beat it fiercely against his knee. Then, with both mittened hands, he scooped the bunch of matches, along with much snow, into his lap. Yet he was no better off.

After some manipulation he managed to get the bunch between the heels of his mittened hands. In this fashion he carried it to his mouth. The ice crackled and snapped when by a violent effort he opened his mouth. He drew the lower jaw in, curled the upper lip out of the way, and scraped the bunch with his upper teeth in order to separate a match. He succeeded in getting one, which he dropped on his lap. He was no better off. He could not pick it up. Then he devised a way. He picked it up in his teeth and scratched it on his leg. Twenty times he scratched it before he succeeded in lighting it. As it flamed he held it with his teeth to the birch-bark. But the burning brimstone went up his nostrils and into his lungs, causing him to cough spasmodically. The match fell into the snow and went out.

The oldtimer on Sulphur Creek was right, he thought in the moment of controlled despair that ensued: after fifty below, a man should travel with a partner. He beat his hands, but failed in exciting any sensation. Suddenly he bared both hands, removing the mittens with his teeth. He caught the whole bunch between the heels of his hands. His arm-muscles not being frozen enabled him to press the hand-heels tightly against the matches. Then he scratched the bunch along his leg. It flared into flame, seventy sulphur matches at once! There was no wind to blow them out. He kept his head to one side to escape the strangling fumes, and held the blazing bunch to the birch-bark. As he so held it, he became aware of a sensation in his hand. His flesh was burning. He could smell it. Deep down below the surface he could feel it. The sensation developed into pain that grew acute. And still he endured it, holding the flame of the matches clumsily to the bark that would not light readily because his own burning hands were in the way, absorbing most of the flame.

At last, when he could endure no more, he jerked his hands apart. The blazing matches fell sizzling into the snow, but the birch-bark was alight. He began laying dry grasses and the tiniest twigs on the flame. He could not pick and choose, for he had to lift the fuel between the heels of his hands. Small pieces of rotten wood and green moss clung to the twigs, and he bit them off as well as he could with his teeth. He cherished the flame carefully and awkwardly. It meant life, and it must not perish. The withdrawal of blood from the surface of his body now made him begin to shiver, and he grew more awkward. A large piece of green moss fell squarely on the little fire. He tried to poke it out with his fingers, but his shivering frame made him poke too far, and he disrupted the nucleus of the little fire, the burning grasses and tiny twigs, separating and scattering. He tried to poke them together again, but in spite of the tenseness of the effort, his shivering got away from him, and the twigs were hopelessly scattered. Each twig gushed a puff of smoke and went out. The fire-provider had failed. As he looked apathetically about him, his eyes chanced on the dog, sitting across the ruins of the fire from him, in the snow, making restless, hunching movements, slightly lifting one forefoot and then the other, shifting its weight back and forth on them with wistful eagerness and eyeing the fire-provider expectantly.

The sight of the dog put a wild idea into his head. He remembered the tale of the man, caught in a blizzard, who killed a steer, and crawled inside the carcass, and so was saved. He would kill the dog and bury his hands in the warm body until the numbness went out of them. Then he could build another fire. He spoke to the dog, calling it to him; but in his voice was a strange note of fear that frightened the animal, who had never known the man to speak in such a way before. Something was the matter, and its suspicious nature sensed danger—it knew not what danger, but somewhere, somehow, in its brain arose an apprehension of the man. It flattened its ears down at the sound of the man's voice, and its restless, hunching movements and the liftings and shiftings of its forefeet became more pronounced; but it would not come to the man. He got on his hands and knees and crawled toward the dog. This unusual posture again excited suspicion, and the animal sidled mincingly away.

The man sat up in the snow for a moment and struggled for calmness. Then he pulled on his mittens, by means of his teeth, and got upon his feet. He glanced down at first in order to assure himself that he was really standing up, for the absence of sensation in his feet left him unrelated to the earth. His erect position in itself started to drive the webs of suspicion from the dog's mind; and when he spoke peremptorily, with the sound of whip-lashes in his voice, the dog rendered its customary allegiance and came to him. As it came within reaching distance, the man lost his control. His arms flashed out to the dog, and he experienced genuine surprise when he discovered that his hands could not clutch, that there was neither bend nor feeling in the fingers. He had forgotten for the moment that they were frozen and that they were freezing more and more. All this happened quickly, and before the animal could get away, he encircled its body with his arms. He sat down in the snow, and in this fashion held the dog, while it snarled and whined and struggled.

But it was all he could do, hold its body encircled in his arms and sit there. He realized that he could not kill the dog. There was no way to do it. With his helpless hand he could neither draw nor hold his sheath-knife nor throttle the animal. He released it, and it plunged wildly away, with tail between its legs, and still snarling. It halted forty feet away and surveyed him curiously, with ears sharply pricked forward. The man looked down at his hands in order to locate them, and found them hanging on the ends of his arms. It struck him as curious that one should have to use his eyes in order to find out where his hands were. He began threshing his arms back and forth, beating the mittened hands against his sides. He did this for five minutes, violently, and his heart pumped enough blood up to the surface to put a stop to his shivering. But no sensation was aroused in the hands. He had an impression that they hung like weights on the ends of his arms, but when he tried to run the impression down, he could not find it.

A certain fear of death, dull and oppressive, came to him. This fear quickly became poignant as he realized that it was no longer a mere matter of freezing his fingers and toes, or of losing his hands and feet, but that it was a matter of life and death, with the chances against him. This threw him into a panic, and he turned and ran up the creek-bed along the old, dim trail. The dog joined in behind and kept up with him. He ran blindly, without intention, in fear such as he had never known in his life. Slowly, as he ploughed and floundered through the snow, he began to see things again—the banks of the creek, the old timber-jams, the leafless aspens, and the sky. The running made him feel better. He did not shiver. Maybe, if he ran on, his feet would thaw out; and, anyway, if he ran far enough, he would reach camp and the boys. Without doubt he would lose some fingers and toes and some of his face; but the boys would take care of him, and save the rest of him when he got there. And at the same time there was another thought in his mind that said he would never get to the camp and the boys; that it was too many miles away, that the freezing had too great a start on him, and that he would soon be stiff and dead. This thought he kept in the background and refused to consider. Sometimes it pushed itself forward and demanded to be heard, but he thrust it back and strove to think of other things.

It struck him as curious that he could run at all on feet so frozen that he could not feel them when they struck the earth and took the weight of his body. He seemed to himself to skim along above the surface, and to have no connection with the earth. Somewhere he had once seen a winged Mercury, and he wondered if Mercury felt as he felt when skimming over the earth.

His theory of running until he reached camp and the boys had one flaw in it: he lacked the endurance. Several times he stumbled, and finally he tottered, crumpled up, and fell. When he tried to rise, he failed. He must sit and rest, he decided, and next time he would merely walk and keep on going. As he sat and regained his breath, he noted that he was feeling quite warm and comfortable. He was not shivering, and it even seemed that a warm glow had come to his chest and trunk. And yet, when he touched his nose or cheeks, there was no sensation. Running would not thaw them out. Nor would it thaw out his hands and feet. Then the thought came to him that the frozen portions of his body must be extending. He tried to keep this thought down, to forget it, to think of something else; he was aware of the panicky feeling that it caused, and he was afraid of the panic. But the thought asserted itself, and persisted, until it produced a vision of his body totally frozen. This was too much, and he made another wild run along the trail. Once he slowed down to a walk, but the thought of the freezing extending itself made him run again.

And all the time the dog ran with him, at his heels. When he fell down a second time, it curled its tail over its forefeet and sat in front of him, facing him, curiously eager and intent. The warmth and security of the animal angered him, and he cursed it till it flattened down its ears appeasingly. This time the shivering came more quickly upon the man. He was losing in his battle with the frost. It was creeping into his body from all sides. The thought of it drove him on, but he ran no more than a hundred feet, when he staggered and pitched headlong. It was his last panic. When he had recovered his breath and control, he sat up and entertained in his mind the conception of meeting death with dignity. However the conception did not come to him in such terms. His idea of it was that he had been making a fool of himself, running around like a chicken with its head cut off—such was the simile that occurred to him. Well, he was bound to freeze anyway, and he might as well take it decently. With this newfound peace of mind came the first glimmerings of drowsiness. A good idea, he thought, to sleep off to death. It was like taking an anaesthetic. Freezing was not so bad as people thought. There were lots worse ways to die.

He pictured the boys finding his body the next day. Suddenly he found himself with them, coming along the trail and looking for himself. And, still with them, he came around a turn in the trail and found himself lying in the snow. He did not belong with himself any more, for even then he was out of himself, standing with the boys and looking at himself in the snow. It certainly was cold, was his thought. When he got back to the States he could tell the folks what real cold was. He drifted on from this to a vision of the oldtimer on Sulphur Creek. He could see him quite clearly, warm and comfortable.

"You were right, old hoss; you were right," the man mumbled to the oldtimer of Sulphur Creek.

Then the man drowsed off into what seemed to him the most comfortable and satisfying sleep he had ever known. The dog sat facing him and waiting. The brief day drew to a close in a long, slow twilight. There were no signs of a fire to be made, and, besides, never in the dog's experience had it known a man to sit like that in the snow and make no fire. As the twilight drew on, its eager yearning for the fire mastered it, and with a great lifting and shifting of forefeet, it whined softly, then flattened its ears down in anticipation of being chidden by the man. But the man remained silent. Later, the dog whined loudly. And still later it crept close to the man and caught the scent of death. This made the animal bristle and back away. A little longer it delayed, howling under the stars that leaped and danced and shone brightly in the cold sky. Then it turned and trotted up the trail in the direction of the camp it knew, where were the other food-providers and fire-providers.

Frank O'Connor

The Man of the House

When I woke, I heard my mother coughing, below in the kitchen. She had been coughing for days, but I had paid no attention. We were living on the Old Youghal Road at the time, the old hilly coaching road into East Cork. The coughing sounded terrible. I dressed and went downstairs in my stocking feet, and in the clear morning light I saw her, unaware that she was being watched, collapsed into a little wickerwork armchair, holding her side. She had made an attempt to light the fire, but it had gone against her. She looked so tired and helpless that my heart turned over with compassion. I ran to her.

"Are you all right, Mum?" I asked.

"I'll be all right in a second," she replied, trying to smile. "The old sticks were wet, and the smoke started me coughing."

"Go back to bed and I'll light the fire," I said.

"Ah, how can I, child?" she said anxiously. "Sure, I have to go to work."

"You couldn't work like that," I said. "I'll stop at home from school and look after you."

It's a funny thing about women, the way they'll take orders from anything in trousers, even if it's only ten.

"If you could make yourself a cup of tea, I might be all right later on," she said guiltily, and she rose, very shakily, and climbed back up the stairs. I knew then she must be feeling really bad.

I got more sticks out of the coalhole, under the stairs. My mother was so economical that she never used enough, and that was why the fire sometimes went against her. I used a whole bundle, and I soon had the fire roaring and the kettle on. I made her toast while I was about it. I was a great believer in hot buttered toast at all hours of the day. Then I made the tea and brought her up a cup on the tray. "Is that all right?" I asked.

"Would you have a sup of boiling water left?" she asked doubtfully.

" 'Tis too strong," I agreed cheerfully, remembering the patience of the saints in their many afflictions. "I'll pour half of it out."

"I'm an old nuisance," she sighed.

" 'Tis my fault," I said, taking the cup. "I can never remember about tea. Put the shawl round you while you're sitting up. Will I shut the skylight?"

"Would you be able?" she asked doubtfully.

" 'Tis no trouble," I said, getting the chair to it. "I'll do the messages after."

I had my own breakfast alone by the window, and then I went out and stood by the front door to watch the kids from the road on their way to school.

"You'd better hurry or you'll be killed, Sullivan," they shouted.

"I'm not going," I said. "My mother is sick, and I have to mind the house."

I wasn't a malicious child, by any means, but I liked to be able to take out my comforts and study them by the light of others' misfortunes. Then I heated another kettle of water and cleared up the breakfast things before I washed my face and came up to the attic with my shopping basket, a piece of paper, and a lead pencil.

"I'll do the messages now if you'll write them down," I said. "Would you like me to get the doctor?"

"Ah," said my mother impatiently, "he'd only want to send me to hospital, and how would I go to hospital? You could call in at the chemist's and ask him to give you a good, strong cough bottle."

"Write it down," I said. "If I haven't it written down, I might forget it. And put 'strong' in big letters. What will I get for the dinner? Eggs?"

As boiled eggs were the only dish I could manage, I more or less knew it would be eggs, but she told me to get sausages as well, in case she could get up.

I passed the school on my way. Opposite it was a hill, and I went up a short distance and stood there for ten minutes in quiet contemplation. The schoolhouse and yard and gate were revealed as in a painted picture, detached and peaceful except for the chorus of voices through the opened windows and the glimpse of Danny Delaney, the teacher, passing the front door with his cane behind his back, stealing a glance at the world outside. I could have stood there all day. Of all the profound and simple pleasures of those days, that was the richest.

When I got home, I rushed upstairs and found Minnie Ryan sitting with my mother. She was a middle-aged woman, very knowledgeable, gossipy, and pious.

"How are you, Mum?" I asked.

"Grand," said my mother, with a smile.

"You can't get up today, though," said Minnie Ryan.

"I'll put the kettle on and make a cup of tea for you," I said.

"Sure I'll do that," said Minnie.

"Ah, don't worry, Miss Ryan," I said lightly. "I can manage it all right."

"Wisha, isn't he very good?" I heard her say in a low voice to my mother.

"As good as gold," said my mother.

"There's not many like that, then," said Minnie. "The most of them that's going now are more like savages than Christians."

In the afternoon, my mother wanted me to run out and play, but I didn't go far. I knew if once I went a certain distance from the house, I was liable to stray into temptation. Below our house, there was a glen, the drill field of the barracks perched high above it on a chalky cliff, and below, in a deep hollow, the millpond and millstream running between wooded hills—the Rockies, the Himalayas, or the Highlands, according to your mood. Once down there, I tended to forget the real world, so I sat on a wall outside the house, running in every half hour to see how the mother was and if there was anything she wanted.

Evening fell; the street lamps were lit, and the paper boy went crying up the road. I bought a paper, lit the lamp in the kitchen and the candle in my mother's attic, and tried to read to her, not very successfully, because I was only at words of one syllable, but I had a great wish to please, and she to be pleased, so we got on quite well, considering.

Later, Minnie Ryan came again, and as she was going, I saw her to the door.

"If she's not better in the morning, I think I'd get the doctor, Flurry," she said over her shoulder.

"Why?" I asked, in alarm. "Do you think is she worse, Miss Ryan."

"Ah, I wouldn't say so," she replied with affected nonchalance, "but I'd be frightened she might get pneumonia."

"But wouldn't he send her to hospital, Miss Ryan?"

"Wisha, he mightn't," she said with a shrug, pulling her old shawl about her. "But even if he did, wouldn't it be better than neglecting it? Ye wouldn't have a drop of whiskey in the house?"

"I'll get it," I said at once. I knew what might happen to people who got pneumonia, and what was bound to happen afterward to their children.

"If you could give it to her hot, with a squeeze of lemon in it, it might help her to shake it off," said Minnie.

My mother said she didn't want the whiskey, dreading the expense, but I had got such a fright that I wouldn't be put off. When I went to the public house, it was full of men, who drew aside to let me reach the bar. I had never been in a public house before, and I was frightened.

"Hullo, my old flower," said one man, grinning diabolically at me. "It must be ten years since I seen you last. What are you having?"

My pal, Bob Connell, had told me how he once asked a drunk man for a half crown and the man gave it to him. I always wished I could bring myself to do the same, but I didn't feel like it just then.

"I want a half glass of whiskey for my mother," I said.

"Oh, the thundering ruffian!" said the man. "Pretending 'tis for his mother, and the last time I seen him he had to be carried home."

"I had not," I shouted indignantly. "And *'tis* for my mother. She's sick."

"Ah, let the child alone, Johnnie," said the barmaid. She gave me the whiskey, and then, still frightened of the men in the public house, I went off to a shop for a lemon.

When my mother had drunk the hot whiskey, she fell asleep, and I quenched the lights and went to bed, but I couldn't sleep very well. I was regretting I hadn't asked the man in the pub for a half crown. I was wakened several times by the coughing, and when I went into my mother's room her head felt very hot, and she was rambling in her talk. It frightened me more than anything else when she didn't know me, and I lay awake, thinking of what would happen to me if it were really pneumonia.

The depression was terrible when, next morning, my mother seemed not to be any better. I had done all I could do, and I felt helpless. I lit the fire and got her breakfast, but this time I didn't stand at the front door to see the other fellows on their way to school. I should have been too inclined to envy them. Instead, I went over to Minnie Ryan and reported.

"I'd go for the doctor," she said firmly. "Better be sure than sorry."

I had first to go to the house of a Poor Law Guardian, for a ticket to show we couldn't pay. Then I went down to the dispensary, which was in a deep hollow beyond the school. After that I had to go back to ready the house for the doctor. I had to have a basin of water and soap and a clean towel laid out for him, and I had to get the dinner, too.

It was after dinner when he called. He was a fat, loudvoiced man and, like all the drunks of the medical profession, supposed to be "the cleverest doctor in Cork, if only he'd mind himself." He hadn't been minding himself much that morning, it seemed.

"How are you going to get this now?" he grumbled, sitting on the bed with the prescription pad on his knee. "The only place open is the North Dispensary."

"I'll go, Doctor," I said at once, relieved that he had said nothing about hospital.

" 'Tis a long way," he said, doubtfully. "Do you know where it is?"

"I'll find it," I said.

"Isn't he a great little fellow?" he said to my mother.

"Oh, the best in the world, Doctor!" she said. "A daughter couldn't be better to me."

"That's right," said the doctor. "Look after your mother; she'll be the best for you in the long run. We don't mind them when we have them," he added, to my mother, "and then we spend the rest of our lives regretting it."

I wished he hadn't said that; it tuned in altogether too well with my mood. To make it worse, he didn't even use the soap and water I had laid ready for him.

My mother gave me directions how to reach the dispensary, and I set off with a bottle wrapped in brown paper under my arm. The road led uphill, through a thickly populated poor locality, as far as the barracks, which was perched on the very top of the hill, over the city, and then descended, between high walls, till it suddenly almost disappeared in a stony path, with red brick corporation houses to one side of it, that dropped steeply, steeply, to the valley of the little river, where a brewery stood, and the opposite hillside, a murmuring honeycomb of houses, rose to the gently rounded top, on which stood the purple sandstone tower of the cathedral and the limestone spire of Shandon church, on a level with your eye.

It was so wide a view that it was never all lit up together, and the sunlight wandered across it as across a prairie, picking out first a line of roofs with a brightness like snow, and then delving into the depth of some dark street and outlining in shadow figures of climbing carts and straining horses. I leaned on the low wall and thought how happy a fellow could be, looking at that, if he had nothing to trouble him. I tore myself from it with a sigh, slithered without stopping to the bottom of the hill, and climbed up a series of shadowy and stepped lanes around the back of the cathedral, which now seemed enormous. I had a penny, which my mother had given me by way of encouragement, and I made up my mind that when I had done my business, I should go into the cathedral and spend it on a candle to the Blessed Virgin, to make my mother better quick. I felt sure it would be more effective in a really big church like that, so very close to Heaven.

The dispensary was a sordid little hallway with a bench to one side and a window like the one in a railway ticket office at the far end. There was a little girl with a green plaid shawl about her shoulders sitting on the bench. I knocked at the window, and a seedy, angry-looking man opened it. Without waiting for me to finish what I was saying, he grabbed bottle and prescription from me and banged the shutter down again without a word. I waited for a moment and then lifted my hand to knock again.

"You'll have to wait, little boy," said the girl quickly.

"What will I have to wait for?" I asked.

"He have to make it up," she explained. "You might as well sit down."

I did, glad of anyone to keep me company.

"Where are you from?" she asked. "I live in Blarney Lane," she added when I had told her. "Who's the bottle for?"

"My mother," I said.

"What's wrong with her?"

"She have a bad cough."

"She might have consumption," she said thoughtfully. "That's what my sister that died last year had. This is a tonic for my other sister. She have to have tonics all the time. Is it nice where you live?"

I told her about the glen, and then she told me about the river near their place. It seemed to be a nicer place than ours, as she described it. She was a pleasant, talkative little girl, and I didn't notice the time until the window opened again and a red bottle was thrust out.

"Dooley!" shouted the seedy man, and closed the window again.

"That's me," said the little girl. "Yours won't be ready for a good while yet. I'll wait for you."

"I have a penny," I said boastfully.

She waited until my bottle was thrust out, and then she accompanied me as far as the steps leading down to the brewery. On the way, I bought a pennyworth of sweets, and we sat on the other steps, beside the infirmary, to eat them. It was nice there, with the spire of Shandon in shadow behind us, the young trees overhanging the high walls, and the sun, when it came out in great golden blasts, throwing our linked shadows onto the road.

"Give us a taste of your bottle, little boy," she said.

"Why?" I asked. "Can't you taste your own?"

"Mine is awful," she said. "Tonics is awful to taste. You can try it if you like."

I took a taste of it and hastily spat out. She was right; it was awful. After that, I couldn't do less than let her taste mine.

"That's grand," she said enthusiastically, after taking a swig from it. "Cough bottles are nearly always grand. Try it, can't you?"

I did, and saw she was right about that, too. It was very sweet and sticky.

"Give us another," she said excitedly, grabbing at it.

" 'Twill be all gone," I said.

"Erra, 'twon't," she replied with a laugh. "You have gallons of it."

Somehow, I couldn't refuse her. I was swept from my anchorage into an unfamiliar world of spires and towers, trees, steps, shadowy laneways, and little girls with red hair and green eyes. I took a drink myself and gave her another. Then I began to panic. " 'Tis nearly gone," I said. "What am I going to do now?"

"Finish it and say the cork fell out," she replied, and again, as she said it, it sounded plausible enough. We finished the bottle between us, and then, slowly, as I looked at it in my hand, empty as I had brought it, and remembered that I had not kept my word to the Blessed Virgin and had spent her penny on sweets, a terrible despondency swept over me, I had sacrificed everything for the little girl and she didn't even care for me. It was my cough bottle she had coveted all the time. I saw her guile too late. I put my head in my hands and began to cry.

"What are you crying for?" the little girl asked in astonishment.

"My mother is sick, and we're after drinking her medicine," I said.

"Ah, don't be an old crybaby!" she said contemptuously. "You have only to say the cork fell out. Sure, that's a thing could happen to anybody."

"And I promised the Blessed Virgin a candle, and I spent the money on you!" I screamed, and, suddenly grabbing the empty bottle, I ran up the road from her, wailing. Now I had only one refuge and one hope—a miracle. I went back to the cathedral, and, kneeling before the shrine of the Blessed Virgin, I begged her pardon for having spent her penny, and promised her a candle from the next penny I got, if only she would work a miracle and make my mother better before I got back. After that, I crawled miserably homeward, back up the great hill, but now all the light had gone out of the day, and the murmuring hillside had become a vast, alien, cruel world. Besides, I felt very sick. I thought I might be going to die. In one way it would be better.

When I got back into the house, the silence of the kitchen and then the sight of the fire gone out in the grate smote me with the cruel realization that the Blessed Virgin had let me down. There was no miracle, and my mother was still in bed. At once, I began to howl.

"What is it at all, child?" she called in alarm from upstairs.

"I lost the medicine," I bellowed, and rushed up the stairs to throw myself on the bed and bury my face in the clothes.

"Oh, wisha, if that's all that's a trouble to you!" she exclaimed with relief, running her hand through my hair. "Is anything the matter?" she added, after a moment. "You're very hot."

"I drank the medicine," I bawled.

"Ah, what harm?" she murmured soothingly. "You poor, unfortunate child! 'Twas my own fault for letting you go all the way by yourself. And then to have your journey for nothing. Undress yourself now, and you can lie down here."

She got up, put on her slippers and coat, and unlaced my boots while I sat on the bed. But even before she had finished I was fast asleep. I didn't see her dress herself or hear her go out, but some time later I felt a hand on my forehead and saw Minnie Ryan peering down at me, laughing.

"Ah, 'twill be nothing," she said, giving her shawl a pull about her. "He'll sleep it off by morning. The dear knows, Mrs. Sullivan, 'tis you should be in bed."

I knew that was a judgment on me, but I could do nothing about it. Later I saw my mother come in with the candle and her paper, and I smiled up at her. She smiled back. Minnie Ryan might despise me as much as she liked, but there were others who didn't. The miracle had happened, after all.

CHARACTER

Katherine Anne Porter
Theft

She had the purse in her hand when she came in. Standing in the middle of the floor, holding her bathrobe around her and trailing a damp towel in one hand, she surveyed the immediate past and remembered everything clearly. Yes, she had opened the flap and spread it out on the bench after she had dried the purse with her handkerchief.

She had intended to take the Elevated, and naturally she looked in her purse to make certain she had the fare, and was pleased to find forty cents in the coin envelope. She was going to pay her own fare, too, even if Camilo did have the habit of seeing her up the steps and dropping a nickel in the machine before he gave the turnstile a little push and sent her through it with a bow. Camilo by a series of compromises had managed to make effective a fairly complete set of smaller courtesies, ignoring the larger and more troublesome ones. She had walked with him to the station in a pouring rain, because she knew he was almost as poor as she was, and when he insisted on a taxi, she was firm and said, "You know it simply will not do." He was wearing a new hat of a pretty biscuit shade, for it never occurred to him to buy anything of a practical color; he had put it on for the first time and the rain was spoiling it. She kept thinking, "But this is dreadful, where will he get another?" She compared it with Eddie's hats that always seemed to be precisely seven years old and as if they had been quite purposely left out in the rain, and yet they sat with a careless and incidental rightness on Eddie. But Camilo was far different; if he wore a shabby hat it would be merely shabby on him, and he would lose his spirits over it. If she had not feared Camilo would take it badly, for he insisted on the practice of his little ceremonies up to the point he had fixed for them, she would have said to him as they left Thora's house, "Do go home. I can surely reach the station by myself."

"It is written that we must be rained upon tonight," said Camilo, "so let it be together."

At the foot of the platform stairway she staggered slightly—they were both nicely set up on Thora's cocktails—and said: "At least, Camilo, do me the favor not to climb these stairs in your present state, since for you it is only a matter of coming down again at once, and you'll certainly break your neck."

He made three quick bows, he was Spanish, and leaped off through the rainy darkness. She stood watching him, for he was a very graceful young man, thinking that tomorrow morning he would gaze soberly at his spoiled hat and soggy shoes and possibly associate her with his misery. As she watched, he stopped at the far corner and took off his hat and hid it under his overcoat. She felt she had betrayed him by seeing, because he would have been humiliated if he thought she even suspected him of trying to save his hat.

Roger's voice sounded over her shoulder above the clang of the rain falling on the stairway shed, wanting to know what she was doing out in the rain at this time of night, and did she take herself for a duck? His long, imperturbable face was streaming with water, and he tapped a bulging spot on the breast of his button-up overcoat: "Hat," he said. "Come on, let's take a taxi."

She settled back against Roger's arm which he laid around her shoulders, and with the gesture they exchanged a glance full of long amiable associations, then she looked through the window at the rain changing the shapes of everything, and the colors. The taxi dodged in and out between the pillars of the Elevated, skidding slightly on every curve, and she said: "The more it skids the calmer I feel, so I really must be drunk."

"You must be," said Roger. "This bird is a homicidal maniac, and I could do with a cocktail myself this minute."

They waited on the traffic at Fortieth Street and Sixth Avenue, and three boys walked before the nose of the taxi. Under the globes of light they were cheerful scarecrows, all very thin and all wearing very seedy snappy-cut suits and gay neckties. They were not very sober either, and they stood for a moment wobbling in front of the car, and there was an argument going on among them. They leaned toward each other as if they were getting ready to sing, and the first one said: "When I get married it won't be jus' for getting married, I'm gonna marry for *love,* see?" and the second one said, "Aw, gwan and tell that stuff to *her,* why n't yuh?" and the third one gave a kind of hoot, and said, "Hell, dis guy? Wot the hell's he got?" and the first one said: "Aaah, shurrup yuh mush, I got plenty." Then they all squealed and scrambled across the street beating the first one on the back and pushing him around.

"Nuts," commented Roger, "pure nuts."

Two girls went skittering by in short transparent raincoats, one green, one red, their heads tucked against the drive of the rain. One of them was saying to the other, "Yes, I know all about *that.* But what about me? You're always so sorry for *him* . . ." and they ran on with their little pelican legs flashing back and forth.

The taxi backed up suddenly and leaped forward again, and after a while Roger said: "I had a letter from Stella today, and she'll be home on the twenty-sixth, so I suppose she's made up her mind and it's all settled."

"I had a sort of letter today too," she said, "making up my mind for me. I think it is time for you and Stella to do something definite."

When the taxi stopped on the corner of West Fifty-third Street, Roger said, "I've just enough if you'll add ten cents," so she opened her purse and gave him a dime, and he said, "That's beautiful, that purse."

"It's a birthday present," she told him, "and I like it. How's your show coming?"

"Oh, still hanging on, I guess. I don't go near the place. Nothing sold yet. I

mean to keep right on the way I'm going and they can take it or leave it. I'm
through with the argument."

"It's absolutely a matter of holding out, isn't it?"

"Holding out's the tough part."

"Good night, Roger."

"Good night, you should take aspirin and push yourself into a tub of hot
water, you look as though you're catching cold."

"I will."

With the purse under her arm she went upstairs, and on the first landing Bill
heard her step and poked his head out with his hair tumbled and his eyes red,
and he said: "For Christ's sake come in and have a drink with me. I've had some
bad news."

"You're perfectly sopping," said Bill, looking at her drenched feet. They had
two drinks, while Bill told how the director had thrown his play out after the
cast had been picked over twice, and had gone through three rehearsals. "I said to
him, 'I didn't say it was a masterpiece, I said it would make a good show.' And
he said, 'It just doesn't *play,* do you see? It needs a doctor.' So I'm stuck,
absolutely stuck," said Bill, on the edge of weeping again. "I've been crying," he
told her, "in my cups." And he went on to ask her if she realized his wife was
ruining him with her extravagance. "I send her ten dollars every week of my
unhappy life, and I don't really have to. She threatens to jail me if I don't, but
she can't do it. God, let her try it after the way she treated me! She's no right to
alimony and she knows it. She keeps on saying she's got to have it for the baby
and I keep on sending it because I can't bear to see anybody suffer. So I'm way
behind on the piano and the victrola, both—"

"Well, this is a pretty big rug, anyhow," she said.

Bill stared at it and blew his nose. "I got it at Ricci's for ninety-five dollars,"
he said. "Ricci told me it once belonged to Marie Dressler, and cost fifteen
hundred dollars, but there's a burnt place on it, under the divan. Can you beat
that?"

"No," she said. She was thinking about her empty purse and that she could
not possibly expect a check for her latest review for another three days, and her
arrangement with the basement restaurant could not last much longer if she did
not pay something on account. "It's no time to speak of it," she said, "but I've
been hoping you would have by now that fifty dollars you promised for my scene
in the third act. Even if it doesn't play. You were to pay me for the work anyhow
out of your advance."

"Weeping Jesus," said Bill, "you, too?" He gave a loud sob, or hiccough, in
his moist handkerchief. "Your stuff was no better than mine, after all. Think of
that."

"But you got something for it," she said. "Seven hundred dollars."

Bill said, "Do me a favor, will you? Have another drink and forget about it. I
can't, you know I can't, I would if I could, but you know the fix I'm in."

"Let it go, then," she found herself saying almost in spite of herself. She had meant to be quite firm about it. They drank again without speaking, and she went to her apartment on the floor above.

There, she now remembered distinctly, she had taken the letter out of the purse before she spread the purse out to dry.

She had sat down and read the letter over again: but there were phrases that insisted on being read many times, they had a life of their own separate from the others, and when she tried to read past and around them, they moved with the movement of her eyes, and she could not escape them . . . "thinking about you more than I mean to . . . yes, I even talk about you . . . why were you so anxious to destroy . . . even if I could see you now I would not . . . not worth all this abominable . . . the end . . ."

Carefully she tore the letter into narrow strips and touched a lighted match to them in the coal grate.

Early the next morning she was in the bathtub when the janitress knocked and then came in, calling out that she wished to examine the radiators before she started the furnace going for the winter. After moving about the room for a few minutes, the janitress went out, closing the door very sharply.

She came out of the bathroom to get a cigarette from the package in the purse. The purse was gone. She dressed and made coffee, and sat by the window while she drank it. Certainly the janitress had taken the purse, and certainly it would be impossible to get it back without a great deal of ridiculous excitement. Then let it go. With this decision of her mind, there rose coincidentally in her blood a deep murderous anger. She set the cup carefully in the center of the table, and walked steadily downstairs, three long flights and a short hall and a steep short flight into the basement, where the janitress, her face streaked with coal dust, was shaking up the furnace. "Will you please give me back my purse? There isn't any money in it. It was a present, and I don't want to lose it."

The janitress turned without straightening up and peered at her with hot flickering eyes, a red light from the furnace reflected in them. "What do you mean, your purse?"

"The gold cloth purse you took from the wooden bench in my room," she said. "I must have it back."

"Before God I never laid eyes on your purse, and that's the holy truth," said the janitress.

"Oh, well then, keep it," she said, but in a very bitter voice; "keep it if you want it so much." And she walked away.

She remembered how she had never locked a door in her life, on some principle of rejection in her that made her uncomfortable in the ownership of things, and her paradoxical boast before the warnings of her friends, that she had never lost a penny by theft; and she had been pleased with the bleak humility of this concrete example designed to illustrate and justify a certain fixed, otherwise baseless and general faith which ordered the movements of her life without regard to her will in the matter.

In this moment she felt that she had been robbed of an enormous number of valuable things, whether material or intangible: things lost or broken by her own fault, things she had forgotten and left in houses when she moved: books borrowed from her and not returned, journeys she had planned and had not made, words she had waited to hear spoken to her and had not heard, and the words she had meant to answer with; bitter alternatives and intolerable substitutes worse than nothing, and yet inescapable: the long patient suffering of dying friendships and the dark inexplicable death of love—all that she had had, and all that she had missed, were lost together, and were twice lost in this landslide of remembered losses.

The janitress was following her upstairs with the purse in her hand and the same deep red fire flickering in her eyes. The janitress thrust the purse towards her while they were still a half dozen steps apart, and said: "Don't never tell on me. I musta been crazy. I get crazy in the head sometimes, I swear I do. My son can tell you."

She took the purse after a moment, and the janitress went on: "I got a niece who is going on seventeen, and she's a nice girl and I thought I'd give it to her. She needs a pretty purse. I musta been crazy; I thought maybe you wouldn't mind, you leave things around and don't seem to notice much."

She said: "I missed this because it was a present to me from someone . . ."

The janitress said: "He'd get you another if you lost this one. My niece is young and needs pretty things, we oughta give the young ones a chance. She's got young men after her maybe will want to marry her. She oughta have nice things. She needs them bad right now. You're a grown woman, you've had your chance, you ought to know how it is!"

She held the purse out to the janitress saying: "You don't know what you're talking about. Here, take it, I've changed my mind. I really don't want it."

The janitress looked up at her with hatred and said: "I don't want it either now. My niece is young and pretty, she don't need fixin' up to be pretty, she's young and pretty anyhow! I guess you need it worse than she does!"

"It wasn't really yours in the first place," she said, turning away. "You mustn't talk as if I had stolen it from you."

"It's not from me, it's from her you're stealing it," said the janitress, and went back downstairs.

She laid the purse on the table and sat down with the cup of chilled coffee, and thought: I was right not to be afraid of any thief but myself, who will end by leaving me nothing.

Virginia Woolf

The Duchess and the Jeweller

Oliver Bacon lived at the top of a house overlooking the Green Park. He had a flat; chairs jutted out at the right angles—chairs covered in hide. Sofas filled the bays of the windows—sofas covered in tapestry. The windows, the three long windows, had the proper allowance of discreet net and figured satin. The mahogany sideboard bulged discreetly with the right brandies, whiskeys, and liqueurs. And from the middle window he looked down upon the glossy roofs of fashionable cars packed in the narrow straits of Piccadilly. A more central position could not be imagined. And at eight in the morning he would have his breakfast brought in on a tray by a man-servant: the man-servant would unfold his crimson dressing-gown; he would rip his letters open with his long pointed nails and would extract thick white cards of invitation upon which the engraving stood up roughly from duchesses, countesses, viscountesses, and Honourable Ladies. Then he would wash; then he would eat his toast; then he would read his paper by the bright burning fire of electric coals.

"Behold Oliver," he would say, addressing himself. "You who began life in a filthy little alley, you who . . ." and he would look down at his legs, so shapely in their perfect trousers; at his boots; at his spats. They were all shapely, shining; cut from the best cloth by the best scissors in Savile Row. But he dismantled himself often and became again a little boy in a dark alley. He had once thought that the height of his ambition—selling stolen dogs to fashionable women in Whitechapel. And once he had been done. "Oh, Oliver," his mother had wailed. "Oh, Oliver! When will you have sense, my son?" . . . Then he had gone behind a counter; had sold cheap watches; then he had taken a wallet to Amsterdam. . . . At that memory he would chuckle—the old Oliver remembering the young. Yes, he had done well with the three diamonds; also there was the commission on the emerald. After that he went into the private room behind the shop in Hatton Garden; the room with the scales, the safe, the thick magnifying glasses. And then . . . and then. . . . He chuckled. When he passed through the knots of jewellers in the hot evening who were discussing prices, gold mines, diamonds, reports from South Africa, one of them would lay a finger to the side of his nose and murmur, "Hum-m-m," as he passed. It was no more than a murmur; no more than a nudge on the shoulder, a finger on the nose, a buzz that ran through the cluster of jewellers in Hatton Garden on a hot afternoon—oh, many years ago now! But still Oliver felt it purring down his spine, the nudge, the murmur that meant, "Look at him—young Oliver, the young jeweller—there he goes." Young he was then. And he dressed better and better; and had, first a hansom cab; then a car; and first he went up to the dress circle, then down into the stalls. And he had a villa at Richmond, overlooking the river, with trellises of

From *A Haunted House and Other Stories* by Virginia Woolf. Copyright, 1944, by Harcourt, Brace and Company, Inc. Used by permission of Harcourt, Brace and Company, Inc. and Leonard Woolf.

red roses; and Mademoiselle used to pick one every morning and stick it in his buttonhole.

"So," said Oliver Bacon, rising and stretching his legs. "So . . ."

And he stood beneath the picture of an old lady on the mantelpiece and raised his hands. "I have kept my word," he said, laying his hands together, palm to palm, as if he were doing homage to her. "I have won my bet." That was so; he was the richest jeweller in England; but his nose, which was long and flexible, like an elephant's trunk, seemed to say by its curious quiver at the nostrils (but it seemed as if the whole nose quivered, not only the nostrils) that he was not satisfied yet; still smelt something under the ground a little further off. Imagine a giant hog in a pasture rich with truffles; after unearthing this truffle and that, still it smells a bigger, a blacker truffle under the ground further off. So Oliver snuffed always in the rich earth of Mayfair another truffle, a blacker, a bigger further off.

Now then he straightened the pearl in his tie, cased himself in his smart blue overcoat; took his yellow gloves and his cane; and swayed as he descended the stairs and half snuffed, half sighed through his long sharp nose as he passed out into Piccadilly. For was he not still a sad man, a dissatisfied man, a man who seeks something that is hidden, though he had won his bet?

He swayed slightly as he walked, as the camel at the zoo sways from side to side when it walks along the asphalt paths laden with grocers and their wives eating from paper bags and throwing little bits of silver paper crumpled up on to the path. The camel despises the grocers; the camel is dissatisfied with its lot; the camel sees the blue lake and the fringe of palm trees in front of it. So the great jeweller, the greatest jeweller in the whole world, swung down Piccadilly, perfectly dressed, with his gloves, with his cane; but dissatisfied still, till he reached the dark little shop, that was famous in France, in Germany, in Austria, in Italy, and all over America—the dark little shop in the street off Bond Street.

As usual, he strode through the shop without speaking, though the four men, the two old men, Marshall and Spencer, and the two young men, Hammond and Wicks, stood straight and looked at him, envying him. It was only with one finger of the amber-coloured glove, waggling, that he acknowledged their presence. And he went in and shut the door of his private room behind him.

Then he unlocked the grating that barred the window. The cries of Bond Street came in; the purr of the distant traffic. The light from reflectors at the back of the shop struck upwards. One tree waved six green leaves, for it was June. But Mademoiselle had married Mr. Pedder of the local brewery—no one stuck roses in his buttonhole now.

"So," he half sighed, half snorted, "so—"

Then he touched a spring in the wall and slowly the panelling slid open, and behind it were the steel safes, five, no, six of them, all of burnished steel. He twisted a key; unlocked one; then another. Each was lined with a pad of deep crimson velvet; in each lay jewels—bracelets, necklaces, rings, tiaras, ducal coronets; loose stones in glass shells; rubies, emeralds, pearls, diamonds. All safe, shining, cool, yet burning, eternally, with their own compressed light.

"Tears!" said Oliver, looking at the pearls.

"Heart's blood!" he said, looking at the rubies.

"Gunpowder!" he continued, rattling the diamonds so that they flashed and blazed.

"Gunpowder enough to blow Mayfair—sky high, high, high!" He threw his head back and made a sound like a horse neighing as he said it.

The telephone buzzed obsequiously in a low muted voice on his table. He shut the safe.

"In ten minutes," he said. "Not before." And he sat down at his desk and looked at the heads of the Roman emperors that were graved on his sleeve links. And again he dismantled himself and became once more the little boy playing marbles in the alley where they sell stolen dogs on Sunday. He became that wily astute little boy, with lips like wet cherries. He dabbled his fingers in ropes of tripe; he dipped them in pans of frying fish; he dodged in and out among the crowds. He was slim, lissome, with eyes like licked stones. And now—now—the hands of the clock ticked on, one, two, three, four. . . . The Duchess of Lambourne waited his pleasure; the Duchess of Lambourne, daughter of a hundred Earls. She would wait for ten minutes on a chair at the counter. She would wait his pleasure. She would wait till he was ready to see her. He watched the clock in its shagreen case. The hand moved on. With each tick the clock handed him—so it seemed—pâté de foie gras, a glass of champagne, another of fine brandy, a cigar costing one guinea. The clock laid them on the table beside him as the ten minutes passed. Then he heard soft slow footsteps approaching; a rustle in the corridor. The door opened. Mr. Hammond flattened himself against the wall.

"Her Grace!" he announced.

And he waited there, flattened against the wall.

And Oliver, rising, could hear the rustle of the dress of the Duchess as she came down the passage. Then she loomed up, filling the door, filling the room with the aroma, the prestige, the arrogance, the pomp, the pride of all the Dukes and Duchesses swollen in one wave. And as a wave breaks, she broke, as she sat down, spreading and splashing and falling over Oliver Bacon, the great jeweller, covering him with sparkling bright colours, green, rose, violet; and odours; and iridescences; and rays shooting from fingers, nodding from plumes, flashing from silk; for she was very large, very fat, tightly girt in pink taffeta, and past her prime. As a parasol with many flounces, as a peacock with many feathers, shuts its flounces, folds its feathers, so she subsided and shut herself as she sank down in the leather armchair.

"Good morning, Mr. Bacon," said the Duchess. And she held out her hand which came through the slit of her white glove. And Oliver bent low as he shook it. And as their hands touched the link was forged between them once more. They were friends, yet enemies; he was master, she was mistress; each cheated the other, each needed the other, each feared the other, each felt this and knew this every time they touched hands thus in the little back room with the white light outside, and the tree with its six leaves, and the sound of the street in the distance and behind them the safes.

"And today, Duchess—what can I do for you today?" said Oliver, very softly.

The Duchess opened her heart, her private heart, gaped wide. And with a sigh but no word she took from her bag a long wash-leather pouch—it looked like a lean yellow ferret. And from a slit in the ferret's belly she dropped pearls—ten pearls. They rolled from the slit in the ferret's belly—one, two, three, four—like the eggs of some heavenly bird.

"All that's left me, dear Mr. Bacon," she moaned. Five, six, seven—down they rolled, down the slopes of the vast mountain sides that fell between her knees into one narrow valley—the eighth, the ninth, and the tenth. There they lay in the glow of the peach-blossom taffeta. Ten pearls.

"From the Appleby cincture," she mourned. "The last . . . the last of them all."

Oliver stretched out and took one of the pearls between finger and thumb. It was round, it was lustrous. But real was it, or false? Was she lying again? Did she dare?

She laid her plump padded finger across her lips. "If the Duke knew . . ." she whispered. "Dear Mr. Bacon, a bit of bad luck . . ."

Been gambling again, had she?

"That villain! That sharper!" she hissed.

The man with the chipped cheek bone? A bad'un. And the Duke was straight as a poker; with side whiskers; would cut her off, shut her up down there if he knew—what I know, thought Oliver, and glanced at the safe.

"Araminta, Daphne, Diana," she moaned. "It's for *them*."

The ladies Araminta, Daphne, Diana—her daughters. He knew them; adored them. But it was Diana he loved.

"You have all my secrets," she leered. Tears slid; tears fell; tears, like diamonds, collecting powder in the ruts of her cherry blossom cheeks.

"Old friend," she murmured, "old friend."

"Old friend," he repeated, "old friend," as if he licked the words.

"How much?" he queried.

She covered the pearls with her hand.

"Twenty thousand," she whispered.

But was it real or false, the one he held in his hand? The Appleby cincture—hadn't she sold it already? He would ring for Spencer or Hammond. "Take it and test it," he would say. He stretched to the bell.

"You will come down tomorrow?" she urged, she interrupted. "The Prime Minister—His Royal Highness . . ." She stopped. "And Diana . . ." she added.

Oliver took his hand off the bell.

He looked past her, at the backs of the houses in Bond Street. But he saw, not the houses in Bond Street, but a dimpling river; and trout rising and salmon; and the Prime Minister; and himself too, in white waistcoat; and then, Diana. He looked down at the pearl in his hand. But how could he test it, in the light of the river, in the light of the eyes of Diana? But the eyes of the Duchess were on him.

"Twenty thousand," she moaned. "My honour!"

The honour of the mother of Diana! He drew his cheque book towards him; he took out his pen.

"Twenty—" he wrote. Then he stopped writing. The eyes of the old woman in the picture were on him—of the old woman his mother.

"Oliver!" she warned him. "Have sense! Don't be a fool!"

"Oliver!" the Duchess entreated—it was "Oliver" now, not "Mr. Bacon." "You'll come for a long week-end?"

Alone in the woods with Diana! Riding alone in the woods with Diana!

"Thousand," he wrote, and signed it.

"Here you are," he said.

And there opened all the flounces of the parasol, all the plumes of the peacock, the radiance of the wave, the swords and spears of Agincourt, as she rose from her chair. And the two old men and the two young men, Spencer and Marshall, Wicks and Hammond, flattened themselves behind the counter envying him as he led her through the shop to the door. And he waggled his yellow glove in their faces, and she held her honour—a cheque for twenty thousand pounds with his signature—quite firmly in her hands.

"Are they false or are they real?" asked Oliver, shutting his private door. There they were, ten pearls on the blotting-paper on the table. He took them to the window. He held them under his lens to the light. . . . This, then, was the truffle he had routed out of the earth! Rotten at the centre—rotten at the core!

"Forgive me, oh, my mother!" he sighed, raising his hand as if he asked pardon of the old woman in the picture. And again he was a little boy in the alley where they sold dogs on Sunday.

"For," he murmured, laying the palms of his hands together, "it is to be a long week-end."

James Joyce

Counterparts

The bell rang furiously and, when Miss Parker went to the tube, a furious voice called out in a piercing North of Ireland accent:

"Send Farrington here!"

Miss Parker returned to her machine, saying to a man who was writing at a desk:

From *Dubliners* by James Joyce. Reprinted by permission of The Viking Press, Inc.

"Mr. Alleyne wants you upstairs."

The man muttered *"Blast* him!" under his breath and pushed back his chair to stand up. When he stood up he was tall and of great bulk. He had a hanging face, dark wine-coloured, with fair eyebrows and moustache: his eyes bulged forward slightly and the whites of them were dirty. He lifted up the counter and, passing by the clients, went out of the office with a heavy step.

He went heavily upstairs until he came to the second landing, where a door bore a brass plate with the inscription *Mr. Alleyne.* Here he halted, puffing with labour and vexation, and knocked. The shrill voice cried:

"Come in!"

The man entered Mr. Alleyne's room. Simultaneously Mr. Alleyne, a little man wearing gold-rimmed glasses on a clean-shaven face, shot his head up over a pile of documents. The head itself was so pink and hairless it seemed like a large egg reposing on the papers. Mr. Alleyne did not lose a moment:

"Farrington? What is the meaning of this? Why have I always to complain of you? May I ask you why you haven't made a copy of that contract between Bodley and Kirwan? I told you it must be ready by four o'clock."

"But Mr. Shelley said, sir—"

"Mr. Shelley said, sir. . . . Kindly attend to what I say and not to what *Mr. Shelley says, sir.* You have always some excuse or another for shirking work. Let me tell you that if the contract is not copied before this evening I'll lay the matter before Mr. Crosbie. . . . Do you hear me now?"

"Yes, sir."

"Do you hear me now? . . . Ay and another little matter! I might as well be talking to the wall as talking to you. Understand once for all that you get a half an hour for your lunch and not an hour and a half. How many courses do you want, I'd like to know. . . . Do you mind me now?"

"Yes, sir."

Mr. Alleyne bent his head again upon his pile of papers. The man stared fixedly at the polished skull which directed the affairs of Crosbie & Alleyne, gauging its fragility. A spasm of rage gripped his throat for a few moments and then passed, leaving after it a sharp sensation of thirst. The man recognised the sensation and felt that he must have a good night's drinking. The middle of the month was passed and, if he could get the copy done in time, Mr. Alleyne might give him an order on the cashier. He stood still, gazing fixedly at the head upon the pile of papers. Suddenly Mr. Alleyne began to upset all the papers, searching for something. Then, as if he had been unaware of the man's presence till that moment, he shot up his head again, saying:

"Eh? Are you going to stand there all day? Upon my word, Farrington, you take things easy!"

"I was waiting to see . . ."

"Very good, you needn't wait to see. Go downstairs and do your work."

The man walked heavily towards the door and, as he went out of the room, he heard Mr. Alleyne cry after him that if the contract was not copied by evening Mr. Crosbie would hear of the matter.

He returned to his desk in the lower office and counted the sheets which remained to be copied. He took up his pen and dipped it in the ink but he continued to stare stupidly at the last words he had written: *In no case shall the said Bernard Bodley be* . . . The evening was falling and in a few minutes they would be lighting the gas: then he could write. He felt that he must slake the thirst in his throat. He stood up from his desk and, lifting the counter as before, passed out of the office. As he was passing out the chief clerk looked at him inquiringly.

"It's all right, Mr. Shelley," said the man, pointing with his finger to indicate the objective of his journey.

The chief clerk glanced at the hat-rack, but, seeing the row complete, offered no remark. As soon as he was on the landing the man pulled a shepherd's plaid cap out of his pocket, put it on his head and ran quickly down the rickety stairs. From the street door he walked on furtively on the inner side of the path towards the corner and all at once dived into a doorway. He was now safe in the dark snug of O'Neill's shop, and filling up the little window that looked into the bar with his inflamed face, the colour of dark wine or dark meat, he called out:

"Here, Pat, give us a g.p., like a good fellow."

The curate brought him a glass of plain porter. The man drank it at a gulp and asked for a caraway seed. He put his penny on the counter and, leaving the curate to grope for it in the gloom, retreated out of the snug as furtively as he had entered it.

Darkness, accompanied by a thick fog, was gaining upon the dusk of February and the lamps in Eustace Street had been lit. The man went up by the houses until he reached the door of the office, wondering whether he could finish his copy in time. On the stairs a moist pungent odour of perfumes saluted his nose: evidently Miss Delacour had come while he was out in O'Neill's. He crammed his cap back again into his pocket and re-entered the office, assuming an air of absentmindedness.

"Mr. Alleyne has been calling for you," said the chief clerk severely. "Where were you?"

The man glanced at the two clients who were standing at the counter as if to intimate that their presence prevented him from answering. As the clients were both male the chief clerk allowed himself a laugh.

"I know that game," he said. "Five times in one day is a little bit . . . Well, you better look sharp and get a copy of our correspondence in the Delacour case for Mr. Alleyne."

This address in the presence of the public, his run upstairs and the porter he had gulped down so hastily confused the man and, as he sat down at his desk to get what was required, he realised how hopeless was the task of finishing his copy of the contract before half past five. The dark damp night was coming and he longed to spend it in the bars, drinking with his friends amid the glare of gas and the clatter of glasses. He got out the Delacour correspondence and passed out of the office. He hoped Mr. Alleyne would not discover that the last two letters were missing.

The moist pungent perfume lay all the way up to Mr. Alleyne's room. Miss Delacour was a middle-aged woman of Jewish appearance. Mr. Alleyne was said to be sweet on her or on her money. She came to the office often and stayed a long time when she came. She was sitting beside his desk now in an aroma of perfumes, smoothing the handle of her umbrella and nodding the great black feather in her hat. Mr. Alleyne had swivelled his chair round to face her and thrown his right foot jauntily upon his left knee. The man put the correspondence on the desk and bowed respectfully but neither Mr. Alleyne nor Miss Delacour took any notice of his bow. Mr. Alleyne tapped a finger on the correspondence and then flicked it towards him as if to say: *"That's all right: you can go."*

The man returned to the lower office and sat down again at his desk. He stared intently at the incomplete phrase: *In no case shall the said Bernard Bodley be* . . . and thought how strange it was that the last three words began with the same letter. The chief clerk began to hurry Miss Parker, saying she would never have the letters typed in time for post. The man listened to the clicking of the machine for a few minutes and then set to work to finish his copy. But his head was not clear and his mind wandered away to the glare and rattle of the public-house. It was a night for hot punches. He struggled on with his copy, but when the clock struck five he had still fourteen pages to write. Blast it! He couldn't finish it in time. He longed to execrate aloud, to bring his fist down on something violently. He was so enraged that he wrote *Bernard Bernard* instead of *Bernard Bodley* and had to begin again on a clean sheet.

He felt strong enough to clear out the whole office singlehanded. His body ached to do something, to rush out and revel in violence. All the indignities of his life enraged him. . . . Could he ask the cashier privately for an advance? No, the cashier was no good, no damn good; he wouldn't give an advance. . . . He knew where he would meet the boys: Leonard and O'Halloran and Nosey Flynn. The barometer of his emotional nature was set for a spell of riot.

His imagination had so abstracted him that his name was called twice before he answered. Mr. Alleyne and Miss Delacour were standing outside the counter and all the clerks had turned round in anticipation of something. The man got up from his desk. Mr. Alleyne began a tirade of abuse, saying that two letters were missing. The man answered that he knew nothing about them, that he had made a faithful copy. The tirade continued: it was so bitter and violent that the man could hardly restrain his fist from descending upon the head of the manikin before him:

"I know nothing about any other two letters," he said stupidly.

"You—know—nothing. Of course you know nothing," said Mr. Alleyne. "Tell me," he added, glancing first for approval to the lady beside him. "do you take me for a fool? Do you think me an utter fool?"

The man glanced from the lady's face to the little egg-shaped head and back again; and, almost before he was aware of it, his tongue had found a felicitous moment:

"I don't think, sir," he said, "that that's a fair question to put to me."

There was a pause in the very breathing of the clerks. Everyone was astounded (the author of the witticism no less than his neighbours) and Miss Delacour, who was a stout amiable person, began to smile broadly. Mr. Alleyne flushed to the hue of a wild rose and his mouth twitched with a dwarf's passion. He shook his fist in the man's face till it seemed to vibrate like the knob of some electric machine:

"You impertinent ruffian! You impertinent ruffian! I'll make short work of you! Wait till you see! You'll apologise to me for your impertinence or you'll quit the office instanter! You'll quit this, I'm telling you, or you'll apologise to me!"

He stood in a doorway opposite the office watching to see if the cashier would come out alone. All the clerks passed out and finally the cashier came out with the chief clerk. It was no use trying to say a word to him when he was with the chief clerk. The man felt that his position was bad enough. He had been obliged to offer an abject apology to Mr. Alleyne for his impertinence but he knew what a hornet's nest the office would be for him. He could remember the way in which Mr. Alleyne had hounded little Peake out of the office in order to make room for his own nephew. He felt savage and thirsty and revengeful, annoyed with himself and with everyone else. Mr. Alleyne would never give him an hour's rest; his life would be a hell to him. He had made a proper fool of himself this time. Could he not keep his tongue in his cheek? But they had never pulled together from the first, he and Mr. Alleyne, ever since the day Mr. Alleyne had overheard him mimicking his North of Ireland accent to amuse Higgins and Miss Parker: that had been the beginning of it. He might have tried Higgins for the money, but sure Higgins never had anything for himself. A man with two establishments to keep up, of course he couldn't. . . .

He felt his great body again aching for the comfort of the public-house. The fog had begun to chill him and he wondered could he touch Pat in O'Neill's. He could not touch him for more than a bob—and a bob was no use. Yet he must get money somewhere or other: he had spent his last penny for the g.p. and soon it would be too late for getting money anywhere. Suddenly, as he was fingering his watch-chain, he thought of Terry Kelly's pawn-office in Fleet Street. That was the dart! Why didn't he think of it sooner?

He went through the narrow alley of Temple Bar quickly, muttering to himself that they could all go to hell because he was going to have a good night of it. The clerk in Terry Kelly's said *A crown!* but the consignor held out for six shillings; and in the end the six shillings was allowed him literally. He came out of the pawn-office joyfully, making a little cylinder of the coins between his thumb and fingers. In Westmoreland Street the footpaths were crowded with young men and women returning from business and ragged urchins ran here and there yelling out the names of the evening editions. The man passed through the crowd, looking on the spectacle generally with proud satisfaction and staring masterfully at the office-girls. His head was full of the noises of tram-gongs and swishing trolleys and his nose already sniffed the curling fumes of punch. As he walked on he preconsidered the terms in which he would narrate the incident to the boys:

"So, I just looked at him—coolly, you know, and looked at her. Then I looked back at him again—taking my time, you know. 'I don't think that that's a fair question to put to me,' says I."

Nosey Flynn was sitting up in his usual corner of Davy Byrne's and, when he heard the story, he stood Farrington a half-one, saying it was as smart a thing as ever he heard. Farrington stood a drink in his turn. After a while O'Halloran and Paddy Leonard came in and the story was repeated to them. O'Halloran stood tailors of malt, hot, all round and told the story of the retort he had made to the chief clerk when he was in Callan's of Fownes's Street; but, as the retort was after the manner of the liberal shepherds in the eclogues, he had to admit that it was not as clever as Farrington's retort. At this Farrington told the boys to polish off that and have another.

Just as they were naming their poisons who should come in but Higgins! Of course he had to join in with the others. The men asked him to give his version of it, and he did so with great vivacity for the sight of five small hot whiskies was very exhilarating. Everyone roared laughing when he showed the way in which Mr. Alleyne shook his fist in Farrington's face. Then he imitated Farrington, saying, *"And here was my nabs, as cool as you please,"* while Farrington looked at the company out of his heavy dirty eyes, smiling and at times drawing forth stray drops of liquor from his moustache with the aid of his lower lip.

When that round was over there was a pause. O'Halloran had money but neither of the other two seemed to have any; so the whole party left the shop somewhat regretfully. At the corner of Duke Street Higgins and Nosey Flynn bevelled off to the left while the other three turned back towards the city. Rain was drizzling down on the cold streets and, when they reached the Ballast Office, Farrington suggested the Scotch House. The bar was full of men and loud with the noise of tongues and glasses. The three men pushed past the whining match-sellers at the door and formed a little party at the corner of the counter. They began to exchange stories. Leonard introduced them to a young fellow named Weathers who was performing at the Tivoli as an acrobat and knock-about *artiste.* Farrington stood a drink all round. Weathers said he would take a small Irish and Apollinaris. Farrington, who had definite notions of what was what, asked the boys would they have an Apollinaris too; but the boys told Tim to make theirs hot. The talk became theatrical. O'Halloran stood a round and then Farrington stood another round, Weathers protesting that the hospitality was too Irish. He promised to get them in behind the scenes and introduce them to some nice girls. O'Halloran said that he and Leonard would go, but that Farrington wouldn't go because he was a married man; and Farrington's heavy dirty eyes leered at the company in token that he understood he was being chaffed. Weathers made them all have just one little tincture at his expense and promised to meet them later on at Mulligan's in Poolbeg Street.

When the Scotch House closed they went round to Mulligan's. They went into the parlour at the back and O'Halloran ordered small hot specials all round. They were all beginning to feel mellow. Farrington was just standing another round when Weathers came back. Much to Farrington's relief he drank a glass of bitter this time. Funds were getting low but they had enough to keep them going. Presently two young women with big hats and a young man in a check suit came in and sat at a table close by. Weathers saluted them and told the company that they were out of the Tivoli. Farrington's eyes wandered at every moment in the direction of one of the young women. There was something striking in her appearance. An immense scarf of peacock-blue muslin was wound round her hat and knotted in a great bow under her chin; and she wore bright yellow gloves, reaching to the elbow. Farrington gazed admiringly at the plump arm which she moved very often and with much grace; and when, after a little time, she answered his gaze he admired still more her large dark brown eyes. The oblique staring expression in them fascinated him. She glanced at him once or twice and, when the party was leaving the room, she brushed against his chair and said *"O, pardon!"* in a London accent. He watched her leave the room in the hope that she would look back at him, but he was disappointed. He cursed his want of money and cursed all the rounds he had stood, particularly to all the whiskies and Apollinaris which he had stood to Weathers. If there was one thing that he hated it was a sponge. He was so angry that he lost count of the conversation of his friends.

When Paddy Leonard called him he found that they were talking about feats of strength. Weathers was showing his biceps muscle to the company and boasting so much that the other two had called on Farrington to uphold the national honour. Farrington pulled up his sleeve accordingly and showed his biceps muscle to the company. The two arms were examined and compared and finally it was agreed to have a trial of strength. The table was cleared and the two men rested their elbows on it, clasping hands. When Paddy Leonard said *"Go!"* each was to try to bring down the other's hand on to the table. Farrington looked very serious and determined.

The trial began. After about thirty seconds Weathers brought his opponent's hand slowly down on to the table. Farrington's dark wine-coloured face flushed darker still with anger and humiliation at having been defeated by such a stripling.

"You're not to put the weight of your body behind it. Play fair," he said.

"Who's not playing fair?" said the other.

"Come on again. The two best out of three."

The trial began again. The veins stood out on Farrington's forehead, and the pallor of Weathers' complexion changed to peony. Their hands and arms trembled under the stress. After a long struggle Weathers again brought his opponent's hand slowly on to the table. There was a murmur of applause from the spectators. The curate, who was standing beside the table, nodded his red head towards the victor and said with stupid familiarity:

"Ah! that's the knack!"

"What the hell do you know about it?" said Farrington fiercely, turning on the man. "What do you put in your gab for?"

"Sh, sh!" said O'Halloran, observing the violent expression of Farrington's face. "Pony up, boys. We'll have just one little smahan more and then we'll be off."

A very sullen-faced man stood at the corner of O'Connell Bridge waiting for the little Sandymount tram to take him home. He was full of smouldering anger and revengefulness. He felt humiliated and discontented; he did not even feel drunk; and he had only twopence in his pocket. He cursed everything. He had done for himself in the office, pawned his watch, spent all his money; and he had not even got drunk. He began to feel thirsty again and he longed to be back again in the hot reeking public-house. He had lost his reputation as a strong man, having been defeated twice by a mere boy. His heart swelled with fury and, when he thought of the woman in the big hat who had brushed against him and said *Pardon!* his fury nearly choked him.

His tram let him down at Shelbourne Road and he steered his great body along in the shadow of the wall of the barracks. He loathed returning to his home. When he went in by the side-door he found the kitchen empty and the kitchen fire nearly out. He bawled upstairs:

"Ada! Ada!"

His wife was a little sharp-faced woman who bullied her husband when he was sober and was bullied by him when he was drunk. They had five children. A little boy came running down the stairs.

"Who is that?" said the man, peering through the darkness.

"Me, pa."

"Who are you? Charlie?"

"No, pa. Tom."

"Where's your mother?"

"She's out at the chapel."

"That's right. . . . Did she think of leaving any dinner for me?"

"Yes, pa. I—"

"Light the lamp. What do you mean by having the place in darkness? Are the other children in bed?"

The man sat down heavily on one of the chairs while the little boy lit the lamp. He began to mimic his son's flat accent, saying half to himself: *"At the chapel. At the chapel, if you please!"* When the lamp was lit he banged his fist on the table and shouted:

"What's for my dinner?"

"I'm going . . . to cook it, pa," said the little boy.

The man jumped up furiously and pointed to the fire.

"On that fire! You let the fire out! By God, I'll teach you to do that again!"

He took a step to the door and seized the walking-stick which was standing behind it.

"I'll teach you to let the fire out!" he said, rolling up his sleeve in order to give his arm free play.

The little boy cried *"O pa!"* and ran whimpering round the table, but the man followed him and caught him by the coat. The little boy looked about him wildly but, seeing no way of escape, fell upon his knees.

"Now, you'll let the fire out the next time!" said the man, striking at him vigorously with the stick. "Take that, you little whelp!"

The boy uttered a squeal of pain as the stick cut his thigh. He clasped his hands together in the air and his voice shook with fright.

"O, pa!" he cried. "Don't beat me, pa! And I'll . . . I'll say a *Hail Mary* for you. . . . I'll say a *Hail Mary* for you, pa, if you don't beat me. . . . I'll say a *Hail Mary*. . . ."

SYMBOL

Stephen Crane

An Episode of War

The lieutenant's rubber blanket lay on the ground, and upon it he had poured the company's supply of coffee. Corporals and other representatives of the grimy and hot-throated men who lined the breast-work had come for each squad's portion.

The lieutenant was frowning and serious at this task of division. His lips pursed as he drew with his sword various crevices in the heap, until brown squares of coffee, astoundingly equal in size, appeared on the blanket. He was on the verge of a great triumph in mathematics, and the corporals were thronging forward, each to reap a little square, when suddenly the lieutenant cried out and looked quickly at a man near him as if he suspected it was a case of personal assault. The others cried out also when they saw blood upon the lieutenant's sleeve.

He had winced like a man stung, swayed dangerously, and then straightened. The sound of his hoarse breathing was plainly audible. He looked sadly, mystically, over the breastwork at the green face of a wood, where now were many little puffs of white smoke. During this moment the men about him gazed statuelike and silent, astonished and awed by this catastrophe which happened when catastrophes were not expected—when they had leisure to observe it.

Reprinted from *Stephen Crane: An Omnibus,* edited by Robert Wooster Stallman, courtesy of Alfred A. Knopf, Inc.

As the lieutenant stared at the wood, they too swung their heads, so that for another instant all hands, still silent, contemplated the distant forest as if their minds were fixed upon the mystery of a bullet's journey.

The officer had, of course, been compelled to take his sword into his left hand. He did not hold it by the hilt. He gripped it at the middle of the blade, awkwardly. Turning his eyes from the hostile wood, he looked at the sword as he held it there, and seemed puzzled as to what to do with it, where to put it. In short, this weapon had of a sudden become a strange thing to him. He looked at it in a kind of stupefaction, as if he had been endowed with a trident, a sceptre, or a spade.

Finally he tried to sheathe it. To sheathe a sword held by the left hand, at the middle of the blade, in a scabbard hung at the left hip, is a feat worthy of a sawdust ring. This wounded officer engaged in a desperate struggle with the sword and the wobbling scabbard, and during the time of it he breathed like a wrestler.

But at this instant the men, the spectators, awoke from their stone-like poses and crowded forward sympathetically. The orderly-sergeant took the sword and tenderly placed it in the scabbard. At the time, he leaned nervously backward, and did not allow even his finger to brush the body of the lieutenant. A wound gives strange dignity to him who bears it. Well men shy from this new and terrible majesty. It is as if the wounded man's hand is upon the curtain which hangs before the revelations of all existence—the meaning of ants, potentates, wars, cities, sunshine, snow, a feather dropped from a bird's wing; and the power of it sheds radiance upon a bloody form, and makes the other men understand sometimes that they are little. His comrades look at him with large eyes thoughtfully. Moreover, they fear vaguely that the weight of a finger upon him might send him headlong, precipitate the tragedy, hurl him at once into the dim, grey unknown. And so the orderly-sergeant, while sheathing the sword, leaned nervously backward.

There were others who proffered assistance. One timidly presented his shoulder and asked the lieutenant if he cared to lean upon it, but the latter waved him away mournfully. He wore the look of one who knows he is the victim of a terrible disease and understands his helplessness. He again stared over the breast-work at the forest, and then, turning, went slowly rearward. He held his right wrist tenderly in his left hand as if the wounded arm was made of very brittle glass.

And the men in silence stared at the wood, then at the departing lieutenant; then at the wood, then at the lieutenant.

As the wounded officer passed from the line of battle, he was enabled to see many things which as a participant in the fight were unknown to him. He saw a general on a black horse gazing over the lines of blue infantry at the green woods which veiled his problems. An aide galloped furiously, dragged his horse suddenly to a halt, saluted, and presented a paper. It was, for a wonder, precisely like a historical painting.

To the rear of the general and his staff a group, composed of a bugler, two or three orderlies, and the bearer of the corps standard, all upon maniacal horses, were working like slaves to hold their ground, preserve their respectful interval, while the shells boomed in the air about them, and caused their chargers to make furious quivering leaps.

A battery, a tumultuous and shining mass, was swirling toward the right. The wild thud of hoofs, the cries of the riders shouting blame and praise, menace and encouragement, and, last, the roar of the wheels, the slant of the glistening guns, brought the lieutenant to an intent pause. The battery swept in curves that stirred the heart; it made halts as dramatic as the crash of a wave on the rocks, and when it fled onward this aggregation of wheels, levers, motors had a beautiful unity, as if it were a missile. The sound of it was a war-chorus that reached into the depths of man's emotion.

The lieutenant, still holding his arm as if it were of glass, stood watching this battery until all detail of it was lost, save the figures of the riders, which rose and fell and waved lashes over the black mass.

Later, he turned his eyes toward the battle, where the shooting sometimes crackled like bush-fires, sometimes sputtered with exasperating irregularity, and sometimes reverberated like the thunder. He saw the smoke rolling upward and saw crowds of men who ran and cheered, or stood and blazed away at the inscrutable distance.

He came upon some stragglers, and they told him how to find the field hospital. They described its exact location. In fact, these men, no longer having part in the battle, knew more of it than others. They told the performance of every corps, every division, the opinion of every general. The lieutenant, carrying his wounded arm rearward, looked upon them with wonder.

At the roadside a brigade was making coffee and buzzing with talk like a girls' boarding school. Several officers came out to him and inquired concerning things of which he knew nothing. One, seeing his arm, began to scold. "Why, man, that's no way to do. You want to fix that thing." He appropriated the lieutenant and the lieutenant's wound. He cut the sleeve and laid bare the arm, every nerve of which softly fluttered under his touch. He bound his handkerchief over the wound, scolding away in the meantime. His tone allowed one to think that he was in the habit of being wounded every day. The lieutenant hung his head, feeling, in this presence, that he did not know how to be correctly wounded.

The low white tents of the hospital were grouped around an old schoolhouse. There was here a singular commotion. In the foreground two ambulances inter-locked wheels in the deep mud. The drivers were tossing the blame of it back and forth, gesticulating and berating, while from the ambulances, both crammed with wounded, there came an occasional groan. An interminable crowd of bandaged men were coming and going. Great numbers sat under the trees nursing heads or arms or legs. There was a dispute of some kind raging on the steps of the schoolhouse. Sitting with his back against a tree a man with a face as grey as a new army blanket was serenely smoking a corncob pipe. The lieutenant wished to rush forward and inform him that he was dying.

A busy surgeon was passing near the lieutenant. "Good-morning," he said, with a friendly smile. Then he caught sight of the lieutenant's arm, and his face at once changed. "Well, let's have a look at it." He seemed possessed suddenly of a great contempt for the lieutenant. This wound evidently placed the latter on a very low social plane. The doctor cried out impatiently: "What mutton-head had tied it up that way anyhow?" The lieutenant answered, "Oh, a man."

When the wound was disclosed the doctor fingered it disdainfully. "Humph," he said. "You come along with me and I'll 'tend to you." His voice contained the same scorn as if he were saying: "You will 'have to go to jail."

The lieutenant had been very meek, but now his face flushed, and he looked into the doctor's eyes. "I guess I won't have it amputated," he said.

"Nonsense, man! Nonsense! Nonsense!" cried the doctor. "Come along, now. I won't amputate it. Come along. Don't be a baby."

"Let go of me," said the lieutenant, holding back wrathfully, his glance fixed upon the door of the old schoolhouse, as sinister to him as the portals of death.

And this is the story of how the lieutenant lost his arm. When he reached home, his sisters, his mother, his wife, sobbed for a long time at the sight of the flat sleeve. "Oh, well," he said, standing shame-faced amid these tears, "I don't suppose it matters so much as all that."

Herman Melville

The Lightning-Rod Man

What grand irregular thunder, thought I, standing on my hearth-stone among the Acroceraunian hills, as the scattered bolts boomed overhead, and crashed down among the valleys, every bolt followed by zigzag irradiations, and swift slants of sharp rain, which audibly rang, like a charge of spear-points, on my low shingled roof. I suppose, though, that the mountains hereabouts break and churn up the thunder, so that it is far more glorious here than on the plain. Hark!—some one at the door. Who is this that chooses a time of thunder for making calls? And why don't he, man-fashion, use the knocker, instead of making that doleful undertaker's clatter with his fist against the hollow panel? But let him in. Ah, here he comes. "Good day, sir:" an entire stranger. "Pray be seated." What is that strange-looking walking-stick he carries: "A fine thunder-storm, sir."

"Fine?—Awful!"

"You are wet. Stand here on the hearth before the fire."

"Not for worlds!"

The stranger still stood in the exact middle of the cottage, where he had first planted himself. His singularity impelled a closer scrutiny. A lean, gloomy figure. Hair dark and lank, mattedly streaked over his brow. His sunken pitfalls of eyes were ringed by indigo halos, and played with an innocuous sort of lightning: the gleam without the bolt. The whole man was dripping. He stood in a puddle on the bare oak floor: his strange walking-stick vertically resting at his side.

It was a polished copper rod, four feet long, lengthwise attached to a neat wooden staff, by insertion into two balls of greenish glass, ringed with copper bands. The metal rod terminated at the top tripodwise, in three keen tines, brightly gilt. He held the thing by the wooden part alone.

"Sir," said I, bowing politely, "have I the honor of a visit from that illustrious god, Jupiter Tonans? So stood he in the Greek status of old, grasping the lightning-bolt. If you be he, or his viceroy, I have to thank you for this noble storm you have brewed among our mountains. Listen: That was a glorious peal. Ah, to a lover of the majestic, it is a good thing to have the Thunderer himself in one's cottage. The thunder grows finer for that. But pray be seated. This old rush-bottomed arm-chair, I grant, is a poor substitute for your evergreen throne on Olympus; but, condescend to be seated."

While I thus pleasantly spoke, the stranger eyed me, half in wonder, and half in a strange sort of horror; but did not move a foot.

"Do, sir, be seated; you need to be dried ere going forth again."

I planted the chair invitingly on the broad hearth, where a little fire had been kindled that afternoon to dissipate the dampness, not the cold; for it was early in the month of September.

But without heeding my solicitation, and still standing in the middle of the floor, the stranger gazed at me portentously and spoke.

"Sir," said he, "excuse me; but instead of my accepting your invitation to be seated on the hearth there, I solemnly warn *you,* that you had best accept *mine,* and stand with me in the middle of the room. Good heavens!" he cried, start-ing—"there is another of those awful crashes. I warn you, sir, quit the hearth."

"Mr. Jupiter Tonans," said I, quietly rolling my body on the stone, "I stand very well here."

"Are you so horridly ignorant, then," he cried, "as not to know, that by far the most dangerous part of a house, during such a terrific tempest as this, is the fire-place?"

"Nay, I did not know that," involuntarily stepping upon the first board next to the stone.

The stranger now assumed such an unpleasant air of successful admonition, that—quite involuntarily again—I stepped back upon the hearth, and threw myself into the erectest, proudest posture I could command. But I said nothing.

"For Heaven's sake," he cried, with a strange mixture of alarm and intimida-tion—"for Heaven's sake, get off the hearth! Know you not, that the heated air and soot are conductors;—to say nothing of those immense iron fire-dogs? Quit the spot—I conjure—I command you."

"Mr. Jupiter Tonans, I am not accustomed to be commanded in my own house."

"Call me not by the pagan name. You are profane in this time of terror."

"Sir, will you be so good as to tell me your business? If you seek shelter from the storm, you are welcome, so long as you be civil; but if you come on business, open it forthwith. Who are you?"

"I am a dealer in lightning-rods," said the stranger, softening his tone; "my special business is—— Merciful heaven! what a crash!—Have you ever been struck—your premises, I mean? No? It's best to be provided;"—significantly rattling his metallic staff on the floor;—"by nature, there are no castles in thunder-storms; yet, say but the word, and of this cottage I can make a Gibraltar by a few waves of this wand. Hark, what Himalayas of concussions!"

"You interrupted yourself; your special business you were about to speak of."

"My special business is to travel the country for orders for lightning-rods. This is my specimen-rod;" tapping his staff; "I have the best of references"—fumbling in his pockets. "In Criggan last month, I put up three-and-twenty rods on only five buildings."

"Let me see. Was it not at Criggan last week, about midnight on Saturday, that the steeple, the big elm, and the assembly-room cupola were struck? Any of your rods there?"

"Not on the tree and cupola, but the steeple."

"Of what use is your rod, then?"

"Of life-and-death use. But my workman was heedless. In fitting the rod at top to the steeple, he allowed a part of the metal to graze the tin sheeting. Hence the accident. Not my fault, but his. Hark!"

"Never mind. That clap burst quite loud enough to be heard without finger-pointing. Did you hear of the event at Montreal last year? A servant girl struck at her bed-side with a rosary in her hand; the beads being metal. Does your beat extend into the Canadas?"

"No. And I hear that there, iron rods only are in use. They should have *mine,* which are copper. Iron is easily fused. Then they draw out the rod so slender, that it has not body enough to conduct the full electric current. The metal melts; the building is destroyed. My copper rods never act so. Those Canadians are fools. Some of them knob the rod at the top, which risks a deadly explosion, instead of imperceptibly carrying down the current into the earth, as this sort of rod does. *Mine* is the only true rod. Look at it. Only one dollar a foot."

"This abuse of your own calling in another might make one distrustful with respect to yourself."

"Hark! The thunder becomes less muttering. It is nearing us, and nearing the earth, too. Hark! One crammed crash! All the vibrations made one by nearness. Another flash. Hold!"

"What do you?" I said, seeing him now, instantaneously relinquishing his staff, lean intently forward towards the window, with his right fore and middle fingers on his left wrist.

But ere the words had well escaped me, another exclamation escaped him.

"Crash! only three pulses—less than a third of a mile off—yonder, somewhere in that wood. I passed three stricken oaks there, ripped out new and glittering.

The oak draws lightning more than other timber, having iron in solution in its sap. Your floor here seems oak."

"Heart-of-oak. From the peculiar time of your call upon me, I suppose you purposely select stormy weather for your journeys. When the thunder is roaring, you deem it an hour peculiarly favorable for producing impressions favorable to your trade."

"Hark!—Awful!"

"For one who would arm others with fearlessness, you seem unbeseemingly timorous yourself. Common men choose fair weather for their travels: you choose thunder-storms; and yet——"

"That I travel in thunder-storms, I grant; but not without particular precautions, such as only a lightning-rod man may know. Hark! Quick—look at my specimen rod. Only one dollar a foot."

"A very fine rod, I dare say. But what are these particular precautions of yours? Yet first let me close yonder shutters; the slanting rain is beating through the sash. I will bar up."

"Are you mad? Know you not that yon iron bar is a swift conductor? Desist."

"I will simply close the shutters, then, and call my boy to bring me a wooden bar. Pray, touch the bell-pull there."

"Are you frantic? That bell-wire might blast you. Never touch bell wire in a thunder-storm, nor ring a bell of any sort."

"Nor those in belfries? Pray, will you tell me where and how one may be safe in a time like this? Is there any part of my house I may touch with hopes of my life?"

"There is; but not where you now stand. Come away from the wall. The current will sometimes run down a wall, and—a man being a better conductor than a wall—it would leave the wall and run into him. Swoop! *That* must have fallen very nigh. That must have been globular lightning."

"Very probably. Tell me at once, which is, in your opinion, the safest part of this house?"

"This room, and this one spot in it where I stand. Come hither."

"The reasons first."

"Hark!—after the flash the gust—the sashes shiver—the house, the house!— Come hither to me!"

"The reasons, if you please."

"Come hither to me!"

"Thank you again, I think I will try my old stand—the hearth. And now, Mr. Lightning-rod-man, in the pauses of the thunder, be so good as to tell me your reasons for esteeming this one room of the house the safest, and your own one standpoint there the safest spot in it."

There was now a little cessation of the storm for a while. The Lightning-rod man seemed relieved, and replied:—

"Your house is a one-storied house, with an attic and a cellar; this room is between. Hence its comparative safety. Because lightning sometimes passes from the clouds to the earth, and sometimes from the earth to the clouds. Do you comprehend?—and I choose the middle of the room, because, if the lightning should strike the house at all, it would come down the chimney or walls; so, obviously, the further you are from them, the better. Come hither to me, now."

"Presently. Something you just said, instead of alarming me, has strangely inspired confidence."

"What have I said?"

"You said that sometimes lightning flashes from the earth to the clouds."

"Aye, the returning-stroke, as it is called; when the earth, being overcharged with the fluid, flashes its surplus upward."

"The returning-stroke; that is, from earth to sky. Better and better. But come here on the hearth and dry yourself."

"I am better here, and better wet."

"How?"

"It is the safest thing you can do—Hark, again!—to get yourself thoroughly drenched in a thunder-storm. Wet clothes are better conductors than the body; and so, if the lightning strike, it might pass down the wet clothes without touching the body. The storm deepens again. Have you a rug in the house? Rugs are non-conductors. Get one, that I may stand on it here, and you, too. The skies blacken—it is dusk at noon. Hark!—the rug, the rug!"

I gave him one; while the hooded mountains seemed closing and tumbling into the cottage.

"And now, since our being dumb will not help us," said I, resuming my place, "let me hear your precautions in traveling during thunder-storms."

"Wait till this one is passed."

"Nay, proceed with the precautions. You stand in the safest possible place according to your own account. Go on."

"Briefly, then. I avoid pine-trees, high houses, lonely barns, upland pastures, running water, flocks of cattle and sheep, a crowd of men. If I travel on foot—as to-day—I do not walk fast; if in my buggy, I touch not its back or sides; if on horseback, I dismount and lead the horse. But of all things, I avoid tall men."

"Do I dream? Man avoid man? and in danger-time, too."

"Tall men in a thunder-storm I avoid. Are you so grossly ignorant as not to know, that the height of a six-footer is sufficient to discharge an electric cloud upon him? Are not lonely Kentuckians, ploughing, smit in the unfinished furrow? Nay, if the six-footer stand by running water, the cloud will sometimes *select* him as its conductor to that running water. Hark! Sure, yon black pinnacle is split. Yes, a man is a good conductor. The lightning goes through and through a man, but only peels a tree. But sir, you have kept me so long answering your questions, that I have not yet come to business. Will you order one of my rods? Look at this specimen one? See: it is of the best of copper. Copper's the best conductor. Your house is low; but being upon the mountains, that lowness does not one whit depress it. You mountaineers are most exposed. In mountainous countries the lightning-rod man should have most business. Look at the specimen, sir. One rod will answer for a house so small as this. Look over these recommendations. Only one rod, sir; cost, only twenty dollars. Hark! There go all the granite Taconics and Hoosics dashed together like pebbles. By the sound, that must have struck something. An elevation of five feet above the house will protect twenty feet radius all about the rod. Only twenty dollars, sir—a dollar a foot. Hark!—Dreadful!—Will you order? Will you buy? Shall I put down your name? Think of being a heap of charred offal, like a haltered horse burnt in his stall; and all in one flash!"

"You pretended envoy extraordinary and minister plenipotentiary to and from Jupiter Tonans," laughed I; "you mere man who come here to put you and your pipestem between clay and sky, do you think that because you can strike a bit of green light from the Leyden jar, that you can thoroughly evert the supernal bolt? Your rod rusts, or breaks, and where are you? Who has empowered you, you Tetzel, to peddle round your indulgences from divine ordinations? The hairs of our heads are numbered, and the days of our lives. In thunder as in sunshine, I stand at ease in the hands of my God. False negotiator, away! See, the scroll of the storm is rolled back; the house is unharmed; and in the blue heavens I read in the rainbow, that the Deity will not, of purpose, make war on man's earth."

"Impious wretch!" foamed the stranger, blackening in the face as the rainbow beamed, "I will publish your infidel notions."

The scowl grew blacker on his face; the indigo-circles enlarged round his eyes as the storm-rings round the midnight moon. He sprang upon me; his tri-forked thing at my heart.

I seized it; I snapped it; I dashed it; I trod it; and dragging the dark lightning-king out of my door, flung his elbowed, copper sceptre after him.

But spite of my treatment, and spite of my dissuasive talk of him to my neighbors, the Lightning-rod man still dwells in the land; still travels in storm-time, and drives a brave trade with the fears of man.

Nathaniel Hawthorne

Young Goodman Brown

Young Goodman Brown came forth at sunset into the street at Salem village; but put his head back, after crossing the threshold, to exchange a parting kiss with his young wife. And Faith, as the wife was aptly named, thrust her own pretty head into the street, letting the wind play with the pink ribbons of her cap while she called to Goodman Brown.

"Dearest heart," whispered she, softly and rather sadly, when her lips were close to his ear, "prithee put off your journey until sunrise and sleep in your own bed to-night. A lone woman is troubled with such dreams and such thoughts that she's afeared of herself sometimes. Pray tarry with me this night, dear husband, of all nights in the year."

"My love and my Faith," replied young Goodman Brown, "of all nights in the year, this one night must I tarry away from thee. My journey, as thou callest it, forth and back again, must needs be done 'twixt now and sunrise. What, my sweet, pretty wife, dost thou doubt me already, and we but three months married?"

"Then God bless you!" said Faith, with the pink ribbons; "and may you find all well when you come back."

"Amen!" cried Goodman Brown. "Say thy prayers, dear Faith, and go to bed at dusk, and no harm will come to thee."

So they parted; and the young man pursued his way until, being about to turn the corner by the meeting-house, he looked back and saw the head of Faith still peeping after him with a melancholy air, in spite of her pink ribbons.

"Poor little Faith!" thought he, for his heart smote him. "What a wretch am I to leave her on such an errand! She talks of dreams, too. Methought as she spoke there was trouble in her face, as if a dream had warned her what work is to be done tonight. But no, no; 't would kill her to think it. Well, she's a blessed angel on earth; and after this one night I'll cling to her skirts and follow her to heaven."

With this excellent resolve for the future, Goodman Brown felt himself justified in making more haste on his present evil purpose. He had taken a dreary road, darkened by all the gloomiest trees of the forest, which barely stood aside to let the narrow path creep through, and closed immediately behind. It was all as lonely as could be; and there is this peculiarity in such a solitude, that the traveller knows not who may be concealed by the innumerable trunks and the thick boughs overhead; so that with lonely footsteps he may yet be passing through an unseen multitude.

"There may be a devilish Indian behind every tree," said Goodman Brown to himself; and he glanced fearfully behind him as he added, "What if the devil himself should be at my very elbow!"

His head being turned back, he passed a crook of the road, and, looking forward again, beheld the figure of a man, in grave and decent attire, seated at the foot of an old tree. He arose at Goodman Brown's approach and walked onward side by side with him.

"You are late, Goodman Brown," said he. "The clock of the Old South was striking as I came through Boston, and that is full fifteen minutes agone."

"Faith kept me back a while," replied the young man, with a tremor in his voice, caused by the sudden appearance of his companion, though not wholly unexpected.

It was now deep dusk in the forest, and deepest in that part of it where these two were journeying. As nearly as could be discerned, the second traveller was about fifty years old, apparently in the same rank of life as Goodman Brown, and bearing a considerable resemblance to him, though perhaps more in expression than features. Still they might have been taken for father and son. And yet, though the elder person was as simply clad as the younger, and as simple in manner too, he had an indescribable air of one who knew the world, and who would not have felt abashed at the governor's dinner table or in King William's court, were it possible that his affairs should call him thither. But the only thing about him that could be fixed upon as remarkable was his staff, which bore the likeness of a great black snake, so curiously wrought that it might almost be seen to twist and wriggle itself like a living serpent. This, of course, must have been an ocular deception, assisted by the uncertain light.

"Come, Goodman Brown," cried his fellow-traveller, "this is a dull pace for the beginning of a journey. Take my staff, if you are so soon weary."

"Friend," said the other, exchanging his slow pace for a full stop, "having kept covenant by meeting thee here, it is my purpose now to return whence I came. I have scruples touching the matter thou wot'st of."

"Sayest thou so?" replied he of the serpent, smiling apart. "Let us walk on, nevertheless, reasoning as we go; and if I convince thee not thou shalt turn back. We are but a little way in the forest yet."

"Too far! too far!" exclaimed the goodman, unconsciously resuming his walk. "My father never went into the woods on such an errand, nor his father before him. We have been a race of honest men and good Christians since the days of the martyrs; and shall I be the first of the name of Brown that ever took this path and kept——"

"Such company, thou wouldst say," observed the elder person, interpreting his pause. "Well said, Goodman Brown! I have been as well acquainted with your family as with ever a one among the Puritans; and that's no trifle to say. I helped your grandfather, the constable, when he lashed the Quaker woman so smartly through the streets of Salem; and it was I that brought your father a pitch-pine knot, kindled at my own hearth, to set fire to an Indian village, in King Philip's war. They were my good friends, both; and many a pleasant walk have we had along this path, and returned merrily after midnight. I would fain be friends with you for their sake."

"If it be as thou sayest," replied Goodman Brown, "I marvel they never spoke of these matters; or, verily, I marvel not, seeing that the least rumor of the sort would have driven them from New England. We are a people of prayer, and good works to boot, and abide no such wickedness."

"Wickedness or not," said the traveller with the twisted staff, "I have a very general acquaintance here in New England. The deacons of many a church have drunk the communion wine with me; the selectmen of divers towns make me their chairman; and a majority of the Great and General Court are firm supporters of my interest. The governor and I, too—But these are state secrets."

"Can this be so?" cried Goodman Brown, with a stare of amazement at his undisturbed companion. "Howbeit, I have nothing to do with the governor and council; they have their own ways, and are no rule for a simple husbandman like me. But, were I to go on with thee, how should I meet the eye of that good old man, our minister, at Salem village? Oh, his voice would make me tremble both Sabbath day and lecture day."

Thus far the elder traveller had listened with due gravity; but now burst into a fit of irrepressible mirth, shaking himself so violently that his snake-like staff actually seemed to wriggle in sympathy.

"Ha! ha! ha!" shouted he again and again; then composing himself, "Well, go on, Goodman Brown, go on; but, prithee, don't kill me with laughing."

"Well, then, to end the matter at once," said Goodman Brown, considerably nettled, "there is my wife, Faith. It would break her dear little heart; and I'd rather break my own."

"Nay, if that be the case," answered the other, "e'en go thy ways, Goodman Brown. I would not for twenty old women like the one hobbling before us that Faith should come to any harm."

As he spoke he pointed his staff at a female figure on the path, in whom Goodman Brown recognized a very pious and exemplary dame, who had taught him his catechism in youth, and was still his moral and spiritual adviser, jointly with the minister and Deacon Gookin.

"A marvel, truly, that Goody Cloyse should be so far in the wilderness at nightfall," said he. "But with your leave, friend, I shall take a cut through the woods until we have left this Christian woman behind. Being a stranger to you, she might ask whom I was consorting with and whither I was going."

"Be it so," said his fellow-traveller. "Betake you to the woods, and let me keep the path."

Accordingly the young man turned aside, but took care to watch his companion, who advanced softly along the road until he had come within a staff's length of the old dame. She, meanwhile, was making the best of her way, with singular speed for so aged a woman, and mumbling some indistinct words—a prayer, doubtless—as she went. The traveller put forth his staff and touched her withered neck with what seemed the serpent's tail.

"The devil!" screamed the pious old lady.

"Then Goody Cloyse knows her old friend?" observed the traveller, confronting her and leaning on his writhing stick.

"Ah, forsooth, and is it your worship indeed?" cried the good dame. "Yea, truly is it, and in the very image of my old gossip, Goodman Brown, the grandfather of the silly fellow that now is. But—would your worship believe it?—my broomstick hath strangely disappeared, stolen, as I suspect, by that unhanged witch, Goody Cory, and that, too, when I was all anointed with the juice of smallage, and cinquefoil, and wolf's bane—"

"Mingled with fine wheat and the fat of a new-born babe," said the shape of old Goodman Brown.

"Ah, your worship knows the recipe," cried the old lady, cackling aloud. "So, as I was saying, being all ready for the meeting, and no horse to ride on, I made up my mind to foot it; for they tell me there is a nice young man to be taken into communion to-night. But now your good worship will lend me your arm, and we shall be there in a twinkling."

"That can hardly be," answered her friend. "I may not spare you my arm, Goody Cloyse; but here is my staff, if you will."

So saying, he threw it down at her feet, where, perhaps, it assumed life, being one of the rods which its owner had formerly lent to the Egyptian magi. Of this fact, however, Goodman Brown could not take cognizance. He had cast up his eyes in astonishment, and, looking down again, beheld neither Goody Cloyse nor the serpentine staff, but his fellow-traveller alone, who waited for him as calmly as if nothing had happened.

"That old woman taught me my catechism," said the young man; and there was a world of meaning in this simple comment.

They continued to walk onward, while the elder traveller exhorted his companion to make good speed and persevere in the path, discoursing so aptly that his arguments seemed rather to spring up in the bosom of his auditor than to be suggested by himself. As they went, he plucked a branch of maple to serve for a walking stick, and began to strip it of the twigs and little boughs, which were wet with evening dew. The moment his fingers touched them they became strangely withered and dried up as with a week's sunshine. Thus the pair proceeded, at a good free pace, until suddenly, in a gloomy hollow of the road, Goodman Brown sat himself down on the stump of a tree and refused to go any farther.

"Friend," said he, stubbornly, "my mind is made up. Not another step will I budge on this errand. What if a wretched old woman do choose to go to the devil when I thought she was going to heaven: is that any reason why I should quit my dear Faith and go after her?"

"You will think better of this by and by," said his acquaintance, composedly. "Sit here and rest yourself a while; and when you feel like moving again, there is my staff to help you along."

Without more words, he threw his companion the maple stick, and was as speedily out of sight as if he had vanished into the deepening gloom. The young man sat a few moments by the roadside, applauding himself greatly, and thinking with how clear a conscience he should meet the minister in his morning walk, nor shrink from the eye of good old Deacon Gookin. And what calm sleep would be his that very night, which was to have been spent so wickedly, but so purely and sweetly now, in the arms of Faith! Amidst these pleasant and praiseworthy meditations, Goodman Brown heard the tramp of horses along the road, and deemed it advisable to conceal himself within the verge of the forest, conscious of the guilty purpose that had brought him thither, though now so happily turned from it.

On came the hoof tramps and the voices of the riders, two grave old voices conversing soberly as they drew near. These mingled sounds appeared to pass along the road, within a few yards of the young man's hiding-place; but, owing doubtless to the depth of the gloom at that particular spot, neither the travellers nor their steeds were visible. Though their figures brushed the small boughs by the wayside, it could not be seen that they intercepted, even for a moment, the faint gleam from the strip of bright sky athwart which they must have passed. Goodman Brown alternately crouched and stood on tiptoe, pulling aside the branches and thrusting forth his head as far as he durst without discerning so much as a shadow. It vexed him the more, because he could have sworn, were such a thing possible, that he recognized the voices of the minister and Deacon Gookin, jogging along quietly, as they were wont to do, when bound to some ordination or ecclesiastical council. While yet within hearing, one of the riders stopped to pluck a switch.

"Of the two, reverend sir," said the voice like the deacon's, "I had rather miss an ordination dinner than to-night's meeting. They tell me that some of our community are to be here from Falmouth and beyond, and others from Connecticut and Rhode Island, besides several of the Indian powwows, who, after their fashion, know almost as much deviltry as the best of us. Moreover, there is a goodly young woman to be taken into communion."

"Mighty well, Deacon Gookin!" replied the solemn old tones of the minister. "Spur up, or we shall be late. Nothing can be done, you know, until I get on the ground."

The hoofs clattered again; and the voices, talking so strangely in the empty air, passed on through the forest, where no church had ever been gathered or solitary Christian prayed. Whither, then, could these holy men be journeying so deep into the heathen wilderness? Young Goodman Brown caught hold of a tree for support, being ready to sink down on the ground, faint and overburdened with the heavy sickness of his heart. He looked up to the sky, doubting whether there really was a heaven above him. Yet there was the blue arch, and the stars brightening in it.

"With heaven above and Faith below, I will yet stand firm against the devil!" cried Goodman Brown.

While he still gazed upward into the deep arch of the firmament and had lifted his hands to pray, a cloud, though no wind was stirring, hurried across the zenith and hid the brightening stars. The blue sky was still visible, except directly overhead, where this black mass of cloud was sweeping swiftly northward. Aloft in the air, as if from the depths of the cloud, came a confused and doubtful sound of voices. Once the listener fancied that he could distinguish the accents of towns-people of his own, men and women, both pious and ungodly, many of whom he had met at the communion table, and had seen others rioting at the tavern. The next moment, so indistinct were the sounds, he doubted whether he had heard aught but the murmur of the old forest, whispering without a wind. Then came a stronger swell of those familiar tones, heard daily in the sunshine at Salem village, but never until now from a cloud of night. There was one voice of a young woman, uttering lamentations, yet with an uncertain sorrow, and entreating for some favor, which, perhaps, it would grieve her to obtain; and all the unseen multitude, both saints and sinners, seemed to encourage her onward.

"Faith!" shouted Goodman Brown, in a voice of agony and desperation; and the echoes of the forest mocked him, crying, "Faith! Faith!" as if bewildered wretches were seeking her all through the wilderness.

The cry of grief, rage, and terror was yet piercing the night, when the unhappy husband held his breath for a response. There was a scream, drowned immediately in a louder murmur of voices, fading into far-off laughter, as the dark cloud swept away, leaving the clear and silent sky above Goodman Brown. But something fluttered lightly down through the air and caught on the branch of a tree. The young man seized it, and beheld a pink ribbon.

"My Faith is gone!" cried he, after one stupefied moment. "There is no good on earth; and sin is but a name. Come, devil; for to thee is this world given."

And, maddened with despair, so that he laughed loud and long, did Goodman Brown grasp his staff and set forth again, at such a rate that he seemed to fly along the forest path rather than to walk or run. The road grew wilder and drearier and more faintly traced, and vanished at length, leaving him in the heart of the dark wilderness, still rushing onward with the instinct that guides mortal men to evil. The whole forest was peopled with frightful sounds—the creaking of the trees, the howling of wild beasts, and the yell of Indians; while sometimes the wind tolled like a distant church bell, and sometimes gave a broad roar around the traveller, as if all Nature were laughing him to scorn. But he was himself the chief horror of the scene, and shrank not from its other horrors.

"Ha! ha! ha!" roared Goodman Brown when the wind laughed at him. "Let us hear which will laugh loudest. Think not to frighten me with your deviltry. Come witch, come wizard, come Indian powwow, come devil himself, and here comes Goodman Brown. You may as well fear him as he fear you."

In truth, all through the haunted forest there could be nothing more frightful than the figure of Goodman Brown. On he flew among the black pines, brandishing his staff with frenzied gestures, now giving vent to an inspiration of horrid blasphemy, and now shouting forth such laughter as set all the echoes of the forest laughing like demons around him. The fiend in his own shape is less hideous than when he rages in the breast of man. Thus sped the demoniac on his course, until, quivering among the trees, he saw a red light before him, as when the felled trunks and branches of a clearing have been set on fire, and throw up their lurid blaze against the sky, at the hour of midnight. He paused, in a lull of the tempest that had driven him onward, and heard the swell of what seemed a hymn, rolling solemnly from a distance with the weight of many voices. He knew the tune; it was a familiar one in the choir of the village meeting-house. The verse died heavily away, and was lengthened by a chorus, not of human voices, but of all the sounds of the benighted wilderness pealing in awful harmony together. Goodman Brown cried out, and his cry was lost to his own ear by its unison with the cry of the desert.

In the interval of silence he stole forward until the light glared full upon his eyes. At one extremity of an open space, hemmed in by the dark wall of the forest, arose a rock, bearing some rude, natural resemblance either to an altar or a pulpit, and surrounded by four blazing pines, their tops aflame, their stems untouched, like candles at an evening meeting. The mass of foliage that had overgrown the summit of the rock was all on fire, blazing high into the night and fitfully illuminating the whole field. Each pendent twig and leafy festoon was in a blaze. As the red light arose and fell, a numerous congregation alternately shone forth, then disappeared in shadow, and again grew, as it were, out of the darkness, peopling the heart of the solitary woods at once.

"A grave and dark-clad company," quoth Goodman Brown.

In truth they were such. Among them, quivering to and fro between gloom and splendor, appeared faces that would be seen next day at the council board of the province, and others which, Sabbath after Sabbath, looked devoutly heavenward, and benignantly over the crowded pews, from the holiest pulpits in the land. Some affirm that the lady of the governor was there. At least there were high dames well known to her, and wives of honored husbands, and widows, a great multitude, and ancient maidens, all of excellent repute, and fair young girls, who trembled lest their mothers should espy them. Either the sudden gleams of light flashing over the obscure field bedazzled Goodman Brown, or he recognized a score of the church members of Salem village famous for their especial sanctity. Good old Deacon Gookin had arrived, and waited at the skirts of that venerable saint, his revered pastor. But, irreverently consorting with these grave, reputable, and pious people, these elders of the church, these chaste dames and dewy virgins, there were men of dissolute lives and women of spotted fame, wretches given over to all mean and filthy vice, and suspected even of horrid crimes. It was strange to see that the good shrank not from the wicked, nor were the sinners abashed by the saints. Scattered also among their pale-faced enemies were the Indian priests, or powwows, who had often scared their native forest with more hideous incantations than any known to English witchcraft.

"But where is Faith?" thought Goodman Brown; and, as hope came into his heart, he trembled.

Another verse of the hymn arose, a slow and mournful strain, such as the pious love, but joined to words which expressed all that our nature can conceive of sin, and darkly hinted at far more. Unfathomable to mere mortals is the lore of fiends. Verse after verse was sung; and still the chorus of the desert swelled between like the deepest tone of a mighty organ; and with the final peal of that dreadful anthem there came a sound, as if the roaring wind, the rushing streams, the howling beasts, and every other voice of the unconcerted wilderness were mingling and according with the voice of guilty man in homage to the prince of all. The four blazing pines threw up a loftier flame, and obscurely discovered shapes and visages of horror on the smoke wreaths above the impious assembly. At the same moment the fire on the rock shot redly forth and formed a glowing arch above its base, where now appeared a figure. With reverence be it spoken, the figure bore no slight similitude, both in garb and manner, to some grave divine of the New England churches.

"Bring forth the converts!" cried a voice that echoed through the field and rolled into the forest.

At the word, Goodman Brown stepped forth from the shadow of the trees and approached the congregation, with whom he felt a loathful brotherhood by the sympathy of all that was wicked in his heart. He could have well-nigh sworn that the shape of his own dead father beckoned him to advance, looking downward from a smoke wreath, while a woman, with dim features of despair, threw out her hand to warn him back. Was it his mother? But he had no power to retreat one step, nor to resist, even in thought, when the minister and good old Deacon

Gookin seized his arms and led him to the blazing rock. Thither came also the
slender form of a veiled female, led between Goody Cloyse, that pious teacher of
the catechism, and Martha Carrier, who had received the devil's promise to be
queen of hell. A rampant hag was she. And there stood the proselytes beneath the
canopy of fire.

"Welcome, my children," said the dark figure, "to the communion of your
race. Ye have found thus young your nature and your destiny. My children, look
behind you!"

They turned; and flashing forth, as it were, in a sheet of flame, the fiend
worshippers were seen; the smile of welcome gleamed darkly on every visage.

"There," resumed the sable form, "are all whom ye have reverenced from
youth. Ye deemed them holier than yourselves, and shrank from your own sin,
contrasting it with their lives of righteousness and prayerful aspirations heavenward. Yet here are they all in my worshipping assembly. This night it shall be
granted you to know their secret deeds: how hoary-bearded elders of the church
have whispered wanton words to the young maids of their households; how many
a woman, eager for widows' weeds, has given her husband a drink at bedtime
and let him sleep his last sleep in her bosom; how beardless youths have made
haste to inherit their fathers' wealth; and how fair damsels—blush not, sweet
ones—have dug little graves in the garden, and bidden me, the sole guest, to an
infant's funeral. By the sympathy of your human hearts for sin ye shall scent out
all the places—whether in church, bedchamber, street, field, or forest—where
crime has been committed, and shall exult to behold the whole earth one stain of
guilt, one mighty blood spot. Far more than this. It shall be yours to penetrate, in
every bosom, the deep mystery of sin, the fountain of all wicked arts, and which
inexhaustibly supplies more evil impulses than human power—than my power at
its utmost—can make manifest in deeds. And now, my children, look upon each
other."

They did so; and, by the blaze of the hell-kindled torches, the wretched man
beheld his Faith, and the wife her husband, trembling before that unhallowed
altar.

"Lo, there ye stand, my children," said the figure, in a deep and solemn tone,
almost sad with its despairing awfulness, as if his once angelic nature could yet
mourn for our miserable race. "Depending upon one another's hearts, ye had still
hoped that virtue were not all a dream. Now are ye undeceived. Evil is the nature
of mankind. Evil must be your only happiness. Welcome again, my children, to
the communion of your race."

"Welcome," repeated the fiend worshippers, in one cry of despair and triumph.

And there they stood, the only pair, as it seemed, who were yet hesitating on
the verge of wickedness in this dark world. A basin was hollowed, naturally, in
the rock. Did it contain water, reddened by the lurid light? or was it blood? or,
perchance, a liquid flame? Herein did the shape of evil dip his hand and prepare
to lay the mark of baptism upon their foreheads, that they might be partakers of
the mystery of sin, more conscious of the secret guilt of others, both in deed and

thought, than they could now be of their own. The husband cast one look at his pale wife, and Faith at him. What polluted wretches would the next glance show them to each other, shuddering alike at what they disclosed and what they saw!

"Faith! Faith!" cried the husband, "look up to heaven, and resist the wicked one."

Whether Faith obeyed he knew not. Hardly had he spoken when he found himself amid calm night and solitude, listening to a roar of the wind which died heavily away through the forest. He staggered against the rock, and felt it chill and damp; while a hanging twig, that had been all on fire, besprinkled his cheek with the coldest dew.

The next morning young Goodman Brown came slowly into the street of Salem village, staring around him like a bewildered man. The good old minister was taking a walk along the graveyard to get an appetite for breakfast and meditate his sermon, and bestowed a blessing, as he passed, on Goodman Brown. He shrank from the venerable saint as if to avoid an anathema. Old Deacon Gookin was at domestic worship, and the holy words of his prayer were heard through the open window. "What God doth the wizard pray to?" quoth Goodman Brown. Goody Cloyse, that excellent old Christian, stood in the early sunshine at her own lattice, catechizing a little girl who had brought her a pint of morning's milk. Goodman Brown snatched away the child as from the grasp of the fiend himself. Turning the corner by the meeting-house, he spied the head of Faith, with the pink ribbons, gazing anxiously forth, and bursting into such joy at sight of him that she skipped along the street and almost kissed her husband before the whole village. But Goodman Brown looked sternly and sadly into her face, and passed on without a greeting.

Had Goodman Brown fallen asleep in the forest and only dreamed a wild dream of a witch-meeting?

Be it so if you will; but, alas! it was a dream of evil omen for young Goodman Brown. A stern, a sad, a darkly meditative, a distrustful, if not a desperate man did he become from the night of that fearful dream. On the Sabbath day, when the congregation were singing a holy psalm, he could not listen because an anthem of sin rushed loudly upon his ear and drowned all the blessed strain. When the minister spoke from the pulpit with power and fervid eloquence, and, with his hand on the open Bible, of the sacred truths of our religion, and of saint-like lives and triumphant deaths, and of future bliss or misery unutterable, then did Goodman Brown turn pale, dreading lest the roof should thunder down upon the gray blasphemer and his hearers. Often, waking suddenly at midnight, he shrank from the bosom of Faith; and at morning or eventide, when the family knelt down at prayer, he scowled and muttered to himself, and gazed sternly at his wife, and turned away. And when he had lived long, and was borne to his grave a hoary corpse, followed by Faith, an aged woman, and children and grandchildren, a goodly procession, besides neighbors not a few, they carved no hopeful verse upon his tombstone, for his dying hour was gloom.

Katherine Mansfield

Revelations

From eight o'clock in the morning until about half-past eleven Monica Tyrell suffered from her nerves, and suffered so terribly that these hours were—agonizing, simply. It was not as though she could control them. "Perhaps if I were ten years younger . . ." she would say. For now that she was thirty-three she had a queer little way of referring to her age on all occasions, of looking at her friends with grave, childish eyes and saying: "Yes, I remember how twenty years ago . . ." or of drawing Ralph's attention to the girls—real girls—with lovely youthful arms and throats and swift hesitating movements who sat near them in restaurants. "Perhaps if I were ten years younger . . ."

"Why don't you get Marie to sit outside your door and absolutely forbid anybody to come near your room until you ring your bell?"

"Oh, if it were as simple as that!" She threw her little gloves down and pressed her eyelids with her fingers in the way he knew so well. "But in the first place I'd be so conscious of Marie sitting there, Marie shaking her finger at Rudd and Mrs. Moon, Marie as a kind of cross between a wardress and a nurse for mental cases! And then, there's the post. One can't get over the fact that the post comes, and once it has come, who—who—could wait until eleven for the letters?"

His eyes grew bright; he quickly, lightly clasped her. *"My* letters, darling?"

"Perhaps," she drawled, softly, and she drew her hand over his reddish hair, smiling too, but thinking: "Heavens! What a stupid thing to say!"

But this morning she had been awakened by one great slam of the front door. Bang. The flat shook. What was it? She jerked up in bed, clutching the eiderdown; her heart beat. What could it be? Then she heard voices in the passage. Marie knocked, and, as the door opened, with a sharp tearing rip out flew the blind and the curtains, stiffening, flapping, jerking. The tassel of the blind knocked—knocked against the window. "Eh-h, *voilà!"* cried Marie, setting down the tray and running. *"C'est le vent, Madame. C'est un vent insupportable."*

Up rolled the blind; the window went up with a jerk; a whitey-greyish light filled the room. Monica caught a glimpse of a huge pale sky and a cloud like a torn shirt dragging across before she hid her eyes with her sleeve.

"Marie! the curtains! Quick, the curtains!" Monica fell back into the bed and then "Ring-ting-a-ping-ping, ring-ting-a-ping-ping." It was the telephone. The limit of her suffering was reached; she grew quite calm. "Go and see, Marie."

"It is Monsieur. To know if Madame will lunch at Princes' at one-thirty to-day." Yes, it was Monsieur himself. Yes, he had asked that the message be given to Madame immediately. Instead of replying, Monica put her cup down and asked Marie in a small wondering voice what time it was. It was half-past nine. She lay still and half closed her eyes. "Tell Monsieur I cannot come," she said gently. But as the door shut, anger—anger suddenly gripped her close, close, violent, half strangling her. How dared he? How dared Ralph do such a thing when he knew how agonizing her nerves were in the morning! Hadn't she explained and described and even—though lightly, of course; she couldn't say such a thing directly—given him to understand that this was the one unforgivable thing?

And then to choose this frightful windy morning. Did he think it was just a fad of hers, a little feminine folly to be laughed at and tossed aside? Why, only last night she had said: "Ah, but you must take me seriously, too." And he had replied: "My darling, you'll not believe me, but I know you infinitely better than you know yourself. Every delicate thought and feeling I bow to, I treasure. Yes, laugh! I love the way your lip lifts"—and he had leaned across the table—"I don't care who sees that I adore all of you. I'd be with you on a mountain-top and have all the searchlights of the world play upon us."

"Heavens!" Monica almost clutched her head. Was it possible he had really said that? How incredible men were! And she had loved him—how could she have loved a man who talked like that. What had she been doing ever since that dinner party months ago, when he had seen her home and asked if he might come and "see again that slow Arabian smile"? Oh, what nonsense—what utter nonsense—and yet she remembered at the time a strange deep thrill unlike anything she had ever felt before.

"Coal! Coal! Coal! Old iron! Old iron! Old iron!" sounded from below. It was all over. Understand her? He had understood nothing. That ringing her up on a windy morning was immensely significant. Would he understand that? She could almost have laughed. "You rang me up when the person who understood me simply couldn't have." It was the end. And when Marie said: "Monsieur replied he would be in the vestibule in case Madame changed her mind," Monica said: "No, not verbena, Marie. Carnations. Two handfuls."

A wild white morning, a tearing, rocking wind. Monica sat down before the mirror. She was pale. The maid combed back her dark hair—combed it all back—and her face was like a mask, with pointed eyelids and dark red lips. As she stared at herself in the blueish shadowy glass she suddenly felt—oh, the strangest, most tremendous excitement filling her slowly, slowly, until she wanted to fling out her arms, to laugh, to scatter everything, to shock Marie, to cry: "I'm free. I'm free. I'm free as the wind." And now all this vibrating, trembling, exciting, flying world was hers. It was her kingdom. No, no, she belonged to nobody but Life.

"That will do, Marie," she stammered. "My hat, my coat, my bag. And now get me a taxi." Where was she going? Oh, anywhere. She could not stand this silent flat, noiseless Marie, this ghostly, quiet, feminine interior. She must be out; she must be driving quickly—anywhere, anywhere.

"The taxi is there, Madame." As she pressed open the big outer doors of the flats the wild wind caught her and floated her across the pavement. Where to? She got in, and smiling radiantly at the cross, cold-looking driver, she told him to take her to her hairdresser's. What would she have done without her hairdresser? Whenever Monica had nowhere else to go to or nothing on earth to do she drove there. She might just have her hair waved, and by that time she'd have thought out a plan. The cross, cold driver drove at a tremendous pace, and she let herself be hurled from side to side. She wished he would go faster and faster. Oh, to be free of Princes' at one-thirty, of being the tiny kitten in the swansdown basket, of being the Arabian, and the grave, delighted child and the little wild creature. . . . "Never again," she cried aloud, clenching her small fist. But the cab had stopped, and the driver was standing holding the door open for her.

The hairdresser's shop was warm and glittering. It smelled of soap and burnt paper and wallflower brilliantine. There was Madame behind the counter, round, fat, white, her head like a powder-puff rolling on a black satin pin-cushion. Monica always had the feeling that they loved her in this shop and understood her—the real her—far better than many of her friends did. She was her real self here, and she and Madame had often talked—quite strangely—together. Then there was George who did her hair, young, dark, slender George. She was really fond of him.

But to-day—how curious! Madame hardly greeted her. Her face was whiter than ever, but rims of bright red showed round her blue bead eyes, and even the rings on her pudgy fingers did not flash. They were cold, dead, like chips of glass. When she called through the wall-telephone to George there was a note in her voice that had never been there before. But Monica would not believe this. No, she refused to. It was just her imagination. She sniffed greedily the warm, scented air, and passed behind the velvet curtain into the small cubicle.

Her hat and jacket were off and hanging from the peg, and still George did not come. This was the first time he had ever not been there to hold the chair for her, to take her hat and hang up her bag, dangling it in his fingers as though it were something he'd never seen before—something fairy. And how quiet the shop was! There was not a sound even from Madame. Only the wind blew, shaking the old house; the wind hooted, and the portraits of Ladies of the Pompadour Period looked down and smiled, cunning and sly. Monica wished she hadn't come. Oh, what a mistake to have come! Fatal. Fatal. Where was George? If he didn't appear the next moment she would go away. She took off the white kimono. She didn't want to look at herself any more. When she opened a big pot of cream on the glass shelf her fingers trembled. There was a tugging feeling at her heart as though her happiness—her marvellous happiness—were trying to get free.

"I'll go. I'll not stay." She took down her hat. But just at that moment steps sounded, and looking in the mirror, she saw George bowing in the doorway.

How queerly he smiled! It was the mirror of course. She turned round quickly. His lips curled back in a sort of grin, and—wasn't he unshaved?—he looked almost green in the face.

"Very sorry to have kept you waiting," he mumbled, sliding, gliding forward. Oh, no, she wasn't going to stay. "I'm afraid," she began. But he had lighted the gas and laid the tongs across, and was holding out the kimono.

"It's a wind," he said. Monica submitted. She smelled his fresh young fingers pinning the jacket under her chin. "Yes, there is a wind," said she, sinking back into the chair. And silence fell. George took out the pins in his expert way. Her hair tumbled back, but he didn't hold it as he usually did, as though to feel how fine and soft and heavy it was. He didn't say it "was in a lovely condition." He let it fall, and, taking a brush out of a drawer, he coughed faintly, cleared his throat and said dully: "Yes, it's a pretty strong one, I should say it was."

She had no reply to make. The brush fell on her hair. Oh, oh, how mournful, how mournful! It fell quick and light, it fell like leaves; and then it fell heavy, tugging like the tugging at her heart. "That's enough," she cried, shaking herself free.

"Did I do it too much?" asked George. He crouched over the tongs. "I'm sorry." There came the smell of burnt paper—the smell she loved—and he swung the hot tongs round in his hand, staring before him. "I shouldn't be surprised if it rained." He took up a piece of her hair, when—she couldn't bear it any longer—she stopped him. She looked at him; she saw herself looking at him in the white kimono like a nun. "Is there something the matter here? Has something happened?" But George gave a half shrug and a grimace. "Oh, no, Madame. Just a little occurrence." And he took up the piece of hair again. But, oh, she wasn't deceived. That was it. Something awful had happened. The silence—really, the silence seemed to come drifting down like flakes of snow. She shivered. It was cold in the little cubicle, all cold and glittering. The nickel taps and jets and sprays looked somehow almost malignant. The wind rattled the window-frame; a piece of iron banged, and the young man went on changing the tongs, crouching over her. Oh, how terrifying Life was, thought Monica. How dreadful. It is the loneliness which is so appalling. We whirl along like leaves, and nobody knows—nobody cares where we fall, in what black river we float away. The tugging feeling seemed to rise into her throat. It ached, ached; she longed to cry. "That will do," she whispered. "Give me the pins." As he stood beside her, so submissive, so silent, she nearly dropped her arms and sobbed. She couldn't bear any more. Like a wooden man the gay young George still slid, glided, handed her her hat and veil, took the note, and brought back the change. She stuffed it into her bag. Where was she going now?

George took a brush. "There is a little powder on your coat," he murmured. He brushed it away. And then suddenly he raised himself and, looking at Monica, gave a strange wave with the brush and said: "The truth is, Madame, since you are an old customer—my little daughter died this morning. A first child"—and then his white face crumpled like paper, and he turned his back on her and began brushing the cotton kimono. "Oh, oh," Monica began to cry. She

ran out of the shop into the taxi. The driver, looking furious, swung off the seat
and slammed the door again. "Where to?"

"Princes'," she sobbed. And all the way there she saw nothing but a tiny wax
doll with a feather of gold hair, lying meek, its tiny hands and feet crossed. And
then just before she came to Princes' she saw a flower shop full of white flowers.
Oh, what a perfect thought. Lilies-of-the-valley, and white pansies, double white
violets and white velvet ribbon. . . . From an unknown friend. . . . From one
who understands. . . . For a Little Girl. . . . She tapped against the window,
but the driver did not hear; and, anyway, they were at Princes' already.

Isaac Babel

Awakening

All the folk in our circle—brokers, shopkeepers, clerks in banks and
steamship offices—used to have their children taught music. Our fathers, seeing
no other escape from their lot, had thought up a lottery, building it on the bones
of little children. Odessa more than other towns was seized by the craze. And in
fact, in the course of ten years or so our town supplied the concert platforms of
the world with infant prodigies. From Odessa came Mischa Elman, Zimbalist,
Gabrilowitsch. Odessa witnessed the first steps of Jascha Heifetz.

When a lad was four or five, his mother took the puny creature to Zagursky's.
Mr. Zagursky ran a factory of infant prodigies, a factory of Jewish dwarfs in lace
collars and patent-leather pumps. He hunted them out in the slums of the
Moldavanka, in the evil-smelling courtyards of the Old Market. Mr. Zagursky
charted the first course, then the children were shipped off to Professor Auer in
St. Petersburg. A wonderful harmony dwelt in the souls of those wizened creatures with their swollen blue hands. They became famous virtuosi. My father
decided that I should emulate them. Though I had, as a matter of fact, passed the
age limit set for infant prodigies, being now in my fourteenth year, my shortness
and lack of strength made it possible to pass me off as an eight-year-old. Herein
lay father's hope.

I was taken to Zagursky's. Out of respect for my grandfather, Mr. Zagursky
agreed to take me on at the cut rate of a rouble a lesson. My grandfather Leivi-
Itzkhok was the laughingstock of the town, and its chief adornment. He used to
walk about the streets in a top hat and old boots, dissipating doubt in the darkest
of cases. He would be asked what a Gobelin was, why the Jacobins betrayed
Robespierre, how you made artificial silk, what a Caesarean section was. And my
grandfather could answer these questions. Out of respect for his learning and

craziness, Mr. Zagursky only charged us a rouble a lesson. And he had the devil of a time with me, fearing my grandfather, for with me there was nothing to be done. The sounds dripped from my fiddle like iron filings, causing even me excruciating agony, but father wouldn't give in. At home there was no talk save of Mischa Elman, exempted by the Tsar himself from military service. Zimbalist, father would have us know, had been presented to the King of England and had played at Buckingham Palace. The parents of Gabrilowitsch had bought two houses in St. Petersburg. Infant prodigies brought wealth to their parents, but though my father could have reconciled himself to poverty, fame he must have.

"It's not possible," people feeding at his expense would insinuate, "it's just not possible that the grandson of such a grandfather . . ."

But what went on in my head was quite different. Scraping my way through the violin exercises, I would have books by Turgenev or Dumas on my music stand. Page after page I devoured as I deedled away. In the daytime I would relate impossible happenings to the kids next door; at night I would commit them to paper. In our family, composition was a hereditary occupation. Grandfather Leivi-Itzkhok, who went cracked as he grew old, spent his whole life writing a tale entitled "The Headless Man." I took after him.

Three times a week, laden with violin case and music, I made my reluctant way to Zagursky's place on Witte (formerly Dvoryanskaya) Street. There Jewish girls aflame with hysteria sat along the wall awaiting their turn, pressing to their feeble knees violins exceeding in dimensions the exalted persons they were to play to at Buckingham Palace.

The door to the sanctum would open, and from Mr. Zagursky's study there would stagger big-headed, freckled children with necks as thin as flower stalks and an epileptic flush on their cheeks. The door would bang to, swallowing up the next dwarf. Behind the wall, straining his throat, the teacher sang and waved his baton. He had ginger curls and frail legs, and sported a big bow tie. Manager of a monstrous lottery, he populated the Moldavanka and the dark culs-de-sac of the Old Market with the ghosts of pizzicato and cantilena. Afterward old Professor Auer lent these strains a diabolical brilliance.

In this crew I was quite out of place. Though like them in my dwarfishness, in the voice of my forebears I perceived inspiration of another sort.

The first step was difficult. One day I left home laden like a beast of burden with violin case, violin, music, and twelve roubles in cash—payment for a month's tuition. I was going along Nezhin Street; to get to Zagursky's I should have turned into Dvoryanskaya, but instead of that I went up Tiraspolskaya and found myself at the harbor. The allotted time flew past in the part of the port where ships went after quarantine. So began my liberation. Zagursky's saw me no more: affairs of greater moment occupied my thoughts. My pal Nemanov and I got into the habit of slipping aboard the S.S. *Kensington* to see an old salt named Trottyburn. Nemanov was a year younger than I. From the age of eight onward he had been doing the most ingenious business deals you can imagine. He had a wonderful head for that kind of thing, and later on amply fulfilled his youthful promise. Now he is a New York millionaire, director of General Motors, a company no less powerful than Ford. Nemanov took me along with him because I silently obeyed all his orders. He used to buy pipes smuggled in by Mr. Trottyburn. They were made in Lincoln by the old sailor's brother.

"Gen'lemen," Mr. Trottyburn would say to us, "take my word, the pets must be made with your own hands. Smoking a factory-made pipe—might as well shove an enema in your mouth. D'you know who Benvenuto Cellini was? He was a grand lad. My brother in Lincoln could tell you about him. Live and let live is my brother's motto. He's got it into his head that you just has to make the pets with your own hands, and not with no one else's. And who are we to say him no, gen'lemen?"

Nemanov used to sell Trottyburn's pipes to bank-managers, foreign consuls, well-to-do Greeks. He made a hundred percent on them.

The pipes of the Lincolnshire master breathed poetry. In each one of them thought was invested, a drop of eternity. A little yellow eye gleamed in their mouthpieces, and their cases were lined with satin. I tried to picture the life in Old England of Matthew Trottyburn, the last master-pipemaker, who refused to swim with the tide.

"We can't but agree, gen'lemen, that the pets has to be made with your own hands."

The heavy waves by the sea wall swept me further and further away from our house, impregnated with the smell of leeks and Jewish destiny. From the harbor I migrated to the other side of the breakwater. There on a scrap of sandspit dwelt the boys from Primorskaya Street. Trouserless from morn till eve, they dived under wherries, sneaked coconuts for dinner, and awaited the time when boats would arrive from Kherson and Kamenka laden with watermelons, which melons it would be possible to break open against moorings.

To learn to swim was my dream. I was ashamed to confess to those bronzed lads that, born in Odessa, I had not seen the sea till I was ten, and at fourteen didn't know how to swim.

How slow was my acquisition of the things one needs to know! In my childhood, chained to the Gemara, I had led the life of a sage. When I grew up I started climbing trees.

But swimming proved beyond me. The hydrophobia of my ancestors—Spanish rabbis and Frankfurt money-changers—dragged me to the bottom. The waves refused to support me. I would struggle to the shore pumped full of salt water and feeling as though I had been flayed, and return to where my fiddle and music lay. I was fettered to the instruments of my torture, and dragged them about with me. The struggle of rabbis versus Neptune continued till such time as the local water-god took pity on me. This was Yefim Nikitich Smolich, proofreader of the *Odessa News*. In his athletic breast there dwelt compassion for Jewish children, and he was the god of a rabble of rickety starvelings. He used to collect them from the bug-infested joints on the Moldavanka, take them down to the sea, bury them in the sand, do gym with them, dive with them, teach them songs. Roasting in the perpendicular sunrays, he would tell them tales about fishermen and wild beasts. To grownups Nikitich would explain that he was a natural philosopher.

The Jewish kids used to roar with laughter at his tales, squealing and snuggling up to him like so many puppies. The sun would sprinkle them with creeping freckles, freckles of the same color as lizards.

Silently, out of the corner of his eye, the old man had been watching my duel with the waves. Seeing that the thing was hopeless, that I should simply never learn to swim, he included me among the permanent occupants of his heart. That cheerful heart of his was with us there all the time; it never went careering off anywhere else, never knew covetousness and never grew disturbed. With his sunburned shoulders, his superannuated gladiator's head, his bronzed and slightly bandy legs, he would lie among us on the other side of the mole, lord and master of those melon-sprinkled, paraffin-stained waters. I came to love that man, with the love that only a lad suffering from hysteria and headaches can feel for a real man. I was always at his side, always trying to be of service to him.

He said to me:

"Don't you get all worked up. You just strengthen your nerves. The swimming will come of itself. How d'you mean, the water won't hold you? Why shouldn't it hold you?"

Seeing how drawn I was to him, Nikitich made an exception of me alone of all his disciples. He invited me to visit the clean and spacious attic where he lived in an ambience of straw mats, showed me his dogs, his hedgehog, his tortoise, and his pigeons. In return for this wealth I showed him a tragedy I had written the day before.

"I was sure you did a bit of scribbling," said Nikitich. "You've the look. You're looking in *that* direction all the time; no eyes for anywhere else."

He read my writings, shrugged a shoulder, passed a hand through his stiff gray curls, paced up and down the attic.

"One must suppose," he said slowly, pausing after each word, "one must suppose that there's a spark of the divine fire in you."

We went out into the street. The old man halted, struck the pavement with his stick, and fastened his gaze upon me.

"Now what is it you lack? Youth's no matter—it'll pass with the years. What you lack is a feeling for nature."

He pointed with his stick at a tree with a reddish trunk and a low crown.

"What's that tree?"

I didn't know.

"What's growing on that bush?"

I didn't know this either. We walked together across the little square on the Alexandrovsky Prospect. The old man kept poking his stick at trees; he would seize me by the shoulder when a bird flew past, and he made me listen to the various kinds of singing.

"What bird is that singing?"

I knew none of the answers. The names of trees and birds, their division into species, where birds fly away to, on which side the sun rises, when the dew falls thickest—all these things were unknown to me.

"And you dare to write! A man who doesn't live in nature, as a stone does or an animal, will never in all his life write two worthwhile lines. Your landscapes are like descriptions of stage props. In heaven's name, what have your parents been thinking of for fourteen years?"

What *had* they been thinking of? Of protested bills of exchange, of Mischa Elman's mansions. I didn't say anything to Nikitich about that, but just kept mum.

At home, over dinner, I couldn't touch my food. It just wouldn't go down.

"A feeling for nature," I thought to myself. "Goodness, why did that never enter my head? Where am I to find someone who will tell me about the way birds sing and what trees are called? What do *I* know about such things? I might perhaps recognize lilac, at any rate when it's in bloom. Lilac and acacia—there are acacias along De Ribas and Greek Streets."

At dinner father told a new story about Jascha Heifetz. Just before he got to Robinat's he had met Mendelssohn, Jascha's uncle. It appeared that the lad was getting eight hundred roubles a performance. Just work out how much that comes to at fifteen concerts a month!

I did, and the answer was twelve thousand a month. Multiplying and carrying four in my head, I glanced out of the window. Across the cement courtyard, his cloak swaying in the breeze, his ginger curls poking out from under his soft hat, leaning on his cane, Mr. Zagursky, my music teacher, was advancing. It must be admitted he had taken his time in spotting my truancy. More than three months had elapsed since the day when my violin had grounded on the sand by the breakwater.

Mr. Zagursky was approaching the main entrance. I dashed to the back door, but the day before it had been nailed up for fear of burglars. Then I locked myself in the privy. In half an hour the whole family had assembled outside the door. The women were weeping. Aunt Bobka, exploding with sobs, was rubbing her fat shoulder against the door. Father was silent. Finally he started speaking, quietly and distinctly as he had never before spoken in his life.

"I am an officer," said my father. "I own real estate. I go hunting. Peasants pay me rent. I have entered my son in the Cadet Corps. I have no need to worry about my son."

He was silent again. The women were sniffling. Then a terrible blow descended on the privy door. My father was hurling his whole body against it, stepping back and then throwing himself forward.

"I am an officer," he kept wailing. "I go hunting. I'll kill him. This is the end."

The hook sprang from the door, but there was still a bolt hanging onto a single nail. The women were rolling about on the floor, grasping father by the legs. Crazy, he was trying to break loose. Father's mother came over, alerted by the hubbub.

"My child," she said to him in Hebrew, "our grief is great. It has no bounds. Only blood was lacking in our house. I do not wish to see blood in our house."

Father gave a groan. I heard his footsteps retreating. The bolt still hung by its last nail.

I sat it out in my fortress till nightfall. When all had gone to bed, Aunt Bobka took me to grandmother's. We had a long way to go. The moonlight congealed on bushes unknown to me, on trees that had no name. Some anonymous bird emitted a whistle and was extinguished, perhaps by sleep. What bird was it? What was it called? Does dew fall in the evening? Where is the constellation of the Great Bear? On what side does the sun rise?

We were going along Post Office Street. Aunt Bobka held me firmly by the hand so that I shouldn't run away. She was right to. I was thinking of running away.

Henry James

The Tree of Knowledge

It was one of the secret opinions, such as we all have, of Peter Brench that his main success in life would have consisted in his never having committed himself about the work, as it was called, of his friend Morgan Mallow. This was a subject on which it was, to the best of his belief, impossible with veracity to quote him, and it was nowhere on record that he had, in the connexion, on any occasion and in any embarrassment, either lied or spoken the truth. Such a triumph had its honour even for a man of other triumphs—a man who had reached fifty, who had escaped marriage, who had lived within his means, who had been in love with Mrs. Mallow for years without breathing it, and who, last not least, had judged himself once for all. He had so judged himself in fact that he felt an extreme and general humility to be his portion; yet there was nothing that made him think so well of his parts as the course he had steered so often through the shallows just mentioned. It became thus a real wonder that the friends in whom he had most confidence were just those with whom he had most reserves. He couldn't tell Mrs. Mallow—or at least he supposed, excellent man, he couldn't—that she was the one beautiful reason he had never married; any more than he could tell her husband that the sight of the multiplied marbles in that gentleman's studio was an affliction of which even time had never blunted the edge. His victory, however, as I have intimated, in regard to these productions, was not simply in his not having let it out that he deplored them; it was, remarkably, in his not having kept it in by anything else.

The whole situation, among these good people, was verily a marvel, and there was probably not such another for a long way from the spot that engages us—the point at which the soft declivity of Hampstead began at that time to confess in broken accents to Saint John's Wood. He despised Mallow's statues and adored

Reprinted by permission of John Farquharson, Ltd.

Mallow's wife, and yet was distinctly fond of Mallow, to whom, in turn, he was equally dear. Mrs. Mallow rejoiced in the statues—though she preferred, when pressed, the busts; and if she was visibly attached to Peter Brench it was because of his affection for Morgan. Each loved the other moreover for the love borne in each case to Lancelot, whom the Mallows respectively cherished as their only child and whom the friend of their fireside identified as the third—but decidedly the handsomest—of his godsons. Already in the old years it had come to that— that no one, for such a relation, could possibly have occurred to any of them, even to the baby itself, but Peter. There was luckily a certain independence, of the pecuniary sort, all round: the Master could never otherwise have spent his solemn *Wanderjahre* in Florence and Rome, and continued by the Thames as well as by the Arno and the Tiber to add unpurchased group to group and model, for what was too apt to prove in the event mere love, fancyheads of celebrities either too busy or too buried—too much of the age or too little of it—to sit. Neither could Peter, lounging in almost daily, have found time to keep the whole complicated tradition so alive by his presence. He was massive but mild, the depositary of these mysteries—large and loose and ruddy and curly, with deep tones, deep eyes, deep pockets, to say nothing of the habit of long pipes, soft hats and brownish greyish weather-faded clothes, apparently always the same.

He had "written," it was known, but had never spoken, never spoken in particular of that; and he had the air (since, as was believed, he continued to write) of keeping it up in order to have something more—as if he hadn't at the worst enough—to be silent about. Whatever his air, at any rate, Peter's occasional unmentioned prose and verse were quite the result of an impulse to maintain the purity of his taste by establishing still more firmly the right relation of fame to feebleness. The little green door of his domain was in a garden-wall on which the discoloured stucco made patches, and in the small detached villa behind it every-thing was old, the furniture, the servants, the books, the prints, the immemorial habits and the new improvements. The Mallows, at Carrara Lodge, were within ten minutes, and the studio there was on their little land, to which they had added, in their happy faith, for building it. This was the good fortune, if it was not the ill, of her having brought him in marriage a portion that put them in a manner at their ease and enabled them thus, on their side, to keep it up. And they did keep it up—they always had—the infatuated sculptor and his wife, for whom nature had refined on the impossible by relieving them of the sense of the difficult. Morgan had at all events everything of the sculptor but the spirit of Phidias—the brown velvet, the becoming *beretto,* the "plastic" presence, the fine fingers, the beautiful accent in Italian and the old Italian factotum. He seemed to make up for everything when he addressed Egidio with the "tu" and waved him to turn one of the rotary pedestals of which the place was full. They were tremendous Italians at Carrara Lodge, and the secret of the part played by this fact in Peter's life was in a large degree that it gave him, sturdy Briton as he was, just the amount of "going abroad" he could bear. The Mallows were all his Italy, but it was in a measure for Italy he liked them. His one worry was that Lance—to which they had shortened his godson—was, in spite of a public school, perhaps a shade too Italian. Morgan meanwhile looked like somebody's flattering idea of somebody's own person as expressed in the great room provided at the Uffizi Museum for the general illustration of that idea by eminent hands. The Master's sole regret that he hadn't been born rather to the brush than to the chisel sprang from his wish that he might have contributed to that collection.

It appeared with time at any rate to be to the brush that Lance had been born; for Mrs. Mallow, one day when the boy was turning twenty, broke it to their friend, who shared, to the last delicate morsel, their problems and pains, that it seemed as if nothing would really do but that he should embrace the career. It had been impossible longer to remain blind to the fact that he was gaining no glory at Cambridge, where Brench's own college had for a year tempered its tone to him as for Brench's own sake. Therefore why renew the vain form of preparing him for the impossible? The impossible—it had become clear—was that he should be anything but an artist.

"Oh dear, dear!" said poor Peter.

"Don't you believe in it?" asked Mrs. Mallow, who still, at more than forty, had her violet velvet eyes, her creamy satin skin and her silken chestnut hair.

"Believe in what?"

"Why in Lance's passion."

"I don't know what you mean by 'believing in it.' I've never been unaware, certainly, of his disposition, from his earliest time, to daub and draw; but I confess I've hoped it would burn out."

"But why should it," she sweetly smiled, "with his wonderful heredity? Passion is passion—though of course indeed *you,* dear Peter, know nothing of that. Has the Master's ever burned out?"

Peter looked off a little and, in his familiar formless way, kept up for a moment, a sound between a smothered whistle and a subdued hum. "Do you think he's going to be another Master?"

She seemed scarce prepared to go that length, yet she had on the whole a marvellous trust. "I know what you mean by that. Will it be a career to incur the jealousies and provoke the machinations that have been at times almost too much for his father? Well—say it may be, since nothing but clap-trap, in these dreadful days, *can,* it would seem, make its way, and since, with the curse of refinement and distinction, one may easily find one's self begging one's bread. Put it at the worst—say he *has* the misfortune to wing his flight further than the vulgar taste of his stupid countrymen can follow. Think, all the same, of the happiness—the same the Master has had. He'll *know.*"

Peter looked rueful. "Ah but *what* will he know?"

"Quiet joy!" cried Mrs. Mallow, quite impatient and turning away.

II

He had of course before long to meet the boy himself on it and to hear that practically everything was settled. Lance was not to go up again, but to go instead to Paris where, since the die was cast, he would find the best advantages. Peter had always felt he must be taken as he was, but had never perhaps found him so much of that pattern as on this occasion. "You chuck Cambridge then altogether? Doesn't that seem rather a pity?"

Lance would have been like his father, to his friend's sense, had he had less humour, and like his mother had he had more beauty. Yet it was a good middle way for Peter that, in the modern manner, he was, to the eye, rather the young stockbroker than the young artist. The youth reasoned that it was a question of time—there was such a mill to go through, such an awful lot to learn. He had talked with fellows and had judged. "One has got, today," he said, "don't you see? to know."

His interlocutor, at this, gave a groan. "Oh hang it, *don't* know!"

Lance wondered. "Don't? Then what's the use—?"

"The use of what?"

"Why of anything. Don't you think I've talent?"

Peter smoked away for a little in silence; then went on: "It isn't knowledge, it's ignorance that—as we've been beautifully told—is bliss."

"Don't you think I've talent?" Lance repeated.

Peter, with his trick of queer kind demonstrations, passed his arm round his godson and held him a moment. "How do I know?"

"Oh," said the boy, "if it's your own ignorance you're defending—!"

Again, for a pause, on the sofa, his godfather smoked. "It isn't. I've the misfortune to be omniscient."

"Oh, well," Lance laughed again, "if you know *too* much—!"

"That's what I do, and it's why I'm so wretched."

Lance's gaiety grew. "Wretched? Come, I say!"

"But I forgot," his companion went on—"you're not to know about that. It would indeed for you too make the too much. Only I'll tell you what I'll do." And Peter got up from the sofa. "If you'll go up again I'll pay your way at Cambridge."

Lance stared, a little rueful in spite of being still more amused. "Oh Peter! You disapprove so of Paris?"

"Well, I'm afraid of it."

"Ah I see!"

"No, you don't see—yet. But you will—that is you would. And you mustn't."

The young man thought more gravely. "But one's innocence, already—!"

"Is considerably damaged? Ah that won't matter," Peter persisted—"we'll patch it up here."

"Here? Then you want me to stay at home?"

Peter almost confessed to it. "Well, we're so right—we four together—just as we are. We're so safe. Come, don't spoil it."

The boy, who had turned to gravity, turned from this, on the real pressure in his friend's tone, to consternation. "Then what's a fellow to be?"

"My particular care. Come, old man"—and Peter now fairly pleaded—"*I'll* look out for you."

Lance, who had remained on the sofa with his legs out and his hands in his pockets watched him with eyes that showed suspicion. Then he got up. "You think there's something the matter with me—that I can't make a success."

"Well, what do you call a success?"

Lance thought again. "Why the best sort, I suppose, is to please one's self. Isn't that the sort that, in spite of cabals and things, is—in his own peculiar line—the Master's?"

There were so much too many things in this question to be answered at once that they practically checked the discussion, which became particularly difficult in the light of such renewed proof that, though the young man's innocence might, in the course of his studies, as he contended, somewhat have shrunken, the finer essence of it still remained. That was indeed exactly what Peter had assumed and what above all he desired: yet perversely enough it gave him a chill. The boy believed in the cabals and things, believed in the peculiar line, believed, to be brief, in the Master. What happened a month or two later wasn't that he went up again at the expense of his godfather, but that a fortnight after he had got settled in Paris this personage sent him fifty pounds.

He had meanwhile at home, this personage, made up his mind to the worst; and what that might be had never yet grown quite so vivid to him as when, on his presenting himself one Sunday night, as he never failed to do, for supper, the mistress of Carrara Lodge met him with an appeal as to—of all things in the world—the wealth of the Canadians. She was earnest, she was even excited. "Are many of them *really* rich?"

He had to confess he knew nothing about them, but he often thought afterwards of that evening. The room in which they sat was adorned with sundry specimens of the Master's genius, which had the merit of being, as Mrs. Mallow herself frequently suggested, of an unusually convenient size. They were indeed of dimensions not customary in the products of the chisel, and they had the singularity that, if the objects and features intended to be small looked too large, the objects and features intended to be large looked too small. The Master's idea, either in respect to this matter or to any other, had in almost any case, even after years, remained undiscoverable to Peter Brench. The creations that so failed to reveal it stood about on pedestals and brackets, on tables and shelves, a little staring white population, heroic, idyllic, allegoric, mythic, symbolic, in which "scale" had so strayed and lost itself that the public square and the chimney-piece seemed to have changed places, the monumental being all diminutive and the diminutive all monumental; branches at any rate, markedly, of a family in which stature was rather oddly irrespective of function, age and sex. They formed, like the Mallows themselves, poor Brench's own family—having at least to such a degree the note of familiarity. The occasion was one of those he had long ago learnt to know and to name—short flickers of the faint flame, soft gusts of a kinder air. Twice a year regularly the Master believed in his fortune, in addition to believing all the year round in his genius. This time it was to be made by a bereaved couple from Toronto, who had given him the handsomest order for a tomb to three lost children, each of whom they desired to see, in the composition, emblematically and characteristically represented.

Such was naturally the moral of Mrs. Mallow's question: if their wealth was to be assumed, it was clear, from the nature of their admiration, as well as from mysterious hints thrown out (they were a little odd!) as to other possibilities of the same mortuary sort, that their further patronage might be; and not less evident that should the Master become at all known in those climes nothing would be more inevitable than a run of Canadian custom. Peter had been present before at runs of custom, colonial and domestic—present at each of those of which the aggregation had left so few gaps in the marble company round him; but it was his habit never at these junctures to prick the bubble in advance. The fond illusion, while it lasted, eased the wound of elections never won, the long ache of medals and diplomas carried off, on every chance, by every one but the Master; it moreover lighted the lamp that would glimmer through the next eclipse. They lived, however, after all—as it was always beautiful to see—at a height scarce susceptible of ups and downs. They strained a point at times charmingly, strained it to admit that the public was here and there not too bad to buy; but they would have been nowhere without their attitude that the Master was always too good to sell. They were at all events deliciously formed, Peter often said to himself, for their fate; the Master had a vanity, his wife had a loyalty, of which success, depriving these things of innocence, would have diminished the merit and the grace. Any one could be charming under a charm, and as he looked about him at a world of prosperity more void of proportion even than the Master's museum he wondered if he knew another pair that so completely escaped vulgarity.

"What a pity Lance isn't with us to rejoice!" Mrs. Mallow on this occasion sighed at supper.

"We'll drink to the health of the absent," her husband replied, filling his friend's glass and his own and giving a drop to their companion; "but we must hope he's preparing himself for a happiness much less like this of ours this evening—excusable as I grant it to be!—than like the comfort we have always (whatever has happened or has not happened) been able to trust ourselves to enjoy. The comfort," the Master explained leaning back in the pleasant lamplight and firelight, holding up his glass and looking round at his marble family, quartered more or less, a monstrous brood, in every room—"the comfort of art in itself!"

Peter looked a little shyly at his wine. "Well—I don't care what you may call it when a fellow doesn't—but Lance must learn to *sell,* you know. I drink to his acquisition of the secret of a base popularity!"

"Oh yes, *he* must sell," the boy's mother, who was still more, however, this seemed to give out, the Master's wife, rather artlessly allowed.

"Ah," the sculptor after a moment confidently pronounced, "Lance *will.* Don't be afraid. He'll have learnt."

"Which is exactly what Peter," Mrs. Mallow gaily returned—"why in the world were you so perverse, Peter?—wouldn't when he told him hear of."

Peter, when this lady looked at him with accusatory affection—a grace on her part not infrequent—could never find a word; but the Master, who was always all amenity and tact, helped him out now as he had often helped him before. "That's his old idea, you know—on which we've so often differed: his theory that the artist should be all impulse and instinct. *I* go in of course for a certain amount to school. Not too much—but a due proportion. There's where his protest came in," he continued to explain to his wife, "as against what *might,* don't you see? be in question for Lance."

"Ah well"—and Mrs. Mallow turned the violet eyes across the table at the subject of this discourse—"he's sure to have meant of course nothing but good. Only that wouldn't have prevented him, if Lance *had* taken his advice, from being in effect horribly cruel."

They had a sociable way of talking of him to his face as if he had been in the clay or—at most—in the plaster, and the Master was unfailingly generous. He might have been waving Egidio to make him revolve. "Ah but poor Peter wasn't so wrong as to what it may after all come to that he *will* learn."

"Oh but nothing artistically bad," she urged—still, for poor Peter, arch and dewy.

"Why just the little French tricks," said the Master: on which their friend had to pretend to admit, when pressed by Mrs. Mallow, that these aesthetic vices had been the objects of his dread.

III

"I know now," Lance said to him the next year, "why you were so much against it." He had come back supposedly for a mere interval and was looking about him at Carrara Lodge, where indeed he had already on two or three occasions since his expatriation briefly reappeared. This had the air of a longer holiday. "Something rather awful has happened to me. It *isn't* so very good to know."

"I'm bound to say high spirits don't show in your face," Peter was rather ruefully forced to confess. "Still, are you very sure you do know?"

"Well, I at least know about as much as I can bear." These remarks were exchanged in Peter's den, and the young man, smoking cigarettes, stood before the fire with his back against the mantel. Something of his bloom seemed really to have left him.

Poor Peter wondered. "You're clear then as to what in particular I wanted you not to go for?"

"In particular?" Lance thought. "It seems to me that in particular there can have been only one thing."

They stood for a little sounding each other. "Are you quite sure?"

"Quite sure I'm a beastly duffer? Quite—by this time."

"Oh!"—and Peter turned away as if almost with relief.

"It's *that* that isn't pleasant to find out."

"Oh I don't care for 'that,' " said Peter, presently coming round again. "I mean I personally don't."

"Yet I hope you can understand a little that I myself should!"

"Well, what do you mean by it?" Peter sceptically asked.

And on this Lance had to explain—how the upshot of his studies in Paris had inexorably proved a mere deep doubt of his means. These studies had so waked him up that a new light was in his eyes; but what the new light did was really to show him too much. "Do you know what's the matter with me? I'm too horribly intelligent. Paris was really the last place for me. I've learnt what I can't do."

Poor Peter stared—it was a staggerer; but even after they had had, on the subject, a longish talk in which the boy brought out to the full the hard truth of his lesson, his friend betrayed less pleasure than usually breaks into a face to the happy tune of "I told you so!" Poor Peter himself made now indeed so little a point of having told him so that Lance broke ground in a different place a day or two after. "What was it then that—before I went—you were afraid I should find out?" This, however, Peter refused to tell him—on the ground that if he hadn't yet guessed perhaps he never would, and that in any case nothing at all for either of them was to be gained by giving the thing a name. Lance eyed him on this an instant with the bold curiosity of youth—with the air indeed of having in his mind two or three names, of which one or other would be right. Peter nevertheless, turning his back again, offered no encouragement, and when they parted afresh it was with some show of impatience on the side of the boy. Accordingly on their next encounter Peter saw at a glance that he had now, in the interval, divined and that, to sound his note, he was only waiting till they should find themselves alone. This he had soon arranged and he then broke straight out. "Do you know your conundrum has been keeping me awake? But in the watches of the night the answer came over me—so that, upon my honour, I quite laughed out. Had you been supposing I had to go to Paris to learn *that?*" Even now, to see him still so sublimely on his guard, Peter's young friend had to laugh afresh. "You won't give a sign till you're sure? Beautiful old Peter!" But Lance at last produced it. "Why, hang it, the truth about the Master."

It made between them for some minutes a lively passage, full of wonder for each at the wonder of the other. "Then how long have you understood—"

"The true value of his work? I understood it," Lance recalled, "as soon as I began to understand anything. But I didn't begin fully to do that, I admit, till I got *là-bas.*"

"Dear, dear!"—Peter gasped with retrospective dread.

"But for what have you taken me? I'm a hopeless muff—that I *had* to have rubbed in. But I'm not such a muff as the Master!" Lance declared.

"Then why did you never tell me—?"

"That I hadn't, after all"—the boy took him up—"remained such an idiot? Just because I never dreamed *you* knew. But I beg your pardon. I only wanted to spare you. And what I don't now understand is how the deuce then for so long you've managed to keep bottled."

Peter produced his explanation, but only after some delay, and with a gravity not void of embarrassment. "It was for your mother."

"Oh!" said Lance.

"And that's the great thing now—since the murder *is* out. I want a promise from you. I mean"—and Peter almost feverishly followed it up—"a vow from you, solemn and such as you owe me here on the spot, that you'll sacrifice anything rather than let her ever guess—"

"That *I've* guessed?"—Lance took it in. "I see." He evidently after a moment had taken in much. "But what is it you've in mind that I may have a chance to sacrifice?"

"Oh one has always something."

Lance looked at him hard. "Do you mean that *you've* had—?" The look he received back, however, so put the question by that he found soon enough another. "Are you really sure my mother doesn't know?"

Peter, after renewed reflexion, was really sure. "If she does she's too wonderful."

"But aren't we all too wonderful?"

"Yes," Peter granted—"but in different ways. The thing's so desperately important because your father's little public consists only, as you know then," Peter developed—"well, of how many?"

"First of all," the Master's son risked, "of himself. And last of all too. I don't quite see of whom else."

Peter had an approach to impatience. "Of your mother, I say—*always.*"

Lance cast it all up. "You absolutely feel that?"

"Absolutely."

"Well then with yourself that makes three."

"Oh *me!*"—and Peter, with a wag of his kind old head, modestly excused himself. "The number's at any rate small enough for any individual dropping out to be too dreadfully missed. Therefore, to put it in a nutshell, take care, my boy—that's all—that *you're* not!"

"I've got to keep on humbugging?" Lance wailed.

"It's just to warn you of the danger of your failing of that that I've seized this opportunity."

"And what do you regard in particular," the young man asked, "as the danger?"

"Why this certainly: that the moment your mother, who feels so strongly, should suspect your secret—well," said Peter desperately, "the fat would be on the fire."

Lance for a moment seemed to stare at the blaze. "She'd throw me over?"

"She'd throw *him* over."

"And come round to us?"

Peter, before he answered, turned away. "Come round to *you.*" But he had said enough to indicate—and, as he evidently trusted, to avert—the horrid contingency.

IV

Within six months again, none the less, his fear was on more occasions than one all before him. Lance had returned to Paris for another trial; then had reappeared at home and had had, with his father, for the first time in his life, one of the scenes that strike sparks. He described it with much expression to Peter, touching whom (since they had never done so before) it was the sign of a new reserve on the part of the pair at Carrara Lodge that they at present failed, on a matter of intimate interest, to open themselves—if not in joy then in sorrow—to their good friend. This produced perhaps practically between the parties a shade of alienation and a slight intermission of commerce—marked mainly indeed by the fact that to talk at his ease with his old playmate Lance had in general to come to see him. The closest if not quite the gayest relation they had yet known together was thus ushered in. The difficulty for poor Lance was a tension at home—begotten by the fact that his father wished him to be at least the sort of success he himself had been. He hadn't "chucked" Paris—though nothing appeared more vivid to him than that Paris had chucked him: he would go back again because of the fascination in trying, in seeing, in sounding the depths—in learning one's lesson, briefly, even if the lesson were simply that of one's impotence in the presence of one's larger vision. But what did the Master, all aloft in his senseless fluency, know of impotence, and what vision—to be called such— had he in all his blind life ever had? Lance, heated and indignant, frankly appealed to his godparent on this score.

His father, it appeared, had come down on him for having, after so long, nothing to show, and hoped that on his next return this deficiency would be repaired. *The* thing, the Master complacently set forth was—for any artist, however inferior to himself—at least to "do" something. "What can you do? That's all I ask!" *He* had certainly done enough, and there was no mistake about what he had to show. Lance had tears in his eyes when it came thus to letting his old friend know how great the strain might be on the "sacrifice" asked of him. It wasn't so easy to continue humbugging—as from son to parent—after feeling one's self despised for not grovelling in mediocrity. Yet a noble duplicity was what, as they intimately faced the situation, Peter went on requiring; and it was still for a time what his young friend, bitter and sore, managed loyally to comfort him with. Fifty pounds more than once again, it was true, rewarded both in London and in Paris the young friend's loyalty; none the less sensibly, doubtless, at the moment, that the money was a direct advance on a decent sum for which Peter had long since privately prearranged an ultimate function. Whether by these arts or others, at all events, Lance's just resentment was kept for a season— but only for a season—at bay. The day arrived when he warned his companion that he could hold out—or hold in—no longer. Carrara Lodge had had to listen to another lecture delivered from a great height—an infliction really heavier at last than, without striking back or in some way letting the Master have the truth, flesh and blood could bear.

"And what I don't see is," Lance observed with a certain irritated eye for what was after all, if it came to that, owing to himself too; "what I don't see is, upon my honour, how *you,* as things are going, can keep the game up."

"Oh the game for me is only to hold my tongue," said placid Peter. "And I have my reason."

"Still my mother?"

Peter showed a queer face as he had often shown it before—that is by turning it straight away. "What will you have? I haven't ceased to like her."

"She's beautiful—she's a dear of course," Lance allowed; "but what is she to you, after all, and what is it to you that, as to anything whatever, she should or she shouldn't?"

Peter, who had turned red, hung fire a little. "Well—it's all simply what I make of it."

There was now, however, in his young friend a strange, an adopted insistence. "What are you after all to *her?*"

"Oh nothing. But that's another matter."

"She cares only for my father," said Lance the Parisian.

"Naturally—and that's just why."

"Why you've wished to spare her?"

"Because she cares so tremendously much."

Lance took a turn about the room, but with his eyes still on his host. "How awfully—always—you must have liked her!"

"Awfully. Always," said Peter Brench.

The young man continued for a moment to muse—then stopped again in front of him. "Do you know how much she cares?" Their eyes met on it, but Peter, as if his own found something new in Lance's, appeared to hesitate, for the first time in an age, to say he did know. "*I've* only just found out," said Lance. "She came to my room last night, after being present, in silence and only with her eyes on me, at what I had had to take from him: she came—and she was with me an extraordinary hour."

He had paused again and they had again for a while sounded each other. Then something—and it made him suddenly turn pale—came to Peter. "She *does* know?"

"She does know. She let it all out to me—so as to demand of me no more than 'that,' as she said, of which she herself had been capable. She has always, always known," said Lance without pity.

Peter was silent a long time, during which his companion might have heard him gently breathe, and on touching him might have felt within him the vibration of a long low sound suppressed. By the time he spoke at last he had taken everything in. "Then I do see how tremendously much."

"Isn't it wonderful?" Lance asked.

"Wonderful," Peter mused.

"So that if your original effort to keep me from Paris was to keep me from knowledge—!" Lance exclaimed as if with a sufficient indication of this futility.

It might have been at the futility Peter appeared for a little to gaze. "I think it must have been—without my quite at the time knowing it—to keep *me!*" he replied at last as he turned away.

STORIES FOR FURTHER READING

Anton Chekhov

The Chorus Girl

One day when she was younger and better-looking, and when her voice was stronger, Nikolay Petrovitch Kolpakov, her adorer, was sitting in the outer room in her summer villa. It was intolerably hot and stifling. Kolpakov, who had just dined and drunk a whole bottle of inferior port, felt ill-humoured and out of sorts. Both were bored and waiting for the heat of the day to be over in order to go for a walk.

All at once there was a sudden ring at the door. Kolpakov, who was sitting with his coat off, in his slippers, jumped up and looked inquiringly at Pasha.

"It must be the postman or one of the girls," said the singer.

Kolpakov did not mind being found by the postman or Pasha's lady friends, but by way of precaution gathered up his clothes and went into the next room, while Pasha ran to open the door. To her great surprise in the doorway stood, not the postman and not a girl friend, but an unknown woman, young and beautiful, who was dressed like a lady, and from all outward signs was one.

The stranger was pale and was breathing heavily as though she had been running up a steep flight of stairs.

"What is it?" asked Pasha.

The lady did not at once answer. She took a step forward, slowly looked about the room, and sat down in a way that suggested that from fatigue, or perhaps illness, she could not stand; then for a long time her pale lips quivered as she tried in vain to speak.

"Is my husband here?" she asked at last, raising to Pasha her big eyes with their red tear-stained lids.

"Husband?" whispered Pasha, and was suddenly so frightened that her hands and feet turned cold. "What husband?" she repeated, beginning to tremble.

From *The Chorus Girl and Other Stories,* by Anton Chekhov, translated by Constance Garnett. Reprinted by permission of The Macmillan Company and Chatto and Windus, Ltd.

"My husband. . . . Nikolay Petrovitch Kolpakov."

"N . . . no, madam. . . . I . . . I don't know any husband."

A minute passed in silence. The stranger several times passed her handkerchief over her pale lips and held her breath to stop her inward trembling, while Pasha stood before her motionless, like a post, and looked at her with astonishment and terror.

"So you say he is not here?" the lady asked, this time speaking with a firm voice and smiling oddly.

"I . . . I don't know who it is you are asking about."

"You are horrid, mean, vile . . ." the stranger muttered, scanning Pasha with hatred and repulsion. "Yes, yes . . . you are horrid. I am very, very glad that at last I can tell you so!"

Pasha felt that on this lady in black with the angry eyes and white slender fingers she produced the impression of something horrid and unseemly, and she felt ashamed of her chubby red cheeks, the pock-mark on her nose, and the fringe on her forehead, which never could be combed back. And it seemed to her that if she had been thin, and had had no powder on her face and no fringe on her forehead, then she could have disguised the fact that she was not "respectable," and she would not have felt so frightened and ashamed to stand facing this unknown, mysterious lady.

"Where is my husband?" the lady went on. "Though I don't care whether he is here or not, but I ought to tell you that the money has been missed, and they are looking for Nikolay Petrovitch. . . . They mean to arrest him. That's your doing!"

The lady got up and walked about the room in great excitement. Pasha looked at her and was so frightened that she could not understand.

"He'll be found and arrested to-day," said the lady, and she gave a sob, and in that sound could be heard her resentment and vexation. "I know who has brought him to this awful position! Low, horrid creature! Loathsome, mercenary hussy!" The lady's lips worked and her nose wrinkled up with disgust. "I am helpless, do you hear, you low woman? . . . I am helpless; you are stronger than I am, but there is One to defend me and my children! God sees all! He is just! He will punish you for every tear I have shed, for all my sleepless nights! The time will come; you will think of me! . . ."

Silence followed again. The lady walked about the room and wrung her hands, while Pasha still gazed blankly at her in amazement, not understanding and expecting something terrible.

"I know nothing about it, madam," she said, and suddenly burst into tears.

"You are lying!" cried the lady, and her eyes flashed angrily at her. "I know all about it! I've known you a long time. I know that for the last month he has been spending every day with you!"

"Yes. What then? What of it? I have a great many visitors, but I don't force anyone to come. He is free to do as he likes."

"I tell you they have discovered that money is missing! He has embezzled money at the office! For the sake of such a . . . creature as you, for your sake he has actually committed a crime. Listen," said the lady in a resolute voice, stopping short, facing Pasha. "You can have no principles; you live simply to do harm—that's your object; but one can't imagine you have fallen so low that you have no trace of human feeling left! He has a wife, children. . . . If he is condemned and sent into exile we shall starve, the children and I. . . . Understand that! And yet there is a chance of saving him and us from destitution and disgrace. If I take them nine hundred roubles to-day they will let him alone. Only nine hundred roubles!"

"What nine hundred roubles?" Pasha asked softly. "I . . . I don't know. . . . I haven't taken it."

"I am not asking you for nine hundred roubles. . . . You have no money, and I don't want your money. I ask you for something else. . . . Men usually give expensive things to women like you. Only give me back the things my husband has given you!"

"Madam, he has never made me a present of anything!" Pasha wailed, beginning to understand.

"Where is the money? He has squandered his own and mine and other people's. . . . What has become of it all? Listen, I beg you! I was carried away by indignation and said a lot of nasty things to you, but I apologize. You must hate me, I know, but if you are capable of sympathy, put yourself in my position! I implore you to give me back the things!"

"H'm!" said Pasha, and she shrugged her shoulders. "I would with pleasure, but, God is my witness, he never made me a present of anything. Believe me, on my conscience. However, you are right, though," said the singer in confusion, "he did bring me two little things. Certainly I will give them back, if you wish it."

Pasha pulled out one of the drawers in the toilet-table and took out of it a hollow gold bracelet and a thin ring with a ruby in it.

"Here, madam!" she said, handing the visitor these articles.

The lady flushed and her face quivered. She was offended.

"What are you giving me?" she said. "I am not asking for charity, but for what does not belong to you . . . what you have taken advantage of your position to squeeze out of my husband . . . that weak, unhappy man. . . . On Thursday, when I saw you with my husband at the harbour you were wearing expensive brooches and bracelets. So it's no use your playing the innocent lamb to me! I ask you for the last time: will you give me the things, or not?"

"You are a queer one, upon my word," said Pasha, beginning to feel offended. "I assure you that, except the bracelet and this little ring, I've never seen a thing from your Nikolay Petrovitch. He brings me nothing but sweet cakes."

"Sweet cakes!" laughed the stranger. "At home the children have nothing to eat, and here you have sweet cakes. You absolutely refuse to restore the presents?"

Receiving no answer, the lady sat down and stared into space, pondering.

"What's to be done now?" she said. "If I don't get nine hundred roubles, he is ruined, and the children and I are ruined, too. Shall I kill this low woman or go down on my knees to her?"

The lady pressed her handkerchief to her face and broke into sobs.

"I beg you!" Pasha heard through the stranger's sobs. "You see you have plundered and ruined my husband. Save him. . . . You have no feeling for him, but the children . . . the children. . . . What have the children done?"

Pasha imagined little children standing in the street, crying with hunger, and she, too, sobbed.

"What can I do, madam?" she said. "You say that I am a low woman and that I have ruined Nikolay Petrovitch, and I assure you . . . before God Almighty, I have had nothing from him whatever. . . . There is only one girl in our chorus who has a rich admirer: all the rest of us live from hand to mouth on bread and kvass. Nikolay Petrovitch is a highly educated, refined gentleman, so I've made him welcome. We are bound to make gentlemen welcome."

"I ask you for the things! Give me the things! I am crying. . . . I am humiliating myself. . . . If you like I will go down on my knees! If you wish it!"

Pasha shrieked with horror and waved her hands. She felt that this pale, beautiful lady who expressed herself so grandly, as though she were on the stage, really might go down on her knees to her, simply from pride, from grandeur, to exalt herself and humiliate the chorus girl.

"Very well, I will give you things!" said Pasha, wiping her eyes and bustling about. "By all means. Only they are not from Nikolay Petrovitch. . . . I got these from other gentlemen. As you please. . . ."

Pasha pulled out the upper drawer of the chest, took out a diamond brooch, a coral necklace, some rings and bracelets, and gave them all to the lady.

"Take them if you like, only I've never had anything from your husband. Take them and grow rich," Pasha went on, offended at the threat to go down on her knees. "And if you are a lady . . . his lawful wife, you should keep him to yourself. I should think so! I did not ask him to come; he came of himself."

Through her tears the lady scrutinized the articles given her and said:

"This isn't everything. . . . There won't be five hundred roubles' worth here."

Pasha impulsively flung out of the chest a gold watch, a cigar-case and studs, and said, flinging up her hands:

"I've nothing else left. . . . You can search!"

The visitor gave a sigh, with trembling hands twisted the things up in her handkerchief, and went out without uttering a word, without even nodding her head.

The door from the next room opened and Kolpakov walked in. He was pale and kept shaking his head nervously, as though he had swallowed something very bitter; tears were glistening in his eyes.

"What presents did you make me?" Pasha asked, pouncing upon him. "When did you, allow me to ask you?"

"Presents . . . that's no matter!" said Kolpakov, and he tossed his head. "My God! She cried before you, she humbled herself. . . ."

"I am asking you, what presents did you make me?" Pasha cried.

"My God! She, a lady, so proud, so pure. . . . She was ready to go down on her knees to . . . to this wench! And I've brought her to this! I've allowed it!"

He clutched his head in his hands and moaned.

"No, I shall never forgive myself for this! I shall never forgive myself! Get away from me . . . you low creature!" he cried with repulsion, backing away from Pasha, and thrusting her off with trembling hands. "She would have gone down on her knees, and . . . and to you! Oh, my God!"

He rapidly dressed, and pushing Pasha aside contemptuously, made for the door and went out.

Pasha lay down and began wailing aloud. She was already regretting her things which she had given away so impulsively, and her feelings were hurt. She remembered how three years ago a merchant had beaten her for no sort of reason, and she wailed more loudly than ever.

Guy de Maupassant

The String

Along all the roads around Goderville the peasants and their wives were coming toward the little town, for it was market day. The men were proceeding with slow steps, the whole body bent forward at each movement of their long twisted legs, deformed by their hard work, by the weight on the plough which, at the same time, raised the left shoulder and distorted the figure, by the reaping of the wheat which made them spread their knees to get a firm stand, by all the slow and painful labours of the country. Their blouses, blue, starched, shining as if varnished, ornamented with a little design in white at the neck and wrists, puffed about their bony bodies, seemed like balloons ready to carry them off. From each of them a head, two arms, and two feet protruded.

Some led a cow or a calf at the end of a rope, and their wives, walking behind the animal, whipped its haunches with a leafy branch to hasten its progress. They carried large baskets on their arms from which, in some cases, chickens and, in others, ducks thrust out their heads. And they walked with a quicker, livelier step than their husbands. Their spare straight figures were wrapped in a scanty little shawl, pinned over their flat bosoms, and their heads were enveloped in a piece of white linen tightly pressed on the hair and surmounted by a cap.

Then a wagon passed at the jerky trot of a nag, shaking strangely, two men seated side by side and a woman in the bottom of the vehicle, the latter holding on to the sides to lessen the hard jolts.

In the square of Goderville there was a crowd, a throng of human beings and

From *Miss Harriet and Other Stories*, by Guy de Maupassant, translated by Ernest Boyd. Copyright 1923 by Alfred A. Knopf, Inc. Used by permission of Alfred A. Knopf, Inc.

animals mixed together. The horns of the cattle, the tall hats with a long nap of the rich peasant, and the headgear of the peasant women rose above the surface of the crowd. And the clamorous, shrill, screaming voices made a continuous and savage din which sometimes was dominated by the robust lungs of some country-man's laugh, or the long lowing of a cow tied to the wall of a house.

It all smacked of the stable, the dairy and the manure heap, of hay and sweat, giving forth that unpleasant odour, human and animal, peculiar to the people of the fields.

Maître Hauchecorne, of Bréauté, had just arrived at Goderville, and he was directing his steps toward the public square, when he perceived upon the ground a little piece of string. Maître Hauchecorne, economical like a true Norman, thought that everything useful ought to be picked up, and he stooped painfully, for he suffered from rheumatism. He took the bit of thin cord from the ground and was beginning to roll it carefully when he noticed Maître Malandain, the harness-maker, on the threshold of his door, looking at him. They had heretofore had business together on the subject of a halter, and they were on bad terms, being both good haters. Maître Hauchecorne was seized with a sort of shame to be seen thus by his enemy, picking a bit of string out of the dirt. He concealed his find quickly under his blouse, then in his trousers pocket; then he pretended to be still looking on the ground for something which he did not find, and he went towards the market, his head thrust forward, bent double by his pains.

He was soon lost in the noisy and slowly moving crowd, which was busy with interminable bargainings. The peasants looked at cows, went and came, per-plexed, always in fear of being cheated, not daring to decide, watching the vender's eye, ever trying to find the trick in the man and the flaw in the beast.

The women, having placed their great baskets at their feet, had taken out the poultry, which lay upon the ground, tied together by the feet, with terrified eyes and scarlet crests.

They heard offers, stated their prices with a dry air and impassive face, or perhaps, suddenly deciding on some proposed reduction, shouted to the customer who was slowly going away: "All right, Maître Anthime, I'll give it to you for that."

Then little by little the square was deserted, and the Angelus ringing at noon, those who lived too far away went to the different inns.

At Jourdain's the great room was full of people eating, as the big yard was full of vehicles of all kinds, carts, gigs, wagons, nondescript carts, yellow with dirt, mended and patched, raising their shafts to the sky like two arms, or perhaps with their shafts in the ground and their backs in the air.

Very near the diners seated at the table, the immense fireplace, filled with bright flames, cast a lively heat on the backs of the row on the right. Three spits were turning on which were chickens, pigeons, and legs of mutton; and an appetizing odour of roast meat and gravy dripping over the nicely browned skin rose from the hearth, increased the jovialness, and made everybody's mouth water.

All the aristocracy of the plough ate there, at Maître Jourdain's, tavern keeper and horse dealer, a clever fellow who had money.

The dishes were passed and emptied, as were the jugs of yellow cider. Everyone told his affairs, his purchases, and sales. They discussed the crops. The weather was favorable for the green things, but rather damp for the wheat.

Suddenly the drum began to beat in the yard, before the house. Everybody rose, except a few indifferent persons, and ran to the door, or to the windows, their mouths still full and napkins in their hands.

After the public crier had ceased his drum-beating, he called out in a jerky voice, speaking his phrases irregularly:

"It is hereby made known to the inhabitants of Goderville, and in general to all persons present at the market, that there was lost this morning, on the road to Benzeville, between nine and ten o'clock, a black leather pocketbook containing five hundred francs and some business papers. The finder is requested to return same to the mayor's office or to Maître Fortuné Houlbrèque of Manneville. There will be twenty francs reward."

Then the man went away. The heavy roll of the drum and the crier's voice were again heard at a distance.

Then they began to talk of this event discussing the chances that Maître Houlbrèque had of finding or not finding his pocketbook.

And the meal concluded. They were finishing their coffee when the chief of the gendarmes appeared upon the threshold.

He inquired:

"Is Maître Hauchecorne, of Bréauté, here?"

Maître Hauchecorne, seated at the other end of the table, replied:

"Here I am."

And the officer resumed:

"Maître Hauchecorne, will you have the goodness to accompany me to the mayor's office? The mayor would like to talk to you."

The peasant, surprised and disturbed, swallowed at a draught his tiny glass of brandy, rose, and, even more bent than in the morning, for the first steps after each rest were specially difficult, set out, repeating: "Here I am, here I am."

The mayor was awaiting him, seated on an armchair. He was the notary of the vicinity, a stout, serious man, with pompous phrases.

"Maître Hauchecorne," said he, "you were seen this morning picking up, on the road to Benzeville, the pocketbook lost by Maître Houlbrèque, of Manneville."

The countryman looked at the mayor in astonishment, already terrified by this suspicion resting on him without his knowing why.

"Me? Me? I picked up the pocketbook?"

"Yes, you, yourself."

"On my word of honour, I never heard of it."

"But you were seen."

"I was seen, me? Who says he saw me?"

"Monsieur Malandain, the harness-maker."

The old man remembered, understood, and flushed with anger.

"Ah, he saw me, the clodhopper, he saw me pick up this string, here, Mr. Mayor." And rummaging in his pocket he drew out the little piece of string.

But the mayor, incredulous, shook his head.

"You will not make me believe, Maître Hauchecorne, that Monsieur Malandain, who is a man we can believe, mistook this cord for a pocketbook."

The peasant, furious, lifted his hand, spat at one side to attest his honour, repeating:

"It is nevertheless the truth of the good God, the sacred truth, Mr. Mayor. I repeat it on my soul and my salvation."

The mayor resumed:

"After picking up the object, you stood like a stilt, looking a long while in the mud to see if any piece of money had fallen out."

The old chap choked with indignation and fear.

"How anyone can tell—how anyone can tell—such lies to take away an honest man's reputation! How can anyone—"

There was no use in his protesting, nobody believed him. He was confronted with Monsieur Malandain, who repeated and maintained his affirmation. They abused each other for an hour. At his own request, Maître Hauchecorne was searched; nothing was found on him.

Finally the mayor, very much perplexed, discharged him with the warning that he would consult the public prosecutor and ask for further orders.

The news had spread. As he left the mayor's office, the old man was surrounded and questioned with a serious or bantering curiosity, in which there was no indignation. He began to tell the story of the string. No one believed him. They laughed at him.

He went along, stopping his friends, beginning endlessly his statement and his protestations, showing his pockets turned inside out, to prove that he had nothing.

They said:

"Old rascal, get out!"

And he grew angry, becoming exasperated, hot, and distressed at not being believed, not knowing what to do and always repeating himself.

Night came. He must depart. He started on his way with three neighbours to whom he pointed out the place where he had picked up the bit of string; and all along the road he spoke of his adventure.

In the evening he took a turn in the village of Bréauté, in order to tell it to everybody. He only met with incredulity.

It made him ill all night.

The next day about one o'clock in the afternoon, Marius Paumelle, a hired man in the employ of Maître Breton, husbandman at Ymauville, returned the pocketbook and its contents to Maître Houlbrèque of Manneville.

This man claimed to have found the object in the road; but not knowing how to read, he had carried it to the house and given it to his employer.

The news spread through the neighbourhood. Maître Hauchecorne was informed of it. He immediately went the circuit and began to recount his story completed by the happy climax. He triumphed.

"What grieved me so much was not the thing itself, as the lying. There is nothing so shameful as to be placed under a cloud on account of a lie."

He talked of his adventure all day long, he told it on the highway to people who were passing by, in the inn to people who were drinking there, and to persons coming out of church the following Sunday. He stopped strangers to tell them about it. He was calm now, and yet something disturbed him without his knowing exactly what it was. People had the air of joking while they listened. They did not seem convinced. He seemed to feel that remarks were being made behind his back.

On Tuesday of the next week he went to the market at Goderville, urged solely by the necessity he felt of discussing the case.

Malandain, standing at his door, began to laugh on seeing him pass. Why?

He approached a farmer from Criquetot, who did not let him finish, and giving him a thump in the stomach said to his face:

"You clever rogue."

Then he turned his back on him.

Maître Hauchecorne was confused. Why was he called a clever rogue?

When he was seated at the table in Jourdain's tavern, he commenced to explain "the affair."

A horse dealer from Monvilliers called to him:

"Come, come, old sharper, that's an old trick; I know all about your piece of string!"

Hauchecorne stammered:

"But since the pocketbook was found . . ."

But the other man replied:

"—Shut up, papa, there is one that finds, and there is one that brings back. No one is any the wiser, so you get out of it."

The peasant stood choking. He understood. They accused him of having had the pocketbook returned by a confederate, by an accomplice.

He tried to protest. All the table began to laugh.

He could not finish his dinner and went away, in the midst of jeers.

He went home ashamed and indignant, choking with anger and confusion, the more dejected that he was capable with his Norman cunning of doing what they had accused him of, and even of boasting of it as of a good trick. His innocence to him, in a confused way, was impossible to prove, as his sharpness was known. And he was stricken to the heart by the injustice of the suspicion.

Then he began to recount the adventure again, enlarging his story every day, adding each time, new reasons, more energetic protestations, more solemn oaths which he imagined and prepared in his hours of solitude, his whole mind given up to the story of the string. He was believed so much the less as his defense was more complicated and his arguing more subtle.

"Those are lying excuses," they said behind his back.

He felt it, consumed his heart over it, and wore himself out with useless efforts. He was visibly wasting away.

The wags now made him tell about the string to amuse them, as they make a soldier who has been on a campaign tell about his battles. His mind, seriously affected, began to weaken.

Towards the end of December he took to his bed.

He died in the first days of January, and in the delirium of his death struggles he kept claiming his innocence, reiterating:

"A piece of string, a piece of string—look—here it is, Mr. Mayor."

Shirley Jackson

After You, My Dear Alphonse

Mrs. Wilson was just taking the gingerbread out of the oven when she heard Johnny outside talking to someone.

"Johnny," she called, "you're late. Come in and get your lunch."

"Just a minute, Mother," Johnny said. "After you, my dear Alphonse."

"After *you*, my dear Alphonse," another voice said.

"No, after *you*, my dear Alphonse," Johnny said.

Mrs. Wilson opened the door. "Johnny," she said, "you come in this minute and get your lunch. You can play after you've eaten."

Johnny came in after her, slowly. "Mother," he said, "I brought Boyd home for lunch with me."

"Boyd?" Mrs. Wilson thought for a moment. "I don't believe I've met Boyd. Bring him in, dear, since you've invited him. Lunch is ready."

"Boyd!" Johnny yelled. "Hey, Boyd, come on in!"

"I'm coming. Just got to unload this stuff."

"Well, hurry, or my mother'll be sore."

"Johnny, that's not very polite to either your friend or your mother," Mrs. Wilson said. "Come sit down, Boyd."

As she turned to show Boyd where to sit, she saw he was a Negro boy, smaller than Johnny but about the same age. His arms were loaded with split kindling wood. "Where'll I put this stuff, Johnny?" he asked.

Mrs. Wilson turned to Johnny, "Johnny," she said, "What is that wood?"

"Dead Japanese," Johnny said mildly. "We stand them in the ground and run over them with tanks."

Reprinted from *The Lottery* by Shirley Jackson, by permission of Farrar, Straus & Giroux, Inc. Copyright 1943, 1949 by Shirley Jackson. First published in *The New Yorker*.

"How do you do, Mrs. Wilson?" Boyd said.

"How do you do, Boyd? You shouldn't let Johnny make you carry all that wood. Sit down now and eat lunch, both of you."

"Why shouldn't he carry the wood, Mother? It's his wood. We got it at his place."

"Johnny," Mrs. Wilson said, "go on and eat your lunch."

"Sure," Johnny said. He held out the dish of scrambled eggs to Boyd. "After you, my dear Alphonse."

"After *you*, my dear Alphonse," Boyd said.

"After *you*, my dear Alphonse," Johnny said. They began to giggle.

"Are you hungry, Boyd?" Mrs. Wilson asked.

"Yes, Mrs. Wilson."

"Well, don't you let Johnny stop you. He always fusses about eating, so you just see that you get a good lunch. There's plenty of food here for you to have all you want."

"Thank you, Mrs. Wilson."

"Come on, Alphonse," Johnny said. He pushed half the scrambled eggs on to Boyd's plate. Boyd watched while Mrs. Wilson put a dish of stewed tomatoes beside his plate.

"Boyd don't eat tomatoes, do you, Boyd?" Johnny said.

"*Doesn't* eat tomatoes, Johnny. And just because you don't like them, don't say that about Boyd. Boyd will eat *anything*."

"Bet he won't," Johnny said, attacking his scrambled eggs.

"Boyd wants to grow up and be a big strong man so he can work hard," Mrs. Wilson said. "I'll bet Boyd's father eats stewed tomatoes."

"My father eats anything he wants to," Boyd said.

"So does mine," Johnny said. "Sometimes he doesn't eat hardly anything. He's a little guy, though. Wouldn't hurt a flea."

"Mine's a little guy, too," Boyd said.

"I'll bet he's strong, though," Mrs. Wilson said. She hesitated. "Does he . . . work?"

"Sure," Johnny said. "Boyd's father works in a factory."

"There, you see?" Mrs. Wilson said. "And he certainly has to be strong to do that—all that lifting and carrying at a factory."

"Boyd's father doesn't have to," Johnny said. "He's a foreman."

Mrs. Wilson felt defeated. "What does your mother do, Boyd?"

"My mother?" Boyd was surprised. "She takes care of us kids."

"Oh. She doesn't work, then?"

"Why should she?" Johnny said through a mouthful of eggs. "You don't work."

"You really don't want any stewed tomatoes, Boyd?"

"No, thank you, Mrs. Wilson," Boyd said.

"No, thank you, Mrs. Wilson, no, thank you, Mrs. Wilson, no, thank you, Mrs. Wilson," Johnny said. "Boyd's sister's going to work, though. She's going to be a teacher."

"That's a very fine attitude for her to have, Boyd." Mrs. Wilson restrained an impulse to pat Boyd on the head. "I imagine you're all very proud of her?"

"I guess so," Boyd said.

"What about all your other brothers and sisters? I guess all of you want to make just as much of yourselves as you can."

"There's only me and Jean," Boyd said. "I don't know yet what I want to be when I grow up."

"We're going to be tank drivers, Boyd and me," Johnny said. "Zoom." Mrs. Wilson caught Boyd's glass of milk as Johnny's napkin ring, suddenly transformed into a tank plowed heavily across the table.

"Look, Johnny," Boyd said. "Here's a foxhole. I'm shooting at you."

Mrs. Wilson, with the speed born of long experience, took the gingerbread off the shelf and placed it carefully between the tank and the foxhole.

"Now eat as much as you want to, Boyd," she said. "I want to see you get filled up."

"Boyd eats a lot, but not as much as I do," Johnny said. "I'm bigger than he is."

"You're not much bigger," Boyd said. "I can beat you running."

Mrs. Wilson took a deep breath. "Boyd," she said. Both boys turned to her. "Boyd, Johnny has some suits that are a little too small for him, and a winter coat. It's not new, of course, but there's lots of wear in it still. And I have a few dresses that your mother or sister could probably use. Your mother can make them over into lots of things for all of you, and I'd be very happy to give them to you. Suppose before you leave I make up a big bundle and then you and Johnny can take it over to your mother right away . . ." Her voice trailed off as she saw Boyd's puzzled expression.

"But I have plenty of clothes, thank you," he said. "And I don't think my mother knows how to sew very well, and anyway I guess we buy about everything we need. Thank you very much though."

"We don't have time to carry that old stuff around, Mother," Johnny said. "We got to play tanks with the kids today."

Mrs. Wilson lifted the plate of gingerbread off the table as Boyd was about to take another piece. "There are many little boys like you, Boyd, who would be grateful for the clothes someone was kind enough to give them."

"Boyd will take them if you want him to, Mother," Johnny said.

"I didn't mean to make you mad, Mrs. Wilson," Boyd said.

"Don't think I'm angry, Boyd. I'm just disappointed in you, that's all. Now let's not say anything more about it."

She began clearing the plates off the table, and Johnny took Boyd's hand and pulled him to the door. "'Bye, Mother," Johnny said. Boyd stood for a minute, staring at Mrs. Wilson's back.

"After you, my dear Alphonse," Johnny said, holding the door open.

"Is your mother still mad?" Mrs. Wilson heard Boyd ask in a low voice.

"I don't know," Johnny said. "She's screwy sometimes."

"So's mine," Boyd said. He hesitated. "After *you*, my dear Alphonse."

William Carlos Williams

The Use of Force

They were new patients to me, all I had was the name Olson. Please come down as soon as you can, my daughter is very sick.

When I arrived I was met by the mother, a big startled looking woman, very clean and apologetic who merely said, Is this the doctor? and let me in. In the back, she added. You must excuse us, doctor, we have her in the kitchen where it is warm. It is very damp here sometimes.

The child was fully dressed and sitting on her father's lap near the kitchen table. He tried to get up, but I motioned for him not to bother, took off my overcoat and started to look things over. I could see that they were all very nervous, eyeing me up and down distrustfully. As often, in such cases, they weren't telling me more than they had to, it was up to me to tell them: that's why they were spending three dollars on me.

The child was fairly eating me up with her cold, steady eyes, and no expression to her face whatever. She did not move and seemed, inwardly, quiet; an unusually attractive little thing, and as strong as a heifer in appearance. But her face was flushed, she was beathing rapidly, and I realized that she had a high fever. She had magnificent blonde hair, in profusion. One of those picture children often reproduced in advertising leaflets and the photogravure sections of the Sunday papers.

She's had a fever for three days, began the father and we don't know what it comes from. My wife has given her things, you know, like people do, but it don't do no good. And there's been a lot of sickness around. So we tho't you'd better look her over and tell us what is the matter.

As doctors often do I took a trial shot at it as a point of departure. Has she had a sore throat?

Both parents answered me together. No . . . No, she says her throat don't hurt her.

Does your throat hurt you? added the mother to the child. But the little girl's expression didn't change nor did she move her eyes from my face.

Have you looked?

I tried to, said the mother, but I couldn't see.

As it happens we had been having a number of cases of diphtheria in the school to which this child went during that month and we were all, quite apparently, thinking of that, though no one had as yet spoken of the thing.

Well, I said, suppose we take a look at the throat first. I smiled in my best professional manner and asking for the child's first name I said, come on, Mathilda, open your mouth and let's take a look at your throat.

Nothing doing.

Aw, come on, I coaxed, just open your mouth wide and let me take a look. Look, I said opening both hands wide, I haven't anything in my hands. Just open up and let me see.

Such a nice man, put in the mother. Look how kind he is to you. Come on, do what he tells you to. He won't hurt you.

At that I ground my teeth in disgust. If only they wouldn't use the word "hurt" I might be able to get somewhere. But I did not allow myself to be hurried or disturbed but speaking quietly and slowly I approached the child again.

As I moved my chair a little nearer suddenly with one catlike movement both her hands clawed instinctively for my eyes and she almost reached them too. In fact she knocked my glasses flying and they fell, though unbroken, several feet away from me on the kitchen floor.

Both the mother and father almost turned themselves inside out in embarrassment and apology. You bad girl, said the mother, taking her and shaking her by one arm. Look what you've done. The nice man . . .

For heaven's sake, I broke in. Don't call me a nice man to her. I'm here to look at her throat on the chance that she might have diphtheria and possibly die of it. But that's nothing to her. Look here, I said to the child, we're going to look at your throat. You're old enough to understand what I'm saying. Will you open it now by yourself or shall we have to open it for you?

Not a move. Even her expression hadn't changed. Her breaths however were coming faster and faster. Then the battle began. I had to do it. I had to have a throat culture for her own protection. But first I told the parents that it was entirely up to them. I explained the danger but said that I would not insist on a throat examination so long as they would take the responsibility.

If you don't do what the doctor says you'll have to go to the hospital, the mother admonished her severely.

Oh yeah? I had to smile to myself. After all, I had already fallen in love with the savage brat, the parents were contemptible to me. In the ensuing struggle they grew more and more abject, crushed, exhausted while she surely rose to magnificent heights of insane fury of effort bred of her terror of me.

The father tried his best, and he was a big man but the fact that she was his daughter, his shame at her behavior and his dread of hurting her made him release her just at the critical times when I had almost achieved success, till I wanted to kill him. But his dread also that she might have diphtheria made him tell me to go on, go on though he himself was almost fainting, while the mother moved back and forth behind us raising and lowering her hands in an agony of apprehension.

Put her in front of you on your lap, I ordered, and hold both her wrists.

But as soon as he did the child let out a scream. Don't, you're hurting me. Let go of my hands. Let them go I tell you. Then she shrieked terrifyingly, hysterically. Stop it! Stop it! You're killing me!

Do you think she can stand it, doctor! said the mother.

You get out, said the husband to his wife. Do you want her to die of diphtheria?

Come on now, hold her, I said.

Then I grasped the child's head with my left hand and tried to get the wooden tongue depressor between her teeth. She fought, with clenched teeth, desperately! But now I also had grown furious—at a child. I tried to hold myself down but I couldn't. I know how to expose a throat for inspection. And I did my best. When finally I got the wooden spatula behind the last teeth and just the point of it into the mouth cavity, she opened up for an instant but before I could see anything she came down again and gripping the wooden blade between her molars she reduced it to splinters before I could get it out again.

Aren't you ashamed, the mother yelled at her. Aren't you ashamed to act like that in front of the doctor?

Get me a smooth-handled spoon of some sort, I told the mother. We're going through with this. The child's mouth was already bleeding. Her tongue was cut and she was screaming in wild hysterical shrieks. Perhaps I should have desisted and come back in an hour or more. No doubt it would have been better. But I have seen at least two children lying dead in bed of neglect in such cases, and feeling that I must get a diagnosis now or never I went at it again. But the worst of it was that I too had got beyond reason. I could have torn the child apart in my own fury and enjoyed it. It was a pleasure to attack her. My face was burning with it.

The damned little brat must be protected against her own idiocy, one says to one's self at such times. Others must be protected against her. It is a social necessity. And all these things are true. But a blind fury, a feeling of adult shame, bred of a longing for muscular release are the operatives. One goes on to the end.

In a final unreasoning assault I overpowered the child's neck and jaws. I forced the heavy silver spoon back of her teeth and down her throat till she gagged. And there it was—both tonsils covered with membrane. She had fought valiantly to keep me from knowing her secret. She had been hiding that sore throat for three days at least and lying to her parents in order to escape just such an outcome as this.

Now truly she was furious. She had been on the defensive before but now she attacked. Tried to get off her father's lap and fly at me while tears of defeat blinded her eyes.

John Updike

Should Wizard Hit Mommy?

In the evenings and for Saturday naps like today's, Jack told his daughter Jo a story out of his head. This custom, begun when she was two, was itself now nearly two years old, and his head felt empty. Each new story was a slight variation of a basic tale: a small creature, usually named Roger (Roger Fish, Roger Squirrel, Roger Chipmunk), had some problem and went with it to the wise old owl. The owl told him to go to the wizard, and the wizard performed a magic spell that solved the problem, demanding in payment a number of pennies greater than the number Roger Creature had but in the same breath directing the animal to a place where the extra pennies could be found. Then Roger was so happy he played many games with other creatures, and went home to his mother just in time to hear the train whistle that brought his daddy home from Boston. Jack described their supper, and the story was over. Working his way through this scheme was especially fatiguing on Saturday, because Jo never fell asleep in naps any more, and knowing this made the rite seem futile.

The little girl (not so little any more; the bumps her feet made under the covers were halfway down the bed, their big double bed that they let her be in for naps and when she was sick) had at last arranged herself, and from the way her fat face deep in the pillow shone in the sunlight sifting through the drawn shades, it did not seem fantastic that something magic would occur, and she would take her nap like an infant of two. Her brother, Bobby, was two, and already asleep with his bottle. Jack asked, "Who shall the story be about today?"

"Roger . . ." Jo squeezed her eyes shut and smiled to be thinking she was thinking. Her eyes opened, her mother's blue. "Skunk," she said firmly.

A new animal; they must talk about skunks at nursery school. Having a fresh hero momentarily stirred Jack to creative enthusiasm. "All right," he said. "Once upon a time, in the deep dark woods, there was a tiny little creature name of Roger Skunk. And he smelled very bad—"

"Yes," Jo said.

"He smelled so bad none of the other little woodland creatures would play with him." Jo looked at him solemnly; she hadn't foreseen this. "Whenever he would go out to play," Jack continued with zest, remembering certain humiliations of his own childhood, "all of the other tiny animals would cry, 'Uh-oh, here comes Roger Stinky Skunk,' and they would run away, and Roger Skunk would stand there all alone, and two little round tears would fall from his eyes." The corners of Jo's mouth drooped down and her lower lip bent forward as he traced with a forefinger along the side of her nose the course of one of Roger Skunk's tears.

"Won't he see the owl?" she asked in a high and faintly roughened voice.

Sitting on the bed beside her, Jack felt the covers tug as her legs switched tensely. He was pleased with this moment—he was telling her something true, something she must know—and had no wish to hurry on. But downstairs a chair scraped, and he realized he must get down to help Clare paint the living-room woodwork.

"Well, he walked along very sadly and came to a very big tree, and in the tiptop of the tree was an enormous wise old owl."

"Good."

" 'Mr. Owl,' Roger Skunk said, 'all the other little animals run away from me because I smell so bad.' 'So you do,' the owl said. 'Very, very bad.' 'What can I do?' Roger Skunk said, and he cried very hard."

"The wizard, the wizard," Jo shouted, and sat right up, and a Little Golden Book spilled from the bed.

"Now, Jo. Daddy's telling the story. Do you want to tell Daddy the story?"

"No. You tell me."

"Then lie down and be sleepy."

Her head relapsed onto the pillow and she said, "Out of your head."

"Well. The owl thought and thought. At last he said, 'Why don't you go see the wizard?' "

"Daddy?"

"What?"

"Are magic spells *real*?" This was a new phase, just this last month, a reality phase. When he told her spiders eat bugs, she turned to her mother and asked, "Do they *really*?" and when Clare told her God was in the sky and all around them, she turned to her father and insisted, with a sly yet eager smile, "Is He *really*?"

"They're real in stories," Jack answered curtly. She had made him miss a beat in the narrative. "The owl said, 'Go through the dark woods, under the apple trees, into the swamp, over the crick—' "

"What's a crick?"

"A little river. 'Over the crick, and there will be the wizard's house.' And that's the way Roger Skunk went, and pretty soon he came to a little white house, and he rapped on the door." Jack rapped on the window sill, and under the covers Jo's tall figure clenched in an infantile thrill. "And then a tiny little old man came out, with a long white beard and a pointed blue hat, and said, 'Eh? Whatzis? Whatcher want? You smell awful.' " The wizard's voice was one of Jack's own favorite effects; he did it by scrunching up his face and somehow whining through his eyes, which felt for the interval rheumy. He felt being an old man suited him.

" 'I know it,' Roger Skunk said, 'and all the little animals run away from me. The enormous wise owl said you could help me.'

" 'Eh? Well, maybe. Come on in. Don't git too close.' Now, inside, Jo, there were all these magic things, all jumbled together in a big dusty heap, because the wizard did not have any cleaning lady."

"Why?"

"Why? Because he was a wizard, and a very old man."

"Will he die?"

"No. Wizards don't die. Well, he rummaged around and found an old stick called a magic wand and asked Roger Skunk what he wanted to smell like. Roger thought and thought and said, 'Roses.' "

"Yes. Good," Jo said smugly.

Jack fixed her with a trancelike gaze and chanted in the wizard's elderly irritable voice:

" 'Abracadabry, hocus-poo,
Roger Skunk, how do you do,
Roses, boses, pull an ear,
Roger Skunk, you never fear:
Bingo!' "

He paused as a rapt expression widened out from his daughter's nostrils,
forcing her eyebrows up and her lower lip down in a wide noiseless grin, an
expression in which Jack was startled to recognize his wife feigning pleasure at
cocktail parties. "And all of a sudden," he whispered, "the whole inside of the
wizard's house was full of the smell of—*roses!* 'Roses!' Roger Fish cried. And
the wizard said, very cranky, 'That'll be seven pennies.' "

"Daddy."

"What?"

"Roger *Skunk*. You said Roger Fish."

"Yes. Skunk."

"You said Roger *Fish*. Wasn't that silly?"

"Very silly of your stupid old daddy. Where was I? Well, you know about the
pennies."

"Say it."

"O.K. Roger Skunk said, 'But all I have is four pennies,' and he began to
cry." Jo made the crying face again, but this time without a trace of sincerity.
This annoyed Jack. Downstairs some more furniture rumbled. Clare shouldn't
move heavy things; she was six months pregnant. It would be their third.

"So the wizard said, 'Oh, very well. Go to the end of the lane and turn around
three times and look down the magic well and there you will find three pennies.
Hurry up.' So Roger Skunk went to the end of the lane and turned around three
times and there in the magic well were *three pennies!* So he took them back to
the wizard and was very happy and ran out into the woods and all the other little
animals gathered around him because he smelled so good. And they played tag,
baseball, football, basketball, lacrosse, hockey, soccer, and pick-up-sticks."

"What's pick-up-sticks?"

"It's a game you play with sticks."

"Like the wizard's magic wand?"

"Kind of. And they played games and laughed all afternoon and then it began
to get dark and they all ran home to their mommies."

Jo was starting to fuss with her hands and look out of the window, at the
crack of day that showed under the shade. She thought the story was all over.
Jack didn't like women when they took anything for granted; he liked them
apprehensive, hanging on his words. "Now, Jo, are you listening?"

"Yes."

"Because this is very interesting. Roger Skunk's mommy said, 'What's that
awful smell?' "

"Wha-at?"

"And Roger Skunk said, 'It's me, Mommy. I smell like roses.' And she said,

'Who made you smell like that?' And he said, 'The wizard,' and she said, 'Well, of all the nerve. You come with me and we're going right back to that very awful wizard.' "

Jo sat up, her hands dabbling in the air with genuine fright. "But Daddy, then he said about the other little aminals run *away!*" Her hands skittered off, into the underbrush.

"All right. He said, 'But Mommy, all the other little animals run away,' and she said, 'I don't care. You smelled the way a little skunk should have and I'm going to take you right back to that wizard,' and she took an umbrella and went back with Roger Skunk and hit that wizard right over the head."

"No," Jo said, and put her hand out to touch his lips, yet even in her agitation did not quite dare to stop the source of truth. Inspiration came to her. "Then the wizard hit *her* on the head and did not change that little skunk back."

"No," he said. "The wizard said 'O.K.' and Roger Skunk did not smell of roses any more. He smelled very bad again."

"But the other little amum—*oh!*—amum—"

"Joanne. It's Daddy's story. Shall Daddy not tell you any more stories?" Her broad face looked at him through sifted light, astounded. "This is what happened, then. Roger Skunk and his mommy went home and they heard *Woo-oo, woooo-oo* and it was the choo-choo train bringing Daddy Skunk home from Boston. And they had lima beans, pork chops, celery, liver, mashed potatoes, and Pie-Oh-My for dessert. And when Roger Skunk was in bed Mommy Skunk came up and hugged him and said he smelled like her little baby skunk again and she loved him very much. And that's the end of the story."

"But Daddy."

"What?"

"Then did the other little ani-mals run away?"

"No, because eventually they got used to the way he was and did not mind it at all."

"What's evenshiladee?"

"In a little while."

"That was a stupid mommy."

"It was *not*," he said with rare emphasis, and believed, from her expression, that she realized he was defending his own mother to her, or something as odd. "Now I want you to put your big heavy head in the pillow and have a good long nap." He adjusted the shade so not even a crack of day showed, and tiptoed to the door, in the pretense that she was already asleep. But when he turned, she was crouching on top of the covers and staring at him. "Hey. Get under the covers and fall faaast asleep. Bobby's asleep."

She stood up and bounced gingerly on the springs. "Daddy."

"What?"

"Tomorrow, I want you to tell me the story that that wizard took that magic wand and hit that mommy"—her plump arms chopped fiercely—"right over the head."

"No. That's not the story. The point is that the little skunk loved his mommy more than he loved aaalll the other animals and she knew what was right."

"No. Tomorrow you say he hit that mommy. Do it." She kicked her legs up and sat down on the bed with a great heave and complaint of springs, as she had done hundreds of times before, except that this time she did not laugh. "Say it, Daddy."

"Well, we'll see. Now at least have a rest. Stay on the bed. You're a good girl."

He closed the door and went downstairs. Clare had spread the newspapers and opened the paint can and, wearing an old shirt of his on top of her maternity smock, was stroking the chair rail with a dipped brush. Above him footsteps vibrated and he called, *"Joanne*. Shall I come up there and spank you?" The footsteps hesitated.

"That was a long story," Clare said.

"The poor kid," he answered, and with utter weariness watched his wife labor. The woodwork, a cage of moldings and rails and baseboards all around them, was half old tan and half new ivory and he felt caught in an ugly middle position, and though he as well felt his wife's presence in the cage with him, he did not want to speak with her, work with her, touch her, anything.

Ernest Hemingway

In Another Country

In the fall the war was always there, but we did not go to it any more. It was cold in the fall in Milan and the dark came very early. Then the electric lights came on, and it was pleasant along the streets looking in the windows. There was much game hanging outside the shops, and the snow powdered in the fur of the foxes and the wind blew their tails. The deer hung stiff and heavy and empty, and small birds blew in the wind and the wind turned their feathers. It was a cold fall and the wind came down from the mountains.

We were all at the hospital every afternoon, and there were different ways of walking across the town through the dusk to the hospital. Two of the ways were alongside canals, but they were long. Always, though, you crossed a bridge across a canal to enter the hospital. There was a choice of three bridges. On one of them a woman sold roasted chestnuts. It was warm, standing in front of her charcoal fire, and the chestnuts were warm afterward in your pocket. The hospital was very old and very beautiful, and you entered through a gate and walked across a courtyard and out a gate on the other side. There were usually funerals starting from the courtyard. Beyond the old hospital were the new brick pavilions, and there we met every afternoon and were all very polite and interested in what was the matter, and sat in the machines that were to make so much difference.

The doctor came up to the machine where I was sitting and said: "What did you like best to do before the war? Did you practise a sport?"

I said: "Yes, football."

"Good," he said. "You will be able to play football again better than ever."

My knee did not bend and the leg dropped straight from the knee to the ankle without a calf, and the machine was to bend the knee and make it move as in riding a tricycle. But it did not bend yet, and instead the machine lurched when it came to the bending part. The doctor said: "That will all pass. You are a fortunate young man. You will play football again like a champion."

In the next machine was a major who had a little hand like a baby's. He winked at me when the doctor examined his hand, which was between two leather straps that bounced up and down and flapped the stiff fingers, and said: "And will I too play football, captain-doctor?" He had been a very great fencer, and before the war the greatest fencer in Italy.

The doctor went to his office in a back room and brought a photograph which showed a hand that had been withered almost as small as the major's, before it had taken a machine course, and after was a little larger. The major held the photograph with his good hand and looked at it very carefully. "A wound?" he asked.

"An industrial accident," the doctor said.

"Very interesting, very interesting," the major said, and handed it back to the doctor.

"You have confidence?"

"No," said the major.

There were three boys who came each day who were about the same age I was. They were all three from Milan, and one of them was to be a lawyer, and one was to be a painter, and one had intended to be a soldier, and after we were finished with the machines, sometimes we walked back together to the Café Cova, which was next door to the Scala. We walked the short way through the communist quarter because we were four together. The people hated us because we were officers, and from a wine-shop some one called out. "A basso gli ufficiali!" as we passed. Another boy who walked with us sometimes and made us five wore a black silk handkerchief across his face because he had no nose then and his face was to be rebuilt. He had gone out to the front from the military academy and been wounded within an hour after he had gone into the front line for the first time. They rebuilt his face, but he came from a very old family and they could never get the nose exactly right. He went to South America and worked in a bank. But this was a long time ago, and then we did not any of us know how it was going to be afterward. We only knew then that there was always the war, but that we were not going to it any more.

We all had the same medals, except the boy with the black silk bandage across his face, and he had not been at the front long enough to get any medals. The tall boy with a very pale face who was to be a lawyer had been a lieutenant of Arditi and had three medals of the sort we each had only one of. He had lived a very long time with death and was a little detached. We were all a little detached, and there was nothing that held us together except that we met every afternoon at the hospital. Although, as we walked to the Cova through the tough part of town, walking in the dark, with light and singing coming out of the wine-shops, and sometimes having to walk into the street when the men and women would crowd together on the sidewalk so that we would have had to jostle them to get by, we felt held together by there being something that had happened that they, the people who disliked us, did not understand.

We ourselves all understood the Cova, where it was rich and warm and not too brightly lighted, and noisy and smoky at certain hours, and there were always girls at the tables and the illustrated papers on a rack on the wall. The girls at the Cova were very patriotic, and I found that the most patriotic people in Italy were the café girls—and I believe they are still patriotic.

The boys at first were very polite about my medals and asked me what I had done to get them. I showed them the papers, which were written in very beautiful language and full of *fratellanza* and *abnegazione,* but which really said, with the adjectives removed, that I had been given the medals because I was an American. After that their manner changed a little toward me, although I was their friend against outsiders. I was a friend, but I was never really one of them after they had read the citations, because it had been different with them and they had done very different things to get their medals. I had been wounded, it was true; but we all knew that being wounded, after all, was really an accident. I was never ashamed of the ribbons, though, and sometimes, after the cocktail hour, I would imagine myself having done all the things they had done to get their medals; but walking home at night through the empty streets with the cold wind and all the shops closed, trying to keep near the street lights, I knew that I would never have done such things, and I was very much afraid to die, and often lay in bed at night by myself, afraid to die and wondering how I would be when I went back to the front again.

The three with the medals were like hunting-hawks; and I was not a hawk, although I might seem a hawk to those who had never hunted; they, the three, knew better and so we drifted apart. But I stayed good friends with the boy who had been wounded his first day at the front, because he would never know now how he would have turned out; so he could never be accepted either, and I liked him because I thought perhaps he would not have turned out to be a hawk either.

The major, who had been the great fencer, did not believe in bravery, and spent much time while we sat in the machines correcting my grammar. He had complimented me on how I spoke Italian, and we talked together very easily. One day I had said that Italian seemed such an easy language to me that I could not take a great interest in it; everything was so easy to say. "Ah, yes," the major said. "Why, then, do you not take up the use of grammar?" So we took up the use of grammar, and soon Italian was such a difficult language that I was afraid to talk to him until I had the grammar straight in my mind.

The major came very regularly to the hospital. I do not think he ever missed a day, although I am sure he did not believe in the machines. There was a time when none of us believed in the machines, and one day the major said it was all nonsense. The machines were new then and it was we who were to prove them. It was an idiotic idea, he said, "a theory, like another." I had not learned my grammar, and he said I was a stupid impossible disgrace, and he was a fool to have bothered with me. He was a small man and he sat straight up in his chair with his right hand thrust into the machine and looked straight ahead at the wall while the straps thumped up and down with his fingers in them.

"What will you do when the war is over if it is over?" he asked me. "Speak grammatically!"

"I will go to the States."

"Are you married?"

"No, but I hope to be."

"The more of a fool you are," he said. He seemed very angry. "A man must not marry."

"Why, Signor Maggiore?"

"Don't call me 'Signor Maggiore.' "

"Why must not a man marry?"

"He cannot marry. He cannot marry," he said angrily. "If he is to lose everything, he should not place himself in a position to lose that. He should not place himself in a position to lose. He should find things he cannot lose."

He spoke very angrily and bitterly, and looked straight ahead while he talked.

"But why should he necessarily lose it?"

"He'll lose it," the major said. He was looking at the wall. Then he looked down at the machine and jerked his little hand out from between the straps and slapped it hard against his thigh. "He'll lose it," he almost shouted. "Don't argue with me!" Then he called to the attendant who ran the machines. "Come and turn this damned thing off."

He went back into the other room for the light treatment and the massage. Then I heard him ask the doctor if he might use his telephone and he shut the door. When he came back into the room, I was sitting in another machine. He was wearing his cape and had his cap on, and he came directly toward my machine and put his arm on my shoulder.

"I am so sorry," he said, and patted me on the shoulder with his good hand. "I would not be rude. My wife has just died. You must forgive me."

"Oh—" I said, feeling sick for him. "I am so sorry."

He stood there biting his lower lip. "It is very difficult," he said. "I cannot resign myself."

He looked straight past me and out through the window. Then he began to cry. "I am utterly unable to resign myself," he said and choked. And then crying, his head up looking at nothing, carrying himself straight and soldierly, with tears on both his cheeks and biting his lips, he walked past the machines and out the door.

The doctor told me that the major's wife, who was very young and whom he had not married until he was definitely invalided out of the war, had died of pneumonia. She had been sick only a few days. No one expected her to die. The major did not come to the hospital for three days. Then he came at the usual hour, wearing a black band on the sleeve of his uniform. When he came back, there were large framed photographs around the wall, of all sorts of wounds before and after they had been cured by the machines. In front of the machine the major used were three photographs of hands like his that were completely restored. I do not know where the doctor got them. I always understood we were the first to use the machines. The photographs did not make much difference to the major because he only looked out of the window.

James B. Hall

Up in the Yards

The next day I was being drafted, so in the way of a very young man, I walked out my mother's back door and across a meadow where once I flew kites, to the railroad siding. Perhaps this was a way of viewing my own past, before I moved on: from civilian to soldier, from boy to man. I felt it was one final walk across the landscape of my youth.

The right of way was a slash of industry across the warm, flat countryside. The section gang's tool shed still squatted beside the empty cattle pens; the creosote was black and glistened on a pile of crossties. West of town the rails spread outward into a broad delta of ballast rock and switch frogs and lonely, empty freight cars. At the end of the yards, a mile away, the tracks singled up once more and finally became a single glint of light on the horizon. At noon the yards were without noise, except beyond the right of way the engine of a tractor grew louder, then faded. Spring. Somewhere a farmer was plowing.

I could not believe it: in the yards, on the same crosstie, at the identical switch, I saw a wad of black, greasy waste, the kind that is packed around the axle of a freight car. Perhaps you have seen this packing on fire, or smoking, as you waited at a crossing for a slow train to pass.

I saw the greasy waste and at the identical moment I heard a faint *scruump*, the noise of many clubs, or gun butts, dropping to the ground. This small noise was only an engine being turned off inside a feed mill, far down the tracks. But the piece of waste lying in the sun, and the noise of a turned-off engine brought back that afternoon and that night.

I was ten years old. The hot sun of June rumbled like a freight train overhead. Winter had melted into ponds or had flowed down the creeks, or was held, still, in the leaf-rotted pools in Simpkin Woods. There must have been a few pools in the deeper woods because the frogs croaked in their old primitive way, calling boys into the swamps.

I was "helping" my father, for one of our fields joined the railroad's land, near a siding.

"Well, you have done good," my father said at the end of a row, for he noticed I was beginning to play.

"That so?" I said, and tried to sound something like him when he was given a compliment. In the country a boy learns to turn praise away, lest it appear a boast.

My father smiled, "Hell-yes, you done good," and then added, "Go on over there, if you want to." He was the best-hearted man in the world.

As I climbed over the fence to railroad property he called, "Watch out for trains."

I was going to boil a potato. I had one saved out in each pocket, and cattle salt in an empty tobacco tin.

To boil a potato up in the yards was more than simply wasting time. I think my father—who was a hunter while he lived—understood the savage appeal of fire to a boy. Or perhaps to start your own fire was to pretend, briefly, to manhood. To ride a freight train, alone, might come later, but now all I wanted was fire, and to cook food under the sky.

At a dump, where people from Sedley carted their refuse, I found an enameled store sign: Pay Car Tobacco. There was a clean half-gallon tin, and settled water in the ditch.

With the sign, I scooped a hole the size of a small dog from the bank along the siding. The sign over the hole made a furnace; in the gravel bank was an opening for a smoke hole. Not far away a refrigerator car was empty, its doors open. Inside a reefer there is always wood.

On the same car, I opened the little door on the axle housing and took out the black, greasy waste. In a minute the black smoke poured upward from the dog-hole furnace, and I was staring into the core of a fire where pieces of lath writhed in the flames. The water in the can boiled. Suddenly I was hungry.

The world beyond the lovely, industrial hum of the telegraph poles, and the encircling woods, all those places I had not yet traveled, came into my daydreams; yet I also heard the steady *caarp-caaarp* of the frogs calling through the scrub oak, sumac, and the rustling pawpaw trees.

I thought—at first—a dog jumped from the refrigerator car. But it was the man's olive-drab blanket roll. The blanket roll leaped from the boxcar door, then lay flat and lifeless beside a crosstie.

The man himself was a shadow in the shadows of the reefer car, but he was so incredibly tall he seemed to fill the whole door. He thrust his head out of the darkness and I saw his face. In the sunlight his whiskers seemed on fire. He turned his face each way in the sunshine, and then seemed to calculate the distance to the main crossing in Sedley, a half mile below the yards. The man spat toward his own blanket roll, then jumped, stiff-legged, to the gravel. I did not want to think he noticed me, but he did. He looked once at the sky, and then at me. We were alone. I thought of all the rabbits I had surprised in a certain fence corner not far away.

As he came closer his shoes sent small rocks flying. His shoes, which had steel safety caps on the toes, came close to my fire, and stopped. Only then did I look up.

The man was dressed in wool, the kind soldiers wear: olive-drab shirt, a belt of old harness leather, olive-drab trousers. On his head was a square, black, quilted cap, with a tiny visor, the kind a fireman on a steam pile driver might wear.

"You woke me up," he said. "When you made them lath."

The inside of the refrigerator car had been dark.

"Don't you know that's stealing?"

"That so?" was all I could say, and I would have made a run for it except the man in the old army clothes began to laugh. That is, he raised his head and showed his flat, chipped teeth.

"Take all you can off'num," he said. "Elst they will take it off of you."

Without saying anything else the man squatted down before my dog-hole furnace and held his hands toward the fire. This seemed to make us in league, bonded by our past, common crimes. The fire felt good on the tips of his fingers. The potato skins were already cracking in the steam.

A knife appeared in his hand. The blade snapped open. The blade was thin, and leather-stropped. All day he must have whetted the blade on his own shoe leather while he rode the freights. With a quick stabbing motion above the fire, he caught one of the potatoes on his knife.

"Our spuds is about done."

"You take them," I said. "I was . . . fooling around."

"Fool around while you can, elst they . . ." He looked down the rails toward town, as though he expected to see someone coming along the right of way. He rubbed the back of his hand across his lips.

He laid both potatoes on the overhanging edge of the sign, and cut them into six even parts. Almost delicately he speared one slice, and when the steam was gone he touched the potato to my pile of cattle salt. Then he ate.

"I've et worse for breakfast," he said. "And Kid, so will you."

"Wheeling," he said when I finally asked him. "Wheeling, West Virginia. Sister there."

"These clothes? Why you might say I collected them, for this little trip to Wheeling."

I had asked him because the old army clothes made me think he might have been Over There, a doughboy in France, had fought The Hun. Memorial Day was just past, and the Drum and Bugle Corps had marched to the cemetery. All of that was fresh in my mind.

Suddenly, above us on the bank, above my dog-hole furnace, I saw Foskett.

Foskett was the railroad's detective, for this Division. He lived in Sedley, with his wife. No children. If there was trouble anywhere along the line, Foskett had to investigate. They say Foskett once shot a car robber near Oakley, but even when there was a depression, when there were so many men on the road, they say Foskett never threw a man off a moving train. He did not carry a blackjack. The gun, however, was always in his shoulder holster, a 38 Special, well known. Foskett had been up in our yards, and I had not seen him walking toward the fire between the two cuts of cars.

Foskett stood on the bank, looking down. I noticed his hair was parted on the extreme right, and was the glistening black of creosote on new crossties. He worked in a faded blue denim jacket, and except for the holster, Foskett looked much like an ordinary brakeman.

"You boys eating a bite?" Foskett said, and he looked closely at the man who squatted beside my fire.

The man did not look up, but he stabbed at three more chunks of potato, as though to harvest them quickly.

"Yes, you are," Foskett said. "You are eating a bite. I saw that black greasy smoke from down the way.

"Would you have took some car packing to start your fire, Billy?"

He was talking to me.

At first I thought he was pretending he did not know me or my father and all of my relatives. I liked being called "you boys" as though I were also on the road. But it was the first time The Law ever addressed me.

The man in olive drab stood up.

"My fire," the man said. "The kid had potatoes, and I had me a fire. Like you said, just eating a bite."

Foskett looked off in the direction of our field. Perhaps from the bank he could see my father working.

"Would I have seen you on Number Twelve, at Urbancrest?"

The man did not answer. He began to kick gravel into the embers of the fire. I stood up also. The man seemed even larger as he threshed his shoes in the ballast, kicking even larger rocks into the hole. His face did not change expression, but he was leaving.

"Oh, finish your bite to eat," Foskett told the man, and then Foskett made a gesture with his thumb toward the fence that divided railroad property from the farms beyond. Foskett's thumb was an order for the man to move on.

Foskett turned to walk down through the yards toward town. But he stopped to call back, "Billy, your dad is looking for you."

I turned and ran.

My father was still at work in our two-acre patch, not far from the railroad.

"Back in the same day," my father said, as I climbed over the fence to his side. I felt better.

I took my hoe and began working along an open furrow. My father believed a good crop came from earth that was already warm. He always held off planting until after Memorial Day—considered too late, by some. He always put the eyes in the potato chunks facing the sky. This, however, was only superstition. Of all the potato growers around Sedley, my father was one of the best.

As I worked I kept remembering my fire. The man had said it was his fire, started with greasy waste, when it was not. Yet there was no reason to lie, because Foskett knew me and my father.

When I got to the end of the row, my father was standing beside the fence. He was listening to the man in old army woolens.

The man had followed me. Now I was near my father and I thought the man had come because he had some claim.

"Well," my father said to the man, "will you work?"

The man threw the blanket roll across the fence to our side. He showed his flat chipped teeth and said, "I'll work."

The man balanced himself on the fence, and then crashed into the brush on our side. My father therefore knew the man was not from the country, and never had been.

"Take Billy's hoe for a couple of hours. He's just put in one hullva day. Up since daylight."

This was my father's good-natured way of letting me go home during the heat of the afternoon. He did not like to see his only son working all day, too soon. Life, he always said, was too short for that.

The man ignored me. He picked up my hoe and then, impulsively, chopped into the warm, dry soil. He pulled the black loam over the eyes of a potato chunk—then back—then tamped it with a surprisingly gentle tap of the hoe.

"Is that it?" he asked, and looked at my father, as though there were a secret, as though the soil would suddenly let out a chime of music, from below the surface, if everything were done just so.

Father nodded, "Just go on to the next one."

Quickly, even delicately, the man covered a half dozen more hills.

He was already sweating through the army woolens, so he came back to his bedroll to strip. Underneath the woolen shirt was another shirt of faded blue denim, something like Foskett's faded jacket.

"I like this," he said and showed his flat teeth which were chipped all the way back into his mouth—from opening bottles with his teeth.

"I wouldn't mind at all, doing this."

Then he and my father turned. Each in a row, they worked to the far end of the field. This was only a patch, the point rows of a back field, but it was real potato land: well-drained loam that broke up almost like ashes. At the far end the two men turned and came back; as a matter of courtesy my father let the new man lead out at his own pace. Back and forth they swung, in easy unison, their hoes making a *chuk-chuk* as they covered the rows which were straight as gun barrels.

At the end of fifty minutes, my father stopped. This was courtesy to a new man, to let him blow and get his second wind.

"Jesus, I wouldn't mind doing this *all* the time," the man said again, and began to take off his denim shirt. Underneath was his underwear, surprisingly white, of summer weight. In the sun, his skin was almost transparent as though he had never before been exposed to light. The man held his arms out straight and looked at the black ring near his wrists, where his hands began.

". . . If I was able, I would like it all the time. If I was steady."

My father looked across the right of way, toward the yards. It was not customary to inquire at once about a man's past, nor about his immediate health, unless there was something anyone must notice: an arm in a sling, or a pair of crutches. Therefore my father remained silent. If a man said he was not a steady worker, it could mean anything. But to me, just after Memorial Day, it could mean only one thing. War.

From the little den I had hollowed out of the brush of the fence row, I said:

"Were you in the War? At the Front?"

The man dropped his hoe, and stamped one huge, steel-capped shoe down into the furrow. Suddenly, in a spasm of anger, he seemed to shake hands with himself. He took one step down the row he had just covered, and stamped his foot again, as though to drive the buried potato chunk into the center of the earth.

"Bell-ow Woods," he told my father, who had not moved. "And Cap'n, they ordered us to attack, and then they opened up on us from a hill . . ."

"Yes," my father said, and hesitated to say more. When the man turned, my father saw a number stenciled plainly across the back of the undershirt.

"Would they have let you out of the Vets' Hospital, up the line?"

The man calmed down at once. He picked up the hoe, and looked down along another furrow. He knew my father was goodhearted for he said, "Yes. You might say they let me go."

"But I went through it all," the man added. "And last night they kicked me off a freight. A brakeman done it."

He looked across the yards, and swore.

"Billy," my father said as he turned to his next row, "your mother is looking for you."

As I walked past the huge man, he took off his fireman's cap. From behind the cap, I heard him say very softly, "Never get in bad, Kid."

The quilted cap covered up the sounds, but I had not thought his hair could be so gray.

My father got home earlier than usual.

Together they had finished out the point rows. After the last row the man had put on his two shirts, and my father had given him wages, and a dollar extra.

That was the spring my father allowed me to ride a bicycle after dark. To ride at night was something like climbing the fence to the right of way. While Father listened to the early news, and while Mother was in the kitchen, I pedaled into the evening, hearing, still, my father's voice as I left, ". . . Watch out for automobiles."

By nine I had pedaled the back roads, past Simpkin Woods, where gravel hissed in the darkness under the bicycle wheels. At the crossing in town there was a crowd under a street light.

"I got the necktie," a boy said. He was holding up a four-in-hand, under the street light. The knot was sliced in two. The ends of the tie might fit around a man's neck, except the knot was slashed.

"Foskett dropped it. He made it to the restaurant, and dropped his necktie."

Up in the yards, where once you saw the green and red and amber switch lights, or the moonbeams adrift on the rails, I saw their flashlights. Two dozen beams tracked in the darkness. First on the ground, then whetting against one another as they pointed toward the clouds. The men already had gone into the yards. The flashlights were pointing under, then on top of the boxcars along the siding.

For the first time I noticed all the people under the street light, drawing back from the slashed necktie, all of them boys. Some my age; some nearly grown.

The flashlights in the yards converged on the ground, all on one spot.

"They got him," said the boy who had picked up Foskett's tie. "We better go see it."

I went, too, stumbling over the rails in the darkness. The boys talked as we stumbled along . . .

". . . He got more wine, and was walking up and down. A rock in his hand . . ."

"He asked the Bailey girl did she want to go up in the woods. To have her picture taken . . ."

In the yards, the circle of men with flashlights was gathered around a switch tie. They carried a flashlight in one hand, a shotgun or a club in the other.

The circle drew closer. I pushed, and was pushed from behind. I entered the middle of the circle of light on the ground.

First I saw the blanket roll. Then I saw the black, quilted cap. In the center of the wool shirt I saw the hopeless, cold brown splotches. Bullet holes. The face was staring upward into the hard, low clouds.

Near at hand, where the knife lay, above his head, was a piece of dark greasy waste. Someone had dropped it there during the winter. A clot of waste on the end of a switch tie.

Their flashlights went out. There was the sudden silence of a man's held breath in the darkness. Then, faintly, *scruuump:* together the men dropped their gun butts and clubs to the gravel.

The next day my father took it on himself to find the next of kin, but no one ever did come from Wheeling, West Virginia. We found out the man bought the wine with what he earned, and then spent the extra dollar on rubbing alcohol. Foskett met him again in the yards and was about to tell him once more to get off the right of way.

"No, Billy," my father said. "The dollar beyond wages didn't likely make the difference. He brought it on himself. If you saw Foskett's neck, you know he had to do it. The necktie knot saved Foskett's jugular."

When I asked if the man really was an old soldier and had been Over There, my father said he did not really know. "But he was a veteran, Billy. Or they wouldn't have kept him at the Vets' Hospital. Up the line."

. . . A wad of black, greasy waste on a switch tie. A turned-off engine, and the silence, except for a tractor plowing, which first seemed far away, then near . . .

Within two years, my father died, of natural causes. When the war in Europe came on my mother sold the farm and we moved to a smaller house in Sedley, not far from the railroad. As my father was too young for the First War, so was I too young for Korea by three months. Now it was my turn to go in the peacetime draft, and I wanted to get it over.

So I thought I never again would hear the noise of clubs or gun butts dropping to the ground, almost at the same time, but I did.

When a training battalion is assembled in the center of an infantry camp, in Texas, and when you have been on the firing range all day, and when the entire battalion stands too long at present arms, you hear that identical noise, the noise of hands slapping the taut slings of rifles, hundreds of hands slapping taut leather almost at the same instant, for order arms, when the sun is going down.

That identical noise, except fainter, and the hopeless splotch of waste on a switch tie brought more than a memory. As I turned back to my mother's house, I suddenly knew I would ask the first nice girl—even if she was not entirely pretty, but if she was nice—I would ask her to marry me. I would ask her against the day when the world was a freight yard.

And that is what happened.

I met my sergeant's daughter one evening in Texas, after the sun went down. We were standing on her porch, and love is what I called it, and after a minute she said, yes. Yes. Through the window I saw the half-averted profile of her father. The sergeant from habit was erect in his customary chair, his khaki shirt still pressed, glittering from starch in the bright parade ground light inside the room. His profile was someone I remembered—of Foskett, yes, and my father too. But, for the moment he was looking the other way, and so I kissed her.

John Steinbeck

The Promise

In a mid-afternoon of spring, the little boy Jody walked martially along the brushlined road toward his home ranch. Banging his knee against the golden lard bucket he used for school lunch, he contrived a good bass drum, while his tongue fluttered sharply against his teeth to fill in snare drums and occasional trumpets. Some time back the other members of the squad that walked so smartly from the school had turned into the various little canyons and taken the wagon roads to their own home ranches. Now Jody marched seemingly alone, with high-lifted knees and pounding feet; but behind him there was a phantom army with great flags and swords, silent but deadly.

The afternoon was green and gold with spring. Underneath the spread branches of the oaks the plants grew pale and tall, and on the hills the feed was smooth and thick. The sage-brushes shone with new silver leaves and the oaks wore hoods of golden green. Over the hills there hung such a green odor that the horses on the flats galloped madly, and then stopped, wondering; lambs, and even old sheep, jumped in the air unexpectedly and landed on stiff legs, and went on eating; young clumsy calves butted their heads together and drew back and butted again.

As the grey and silent army marched past, led by Jody, the animals stopped their feeding and their play and watched it go by.

Suddenly Jody stopped. The grey army halted, bewildered and nervous. Jody went down on his knees. The army stood in long uneasy ranks for a moment, and then, with a soft sigh of sorrow, rose up in a faint grey mist and disappeared. Jody had seen the thorny crown of a horny-toad moving under the dust of the road. His grimy hand went out and grasped the spiked halo and held firmly while the little beast struggled. Then Jody turned the horny-toad over, exposing its pale gold stomach. With a gentle forefinger he stroked the throat and chest until the horny-toad relaxed, until its eyes closed and it lay languorous and asleep.

Jody opened his lunch pail and deposited the first game inside. He moved on now, his knees bent slightly, his shoulders crouched; his bare feet were wise and silent. In his right hand there was a long grey rifle. The brush along the road stirred restively under a new and unexpected population of grey tigers and grey bears. The hunting was very good, for by the time Jody reached the fork of the road where the mail box stood on a post, he had captured two more horny-toads, four little grass lizards, a blue snake, sixteen yellow-winged grasshoppers and a brown damp newt from under a rock. This assortment scrabbled unhappily against the tin of the lunch bucket.

At the road fork the rifle evaporated and the tigers and bears melted from the hillsides. Even the moist and uncomfortable creatures in the lunch pail ceased to exist, for the little red metal flag was up on the mail box, signifying that some postal matter was inside. Jody set his pail on the ground and opened the letter box. There was a Montgomery Ward catalog and a copy of the Salinas Weekly Journal. He slammed the box, picked up his lunch pail and trotted over the ridge and down into the cup of the ranch. Past the barn he ran, and past the used-up haystack and the bunkhouse and the cypress tree. He banged through the front screen door of the ranch house calling, "Ma'am, ma'am, there's a catalog."

Mrs. Tiflin was in the kitchen spooning clabbered milk into a cotton bag. She put down her work and rinsed her hands under the tap. "Here in the kitchen, Jody. Here I am."

He ran in and clattered his lunch pail on the sink. "Here it is. Can I open the catalog, ma'am?"

Mrs. Tiflin took up the spoon again and went back to her cottage cheese. "Don't lose it, Jody. Your father will want to see it." She scraped the last of the milk into the bag. "Oh, Jody, your father wants to see you before you go to your chores." She waved a cruising fly from the cheese bag.

Jody closed the new catalog in alarm. "Ma'am?"

"Why don't you ever listen? I say your father wants to see you."

The boy laid the catalog gently on the sink board. "Do you—is it something I did?"

Mrs. Tiflin laughed. "Always a bad conscience. What did you do?"

"Nothing, ma'am," he said lamely. But he couldn't remember, and besides it was impossible to know what action might later be construed as a crime.

His mother hung the full bag on a nail where it could drip into the sink. "He just said he wanted to see you when you got home. He's somewhere down by the barn."

Jody turned and went out the back door. Hearing his mother open the lunch pail and then gasp with rage, a memory stabbed him and he trotted away toward the barn, conscientiously not hearing the angry voice that called him from the house.

Carl Tiflin and Billy Buck, the ranch hand, stood against the lower pasture fence. Each man rested one foot on the lowest bar and both elbows on the top bar. They were talking slowly and aimlessly. In the pasture half a dozen horses nibbled contentedly at the sweet grass. The mare, Nellie, stood backed up against the gate, rubbing her buttocks on the heavy post.

Jody sidled uneasily near. He dragged one foot to give an impression of great innocence and nonchalance. When he arrived beside the men he put one foot on the lowest fence rail, rested his elbows on the second bar and looked into the pasture too. The two men glanced sideways at him.

"I wanted to see you," Carl said in the stern tone he reserved for children and animals.

"Yes, sir," said Jody guiltily.

"Billy, here, says you took good care of the pony before it died."

No punishment was in the air. Jody grew bolder. "Yes, sir, I did."

"Billy says you have a good patient hand with horses."

Jody felt a sudden warm friendliness for the ranch hand.

Billy put in, "He trained that pony as good as anybody I ever seen."

Then Carl Tiflin came gradually to the point. "If you could have another horse would you work for it?"

Jody shivered. "Yes, sir."

"Well, look here, then. Billy says the best way for you to be a good hand with horses is to raise a colt."

"It's the only good way," Billy interrupted.

"Now, look here, Jody," continued Carl. "Jess Taylor, up to the ridge ranch, has a fair stallion, but it'll cost five dollars. I'll put up the money, but you'll have to work it out all summer. Will you do that?"

Jody felt that his insides were shriveling. "Yes, sir," he said softly.

"And no complaining? And no forgetting when you're told to do something?"

"Yes, sir."

"Well, all right, then. Tomorrow morning you take Nellie up to the ridge ranch and get her bred. You'll have to take care of her, too, till she throws the colt."

"Yes, sir."

"You better get to the chickens and the wood now."

Jody slid away. In passing behind Billy Buck he very nearly put out his hand to touch the blue-jeaned legs. His shoulders swayed a little with maturity and importance.

He went to his work with unprecedented seriousness. This night he did not dump the can of grain to the chickens so that they had to leap over each other and struggle to get it. No, he spread the wheat so far and so carefully that the hens couldn't find some of it at all. And in the house, after listening to his mother's despair over boys who filled their lunch pails with slimy, suffocated reptiles, and bugs, he promised never to do it again. Indeed, Jody felt that all such foolishness was lost in the past. He was far too grown up ever to put horny-toads in his lunch pail any more. He carried in so much wood and built such a high structure with it that his mother walked in fear of an avalanche of oak. When he was done, when he had gathered eggs that had remained hidden for weeks, Jody walked down again past the cypress tree, and past the bunk house toward the pasture. A fat warty toad that looked out at him from under the watering trough had no emotional effect on him at all.

Carl Tiflin and Billy Buck were not in sight, but from a metallic ringing on the other side of the barn Jody knew that Billy Buck was just starting to milk a cow.

The other horses were eating toward the upper end of the pasture, but Nellie continued to rub herself nervously against the post. Jody walked slowly near, saying, "So, girl, so-o, Nellie." The mare's ears went back naughtily and her lips drew away from her yellow teeth. She turned her head around; her eyes were glazed and mad. Jody climbed to the top of the fence and hung his feet over and looked paternally down on the mare.

The evening hovered while he sat there. Bats and night-hawks flicked about. Billy Buck, walking toward the house carrying a full milk bucket, saw Jody and stopped. "It's a long time to wait," he said gently. "You'll get awful tired waiting."

"No I won't, Billy. How long will it be?"

"Nearly a year."

"Well, I won't get tired."

The triangle at the house rang stridently. Jody climbed down from the fence and walked to supper beside Billy Buck. He even put out his hand and took hold of the milk bucket to help carry it.

The next morning after breakfast Carl Tiflin folded a five-dollar bill in a piece of newspaper and pinned the package in the bib pocket of Jody's overalls. Billy Buck haltered the mare Nellie and led her out of the pasture.

"Be careful now," he warned. "Hold her up short here so she can't bite you. She's crazy as a coot."

Jody took hold of the halter leather itself and started up the hill toward the ridge ranch with Nellie skittering and jerking behind him. In the pasturage along the road the wild oat heads were just clearing their scabbards. The warm morning sun shone on Jody's back so sweetly that he was forced to take a serious stiff-legged hop now and then in spite of his maturity. On the fences the shiny blackbirds with red epaulets clicked their dry call. The meadowlarks sang like water, and the wild doves, concealed among the bursting leaves of the oaks, made a sound of restrained grieving. In the fields the rabbits sat sunning themselves, with only their forked ears showing above the grass heads.

After an hour of steady uphill walking, Jody turned into a narrow road that led up a steeper hill to the ridge ranch. He could see the red roof of the barn sticking up above the oak trees, and he could hear a dog barking unemotionally near the house.

Suddenly Nellie jerked back and nearly freed herself. From the direction of the barn Jody heard a shrill whistling scream and a splintering of wood, and then a man's voice shouting. Nellie reared and whinnied. When Jody held to the halter rope she ran at him with bared teeth. He dropped his hold and scuttled out of the way, into the brush. The high scream came from the oaks again, and Nellie answered it. With hoofs battering the ground the stallion appeared and charged down the hill trailing a broken halter rope. His eyes glittered feverishly. His stiff, erected nostrils were as red as flame. His black, sleek hide shone in the sunlight. The stallion came on so fast that he couldn't stop when he reached the mare. Nellie's ears went back; she whirled and kicked at him as he went by. The stallion spun around and reared. He struck the mare with his front hoof, and while she staggered under the blow, his teeth raked her neck and drew an ooze of blood.

Instantly Nellie's mood changed. She became coquettishly feminine. She nibbled his arched neck with her lips. She edged around and rubbed her shoulder against his shoulder. Jody stood half-hidden in the brush and watched. He heard the step of a horse behind him, but before he could turn, a hand caught him by the overall straps and lifted him off the ground. Jess Taylor sat the boy behind him on the horse.

"You might have got killed," he said. "Sundog's a mean devil sometimes. He busted his rope and went right through a gate."

Jody sat quietly, but in a moment he cried, "He'll hurt her, he'll kill her. Get him away!"

Jess chuckled. "She'll be all right. Maybe you'd better climb off and go up to the house for a little. You could get maybe a piece of pie up there."

But Jody shook his head. "She's mine, and the colt's going to be mine. I'm going to raise it up."

Jess nodded. "Yes, that's a good thing. Carl has good sense sometimes."

In a little while the danger was over. Jess lifted Jody down and then caught the stallion by its broken halter rope. And he rode ahead, while Jody followed, leading Nellie.

It was only after he had unpinned and handed over the five dollars, and after he had eaten two pieces of pie, that Jody started for home again. And Nellie followed docilely after him. She was so quiet that Jody climbed on a stump and rode her most of the way home.

The five dollars his father had advanced reduced Jody to peonage for the whole late spring and summer. When the hay was cut he drove a rake. He led the horse that pulled on the Jackson-fork tackle, and when the baler came he drove the circling horse that put pressure on the bales. In addition, Carl Tiflin taught him to milk and put a cow under his care, so that a new chore was added night and morning.

The bay mare Nellie quickly grew complacent. As she walked about the yellowing hillsides or worked at easy tasks, her lips were curled in a perpetual fatuous smile. She moved slowly, with the calm importance of an empress. When she was put to a team, she pulled steadily and unemotionally. Jody went to see her every day. He studied her with critical eyes and saw no change whatever.

One afternoon Billy Buck leaned the many-tined manure fork against the barn wall. He loosened his belt and tucked in his shirt-tail and tightened the belt again. He picked one of the little straws from his hatband and put it in the corner of his mouth. Jody, who was helping Doubletree Mutt, the big serious dog, to dig out a gopher, straightened up as the ranch hand sauntered out of the barn.

"Let's go up and have a look at Nellie," Billy suggested.

Instantly Jody fell into step with him. Doubletree Mutt watched them over his shoulder; then he dug furiously, growled, sounded little sharp yelps to indicate that the gopher was practically caught. When he looked over his shoulder again, and saw that neither Jody nor Billy was interested, he climbed reluctantly out of the hole and followed them up the hill.

The wild oats were ripening. Every head bent sharply under its load of grain, and the grass was dry enough so that it made a swishing sound as Jody and Billy stepped through it. Halfway up the hill they could see Nellie and the iron-grey gelding, Pete, nibbling the heads from the wild oats. When they approached, Nellie looked at them and backed her ears and bobbed her head up and down rebelliously. Billy walked to her and put his hand under her mane and patted her neck, until her ears came forward again and she nibbled delicately at his shirt.

Jody asked, "Do you think she's really going to have a colt?"

Billy rolled the lids back from the mare's eyes with his thumb and forefinger. He felt the lower lip and fingered the black, leathery teats. "I wouldn't be surprised," he said.

"Well, she isn't changed at all. It's three months gone."

Billy rubbed the mare's flat forehead with his knuckle while she grunted with pleasure. "I told you you'd get tired waiting. It'll be five months more before you can even see a sign, and it'll be at least eight months more before she throws the colt, about next January."

Jody sighed deeply. "It's a long time, isn't it?"

"And then it'll be about two years more before you can ride."

Jody cried out in despair, "I'll be grown up."

"Yep, you'll be an old man," said Billy.

"What color do you think the colt'll be?"

"Why, you can't ever tell. The stud is black and the dam is bay. Colt might be black or bay or grey or dapple. You can't tell. Sometimes a black dam might have a white colt."

"Well, I hope it's black, and a stallion."

"If it's a stallion, we'll have to geld it. Your father wouldn't let you have a stallion."

"Maybe he would," Jody said. "I could train him not to be mean."

Billy pursed his lips, and the little straw that had been in the corner of his mouth rolled down to the center. "You can't ever trust a stallion," he said critically. "They're mostly fighting and making trouble. Sometimes when they're feeling funny they won't work. They make the mares uneasy and kick hell out of the geldings. Your father wouldn't let you keep a stallion."

Nellie sauntered away, nibbling the drying grass. Jody skinned the grain from a grass stem and threw the handful into the air, so that each pointed, feathered seed sailed out like a dart. "Tell me how it'll be, Billy. Is it like when the cows have calves?"

"Just about. Mares are a little more sensitive. Sometimes you have to be there to help the mare. And sometimes if it's wrong, you have to——" he paused.

"Have to what, Billy?"

"Have to tear the colt to pieces to get it out, or the mare'll die."

"But it won't be that way this time, will it Billy?"

"Oh, no. Nellie's thrown good colts."

"Can I be there, Billy? Will you be certain to call me? It's my colt."

"Sure, I'll call you. Of course I will."

"Tell me how it'll be."

"Why, you've seen the cows calving. It's almost the same. The mare starts groaning and stretching, and then, if it's a good right birth, the head and forefeet come out, and the front hoofs kick a hole just the way the calves do. And the colt starts to breathe. It's good to be there, 'cause if its feet aren't right maybe he can't break the sack, and then he might smother."

Jody whipped his leg with a bunch of grass. "We'll have to be there, then, won't we?"

"Oh, we'll be there, all right."

They turned and walked slowly down the hill toward the barn. Jody was tortured with a thing he had to say, although he didn't want to. "Billy," he began miserably, "Billy, you won't let anything happen to the colt, will you?"

And Billy knew he was thinking of the red pony, Gabilan, and of how it died of strangles. Billy knew he had been infallible before that, and now he was capable of failure. This knowledge made Billy much less sure of himself than he had been. "I can't tell," he said roughly. "All sorts of things might happen, and they wouldn't be my fault. I can't do everything." He felt badly about his lost prestige, and so he said, meanly, "I'll do everything I know, but I won't promise anything. Nellie's a good mare. She's thrown good colts before. She ought to this time." And he walked away from Jody and went into the saddle-room beside the barn, for his feelings were hurt.

Jody traveled often to the brushline behind the house. A rusty iron pipe ran a thin stream of spring water into an old green tub. Where the water spilled over and sank into the ground there was a patch of perpetually green grass. Even when the hills were brown and baked in the summer that little patch was green. The water whined softly into the trough all the year round. This place had grown to be a center-point for Jody. When he had been punished the cool green grass and the singing water soothed him. When he had been mean the biting acid of meanness left him at the brushline. When he sat in the grass and listened to the purling stream, the barriers set up in his mind by the stern day went down to ruin.

On the other hand, the black cypress tree by the bunkhouse was as repulsive as the water-tub was dear; for to this tree all the pigs came, sooner or later, to be slaughtered. Pig killing was fascinating, with the screaming and the blood, but it made Jody's heart beat so fast that it hurt him. After the pigs were scalded in the big iron tripod kettle and their skins were scraped and white, Jody had to go to the water-tub to sit in the grass until his heart grew quiet. The water-tub and the black cypress were opposites and enemies.

When Billy left him and walked angrily away, Jody turned up toward the house. He thought of Nellie as he walked, and of the little colt. Then suddenly he saw that he was under the black cypress, under the very singletree where the pigs were hung. He brushed his dry-grass hair off his forehead and hurried on. It seemed to him an unlucky thing to be thinking of his colt in the very slaughter place, especially after what Billy had said. To counteract any evil result of that bad conjunction he walked quickly past the ranch house, through the chicken yard, through the vegetable patch, until he came at last to the brushline.

He sat down in the green grass. The trilling water sounded in his ears. He looked over the farm buildings and across at the round hills, rich and yellow with grain. He could see Nellie feeding on the slope. As usual the water place eliminated time and distance. Jody saw a black, long-legged colt, butting against Nellie's flanks, demanding milk. And then he saw himself breaking a large colt to halter. All in a few moments the colt grew to be a magnificent animal, deep of chest, with a neck as high and arched as a sea-horse's neck, with a tail that tongued and rippled like black flame. This horse was terrible to everyone but Jody. In the schoolyard the boys begged rides, and Jody smilingly agreed. But no sooner were they mounted than the black demon pitched them off. Why, that was his name, Black Demon! For a moment the trilling water and the grass and the sunshine came back, and then . . .

Sometimes in the night the ranch people, safe in their beds, heard a roar of hoofs go by. They said, "It's Jody, on Demon. He's helping out the sheriff again." And then . . .

The golden dust filled the air in the arena at the Salinas Rodeo. The announcer called the roping contests. When Jody rode the black horse to the starting chute the other contestants shrugged and gave up first place, for it was well known that Jody and Demon could rope and throw and tie a steer a great deal quicker than any roping team of two men could. Jody was not a boy any more, and Demon was not a horse. The two together were one glorious individual. And then . . .

The President wrote a letter and asked them to help catch a bandit in Washington. Jody settled himself comfortably in the grass. The little stream of water whined into the mossy tub.

The year passed slowly on. Time after time Jody gave up his colt for lost. No change had taken place in Nellie. Carl Tiflin still drove her to a light cart, and she pulled on a hay rake and worked the Jackson-fork tackle when the hay was being put into the barn.

The summer passed, and the warm bright autumn. And then the frantic morning winds began to twist along the ground, and a chill came into the air, and the poison oak turned red. One morning in September, when he had finished his breakfast, Jody's mother called him into the kitchen. She was pouring boiling water into a bucket full of dry middlings and stirring the materials to a steaming paste.

"Yes, ma'am?" Jody asked.

"Watch how I do it. You'll have to do it after this every other morning."

"Well, what is it?"

"Why, it's warm mash for Nellie. It'll keep her in good shape."

Jody rubbed his forehead with a knuckle. "Is she all right?" he asked timidly.

Mrs. Tiflin put down the kettle and stirred the mash with a wooden paddle. "Of course she's all right, only you've got to take better care of her from now on. Here, take this breakfast out to her!"

Jody seized the bucket and ran, down past the bunkhouse, past the barn, with the heavy bucket banging against his knees. He found Nellie playing with the water in the trough, pushing waves and tossing her head so that the water slopped out on the ground.

Jody climbed the fence and set the bucket of steaming mash beside her. Then he stepped back to look at her. And she was changed. Her stomach was swollen. When she moved, her feet touched the ground gently. She buried her nose in the bucket and gobbled the hot breakfast. And when she had finished and had pushed the bucket around the ground with her nose a little, she stepped quietly over to Jody and rubbed her cheek against him.

Billy Buck came out of the saddle-room and walked over. "Starts fast when it starts, doesn't it?"

"Did it come all at once?"

"Oh, no, you just stopped looking for a while." He pulled her head around toward Jody. "She's goin' to be nice, too. See how nice her eyes are! Some mares get mean, but when they turn nice, they just love everything." Nellie slipped her head under Billy's arm and rubbed her neck up and down between his arm and his side. "You better treat her awful nice now," Billy said.

"How long will it be?" Jody demanded breathlessly.

The man counted in whispers on his fingers. "About three months," he said aloud. "You can't tell exactly. Sometimes it's eleven months to the day, but it might be two weeks early, or a month late, without hurting anything."

Jody looked hard at the ground. "Billy," he began nervously, "Billy, you'll call me when it's getting born, won't you? You'll let me be there won't you?"

Billy bit the tip of Nellie's ear with his front teeth. "Carl says he wants you to start right at the start. That's the only way to learn. Nobody can tell you anything. Like my old man did with me about the saddle blanket. He was a government packer when I was your size, and I helped him some. One day I left a wrinkle in my saddle blanket and made a saddle-sore. My old man didn't give me hell at all. But the next morning he saddled me up with a forty-pound stock saddle. I had to lead my horse and carry that saddle over a whole damn mountain in the sun. It darn near killed me, but I never left no wrinkles in a blanket again. I couldn't. I never in my life since then put on a blanket but I felt that saddle on my back."

Jody reached up a hand and took hold of Nellie's mane. "You'll tell me what to do about everything, won't you? I guess you know everything about horses, don't you?"

Billy laughed. "Why I'm half horse myself, you see," he said. "My ma died when I was born, and being my old man was a government packer in the mountains, and no cows around most of the time, why he just gave me mostly mare's milk." He continued seriously. "And horses know that. Don't you know it, Nellie?"

The mare turned her head and looked full into his eyes for a moment, and this is a thing horses practically never do. Billy was proud and sure of himself now. He boasted a little. "I'll see you get a good colt. I'll start you right. And if you do like I say, you'll have the best horse in the country."

That made Jody feel warm and proud, too; so proud that when he went back to the house he bowed his legs and swayed his shoulders as horsemen do. And he whispered, "Whoa, you Black Demon, you! Steady down there and keep your feet on the ground."

The winter fell sharply. A few preliminary gusty showers, and then a strong steady rain. The hills lost their straw color and blackened under the water, and the winter streams scrambled noisily down the canyons. The mushrooms and puffballs popped up and the new grass started before Christmas.

But this year Christmas was not the central day to Jody. Some undetermined time in January had become the axis day around which the months swung. When the rains fell, he put Nellie in a box stall and fed her warm food every morning and curried her and brushed her.

The mare was swelling so greatly that Jody became alarmed. "She'll pop wide open," he said to Billy.

Billy laid his strong hand against Nellie's swollen abdomen. "Feel here," he said quietly. "You can feel it move. I guess it would surprise you if there were twin colts."

"You don't think so?" Jody cried. "You don't think it will be twins, do you, Billy?"

"No, I don't, but it does happen, sometimes."

During the first two weeks of January it rained steadily.

Jody spent most of his time, when he wasn't in school, in the box stall with Nellie. Twenty times a day he put his hand on her stomach to feel the colt move. Nellie became more and more gentle and friendly to him. She rubbed her nose on him. She whinnied softly when he walked into the barn.

Carl Tiflin came to the barn with Jody one day. He looked admiringly at the groomed bay coat, and he felt the firm flesh over ribs and shoulders. "You've done a good job," he said to Jody. And this was the greatest praise he knew how to give. Jody was tight with pride.

The fifteenth of January came, and the colt was not born. And the twentieth came; a lump of fear began to form in Jody's stomach. "Is it all right?" he demanded of Billy.

"Oh, sure."

And again, "Are you sure it's going to be all right?"

Billy stroked the mare's neck. She swayed her head uneasily. "I told you it wasn't always the same time, Jody. You just have to wait."

When the end of the month arrived with no birth, Jody grew frantic. Nellie was so big that her breath came heavily, and her ears were close together and straight up, as though her head ached. Jody's sleep grew restless, and his dreams confused.

On the night of the second of February he awakened crying. His mother called to him, "Jody, you're dreaming. Wake up and start over again."

But Jody was filled with terror and desolation. He lay quietly a few moments, waiting for his mother to go back to sleep, and then he slipped his clothes on, and crept out in his bare feet.

The night was black and thick. A little misting rain fell. The cypress tree and the bunkhouse loomed and then dropped back into the mist. The barn door screeched as he opened it, a thing it never did in the daytime. Jody went to the rack and found a lantern and a tin box of matches. He lighted the wick and walked down the long straw-covered aisle to Nellie's stall. She was standing up. Her whole body weaved from side to side. Jody called to her, "So, Nellie, so-o, Nellie," but she did not stop her swaying nor look around. When he stepped into the stall and touched her on the shoulder she shivered under his hand. Then Billy Buck's voice came from the hayloft right above the stall.

"Jody, what are you doing?"

Jody started back and turned miserable eyes up toward the nest where Billy was lying in the hay. "Is she all right, do you think?"

"Why sure, I think so."

"You won't let anything happen, Billy, you're sure you won't?"

Billy growled down at him, "I told you I'd call you, and I will. Now you get back to bed and stop worrying that mare. She's got enough to do without you worrying her."

Jody cringed, for he had never heard Billy speak in such a tone. "I only thought I'd come and see," he said, "I woke up."

Billy softened a little then. "Well, you get to bed. I don't want you bothering her. I told you I'd get you a good colt. Get along now."

Jody walked slowly out of the barn. He blew out the lantern and set it in the rack. The blackness of the night, and the chilled mist struck him and enfolded him. He wished he believed everything Billy said as he had before the pony died. It was a moment before his eyes, blinded by the feeble lantern-flame, could make any form of the darkness. The damp ground chilled his bare feet. At the cypress tree the roosting turkeys chattered a little in alarm, and the two good dogs responded to their duty and came charging out, barking to frighten away the coyotes they thought were prowling under the tree.

As he crept through the kitchen, Jody stumbled over a chair. Carl called from his bedroom. "Who's there? What's the matter there?"

And Mrs. Tiflin said sleepily, "What's the matter, Carl?"

The next second Carl came out of the bedroom carrying a candle, and found Jody before he could get into bed. "What are you doing out?"

Jody turned shyly away. "I was down to see the mare."

For a moment anger at being awakened fought with approval in Jody's father. "Listen," he said, finally, "there's not a man in this country that knows more about colts than Billy. You leave it to him."

Words burst out of Jody's mouth. "But the pony died——"

"Don't you go blaming that on him," Carl said sternly. "If Billy can't save a horse, it can't be saved."

Mrs. Tiflin called, "Make him clean his feet and go to bed, Carl. He'll be sleepy all day tomorrow."

It seemed to Jody that he had just closed his eyes to try to go to sleep when he was shaken violently by the shoulder. Billy Buck stood beside him, holding a lantern in his hand. "Get up," he said. "Hurry up." He turned and walked quickly out of the room.

Mrs. Tiflin called, "What's the matter? Is that you, Billy?"

"Yes, ma'am."

"Is Nellie ready?"

"Yes, ma'am."

"All right, I'll get up and heat some water in case you need it."

Jody jumped into his clothes so quickly that he was out the back door before Billy's swinging lantern was halfway to the barn. There was a rim of dawn on the mountaintops, but no light had penetrated into the cup of the ranch yet. Jody ran frantically after the lantern and caught up to Billy just as he reached the barn. Billy hung the lantern to a nail on the stall-side and took off his blue denim coat. Jody saw that he wore only a sleeveless shirt under it.

Nellie was standing rigid and stiff. While they watched, she crouched. Her whole body was wrung with a spasm. The spasm passed. But in a few moments it started all over again, and passed.

Billy muttered nervously, "There's something wrong." His bare hand disappeared. "Oh, Jesus," he said. "It's wrong."

The spasm came again, and this time Billy strained, and the muscles stood out on his arm and shoulder. He heaved strongly, his forehead beaded with perspiration. Nellie cried with pain. Billy was muttering, "It's wrong. I can't turn it. It's way wrong. It's turned all around wrong."

He glared wildly toward Jody. And then his fingers made a careful, careful diagnosis. His cheeks were growing tight and grey. He looked for a long questioning minute at Jody standing back of the stall. Then Billy stepped to the rack under the manure window and picked up a horseshoe hammer with his wet right hand.

"Go outside, Jody," he said.

The boy stood still and stared dully at him.

"Go outside, I tell you. It'll be too late."

Jody didn't move.

Then Billy walked quickly to Nellie's head. He cried, "Turn your face away, damn you, turn your face."

This time Jody obeyed. His head turned sideways. He heard Billy whispering hoarsely in the stall. And then he heard a hollow crunch of bone. Nellie chuckled shrilly. Jody looked back in time to see the hammer rise and fall again on the flat forehead. Then Nellie fell heavily to her side and quivered for a moment.

Billy jumped to the swollen stomach; his big pocket-knife was in his hand. He lifted the skin and drove the knife in. He sawed and ripped at the tough belly. The air filled with the sick odor of warm living entrails. The other horses reared back against their halter chains and squealed and kicked.

Billy dropped the knife. Both of his arms plunged into the terrible ragged hole and dragged out a big, white, dripping bundle. His teeth tore a hole in the covering. A little black head appeared through the tear, and little slick, wet ears. A gurgling breath was drawn, and then another. Billy shucked off the sac and found his knife and cut the string. For a moment he held the little black colt in his arms and looked at it. And then he walked slowly over and laid it in the straw at Jody's feet.

Billy's face and arms and chest were dripping red. His body shivered and his teeth chattered. His voice was gone; he spoke in a throaty whisper. "There's your colt. I promised. And there it is. I had to do it—had to." He stopped and looked over his shoulder into the box stall. "Go get hot water and a sponge," he whispered. "Wash him and dry him the way his mother would. You'll have to feed him by hand. But there's your colt, the way I promised."

Jody stared stupidly at the wet, panting foal. It stretched out its chin and tried to raise its head. Its blank eyes were navy blue.

"God damn you," Billy shouted, "will you go now for the water? Will you go?"

Then Jody turned and trotted out of the barn into the dawn. He ached from his throat to his stomach. His legs were stiff and heavy. He tried to be glad because of the colt, but the bloody face, and the haunted, tired eyes of Billy Buck hung in the air ahead of him.

William Faulkner

Wash

Sutpen stood above the pallet bed on which the mother and child lay. Between the shrunken planking of the wall the early sunlight fell in long pencil strokes, breaking upon his straddled legs and upon the riding whip in his hand, and lay across the still shape of the mother, who lay looking up at him from still, inscrutable, sullen eyes, the child at her side wrapped in a piece of dingy though clean cloth. Behind them an old Negro woman squatted beside the rough hearth where a meager fire smoldered.

"Well, Milly," Sutpen said, "too bad you're not a mare. Then I could give you a decent stall in the stable."

Still the girl on the pallet did not move. She merely continued to look up at him without expression, with a young, sullen, inscrutable face still pale from recent travail. Sutpen moved, bringing into the splintered pencils of sunlight the face of a man of sixty. He said quietly to the squatting Negress, "Griselda foaled this morning."

"Horse or mare?" the Negress said.

"A horse. A damned fine colt. . . . What's this?" He indicated the pallet with the hand which held the whip.

From *Doctor Martino and Other Stories*, by William Faulkner. Copyright 1934 by William Faulkner. Reprinted from *Collected Short Stories of William Faulkner* by permission of Random House, Inc.

"That un's a mare, I reckon."

"Hah," Sutpen said. "A damned fine colt. Going to be the spit and image of old Rob Roy when I rode him North in '61. Do you remember?"

"Yes, Marster."

"Hah." He glanced back towards the pallet. None could have said if the girl still watched him or not. Again his whip hand indicated the pallet. "Do whatever they need with whatever we've got to do it with." He went out, passing out the crazy doorway and stepping down into the rank weeds (there yet leaned rusting against the corner of the porch the scythe which Wash had borrowed from him three months ago to cut them with) where his horse waited, where Wash stood holding the reins.

When Colonel Sutpen rode away to fight the Yankees, Wash did not go. "I'm looking after the Kernel's place and niggers," he would tell all who asked him and some who had not asked—a gaunt, malaria-ridden man with pale, questioning eyes, who looked about thirty-five, though it was known that he had not only a daughter but an eight-year-old granddaughter as well. This was a lie, as most of them—the few remaining men between eighteen and fifty—to whom he told it, knew, though there were some who believed that he himself really believed it, though even these believed that he had better sense than to put it to the test with Mrs. Sutpen or the Sutpen slaves. Knew better or was just too lazy and shiftless to try it, they said, knowing that his sole connection with the Sutpen plantation lay in the fact that for years now Colonel Sutpen had allowed him to squat in a crazy shack on a slough in the river bottom on the Sutpen place, which Sutpen had built for a fishing lodge in his bachelor days and which had since fallen in dilapidation from disuse, so that now it looked like an aged or sick wild beast crawled terrifically there to drink in the act of dying.

The Sutpen slaves themselves heard of his statement. They laughed. It was not the first time they had laughed at him, calling him white trash behind his back. They began to ask him themselves, in groups, meeting him in the faint road which led up from the slough and the old fish camp, "Why ain't you at de war, white man?"

Pausing, he would look about the ring of black faces and white eyes and teeth behind which derision lurked. "Because I got a daughter and family to keep," he said. "Git out of my road, niggers."

"Niggers?" they repeated; "niggers?" laughing now. "Who him, calling us niggers?"

"Yes," he said. "I ain't got no niggers to look after my folks if I was gone."

"Nor nothing else but dat shack down yon dat Cunnel wouldn't *let* none of us live in."

Now he cursed them; sometimes he rushed at them, snatching up a stick from the ground while they scattered before him, yet seeming to surround him still with that black laughing, derisive, evasive, inescapable, leaving him panting and impotent and raging. Once it happened in the very back yard of the big house itself. This was after bitter news had come down from the Tennessee mountains and from Vicksburg, and Sherman had passed through the plantation, and most of the Negroes had followed him. Almost everything else had gone with the Federal troops, and Mrs. Sutpen had sent word to Wash that he could have the scuppernongs ripening in the arbor in the back yard. This time it was a house servant, one of the few Negroes who remained; this time the Negress had to retreat up the kitchen steps, where she turned, "Stop right dar, white man. Stop right whar you is. You ain't never crossed dese steps whilst Cunnel here, and you ain't ghy' do hit now."

This was true. But there was this of a kind of pride: he had never tried to enter the big house, even though he believed that if he had, Sutpen would have received him, permitted him. "But I ain't going to give no black nigger the chance to tell me I can't go nowhere," he said to himself. "I ain't even going to give Kernel the chance to have to cuss a nigger on my account." This, though he and Sutpen had spent more than one afternoon together on those rare Sundays when there would be no company in the house. Perhaps his mind knew that it was because Sutpen had nothing else to do, being a man who could not bear his own company. Yet the fact remained that the two of them would spend whole afternoons in the scuppernong arbor, Sutpen in the hammock and Wash squatting against a post, a pail of cistern water between them, taking drink for drink from the same demijohn. Meanwhile on weekdays he would see the fine figure of the man—they were the same age almost to a day, though neither of them (perhaps because Wash had a grandchild while Sutpen's son was a youth in school) ever thought of himself as being so—on the fine figure of the black stallion, galloping about the plantation. For that moment his heart would be quiet and proud. It would seem to him that that world in which Negroes, whom the Bible told him had been created and cursed by God to be brute and vassal to all men of white skin, were better found and housed and even clothed than he and his; that world in which he sensed always about him mocking echoes of black laughter was but a dream and an illusion, and that the actual world was this one across which his own lonely apotheosis seemed to gallop on the black thoroughbred, thinking how the Book said also that all men were created in the image of God and hence all men made the same image in God's eyes at least; so that he could say, as though speaking of himself, "A fine proud man. If God Himself was to come down and ride the natural earth, that's what He would aim to look like."

Sutpen returned in 1865, on the black stallion. He seemed to have aged ten years. His son had been killed in action the same winter in which his wife had died. He returned with his citation for gallantry from the hand of General Lee to a ruined plantation, where for a year now his daughter had subsisted partially on the meager bounty of the man to whom fifteen years ago he had granted permission to live in that tumbledown fishing camp whose very existence he had at the time forgotten. Wash was there to meet him, unchanged: still gaunt, still ageless, with his pale, questioning gaze, his air diffident, a little servile, a little familiar.

"Well Kernel," Wash said, "they kilt us but they ain't whupped us yit, air they?"

That was the tenor of their conversation for the next five years. It was inferior whisky which they drank now together from a stoneware jug, and it was not in the scuppernong arbor. It was in the rear of the little store which Sutpen managed to set up on the highroad: a frame shelved room where, with Wash for clerk and porter, he dispensed kerosene and staple foodstuffs and stale gaudy candy and cheap beads and ribbons to Negroes or poor whites of Wash's own kind, who came afoot or on gaunt mules to haggle tediously for dimes and quarters with a man who at one time could gallop (the black stallion was still alive; the stable in which his jealous get lived was in better repair than the house where the master himself lived) for ten miles across his own fertile land and who had led troops gallantly in battle; until Sutpen in fury would empty the store, close and lock the doors from the inside. Then he and Wash would repair to the rear and the jug. But the talk would not be quiet now, as when Sutpen lay in the hammock, delivering an arrogant monologue while Wash squatted guffawing against his post. They both sat now, though Sutpen had the single chair while Wash used whatever box or keg was handy, and even this for just a little while, because soon Sutpen would reach that stage of impotent and furious undefeat in which he would rise, swaying and plunging, and declare again that he would take his pistol and the black stallion and ride single-handed into Washington and kill Lincoln, dead now, and Sherman, now a private citizen. "Kill them!" he would shout. "Shoot them down like the dogs they are—"

"Sho, Kernel; sho, Kernel," Wash would say, catching Sutpen as he fell. Then he would commandeer the first passing wagon or, lacking that, he would walk the mile to the nearest neighbor and borrow one and return and carry Sutpen home. He entered the house now. He had been doing so for a long time, taking Sutpen home in whatever borrowed wagon might be, talking him into locomotion with cajoling murmurs as though he were a horse, a stallion himself. The daughter would meet them and hold open the door without a word. He would carry his burden through the once white formal entrance, surmounted by a fanlight imported piece by piece from Europe and with a board now nailed over a missing pane, across a velvet carpet from which all nap was now gone, and up a formal stairs, now but a fading ghost of bare boards between two strips of fading paint, and into the bedroom. It would be dusk by now, and he would let his burden sprawl onto the bed and undress it and then he would sit quietly in a chair beside. After a time the daughter would come to the door. "We're all right now," he would tell her. "Don't you worry none, Miss Judith."

Then it would become dark, and after a while he would lie down on the floor beside the bed, though not to sleep, because after a time—sometimes before midnight—the man on the bed would stir and groan and then speak. "Wash?"

"Hyer I am, Kernel. You go back to sleep. We ain't whupped yit, air we? Me and you kin do hit."

Even then he had already seen the ribbon about his granddaughter's waist. She was now fifteen, already mature, after the early way of her kind. He knew where the ribbon came from; he had been seeing it and its kind daily for three years, even if she had lied about where she got it, which she did not, at once bold, sullen, and fearful. "Sho now," he said. "Ef Kernel wants to give hit to you, I hope you minded to thank him."

His heart was quiet, even when he saw the dress, watching her secret, defiant, frightened face when she told him that Miss Judith, the daughter, had helped her to make it. But he was quite grave when he approached Sutpen after they closed the store that afternoon, following the other to the rear.

"Get the jug," Sutpen directed.

"Wait," Wash said. "Not yit for a minute."

Neither did Sutpen deny the dress. "What about it?" he said.

But Wash met his arrogant stare; he spoke quietly. "I've knowed you for going on twenty years. I ain't never yit denied to do what you told me to do. And I'm a man nigh sixty. And she ain't nothing but a fifteen-year-old gal."

"Meaning that I'd harm a girl? I, a man as old as you are?"

"If you was ara other man, I'd say you was as old as me. And old or no old, I wouldn't let her keep that dress nor nothing else that come from your hand. But you are different."

"How different?" But Wash merely looked at him with his pale, questioning, sober eyes. "So that's why you are afraid of me?"

Now Wash's gaze no longer questioned. It was tranquil, serene. "I ain't afraid. Because you air brave. It ain't that you were a brave man at one minute or day of your life and got a paper to show hit from General Lee. But you air brave, the same as you air alive and breathing. That's where hit's different. Hit don't need no ticket from nobody to tell me that. And I know that whatever you handle or tech, whether hit's a regiment of men or a ignorant gal or just a hound dog, that you will make hit right."

Now it was Sutpen who looked away, turning suddenly, brusquely. "Get the jug," he said sharply.

"Sho, Kernel," Wash said.

So on that Sunday dawn two years later, having watched the Negro midwife, which he had walked three miles to fetch, enter the crazy door beyond which his granddaughter lay wailing, his heart was still quiet though concerned. He knew what they had been saying—the Negroes in cabins about the land, the white men who loafed all day long about the store, watching quietly the three of them: Sutpen, himself, his granddaughter with her air of brazen and shrinking defiance as her condition became daily more and more obvious, like three actors that came and went upon a stage. "I know what they say to one another," he thought. "I can almost hyear them: *Wash Jones has fixed old Sutpen at last. Hit taken him twenty years, but he has done hit at last.*"

It would be dawn after a while, though not yet. From the house, where the lamp shone dim beyond the warped doorframe, his granddaughter's voice came steadily as though run by a clock, while thinking went slowly and terrifically, fumbling, involved somehow with a sound of galloping hooves, until there broke suddenly free in mid-gallop the fine proud figure of the man on the fine proud stallion, galloping; and then that at which thinking fumbled, broke free too and quite clear, not in justification nor even explanation, but as the apotheosis, lonely, explicable, beyond all fouling by human touch: "He is bigger than all them Yankees that kilt his son and his wife and taken his niggers and ruined his land, bigger than this hyer durn country that he fit for and that has denied him into keeping a little country store; bigger than the denial which hit helt to his lips like the bitter cup in the Book. And how could I have lived this nigh to him for twenty years without being teched and changed by him? Maybe I ain't as big as him and maybe I ain't done none of the galloping. But at least I done been drug along. Me and him kin do hit, if so be he will show me what he aims for me to do."

Then it was dawn. Suddenly he could see the house, and the old Negress in the door looking at him. Then he realized that his granddaughter's voice had ceased. "It's a girl," the Negress said. "You can go tell him if you want to." She reëntered the house.

"A girl," he repeated; "a girl"; in astonishment, hearing the galloping hooves, seeing the proud galloping figure emerge again. He seemed to watch it pass, galloping through avatars which marked the accumulation of years, time, to the climax where it galloped beneath a brandished saber and a shot-torn flag rushing down a sky in color like thunderous sulphur, thinking for the first time in his life that perhaps Sutpen was an old man like himself. "Gittin a gal," he thought in that astonishment; then he thought with the pleased surprise of a child: "Yes, sir. Be dawg if I ain't lived to be a great-grandpaw after all."

He entered the house. He moved clumsily, on tiptoe, as if he no longer lived there, as if the infant which had just drawn breath and cried in light had dispossessed him, be it of his own blood too though it might. But even above the pallet he could see little save the blur of his granddaughter's exhausted face. Then the Negress squatting at the hearth spoke, "You better gawn tell him if you going to. Hit's daylight now."

But this was not necessary. He had no more than turned the corner of the porch where the scythe leaned which he had borrowed three months ago to clear away the weeds through which he walked, when Sutpen himself rode up on the old stallion. He did not wonder how Sutpen had got the word. He took it for granted that this was what had brought the other out at this hour on Sunday morning, and he stood while the other dismounted, and he took the reins from Sutpen's hand, an expression on his gaunt face almost imbecile with a kind of weary triumph, saying, "Hit's a gal, Kernel. I be dawg if you ain't as old as I am—" until Sutpen passed him and entered the house. He stood there with the reins in his hand and heard Sutpen cross the floor to the pallet. He heard what Sutpen said, and something seemed to stop dead in him before going on.

The sun was now up, the swift sun of Mississippi latitudes, and it seemed to him that he stood beneath a strange sky, in a strange scene, familiar only as things are familiar in dreams, like the dreams of falling to one who has never climbed. "I kain't have heard what I thought I heard," he thought quietly. "I know I kain't." Yet the voice, the familiar voice which had said the words was still speaking, talking now to the old Negress about a colt foaled that morning. "That's why he was up so early," he thought. "That was hit. Hit ain't me and mine. Hit ain't even hisn that got him outen bed."

Sutpen emerged. He descended into the weeds, moving with that heavy deliberation which would have been haste when he was younger. He had not yet looked full at Wash. He said, "Dicey will stay and tend to her. You better—" Then he seemed to see Wash facing him and paused. "What?" he said.

"You said—" To his own ears Wash's voice sounded flat and ducklike, like a deaf man's. "You said if she was a mare, you could give her a good stall in the stable."

"Well?" Sutpen said. His eyes widened and narrowed, almost like a man's fists flexing and shutting, as Wash began to advance towards him, stooping a little. Very astonishment kept Sutpen still for the moment, watching that man whom in twenty years he had no more known to make any motion save at command than he had the horse which he rode. Again his eyes narrowed and widened; without moving he seemed to rear suddenly upright. "Stand back," he said suddenly and sharply. "Don't you touch me."

"I'm going to tech you, Kernel," Wash said in that flat, quiet, almost soft voice, advancing.

Sutpen raised the hand which held the riding whip; the old Negress peered around the crazy door with her black gargoyle face of a worn gnome. "Stand back, Wash," Sutpen said. Then he struck. The old Negress leaped down into the weeds with the agility of a goat and fled. Sutpen slashed Wash again across the face with the whip, striking him to his knees. When Wash rose and advanced once more he held in his hands the scythe which he had borrowed from Sutpen three months ago and which Sutpen would never need again.

When he reëntered the house his granddaughter stirred on the pallet bed and called his name fretfully. "What was that?" she said.

"What was what, honey?"

"That ere racket out there."

" 'Twarn't nothing," he said gently. He knelt and touched her hot forehead clumsily. "Do you want ara thing?"

"I want a sup of water," she said querulously. "I been laying here wanting a sup of water a long time, but don't nobody care enough to pay me no mind."

"Sho now," he said soothingly. He rose stiffly and fetched the dipper of water and raised her head to drink and laid her back and watched her turn to the child with an absolutely stonelike face. But a moment later he saw that she was crying quietly. "Now, now," he said, "I wouldn't do that. Old Dicey says hit's a right fine gal. Hit's all right now. Hit's all over now. Hit ain't no need to cry now."

But she continued to cry quietly, almost sullenly, and he rose again and stood uncomfortably above the pallet for a time, thinking as he had thought when his own wife lay so and then his daughter in turn: "Women. Hit's a mystry to me. They seem to want em, and yit when they git em they cry about hit. Hit's a

mystry to me. To ara man." Then he moved away and drew a chair up to the
window and sat down.

Through all that long, bright, sunny forenoon he sat at the window, waiting.
Now and then he rose and tiptoed to the pallet. But his granddaughter slept now,
her face sullen and calm and weary, the child in the crook of her arm. Then he
returned to the chair and sat again, waiting, wondering why it took them so
long, until he remembered that it was Sunday. He was sitting there at mid-
afternoon when a half-grown white boy came around the corner of the house
upon the body and gave a choked cry and looked up and glared for a mesmerized
instant at Wash in the window before he turned and fled. Then Wash rose and
tiptoed again to the pallet.

The granddaughter was awake now, wakened perhaps by the boy's cry without
hearing it. "Milly," he said, "air you hungry?" She didn't answer, turning her
face away. He built up the fire on the hearth and cooked the food which he had
brought home the day before: fatback it was, and cold corn pone; he poured
water into the stale coffee pot and heated it. But she would not eat when he
carried the plate to her, so he ate himself, quietly, alone, and left the dishes as
they were and returned to the window.

Now he seemed to sense, feel, the men who would be gathering with horses
and guns and dogs—the curious, and the vengeful: men of Sutpen's own kind,
who had made the company about Sutpen's table in the time when Wash himself
had yet to approach nearer to the house than the scuppernong arbor—men who
had also shown the lesser ones how to fight in battle, who maybe also had signed
papers from the generals saying that they were among the first of the brave; who
had also galloped in the old days arrogant and proud on the fine horses across the
fine plantations—symbols also of admiration and hope; instruments too of
despair and grief.

That was whom they would expect him to run from. It seemed to him that he
had no more to run from than he had to run to. If he ran, he would merely be
fleeing one set of bragging and evil shadows for another just like them, since they
were all of a kind throughout all the earth which he knew, and he was old, too
old to flee far even if he were to flee. He could never escape them, no matter how
much or how far he ran: a man going on sixty could not run that far. Not far
enough to escape beyond the boundaries of earth where such men lived, set the
order and the rule of living. It seemed to him that he now saw for the first time,
after five years, how it was that Yankees or any other living armies had managed
to whip them: the gallant, the proud, the brave; the acknowledged and chosen
best among them all to carry courage and honor and pride. Maybe if he had gone
to the war with them he would have discovered them sooner. But if he had
discovered them sooner, what would he have done with his life since? How could
he have borne to remember for five years what his life had been before?

Now it was getting toward sunset. The child had been crying; when he went to
the pallet he saw his granddaughter nursing it, her face still bemused, sullen,
inscrutable. "Air you hungry yit?" he said.

"I don't want nothing."

"You ought to eat."

This time she did not answer at all, looking down at the child. He returned to his chair and found that the sun had set. "Hit kain't be much longer," he thought. He could feel them quite near now, the curious and the vengeful. He could even seem to hear what they were saying about him, the undercurrent of believing beyond the immediate fury: *Old Wash Jones he come a tumble at last. He thought he had Sutpen, but Sutpen fooled him. He thought he had Kernel where he would have to marry the gal or pay up. And Kernel refused.* "But I never expected that, Kernel!" he cried aloud, catching himself at the sound of his own voice, glancing quickly back to find his granddaughter watching him.

"Who you talking to now?" she said.

"Hit ain't nothing. I was just thinking and talked out before I knowed hit."

Her face was becoming indistinct again, again a sullen blur in the twilight. "I reckon so. I reckon you'll have to holler louder than that before he'll hear you, up yonder at that house. And I reckon you'll need to do more than holler before you get him down here too."

"Sho now," he said. "Don't you worry none." But already thinking was going smoothly on: "You know I never. You know how I ain't never expected or asked nothing from ara living man but what I expected from you. And I never asked that. I didn't think hit would need. I said, *I don't need to. What need has a fellow like Wash Jones to question or doubt the man that General Lee himself says in a handwrote ticket that he was brave?* Brave," he thought. "Better if nara one of them had never rid back home in '65"; thinking *Better if his kind and mine too had never drawn the breath of life on this earth. Better that all who remain of us be blasted from the face of earth than that another Wash Jones should see his whole life shredded from him and shrivel away like a dried shuck thrown onto the fire.*

He ceased, became still. He heard the horses, suddenly and plainly; presently he saw the lantern and the movement of men, the glint of gun barrels, in its moving light. Yet he did not stir. It was quite dark now, and he listened to the voices and the sounds of underbrush as they surrounded the house. The lantern itself came on; its light fell upon the quiet body in the weeds and stopped, the horses tall and shadowy. A man descended and stooped in the lantern light, above the body. He held a pistol; he rose and faced the house. "Jones," he said.

"I'm here," Wash said quietly from the window. "That you, Major?"

"Come out."

"Sho," he said quietly. "I just want to see to my granddaughter."

"We'll see to her. Come on out."

"Sho, Major. Just a minute."

"Show a light. Light your lamp."

"Sho. In just a minute." They could hear his voice retreat into the house, though they could not see him as he went swiftly to the crack in the chimney where he kept the butcher knife: the one thing in his slovenly life and house in which he took pride, since it was razor sharp. He approached the pallet, his granddaughter's voice:

"Who is it? Light the lamp, Grandpaw."

"Hit won't need no light, honey. Hit won't take but a minute," he said, kneeling, fumbling toward her voice, whispering now, "Where air you?"

"Right here," she said fretfully. "Where would I be? What is . . ." His hand touched her face. "What is . . . Grandpaw! Grand. . . ."

"Jones!" the sheriff said. "Come out of there!"

"In just a minute, Major," he said. Now he rose and moved swiftly. He knew where in the dark the can of kerosene was, just as he knew that it was full, since it was not two days ago that he had filled it at the store and held it there until he got a ride home with it, since the five gallons were heavy. There were still coals on the hearth; besides, the crazy building itself was like tinder: the coals, the hearth, the walls exploding in a single blue glare. Against it the waiting men saw him in a wild instant springing toward them with the lifted scythe before the horses reared and whirled. They checked the horses and turned them back toward the glare, yet still in wild relief against it the gaunt figure ran toward them with the lifted scythe.

"Jones!" the sheriff shouted; "stop! Stop, or I'll shoot. Jones! *Jones!*" Yet still the gaunt, furious figure came on against the glare and roar of the flames. With the scythe lifted, it bore down upon them, upon the wild glaring eyes of the horses and the swinging glints of gun barrels, without any cry, any sound.

Graham Greene

A Drive in the Country

As every other night she listened to her father going round the house, locking the doors and windows. He was head clerk at Bergson's Export Agency, and lying in bed she would think with dislike that his home was like his office, run on the same lines, its safety preserved with the same meticulous care, so that he could present a faithful steward's account to the managing director. Regularly every Sunday he presented the account, accompanied by his wife and two daughters, in the little neo-Gothic church in Park Road. They always had the same pew, they were always five minutes early, and her father sang loudly with no sense of tune, holding an out-size prayer book on the level of his eyes "Singing songs of exultation"—he was presenting the week's account (one household duly safeguarded)—"marching to the Promised Land." When they came out of church, she looked carefully from the corner by the Bricklayers' Arms where Fred

From *Nineteen Stories*, by Graham Greene. Copyright 1947 by Graham Greene. Reprinted by permission of the Viking Press, Inc., and William Heinemann, Ltd.

always stood, a little lit because the Arms had been open for half an hour, with his air of unbalanced exultation.

She listened: the back door closed, she could hear the catch of the kitchen window click, and the restless pad of his feet going back to try the front door. It wasn't only the outside doors he locked: he locked the empty rooms, the bathroom, the lavatory. He was locking something out, but obviously it was something capable of penetrating his first defences. He raised his second line all the way up to bed.

She laid her ear against the thin wall of the jerry-built villa and could hear the faint voices from the neighboring room; as she listened they came clearer as though she were turning the screw of a wireless set. Her mother said ". . . margarine in the cooking . . ." and her father said ". . . much easier in fifteen years." Then the bed creaked and there were dim sounds of tenderness and comfort between the two middle-aged strangers in the next room. In fifteen years, she thought unhappily, the house will be his; he had paid twenty-five pounds down and the rest he was paying month by month as rent. "Of course," he was in the habit of saying after a good meal, "I've improved the property," and he expected at least one of them to follow him into his study. "I've wired this room for power," he padded back past the little downstairs lavatory, "this radiator," the final stroke of satisfaction, "the garden," and if it was a fine evening he would fling the french window of the dining-room open on a little carpet of grass as carefully kept as a college lawn. "A pile of bricks," he'd say, "that's all it was." Five years of Saturday afternoons and fine Sundays had gone into the patch of turf, the surrounding flower-bed, the one apple tree which regularly produced one crimson tasteless apple more each year.

"Yes," he said, "I've improved the property," looking round for a nail to drive in, a weed to be uprooted. "If we had to sell now, we should get more than I've paid back from the society." It was more than a sense of property, it was a sense of honesty. Some people who bought their houses through the society let them go to rack and ruin and then cleared out.

She stood with her ear against the wall, a small, dark, furious, immature figure. There was no more to be heard from the other room; but in her inner ear she still heard the chorus of a property owner, the tap-tap of a hammer, the scrape of a spade, the whistle of radiator steam, a key turning, a bolt pushed home, the little trivial sounds of men building barricades. She stood planning her treachery.

It was a quarter-past ten; she had an hour in which to leave the house, but it did not take so long. There was really nothing to fear. They had played their usual rubber of three-handed bridge while her sister altered a dress for the local hop next night; after the rubber she had boiled a kettle and brought in a pot of tea; then she had filled the hot-water bottles and put them in the beds while her father locked up. He had no idea whatever that she was an enemy.

She put on a hat and a heavy coat because it was still cold at night; the spring was late that year, as her father commented, watching for the buds on the apple tree. She didn't pack a suitcase; that would have reminded her too much of week-ends at the sea, a family expedition to Ostend from all of which one returned; she wanted to match the odd reckless quality of Fred's mind. This time she wasn't going to return. She went softly downstairs into the little crowded hall, unlocked the door. All was quiet upstairs, and she closed the door behind her.

She was touched by a faint feeling of guilt because she couldn't lock it from the outside. But it had vanished by the time she reached the end of the crazy paved path and turned to the left down the road which after five years was still half-made, past the gaps between the villas where the wounded fields remained grimly alive in the form of thin grass and heaps of clay and dandelions.

She walked fast, passing a long line of little garages like the graves in a Portuguese cemetery where the coffin lies forever below the fading photograph of its occupant. The cold night air touched her with exhilaration. She was ready for anything, as she turned by the Belisha beacon into the shuttered shopping street; she was like a recruit in the first months of a war. The choice made, she could surrender her will to the strange, the exhilarating, the gigantic event.

Fred, as he had promised, was at the corner where the road turned down towards the church; she could taste the spirit on his lips as they kissed, and she was satisfied that no one else could have so adequately matched the occasion; his face was bright and reckless in the lamplight, he was as exciting and strange to her as the adventure. He took her arm and ran her into a blind unlighted alley, then left her for a moment until two headlamps beamed softly at her out of the cavern. She cried with astonishment, "You've got a car?" and felt the jerk of his nervous hand urging her towards it. "Yes," he said, "do you like it?" grinding into second gear, changing clumsily into top as they came out between the shuttered windows.

She said, "It's lovely. Let's drive a long way."

"We will," he said, watching the speedometer needle go quivering to forty-five.

"Does it mean you've got a job?"

"There are no jobs," he said, "they don't exist any more than the Dodo. Did you see that bird?" he asked sharply, turning his headlights full on as they passed the turning to the housing estate and quite suddenly came out into the country between a café ("Draw in here"), a bootshop ("Buy the shoes worn by your favourite film star"), and an undertaker's with a large white angel lit by a neon light.

"I didn't see any bird."

"Not flying at the windscreen?"

"No."

"I nearly hit it," he said. "It would have made a mess. Bad as those fellows who run someone down and don't stop. Should *we* stop?" he asked, turning out his switchboard light so that they couldn't see the needle vibrate downwards to sixty.

"Whatever you say," she said, sitting deep in a reckless dream.

"You going to love me tonight?"

"Of course I am."

"Never going back there?"

"No," she said, abjuring the tap of hammer, the click of latch, the pad of slippered feet making the rounds.

"Want to know where we are going?"

"No." A little flat cardboard copse ran forward into the green light and darkly by. A rabbit turned its scut and vanished into a hedge.

He said, "Have you any money?"

"Half a crown."

"Do you love me?" For a long time she expended on his lips all she had patiently had to keep in reserve, looking the other way on Sunday mornings, saying nothing when his name came up at meals with disapproval. She expended herself against dry unresponsive lips as the car leapt ahead and his foot trod down on the accelerator. He said, "It's the hell of a life."

She echoed him, "The hell of a life."

He said, "There's a bottle in my pocket. Have a drink."

"I don't want one."

"Give me one then. It has a screw top," and with one hand on her and one on the wheel he tipped his head, so that she could pour a little whisky into his mouth out of the quarter bottle. "Do you mind?" he said.

"Of course I don't mind."

"You can't save," he said, "on ten shillings a week pocket-money. I lay it out the best I can. It needs a hell of a lot of thought. To give variety. Half a crown on Weights. Three and six on whisky. A shilling on the pictures. That leaves three shillings for beer. I take my fun once a week and get it over."

The whisky had dribbled on to his tie and the smell filled the small coupé. It pleased her. It was *his* smell. He said, "They grudge it me. They think I ought to get a job. When you're that age you don't realize there aren't any jobs for some of us—any more for ever."

"I know," she said. "They are old."

"How's your sister?" he asked abruptly; the bright glare swept the road ahead of them clean of small scurrying birds and animals.

"She's going to the hop tomorrow. I wonder where we shall be."

He wouldn't be drawn; he had his own idea and kept it to himself.

"I'm loving this."

He said, "There's a club out this way. At a road-house. Mick made me a member. Do you know Mick?"

"No."

"Mick's all right. If they know you, they'll serve you drinks till midnight. We'll look in there. Say hullo to Mick. And then in the morning—we'll decide that later when we've had a few drinks."

"Have you the money?" A small village, a village fast asleep already behind closed doors and windows, sailed down the hill towards them as if it were being carried smoothly by a landslide into the scarred plain from which they'd come. A long grey Norman church, an inn without a sign, a clock striking eleven. He said, "Look in the back. There's a suitcase there."

"It's locked."

"I forgot the key," he said.

"What's in it?"

"A few things," he said vaguely. "We could pop them for drinks."

"What about a bed?"

"There's the car. You aren't scared, are you?"

"No," she said. "I'm not scared. This is—" but she hadn't words for the damp cold wind, the darkness, the strangeness, the smell of whisky and the rushing car. "It moves," she said. "We must have gone a long way already. This is real country," seeing an owl sweep low on furry wings over a ploughed field.

"You've got to go farther than this for real country," he said. "You won't find it yet on *this* road. We'll be at the road-house soon."

She discovered in herself a nostalgia for their dark windy solitary progress. She said, "Need we go to the club? Can't we go farther into the country?"

He looked sideways at her; he had always been open to *any* suggestion: like some meteorological instrument, he was only made for the winds to blow through. "Of course," he said, "anything you like." He didn't give the club a second thought; they swept past it a moment later, a long lit Tudor bungalow, a crash of voices, a bathing pool filled for some reason with hay. It was immediately behind them, a patch of light whipping round a corner out of sight.

He said, "I suppose this is country now. They none of them get farther than the club. We're quite alone now. We could lie in these fields till doomsday as far as *they* are concerned, though I suppose a ploughman . . . if they do plough here." He raised his foot from the accelerator and let the car's speed gradually diminish. Somebody had left a wooden gate open into a field and he turned the car in; they jolted a long way down the field beside the hedge and came to a standstill. He turned out the headlamps and they sat in the tiny glow of the switchboard light. "Peaceful," he said uneasily; and they heard a screech owl hunting overhead and a small rustle in the hedge where something went to hiding. They belonged to the city; they hadn't a name for anything round them; the tiny buds breaking in the bushes were nameless. He nodded at a group of dark trees at the hedge end. "Oaks?"

"Elms?" she asked and their mouths went together in a mutual ignorance. The touch excited her; she was ready for the most reckless act; but from his mouth, the dry spiritous lips, she gained a sense that he was less excited than he had hoped to be.

She said, to reassure herself, "It's good to be here—miles away from anyone we know."

"I dare say Mick's there. Down the road."

"Does he know?"

"Nobody knows."

She said, "That's how I want it. How did you get this car?"

He grinned at her with unbalanced amusement. "I saved from the ten shillings."

"No, but how? Did someone lend it you?"

"Yes," he said. He suddenly pushed the door open and said, "Let's take a walk."

"We've never walked in the country before." She took his arm, and she could feel the tense nerves responding to her touch. It was what she liked; she couldn't tell what he would do next. She said, "My father calls you crazy. I like you crazy. What's all this stuff?" kicking at the ground.

"Clover," he said, "isn't it? I don't know." It was like being in a foreign city where you can't understand the names on shops, the traffic signs: nothing to catch hold of, to hold you down to this and that, adrift together in a dark vacuum. "Shouldn't you turn on the headlamps?" she said. "It won't be easy finding our way back. There's not much moon." Already they seemed to have gone a long way from the car; she couldn't see it clearly any longer.

"We'll find our way," he said. "Somehow. Don't worry." At the hedge end they came to the trees. He pulled a twig down and felt the sticky buds. "What is it? Beech?"

"I don't know."

He said, "If it had been warmer, we could have slept out here. You'd think we might have had that much luck, tonight of all nights. But it's cold and it's going to rain."

"Let's come in the summer," but he didn't answer. Some other wind had blown, she could tell it, and already he had lost interest in her. There was something hard in his pocket; it hurt her side; she put her hand in. The metal chamber had absorbed all the cold there had been in the windy ride. She whispered fearfully, "Why are you carrying that?" She had always before drawn a line round his recklessness. When her father had said he was crazy she had secretly and possessively smiled because she thought she knew the extent of his craziness. Now, while she waited for him to answer her, she could feel his craziness go on and on and out of her reach, out of her sight; she couldn't see where it ended; it had no end, she couldn't possess it any more than she could possess a darkness or a desert.

"Don't be scared," he said. "I didn't mean you to find that tonight." He suddenly became more tender than he had ever been; he put his hand on her breast; it came from his fingers, a great soft meaningless flood of tenderness. He said, "Don't you see? Life's hell. There's nothing we can do." He spoke very gently, but she had never been more aware of his recklessness: he was open to every wind, but the wind now seemed to have set from the east: it blew like sleet through his words. "I haven't a penny," he said. "We can't live on nothing. It's no good hoping that I'll get a job." He repeated, "There aren't any more jobs any more. And every year, you know, there's less chance, because there are more people younger than I am."

"But why," she said, "have we come—?"

He became softly and tenderly lucid. "We do love each other, don't we? We can't live without each other. It's no good hanging around, is it, waiting for our luck to change. We don't even get a fine night," he said, feeling for rain with his hand. "We can have a good time tonight—in the car—and then—in the morn-ing—"

"No, no," she said. She tried to get away from him. "I couldn't. It's horrible. I never said—"

"You wouldn't know anything," he said gently and inexorably. Her words, she could realize now, had never made any real impression; he was swayed by them but no more than he was swayed by anything: now that the wind had set, it was like throwing scraps of paper towards the sky to speak at all, or to argue. He said, "Of course we neither of us believe in God, but there may be a chance, and it's company, going together like that." He added with pleasure, "It's a gamble," and she remembered more occasions than she could count when their last coppers had gone ringing down in slot machines.

He pulled her closer and said with complete assurance, "We love each other. It's the only way, you know. You can trust me." He was like a skilled logician; he knew all the stages of the argument. She despaired at catching him out on any point but the promise: we love each other. *That* she doubted for the first time, faced by the mercilessness of his egotism. He repeated, "It will be company."

She said, "There must be some way . . ."

"Why *must?*"

"Otherwise people would be doing it all the time—everywhere!"

"They are," he said triumphantly, as if it were more important for him to find his argument flawless than to find—well, a way, a way to go on living. "You've only got to read the papers," he said. He whispered gently, endearingly, as if he thought the very sound of the words tender enough to dispel all fear. "They call it a suicide pact. It's happening all the time."

"I couldn't. I haven't the nerve."

"You needn't do anything," he said, "I'll do it all."

His calmness horrified her. "You mean—you'd kill me?"

He said, "I love you enough for that. I promise it won't hurt you." He might have been persuading her to play some trivial and uncongenial game. "We shall be together always." He added rationally, "Of course, if there *is* an always," and suddenly she saw his love as a mere flicker of gas flame playing on the marshy depth of his irresponsibility. She had loved his irresponsibility, but now she realized that it was without any limit at all; it closed over the head. She pleaded, "There are things we can sell. That suitcase."

She knew that he was watching her with amusement, that he had rehearsed all her arguments and had an answer; he was only pretending to take her seriously. "We might get fifteen shillings," he said. "We could live a day on that—but we shouldn't have much fun."

"The things inside it?"

"Ah, that's another gamble. They might be worth thirty shillings. Three days, that would give us—with economy."

"We might get a job."

"I've been trying for a good many years now."

"Isn't there the dole?"

"I'm not an insured worker. I'm one of the ruling class."

"Your people, they'd give us something."

"But we've got our pride, haven't we?" he said with remorseless conceit.

"The man who lent you the car?"

He said, "You remember Cortez, the fellow who burnt his boats? I've burnt mine. I've *got* to kill myself. You see, I stole that car. We'd be stopped in the next town. It's too late even to go back." He laughed; he had reached the climax of his argument and there was nothing more to dispute about. She could tell that he was perfectly satisfied and perfectly happy. It infuriated her. *"You've* got to, maybe. But I haven't. Why should I kill myself? What right have you—?" She dragged herself away from him and felt against her back the rough massive trunk of the living tree.

"Oh," he said in an irritated tone, "of course if you like to go on without me." She had admired his conceit; he had always carried his unemployment with a manner: now you could no longer call it conceit: it was a complete lack of any values. "You can go home," he said, "though I don't quite know how—I can't drive you back because I'm staying here. You'll be able to go to the hop tomorrow night. And there's a whist-drive, isn't there, in the church hall? My dear, I wish you joy of home."

There was a savagery in his manner. He took security, peace, order, in his teeth and worried them so that she couldn't help feeling a little pity for what they had joined in despising: a hammer tapped at her heart, driving in a nail here and a nail there. She tried to think of a bitter retort, for after all there was something to be said for the negative virtues of doing no injury, of simply going on, as her father was going on for another fifteen years. But the next moment she felt no anger. They had trapped each other. He had always wanted this: the dark field, the weapon in his pocket, the escape and the gamble; and she less honestly had wanted a little of both worlds: irresponsibility and a safe love, danger and a secure heart.

He said, "I'm going now. Are you coming?"

"No," she said. He hesitated; the recklessness for a moment wavered; a sense of something lost and bewildered came to her through the dark. She wanted to say, Don't be a fool. Leave the car where it is. Walk back with me, and we'll get a lift home, but she knew any thought of hers had occurred to him and been answered already: ten shillings a week, no job, getting older. Endurance was a virtue of one's fathers.

He suddenly began to walk fast down the hedge; he couldn't see where he was going; he stumbled on a root and she heard him swear. "Damnation"—the little commonplace sound in the darkness overwhelmed her with pain and sorrow. She cried out, "Fred. Fred. Don't do it," and began to run in the opposite direction. She couldn't stop him and she wanted to be out of hearing. A twig broke under her foot like a shot, and the owl screamed across the ploughed field beyond the hedge. It was like a rehearsal with sound effects. But when the real shot came, it was quite different: a thud like a gloved hand striking a door and no cry at all.

She didn't notice it at first and afterwards she thought that she had never been conscious of the exact moment when her lover ceased to exist.

She bruised herself against the car, running blindly; a blue-spotted Woolworth handkerchief lay on the seat in the light of the switchboard bulb. She nearly took it, but no, she thought, no one must know that I have been here. She turned out the light and picked her way as quietly as she could across the clover. She could begin to be sorry when she was safe. She wanted to close a door behind her, thrust a bolt down, hear the catch grip.

It wasn't ten minutes' walk down the deserted lane to the roadhouse. Tipsy voices spoke a foreign language, though it was the language Fred had spoken. She could hear the clink of coins in slot machines, the hiss of soda; she listened to these sounds like an enemy, planning her escape. They frightened her like something mindless: there was no appeal one could make to that egotism. It was simply a Want to be satisfied; it gaped at her like a mouth. A man was trying to wind up his car; the self-starter wouldn't work; he said, "I'm a Bolshie. Of course I'm a Bolshie. I believe—"

A thin girl with red hair sat on the step and watched him. "You're all wrong," she said.

"I'm a Liberal Conservative."

"You *can't* be a Liberal Conservative."

"Do you love me?"

"I love Joe."

"You *can't* love Joe."

"Let's go home, Mick."

The man tried to wind up the car again, and she came up to them as if she'd come out of the club and said, "Give me a lift?"

"Course. Delighted. Get in."

"Won't the car go?"

"No."

"Have you flooded—?"

"Tha's an idea." He lifted the bonnet and she pressed the self-starter. It began to rain slowly and heavily and drenchingly, the kind of rain you always expect to fall on graves, and her thoughts went down the lane towards the field, the hedge, the trees—oak, beech, elm? She imagined the rain on his face, the pool collecting in each eye-socket and streaming down on either side the nose. But she could feel nothing but gladness because she had escaped from him.

"Where are you going?" she said.

"Devizes."

"I thought you might be going to London."

"Where do *you* want to go to?"

"Golding's Park."

"Le's go to Golding's Park."

The red-haired girl said, "I'm going in, Mick. It's raining."

"Aren't you coming?"

"I'm going to find Joe."

"All right." He smashed his way out of the little car park, bending his mudguard on a wooden post, scraping the paint of another car.

"That's the wrong way," she said.

"We'll turn." He backed the car into a ditch and out again. "Was a good party," he said. The rain came down harder; it blinded the windscreen and the electric wiper wouldn't work, but her companion didn't care. He drove straight on at forty miles an hour; it was an old car, it wouldn't do any more; it leaked through the hood. He said, "Twis' that knob. Have a tune," and when she turned it and the dance music came through, he said, "That's Harry Roy. Know him anywhere," driving into the thick wet night carrying the hot music with them. Presently he said, "A friend of mine, one of the best, you'd know him, Peter Weatherall. You know him."

"No."

"You must know Peter. Haven't seen him about lately. Goes off on the drink for weeks. They sent out an SOS for Peter once in the middle of the dance music. 'Missing from Home.' We were in the car. We had a laugh about that."

She said, "Is that what people do—when people are missing?"

"Know this tune," he said. "This isn't Harry Roy. This is Alf Cohen."

She said suddenly, "You're Mick, aren't you? Wouldn't *you* lend—"

He sobered up. "Stony broke," he said. "Comrades in misfortune. Try Peter. Why do you want to go to Gulding's Park?"

"My home."

"You mean you live there?"

"Yes." She said, "Be careful. There's a speed limit here." He was perfectly obedient. He raised his foot and let the car crawl at fifteen miles an hour. The lamp standards marched unsteadily to meet them and lit his face: he was quite old, forty if a day, ten years older than Fred. He wore a striped tie and she could see his sleeve was frayed. He had more than ten shillings a week, but perhaps not so very much more. His hair was going thin.

"You can drop me here," she said. He stopped the car and she got out and the rain went on. He followed her on to the road. "Let me come in?" he said. She shook her head; the rain wetted them through; behind her was the pillar-box, the Belisha beacon, the road through the housing estate. "Hell of a life," he said politely, holding her hand, while the rain drummed on the hood of the cheap car and ran down his face, across his collar and the school tie. But she felt no pity, no attraction, only a faint horror and repulsion. A kind of dim recklessness gleamed in his wet eye, as the hot music of Alf Cohen's band screamed from the car, a faded irresponsibility. "Le's go back," he said, "le's go somewhere. Le's go for a ride in the country. Le's go to Maidenhead," holding her hand limply.

She pulled it away, he didn't resist, and walked down the half-made road to No. 64. The crazy paving in the front garden seemed to hold her feet firmly up. She opened the door and heard through the dark and the rain a car grind into second gear and drone away—certainly not towards Maidenhead or Devizes or the country. Another wind must have blown.

Her father called down from the first landing, "Who's there?"

"It's me," she said. She explained, "I had a feeling you'd left the door unbolted."

"And had I?"

"No," she said gently, "it's bolted all right," driving the bolt softly and firmly home. She waited till his door closed; she touched the radiator to warm her fingers—he had put it in himself, he had improved the property; in fifteen years, she thought, it will be ours. She was quite free from pain, listening to the rain on the roof; he had been over the whole roof that winter inch by inch; there was nowhere for the rain to enter. It was kept outside, drumming on the shabby hood, pitting the clover field. She stood by the door, feeling only the faint repulsion she always had for things weak and crippled, thinking, "It isn't tragic at all," and looking down with an emotion like tenderness at the flimsy bolt from a sixpenny store any man could have broken, but which a Man had put in, the head clerk of Bergson's.

Carson McCullers

A Domestic Dilemma

On Thursday Martin Meadows left the office early enough to make the first express bus home. It was the hour when the evening lilac glow was fading in the slushy streets, but by the time the bus had left the Mid-town terminal the bright city night had come. On Thursdays the maid had a half-day off and Martin liked to get home as soon as possible, since for the past year his wife had not been—well. This Thursday he was very tired and, hoping that no regular commuter would single him out for conversation, he fastened his attention to the newspaper until the bus had crossed the George Washington Bridge. Once on 9-W Highway Martin always felt that the trip was halfway done, he breathed deeply, even in cold weather when only ribbons of draught cut through the smoky air of the bus, confident that he was breathing country air. It used to be that at this point he would relax and begin to think with pleasure of his home. But in this last year nearness brought only a sense of tension and he did not anticipate the journey's end. This evening Martin kept his face close to the window and watched the barren fields and lonely lights of passing townships. There was a moon, pale on the dark earth and areas of late, porous snow; to Martin the countryside seemed vast and somehow desolate that evening. He took his hat from the rack and put his folded newspaper in the pocket of his overcoat a few minutes before time to pull the cord.

The cottage was a block from the bus stop, near the river but not directly on the shore; from the living-room window you could look across the street and opposite yard and see the Hudson. The cottage was modern, almost too white and new on the narrow plot of yard. In summer the grass was soft and bright and Martin carefully tended a flower border and a rose trellis. But during the cold, fallow months the yard was bleak and the cottage seemed naked. Lights were on that evening in all the rooms in the little house and Martin hurried up the front walk. Before the steps he stopped to move a wagon out of the way.

The children were in the living room, so intent on play that the opening of the front door was at first unnoticed. Martin stood looking at his safe, lovely children. They had opened the bottom drawer of the secretary and taken out the Christmas decorations. Andy had managed to plug in the Christmas tree lights and the green and red bulbs glowed with out-of-season festivity on the rug of the living room. At the moment he was trying to trail the bright cord over Marianne's rocking horse. Marianne sat on the floor pulling off an angel's wings. The children wailed a startling welcome. Martin swung the fat little baby girl up to his shoulder and Andy threw himself against his father's legs.

"Daddy, Daddy, Daddy!"

Martin sat down the little girl carefully and swung Andy a few times like a pendulum. Then he picked up the Christmas tree cord.

"What's all this stuff doing out? Help me put it back in the drawer. You're not to fool with the light socket. Remember I told you that before. I mean it, Andy."

The six-year-old child nodded and shut the secretary drawer. Martin stroked his fair soft hair and his hand lingered tenderly on the nape of the child's frail neck.

"Had supper yet, Bumpkin?"

"It hurt. The toast was hot."

The baby girl stumbled on the rug and, after the first surprise of the fall, began to cry; Martin picked her up and carried her in his arms back to the kitchen.

"See, Daddy," said Andy. "The toast—"

Emily had laid the children's supper on the uncovered porcelain table. There were two plates with the remains of cream-of-wheat and eggs and silver mugs that had held milk. There was also a platter of cinnamon toast, untouched, except for one tooth-marked bite. Martin sniffed the bitten piece and nibbled gingerly. Then he put the toast into the garbage pail.

"Hoo—phui—What on earth!"

Emily had mistaken the tin of cayenne for the cinnamon.

"I like to have burnt up," Andy said. "Drank water and ran outdoors and opened my mouth. Marianne didn't eat none."

"Any," corrected Martin. He stood helpless, looking around the walls of the kitchen. "Well, that's that, I guess," he said finally. "Where is your mother now?"

"She's up in you alls' room."

Martin left the children in the kitchen and went up to his wife. Outside the door he waited for a moment to still his anger. He did not knock and once inside the room he closed the door behind him.

Emily sat in the rocking chair by the window of the pleasant room. She had been drinking something from a tumbler and as he entered she put the glass hurriedly on the floor behind the chair. In her attitude there was confusion and guilt which she tried to hide by a show of spurious vivacity.

"Oh, Marty! You home already? The time slipped up on me. I was just going down—" She lurched to him and her kiss was strong with sherry. When he stood unresponsive she stepped back a pace and giggled nervously.

"What's the matter with you? Standing there like a barber pole. Is anything wrong with you?"

"Wrong with *me*?" Martin bent over the rocking chair and picked up the tumbler from the floor. "If you could only realize how sick I am—how bad it is for all of us."

Emily spoke in a false, airy voice that had become too familiar to him. Often at such times she affected a slight English accent copying perhaps some actress she admired. "I haven't the vaguest idea what you mean. Unless you are referring to the glass I used for a spot of sherry. I had a finger of sherry—maybe two. But what is the crime in that, pray tell me? Quite all right."

"So anyone can see."

As she went into the bathroom Emily walked with careful gravity. She turned on the cold water and dashed some on her face with her cupped hands, then patted herself dry with the corner of a bath towel. Her face was delicately featured and young, unblemished.

"I was just going down to make dinner." She tottered and balanced herself by holding to the door frame.

"I'll take care of dinner. You stay up here. I'll bring it up."

"I'll do nothing of the sort. Why, whoever heard of such a thing?"

"Please," Martin said.

"Leave me alone. I'm quite all right. I was just on the way down—"

"Mind what I say."

"Mind your grandmother."

She lurched toward the door, but Martin caught her by the arm. "I don't want the children to see you in this condition. Be reasonable."

"Condition!" Emily jerked her arm. Her voice rose angrily. "Why, because I drink a couple of sherries in the afternoon you're trying to make me out a drunkard. Condition! Why, I don't even touch whiskey. As well you know. *I* don't swill liquor at bars. And that's more than you can say. I don't even have a cocktail at dinner-time. I only sometimes have a glass of sherry. What, I ask you, is the disgrace of that? Condition!"

Martin sought words to calm his wife. "We'll have a quiet supper by ourselves up here. That's a good girl." Emily sat on the side of the bed and he opened the door for a quick departure.

"I'll be back in a jiffy."

As he busied himself with the dinner downstairs he was lost in the familiar question as to how this problem had come upon his home. He himself had always enjoyed a good drink. When they were still living in Alabama they had served long drinks or cocktails as a matter of course. For years they had drunk one or two—possibly three drinks before dinner, and at bedtime a long nightcap. Evenings before holidays they might get a buzz on, might even become a little tight. But alcohol had never seemed a problem to him, only a bothersome expense that with the increase in the family they could scarcely afford. It was only after his company had transferred him to New York that Martin was aware that certainly his wife was drinking too much. She was tippling, he noticed, during the day.

The problem acknowledged, he tried to analyze the source. The change from Alabama to New York had somehow disturbed her; accustomed to the idle warmth of a small Southern town, the matrix of the family and cousinship and childhood friends, she had failed to accommodate herself to the stricter, lonelier mores of the North. The duties of motherhood and housekeeping were onerous to her. Homesick for Paris City, she had made no friends in the suburban town. She read only magazines and murder books. Her interior life was insufficient without the artifice of alcohol.

The revelations of incompetence insidiously undermined his previous conceptions of his wife. There were times of unexplainable malevolence, times when the alcoholic fuse caused an explosion of unseemly anger. He encountered a latent coarseness in Emily, inconsistent with her natural simplicity. She lied about drinking and deceived him with unsuspected stratagems.

Then there was an accident. Coming home from work one evening about a year ago, he was greeted with screams from the children's room. He found Emily holding the baby, wet and naked from her bath. The baby had been dropped, her frail, frail skull striking the table edge, so that a thread of blood was soaking into the gossamer hair. Emily was sobbing and intoxicated. As Martin cradled the hurt child, so infinitely precious at that moment, he had an affrighted vision of the future.

The next day Marianne was all right. Emily vowed that never again would she touch liquor, and for a few weeks she was sober, cold and downcast. Then gradually she began—not whiskey or gin—but quantities of beer, or sherry, or outlandish liqueurs; once he had come across a hatbox of empty crème de menthe bottles. Martin found a dependable maid who managed the household competently. Virgie was also from Alabama and Martin had never dared tell Emily the wage scale customary in New York. Emily's drinking was entirely secret now, done before he reached the house. Usually the effects were almost imperceptible— a looseness of movement or the heavy-lidded eyes. The times of irresponsibilities, such as the cayenne-pepper toast were rare, and Martin could dismiss his worries when Virgie was at the house. But, nevertheless, anxiety was always latent, a threat of undefined disaster that underlaid his days.

"Marianne!" Martin called, for even the recollection of that time brought the need for reassurance. The baby girl, no longer hurt, but no less precious to her father, came into the kitchen with her brother. Martin went on with the preparations for the meal. He opened a can of soup and put two chops in the frying pan. Then he sat down by the table and took Marianne on his knees for a pony ride. Andy watched them, his fingers wobbling the tooth that had been loose all that week.

"Andy-the-candyman!" Martin said. "Is that old critter still in your mouth? Come closer, let Daddy have a look."

"I got a string to pull it with." The child brought from his pocket a tangled thread. "Virgie said to tie it to the tooth and tie the other end to the doorknob and shut the door real suddenly."

Martin took out a clean handkerchief and felt the loose tooth carefully. "That tooth is coming out of my Andy's mouth tonight. Otherwise I'm awfully afraid we'll have a tooth tree in the family."

"A what?"

"A tooth tree," Martin said. "You'll bite into something and swallow that tooth. And the tooth will take root in poor Andy's stomach and grow into a tooth tree with sharp little teeth instead of leaves."

"Shoo, Daddy," Andy said. But he held the tooth firmly between his grimy little thumb and forefinger. "There ain't any tree like that. I never seen one."

"There *isn't* any tree like that and I never *saw* one."

Martin tensed suddenly. Emily was coming down the stairs. He listened to her fumbling footsteps, his arm embracing the little boy with dread. When Emily came into the room he saw from her movements and her sullen face that she had again been at the sherry bottle. She began to yank open drawers and set the table.

"Condition!" she said in a furry voice. "You talk to me like that. Don't think I'll forget. I remember every dirty lie you say to me. Don't you think for a minute that I forget."

"Emily!" he begged. "The children—"

"The children—yes! Don't think I don't see through your dirty plots and schemes. Down here trying to turn my own children against me. Don't think I don't see and understand."

"Emily! I beg you—please go upstairs."

"So you can turn my children—my very own children—" Two large tears coursed rapidly down her cheeks. "Trying to turn my little boy, my Andy, against his own mother."

With drunken impulsiveness Emily knelt on the floor before the startled child. Her hands on his shoulders balanced her. "Listen, my Andy—you wouldn't listen to any lies your father tells you? You wouldn't believe what he says? Listen, Andy, what was your father telling you before I came downstairs?" Uncertain, the child sought his father's face. "Tell me. Mama wants to know."

"About the tooth tree."

"What?"

The child repeated the words and she echoed them with unbelieving terror. "The tooth tree!" She swayed and renewed her grasp on the child's shoulder. "I don't know what you're talking about. But listen, Andy, Mama is all right, isn't she?" The tears were spilling down her face and Andy drew back from her, for he was afraid. Grasping the table edge, Emily stood up.

"See! You have turned my child against me."

Marianne began to cry, and Martin took her in his arms.

"That's all right, you can take *your* child. You have always shown partiality from the very first. I don't mind, but at least you can leave me my little boy."

Andy edged close to his father and touched his leg. "Daddy," he wailed.

Martin took the children to the foot of the stairs. "Andy, you take up Marianne and Daddy will follow you in a minute."

"But Mama?" the child asked, whispering.

"Mama will be all right. Don't worry."

Emily was sobbing at the kitchen table, her face buried in the crook of her arm. Martin poured a cup of soup and set it before her. Her rasping sobs unnerved him; the vehemence of her emotion, irrespective of the source, touched in him a strain of tenderness. Unwillingly he laid his hand on her dark hair. "Sit up and drink the soup." Her face as she looked up at him was chastened and imploring. The boy's withdrawal or the touch of Martin's hand had turned the tenor of her mood.

"Ma-Martin," she sobbed. "I'm so ashamed."

"Drink the soup."

Obeying him, she drank between gasping breaths. After a second cup she allowed him to lead her up to their room. She was docile now and more restrained. He laid her nightgown on the bed and was about to leave the room when a fresh round of grief, the alcoholic tumult, came again.

"He turned away. My Andy looked at me and turned away."

Impatience and fatigue hardened his voice, but he spoke warily. "You forget that Andy is still a little child—he can't comprehend the meaning of such scenes."

"Did I make a scene? Oh, Martin, did I make a scene before the children?"

Her horrified face touched and amused him against his will. "Forget it. Put on your nightgown and go to sleep."

"My child turned away from me. Andy looked at his mother and turned away. The children—"

She was caught in the rhythmic sorrow of alcohol. Martin withdrew from the room, saying: "For God's sake go to sleep. The children will forget by tomorrow."

As he said this he wondered if it was true. Would the scene glide so easily from memory—or would it root in the unconscious to fester in the after-years? Martin did not know, and the last alternative sickened him. He thought of Emily, foresaw the morning-after humiliation: the shards of memory, the lucidities that glared from the obliterating darkness of shame. She would call the New York office twice—possibly three or four times. Martin anticipated his own embarrassment, wondering if the others at the office could possibly suspect. He felt that his secretary had divined the trouble long ago and that she pitied him. He suffered a moment of rebellion against his fate, he hated his wife.

Once in the children's room he closed the door and felt secure for the first time that evening. Marianne fell down on the floor, picked herself up and calling: "Daddy, watch me," fell again, got up, and continued the falling-calling routine. Andy sat in the child's low chair, wobbling the tooth. Martin ran the water in the tub, washed his own hands in the lavatory, and called the boy into the bathroom.

"Let's have another look at that tooth." Martin sat on the toilet, holding Andy between his knees. The child's mouth gaped and Martin grasped the tooth. A wobble, a quick twist and the nacreous milk tooth was free. Andy's face was for the first moment split between terror, astonishment, and delight. He mouthed a swallow of water and spat into the lavatory.

"Look, Daddy? It's blood. Marianne!"

Martin loved to bathe his children, loved inexpressibly the tender, naked bodies as they stood in the water so exposed. It was not fair of Emily to say that he showed partiality. As Martin soaped the delicate boy-body of his son he felt that further love would be impossible. Yet he admitted the difference in the quality of his emotions for the two children. His love for his daughter was graver, touched with a strain of melancholy, a gentleness that was akin to pain. His pet names for the little boy were the absurdities of daily inspiration—he called the little girl always Marianne, and his voice as he spoke it was a caress. Martin patted dry the fat baby stomach and the sweet little genital fold. The washed child faces were radiant as flower petals, equally loved.

"I'm putting the tooth under my pillow. I'm supposed to get a quarter."

"What for?"

"*You* know, Daddy. Johnny got a quarter for his tooth."

"Who puts the quarter there?" asked Martin. "I used to think the fairies left it in the night. It was a dime in my day, though."

"That's what they say in kindergarten."

"Who does put it there?"

"Your parents," Andy said. "You!"

Martin was pinning the cover on Marianne's bed. His daughter was already asleep. Scarcely breathing, Martin bent over and kissed her forehead, kissed again the tiny hand that lay palm-upward, flung in slumber beside her head.

"Good night, Andy-man."

The answer was only a drowsy murmur. After a minute Martin took out his change and slid a quarter underneath the pillow. He left a night light in the room.

As Martin prowled about the kitchen making a late meal, it occurred to him that the children had not once mentioned their mother or the scene that must have seemed to them incomprehensible. Absorbed in the instant—the tooth, the bath, the quarter—the fluid passage of child-time had borne these weightless episodes like leaves in the swift current of a shallow stream while the adult enigma was beached and forgotten on the shore. Martin thanked the Lord for that.

But his own anger, repressed and lurking, rose again. His youth was being frittered by a drunkard's waste, his very manhood subtly undermined. And the children, once the immunity of incomprehension passed—what would it be like in a year or so? With his elbows on the table he ate his food brutishly, untasting. There was no hiding the truth—soon there would be gossip in the office and in the town; his wife was a dissolute woman. Dissolute. And he and his children were bound to a future of degradation and slow ruin.

Martin pushed away from the table and stalked into the living room. He followed the lines of a book with his eyes but his mind conjured miserable images: he saw his children drowned in the river, his wife a disgrace on the public street. By bedtime the dull, hard anger was like a weight upon his chest and his feet dragged as he climbed the stairs.

The room was dark except for the shafting light from the half-opened bathroom door. Martin undressed quietly. Little by little, mysteriously, there came in him a change. His wife was asleep, her peaceful respiration sounding gently in the room. Her high-heeled shoes with the carelessly dropped stockings made to him a mute appeal. Her underclothes were flung in disorder on the chair. Martin picked up the girdle and the soft, silk brassière and stood for a moment with them in his hands. For the first time that evening he looked at his wife. His eyes rested on the sweet forehead, the arch of the fine brow. The brow had descended to Marianne, and the tilt at the end of the delicate nose. In his son he could trace the high cheekbones and pointed chin. Her body was full-bosomed, slender and undulant. As Martin watched the tranquil slumber of his wife the ghost of the old anger vanished. All thoughts of blame or blemish were distant from him now. Martin put out the bathroom light and raised the window. Careful not to awaken Emily he slid into the bed. By moonlight he watched his wife for the last time. His hand sought the adjacent flesh and sorrow paralleled desire in the immense complexity of love.

Bernard Malamud

The Bill

Though the street was somewhere near a river, it was landlocked and narrow, a crooked row of aged brick tenement buildings. A child throwing a ball straight up saw a bit of pale sky. On the corner, opposite the blackened tenement where Willy Schlegel worked as janitor, stood another like it except that this included the only store on the street—going down five stone steps into the basement, a small, dark delicatessen owned by Mr. and Mrs. F. Panessa, really a hole in the wall.

They had just bought it with the last of their money, Mrs. Panessa told the janitor's wife, so as not to have to depend on either of their daughters, both of whom, Mrs. Schlegel understood, were married to selfish men who had badly affected their characters. To be completely independent of them, Panessa, a retired factory worker, withdrew his three thousands of savings and bought this little delicatessen store. When Mrs. Schlegel, looking around—though she knew the delicatessen quite well for the many years she and Willy had been janitors across the way—when she asked, "Why did you buy this one?" Mrs. Panessa cheerfully replied because it was a small place and they would not have to overwork; Panessa was sixty-three. They were not here to coin money but to support themselves without working too hard. After talking it over many nights and days, they had decided that the store would at least give them a living. She gazed into Etta Schlegel's gaunt eyes and Etta said she hoped so.

She told Willy about the new people across the street who had bought out the Jew, and said to buy there if there was a chance; she meant by that they would continue to shop at the self-service, but when there was some odd or end to pick up, or something they had forgotten to buy, they could go to Panessa's. Willy did as he was told. He was tall and broad-backed, with a heavy face seamed dark from the coal and ashes he shoveled around all winter, and his hair often looked gray from the dust the wind whirled up at him out of the ash cans when he was lining them up for the sanitation truck. Always in overalls—he complained he never stopped working—he would drift across the street and down the steps when something was needed, and lighting his pipe, would stand around talking to Mrs. Panessa as her husband, a small bent man with a fitful smile, stood behind the counter waiting for the janitor after a long interval of talk to ask, upon reflection, for a dime's worth of this or that, the whole business never amounting to more than half a dollar. Then one day Willy got to talking about how the tenants goaded him all the time and what the cruel and stingy landlord could think up for him to do in that smelly five-floor dungeon. He was absorbed by what he was saying and before he knew it had run up a three-dollar order, though all he had on him was fifty cents. Willy looked like a dog that had just had a licking, but Mr. Panessa, after clearing his throat, chirped up it didn't matter, he could pay the rest whenever he wanted. He said that everything was run on credit, business and everything else, because after all what was credit but the fact that people were human beings, and if you were really a human being you gave credit to somebody else and he gave credit to you. That surprised Willy because he had never heard a storekeeper say it before. After a couple of days he paid the two fifty, but when Panessa said he could trust whenever he felt like it, Willy sucked a flame into his pipe, then began to order all sorts of things.

When he brought home two large bagfuls of stuff, Etta shouted he must be crazy. Willy answered he had charged everything and paid no cash.

"But we have to pay sometime, don't we?" Etta shouted. "And we have to pay higher prices than in the self-service." She said then what she always said, "We're poor people, Willy. We can't afford too much."

Though Willy saw the justice of her remarks, despite her scolding he still went across the street and trusted. Once he had a crumpled ten-dollar bill in his pants pocket and the amount came to less than four, but he didn't offer to pay, and let Panessa write it in the book. Etta knew he had the money so she screamed when he admitted he had bought on credit.

"Why are you doing it for? Why don't you pay if you have the money?"

He didn't answer but after a time he said there were other things he had to buy once in a while. He went into the furnace room and came out with a wrapped package which he opened, and it contained a beaded black dress.

Etta cried over the dress and said she would never wear it because the only time he ever brought her anything was when he had done something wrong. Thereafter she let him do all the grocery shopping and she did not speak when he bought on trust.

Willy continued to buy at Panessa's. It seemed they were always waiting for him to come in. They lived in three tiny rooms on the floor above the store, and when Mrs. Panessa saw him out of her window, she ran down to the store. Willy came up from his basement, crossed the street and went down the steps into the delicatessen, looming large as he opened the door. Every time he bought, it was never less than two dollars' worth and sometimes it would go as high as five. Mrs. Panessa would pack everything into a deep double bag, after Panessa had called off each item and written the price with a smeary black pencil into his looseleaf notebook. Whenever Willy walked in, Panessa would open the book, wet his finger tip and flip through a number of blank pages till he found Willy's account in the center of the book. After the order was packed and tied up, Panessa added the amount, touching each figure with his pencil, hissing to himself as he added, and Mrs. Panessa's bird eyes would follow the figuring until Panessa wrote down a sum, and the new total sum (after Panessa had glanced up at Willy and saw that Willy was looking) was twice underscored and then Panessa shut the book. Willy, with his loose unlit pipe in his mouth, did not move until the book was put away under the counter; then he roused himself and embracing the bundle—with which they offered to help him across the street though he always refused—plunged out of the store.

One day when the sum total came to eighty-three dollars and some cents, Panessa, lifting his head and smiling, asked Willy when he could pay something on account. The very next day Willy stopped buying at Panessa's and after that Etta, with her cord market bag, began to shop again at the self-service, and neither of them went across the street for as much as a pound of prunes or box of salt they had meant to buy but had forgotten.

Etta, when she returned from shopping at the self-service, scraped the wall on her side of the street to get as far away as possible from Panessa's.

Later she asked Willy if he had paid them anything.

He said no.

"When will you?"

He said he didn't know.

A month went by, then Etta met Mrs. Panessa around the corner, and though Mrs. Panessa, looking unhappy, said nothing about the bill, Etta came home and reminded Willy.

"Leave me alone," he said, "I got enough trouble of my own."

"What kind of trouble have you got, Willy?"

"The goddam tenants and the goddam landlord," he shouted and slammed the door.

When he returned he said, "What have I got that I can pay? Ain't I been a poor man every day of my life?"

She was sitting at the table and lowered her arms and put her head down on them and wept.

"With what?" he shouted, his face lit up dark and webbed. "With the meat off of my bones?

"With the ashes in my eyes. With the piss I mop up on the floors. With the cold in my lungs when I sleep."

He felt for Panessa and his wife a grating hatred and vowed never to pay because he hated them so much, especially the humpback behind the counter. If he ever smiled at him again with those goddam eyes he would lift him off the floor and crack his bent bones.

That night he went out and got drunk and lay till morning in the gutter. When he returned, with filthy clothes and bloodied eyes, Etta held up to him the picture of their four-year-old son who had died from diphtheria, and Willy weeping splashy tears, swore he would never touch another drop.

Each morning he went out to line up the ash cans, he never looked the full way across the street.

"Give credit," he mimicked, "give credit."

Hard times set in. The landlord ordered cut down on heat, cut down on hot water. He cut down on Willy's expense money and wages. The tenants were angered. All day they pestered Willy like clusters of flies and he told them what the landlord had ordered. Then they cursed Willy and Willy cursed them. They telephoned the Board of Health but when the inspectors arrived they said the temperature was within the legal minimum though the house was drafty. However the tenants still complained they were cold and goaded Willy about it all day but he said he was cold too. He said he was freezing but no one believed him.

One day he looked up from lining up four ash cans for the truck to remove and saw Mr. and Mrs. Panessa staring at him from the store. They were staring up through the glass front door and when he looked at them at first his eyes blurred and they appeared to be two scrawny, loose-feathered birds.

He went down the block to get a wrench from another janitor, and when he got back they then reminded him of two skinny leafless bushes sprouting up through the wooden floor. He could see through the bushes to the empty shelves.

In the spring, when the grass shoots were sticking up from the cracks in the sidewalk, he told Etta, "I'm only waiting till I can pay it all."

"How, Willy?"

"We can save up."

"How?"

"How much do we save a month?"

"Nothing."

"How much have you got hid away?"

"Nothing any more."

"I'll pay them bit by bit. I will, by Jesus."

The trouble was there was no place they could get the money. Sometimes when he was trying to think of the different ways there were to get money his thoughts ran ahead and he saw what it would be like when he paid. He would wrap the wad of bills with a thick rubber band and then go up the stairs and cross the street and go down the five steps into the store. He would say to Panessa, "Here it is, little old man, and I bet you didn't think I would do it, and I don't suppose nobody else did and sometimes me myself, but here it is in bucks all held together by a fat rubber band." After hefting the wad a little, he placed it, like making a move on a checkerboard, squarely in the center of the counter, and the diminutive man and his wife both unpeeled it, squeaking and squealing over each blackened buck, and marveling that so many ones had been tied together into such a small pack.

Such was the dream Willy dreamed but he could never make it come true.

He worked hard to. He got up early and scrubbed the stairs from cellar to roof with soap and a hard brush then went over that with a wet mop. He cleaned the woodwork too and oiled the bannister till it shone the whole zigzag way down and rubbed the mailboxes in the vestibule with metal polish and a soft rag until you could see your face in them. He saw his own heavy face with a surprising yellow mustache he had recently grown and the tan felt cap he wore that a tenant had left behind in a closetful of junk when he had moved. Etta helped him and they cleaned the whole cellar and the dark courtyard under the crisscrossed clotheslines, and they were quick to respond to any kind of request, even from tenants they didn't like, for sink or toilet repairs. Both worked themselves to exhaustion every day, but as they knew from the beginning, no extra money came in.

One morning when Willy was shining up the mailboxes, he found in his own a letter for him. Removing his cap, he opened the envelope and held the paper to the light as he read the trembling writing. It was from Mrs. Panessa, who wrote her husband was sick across the street, and she had no money in the house so could he pay her just ten dollars and the rest could wait for later.

He tore the letter into bits and hid all day in the cellar. That night, Etta, who had been searching for him in the streets, found him behind the furnace amid the pipes, and she asked him what he was doing there.

He explained about the letter.

"Hiding won't do you any good at all," she said hopelessly.

"What should I do then?"

"Go to sleep, I guess."

He went to sleep but the next morning burst out of his covers, pulled on his overalls and ran out of the house with an overcoat flung over his shoulders. Around the corner he found a pawnshop, where he got ten dollars for the coat and was gleeful.

But when he ran back, there was a hearse or something across the street, and two men in black were carrying this small and narrow pine box out of the house.

"Who's dead, a child?" he asked one of the tenants.

"No, a man named Mr. Panessa."

Willy couldn't speak. His throat had turned to bone.

After the pine box was squeezed through the vestibule doors, Mrs. Panessa, grieved all over, tottered out alone. Willy turned his head away although he thought she wouldn't recognize him because of his new mustache and tan cap.

"What'd he die of?" he whispered to the tenant.

"I really couldn't say."

But Mrs. Panessa, walking behind the box, had heard.

"Old age," she shrilly called back.

He tried to say some sweet thing but his tongue hung in his mouth like dead fruit on a tree, and his heart was a black-painted window.

Mrs. Panessa moved away to live first with one stone-faced daughter, then with the other. And the bill was never paid.

J. F. Powers

Dawn

Father Udovic placed the envelope before the Bishop and stepped back. He gave the Bishop more than enough time to read what was written on the envelope, time to digest *The Pope* and, down in the corner, the *Personal,* and then he stepped forward. "It was in the collection yesterday," he said. "At Cathedral."

"Peter's Pence, Father?"

Father Udovic nodded. He'd checked that. It had been in with the special Peter's Pence envelopes, and not with the regular Sunday ones.

"Well, then . . ." The Bishop's right hand opened over the envelope, then stopped, and came to roost again, uneasily, on the edge of the desk.

Father Udovic shifted a foot, popped a knuckle in his big toe. The envelope was a bad thing all right. They'd never received anything like it. The Bishop was doing what Father Udovic had done when confronted by the envelope, thinking twice, which was what Monsignor Renton at Cathedral had done, and his curates before him, and his housekeeper who counted the collection. In the end, each had seen the envelope as a hot potato and passed it on. But the Bishop couldn't do that. He didn't know *what* might be inside. Even Father Udovic, who had held it up to a strong light, didn't know. That was the hell of it.

The Bishop continued to stare at the envelope. He still hadn't touched it.

"It beats me," said Father Udovic, moving backwards. He sank down on the leather sofa.

"Was there something else, Father?"

Father Udovic got up quickly and went out of the office—wondering how the Bishop would handle the problem, disappointed that he evidently meant to handle it by himself. In a way, Father Udovic felt responsible. It had been his idea to popularize the age-old collection—"to personalize Peter's Pence"—by moving the day for it ahead a month so that the Bishop, who was going to Rome, would be able to present the proceeds to the Holy Father personally. There had been opposition from the very first. Monsignor Renton, the rector at Cathedral, and one of those at table when Father Udovic proposed his plan, was ill-disposed to it (as he was to Father Udovic himself) and had almost killed it with his comment, "Smart promotion, Bruno." (Monsignor Renton's superior attitude was understandable. He'd had Father Udovic's job, that of chancellor of the diocese, years ago, under an earlier bishop.) But Father Udovic had won out. The Bishop had written a letter incorporating Father Udovic's idea. The plan had been poorly received in some rectories, which was to be expected since it disturbed the routine schedule of special collections. Father Udovic, however, had been confident that the people, properly appealed to, could do better than in the past with Peter's Pence. And the first returns, which had reached him that afternoon, were reassuring—whatever the envelope might be.

It was still on the Bishop's desk the next day, off to one side, and it was there on the day after. On the following day, Thursday, it was in the "In" section of his file basket. On Friday it was still there, buried. Obviously the Bishop was stumped.

On Saturday morning, however, it was back on the desk. Father Udovic, called in for consultation, had a feeling, a really satisfying feeling, that the Bishop might have need of him. If so, he would be ready. He had a plan. He sat down on the sofa.

"It's about this," the Bishop said, glancing down at the envelope before him. "I wonder if you can locate the sender."

"I'll do my best," said Father Udovic. He paused to consider whether it would be better just to go and do his best, or to present his plan of operation to the Bishop for approval. But the Bishop, not turning to him at all, was outlining what he wanted done. And it was Father Udovic's own plan! The Cathedral priests at their Sunday Masses should request the sender of the envelope to report to the sacristy afterwards. The sender should be assured that the contents would be turned over to the Holy Father, if possible.

"Providing, of course," said Father Udovic, standing and trying to get into the act, "it's not something . . ."

"Providing it's possible to do so."

Father Udovic tried not to look sad. The Bishop might express himself better, but he was saying nothing that hadn't occurred to Father Udovic first, days before. It was pretty discouraging.

He retreated to the outer office and went to work on a memo of their conversation. Drafting letters and announcements was the hardest part of his job for him. He tended to go astray without a memo, to take up with the tempting clichés that came to him in the act of composition and sometimes perverted the Bishop's true meaning. Later that morning he called Monsignor Renton and read him the product of many revisions, the two sentences.

"Okay," said Monsignor Renton. "I'll stick it in the bulletin. Thanks a lot."

As soon as Father Udovic hung up, he doubted that that was what the Bishop wished. He consulted the memo. The Bishop was very anxious that "not too much be made of this matter." Naturally, Monsignor Renton wanted the item for his parish bulletin. He was hard up. At one time he had produced the best bulletin in the diocese, but now he was written out, quoting more and more from the magazines and even from the papal encyclicals. Father Udovic called Monsignor Renton back and asked that the announcement be kept out of print. It would be enough to read it once over lightly from the pulpit, using Father Udovic's version because it said enough without saying too much and was, he implied, authorized by the Bishop. Whoever the announcement concerned would comprehend it. If published, the announcement would be subject to study and private interpretation. "Announcements from the pulpit are soon forgotten," Father Udovic said. "I mean—by the people they don't concern."

"You were right the first time, Bruno," said Monsignor Renton. He sounded sore.

The next day—Sunday—Father Udovic stayed home, expecting a call from Monsignor Renton, or possibly even a visit. There was nothing. That evening he called the Cathedral rectory and got one of the curates. Monsignor Renton wasn't expected in until very late. The curate had made the announcement at his two Masses, but no one had come to him about it. "Yes, Father, as you say, it's quite possible someone came to Monsignor about it. Probably he didn't consider it important enough to call you about."

"*Not important!*"

"Not important enough to call *you* about, Father. On *Sunday.*"

"I see," said Father Udovic mildly. It was good to know that the curate, after almost a year of listening to Monsignor Renton, was still respectful. Some of the men out in parishes said Father Udovic's job was a snap and maintained that he'd landed it only because he employed the touch system of typing. Before hanging up, Father Udovic stressed the importance of resolving the question of the envelope, but somehow (words played tricks on him) he sounded as though he were accusing the curate of indifference. What a change! The curate didn't take criticism very well, as became all too clear from his sullen silence, and he wasn't very loyal. When Father Udovic suggested that Monsignor Renton might have neglected to make the announcement at his Masses, the curate readily agreed. "Could've slipped his mind all right. I guess you know what that's like."

Early the next morning Father Udovic was in touch with Monsignor Renton, beginning significantly with a glowing report on the Peter's Pence collection, but the conversation languished, and finally he had to ask about the announcement.

"Nobody showed," Monsignor Renton said in an annoyed voice. "What d'ya want to do about it?"

"Nothing right now," said Father Udovic, and hung up. If there had been a failure in the line of communication, he thought he knew where it was.

The envelope had reposed on the Bishop's desk over the weekend and through most of Monday. But that afternoon Father Udovic, on one of his appearances in the Bishop's office, noticed that it was gone. As soon as the Bishop left for the day, Father Udovic rushed in, looking first in the wastebasket, then among the sealed outgoing letters, for a moment actually expecting to see a fat one addressed in the Bishop's hand to the Apostolic Delegate. When he uncovered the envelope in the "Out" section of the file basket, he wondered at himself for looking in the other places first. The envelope had to be filed somewhere—a separate folder would be best—but Father Udovic didn't file it. He carried it to his desk. There, sitting down to it in the gloom of the outer office, weighing, feeling, smelling the envelope, he succumbed entirely to his first fears. He remembered the parable of the cockle. "An enemy hath done this." An enemy was plotting to disturb the peace of the diocese, to employ the Bishop as an agent against himself, or against some other innocent person, some unsuspecting priest or nun—yes, against Father Udovic. Why him? Why not? Only a diseased mind would contemplate such a scheme, Father Udovic thought, but that didn't make it less likely. And the sender, whoever he was, doubtless anonymous and judging others by himself, would assume that the envelope had already been opened and that the announcement was calculated to catch him. Such a person would never come forward.

Father Udovic's fingers tightened on the envelope. He could rip it open, but he wouldn't. That evening, enjoying instant coffee in his room, he could steam it open. But he wouldn't. In the beginning, the envelope might have been opened. It would have been so easy, pardonable then. Monsignor Renton's housekeeper might have done it. With the Bishop honoring the name on the envelope and the intentions of whoever wrote it, up to a point anyway, there was now a principle operating that just couldn't be bucked. Monsignor Renton could have it his way.

That evening Father Udovic called him and asked that the announcement appear in the bulletin.

"Okay. I'll stick it in. It wouldn't surprise me if we got some action now."

"I hope so," said Father Udovic, utterly convinced that Monsignor Renton had failed him before. "Do you mind taking it down verbatim this time?"

"Not at all."

In the next bulletin, an advance copy of which came to Father Udovic through the courtesy of Monsignor Renton, the announcement appeared in an expanded, unauthorized version.

The result on Sunday was no different.

During the following week, Father Udovic considered the possibility that the sender was a floater and thought of having the announcement broadcast from every pulpit in the diocese. He would need the Bishop's permission for that, though, and he didn't dare to ask for something he probably wouldn't get. The Bishop had instructed him not to make too much of the matter. The sender would have to be found at Cathedral, or not at all. If not at all, Father Udovic, having done his best, would understand that he wasn't supposed to know any more about the envelope than he did. He would file it away, and some other chancellor, some other bishop, perhaps, would inherit it. The envelope was most likely harmless anyway, but Father Udovic wasn't so much relieved as bored by the probability that some poor soul was trusting the Bishop to put the envelope into the hands of the Holy Father, hoping for rosary beads blessed by him, or for his autographed picture, and enclosing a small offering, perhaps a spiritual bouquet. Toward the end of the week, Father Udovic told the Bishop that he liked to think that the envelope contained a spiritual bouquet from a little child, and that its contents had already been delivered, so to speak, its prayers and communions already credited to the Holy Father's account in heaven.

"I must say I hadn't thought of that," said the Bishop.

Unfortunately for his peace of mind Father Udovic wasn't always able to believe that the sender was a little child.

The most persistent of those coming to him in reverie was a middle-aged woman saying she hadn't received a special Peter's Pence envelope, had been out of town a few weeks, and so hadn't heard or read the announcement. When Father Udovic tried her on the meaning of the *Personal* on the envelope, however, the woman just went away, and so did all the other suspects under questioning—except one. This was a rich old man suffering from scrupulosity. He wanted his alms to be in secret, as it said in Scripture, lest he be deprived of his eternal reward, but not *entirely* in secret. That was as far as Father Udovic could figure the old man. Who was he? An audacious old Protestant who hated communism, or could some future Knight of St. Gregory be taking his first awkward step? The old man was pretty hard to believe in, and the handwriting on the envelope sometimes struck Father Udovic as that of a woman. This wasn't necessarily bad. Women controlled the nation's wealth. He'd seen the figures on it. The explanation was simple: widows. Perhaps they hadn't taken the right tone in the announcement. Father Udovic's version had been safe and cold, Monsignor Renton's like a summons. It might have been emphasized that the Bishop, under certain circumstances, would *gladly* undertake to deliver the envelope. That might have made a difference. The sender would not only have to appreciate the difficulty of the Bishop's position, but abandon his own. That wouldn't be easy for the sort of person Father Udovic had in mind. He had a feeling that it wasn't going to happen. The Bishop would leave for Rome on the following Tuesday.

So time was running out. The envelope could contain a check—quite the cruelest thought—on which payment would be stopped after a limited time by the donor, whom Father Udovic persistently saw as an old person not to be dictated to, or it could be nullified even sooner by untimely death. God, what a shame! In Rome, where the needs of the world, temporal as well as spiritual, were so well known, the Bishop would've been welcome as the flowers in May.

And then, having come full circle, Father Udovic would be hard on himself for dreaming and see the envelope as a whited sepulcher concealing all manner of filth, spelled out in letters snipped from newsprint and calculated to shake Rome's faith in him. It was then that he particularly liked to think of the sender as a little child. But soon the middle-aged woman would be back, and all the others, among whom the hottest suspect was a feeble-minded nun—devils all to pester him, and the last was always worse than the first. For he always ended up with the old man—and what if there was such an old man?

On Saturday, Father Udovic called Monsignor Renton and asked him to run the announcement again. It was all they could do, he said, and admitted that he had little hope of success.

"Don't let it throw you, Bruno. It's always darkest before dawn."

Father Udovic said he no longer cared. He said he liked to think that the envelope contained a spiritual bouquet from a little child, that its contents had already been delivered, its prayers and communions already. . . .

"You should've been a nun, Bruno."

"Not sure I know what you mean," Father Udovic said, and hung up. He wished it were in his power to do something about Monsignor Renton. Some of the old ones got funny when they stayed too long in one place.

On Sunday, after the eight o'clock Mass, Father Udovic received a call from Monsignor Renton. "I told 'em if somebody didn't own up to the envelope, we'd open it. I guess I got carried away." But it had worked. Monsignor Renton had just talked with the party responsible for the envelope—a Mrs. Anton—and she was on the way over to see Father Udovic.

"A woman, huh?"

"A widow. That's about all I know about her."

"A widow, huh? Did she say what was in it?"

"I'm afraid it's not what you thought, Bruno. It's money."

Father Udovic returned to the front parlor, where he had left Mrs. Anton. "The Bishop'll see you," he said, and sat down. She wasn't making a good impression on him. She could've used a shave. When she'd asked for the Bishop, Father Udovic had replied instinctively, "He's busy," but it hadn't convinced her. She had appeared quite capable of walking out on him. He invoked the Bishop's name again. "Now one of the things the Bishop'll want to know is why you didn't show up before this."

Mrs. Anton gazed at him, then past him, as she had when he'd tried to question her. He saw her starting to get up, and thought he was about to lose her. He hadn't heard the Bishop enter the room.

The Bishop waved Mrs. Anton down, seated himself near the doorway at some distance from them, and motioned to Father Udovic to continue.

To the Bishop it might sound like browbeating, but Father Udovic meant to go on being firm with Mrs. Anton. He hadn't forgotten that she'd responded to Monsignor Renton's threats. "Why'd you wait so long? You listen to the Sunday announcements, don't you?" If she persisted in ignoring him, she could make him look bad, of course, but he didn't look for her to do that, with the Bishop present.

Calmly Mrs. Anton spoke, but not to Father Udovic. "Call off your trip?"

The Bishop shook his head.

In Father Udovic's opinion, it was one of his functions to protect the Bishop from directness of that sort. "How do we know what's in here?" he demanded. Here, unfortunately, he reached up the wrong sleeve of his cassock for the envelope. Then he had it. "What's in here? Money?" He knew from Monsignor Renton that the envelope contained money, but he hadn't told the Bishop, and so it probably sounded rash to him. Father Udovic could feel the Bishop disapproving of him, and Mrs. Anton still hadn't answered the question.

"Maybe you should return the envelope to Mrs. Anton, Father," said the Bishop.

That did it for Mrs. Anton. "It's got a dollar in it," she said.

Father Udovic glanced at the Bishop. The Bishop was adjusting his cuffs. This was something he did at funerals and public gatherings. It meant that things had gone on too long. Father Udovic's fingers were sticking to the envelope. He still couldn't believe it. "Feels like there's more than that," he said.

"I wrapped it up good in paper."

"You didn't write a letter or anything?"

"Was I supposed to?"

Father Udovic came down on her. "You were supposed to do what everybody else did. You were supposed to use the envelopes we had printed up for the purpose." He went back a few steps in his mind. "You told Monsignor Renton what was in the envelope?"

"Yes."

"Did you tell him how much?"

"No."

"Why not?"

"*He* didn't ask me."

And *he* didn't have to, thought Father Udovic. One look at Mrs. Anton and Monsignor Renton would know. Parish priests got to know such things. They were like weight-guessers, for whom it was only a question of ounces. Monsignor Renton shouldn't have passed Mrs. Anton on. He had opposed the plan to personalize Peter's Pence, but who would have thought he'd go to such lengths to get even with Father Udovic? It was sabotage. Father Udovic held out the envelope and pointed to the *Personal* on it. "What do you mean by that?" Here was where the creatures of his dreams had always gone away. He leaned forward for the answer.

Mrs. Anton leaned forward to give it. "I mean I don't want somebody else takin' all the credit with the Holy Father!"

Father Udovic sank back. It had been bad before, when she'd ignored him, but now it was worse. She was attacking the Bishop. If there were only a way to *prove* she was out of her mind, if only she'd say something that would make all her remarks acceptable in retrospect . . . "How's the Holy Father gonna know who this dollar came from if you didn't write anything?"

"I wrote my name and address on it. In ink."

"All right, Father," said the Bishop. He stood up and almost went out of the room before he stopped and looked back at Mrs. Anton. "Why don't you send it by regular mail?"

"He'd never see it! That's why! Some flunky'd get hold of it! Same as here! Oh, don't I know!"

The Bishop walked out, leaving them together—with the envelope.

In the next few moments, although Father Udovic knew he had an obligation to instruct Mrs. Anton, and had the text for it—"When thou dost an alms-deed, sound not a trumpet before thee"—he despaired. He realized that they had needed each other to arrive at their sorry state. It seemed to him, sitting there saying nothing, that they saw each other as two people who'd sinned together on earth might see each other in hell, unchastened even then, only blaming each other for what had happened.

Albert Camus

The Guest

The schoolmaster was watching the two men climb toward him. One was on horseback, the other on foot. They had not yet tackled the abrupt rise leading to the schoolhouse built on the hillside. They were toiling onward, making slow progress in the snow, among the stones, on the vast expanse of the high, deserted plateau. From time to time the horse stumbled. Without hearing anything yet, he could see the breath issuing from the horse's nostrils. One of the men, at least, knew the region. They were following the trail although it had disappeared days ago under a layer of dirty white snow. The schoolmaster calculated that it would take them half an hour to get onto the hill. It was cold; he went back into the school to get a sweater.

He crossed the empty, frigid classroom. On the blackboard the four rivers of France, drawn with four different colored chalks, had been flowing toward their estuaries for the past three days. Snow had suddenly fallen in mid-October after eight months of drought without the transition of rain, and the twenty pupils, more or less, who lived in the villages scattered over the plateau had stopped coming. With fair weather they would return. Daru now heated only the single room that was his lodging, adjoining the classroom and giving also onto the plateau to the east. Like the class windows, his window looked to the south too. On that side the school was a few kilometers from the point where the plateau began to slope toward the south. In clear weather could be seen the purple mass of the mountain range where the gap opened onto the desert.

Somewhat warmed, Daru returned to the window from which he had first seen the two men. They were no longer visible. Hence they must have tackled the rise. The sky was not so dark, for the snow had stopped falling during the night. The morning had opened with a dirty light which had scarcely become brighter as the ceiling of clouds lifted. At two in the afternoon it seemed as if the day were merely beginning. But still this was better than those three days when the thick snow was falling amidst unbroken darkness with little gusts of wind that rattled the double door of the classroom. Then Daru had spent long hours in his room, leaving it only to go to the shed and feed the chickens or get some coal. Fortunately the delivery truck from Tadjid, the nearest village to the north, had brought his supplies two days before the blizzard. It would return in forty-eight hours.

Besides, he had enough to resist a siege, for the little room was cluttered with bags of wheat that the administration left as a stock to distribute to those of his pupils whose families had suffered from the drought. Actually they had all been victims because they were all poor. Every day Daru would distribute a ration to the children. They had missed it, he knew, during these bad days. Possibly one of the fathers or big brothers would come this afternoon and he could supply them with grain. It was just a matter of carrying them over to the next harvest. Now shiploads of wheat were arriving from France and the worst was over. But it would be hard to forget that poverty, that army of ragged ghosts wandering in the sunlight, the plateaus burned to a cinder month after month, the earth shriveled up little by little, literally scorched, every stone bursting into dust under one's foot. The sheep had died then by thousands and even a few men, here and there, sometimes without anyone's knowing.

In contrast with such poverty, he who lived almost like a monk in his remote schoolhouse, nonetheless satisfied with the little he had and with the rough life, had felt like a lord with his whitewashed walls, his narrow couch, his unpainted shelves, his well, and his weekly provision of water and food. And suddenly this snow, without warning, without the foretaste of rain. This is the way the region was, cruel to live in, even without men—who didn't help matters either. But Daru had been born here. Everywhere else, he felt exiled.

He stepped out onto the terrace in front of the schoolhouse. The two men were now halfway up the slope. He recognized the horseman as Balducci, the old gendarme he had known for a long time. Balducci was holding on the end of a rope an Arab who was walking behind him with hands bound and head lowered. The gendarme waved a greeting to which Daru did not reply, lost as he was in contemplation of the Arab dressed in a faded blue jellaba, his feet in sandals but covered with socks of heavy raw wool, his head surmounted by a narrow, short *chèche*. They were approaching. Balducci was holding back his horse in order not to hurt the Arab, and the group was advancing slowly.

Within earshot, Balducci shouted: "One hour to do the three kilometers from El Ameur!" Daru did not answer. Short and square in his thick sweater, he watched them climb. Not once had the Arab raised his head. "Hello," said Daru when they got up onto the terrace. "Come in and warm up." Balducci painfully got down from his horse without letting go of the rope. From under his bristling moustache he smiled at the schoolmaster. His little dark eyes, deep set under a tanned forehead, and his mouth surrounded with wrinkles made him look attentive and studious. Daru took the bridle, led the horse to the shed, and came back to the two men, who were now waiting for him in the school. He led them into his room. "I am going to heat up the classroom," he said. "We'll be more comfortable there." When he entered the room again, Balducci was on the couch. He had undone the rope tying him to the Arab, who had squatted near the stove. His hands still bound, the *chèche* pushed back on his head, he was looking toward the window. At first Daru noticed only his huge lips, fat, smooth, almost Negroid; yet his nose was straight, his eyes were dark and full of fever. The *chèche* revealed an obstinate forehead and, under the weathered skin now rather discolored by the cold, the whole face had a restless and rebellious look that struck Daru when the Arab, turning his face toward him, looked him straight in the eyes. "Go into the other room," said the schoolmaster, "and I'll make you some mint tea." "Thanks," Balducci said. "What a chore! How I long for retirement." And addressing his prisoner in Arabic: "Come on, you." The Arab got up and, slowly, holding his bound wrists in front of him, went into the classroom.

With the tea, Daru brought a chair. But Balducci was already enthroned on the nearest pupil's desk and the Arab had squatted against the teacher's platform facing the stove, which stood between the desk and the window. When he held out the glass of tea to the prisoner, Daru hesitated at the sight of his bound hands. "He might perhaps be untied." "Sure," said Balducci. "That was for the trip." He started to get to his feet. But Daru, setting the glass on the floor, had knelt beside the Arab. Without saying anything, the Arab watched him with his feverish eyes. Once his hands were free, he rubbed his swollen wrists against each other, took the glass of tea, and sucked up the burning liquid in swift little sips.

"Good," said Daru. "And where are you headed?"

Balducci withdrew his moustache from the tea. "Here, son."

"Odd pupils! And you're spending the night?"

"No. I'm going back to El Ameur. And you will deliver this fellow to Tinguit. He is expected at police headquarters."

Balducci was looking at Daru with a friendly little smile.

"What's this story?" asked the schoolmaster. "Are you pulling my leg?"

"No, son. Those are the orders."

"The orders? I'm not . . ." Daru hesitated, not wanting to hurt the old Corsican. "I mean, that's not my job."

"What! What's the meaning of that? In wartime people do all kinds of jobs."

"Then I'll wait for the declaration of war!"

Balducci nodded.

"O.K. But the orders exist and they concern you too. Things are brewing, it appears. There is talk of a forthcoming revolt. We are mobilized, in a way."

Daru still had his obstinate look.

"Listen, son," Balducci said. "I like you and you must understand. There's only a dozen of us at El Ameur to patrol throughout the whole territory of a small department and I must get back in a hurry. I was told to hand this guy over to you and return without delay. He couldn't be kept there. His village was beginning to stir; they wanted to take him back. You must take him to Tinguit tomorrow before the day is over. Twenty kilometers shouldn't faze a husky fellow like you. After that, all will be over. You'll come back to your pupils and your comfortable life."

Behind the wall the horse could be heard snorting and pawing the earth. Daru was looking out the window. Decidedly, the weather was clearing and the light was increasing over the snowy plateau. When all the snow was melted, the sun would take over again and once more would burn the fields of stone. For days, still, the unchanging sky would shed its dry light on the solitary expanse where nothing had any connection with man.

"After all," he said, turning around toward Balducci, "what did he do?" And, before the gendarme had opened his mouth, he asked: "Does he speak French?"

"No, not a word. We had been looking for him for a month, but they were hiding him. He killed his cousin."

"Is he against us?"

"I don't think so. But you can never be sure."

"Why did he kill?"

"A family squabble, I think. One owed the other grain, it seems. It's not at all clear. In short, he killed his cousin with a billhook. You know, like a sheep, *kreezk!*"

Balducci made the gesture of drawing a blade across his throat and the Arab, his attention attracted, watched him with a sort of anxiety. Daru felt a sudden wrath against the man, against all men with their rotten spite, their tireless hates, their blood lust.

But the kettle was singing on the stove. He served Balducci more tea, hesitated, then served the Arab again, who, a second time, drank avidly. His raised arms made the jellaba fall open and the schoolmaster saw his thin, muscular chest.

"Thanks, kid," Balducci said. "And now, I'm off."

He got up and went toward the Arab, taking a small rope from his pocket.

"What are you doing?" Daru asked dryly.

Balducci, disconcerted, showed him the rope.

"Don't bother."

The old gendarme hesitated. "It's up to you. Of course, you are armed?"

"I have my shotgun."

"Where?"

"In the trunk."

"You ought to have it near your bed."

"Why? I have nothing to fear."

"You're crazy, son. If there's an uprising, no one is safe, we're all in the same boat."

"I'll defend myself. I'll have time to see them coming."

Balducci began to laugh, then suddenly the moustache covered the white teeth. "You'll have time? O.K. That's just what I was saying. You have always been a little cracked. That's why I like you, my son was like that."

At the same time he took out his revolver and put it on the desk.

"Keep it; I don't need two weapons from here to El Ameur."

The revolver shone against the black paint of the table. When the gendarme turned toward him, the schoolmaster caught the smell of leather and horseflesh.

"Listen, Balducci," Daru said suddenly, "every bit of this disgusts me, and first of all your fellow here. But I won't hand him over. Fight, yes, if I have to. But not that."

The old gendarme stood in front of him and looked at him severely.

"You're being a fool," he said slowly. "I don't like it either. You don't get used to putting a rope on a man even after years of it, and you're even ashamed—yes, ashamed. But you can't let them have their way."

"I won't hand him over," Daru said again.

"It's an order, son, and I repeat it."

"That's right. Repeat to them what I've said to you: I won't hand him over."

Balducci made a visible effort to reflect. He looked at the Arab and at Daru. At last he decided.

"No, I won't tell them anything. If you want to drop us, go ahead; I'll not denounce you. I have an order to deliver the prisoner and I'm doing so. And now you'll just sign this paper for me."

"There's no need. I'll not deny that you left him with me."

"Don't be mean with me. I know you'll tell the truth. You're from hereabouts and you are a man. But you must sign, that's the rule."

Daru opened his drawer, took out a little square bottle of purple ink, the red wooden penholder with the "sergeant-major" pen he used for making models of penmanship, and signed. The gendarme carefully folded the paper and put it into his wallet. Then he moved toward the door.

"I'll see you off," Daru said.

"No," said Balducci. "There's no use being polite. You insulted me."

He looked at the Arab, motionless in the same spot, sniffed peevishly, and turned away toward the door. "Good-by, son," he said. The door shut behind him. Balducci appeared suddenly outside the window and then disappeared. His footsteps were muffled by the snow. The horse stirred on the other side of the wall and several chickens fluttered in fright. A moment later Balducci reappeared outside the window leading the horse by the bridle. He walked toward the little rise without turning around and disappeared from sight with the horse following him. A big stone could be heard bouncing down. Daru walked back toward the prisoner, who, without stirring, never took his eyes off him. "Wait," the schoolmaster said in Arabic and went toward the bedroom. As he was going through the door, he had a second thought, went to the desk, took the revolver, and stuck it in his pocket. Then, without looking back, he went into his room.

For some time he lay on his couch watching the sky gradually close over, listening to the silence. It was this silence that had seemed painful to him during the first days here, after the war. He had requested a post in the little town at the base of the foothills separating the upper plateaus from the desert. There, rocky walls, green and black to the north, pink and lavender to the south, marked the frontier of eternal summer. He had been named to a post farther north, on the plateau itself. In the beginning, the solitude and the silence had been hard for him on these wastelands peopled only by stones. Occasionally, furrows suggested cultivation, but they had been dug to uncover a certain kind of stone good for building. The only plowing here was to harvest rocks. Elsewhere a thin layer of soil accumulated in the hollows would be scraped out to enrich paltry village gardens. This is the way it was: bare rock covered three quarters of the region. Towns sprang up, flourished, then disappeared; men came by, loved one another or fought bitterly, then died. No one in this desert, neither he nor his guest, mattered. And yet, outside this desert neither of them, Daru knew, could have really lived.

When he got up, no noise came from the classroom. He was amazed at the unmixed joy he derived from the mere thought that the Arab might have fled and that he would be alone with no decision to make. But the prisoner was there. He had merely stretched out between the stove and the desk. With eyes open, he was staring at the ceiling. In that position, his thick lips were particularly noticeable, giving him a pouting look. "Come," said Daru. The Arab got up and followed him. In the bedroom, the schoolmaster pointed to a chair near the table under the window. The Arab sat down without taking his eyes off Daru.

"Are you hungry?"

"Yes," the prisoner said.

Daru set the table for two. He took flour and oil, shaped a cake in a frying-pan, and lighted the little stove that functioned on bottled gas. While the cake was cooking, he went out to the shed to get cheese, eggs, dates, and condensed milk. When the cake was done he set it on the window sill to cool, heated some condensed milk diluted with water, and beat up the eggs into an omelette. In one of his motions he knocked against the revolver stuck in his right pocket. He set the bowl down, went into the classroom, and put the revolver in his desk drawer. When he came back to the room, night was falling. He put on the light and served the Arab. "Eat," he said. The Arab took a piece of the cake, lifted it eagerly to his mouth, and stopped short.

"And you?" he asked.

"After you. I'll eat too."

The thick lips opened slightly. The Arab hesitated, then bit into the cake determinedly.

The meal over, the Arab looked at the schoolmaster. "Are you the judge?"

"No, I'm simply keeping you until tomorrow."

"Why do you eat with me?"

"I'm hungry."

The Arab fell silent. Daru got up and went out. He brought back a folding bed from the shed, set it up between the table and the stove, perpendicular to his own bed. From a large suitcase which, upright in a corner, served as a shelf for papers, he took two blankets and arranged them on the camp bed. Then he stopped, felt useless, and sat down on his bed. There was nothing more to do or to get ready. He had to look at this man. He looked at him, therefore, trying to imagine his face bursting with rage. He couldn't do so. He could see nothing but the dark yet shining eyes and the animal mouth.

"Why did you kill him?" he asked in a voice whose hostile tone surprised him.

The Arab looked away. "He ran away. I ran after him."

He raised his eyes to Daru again and they were full of a sort of woeful interrogation. "Now what will they do to me?"

"Are you afraid?"

He stiffened, turning his eyes away.

"Are you sorry?"

The Arab stared at him openmouthed. Obviously he did not understand. Daru's annoyance was growing. At the same time he felt awkward and self-conscious with his big body wedged between the two beds.

"Lie down there," he said impatiently. "That's your bed."

The Arab didn't move. He called to Daru:

"Tell me!"

The schoolmaster looked at him.

"Is the gendarme coming back tomorrow?"

"I don't know."

"Are you coming with us?"

"I don't know. Why?"

The prisoner got up and stretched out on top of the blankets, his feet toward the window. The light from the electric bulb shone straight into his eyes and he closed them at once.

"Why?" Daru repeated, standing beside the bed.

The Arab opened his eyes under the blinding light and looked at him, trying not to blink.

"Come with us," he said.

In the middle of the night, Daru was still not asleep. He had gone to bed after undressing completely; he generally slept naked. But when he suddenly realized that he had nothing on, he hesitated. He felt vulnerable and the temptation came to him to put his clothes back on. Then he shrugged his shoulders; after all, he wasn't a child and, if need be, he could break his adversary in two. From his bed he could observe him, lying on his back, still motionless with his eyes closed under the harsh light. When Daru turned out the light, the darkness seemed to coagulate all of a sudden. Little by little, the night came back to life in the window where the starless sky was stirring gently. The schoolmaster soon made out the body lying at his feet. The Arab still did not move, but his eyes seemed open. A faint wind was prowling around the schoolhouse. Perhaps it would drive away the clouds and the sun would reappear.

During the night the wind increased. The hens fluttered a little and then were silent. The Arab turned over on his side with his back to Daru, who thought he heard him moan. Then he listened for his guest's breathing, become heavier and more regular. He listened to that breath so close to him and mused without being able to go to sleep. In this room where he had been sleeping alone for a year, this presence bothered him. But it bothered him also by imposing on him a sort of brotherhood he knew well but refused to accept in the present circumstances. Men who share the same rooms, soldiers or prisoners, develop a strange alliance as if, having cast off their armor with their clothing, they fraternized every evening, over and above their differences, in the ancient community of dream and fatigue. But Daru shook himself; he didn't like such musings, and it was essential to sleep.

A little later, however, when the Arab stirred slightly, the schoolmaster was still not asleep. When the prisoner made a second move, he stiffened, on the alert. The Arab was lifting himself slowly on his arms with almost the motion of a sleepwalker. Seated upright in bed, he waited motionless without turning his head toward Daru, as if he were listening attentively. Daru did not stir; it had just occurred to him that the revolver was still in the drawer of his desk. It was better to act at once. Yet he continued to observe the prisoner, who, with the same slithery motion, put his feet on the ground, waited again, then began to stand up slowly. Daru was about to call out to him when the Arab began to walk, in a quite natural but extraordinary silent way. He was heading toward the door at the end of the room that opened into the shed. He lifted the latch with precaution and went out, pushing the door behind him but without shutting it. Daru had not stirred. "He is running away," he merely thought. "Good riddance!" Yet he listened attentively. The hens were not fluttering; the guest must be on the plateau. A faint sound of water reached him, and he didn't know what it was until the Arab again stood framed in the doorway, closed the door carefully, and came back to bed without a sound. Then Daru turned his back on him and fell asleep. Still later he seemed, from the depths of his sleep, to hear furtive steps around the schoolhouse. "I'm dreaming! I'm dreaming!" he repeated to himself. And he went on sleeping.

When he awoke, the sky was clear; the loose window let in a cold, pure air. The Arab was asleep, hunched up under the blankets now, his mouth open, utterly relaxed. But when Daru shook him, he started dreadfully, staring at Daru with wild eyes as if he had never seen him and such a frightened expression that the schoolmaster stepped back. "Don't be afraid. It's me. You must eat." The Arab nodded his head and said yes. Calm had returned to his face, but his expression was vacant and listless.

The coffee was ready. They drank it seated together on the folding bed as they munched their pieces of the cake. Then Daru led the Arab under the shed and showed him the faucet where he washed. He went back into the room, folded the blankets and the bed, made his own bed and put the room in order. Then he went through the classroom and out onto the terrace. The sun was already rising in the blue sky; a soft, bright light was bathing the deserted plateau. On the ridge the snow was melting in spots. The stones were about to reappear. Crouched on the edge of the plateau, the schoolmaster looked at the deserted expanse. He thought of Balducci. He had hurt him, for he had sent him off in a way as if he didn't want to be associated with him. He could still hear the gendarme's farewell and, without knowing why, he felt strangely empty and vulnerable. At that moment, from the other side of the schoolhouse, the prisoner coughed. Daru listened to him almost despite himself and then, furious, threw a pebble that whistled through the air before sinking into the snow. That man's stupid crime revolted him, but to hand him over was contrary to honor. Merely thinking of it made him smart with humiliation. And he cursed at one and the same time his own people who had sent him this Arab and the Arab too who had dared to kill and not managed to get away. Daru got up, walked in a circle on the terrace, waited motionless, and then went back into the schoolhouse.

The Arab, leaning over the cement floor of the shed, was washing his teeth with two fingers. Daru looked at him and said: "Come." He went back into the room ahead of the prisoner. He slipped a hunting-jacket on over his sweater and put on walking-shoes. Standing, he waited until the Arab had put on his *chèche* and sandals. They went into the classroom and the schoolmaster pointed to the exit, saying: "Go ahead." The fellow didn't budge. "I'm coming," said Daru. The Arab went out. Daru went back into the room and made a package of pieces of rusk, dates, and sugar. In the classroom, before going out, he hesitated a second in front of his desk, then crossed the threshold and locked the door. "That's the way," he said. He started toward the east, followed by the prisoner. But, a short distance from the schoolhouse, he thought he heard a slight sound behind them. He retraced his steps and examined the surroundings of the house;

there was no one there. The Arab watched him without seeming to understand. "Come on," said Daru.

They walked for an hour and rested beside a sharp peak of limestone. The snow was melting faster and faster and the sun was drinking up the puddles at once, rapidly cleaning the plateau, which gradually dried and vibrated like the air itself. When they resumed walking, the ground rang under their feet. From time to time a bird rent the space in front of them with a joyful cry. Daru breathed in deeply the fresh morning light. He felt a sort of rapture before the vast familiar expanse, now almost entirely yellow under its dome of blue sky. They walked an hour more, descending toward the south. They reached a level height made up of crumbly rocks. From there on, the plateau sloped down, eastward toward a low plain where there were a few spindly trees and, to the south, toward outcroppings of rock that gave the landscape a chaotic look.

Daru surveyed the two directions. There was nothing but the sky on the horizon. Not a man could be seen. He turned toward the Arab, who was looking at him blankly. Daru held out the package to him. "Take it," he said. "There are dates, bread, and sugar. You can hold out for two days. Here are a thousand francs too." The Arab took the package and the money but kept his full hands at chest level as if he didn't know what to do with what was being given him. "Now look," the schoolmaster said as he pointed in the direction of the east, "there's the way to Tinguit. You have a two-hour walk. At Tinguit you'll find the administration and the police. They are expecting you." The Arab looked toward the east, still holding the package and the money against his chest. Daru took his elbow and turned him rather roughly toward the south. At the foot of the height on which they stood could be seen a faint path. "That's the trail across the plateau. In a day's walk from here you'll find pasturelands and the first nomads. They'll take you in and shelter you according to their law." The Arab had now turned toward Daru and a sort of panic was visible in his expression. "Listen," he said. Daru shook his head: "No, be quiet. Now I'm leaving you." He turned his back on him, took two long steps in the direction of the school, looked hesitantly at the motionless Arab, and started off again. For a few minutes he heard nothing but his own step resounding on the cold ground and did not turn his head. A moment later, however, he turned around. The Arab was still there on the edge of the hill, his arms hanging now, and he was looking at the schoolmaster. Daru felt something rise in his throat. But he swore with impatience, waved vaguely, and started off again. He had already gone some distance when he again stopped and looked. There was no longer anyone on the hill.

Daru hesitated. The sun was now rather high in the sky and was beginning to beat down on his head. The schoolmaster retraced his steps, at first somewhat uncertainly, then with decision. When he reached the little hill, he was bathed in sweat. He climbed it as fast as he could and stopped, out of breath, at the top. The rock-fields to the south stood out sharply against the blue sky, but on the plain to the east a steamy heat was already rising. And in that slight haze, Daru, with heavy heart, made out the Arab walking slowly on the road to prison.

A little later, standing before the window of the classroom, the schoolmaster was watching the clear light bathing the whole surface of the plateau, but he hardly saw it. Behind him on the blackboard, among the winding French rivers, sprawled the clumsily chalked-up words he had just read: "You handed over our brother. You will pay for this." Daru looked at the sky, the plateau, and, beyond, the invisible lands stretching all the way to the sea. In this vast landscape he had loved so much, he was alone.

Drama

A written script is no more than a plan for giving a play actual existence through a performance. It is a framework to which the various artists and craftsmen involved in its production, such as actors, directors, scene-designers, costumers, and lighting technicians, are expected to give body and substance. A play seen in the theater creates a powerful illusion that appeals to many senses, one of the most moving and absorbing of all the art forms. The reading of a play is, in comparison, a pale and unexciting experience, and the reader must try to compensate for the absence of the physical stimuli offered by an actual performance by using his imagination to picture the characters and scenes as they would appear on the stage.

In some respects, however, the reader of a play has an advantage over a member of the theater audience. He can analyze and examine the drama carefully, as the theater audience is unable to do, and in the case of notable works of the theater, like those in this section, a detailed study of moral and structural elements is always worthwhile. Thus, although he must do without the vivid impressions and exciting moments of climax and suspense characteristic of the dramatic experience, he can enter more fully into the crucial qualities that distinguish great plays from ordinary ones.

The literary form most closely resembling drama is fiction, but there are significant differences between the two. Plays have certain natural limitations that do not apply to novels or stories. They have to be comparatively short, for performances cannot run for a longer time than the audience can be expected to remain in a theater and to keep its attention focused on the stage. The scene of action cannot move from one place to another as freely as it may in fiction, although the conventions of Shakespeare's theater went far toward overcoming this disadvantage. The playwright cannot directly give the audience information, as the novelist can, about the past of his characters, offstage events, or other facts relevant to the action. The objectivity of the dramatic form prevents him from discussing what is going on or showing his attitude toward it. Most important of all, he cannot reveal any more about the minds of his characters than they reveal themselves.

The playwright must convey everything he wants his audience to know through dialogue or through the costumes and settings of the play. The technical term for the information necessary to the audience's understanding of plays is *exposition.* But the playwright cannot take time out to present his exposition. From the moment the first curtain rises, he must keep the situations of his play moving and developing, for the theater audience must have a sense of continuous action. The exposition must therefore be presented in an unobtrusive way in the course of the action. An excellent example of this occurs in *Oedipus,* where the vital facts about Oedipus' parentage and earlier actions emerge as the mystery of Laïos' death is being unraveled. A more common instance is the first scene of *Henry IV, Part I,* where the recent events in the Scottish and Welsh wars are described as background for the king's disagreement with Hotspur.

These limitations do not mean that the drama is inferior to the novel or short story, but only that its formal demands are somewhat more stringent. The interesting thing about the limitations of drama is that the dramatist usually directs his efforts, not toward overcoming them, but toward making use of them in order to interest and involve his audience. In *Arms and the Man,* for example, the audience does not know whether or not Raina is in love with Bluntschli. Instead of trying to reveal her feelings about him, Shaw manipulates the unknown element in order to arouse and sustain the attitude of active curiosity which is called *suspense.* When the audience learns that Raina has left a photograph of herself in the coat she loaned Bluntschli, it receives a strong indication that she is interested in him, and it wonders how this will affect her feeling for Sergius. In the same way, in *Oedipus,* the playwright's inability to give the facts about his hero's parentage turns out to be an advantage, for the gradual discovery of those facts and their significance provides the exciting action of the play.

The most important elements of the drama, however, are those it has in common with the novel or the short story, including plot, character, setting, theme, and conflict. Of these, the two that are most concerned with the peculiarities of drama are plot and character. Like the novelist, the dramatist has the task of presenting the spectacle of people performing actions in order to meet the problems and challenges they encounter. Although he cannot tell us about his people directly, as the writer of fiction can, the playwright has other means of characterization at his disposal. Exploiting the fact that everything a person says or does is, if properly understood, a reflection of personality, he projects his characters through their speeches, their actions, and their relations with each other. There is probably no more splendid exhibition of character in all drama than the scene in *Henry IV, Part I,* where Hotspur, after demanding some of the land allotted to Glendower, withdraws his demand once he has won Glendower's agreement to it. In this scene we learn about Hotspur's aggressive pride, not through having it described, but through witnessing it in action. Such methods, especially when augmented with the resources of voice, gesture, and bearing that a skillful actor can bring to them, can portray very full and vivid conceptions of character.

The plot of a play, like that of a narrative, can be usefully analyzed in terms of such concepts as conflict, climax, and resolution. It is a part of the dramatic form to lay considerable emphasis upon the clash between the forces of the play and upon the turning-points of the action. Hence, when Sergius accuses Raina of deceiving him with Bluntschli in *Arms and the Man,* they argue face to face, and a turning-point comes when Raina learns that Sergius has been flirting with the servant, thus forcing him into a defensive position. When Oedipus learns the truth of his birth, the change in his situation is heavily underlined by his reaction and that of the chorus. Like a story, a play has a theme or central idea of importance to which its other elements are related. The author of a story is free to state his theme in his own words (though, in modern fiction, it is considered very bad form to do so), but the playwright can express it directly only by having one of the characters say it. In the Greek tragedies, one of the main functions of the chorus was that of plainly stating the theme illustrated by the action of the play.

Yeats' *Purgatory* does not belong to any well-defined class of drama; it is simply a short poetic treatment of a dramatic situation, the one made famous by *Oedipus Rex.* Of the other three plays in this section, two represent the most established types of drama, tragedy and comedy, and the third is an example of the mixture of styles and tones typical of English drama, and particularly characteristic of Shakespeare. Tragedy, an invention of the Athenian dramatists, portrays man in his struggle against the superior powers that control the universe, a struggle that is, of course, bound to end in failure. The definitive comments on tragedy, made by Aristotle, who had Sophocles' *Oedipus* in mind as his example, describe it as a series of events brought about, not through chance, but through logical causes, in which the tragic hero is destroyed through a failing in his own character, providing a spectacle that arouses the emotions of pity and terror in the audience. In general, tragedy is a way of showing both the greatness and the limitations of man's position in the moral universe.

Comedy is not so much the opposite of tragedy as the result of a different approach to life. Where tragedy is concerned with man's relation to God or the gods, comedy is judged, not by moral absolutes, but by the codes and conventions of the society in which the play has its context. Raina's boast in *Arms and the Man* that refined Bulgarians wash their hands nearly every day and her father's observation that Englishmen bathe so often because their climate is dirty are amusing only in relation to modern Western standards of cleanliness. The comic dramatist is interested in character as it reveals itself in the social sphere and in the varied activities and situations of people trying to make their way in the world. Though comedy often produces laughter and has a happy ending, these features are merely incidental to its real purpose, which is the examination of men's relations with each other.

Sophocles

Oedipus Rex

PERSONS REPRESENTED

OEDIPUS	IOCASTE
A PRIEST	MESSENGER
CREON	SHEPHERD OF LAÏOS
TEIRESIAS	SECOND MESSENGER
CHORUS OF THEBAN ELDERS	

THE SCENE: *Before the palace of* OEDIPUS, *King of Thebes. A central door and two lateral doors open onto a platform which runs the length of the façade. On the platform, right and left, are altars; and three steps lead down into the "orchestra," or chorus-ground. At the beginning of the action these steps are crowded by suppliants who have brought branches and chaplets of olive leaves and who lie in various attitudes of despair.* OEDIPUS *enters.*

PROLOGUE

OEDIPUS. My children, generations of the living
In the line of Kadmos, nursed at his ancient hearth:
Why have you strewn yourselves before these altars
In supplication, with your boughs and garlands?
The breath of incense rises from the city
With a sound of prayer and lamentation.
         Children,
I would not have you speak through messengers,
And therefore I have come myself to hear you—
I, Oedipus, who bear the famous name.

              (*To a* PRIEST.)

You, there, since you are eldest in the company,
Speak for them all, tell me what preys upon you,
Whether you come in dread, or crave some blessing:
Tell me, and never doubt that I will help you
In every way I can; I should be heartless
Were I not moved to find you suppliant here.
 PRIEST. Great Oedipus, O powerful King of Thebes!
You see how all the ages of our people

Cling to your altar steps: here are boys
Who can barely stand alone, and here are priests
By weight of age, as I am a priest of God,
And young men chosen from those yet unmarried;
As for the others, all that multitude,
They wait with olive chaplets in the squares,
At the two shrines of Pallas, and where Apollo
Speaks in the glowing embers.

                    Your own eyes
Must tell you: Thebes is in her extremity
And can not lift her head from the surge of death.
A rust consumes the buds and fruits of the earth;
The herds are sick; children die unborn,
And labor is vain. The god of plague and pyre
Raids like detestable lightning through the city,
And all the house of Kadmos is laid waste,
All emptied, and all darkened: Death alone
Battens upon the misery of Thebes.

You are not one of the immortal gods, we know;
Yet we have come to you to make our prayer
As to the man of all men best in adversity
And wisest in the ways of God. You saved us
From the Sphinx, that flinty singer, and the tribute
We paid to her so long; yet you were never
Better informed than we, nor could we teach you:
It was some god breathed in you to set us free.

Therefore, O mighty King, we turn to you:
Find us our safety, find us a remedy,
Whether by counsel of the gods or men.
A king of wisdom tested in the past
Can act in a time of troubles, and act well.
Noblest of men, restore
Life to your city! Think how all men call you
Liberator for your triumph long ago;
Ah, when your years of kingship are remembered,
Let them not say *We rose, but later fell*—
Keep the State from going down in the storm!
Once, years ago, with happy augury,
You brought us fortune; be the same again!
No man questions your power to rule the land:
But rule over men, not over a dead city!
Ships are only hulls, citadels are nothing,
When no life moves in the empty passageways.

    OEDIPUS. Poor children! You may be sure I know

All that you longed for in your coming here.
I know that you are deathly sick; and yet,
Sick as you are, not one is as sick as I.
Each of you suffers in himself alone
His anguish, not another's; but my spirit
Groans for the city, for myself, for you.

I was not sleeping, you are not waking me.
No, I have been in tears for a long while
And in my restless thought walked many ways.
In all my search, I found one helpful course,
And that I have taken: I have sent Creon,
Son of Menoikeus, brother of the Queen,
To Delphi, Apollo's place of revelation,
To learn there, if he can,
What act or pledge of mine may save the city.
I have counted the days, and now, this very day,
I am troubled, for he has overstayed his time.
What is he doing? He has been gone too long.
Yet whenever he comes back, I should do ill
To scant whatever hint the god may give.
    PRIEST. It is a timely promise. At this instant
They tell me Creon is here.
    OEDIPUS.   O Lord Apollo!
May his news be fair as his face is radiant!
    PRIEST. It could not be otherwise: he is crowned with bay,
The chaplet is thick with berries.
    OEDIPUS.   We shall soon know;
He is near enough to hear us now.
                   (*Enter* CREON.)
                 O Prince:
Brother: son of Menoikeus:
What answer do you bring us from the god?
    CREON. It is favorable. I can tell you, great afflictions
Will turn out well, if they are taken well.
    OEDIPUS. What was the oracle? These vague words
Leave me still hanging between hope and fear.
    CREON. Is it your pleasure to hear me with all these
Gathered around us? I am prepared to speak,
But should we not go in?
    OEDIPUS.   Let them all hear it.
It is for them I suffer, more than for myself.
    CREON. Then I will tell you what I heard at Delphi.

In plain words
The god commands us to expel from the land of Thebes

An old defilement that it seems we shelter.
It is a deathly thing, beyond expiation.
We must not let it feed upon us longer.
   OEDIPUS. What defilement? How shall we rid ourselves of it?
   CREON. By exile or death, blood for blood. It was
Murder that brought the plague-wind on the city.
   OEDIPUS. Murder of whom? Surely the god has named him?
   CREON. My lord: long ago Laïos was our king,
Before you came to govern us.
   OEDIPUS.   I know;
I learned of him from others; I never saw him.
   CREON. He was murdered; and Apollo commands us now
To take revenge upon whoever killed him.
   OEDIPUS. Upon whom? Where are they? Where shall we find a clue
To solve that crime, after so many years?
   CREON. Here in this land, he said.
                           If we make enquiry,
We may touch things that otherwise escape us.
   OEDIPUS. Tell me: Was Laïos murdered in his house,
Or in the fields, or in some foreign country?
   CREON. He said he planned to make a pilgrimage.
He did not come home again.
   OEDIPUS.   And was there no one,
No witness, no companion, to tell what happened?
   CREON. They were all killed but one, and he got away
So frightened that he could remember one thing only.
   OEDIPUS. What was that one thing? One may be the key
To everything, if we resolve to use it.
   CREON. He said that a band of highwaymen attacked them,
Outnumbered them, and overwhelmed the King.
   OEDIPUS. Strange, that a highwayman should be so daring—
Unless some faction here bribed him to do it.
   CREON. We thought of that. But after Laïos' death
New troubles arose and we had no avenger.
   OEDIPUS. What troubles could prevent your hunting down the killers?
   CREON. The riddling Sphinx's song
Made us deaf to all mysteries but her own.
   OEDIPUS. Then once more I must bring what is dark to light.
It is most fitting that Apollo shows,
As you do, this compunction for the dead.
You shall see how I stand by you, as I should,
To avenge the city and the city's god,
And not as though it were for some distant friend,
But for my own sake, to be rid of evil.
Whoever killed King Laïos might—who knows?—

Decide at any moment to kill me as well.
By avenging the murdered king I protect myself.
Come, then, my children: leave the altar steps,
Lift up your olive boughs!
                              One of you go
And summon the people of Kadmos to gather here.
I will do all that I can; you may tell them that.

                                                        (*Exit a* PAGE.)

So, with the help of God,
We shall be saved—or else indeed we are lost.
    PRIEST. Let us rise, children. It was for this we came,
And now the King has promised it himself.
Phoibos has sent us an oracle; may he descend
Himself to save us and drive out the plague.
(*Exeunt* OEDIPUS *and* CREON *into the palace by the central door. The* PRIEST
and the SUPPLIANTS *disperse R and L. After a short pause the* CHORUS *enters
                              the orchestra.*)

PARODOS

    CHORUS. What is God singing in his profound   [STROPHE 1
Delphi of gold and shadow?
What oracle for Thebes, the sunwhipped city?
Fear unjoints me, the roots of my heart tremble.
Now I remember, O Healer, your power, and wonder;
Will you send doom like a sudden cloud, or weave it
Like nightfall of the past?
Speak, speak to us, issue of holy sound:
Dearest to our expectancy: be tender!

Let me pray to Athenê, the immortal daughter of Zeus,   [ANTISTROPHE 1
And to Artemis her sister
Who keeps her famous throne in the market ring,
And to Apollo, bowman at the far butts of heaven—

O gods, descend! Like three streams leap against
The fires of our grief, the fires of darkness;
Be swift to bring us rest!

As in the old time from the brilliant house
Of air you stepped to save us, come again!

Now our afflictions have no end,   [STROPHE 2
Now all our stricken host lies down
And no man fights off death with his mind;

The noble plowland bears no grain,
And groaning mothers can not bear—

See, how our lives like birds take wing,
Like sparks that fly when a fire soars,
To the shore of the god of evening.

The plague burns on, it is pitiless,   [ANTISTROPHE 2
Though pallid children laden with death
Lie unwept in the stony ways,

And old gray women by every path
Flock to the strand about the altars

There to strike their breasts and cry
Worship of Phoibos in wailing prayers:
Be kind, God's golden child!

There are no swords in this attack by fire,   [STROPHE 3
No shields, but we are ringed with cries.
Send the besieger plunging from our homes
Into the vast sea-room of the Atlantic
Or into the waves that foam eastward of Thrace—
For the day ravages what the night spares—

Destroy our enemy, lord of the thunder!
Let him be riven by lightning from heaven!

Phoibos Apollo, stretch the sun's bowstring,   [ANTISTROPHE 3
That golden cord, until it sing for us,
Flashing arrows in heaven!
                        Artemis, Huntress,
Race with flaring lights upon our mountains!

O scarlet god, O golden-banded brow,
O Theban Bacchos in a storm of Maenads,
                    (*Enter* OEDIPUS, *C.*)
Whirl upon Death, that all the Undying hate!
Come with blinding cressets, come in joy!

SCENE I

OEDIPUS. Is this your prayer? It may be answered. Come,
Listen to me, act as the crisis demands,
And you shall have relief from all these evils.

Until now I was a stranger to this tale,
As I had been a stranger to the crime.
Could I track down the murderer without a clue?
But now, friends,
As one who became a citizen after the murder,

I make this proclamation to all Thebans:
If any man knows by whose hand Laïos, son of Labdakos,
Met his death, I direct that man to tell me everything,
No matter what he fears for having so long withheld it.
Let it stand as promised that no further trouble
Will come to him, but he may leave the land in safety.

Moreover: If anyone knows the murderer to be foreign,
Let him not keep silent: he shall have his reward from me.
However, if he does conceal it; if any man
Fearing for his friend or for himself disobeys this edict,
Hear what I propose to do:

I solemnly forbid the people of this country,
Where power and throne are mine, ever to receive that man
Or speak to him, no matter who he is, or let him
Join in sacrifice, lustration, or in prayer.
I decree that he be driven from every house,
Being, as he is, corruption itself to us: the Delphic
Voice of Zeus has pronounced this revelation.
Thus I associate myself with the oracle
And take the side of the murdered king.

As for the criminal, I pray to God—
Whether it be a lurking thief, or one of a number—
I pray that that man's life be consumed in evil and wretchedness.
And as for me, this curse applies no less
If it should turn out that the culprit is my guest here,
Sharing my hearth.
                    You have heard the penalty.
I lay it on you now to attend to this
For my sake, for Apollo's, for the sick
Sterile city that heaven has abandoned.
Suppose the oracle had given you no command:
Should this defilement go uncleansed for ever?
You should have found the murderer: your king,
A noble king, had been destroyed!
                    Now I,
Having the power that he held before me,
Having his bed, begetting children there
Upon his wife, as he would have, had he lived—
Their son would have been my children's brother,
If Laïos had had luck in fatherhood!
(But surely ill luck rushed upon his reign)—
I say I take the son's part, just as though

I were his son, to press the fight for him
And see it won! I'll find the hand that brought
Death to Labdakos' and Polydoros' child,
Heir of Kadmos' and Agenor's line.
And as for those who fail me,
May the gods deny them the fruit of the earth,
Fruit of the womb, and may they rot utterly!
Let them be wretched as we are wretched, and worse!

For you, for loyal Thebans, and for all
Who find my actions right, I pray the favor
Of justice, and of all the immortal gods.
CHORAGOS. Since I am under oath, my lord, I swear
I did not do the murder, I can not name
The murderer. Might not the oracle
That has ordained the search tell where to find him?
OEDIPUS. An honest question. But no man in the world
Can make the gods do more than the gods will.
CHORAGOS. There is one last expedient—
OEDIPUS.   Tell me what it is.
Though it seem slight, you must not hold it back.
CHORAGOS. A lord clairvoyant to the lord Apollo,
As we all know, is the skilled Teiresias.
One might learn much about this from him, Oedipus.
OEDIPUS. I am not wasting time:
Creon spoke of this, and I have sent for him—
Twice, in fact; it is strange that he is not here.
CHORAGOS. The other matter—that old report—seems useless.
OEDIPUS. Tell me. I am interested in all reports.
CHORAGOS. The King was said to have been killed by highwaymen.
OEDIPUS. I know. But we have no witnesses to that.
CHORAGOS. If the killer can feel a particle of dread,
Your curse will bring him out of hiding!
OEDIPUS.   No.
The man who dared that act will fear no curse.
                    (Enter the blind seer TEIRESIAS, led by a PAGE.)
CHORAGOS. But there is one man who may detect the criminal.
This is Teiresias, this is the holy prophet
In whom, alone of all men, truth was born.
OEDIPUS. Teiresias: seer: student of mysteries,
Of all that's taught and all that no man tells,
Secrets of Heaven and secrets of the earth:
Blind though you are, you know the city lies
Sick with plague; and from this plague, my lord,

We find that you alone can guard or save us.
Possibly you did not hear the messengers?
Apollo, when we sent to him,
Sent us back word that this great pestilence
Would lift, but only if we established clearly
The identity of those who murdered Laïos.
They must be killed or exiled.

                        Can you use
Birdflight or any art of divination
To purify yourself, and Thebes, and me
From this contagion? We are in your hands.
There is no fairer duty
Than that of helping others in distress.

    TEIRESIAS. How dreadful knowledge of the truth can be
When there's no help in truth! I knew this well,
But did not act on it: else I should not have come.

    OEDIPUS. What is troubling you? Why are your eyes so cold?

    TEIRESIAS. Let me go home. Bear your own fate, and I'll
Bear mine. It is better so: trust what I say.

    OEDIPUS. What you say is ungracious and unhelpful
To your native country. Do not refuse to speak.

    TEIRESIAS. When it comes to speech, your own is neither temperate
Nor opportune. I wish to be more prudent.

    OEDIPUS. In God's name, we all beg you—

    TEIRESIAS.   You are all ignorant.
No; I will never tell you what I know.
Now it is my misery; then, it would be yours.

    OEDIPUS. What! You do know something, and will not tell us?
You would betray us all and wreck the State?

    TEIRESIAS. I do not intend to torture myself, or you.
Why persist in asking? You will not persuade me.

    OEDIPUS. What a wicked old man you are! You'd try a stone's
Patience! Out with it! Have you no feeling at all?

    TEIRESIAS. You call me unfeeling. If you could only see
The nature of your own feelings . . .

    OEDIPUS.   Why,
Who would not feel as I do? Who could endure
Your arrogance toward the city?

    TEIRESIAS.   What does it matter!
Whether I speak or not, it is bound to come.

    OEDIPUS. Then, if "it" is bound to come, you are bound to tell me.

    TEIRESIAS. No, I will not go on. Rage as you please.

    OEDIPUS. Rage? Why not!
                    And I'll tell you what I think:
You planned it, you had it done, you all but

Killed him with your own hands: if you had eyes,
I'd say the crime was yours, and yours alone.

TEIRESIAS. So? I charge you, then,
Abide by the proclamation you have made:
From this day forth
Never speak again to these men or to me;
You yourself are the pollution of this country.

OEDIPUS. You dare say that! Can you possibly think you have
Some way of going free, after such insolence?

TEIRESIAS. I have gone free. It is the truth sustains me.

OEDIPUS. Who taught you shamelessness? It was not your craft.

TEIRESIAS. You did. You made me speak. I did not want to.

OEDIPUS. Speak what? Let me hear it again more clearly.

TEIRESIAS. Was it not clear before? Are you tempting me?

OEDIPUS. I did not understand it. Say it again.

TEIRESIAS. I say that you are the murderer whom you seek.

OEDIPUS. Now twice you have spat out infamy. You'll pay for it!

TEIRESIAS. Would you care for more? Do you wish to be really angry?

OEDIPUS. Say what you will. Whatever you say is worthless.

TEIRESIAS. I say you live in hideous shame with those
Most dear to you. You can not see the evil.

OEDIPUS. It seems you can go on mouthing like this for ever.

TEIRESIAS. I can, if there is power in truth.

OEDIPUS.   There is:
But not for you, not for you,
You sightless, witless, senseless, mad old man!

TEIRESIAS. You are the madman. There is no one here
Who will not curse you soon, as you curse me.

OEDIPUS. You child of endless night! You can not hurt me
Or any other man who sees the sun.

TEIRESIAS. True: it is not from me your fate will come.
That lies within Apollo's competence,
As it is his concern.

OEDIPUS.   Tell me:
Are you speaking for Creon, or for yourself?

TEIRESIAS. Creon is no threat. You weave your own doom.

OEDIPUS. Wealth, power, craft of statesmanship!
Kingly position, everywhere admired!
What savage envy is stored up against these,
If Creon, whom I trusted, Creon my friend,
For this great office which the city once
Put in my hands unsought—if for this power
Creon desires in secret to destroy me!

He has bought this decrepit fortune-teller, this
Collector of dirty pennies, this prophet fraud—

Why, he is no more clairvoyant than I am!

Tell us:

Has your mystic mummery ever approached the truth?
When that hellcat the Sphinx was performing here,
What help were you to these people?
Her magic was not for the first man who came along:
It demanded a real exorcist. Your birds—
What good were they? or the gods, for the matter of that?
But I came by,
Oedipus, the simple man, who knows nothing—
I thought it out for myself, no birds helped me!
And this is the man you think you can destroy,
That you may be close to Creon when he's king!
Well, you and your friend Creon, it seems to me,
Will suffer most. If you were not an old man,
You would have paid already for your plot.

    CHORAGOS. We can not see that his words or yours
Have been spoken except in anger, Oedipus,
And of anger we have no need. How can God's will
Be accomplished best? That is what most concerns us.

    TEIRESIAS. You are a king. But where argument's concerned
I am your man, as much a king as you.
I am not your servant, but Apollo's.
I have no need of Creon to speak for me.

Listen to me. You mock my blindness, do you?
But I say that you, with both your eyes, are blind:
You can not see the wretchedness of your life,
Nor in whose house you live, no, nor with whom.
Who are your father and mother? Can you tell me?
You do not even know the blind wrongs
That you have done them, on earth and in the world below.
But the double lash of your parents' curse will whip you
Out of this land some day, with only night
Upon your precious eyes.
Your cries then—where will they not be heard?
What fastness of Kithairon will not echo them?
And that bridal-descant of yours—you'll know it then,
The song they sang when you came here to Thebes
And found your misguided berthing.
All this, and more, that you can not guess at now,
Will bring you to yourself among your children.

Be angry, then. Curse Creon. Curse my words.
I tell you, no man that walks upon the earth
Shall be rooted out more horribly than you.

OEDIPUS. Am I to bear this from him?—Damnation
Take you! Out of this place! Out of my sight!
   TEIRESIAS. I would not have come at all if you had not asked me.
   OEDIPUS. Could I have told that you'd talk nonsense, that
You'd come here to make a fool of yourself, and of me?
   TEIRESIAS. A fool? Your parents thought me sane enough.
   OEDIPUS. My parents again!—Wait: who were my parents?
   TEIRESIAS. This day will give you a father, and break your heart.
   OEDIPUS. Your infantile riddles! Your damned abracadabra!
   TEIRESIAS. You were a great man once at solving riddles.
   OEDIPUS. Mock me with that if you like; you will find it true.
   TEIRESIAS. It was true enough. It brought about your ruin.
   OEDIPUS. But if it saved this town?
   TEIRESIAS (*to the* PAGE). Boy, give me your hand.
   OEDIPUS. Yes, boy; lead him away.
                    —While you are here
We can do nothing. Go; leave us in peace.
   TEIRESIAS. I will go when I have said what I have to say.
How can you hurt me? And I tell you again:
The man you have been looking for all this time,
The damned man, the murderer of Laïos,
That man is in Thebes. To your mind he is foreignborn,
But it will soon be shown that he is a Theban,
A revelation that will fail to please.
                  A blind man,
Who has his eyes now; a penniless man, who is rich now;
And he will go tapping the strange earth with his staff;
To the children with whom he lives now he will be
Brother and father—the very same; to her
Who bore him, son and husband—the very same
Who came to his father's bed, wet with his father's blood.

Enough. Go think that over.
If later you find error in what I have said,
You may say that I have no skill in prophecy.
       (*Exit* TEIRESIAS, *led by his* PAGE. OEDIPUS *goes into the palace.*)

ODE I

CHORUS. The Delphic stone of prophecies   [STROPHE 1
Remembers ancient regicide
And a still bloody hand.
That killer's hour of flight has come.
He must be stronger than riderless
Coursers of untiring wind,

For the son of Zeus armed with his father's thunder
Leaps in lightning after him;
And the Furies follow him, the sad Furies.

Holy Parnassos' peak of snow   [ANTISTROPHE 1
Flashes and blinds that secret man,
That all shall hunt him down:
Though he may roam the forest shade
Like a bull gone wild from pasture
To rage through glooms of stone.
Doom comes down on him; flight will not avail him;
For the world's heart calls him desolate,
And the immortal Furies follow, for ever follow.

But now a wilder thing is heard   [STROPHE 2
From the old man skilled at hearing Fate in the wingbeat of a bird.
Bewildered as a blown bird, my soul hovers and can not find
Foothold in this debate, or any reason or rest of mind.
But no man ever brought—none can bring
Proof of strife between Thebes' royal house,
Labdakos' line, and the son of Polybos;
And never until now has any man brought word
Of Laïos' dark death staining Oedipus the King.

Divine Zeus and Apollo hold   [ANTISTROPHE 2
Perfect intelligence alone of all tales ever told;
And well though this diviner works, he works in his own night;
No man can judge that rough unknown or trust in second sight,
For wisdom changes hands among the wise.
Shall I believe my great lord criminal
At a raging word that a blind old man let fall?
I saw him, when the carrion woman faced him of old,
Prove his heroic mind! These evil words are lies.

SCENE II

CREON. Men of Thebes:
I am told that heavy accusations
Have been brought against me by King Oedipus.

I am not the kind of man to bear this tamely.

If in these present difficulties
He holds me accountable for any harm to him
Through anything I have said or done—why, then,
I do not value life in this dishonor.
It is not as though this rumor touched upon

Some private indiscretion. The matter is grave.
The fact is that I am being called disloyal
To the State, to my fellow citizens, to my friends.
    CHORAGOS. He may have spoken in anger, not from his mind.
    CREON. But did you not hear him say I was the one
Who seduced the old prophet into lying?
    CHORAGOS. The thing was said; I do not know how seriously.
    CREON. But you were watching him! Were his eyes steady?
Did he look like a man in his right mind?
    CHORAGOS.   I do not know.
I can not judge the behavior of great men.
But here is the King himself.
                              (*Enter* OEDIPUS.)
    OEDIPUS.   So you dared come back.
Why? How brazen of you to come to my house,
You murderer!
                Do you think I do not know
That you plotted to kill me, plotted to steal my throne?
Tell me, in God's name: am I coward, a fool,
That you should dream you could accomplish this?
A fool who could not see your slippery game?
A coward, not to fight back when I saw it?
You are the fool, Creon, are you not? hoping
Without support or friends to get a throne?
Thrones may be won or bought: you could do neither.
    CREON. Now listen to me. You have talked; let me talk, too.
You can not judge unless you know the facts.
    OEDIPUS. You speak well: there is one fact; but I find it hard
To learn from the deadliest enemy I have.
    CREON. That above all I must dispute with you.
    OEDIPUS. That above all I will not hear you deny.
    CREON. If you think there is anything good in being stubborn
Against all reason, then I say you are wrong.
    OEDIPUS. If you think a man can sin against his own kind
And not be punished for it, I say you are mad.
    CREON. I agree. But tell me: what have I done to you?
    OEDIPUS. You advised me to send for that wizard, did you not?
    CREON. I did. I should do it again.
    OEDIPUS.   Very well. Now tell me:
How long has it been since Laïos—
    CREON.   What of Laïos?
    OEDIPUS. Since he vanished in that onset by the road?
    CREON. It was long ago, a long time.
    OEDIPUS.   And this prophet,
Was he practicing here then?

CREON. He was; and with honor, as now.

OEDIPUS. Did he speak of me at that time?

CREON. He never did;
At least, not when I was present.

OEDIPUS. But . . . the enquiry?
I suppose you held one?

CREON. We did, but we learned nothing.

OEDIPUS. Why did the prophet not speak against me then?

CREON. I do not know; and I am the kind of man
Who holds his tongue when he has no facts to go on.

OEDIPUS. There's one fact that you know, and you could tell it.

CREON. What fact is that? If I know it, you shall have it.

OEDIPUS. If he were not involved with you, he could not say
That it was I who murdered Laïos.

CREON. If he says that, you are the one that knows it!—
But now it is my turn to question you.

OEDIPUS. Put your questions. I am no murderer.

CREON. First, then: You married my sister?

OEDIPUS. I married your sister.

CREON. And you rule the kingdom equally with her?

OEDIPUS. Everything that she wants she has from me.

CREON. And I am the third, equal to both of you?

OEDIPUS. That is why I call you a bad friend.

CREON. No. Reason it out, as I have done.
Think of this first: Would any sane man prefer
Power, with all a king's anxieties,
To that same power and the grace of sleep?
Certainly not I.
I have never longed for the king's power—only his rights.
Would any wise man differ from me in this?
As matters stand, I have my way in everything
With your consent, and no responsibilities.
If I were king, I should be a slave to policy.

How could I desire a scepter more
Than what is now mine—untroubled influence?
No, I have not gone mad; I need no honors,
Except those with the perquisites I have now.
I am welcome everywhere; every man salutes me,
And those who want your favor seek my ear,
Since I know how to manage what they ask.
Should I exchange this ease for that anxiety?
Besides, no sober mind is treasonable.
I hate anarchy
And never would deal with any man who likes it.

Test what I have said. Go to the priestess
At Delphi, ask if I quoted her correctly.
And as for this other thing: if I am found
Guilty of treason with Teiresias,
Then sentence me to death! You have my word
It is a sentence I should cast my vote for—
But not without evidence!

                      You do wrong
When you take good men for bad, bad men for good.
A true friend thrown aside—why, life itself
Is not more precious!

                 In time you will know this well:
For time, and time alone, will show the just man,
Though scoundrels are discovered in a day.

    CHORAGOS. This is well said, and a prudent man would ponder it.
Judgments too quickly formed are dangerous.

    OEDIPUS. But is he not quick in his duplicity?
And shall I not be quick to parry him?
Would you have me stand still, hold my peace, and let
This man win everything, through my inaction?

    CREON. And you want—what is it, then? To banish me?

    OEDIPUS. No, not exile. It is your death I want,
So that all the world may see what treason means.

    CREON. You will persist, then? You will not believe me?

    OEDIPUS. How can I believe you?

    CREON.   Then you are a fool.

    OEDIPUS. To save myself?

    CREON.   In justice, think of me.

    OEDIPUS. You are evil incarnate.

    CREON.   But suppose that you are wrong?

    OEDIPUS. Still I must rule.

    CREON.   But not if you rule badly.

    OEDIPUS. O city, city!

    CREON.   It is my city, too!

    CHORAGOS. Now, my lords, be still. I see the Queen,
Iocastê, coming from her palace chambers;
And it is time she came, for the sake of you both.
This dreadful quarrel can be resolved through her.

                (*Enter* IOCASTE.)

    IOCASTE. Poor foolish men, what wicked din is this?
With Thebes sick to death, is it not shameful
That you should rake some private quarrel up?

                            (*To* OEDIPUS.)

Come into the house.

—And you, Creon, go now:
Let us have no more of this tumult over nothing.
    CREON. Nothing? No, sister: what your husband plans for me
Is one of two great evils: exile or death.
    OEDIPUS. He is right.
                       Why, woman I have caught him squarely
Plotting against my life.
    CREON.   No! Let me die
Accurst if ever I have wished you harm!
    IOCASTE. Ah, believe it, Oedipus!
In the name of the gods, respect this oath of his
For my sake, for the sake of these people here!

                                               [STROPHE 1

    CHORAGOS. Open your mind to her, my lord. Be ruled by her, I beg you!
    OEDIPUS. What would you have me do?
    CHORAGOS. Respect Creon's word. He has never spoken like a fool,
And now he has sworn an oath.
    OEDIPUS.   You know what you ask?
    CHORAGOS.   I do.
    OEDIPUS.   Speak on, then.
    CHORAGOS. A friend so sworn should not be baited so,
In blind malice, and without final proof.
    OEDIPUS. You are aware, I hope, that what you say
Means death for me, or exile at the least.
    CHORAGOS. No, I swear by Helios, first in Heaven!   [STROPHE 2
May I die friendless and accurst,
The worst of deaths, if ever I meant that!
        It is the withering fields
            That hurt my sick heart:
        Must we bear all these ills,
            And now your bad blood as well?
    OEDIPUS. Then let him go. And let me die, if I must,
Or be driven by him in shame from the land of Thebes.
It is your unhappiness, and not his talk,
That touches me.
             As for him—
Wherever he is, I will hate him as long as I live.
    CREON. Ugly in yielding, as you were ugly in rage!
Natures like yours chiefly torment themselves.
    OEDIPUS. Can you not go? Can you not leave me?
    CREON.   I can.
You do not know me; but the city knows me,
And in its eyes I am just, if not in yours.

                                              (*Exit* CREON.)

[ANTISTROPHE 1

CHORAGOS. Lady Iocastê, did you not ask the King to go to his chambers?

IOCASTE. First tell me what has happened.

CHORAGOS. There was suspicion without evidence; yet it rankled
As even false charges will.

IOCASTE.   On both sides?

CHORAGOS.   On both.

IOCASTE.   But what was said?

CHORAGOS. Oh let it rest, let it be done with!
Have we not suffered enough?

OEDIPUS. You see to what your decency has brought you:
You have made difficulties where my heart saw none.

[ANTISTROPHE 2

CHORAGOS. Oedipus, it is not once only I have told you—
    You must know I should count myself unwise
To the point of madness, should I now forsake you—
        You, under whose hand,
            In the storm of another time,
        Our dear land sailed out free.
            But now stand fast at the helm!

IOCASTE. In God's name, Oedipus, inform your wife as well:
Why are you so set in this hard anger?

OEDIPUS. I will tell you, for none of these men deserves
My confidence as you do. It is Creon's work,
His treachery, his plotting against me.

IOCASTE. Go on, if you can make this clear to me.

OEDIPUS. He charges me with the murder of Laïos.

IOCASTE. Has he some knowledge? Or does he speak from hearsay?

OEDIPUS. He would not commit himself to such a charge,
But he has brought in that damnable soothsayer
To tell his story.

IOCASTE.   Set your mind at rest.
If it is a question of soothsayers, I tell you
That you will find no man whose craft gives knowledge
Of the unknowable.

                Here is my proof:

An oracle was reported to Laïos once
(I will not say from Phoibos himself, but from
His appointed ministers, at any rate)
That his doom would be death at the hands of his own son—
His son, born of his flesh and of mine!

Now, you remember the story: Laïos was killed
By marauding strangers where three highways meet;

But his child had not been three days in this world
Before the King had pierced the baby's ankles
And left him to die on a lonely mountainside.

Thus, Apollo never caused that child
To kill his father, and it was not Laïos' fate
To die at the hands of his son, as he had feared.
This is what prophets and prophecies are worth!
Have no dread of them.
                    It is God himself
Who can show us what he wills, in his own way.
    OEDIPUS. How strange a shadowy memory crossed my mind,
Just now while you were speaking; it chilled my heart.
      IOCASTE. What do you mean? What memory do you speak of?
      OEDIPUS. If I understand you, Laïos was killed
At a place where three roads meet.
      IOCASTE.   So it was said;
We have no later story.
      OEDIPUS.   Where did it happen?
      IOCASTE. Phokis, it is called: at a place where the Theban Way
Divides into the roads towards Delphi and Daulia.
      OEDIPUS. When?
      IOCASTE.   We had the news not long before you came
And proved the right to your succession here.
      OEDIPUS. Ah, what net has God been weaving for me?
      IOCASTE. Oedipus! Why does this trouble you?
      OEDIPUS.   Do not ask me yet.
First, tell me how Laïos looked, and tell me
How old he was.
      IOCASTE.   He was tall, his hair just touched
With white; his form was not unlike your own.
      OEDIPUS. I think that I myself may be accurst
By my own ignorant edict.
      IOCASTE.   You speak strangely.
It makes me tremble to look at you, my King.
      OEDIPUS. I am not sure that the blind man can not see.
But I should know better if you were to tell me—
      IOCASTE. Anything—though I dread to hear you ask it.
      OEDIPUS. Was the King lightly escorted, or did he ride
With a large company, as a ruler should?
      IOCASTE. There were five men with him in all: one was a herald;
And a single chariot, which he was driving.
      OEDIPUS. Alas, that makes it plain enough!
                              But who—
Who told you how it happened?
      IOCASTE.   A household servant,

The only one to escape.

  OEDIPUS.   And is he still
A servant of ours?

  IOCASTE.   No; for when he came back at last
And found you enthroned in the place of the dead king,
He came to me, touched my hand with his, and begged
That I would send him away to the frontier district
Where only the shepherds go—
As far away from the city as I could send him.
I granted his prayer; for although the man was a slave,
He had earned more than this favor at my hands.

  OEDIPUS. Can he be called back quickly?

  IOCASTE.   Easily.
But why?

  OEDIPUS. I have taken too much upon myself
Without enquiry; therefore I wish to consult him.

  IOCASTE. Then he shall come.

        But am I not one also
To whom you might confide these fears of yours?

  OEDIPUS. That is your right; it will not be denied you,
Now least of all; for I have reached a pitch
Of wild foreboding. Is there anyone
To whom I should sooner speak?
Polybos of Corinth is my father.
My mother is a Dorian: Meropê.
I grew up chief among the men of Corinth
Until a strange thing happened—
Not worth my passion, it may be, but strange.

At a feast, a drunken man maundering in his cups
Cries out that I am not my father's son!

I contained myself that night, though I felt anger
And a sinking heart. The next day I visited
My father and mother, and questioned them. They stormed,
Calling it all the slanderous rant of a fool;
And this relieved me. Yet the suspicion
Remained always aching in my mind;
I knew there was talk; I could not rest;
And finally, saying nothing to my parents,
I went to the shrine at Delphi.
The god dismissed my question without reply;
He spoke of other things.

      Some were clear,
Full of wretchedness, dreadful, unbearable:
As, that I should lie with my own mother, breed

Children from whom all men would turn their eyes;
And that I should be my father's murderer.

I heard all this, and fled. And from that day
Corinth to me was only in the stars
Descending in that quarter of the sky,
As I wandered farther and farther on my way
To a land where I should never see the evil
Sung by the oracle. And I came to this country
Where, so you say, King Laïos was killed.

I will tell you all that happened there, my lady.

There were three highways
Coming together at a place I passed;
And there a herald came towards me, and a chariot
Drawn by horses, with a man such as you describe
Seated in it. The groom leading the horses
Forced me off the road at his lord's command;
But as this charioteer lurched over towards me
I struck him in my rage. The old man saw me
And brought his double goad down upon my head
As I came abreast.

           He was paid back, and more!
Swinging my club in this right hand I knocked him
Out of his car, and he rolled on the ground.

                             I killed him.

I killed them all.
Now if that stranger and Laïos were—kin,
Where is a man more miserable than I?
More hated by the gods? Citizen and alien alike
Must never shelter me or speak to me—
I must be shunned by all.

                      And I myself
Pronounced this malediction upon myself!

Think of it: I have touched you with these hands,
These hands that killed your husband. What defilement!

Am I all evil, then? It must be so,
Since I must flee from Thebes, yet never again
See my own countrymen, my own country,
For fear of joining my mother in marriage
And killing Polybos, my father.

                Ah,
If I was created so, born to this fate,
Who could deny the savagery of God?

O holy majesty of heavenly powers!
May I never see that day! Never!
Rather let me vanish from the race of men
Than know the abomination destined me!
   CHORAGOS. We too, my lord, have felt dismay at this.
But there is hope: you have yet to hear the shepherd.
   OEDIPUS. Indeed, I fear no other hope is left me.
   IOCASTE. What do you hope from him when he comes?
   OEDIPUS.   This much:
If his account of the murder tallies with yours,
Then I am cleared.
   IOCASTE.   What was it that I said
Of such importance?
   OEDIPUS.   Why, "marauders," you said,
Killed the King, according to this man's story.
If he maintains that still, if there were several,
Clearly the guilt is not mine: I was alone.
But if he says one man, singlehanded, did it,
Then the evidence all points to me.
   IOCASTE. You may be sure that he said there were several;
And can he call back that story now? He cán not.
The whole city heard it as plainly as I.
But suppose he alters some detail of it:
He can not ever show that Laïos' death
Fulfilled the oracle: for Apollo said
My child was doomed to kill him; and my child—
Poor baby!—it was my child that died first.

No. From now on, where oracles are concerned,
I would not waste a second thought on any.
   OEDIPUS. You may be right.
                But come: let someone go
For the shepherd at once. This matter must be settled.
   IOCASTE. I will send for him.
I would not wish to cross you in anything,
And surely not in this.—Let us go in.

                        (*Exeunt into the palace.*)

ODE II

   CHORUS. Let me be reverent in the ways of right,   [STROPHE I
Lowly the paths I journey on;
Let all my words and actions keep

The laws of the pure universe
From highest Heaven handed down.
For Heaven is their bright nurse,
Those generations of the realms of light;
Ah, never of mortal kind were they begot,
Nor are they slaves of memory, lost in sleep:
Their Father is greater than Time, and ages not.

The tyrant is a child of Pride   [ANTISTROPHE 1
Who drinks from his great sickening cup
Recklessness and vanity,
Until from his high crest headlong
He plummets to the dust of hope.
That strong man is not strong.
But let no fair ambition be denied;
May God protect the wrestler for the State
In government, in comely policy,
Who will fear God, and on His ordinance wait.

Haughtiness and the high hand of disdain   [STROPHE 2
Tempt and outrage God's holy law;
And any mortal who dares hold
No immortal Power in awe
Will be caught up in a net of pain:
The price for which his levity is sold.
Let each man take due earnings, then,
And keep his hands from holy things,
And from blasphemy stand apart—
Else the crackling blast of heaven
Blows on his head, and on his desperate heart;
Though fools will honor impious men,
In their cities no tragic poet sings.

Shall we lose faith in Delphi's obscurities,   [ANTISTROPHE 2
We who have heard the world's core
Discredited, and the sacred wood
Of Zeus at Elis praised no more?
The deeds and the strange prophecies
Must make a pattern yet to be understood.
Zeus, if indeed you are lord of all,
Throned in light over night and day,
Mirror this in your endless mind:
Our masters call the oracle
Words on the wind, and the Delphic vision blind!
Their hearts no longer know Apollo,
And reverence for the gods has died away.

Scene III

(*Enter* IOCASTE.)

IOCASTE. Princes of Thebes, it has occurred to me
To visit the altars of the gods, bearing
These branches as a suppliant, and this incense.
Our King is not himself: his noble soul
Is overwrought with fantasies of dread,
Else he would consider
The new prophecies in the light of the old.
He will listen to any voice that speaks disaster,
And my advice goes for nothing.

(*She approaches the altar, R.*)

To you, then, Apollo,
Lycean lord, since you are nearest, I turn in prayer.
Receive these offerings, and grant us deliverance
From defilement. Our hearts are heavy with fear
When we see our leader distracted, as helpless sailors
Are terrified by the confusion of their helmsman.

(*Enter* MESSENGER.)

MESSENGER. Friends, no doubt you can direct me:
Where shall I find the house of Oedipus,
Or, better still, where is the King himself?

CHORAGOS. It is this very place, stranger; he is inside.
This is his wife and mother of his children.

MESSENGER. I wish her happiness in a happy house,
Blest in all the fulfillment of her marriage.

IOCASTE. I wish as much for you: your courtesy
Deserves a like good fortune. But now, tell me:
Why have you come? What have you to say to us?

MESSENGER. Good news, my lady, for your house and your husband.

IOCASTE. What news? Who sent you here?

MESSENGER.   I am from Corinth.
The news I bring ought to mean joy for you,
Though it may be you will find some grief in it.

IOCASTE. What is it? How can it touch us in both ways?

MESSENGER. The people of Corinth, they say,
Intend to call Oedipus to be their king.

IOCASTE. But old Polybos—is he not reigning still?

MESSENGER. No. Death holds him in his sepulchre.

IOCASTE. What are you saying? Polybos is dead?

MESSENGER. If I am not telling the truth, may I die myself.

IOCASTE (*to a* MAIDSERVANT). Go in, go quickly; tell this to your master.

O riddlers of God's will, where are you now!
This was the man whom Oedipus, long ago,
Feared so, fled so, in dread of destroying him—
But it was another fate by which he died.

(*Enter* OEDIPUS, *C.*)

OEDIPUS. Dearest Iocastê, why have you sent for me?

IOCASTE. Listen to what this man says, and then tell me
What has become of the solemn prophecies.

OEDIPUS. Who is this man? What is his news for me?

IOCASTE. He has come from Corinth to announce your father's death!

OEDIPUS. Is it true, stranger? Tell me in your own words.

MESSENGER. I can not say it more clearly: the King is dead.

OEDIPUS. Was it by treason? Or by an attack of illness?

MESSENGER. A little thing brings old men to their rest.

OEDIPUS. It was sickness, then?

MESSENGER.   Yes, and his many years.

OEDIPUS. Ah!

Why should a man respect the Pythian hearth, or
Give heed to the birds that jangle above his head?
They prophesied that I should kill Polybos,
Kill my own father; but he is dead and buried,
And I am here— I never touched him, never,
Unless he died of grief for my departure,
And thus, in a sense, through me. No. Polybos
Has packed the oracles off with him underground.
They are empty words.

IOCASTE.   Had I not told you so?

OEDIPUS. You had; it was my faint heart that betrayed me.

IOCASTE. From now on never think of those things again.

OEDIPUS. And yet—must I not fear my mother's bed?

IOCASTE. Why should anyone in this world be afraid,
Since Fate rules us and nothing can be foreseen?
A man should live only for the present day.

Have no more fear of sleeping with your mother:
How many men, in dreams, have lain with their mothers!
No reasonable man is troubled by such things.

OEDIPUS. That is true; only—
If only my mother were not still alive!
But she is alive. I can not help my dread.

IOCASTE. Yet this news of your father's death is wonderful.

OEDIPUS. Wonderful. But I fear the living woman.

MESSENGER. Tell me, who is this woman that you fear?

OEDIPUS. It is Meropê, man; the wife of King Polybos.

MESSENGER. Meropê? Why should you be afraid of her?

OEDIPUS. An oracle of the gods, a dreadful saying.

MESSENGER. Can you tell me about it or are you sworn to silence?

OEDIPUS. I can tell you, and I will.

Apollo said through his prophet that I was the man
Who should marry his own mother, shed his father's blood
With his own hands. And so, for all these years
I have kept clear of Corinth, and no harm has come —
Though it would have been sweet to see my parents again.

MESSENGER. And is this the fear that drove you out of Corinth?

OEDIPUS. Would you have me kill my father?

MESSENGER.   As for that
You must be reassured by the news I gave you.

OEDIPUS. If you could reassure me, I would reward you.

MESSENGER. I had that in mind, I will confess: I thought
I could count on you when you returned to Corinth.

OEDIPUS. No: I will never go near my parents again.

MESSENGER. Ah, son, you still do not know what you are doing—

OEDIPUS. What do you mean? In the name of God tell me!

MESSENGER. —If these are your reasons for not going home.

OEDIPUS. I tell you, I fear the oracle may come true.

MESSENGER. And guilt may come upon you through your parents?

OEDIPUS. That is the dread that is always in my heart.

MESSENGER. Can you not see that all your fears are groundless?

OEDIPUS. How can you say that? They are my parents, surely?

MESSENGER. Polybos was not your father.

OEDIPUS.   Not my father?

MESSENGER. No more your father than the man speaking to you.

OEDIPUS. But you are nothing to me!

MESSENGER.   Neither was he.

OEDIPUS. Then why did he call me son?

MESSENGER.   I will tell you:
Long ago he had you from my hands, as a gift.

OEDIPUS. Then how could he love me so, if I was not his?

MESSENGER. He had no children, and his heart turned to you.

OEDIPUS. What of you? Did you find me by chance?

MESSENGER. I came upon you in the crooked pass of Kithairon.

OEDIPUS. And what were you doing there?

MESSENGER.   Tending my flocks.

OEDIPUS. A wandering shepherd?

MESSENGER.   But your savior, son, that day.

OEDIPUS. From what did you save me?

MESSENGER.   Your ankles should tell you that.

OEDIPUS. Ah, stranger, why do you speak of that childhood pain?

MESSENGER. I cut the bonds that tied your ankles together.

OEDIPUS. I have had the mark as long as I can remember.

MESSENGER. That was why you were given the name you bear.

OEDIPUS. God! Was it my father or my mother who did it?
Tell me!

MESSENGER. I do not know. The man who gave you to me
Can tell you better than I.

OEDIPUS. It was not you that found me, but another?

MESSENGER. It was another shepherd gave you to me.

OEDIPUS. Who was he? Can you tell me who he was?

MESSENGER. I think he was said to be one of Laïos' people.

OEDIPUS. You mean the Laïos who was king here years ago?

MESSENGER. Yes; King Laïos; and the man was one of his herdsmen.

OEDIPUS. Is he still alive? Can I see him?

MESSENGER.   These men here
Know best about such things.

OEDIPUS.   Does anyone here
Know this shepherd that he is talking about?
Have you seen him in the fields, or in the town?
If you have, tell me. It is time things were made plain.

CHORAGOS. I think the man he means is that same shepherd
You have already asked to see. Iocastê perhaps
Could tell you something.

OEDIPUS.   Do you know anything
About him, Lady? Is he the man we have summoned?
Is that the man this shepherd means?

IOCASTE.   Why think of him?
Forget this herdsman. Forget it all.
This talk is a waste of time.

OEDIPUS.   How can you say that,
When the clues to my true birth are in my hands?

IOCASTE. For God's love, let us have no more questioning!
Is your life nothing to you?
My own is pain enough for me to bear.

OEDIPUS. You need not worry. Suppose my mother a slave,
And born of slaves: no baseness can touch you.

IOCASTE. Listen to me, I beg you: do not do this thing!

OEDIPUS. I will not listen; the truth must be made known.

IOCASTE. Everything that I say is for your own good!

OEDIPUS.   My own good
Snaps my patience, then; I want none of it.

IOCASTE. You are fatally wrong! May you never learn who you are!

OEDIPUS. Go, one of you, and bring the shepherd here.
Let us leave this woman to brag of her royal name.

IOCASTE. Ah, miserable!
That is the only word I have for you now.
That is the only word I can ever have.

(*Exit into the palace.*)

CHORAGOS. Why has she left us, Oedipus? Why has she gone
In such a passion of sorrow? I fear this silence:
Something dreadful may come of it.

OEDIPUS.   Let it come!
However base my birth, I must know about it.
The Queen, like a woman, is perhaps ashamed
To think of my low origin. But I
Am a child of Luck; I can not be dishonored.
Luck is my mother; the passing months, my brothers,
Have seen me rich and poor.

                              If this is so,
How could I wish that I were someone else?
How could I not be glad to know my birth?

ODE III

CHORUS. If ever the coming time were known   [STROPHE
To my heart's pondering,
Kithairon, now by Heaven I see the torches
At the festival of the next full moon,   .
And see the dance, and hear the choir sing
A grace to your gentle shade:
Mountain where Oedipus was found,
O mountain guard of a noble race!
May the god who heals us lend his aid,
And let that glory come to pass
For our king's cradling-ground.

Of the nymphs that flower beyond the years,   [ANTISTROPHE
Who bore you, royal child,
To Pan of the hills or the timberline Apollo,
Cold in delight where the upland clears,
Or Hermês for whom Kyllenê's heights are piled?
Or flushed as evening cloud,
Great Dionysos, roamer of mountains,
He—was it he who found you there,
And caught you up in his own proud
Arms from the sweet god-ravisher
Who laughed by the Muses' fountains?

Scene IV

OEDIPUS. Sirs: though I do not know the man,
I think I see him coming, this shepherd we want:
He is old, like our friend here, and the men
Bringing him seem to be servants of my house.
But you can tell, if you have ever seen him.

(*Enter* SHEPHERD *escorted by servants.*)

CHORAGOS. I know him, he was Laïos' man. You can trust him.

OEDIPUS. Tell me first, you from Corinth: is this the shepherd
We were discussing?

MESSENGER.   This is the very man.

OEDIPUS. (*to* SHEPHERD). Come here. No, look at me. You must answer
Everything I ask.—You belonged to Laïos?

SHEPHERD. Yes: born his slave, brought up in his house.

OEDIPUS. Tell me: what kind of work did you do for him?

SHEPHERD. I was a shepherd of his, most of my life.

OEDIPUS. Where mainly did you go for pasturage?

SHEPHERD. Sometimes Kithairon, sometimes the hills near-by.

OEDIPUS. Do you remember ever seeing this man out there?

SHEPHERD. What would he be doing there? This man?

OEDIPUS. This man standing here. Have you ever seen him before?

SHEPHERD. No. At least, not to my recollection.

MESSENGER. And that is not strange, my lord. But I'll refresh
His memory: he must remember when we two
Spent three whole seasons together, March to September,
On Kithairon or thereabouts. He had two flocks;
I had one. Each autumn I'd drive mine home
And he would go back with his to Laïos' sheepfold.—
Is this not true, just as I have described it?

SHEPHERD. True, yes; but it was all so long ago.

MESSENGER. Well, then: do you remember, back in those days
That you gave me a baby boy to bring up as my own?

SHEPHERD. What if I did? What are you trying to say?

MESSENGER. King Oedipus was once that little child.

SHEPHERD. Damn you, hold your tongue!

OEDIPUS.   No more of that!
It is your tongue needs watching, not this man's.

SHEPHERD. My King, my Master, what is it I have done wrong?

OEDIPUS. You have not answered his question about the boy.

SHEPHERD. He does not know . . . He is only making trouble . . .

OEDIPUS. Come, speak plainly, or it will go hard with you.

SHEPHERD. In God's name, do not torture an old man!

OEDIPUS. Come here, one of you; bind his arms behind him.

SHEPHERD. Unhappy king! What more do you wish to learn?

OEDIPUS. Did you give this man the child he speaks of?

SHEPHERD.   I did.
And I would to God I had died that very day.

OEDIPUS. You will die now unless you speak the truth.

SHEPHERD. Yet if I speak the truth, I am worse than dead.

OEDIPUS. Very well; since you insist upon delaying—

SHEPHERD. No! I have told you already that I gave him the boy.

OEDIPUS. Where did you get him? From your house? From somewhere else?

SHEPHERD. Not from mine, no. A man gave him to me.

OEDIPUS. Is that man here? Do you know whose slave he was?

SHEPHERD. For God's love, my King, do not ask me any more!

OEDIPUS. You are a dead man if I have to ask you again.

SHEPHERD. Then . . . Then the child was from the palace of Laïos.

OEDIPUS. A slave child? or a child of his own line?

SHEPHERD. Ah, I am on the brink of dreadful speech!

OEDIPUS. And I of dreadful hearing. Yet I must hear.

SHEPHERD. If you must be told, then . . .

                                              They said it was Laïos' child,
But it is your wife who can tell you about that.

OEDIPUS. My wife!—Did she give it to you?

SHEPHERD.   My lord, she did.

OEDIPUS. Do you know why?

SHEPHERD.   I was told to get rid of it.

OEDIPUS. An unspeakable mother!

SHEPHERD.   There had been prophecies . . .

OEDIPUS. Tell me.

SHEPHERD.   It was said that the boy would kill his own father.

OEDIPUS. Then why did you give him over to this old man?

SHEPHERD. I pitied the baby, my King,
And I thought that this man would take him far away
To his own country.

                                              He saved him—but for what a fate!
For if you are what this man says you are,
No man living is more wretched than Oedipus.

OEDIPUS. Ah God!
It was true!

                       All the prophecies!

                                              —Now,
O Light, may I look on you for the last time!
I, Oedipus,
Oedipus, damned in his birth, in his marriage damned,
Damned in the blood he shed with his own hand!

                                              (*He rushes into the palace.*)

Ode IV

CHORUS. Alas for the seed of men.　　　　　　　　[STROPHE 1

What measure shall I give these generations
That breathe on the void and are void
And exist and do not exist?

Who bears more weight of joy
Than mass of sunlight shifting in images,
Or who shall make his thoughts stay on
That down time drifts away?

Your splendor is all fallen.

O naked brow of wrath and tears,
O change of Oedipus!
I who saw your days call no man blest—
Your great days like ghósts góne.

That mind was a strong bow.　　　　　　　　[ANTISTROPHE 1

Deep, how deep you drew it then, hard archer,
At a dim fearful range,
And brought dear glory down!

You overcame the stranger—
The virgin with her hooking lion claws—
And though death sang, stood like a tower
To make pale Thebes take heart.

Fortress against our sorrow!

Divine king, giver of laws,
Majestic Oedipus!
No prince in Thebes had ever such renown,
No prince won such grace of power.

And now of all men ever known　　　　　　　　[STROPHE 2
Most pitiful is this man's story:
His fortunes are most changed, his state
Fallen to a low slave's
Ground under bitter fate.

O Oedipus, most royal one!
The great door that expelled you to the light
Gave at night—ah, gave night to your glory:
As to the father, to the fathering son.

All understood too late.

How could that queen whom Laïos won,
The garden that he harrowed at his height,
Be silent when that act was done?

But all eyes fail before time's eye,   [ANTISTROPHE 2
All actions come to justice there.
Though never willed, though far down the deep past,
Your bed, your dread sirings,
Are brought to book at last.
Child by Laïos doomed to die,
Then doomed to lose that fortunate little death,
Would God you never took breath in this air
That with my wailing lips I take to cry:

For I weep the world's outcast.

I was blind, and now I can tell why:
Asleep, for you had given ease of breath
To Thebes, while the false years went by.

EXODOS

(*Enter, from the palace,* SECOND MESSENGER.)
SECOND MESSENGER. Elders of Thebes, most honored in this land,
What horrors are yours to see and hear, what weight
Of sorrow to be endured, if, true to your birth,
You venerate the line of Labdakos!
I think neither Istros nor Phasis, those great rivers,
Could purify this place of the corruption
It shelters now, or soon must bring to light—
Evil not done unconsciously, but willed.

The greatest griefs are those we cause ourselves.
    CHORAGOS. Surely, friend, we have grief enough already;
What new sorrow do you mean?
    SECOND MESSENGER.   The Queen is dead.
    CHORAGOS. Iocastê? Dead? But at whose hand?
    SECOND MESSENGER.   Her own.
The full horror of what happened you can not know,
For you did not see it; but I, who did, will tell you
As clearly as I can how she met her death.

When she had left us,
In passionate silence, passing through the court,
She ran to her apartment in the house,
Her hair clutched by the fingers of both hands.

She closed the doors behind her; then, by that bed
Where long ago the fatal son was conceived—
That son who should bring about his father's death—
We heard her call upon Laïos, dead so many years,
And heard her wail for the double fruit of her marriage,
A husband by her husband, children by her child.

Exactly how she died I do not know:
For Oedipus burst in moaning and would not let us
Keep vigil to the end: it was by him
As he stormed about the room that our eyes were caught.
From one to another of us he went, begging a sword,
Cursing the wife who was not his wife, the mother
Whose womb had carried his own children and himself.
I do not know: it was none of us aided him,
But surely one of the gods was in control!
For with a dreadful cry
He hurled his weight, as though wrenched out of himself,
At the twin doors: the bolts gave, and he rushed in.
And there we saw her hanging, her body swaying
From the cruel cord she had noosed about her neck.
A great sob broke from him, heartbreaking to hear,
As he loosed the rope and lowered her to the ground.

I would blot out from my mind what happened next!
For the King ripped from her gown the golden brooches
That were her ornament, and raised them, and plunged them down
Straight into his own eyeballs, crying, "No more,
No more shall you look on the misery about me,
The horrors of my own doing! Too long you have known
The faces of those whom I should never have seen,
Too long been blind to those for whom I was searching!
From this hour, go in darkness!" And as he spoke,
He struck at his eyes—not once, but many times;
And the blood spattered his beard,
Bursting from his ruined sockets like red hail.

So from the unhappiness of two this evil has sprung,
A curse on the man and woman alike. The old
Happiness of the house of Labdakos
Was happiness enough: where is it today?
It is all wailing and ruin, disgrace, death—all
The misery of mankind that has a name—
And it is wholly and for ever theirs.

    CHORAGOS. Is he in agony still? Is there no rest for him?
    SECOND MESSENGER. He is calling for someone to lead him to the gates
So that all the children of Kadmos may look upon

His father's murderer, his mother's—no,
I can not say it!
                    And then he will leave Thebes,
Self-exiled, in order that the curse
Which he himself pronounced may depart from the house.
He is weak, and there is none to lead him,
So terrible is his suffering.
                    But you will see:
Look, the doors are opening; in a moment
You will see a thing that would crush a heart of stone.
          (*The central door is opened;* OEDIPUS, *blinded, is led in.*)
     CHORAGOS. Dreadful indeed for men to see.
Never have my own eyes
Looked on a sight so full of fear.

Oedipus!
What madness came upon you, what daemon
Leaped on your life with heavier
Punishment than a mortal man can bear?
No: I can not even
Look at you, poor ruined one.
And I would speak, question, ponder,
If I were able. No.
You make me shudder.
     OEDIPUS. God. God.
Is there a sorrow greater?
Where shall I find harbor in this world?
My voice is hurled far on a dark wind.
What has God done to me?
     CHORAGOS. Too terrible to think of, or to see.

     OEDIPUS. O cloud of night,   [STROPHE I
Never to be turned away: night coming on,
I can not tell how: night like a shroud!

My fair winds brought me here.
                    Oh God. Again
The pain of the spikes where I had sight,
The flooding pain
Of memory, never to be gouged out.
     CHORAGOS. This is not strange.
You suffer it all twice over, remorse in pain,
Pain in remorse.

     OEDIPUS. Ah dear friend   [ANTISTROPHE I
Are you faithful even yet, you alone?
Are you still standing near me, will you stay here,

Patient, to care for the blind?
                              The blind man!
Yet even blind I know who it is attends me,
By the voice's tone—
Though my new darkness hide the comforter.
   CHORAGOS. Oh fearful act!
What god was it drove you to rake black
Night across your eyes?

   OEDIPUS. Apollo. Apollo. Dear   [STROPHE 2
Children, the god was Apollo.
He brought my sick, sick fate upon me.
But the blinding hand was my own!
How could I bear to see
When all my sight was horror everywhere?
   CHORAGOS. Everywhere; that is true.
   OEDIPUS. And now what is left?
Images? Love? A greeting even,
Sweet to the senses? Is there anything?
Ah, no, friends: lead me away.
Lead me away from Thebes.
                              Lead the great wreck
And hell of Oedipus, whom the gods hate.
   CHORAGOS. Your fate is clear, you are not blind to that.
Would God you had never found it out!

   OEDIPUS. Death take the man who unbound   [ANTISTROPHE 2
My feet on that hillside
And delivered me from death to life! What life?
If only I had died,
This weight of monstrous doom
Could not have dragged me and my darlings down.
   CHORAGOS. I would have wished the same.
   OEDIPUS. Oh never to have come here
With my father's blood upon me! Never
To have been the man they call his mother's husband!
Oh accurst! Oh child of evil,
To have entered that wretched bed—
                              the selfsame one!
More primal than sin itself, this fell to me.
   CHORAGOS. I do not know how I can answer you.
You were better dead than alive and blind.
   OEDIPUS. Do not counsel me any more. This punishment
That I have laid upon myself is just.
If I had eyes,
I do not know how I could bear the sight

Of my father, when I came to the house of Death,
Or my mother: for I have sinned against them both
So vilely that I could not make my peace
By strangling my own life.
     Or do you think my children,
Born as they were born, would be sweet to my eyes?
Ah never, never! Nor this town with its high walls,
Nor the holy images of the gods.
      For I,
Thrice miserable!—Oedipus, noblest of all the line
Of Kadmos, have condemned myself to enjoy
These things no more, by my own malediction
Expelling that man whom the gods declared
To be a defilement in the house of Laïos.
After exposing the rankness of my own guilt,
How could I look men frankly in the eyes?
No, I swear it,
If I could have stifled my hearing at its source,
I would have done it and made all this body
A tight cell of misery, blank to light and sound:
So I should have been safe in a dark agony
Beyond all recollection.
    Ah Kithairon!
Why did you shelter me? When I was cast upon you,
Why did I not die? Then I should never
Have shown the world my execrable birth.

Ah Polybos! Corinth, city that I believed
The ancient seat of my ancestors: how fair
I seemed, your child! And all the while this evil
Was cancerous within me!
    For I am sick
In my daily life, sick in my origin.

O three roads, dark ravine, woodland and way
Where three roads met: you, drinking my father's blood,
My own blood, spilled by my own hand: can you remember
The unspeakable things I did there, and the things
I went on from there to do?
    O marriage, marriage!
The act that engendered me, and again the act
Performed by the son in the same bed—
     Ah, the net
Of incest, mingling fathers, brothers, sons,
With brides, wives, mothers: the last evil
That can be known by men: no tongue can say

How evil!
    No. For the love of God, conceal me
Somewhere far from Thebes; or kill me; or hurl me
Into the sea, away from men's eyes for ever.

Come, lead me. You need not fear to touch me.
Of all men, I alone can bear this guilt.
        (*Enter* CREON.)
  CHORAGOS. We are not the ones to decide; but Creon here
May fitly judge of what you ask. He only
Is left to protect the city in your place.
  OEDIPUS. Alas, how can I speak to him? What right have I
To beg his courtesy whom I have deeply wronged?
  CREON. I have not come to mock you, Oedipus,
Or to reproach you, either.
                (*To* ATTENDANTS.)

       —You, standing there:
If you have lost all respect for man's dignity,
At least respect the flame of Lord Helios:
Do not allow this pollution to show itself
Openly here, an affront to the earth
And Heaven's rain and the light of day. No, take him
Into the house as quickly as you can.
For it is proper
That only the close kindred see his grief.
  OEDIPUS. I pray you in God's name, since your courtesy
Ignores my dark expectation, visiting
With mercy this man of all men most execrable:
Give me what I ask—for your good, not for mine.
  CREON. And what is it that you would have me do?
  OEDIPUS. Drive me out of this country as quickly as may be
To a place where no human voice can ever greet me.
  CREON. I should have done that before now—only,
God's will had not been wholly revealed to me.
  OEDIPUS. But his command is plain: the parricide
Must be destroyed. I am that evil man.
  CREON. That is the sense of it, yes; but things are,
We had best discover clearly what is to be done.
  OEDIPUS. You would learn more about a man like me?
  CREON. You are ready now to listen to the god.
  OEDIPUS. I will listen. But it is to you
That I must turn for help. I beg you, hear me.

The woman in there—
Give her whatever funeral you think proper:
She is your sister.

—But let me go, Creon!
Let me purge my father's Thebes of the pollution
Of my living here, and go out to the wild hills,
To Kithairon, that has won such fame with me,
The tomb my mother and father appointed for me,
And let me die there, as they willed I should.
And yet I know
Death will not ever come to me through sickness
Or in any natural way: I have been preserved
For some unthinkable fate. But let that be.
As for my sons, you need not care for them.
They are men, they will find some way to live.
But my poor daughters, who have shared my table,
Who never before have been parted from their father—
Take care of them, Creon; do this for me.
And will you let me touch them with my hands
A last time, and let us weep together?
Be kind, my lord,
Great prince, be kind!
                  Could I but touch them,
They would be mine again, as when I had my eyes.
             (*Enter* ANTIGONE *and* ISMENE, *attended.*)
Ah, God!
Is it my dearest children I hear weeping?
Has Creon pitied me and sent my daughters?

    CREON. Yes, Oedipus: I knew that they were dear to you
In the old days, and know you must love them still.

    OEDIPUS. May God bless you for this—and be a friendlier
Guardian to you than he has been to me!

Children, where are you?
Come quickly to my hands: they are your brother's—
Hands that have brought your father's once clear eyes
To this way of seeing—
               Ah dearest ones,
I had neither sight nor knowledge then, your father
By the woman who was the source of his own life!
And I weep for you—having no strength to see you—,
I weep for you when I think of the bitterness
That men will visit upon you all your lives.
What homes, what festivals can you attend
Without being forced to depart again in tears?
And when you come to marriageable age,
Where is the man, my daughters, who would dare
Risk the bane that lies on all my children?

Is there any evil wanting? Your father killed
His father; sowed the womb of her who bore him;
Engendered you at the fount of his own existence!
That is what they will say of you.
                                        Then, whom
Can you ever marry? There are no bridegrooms for you,
And your lives must wither away in sterile dreaming.
O Creon, son of Menoikeus!
You are the only father my daughters have,
Since we, their parents, are both of us gone for ever.
They are your own blood: you will not let them
Fall into beggary and loneliness;
You will keep them from the miseries that are mine!
Take pity on them; see, they are only children,
Friendless except for you. Promise me this,
Great Prince, and give me your hand in token of it.

                              (CREON *clasps his right hand.*)

Children:
I could say much, if you could understand me,
But as it is, I have only this prayer for you:
Live where you can, be as happy as you can—
Happier, please God, than God has made your father!
    CREON. Enough. You have wept enough. Now go within.
    OEDIPUS. I must; but it is hard.
    CREON.   Time eases all things.
    OEDIPUS. But you must promise—
    CREON.   Say what you desire.
    OEDIPUS. Send me from Thebes!
    CREON.   God grant that I may!
    OEDIPUS. But since God hates me . . .
    CREON.   No, he will grant your wish.
    OEDIPUS. You promise?
    CREON.   I can not speak beyond my knowledge.
    OEDIPUS. Then lead me in.
    CREON.   Come now, and leave your children.
    OEDIPUS. No! Do not take them from me!
    CREON.   Think no longer
That you are in command here, but rather think
How, when you were, you served your own destruction.

              (*Exeunt into the house all but the* CHORUS; *the* CHORAGOS *chants
                                        directly to the audience.*)

    CHORAGOS. Men of Thebes: look upon Oedipus.

This is the king who solved the famous riddle
And towered up, most powerful of men.

No mortal eyes but looked on him with envy,
Yet in the end ruin swept over him.

Let every man in mankind's frailty
Consider his last day; and let none
Presume on his good fortune until he find
Life, at his death, a memory without pain.

William Shakespeare

The Chronicle History of King Henry the Fourth

Part one

CHARACTERS

KING HENRY IV	SIR RICHARD VERNON
HENRY, PRINCE OF WALES, ⎤ *sons*	SIR JOHN FALSTAFF
JOHN OF LANCASTER, ⎬ *to the*	SIR MICHAEL, *a friend to the Arch-*
EARL OF WESTMORELAND ⎦ *King.*	*bishop of York*
SIR WALTER BLUNT	POINS
THOMAS PERCY, *Earl of Worcester*	GADSHILL
HENRY PERCY, *Earl of Northumber-*	PETO
land	BARDOLPH
HENRY PERCY, *surnamed* HOTSPUR,	LADY PERCY, *wife to* HOTSPUR, *and*
his son	*sister to* MORTIMER
EDMUND MORTIMER, *Earl of March*	LADY MORTIMER, *daughter to* GLEN-
RICHARD SCROOP, *Archbishop of*	DOWER *and wife to* MORTIMER
York	MISTRESS QUICKLY, *hostess of a tav-*
ARCHIBALD, *Earl of Douglas*	*ern in Eastcheap*
OWEN GLENDOWER	

Lords, Officers, Sheriff, Vintner, Chamberlain, Drawers,
Two Carriers, Travellers, and Attendants.
SCENE: *England and Wales.* TIME: *1402–1403*

ACT I/1   London. The palace.

(*Enter* KING HENRY, LORD JOHN OF LANCASTER, *the* EARL OF WEST-
MORELAND, SIR WALTER BLUNT *with others.*)

KING. So shaken as we are, so wan with care,
Find we a time for frighted Peace to pant
And breathe short-winded accents of new broils

3 *accents:* speech.

To be commenc'd in strands afar remote.
No more the thirsty entrance of this soil   5
Shall daub her lips with her own children's blood;
No more shall trenching war channel her fields,
Nor bruise her flowerets with the armed hoofs
Of hostile paces. Those opposed eyes,
Which, like the meteors of a troubled heaven,   10
All of one nature, of one substance bred,
Did lately meet in the intestine shock
And furious close of civil butchery,
Shall now, in mutual well-beseeming ranks,
March all one way and be no more oppos'd   15
Against acquaintance, kindred, and allies.
The edge of war, like an ill-sheathed knife,
No more shall cut his master. Therefore, friends,
As far as to the sepulchre of Christ,
Whose soldier now under whose blessed cross   20
We are impressed and engag'd to fight,
Forthwith a power of English shall we levy;
Whose arms were moulded in their mothers' womb
To chase these pagans in those holy fields
Over whose acres walk'd those blessed feet   25
Which fourteen hundred years ago were nail'd
For our advantage on the bitter cross.
But this our purpose now is twelve months old,
And bootless 't is to tell you we will go;
Therefore we meet not now. Then let me hear   30
Of you, my gentle cousin Westmoreland,
What yesternight our council did decree
In forwarding this dear expedience.
        WESTMORELAND. My liege, this haste was hot in question,
And many limits of the charge set down   35
But yesternight; when all athwart there came
A post from Wales loaden with heavy news;
Whose worst was that the noble Mortimer,
Leading the men of Herefordshire to fight
Against the irregular and wild Glendower,   40
Was by the rude hands of that Welshman taken,
A thousand of his people butchered;
Upon whose dead corpses there was such misuse,
Such beastly shameless transformation,

7 *trenching: cutting.*   12 *intestine:* internal.   13 *close:* meeting.   21 *impressed:* forced to
serve.   22 *power:* army.   29 *bootless:* useless.   33 *dear expedience:* important undertaking.   35 *limits of the charge:* duties of the task.   36 *all athwart:* inconveniently.
37 *post:* messenger; *heavy:* sad.   44 *transformation:* mutilation.

By those Welshwomen done as may not be   45
Without much shame retold or spoken of.
    KING. It seems then that the tidings of this broil
Brake off our business for the Holy Land.
    WESTMORELAND. This match'd with other did, my gracious lord;
For more uneven and unwelcome news   50
Came from the north, and thus it did import:
On Holy-rood day, the gallant Hotspur there,
Young Harry Percy, and brave Archibald,
That ever-valiant and approved Scot,
At Holmedon met,   55
Where they did spend a sad and bloody hour,
As by discharge of their artillery,
And shape of likelihood, the news was told;
For he that brought them, in the very heat
And pride of their contention did take horse,   60
Uncertain of the issue any way.
    KING. Here is a dear, a true-industrious friend,
Sir Walter Blunt, new lighted from his horse,
Stained with the variation of each soil
Betwixt that Holmedon and this seat of ours;   65
And he hath brought us smooth and welcome news.
The Earl of Douglas is discomfited.
Ten thousand bold Scots, two and twenty knights,
Balk'd in their own blood did Sir Walter see
On Holmedon's plains. Of prisoners, Hotspur took   70
Murdoch Earl of Fife and eldest son
To beaten Douglas; and the Earl of Athole,
Of Murray, Angus, and Menteith:
And is not this an honourable spoil?
A gallant prize, ha, cousin, is it not?   75
    WESTMORELAND. In faith,
It is a conquest for a prince to boast of.
    KING. Yea, there thou mak'st me sad, and mak'st me sin
In envy that my Lord Northumberland
Should be the father to so blest a son,   80
A son who is the theme of Honour's tongue,
Amongst a grove the very straightest plant,
Who is sweet Fortune's minion and her pride;
Whilst I, by looking on the praise of him,
See riot and dishonour stain the brow   85
Of my young Harry. O that it could be prov'd

---

52 *Holy-rood day:* September 14th.   54 *approved:* tested.   58 *shape of likelihood:* probability.   69 *Balk'd:* piled up.   83 *minion:* favorite.

That some night-tripping fairy had exchang'd
In cradle-clothes our children where they lay,
And call'd mine Percy, his Plantagenet!
Then would I have his Harry, and he mine.   90
But let him from my thoughts. What think you, coz,
Of this young Percy's pride? The prisoners,
Which he in this adventure hath surpris'd,
To his own use he keeps; and sends me word,
I shall have none but Murdoch Earl of Fife.   95

    WESTMORELAND. This is his uncle's teaching. This is Worcester,
Malevolent to you in all aspécts;
Which makes him prune himself, and bristle up
The crest of youth against your dignity.

    KING. But I have sent for him to answer this;   100
And for this cause awhile we must neglect
Our holy purpose to Jerusalem.
Cousin, on Wednesday next our council we
Will hold at Windsor; so inform the lords;
But come yourself with speed to us again,   105
For more is to be said and to be done
Than out of anger can be uttered.

    WESTMORELAND. I will, my liege.   (*Exeunt.*)

ACT I/2   London. An apartment of the PRINCE'S.

(*Enter the* PRINCE OF WALES *and* FALSTAFF.)

    FALSTAFF. Now, Hal, what time of day is it, lad?

    PRINCE. Thou art so fat-witted, with drinking of old sack and unbutton-
ing thee after supper and sleeping up on benches after noon, that thou hast
forgotten to demand that truly which thou wouldest truly know. What a
devil hast thou to do with the time of the day? Unless hours were cups of   5
sack, and minutes capons, and the clocks the tongues of bawds, and dials
the signs of leaping-houses, and the blessed sun himself a fair hot wench
in flame-coloured taffeta, I see no reason why thou shouldst be so superfluous to demand the time of the day.

    FALSTAFF. Indeed, you come near me now, Hal; for we that take   10
purses go by the moon and the seven stars, and not by Phoebus, he, "that
wand'ring knight so fair." And, I prithee, sweet wag, when thou art
king, as, God save thy Grace,—Majesty I should say, for grace thou wilt
have none,—

---

89 *Plantagenet:* the family name of the king.   94 *To his own use* etc.: he claims the
ransoms for himself.   98 *prune:* preen.

2 *sack:* a dry white sherry wine.   6 *bawds:* procurers; *dials:* clock-faces.   7 *leaping-houses:*
brothels.   8 *superfluous:* irrelevant.   10 *come near me:* you are right about me.   11 *the
seven stars:* the Big Dipper; *Phoebus:* the sun.

PRINCE. What, none? 15

FALSTAFF. No, by my troth, not so much as will serve to be prologue to an egg and butter.

PRINCE. Well, how then? Come, roundly, roundly.

FALSTAFF. Marry, then, sweet wag, when thou art king, let not us that are squires of the night's body be called thieves of the day's beauty. Let 20 us be Diana's foresters, gentlemen of the shade, minions of the moon; and let men say we be men of good government, being governed, as the sea is, by our noble and chaste mistress the moon, under whose countenance we steal.

PRINCE. Thou say'st well, and it holds well too; for the fortune of us 25 that are the moon's men doth ebb and flow like the sea, being governed, as the sea is, by the moon. As for proof, now: a purse of gold most resolutely snatched on Monday night and most dissolutely spent on Tuesday morning; got with swearing "Lay by" and spent with crying "Bring in"; now in as low an ebb as the foot of the ladder, and by and by in as high 30 a flow as the ridge of the gallows.

FALSTAFF. By the Lord, thou say'st true, lad. And is not my hostess of the tavern a most sweet wench?

PRINCE. As the honey of Hybla, my old lad of the castle. And is not a buff jerkin a most sweet robe of durance? 35

FALSTAFF. How now, how now, mad wag! What, in thy quips and thy quiddities, what a plague have I to do with a buff jerkin?

PRINCE. Why, what a pox have I to do with my hostess of the tavern?

FALSTAFF. Well, thou hast called her to a reckoning many a time and oft.

PRINCE. Did I ever call for thee to pay thy part? 40

FALSTAFF. No; I'll give thee thy due, thou hast paid all there.

PRINCE. Yea, and elsewhere, so far as my coin would stretch; and where it would not, I have used my credit.

FALSTAFF. Yea, and so used it that, were it not here apparent that thou art heir apparent—But, I prithee, sweet wag, shall there be gallows stand- 45 ing in England when thou art king? and resolution thus fobbed as it is with the rusty curb of old father antic the law? Do not thou, when thou art king, hang a thief.

PRINCE. No; thou shalt.

FALSTAFF. Shall I? O rare! By the Lord, I'll be a brave judge. 50

PRINCE. Thou judgest false already. I mean, thou shalt have the hanging of the thieves and so become a rare hangman.

---

17 *an egg and butter:* a small breakfast. 18 *roundly:* directly. 19 *Marry:* an exclamation, meaning, roughly, "Well. . . ." 20 *squires:* attendants; *thieves of the day's beauty:* idlers in the daytime. 21 *Diana:* the moon-goddess. 22 *government:* behavior. 29 *Lay by:* thieves' warning to their victims, meaning "Drop your weapons!" *Bring in:* the call for wine. 30 *the ladder:* the one leading to the gallows. 34 *Hybla:* a region in Sicily famous for honey. 35 *buff jerkin:* a leather jacket, of the kind worn by sheriffs' officers; *durance:* a kind of cloth; also, imprisonment. 37 *quiddities:* verbal jokes. 39 *reckoning:* payment of a bill. 46 *resolution:* courage; *fobbed:* frustrated. 47 *antic:* jester. 50 *brave:* fine.

FALSTAFF. Well, Hal, well; and in some sort it jumps with my humour
as well as waiting in the court, I can tell you.

PRINCE. For obtaining of suits?   55

FALSTAFF. Yea, for obtaining of suits, whereof the hangman hath no
lean wardrobe. 'Sblood, I am as melancholy as a gib cat or a lugged bear.

PRINCE. Or an old lion, or a lover's lute.

FALSTAFF. Yea, or the drone of a Lincolnshire bagpipe.

PRINCE. What sayest thou to a hare, or the melancholy of Moor Ditch?   60

FALSTAFF. Thou hast the most unsavoury similes and art indeed the most
comparative, rascalliest, sweet young prince. But, Hal, I prithee, trouble
me no more with vanity. I would to God thou and I knew where a commodity of good names were to be bought. An old lord of the council rated
me the other day in the street about you, sir, but I marked him not; and   65
yet he talked very wisely, but I regarded him not; and yet he talked wisely,
and in the street too.

PRINCE. Thou didst well; for wisdom cries out in the streets, and no
man regards it.

FALSTAFF. O, thou hast damnable iteration and art indeed able to corrupt   70
a saint. Thou hast done much harm upon me, Hal; God forgive thee for
it! Before I knew thee, Hal, I knew nothing; and now am I, if a man
should speak truly, little better than one of the wicked. I must give over
this life, and I will give it over. By the Lord, an I do not, I am a villain.
I'll be damned for never a king's son in Christendom.   75

PRINCE. Where shall we take a purse tomorrow, Jack?

FALSTAFF. 'Zounds, where thou wilt, lad; I'll make one. An I do not,
call me villain and baffle me.

PRINCE. I see a good amendment of life in thee; from praying to purse-
taking.   80

FALSTAFF. Why, Hal, 't is my vocation, Hal: 't is no sin for a man to
labour in his vocation.

(Enter POINS.*)*

Poins! Now shall we know if Gadshill have set a match. O, if men were
to be saved by merit, what hole in hell were hot enough for him? This is
the most omnipotent villain that ever cried "Stand!" to a true man.   85

PRINCE. Good morrow, Ned.

POINS. Good morrow, sweet Hal. What says Monsieur Remorse? What
says Sir John Sack and Sugar? Jack! how agrees the devil and thee about
thy soul, that thou soldest him on Good Friday last for a cup of Madeira
and a cold capon's leg?   90

---

53 *jumps with my humour:* suits me.   55 *suits:* requests made to the king.   57 *wardrobe:*
the hangman kept the clothes of his victims; *'Sblood:* by God's blood, an oath; *gib cat:*
a tom-cat; *lugged:* dragged.   60 *Moor Ditch:* an open sewer near London.   62
comparative: in the habit of making comparisons.   63 *commodity:* quantity.   64 *rated:*
scolded.   70 *iteration:* quotation.   77 *'Zounds:* by God's wounds, an oath; *make one:*
participate; *An:* if.   78 *baffle:* disgrace.   83 *set a match:* planned a robbery.   85
"Stand!": the thief's warning to his victim.   89 *Madeira:* a red wine.

PRINCE. Sir John stands to his word, the devil shall have his bargain; for he was never yet a breaker of proverbs. He will give the devil his due.

POINS. Then art thou damned for keeping thy word with the devil.

PRINCE. Else he had been damned for cozening the devil.

POINS. But, my lads, my lads, to-morrow morning, by four o'clock, early   95
at Gadshill! There are pilgrims going to Canterbury with rich offerings, and traders riding to London with fat purses. I have vizards for you all; you have horses for yourselves: Gadshill lies tonight in Rochester: I have bespoke supper to-morrow night in Eastcheap: we may do it as secure as sleep. If you will go, I will stuff your purses full of crowns; if you will   100
not, tarry at home and be hanged.

FALSTAFF. Hear ye, Yedward; if I tarry at home and go not, I'll hang you for going.

POINS. You will, chops?

FALSTAFF. Hal, wilt thou make one?   105

PRINCE. Who, I rob? I a thief? Not I, by my faith.

FALSTAFF. There's neither honesty, manhood, nor good fellowship in thee, nor thou cam'st not of the blood royal, if thou dar'st not stand for ten shillings.

PRINCE. Well, then, once in my days I'll be a madcap.   110

FALSTAFF. Why, that's well said.

PRINCE. Well, come what will, I'll tarry at home.

FALSTAFF. By the lord, I'll be a traitor then, when thou art king.

PRINCE. I care not.

POINS. Sir John, I prithee, leave the Prince and me alone. I will lay him   115
down such reasons for this adventure that he shall go.

FALSTAFF. Well, God give thee the spirit of persuasion and him the ears of profiting, that what thou speakest may move and what he hears may be believed, that the true prince may, for recreation sake, prove a false thief; for the poor abuses of the time want countenance. Farewell; you   120
shall find me in Eastcheap.

PRINCE. Farewell, thou latter spring! Farewell, All-hallown summer!

(*Exit* FALSTAFF.)

POINS. Now, my good sweet honey lord, ride with us to-morrow; I have a jest to execute that I cannot manage alone. Falstaff, Bardolph, Peto, and Gadshill shall rob those men that we have already waylaid; yourself and   125
I will not be there; and when they have the booty, if you and I do not rob them, cut this head off from my shoulders.

PRINCE. How shall we part with them in setting forth?

POINS. Why, we will set forth before or after them, and appoint them a

---

94 *cozening:* cheating.   96 *Gadshill:* a hill on the road between London and Canterbury. This name should be distinguished from that of Falstaff's crony, who is mentioned a few lines later.   97 *vizards:* masks.   99 *bespoke:* ordered.   104 *chops:* fat cheeks. 108 *royal:* a ten-shilling coin; *stand:* fight.   120 *countenance:* encouragement. 122 *All-hallown summer:* a November summer. All-hallows day came on November 1st.

place of meeting, wherein it is at our pleasure to fail, and then will they 　130
adventure upon the exploit themselves; which they shall have no sooner
achieved, but we'll set upon them.

PRINCE. Yea, but 't is like that they will know us by our horses, by our
habits, and by every other appointment, to be ourselves.

POINS. Tut! our horses they shall not see; I'll tie them in the wood; our 　135
vizards we will change after we leave them; and, sirrah, I have cases of
buckram for the nonce, to immask our noted outward garments.

PRINCE. Yea, but I doubt they will be too hard for us.

POINS. Well, for two of them, I know them to be as true-bred cowards
as ever turned back; and for the third, if he fight longer than he sees 　140
reason, I'll forswear arms. The virtue of this jest will be the incomprehensible lies that this same fat rogue will tell us when we meet at supper;
how thirty, at least, he fought with; what wards, what blows, what extremities he endured; and in the reproof of this lies the jest.

PRINCE. Well, I'll go with thee: provide us all things necessary and 　145
meet me to-morrow night in Eastcheap; there I'll sup. Farewell.

POINS. Farewell, my lord. 　　　　　　　　　　　　　　　(*Exit.*)

PRINCE. I know you all, and will a while uphold
The unyok'd humour of your idleness;
Yet herein will I imitate the sun, 　　　　　　　　　　　　　　150
Who doth permit the base contagious clouds
To smother up his beauty from the world,
That when he please again to be himself,
Being wanted, he may be more wonder'd at
By breaking through the foul and ugly mists 　　　　　　　　　155
Of vapours that did seem to strangle him.
If all the year were playing holidays,
To sport would be as tedious as to work;
But when they seldom come, they wish'd for come,
And nothing pleaseth but rare accidents. 　　　　　　　　　　160
So, when this loose behaviour I throw off
And pay the debt I never promised,
By how much better than my word I am,
By so much shall I falsify men's hopes;
And like bright metal on a sullen ground, 　　　　　　　　　　165
My reformation, glitt'ring o'er my fault,
Shall show more goodly and attract more eyes
Than that which hath no foil to set it off.
I'll so offend, to make offence a skill,
Redeeming time when men think least I will. 　　　　　(*Exit.*) 　170

---

134 *habits:* clothing. 　136 *sirrah:* "sir," a form of address; *cases:* coverings. 　137 *for
the nonce:* for the time being; *noted:* known. 　141 *forswear:* give up; *incomprehensible:* limitless. 　143 *wards:* parries. 　144 *reproof:* disproof. 　149 *unyok'd:* reckless.
160 *accidents:* events. 　164 *hopes:* expectations. 　165 *sullen:* dark. 　168 *foil:* contrast.

ACT I/3   London. The Palace.

(*Enter the* KING, NORTHUMBERLAND, WORCESTER, HOTSPUR,
SIR WALTER BLUNT, *with others.*)

KING. My blood hath been too cold and temperate,
Unapt to stir at these indignities,
And you have found me; for accordingly
You tread upon my patience. But be sure
I will from henceforth rather be myself,   5
Mighty and to be fear'd, than my condition;
Which hath been smooth as oil, soft as young down,
And therefore lost that title of respect
Which the proud soul ne'er pays but to the proud.
   WORCESTER. Our house, my sovereign liege, little deserves   10
The scourge of greatness to be us'd on it;
And that same greatness too which our own hands
Have holp to make so portly.
   NORTHUMBERLAND. My lord,—
   KING. Worcester, get thee gone; for I do see   15
Danger and disobedience in thine eye.
O, sir, your presence is too bold and peremptory,
And majesty might never yet endure
The moody frontier of a servant brow.
You have good leave to leave us. When we need   20
Your use and counsel, we shall send for you.   (*Exit* WORCESTER.)
You were about to speak.
   NORTHUMBERLAND.   Yea, my good lord.
Those prisoners in your Highness' name demanded,
Which Harry Percy here at Holmedon took,
Were, as he says, not with such strength denied   25
As is delivered to your Majesty.
Either envy, therefore, or misprision
Is guilty of this fault, and not my son.
   HOTSPUR. My liege, I did deny no prisoners.
But I remember, when the fight was done,   30
When I was dry with rage and extreme toil,
Breathless and faint, leaning upon my sword,
Came there a certain lord, neat, and trimly dress'd,
Fresh as a bridegroom; and his chin new reap'd
Show'd like a stubble-land at harvest-home.   35

---

3 *found me:* found me out. 6 *condition:* personality. 11 *scourge:* whip. 13 *holp:* helped. 19 *frontier:* defensive wall; here it refers to the forehead. 27 *misprision:* misunderstanding. 34 *new reap'd:* freshly trimmed.

He was perfumed like a milliner;
And 'twixt his finger and his thumb he held
A pouncet-box, which ever and anon
He gave his nose and took 't away again;
Who therewith angry, when it next came there,   40
Took it in snuff; and still he smil'd and talk'd,
And as the soldiers bore dead bodies by,
He call'd them untaught knaves, unmannerly,
To bring a slovenly unhandsome corse
Betwixt the wind and his nobility.   45
With many holiday and lady terms
He question'd me; amongst the rest, demanded
My prisoners in your Majesty's behalf.
I then, all smarting with my wounds being cold,
To be so pester'd with a popinjay,   50
Out of my grief, and my impatience
Answer'd neglectingly—I know not what,
He should, or he should not; for he made me mad
To see him shine so brisk and smell so sweet
And talk so like a waiting-gentlewoman   55
Of guns and drums and wounds,—God save the mark!—
And telling me the sovereign'st thing on earth
Was parmaceti for an inward bruise;
And that it was great pity, so it was,
This villanous salt-petre should be digg'd   60
Out of the bowels of the harmless earth,
Which many a good tall fellow had destroy'd
So cowardly; and but for these vile guns,
He would himself have been a soldier.
This bald unjointed chat of his, my lord,   65
I answered indirectly, as I said;
And I beseech you, let not his report
Come current for an accusation
Betwixt my love and your high Majesty.
    BLUNT. The circumstance considered, good my lord,   70
Whate'er Lord Harry Percy then had said
To such a person and in such a place,
At such a time, with all the rest retold,
May reasonably die and never rise
To do him wrong or any way impeach   75
What then he said, so he unsay it now.

---

38 *pouncet-box:* perfume box; *ever and anon:* from time to time.   41 *Took it in snuff:*
inhaled it; *still:* continually.   44 *corse:* corpse.   46 *holiday:* affected.   51 *grief:* pain.
58 *parmaceti:* or spermaceti, an ointment derived from the sperm whale.   68 *Come
current:* be accepted.

KING. Why, yet he doth deny his prisoners
But with proviso and exception
That we at our own charge shall ransom straight
His brother-in-law, the foolish Mortimer;   80
Who, on my soul, hath willfully betray'd
The lives of those that he did lead to fight
Against the great magician, damn'd Glendower,
Whose daughter, as we hear, that Earl of March
Hath lately married. Shall our coffers, then,   85
Be emptied to redeem a traitor home?
Shall we buy treason, and indent with fears,
When they have lost and forfeited themselves?
No, on the barren mountains let him starve;
For I shall never hold that man my friend   90
Whose tongue shall ask me for one penny cost
To ransom home revolted Mortimer.
   HOTSPUR. Revolted Mortimer!
He never did fall off, my sovereign liege,
But by the chance of war: to prove that true   95
Needs no more but one tongue for all those wounds,
Those mouthed wounds, which valiantly he took
When on the gentle Severn's sedgy bank,
In single opposition, hand to hand,
He did confound the best part of an hour   100
In changing hardiment with great Glendower.
Three times they breath'd and three times did they drink,
Upon agreement, of swift Severn's flood;
Who then, affrighted with their bloody looks,
Ran fearfully among the trembling reeds,   105
And hid his crisp head in the hollow bank
Bloodstained with these valiant combatants.
Never did base and rotten policy
Colour her working with such deadly wounds;
Nor never could the noble Mortimer   110
Receive so many, and all willingly.
Then let not him be slander'd with revolt.
   KING. Thou dost belie him, Percy, thou dost belie him;
He never did encounter with Glendower.
I tell thee,   115
He durst as well have met the devil alone
As Owen Glendower for an enemy.
Art thou not asham'd? But, sirrah, henceforth

---

87 *indent*: make terms. 94 *fall off*: break faith. 97 *mouthed*: gaping. 100 *confound*: spend. 101 *changing hardiment*: exchanging blows. 106 *crisp*: curly or wavy. 108 *policy*: trickery. 109 *Colour*: disguise. 113 *belie*: lie about.

Let me not hear you speak of Mortimer.
Send me your prisoners with the speediest means,   120
Or you shall hear in such a kind from me
As will displease you. My Lord Northumberland,
We license your departure with your son.
Send us your prisoners or you'll hear of it.

       (*Exeunt* KING HENRY, BLUNT, *and train.*)

 HOTSPUR. An if the devil come and roar for them,   125
I will not send them. I will straight
And tell him so; for I will ease my heart,
Albeit I make a hazard of my head.

 NORTHUMBERLAND. What, drunk with choler? Stay and pause a while.
Here comes your uncle.

      (*Re-enter* WORCESTER.)

 HOTSPUR.   Speak of Mortimer!   130
Zounds, I will speak of him; and let my soul
Want mercy, if I do not join with him.
Yea, on his part I'll empty all these veins,
And shed my dear blood drop by drop in the dust,
But I will lift the down-trod Mortimer   135
As high in the air as this unthankful king,
As this ingrate and canker'd Bolingbroke.

 NORTHUMBERLAND. Brother, the king hath made your nephew mad.

 WORCESTER. Who struck this heat up after I was gone?

 HOTSPUR. He will, forsooth, have all my prisoners;   140
And when I urg'd the ransom once again
Of my wife's brother, then his cheek look'd pale,
And on my face he turn'd an eye of death,
Trembling even at the name of Mortimer.

 WORCESTER. I cannot blame him. Was not he proclaim'd   145
By Richard, that dead is, the next of blood?

 NORTHUMBERLAND. He was; I heard the proclamation.
And then it was when the unhappy king,—
Whose wrongs in us God pardon!—did set forth
Upon his Irish expedition;   150
From whence he intercepted did return
To be depos'd and shortly murdered.

 WORCESTER. And for whose death we in the world's wide mouth
Live scandaliz'd and foully spoken of.

 HOTSPUR. But, soft, I pray you; did King Richard then   155
Proclaim my brother Edmund Mortimer
Heir to the crown?

---

129 *choler:* anger. 137 *canker'd:* diseased; *Bolingbroke:* the name borne by the king
before he came to the throne. 146 *Richard:* Richard II, who was forced from the throne
by Henry IV, and murdered by one of his followers.

NORTHUMBERLAND.   He did; myself did hear it.

HOTSPUR. Nay, then I cannot blame his cousin king,
That wish'd him on the barren mountains starve.
But shall it be, that you, that set the crown   160
Upon the head of this forgetful man
And for his sake wear the detested blot
Of murderous subornation, shall it be,
That you a world of curses undergo,
Being the agents, or base second means,   165
The cords, the ladder, or the hangman rather?
O, pardon me that I descend so low,
To show the line and the predicament
Wherein you range under this subtle king!
Shall it for shame be spoken in these days,   170
Or fill up chronicles in time to come,
That men of your nobility and power
Did gage them both in an unjust behalf,
As both of you—God pardon it!—have done,
To put down Richard, that sweet lovely rose,   175
And plant this thorn, this canker, Bolingbroke?
And shall it in more shame be further spoken,
That you are fool'd, discarded, and shook off
By him for whom these shames ye underwent?
No; yet time serves wherein you may redeem   180
Your banish'd honours and restore yourselves
Into the good thoughts of the world again,
Revenge the jeering and disdain'd contempt
Of this proud king, who studies day and night
To answer all the debt he owes to you   185
Even with the bloody payment of your deaths.
Therefore, I say,—

WORCESTER.   Peace, cousin, say no more;
And now I will unclasp a secret book,
And to your quick-conceiving discontents
I'll read you matter deep and dangerous,   190
As full of peril and adventurous spirit
As to o'er-walk a current roaring loud
On the unsteadfast footing of a spear.

HOTSPUR. If he fall in, good night! or sink or swim.
Send Danger from the east unto the west   195
So Honour cross it from the north to south,
And let them grapple: O, the blood more stirs

---

163 *murderous subornation:* instigation of murder.   173 *gage:* commit.   176 *canker:* wild
rose.   183 *disdain'd:* disdainful.   185 *answer:* repay.   189 *quick-conceiving:* quick in
understanding.   194 *he:* the man walking the spear.

To rouse a lion than to start a hare!

NORTHUMBERLAND. Imagination of some great exploit
Drives him beyond the bounds of patience.   200

HOTSPUR. By heaven, methinks it were an easy leap,
To pluck bright Honour from the pale-fac'd moon,
Or dive into the bottom of the deep,
Where fathom-line could never touch the ground,
And pluck up drowned Honour by the locks;   205
So he that doth redeem her thence might wear
Without corrival all her dignities.
But out upon this half-fac'd fellowship!

WORCESTER. He apprehends a world of figures here,
But not the form of what he should attend.   210
Good cousin, give me audience for a while.

HOTSPUR. I cry you mercy.

WORCESTER.   Those same noble Scots
That are your prisoners,—

HOTSPUR.   I'll keep them all!
By God, he shall not have a Scot of them;
No, if a Scot would save his soul, he shall not!   215
I'll keep them, by this hand.

WORCESTER.   You start away
And lend no ear unto my purposes.
Those prisoners you shall keep.

HOTSPUR.   Nay, I will; that's flat.
He said he would not ransom Mortimer;
Forbad my tongue to speak of Mortimer;   220
But I will find him when he lies asleep,
And in his ear I'll holla "Mortimer!"
Nay,
I'll have a starling shall be taught to speak
Nothing but "Mortimer," and give it him,   225
To keep his anger still in motion.

WORCESTER. Hear you, cousin; a word.

HOTSPUR. All studies here I solemnly defy,
Save how to gall and pinch this Bolingbroke;
And that same sword-and-buckler Prince of Wales,   230
But that I think his father loves him not
And would be glad he met with some mischance,
I would have him poison'd with a pot of ale.

WORCESTER. Farewell, kinsman! I'll talk to you

---

200 *patience:* self-control.   207 *corrival:* rival.   208 *half-fac'd:* half-hearted.   209 *figures:*
imaginary shapes.   212 *I cry you mercy:* I beg your pardon.   228 *defy:* renounce.
230 *sword-and-buckler:* these weapons were not used by gentlemen, but by servants or
ruffians. Hence, Hotspur is putting the Prince in the category of his tavern companions.

When you are better temper'd to attend.   235
   NORTHUMBERLAND. Why, what a wasp-stung and impatient fool
Art thou to break into this woman's mood,
Tying thine ear to no tongue but thine own!
   HOTSPUR. Why, look you, I am whipp'd and scourg'd with rods,
Nettled and stung with pismires, when I hear   240
Of this vile politician, Bolingbroke.
In Richard's time,—what do you call the place?—
A plague upon it, it is in Gloucestershire;
'T was where the madcap duke his uncle kept,
His uncle York; where I first bow'd my knee   245
Unto this king of smiles, this Bolingbroke,—
'Sblood!—
When you and he came back from Ravenspurgh.
   NORTHUMBERLAND. At Berkley castle.
   HOTSPUR. You say true.   250
Why, what a candy deal of courtesy
This fawning greyhound then did proffer me!
Look, "when his infant fortune came to age,"
And "gentle Harry Percy," and "kind cousin;"
O, the devil take such cozeners!—God forgive me!   255
Good uncle, tell your tale; for I have done.
   WORCESTER. Nay, if you have not, to 't again;
We'll stay your leisure.
   HOTSPUR.   I have done, i' faith.
   WORCESTER. Then once more to your Scottish prisoners.
Deliver them up without their ransom straight,   260
And make the Douglas' son your only mean
For powers in Scotland; which, for divers reasons
Which I shall send you written, be assur'd,
Will easily be granted. You, my lord, [*to* NORTHUMBERLAND]
Your son in Scotland being thus employ'd,   265
Shall secretly into the bosom creep
Of that same noble prelate, well belov'd,
The Archbishop.
   HOTSPUR. Of York, is it not?
   WORCESTER. True; who bears hard   270
His brother's death at Bristow, the Lord Scroop.
I speak not this in estimation,
As what I think might be, but what I know
Is ruminated, plotted, and set down,
And only stays but to behold the face   275

240 *pismires:* ants.   244 *kept:* lived.   251 *candy:* sugary.   255 *cozeners:* tricksters.   256
have done: am finished.   261 *mean:* means.   270 *bears hard:* resents.   272 *estimation:*
conjecture.

Of that occasion that shall bring it on.
    HOTSPUR. I smell it. Upon my life, it will do well.
    NORTHUMBERLAND. Before the game 's afoot, thou still let'st slip.
    HOTSPUR. Why, it cannot choose but be a noble plot:
And then the power of Scotland and of York,   280
To join with Mortimer, ha?
    WORCESTER.   And so they shall.
    HOTSPUR. In faith, it is exceedingly well aim'd.
    WORCESTER. And 't is no little reason bids us speed,
To save our heads by raising of a head;
For, bear ourselves as even as we can,   285
The King will always think him in our debt,
And think we think ourselves unsatisfied,
Till he hath found a time to pay us home.
And see already how he doth begin
To make us strangers to his looks of love.   290
    HOTSPUR. He does, he does. We'll be reveng'd on him.
    WORCESTER. Cousin, farewell! No further go in this
Than I by letters shall direct your course.
When time is ripe, which will be suddenly,
I'll steal to Glendower and Lord Mortimer;   295
Where you and Douglas and our powers at once,
As I will fashion it, shall happily meet,
To bear our fortunes in our own strong arms,
Which now we hold at much uncertainty.
    NORTHUMBERLAND. Farewell, good brother! We shall thrive, I trust.   300
    HOTSPUR. Uncle, adieu! O, let the hours be short
Till fields and blows and groans applaud our sport!   (*Exeunt.*)

ACT II/1   Rochester. An inn yard.

(*Enter a* CARRIER *with a lantern in his hand.*)
    FIRST CARRIER. Heigh-ho! an it be not four by the day, I'll be hanged.
Charles' wain is over the new chimney, and yet our horse not packed.
What, ostler!
    OSTLER [*within*]. Anon, anon.
    FIRST CARRIER. I prithee, Tom, beat Cut's saddle, put a few flocks in the   5
point: the poor jade is wrung in the withers out of all cess.
    (*Enter another* CARRIER.)

---

278 *thou still let'st slip:* you always release the hunting dogs too early.   284 *head:* army.
288 *home:* in full.   294 *suddenly:* soon.

1 *carrier:* porter.   2 *Charles' wain:* the Big Dipper.   3 *ostler:* stable attendant.   4 *Anon:*
right away.   5 *flocks:* tufts of wool.   6 *jade:* horse; *out of all cess:* beyond measure.

SECOND CARRIER. Peas and beans are as dank here as a dog, and that is the next way to give poor jades the bots: this house is turned upside down since Robin Ostler died.

FIRST CARRIER. Poor fellow, never joyed since the price of oats rose; it was the death of him.

SECOND CARRIER. I think this be the most villanous house in all London road for fleas: I am stung like a tench.

FIRST CARRIER. Like a tench! by the mass, there is ne'er a king christen could be better bit than I have been since the first cock.

SECOND CARRIER. Why, they will allow us ne'er a jordan, and then we leak in your chimney; and your chamber-lye breeds fleas like a loach.

FIRST CARRIER. What, ostler! come away and be hanged! Come away.

SECOND CARRIER. I have a gammon of bacon and two razes of ginger, to be delivered as far as Charing Cross.

FIRST CARRIER. God's body! the turkeys in my pannier are quite starved. What, ostler! A plague on thee! hast thou never an eye in thy head? Canst not hear? An 't were not as good deed as drink, to break the pate on thee, I am a very villain. Come, and be hanged! Hast no faith in thee?

(*Enter* GADSHILL.)

GADSHILL. Good morrow, carriers. What's o'clock?

FIRST CARRIER. I think it be two o'clock.

GADSHILL. I prithee, lend me thy lantern, to see my gelding in the stable.

FIRST CARRIER. Nay, by God, soft, I know a trick worth two of that, i' faith.

GADSHILL. I pray thee, lend me thine.

SECOND CARRIER. Ay, when? canst tell? Lend me thy lantern, quoth he? Marry, I'll see thee hanged first.

GADSHILL. Sirrah carrier, what time do you mean to come to London?

SECOND CARRIER. Time enough to go to bed with a candle, I warrant thee. Come, neighbour Mugs, we'll call up the gentlemen: they will along with company, for they have great charge.   (*Exeunt* CARRIERS.)

(*Enter* CHAMBERLAIN.)

GADSHILL. What, ho! chamberlain!

CHAMBERLAIN. At hand, quoth pick-purse.

GADSHILL. That's even as fair as—at hand, quoth the chamberlain; for thou variest no more from picking of purses than giving direction doth from labouring; thou lay'st the plot how.

CHAMBERLAIN. Good morrow, Master Gadshill. It holds current that I told you yesternight: there's a franklin in the wild of Kent hath brought three hundred marks with him in gold. I heard him tell it to one of his

7 *Peas and beans:* used for fodder. 8 *next:* quickest; *bots:* worms. 13 *tench:* a fish with red spots resembling flea-bites. 14 *christen:* Christian. 16 *jordan:* chamber-pot. 17 *chamber-lye:* urine; *loach:* a prolific variety of fish. 19 *gammon of bacon:* ham; *razes:* roots. 21 *pannier:* basket. 23 *pate:* head. 36 *charge:* possessions. 41 *lay'st the plot:* give the directions. 43 *franklin:* landowner. 44 *three hundred marks:* about £200.

company last night at supper; a kind of auditor; one that hath abundance   45
of charge too, God knows what. They are up already, and call for eggs and
butter: they will away presently.

GADSHILL. Sirrah, if they meet not with Saint Nicholas' clerks, I'll give
thee this neck.

CHAMBERLAIN. No, I'll none of it. I pray thee, keep that for the hang-   50
man; for I know thou worshippest Saint Nicholas as truly as a man of
falsehood may.

GADSHILL. What talkest thou to me of the hangman? If I hang, I'll make
a fat pair of gallows; for if I hang, old Sir John hangs with me, and
thou knowest he is no starveling. Tut! there are other Troians that thou   55
dream'st not of, the which for sport sake are content to do the profession
some grace, that would, if matters should be looked into, for their own
credit sake, make all whole. I am joined with no foot land-rakers, no long-
staff sixpenny strikers, none of these mad mustachio purple-hued malt-
worms; but with nobility and tranquillity, burgomasters and great oneyers;   60
such as can hold in, such as will strike sooner than speak, and speak sooner
than drink, and drink sooner than pray; and yet, 'zounds, I lie; for they
pray continually to their saint, the commonwealth; or rather, not pray to
her, but prey on her, for they ride up and down on her and make her their
boots.   65

CHAMBERLAIN. What, the commonwealth their boots? Will she hold
out water in foul way?

GADSHILL. She will, she will; justice hath liquored her. We steal as in a
castle, cocksure; we have the receipt of fern-seed, we walk invisible.

CHAMBERLAIN. Nay, by my faith, I think you are more beholding to the   70
night than to fern-seed for your walking invisible.

GADSHILL. Give me thy hand: thou shalt have a share in our purchase, as
I am a true man.

CHAMBERLAIN. Nay, rather let me have it as you are a false thief.

GADSHILL. Go to; *homo* is a common name to all men. Bid the ostler   75
bring my gelding out of the stable. Farewell, you muddy knave.

(*Exeunt.*)

ACT II/2   The highway near Gadshill.

(*Enter* PRINCE HENRY *and* POINS.)

POINS. Come, shelter, shelter! I have removed Falstaff's horse, and he
frets like a gummed velvet.   [*They step back.*]

PRINCE. Stand close.

---

47 *presently:* right away.   48 *Saint Nicholas' clerks:* highwaymen.   55 *Troians:* thieves.
58 *foot land-rakers:* footpads.   59 *sixpenny strikers:* thieves who knocked their victims
down with a staff; *malt-worms:* alcoholics.   60 *oneyers:* officials.   66 *boots:* booty.   67
foul way: wet road.   68 *as in a castle:* without danger.   69 *fern-seed:* it was supposed to
make one invisible.   72 *purchase:* gains.

2 *frets:* is irritated; *gummed velvet:* velvet stiffened with gum.

(*Enter* FALSTAFF.)

FALSTAFF. Poins! Poins, and be hanged! Poins!

PRINCE [*coming forward*]. Peace, ye fat-kidneyed rascal! what a bawl-   5
ing dost thou keep!

FALSTAFF. Where's Poins, Hal?

PRINCE. He is walked up to the top of the hill; I'll go seek him.

[*Withdraws.*]

FALSTAFF. I am accursed to rob in that thief's company: the rascal hath
removed my horse and tied him I know not where. If I travel but four   10
foot by the squire further afoot, I shall break my wind. Well, I doubt not
but to die a fair death for all this, if I scape hanging for killing that rogue.
I have forsworn his company hourly any time this two and twenty years,
and yet I am bewitched with the rogue's company. If the rascal have not
given me medicines to make me love him, I'll be hanged. It could not be   15
else; I have drunk medicines. Poins! Hal! a plague upon you both! Bardolph! Peto! I'll starve ere I'll rob a foot further. An 't were not as good
a deed as drink, to turn true man and to leave these rogues, I am the veriest
varlet that ever chewed with a tooth. Eight yards of uneven ground is three
score and ten miles afoot with me; and the stony-hearted villains know it   20
well enough. A plague upon it when thieves cannot be true one to another!
[*They whistle.*] Whew! A plague upon you all! Give me my horse, you
rogues; give me my horse, and be hanged!

PRINCE [*coming forward*]. Peace ye fat-guts! lie down: lay thine ear
close to the ground and list if thou canst hear the tread of travellers.   25

FALSTAFF. Have you any levers to lift me up again, being down?
'Sblood, I'll not bear mine own flesh so far afoot again for all the coin in
thy father's exchequer. What a plague mean ye to colt me thus?

PRINCE. Thou liest; thou art not colted, thou art uncolted.

FALSTAFF. I prithee, good Prince Hal, help me to my horse, good king's   30
son.

PRINCE. Out, ye rogue! shall I be your ostler?

FALSTAFF. Hang thyself in thine own heir-apparent garters! If I be ta'en,
I'll peach for this. An I have not ballads made on you all and sung to
filthy tunes, let a cup of sack be my poison. When a jest is so forward,   35
and afoot too! I hate it.

(*Enter* GADSHILL, BARDOLPH, *and* PETO.)

GADSHILL. Stand.

FALSTAFF. So I do, against my will.

POINS [*coming forward*]. O, 't is our setter; I know his voice. Bardolph,
what news?   40

BARDOLPH. Case ye, case ye; on with your vizards: there's money of the
King's coming down the hill; 't is going to the King's exchequer.

---

11 *squire*: a foot-long rule.   15 *medicines*: love potions.   19 *varlet*: rogue.   28 *colt*: trick.
33 *ta'en*: arrested.   34 *peach*: inform.   39 *setter*: a scout for thieves.   41 *case ye*:
conceal yourselves.

FALSTAFF. You lie, ye rogue; 't is going to the King's tavern.

GADSHILL. There's enough to make us all.

FALSTAFF. To be hanged.   45

PRINCE. Sirs, you four shall front them in the narrow lane; Ned Poins and I will walk lower: if they scape from your encounter, then they light on us.

PETO. How many be there of them?

GADSHILL. Some eight or ten.   50

FALSTAFF. 'Zounds, will they not rob us?

PRINCE. What, a coward, Sir John Paunch?

FALSTAFF. Indeed, I am not John of Gaunt, your grandfather; but yet no coward, Hal.

PRINCE. Well, we leave that to the proof.   55

POINS. Sirrah Jack, thy horse stands behind the hedge; when thou need'st him, there thou shalt find him. Farewell, and stand fast.

FALSTAFF. Now cannot I strike him, if I should be hanged.

PRINCE [aside]. Ned, where are our disguises?

POINS [aside]. Here, hard by: stand close.   60

(Exeunt PRINCE and POINS.)

FALSTAFF. Now, my masters, happy man be his dole, say I: every man to his business.

(Enter the TRAVELLERS.)

FIRST TRAVELLER. Come, neighbour; the boy shall lead our horses down the hill: we'll walk afoot a while, and ease our legs.

THIEVES. Stand!   65

TRAVELLERS. Jesus bless us!

FALSTAFF. Strike; down with them! Cut the villains' throats! Ah! whoreson caterpillars! bacon-fed knaves! they hate us youth. Down with them! Fleece them!

TRAVELLERS. O, we are undone, both we and ours for ever!   70

FALSTAFF. Hang ye, gorbellied knaves, are ye undone? No, ye fat chuffs; I would your store were here! On, bacons, on! What, ye knaves! young men must live. You are grandjurors, are ye? We'll jure ye, faith.

[Here they rob the travellers and bind them.]

(Exeunt.)

(Re-enter PRINCE HENRY and POINS in buckram suits.)

PRINCE. The thieves have bound the true men. Now, could thou and I rob the thieves and go merrily to London, it would be argument for a   75 week, laughter for a month, and a good jest for ever.

POINS. Stand close; I hear them coming.

(Enter the THIEVES again.)

FALSTAFF. Come, my masters, let us share, and then to horse before day.

---

61 dole: fate.   71 gorbellied: big-bellied.   72 chuffs: misers; your store: all your wealth; bacons: fat men.   73 grandjurors: wealthy citizens.   75 argument: a topic of discussion.

An the Prince and Poins be not two arrant cowards, there's no equity stir-
ring. There's no more valour in that Poins than in a wild-duck.   80
PRINCE. Your money!
POINS. Villains!

> [*As they are sharing, the* PRINCE *and* POINS *set upon
> them; they all run away; and* FALSTAFF, *after a blow or
> two, runs away too, leaving the booty behind them.*]

PRINCE. Got with much ease. Now merrily to horse.
The thieves are all scatter'd and possess'd with fear
So strongly that they dare not meet each other;   85
Each takes his fellow for an officer.
Away, good Ned. Falstaff sweats to death,
And lards the lean earth as he walks along.
Were't not for laughing, I should pity him.
POINS. How the rogue roar'd!   90

(Exeunt.)

ACT II/3   Warkworth Castle.

(*Enter* HOTSPUR, *alone, reading a letter.*)
HOTSPUR. "But, for mine own part, my lord, I could be well contented
to be there, in respect of the love I bear your house." He could be contented: why is he not, then? In respect of the love he bears our house: he
shows in this, he loves his own barn better than he loves our house. Let
me see some more. "The purpose you undertake is dangerous;"—why,   5
that's certain. 'T is dangerous to take a cold, to sleep, to drink; but I tell
you, my lord fool, out of this nettle, danger, we pluck this flower, safety.
"The purpose you undertake is dangerous; the friends you have named
uncertain; the time itself unsorted; and your whole plot too light for the
counterpoise of so great an opposition." Say you so, say you so? I say unto   10
you again, you are a shallow, cowardly hind, and you lie. What a lack-brain
is this! By the Lord, our plot is a good plot as ever was laid; our friends
true and constant: a good plot, good friends, and full of expectation; an
excellent plot, very good friends. What a frosty-spirited rogue is this!
Why, my Lord of York commends the plot and the general course of the   15
action. 'Zounds, an I were now by this rascal, I could brain him with his
lady's fan. Is there not my father, my uncle, and myself? Lord Edmund
Mortimer, my Lord of York, and Owen Glendower? Is there not besides
the Douglas? Have I not all their letters to meet me in arms by the ninth
of the next month? and are they not some of them set forward already?   20
What a pagan rascal is this! an infidel! Ha! you shall see now in very sin-

---

79 *arrant:* thorough; *equity:* fairness.

2 *in respect of:* because of; *house:* family.   9 *unsorted:* inappropriate.   11 *hind:* peasant.
21 *pagan:* lacking faith.

cerity of fear and cold heart, will he to the King and lay open all our proceedings. O, I could divide myself and go to buffets, for moving such a dish of skim-milk with so honourable an action! Hang him! let him tell the King; we are prepared. I will set forward tonight.   25

(*Enter* HOTSPUR'S *wife*.)

How now, Kate! I must leave you within these two hours.

LADY PERCY. O, my good lord, why are you thus alone?
For what offence have I this fortnight been
A banish'd woman from my Harry's bed?
Tell me, sweet lord, what is 't that takes from thee   30
Thy stomach, pleasure, and thy golden sleep?
Why dost thou bend thine eyes upon the earth,
And start so often when thou sit'st alone?
Why hast thou lost the fresh blood in thy cheeks,
And given my treasures and my rights of thee   35
To thick-ey'd musing and curst melancholy?
In thy faint slumbers I by thee have watch'd,
And heard thee murmur tales of iron wars;
Speak terms of manage to thy bounding steed;
Cry "Courage! to the field!" And thou hast talk'd   40
Of sallies and retires, of trenches, tents,
Of palisadoes, frontiers, parapets,
Of basilisks, of cannon, culverin,
Of prisoners' ransom, and of soldiers slain,
And all the currents of a heady fight.   45
Thy spirit within thee hath been so at war
And thus hath so bestirr'd thee in thy sleep,
That beads of sweat have stood upon thy brow,
Like bubbles in a late-disturbed stream;
And in thy face strange motions have appear'd,   50
Such as we see when men restrain their breath
On some great sudden hest. O, what portents are these?
Some heavy business hath my lord in hand,
And I must know it, else he loves me not.

HOTSPUR. What, ho!

(*Enter* SERVANT.)

Is Gilliams with the packet gone?   55

SERVANT. He is, my lord, an hour ago.

HOTSPUR. Hath Butler brought those horses from the sheriff?

SERVANT. One horse, my lord, he brought even now.

HOTSPUR. What horse? A roan, a crop-ear, is it not?

---

23 *buffets*: blows of the fist. 31 *stomach*: appetite. 39 *manage*: horsemanship. 42 *palisadoes*: stakes driven into the ground to stop advancing soldiers; *frontiers*: defensive walls. 43 *basilisks*: heavy cannon; *culverin*: light cannon. 52 *hest*: command. 53 *heavy*: important.

SERVANT. It is, my lord.

HOTSPUR.   That roan shall be my throne   60
Well, I will back him straight. O *Esperance!*
Bid Butler lead him forth into the park.   (*Exit* SERVANT.)

LADY PERCY. But hear you, my lord.

HOTSPUR. What say'st thou, my lady?

LADY PERCY. What is it carries you away?   65

HOTSPUR. Why, my horse, my love, my horse.

LADY PERCY. Out, you mad-headed ape!
A weasel hath not such a deal of spleen
As you are toss'd with. In faith,
I'll know your business, Harry, that I will.   70
I fear my brother Mortimer doth stir
About his title, and hath sent for you
To line his enterprise; but if you go,—

HOTSPUR. So far afoot, I shall be weary, love.

LADY PERCY. Come, come, you paraquito, answer me   75
Directly unto this question that I ask.
In faith, I'll break thy little finger, Harry,
An if thou wilt not tell me all things true.

HOTSPUR. Away,
Away, you trifler! Love! I love thee not,   80
I care not for thee, Kate: this is no world
To play with mammets and to tilt with lips:
We must have bloody noses and crack'd crowns,
And pass them current too. God's me, my horse!
What say'st thou, Kate? What would'st thou have with me?   85

LADY PERCY. Do you not love me? Do you not, indeed?
Well, do not then; for since you love me not,
I will not love myself. Do you not love me?
Nay, tell me if you speak in jest or no.

HOTSPUR. Come, wilt thou see me ride?   90
And when I am a-horseback, I will swear
I love thee infinitely. But hark you, Kate;
I must not have you henceforth question me
Whither I go, nor reason whereabout.
Whither I must, I must; and, to conclude,   95
This evening must I leave you, gentle Kate.
I know you wise; but yet no farther wise
Than Harry Percy's wife. Constant you are,
But yet a woman; and for secrecy,
No lady closer; for I well believe   100

---

61 *Esperance!*: Hotspur's battle cry. It is the French word for "hope." 68 *spleen*: bad
temper. 73 *To line*: to support. 75 *paraquito*: a small parrot. 82 *mammets*: dolls;
tilt: combat.

Thou wilt not utter what thou dost not know;
And so far will I trust thee, gentle Kate.

LADY PERCY. How! so far?

HOTSPUR. Not an inch further. But hark you, Kate:
Whither I go, thither shall you go too;   105
To-day will I set forth, to-morrow you.
Will this content you, Kate?

LADY PERCY.   It must of force.   (*Exeunt.*)

ACT II/4   The Boar's-Head Tavern, Eastcheap.

(*Enter the* PRINCE *and* POINS.)

PRINCE. Ned, prithee, come out of that fat room, and lend me thy hand
to laugh a little.

POINS. Where hast been, Hal?

PRINCE. With three or four loggerheads amongst three or four score
hogsheads. I have sounded the very base-string of humility. Sirrah, I am   5
sworn brother to a leash of drawers; and can call them all by their christen
names, as Tom, Dick, and Francis. They take it already upon their salvation, that though I be but Prince of Wales, yet I am the king of courtesy;
and tell me flatly I am no proud Jack, like Falstaff, but a Corinthian, a lad
of mettle, a good boy (by the Lord, so they call me), and when I am King   10
of England, I shall command all the good lads in Eastcheap. They call
drinking deep, dyeing scarlet; and when you breathe in your watering, they
cry "hem!" and bid you play it off. To conclude, I am so good a proficient
in one quarter of an hour, that I can drink with any tinker in his own
language during my life. I tell thee, Ned, thou hast lost much honour, that   15
thou wert not with me in this action. But, sweet Ned,—to sweeten which
name of Ned, I give thee this pennyworth of sugar, clapped even now into
my hand by an under-skinker, one that never spake other English in his
life than "Eight shillings and sixpence," and "You are welcome," with
this shrill addition, "Anon, anon, sir! Score a pint of bastard in the Half-   20
moon," or so. But, Ned, to drive away the time till Falstaff come, I prithee,
do thou stand in some by-room, while I question my puny drawer to what
end he gave me the sugar; and do thou never leave calling "Francis," that
his tale to me may be nothing but "Anon." Step aside, and I'll show thee
a precedent.   25

POINS. Francis!

107 *of force:* necessarily.

1 *fat room:* vat room.   4 *loggerheads:* numbskulls.   6 *drawers:* waiters.   9 *Corinthian:*
a man of spirit.   12 *breathe:* pause for breath; *watering:* drinking.   13 *play:* drink
18 *under-skinker:* waiter's assistant.   20 *bastard:* sweet Spanish wine; *Half-moon:* the
name of one of the rooms in the tavern.   25 *precedent:* example.

PRINCE. Thou art perfect.

POINS. Francis!   (*Exit* POINS.)

(*Enter* FRANCIS, *a drawer.*)

FRANCIS. Anon, anon, sir. Look down into the Pomgarnet, Ralph.

PRINCE. Come hither, Francis.   30

FRANCIS. My lord?

PRINCE. How long hast thou to serve, Francis?

FRANCIS. Forsooth, five years, and as much as to—

POINS [*within*]. Francis!

FRANCIS. Anon, anon, sir.   35

PRINCE. Five year! by 'r lady, a long lease for the clinking of pewter. But, Francis, darest thou be so valiant as to play the coward with thy indenture and show it a fair pair of heels and run from it?

FRANCIS. O Lord, sir, I'll be sworn upon all the books in England, I could find in my heart—   40

POINS [*within*]. Francis!

FRANCIS. Anon, sir.

PRINCE. How old art thou, Francis?

FRANCIS. Let me see—about Michaelmas next I shall be—

POINS [*within*]. Francis!   45

FRANCIS. Anon, sir. Pray, stay a little, my lord.

PRINCE. Nay, but hark you, Francis: for the sugar thou gavest me, 't was a pennyworth, was 't not?

FRANCIS. O Lord, I would it had been two!

PRINCE. I will give thee for it a thousand pound. Ask me when thou   50
wilt, and thou shalt have it.

POINS [*within*]. Francis!

FRANCIS. Anon, anon.

PRINCE. Anon, Francis? No, Francis; but to-morrow, Francis; or Francis, o' Thursday; or indeed, Francis, when thou wilt. But, Francis!   55

FRANCIS. My lord?

PRINCE. Wilt thou rob this leathern-jerkin crystal-button, not-pated, agate-ring, puke-stocking, caddis-garter, smooth-tongue, Spanish-pouch,—

FRANCIS. O Lord, sir, who do you mean?

PRINCE. Why, then, your brown bastard is your only drink; for look   60
you, Francis, your white canvas doublet will sully. In Barbary, sir, it cannot come to so much.

FRANCIS. What, sir?

POINS [*within*]. Francis!

29 *Pomgarnet:* Pomegranate, the name of another room.   32 *serve:* complete his apprenticeship.   37 *indenture:* agreement of apprenticeship.   57 *leathern-jerkin:* leather-coated;
not-pated: short-haired.   58 *puke:* dark in color; *caddis-garter:* cheap garters made
of wool.   61 *doublet:* jacket; *In Barbary:* the sugar came from Barbary.

PRINCE. Away, you rogue! dost thou not hear them call?   65
> [*Here they both call him; the drawer stands
> amazed, not knowing which way to go.*]

(*Enter* VINTNER.)

VINTNER. What, stand'st thou still, and hear'st such a calling? Look to the guests within. [*Exit* FRANCIS.] My lord, old Sir John with half-a-dozen more are at the door; shall I let them in?

PRINCE. Let them alone a while, and then open the door. [*Exit* VINTNER.] Poins!   70

POINS [*within*]. Anon, anon, sir.

(*Re-enter* POINS.)

PRINCE. Sirrah, Falstaff and the rest of the thieves are at the door; shall we be merry?

POINS. As merry as crickets, my lad. But hark ye; what cunning match have you made with this jest of the drawer? Come, what's the issue?   75

PRINCE. I am now of all humours that have showed themselves humours since the old days of goodman Adam to the pupil age of this present twelve o'clock at midnight.

(*Re-enter* FRANCIS.)

What's o'clock, Francis?

FRANCIS. Anon, anon, sir.   (*Exit.*)   80

PRINCE. That ever this fellow should have fewer words than a parrot, and yet the son of a woman! His industry is upstairs and downstairs; his eloquence the parcel of a reckoning. I am not yet of Percy's mind, the Hotspur of the north; he that kills me some six or seven dozen of Scots at a breakfast, washes his hands, and says to his wife, "Fie upon this quiet life!   85 I want work." "O my sweet Harry," says she, "how many hast thou killed to-day?" "Give my roan horse a drench," says he; and answers, "Some fourteen," an hour after; "a trifle, a trifle." I prithee, call in Falstaff. I'll play Percy, and that damned brawn shall play Dame Mortimer his wife. "Rivo!" says the drunkard. Call in ribs, call in tallow.   90

(*Enter* FALSTAFF, GADSHILL, BARDOLPH, *and* PETO;
FRANCIS *following with wine.*)

POINS. Welcome, Jack! Where hast thou been?

FALSTAFF. A plague of all cowards, I say, and a vengeance too! marry, and amen! Give me a cup of sack, boy. Ere I lead this life long, I'll sew nether stocks, and mend them and foot them too. A plague of all cowards! Give me a cup of sack, rogue. Is there no virtue extant?   [*He drinks.*]   95

PRINCE. Didst thou never see Titan kiss a dish of butter, pitiful-hearted Titan, that melted at the sweet tale of the sun? If thou didst, then behold that compound.

---

74 *match:* game.   77 *pupil age:* the age of youth.   83 *the parcel of a reckoning:* an item on a bill.   87 *drench:* dose of medicine.   89 *brawn:* mass of flesh.   90 *"Rivo":* a drinking cry.   94 *nether stocks:* stockings.   96 *Titan:* the sun.   98 *that compound:* melted butter.

FALSTAFF. You rogue, here's lime in this sack too: there is nothing but roguery to be found in villanous man; yet a coward is worse than a cup of   100
sack with lime in it. A villanous coward! Go thy ways, old Jack; die when thou wilt, if manhood, good manhood, be not forgot upon the face of the earth, then am I a shotten herring. There lives not three good men un-hanged in England; and one of them is fat and grows old. God help the while! a bad world, I say. I would I were a weaver; I could sing psalms or   105
anything. A plague of all cowards, I say still.

PRINCE. How now, wool-sack! what mutter you?

FALSTAFF. A king's son! If I do not beat thee out of thy kingdom with a dagger of lath, and drive all thy subjects afore thee like a flock of wild-geese, I'll never wear hair on my face more. You Prince of Wales!   110

PRINCE. Why, you whoreson round man, what's the matter?

FALSTAFF. Are not you a coward? Answer me to that; and Poins there?

POINS. 'Zounds, ye fat paunch, an ye call me coward, by the Lord, I'll stab thee.

FALSTAFF. I call thee coward! I'll see thee damned ere I call thee   115
coward; but I would give a thousand pound I could run as fast as thou canst. You are straight enough in the shoulders; you care not who sees your back: call you that backing of your friends? A plague upon such back-ing! give me them that will face me. Give me a cup of sack. I am a rogue, if I drunk to-day.   120

PRINCE. O villain! thy lips are scarce wiped since thou drunk'st last.

FALSTAFF. All's one for that. [*He drinks.*] A plague of all cowards, still say I.

PRINCE. What's the matter?

FALSTAFF. What's the matter? There be four of us here have ta'en a   125
thousand pound this day morning.

PRINCE. Where is it, Jack? where is it?

FALSTAFF. Where is it? Taken from us it is; a hundred upon poor four of us.

PRINCE. What, a hundred, man?   130

FALSTAFF. I am a rogue, if I were not at half-sword with a dozen of them two hours together. I have scaped by miracle. I am eight times thrust through the doublet, four through the hose; my buckler cut through and through; my sword hack'd like a hand-saw—*ecce signum!* I never dealt better since I was a man; all would not do. A plague of all cowards! Let   135
them speak; if they speak more or less than truth, they are villains and the sons of darkness.

PRINCE. Speak, sirs; how was it?

---

99 *lime:* an adulterant put into wine to improve the strength or color. 103 *shotten:* without roe, therefore thin. 105 *a weaver:* weavers were reputed to be good singers. 109 *a dagger of lath:* a wooden dagger. 131 *at half-sword:* in close combat. 132 *scaped:* escaped. 133 *hose:* breeches; *buckler:* shield. 134 *ecce signum:* behold the evidence; *dealt:* fought.

GADSHILL. We four set upon some dozen—

FALSTAFF. Sixteen at least, my lord.   140

GADSHILL. And bound them.

PETO. No, no, they were not bound.

FALSTAFF. You rogue, they were bound, every man of them, or I am a
Jew else, an Ebrew Jew.

GADSHILL. As we were sharing, some six or seven fresh men set upon   145
us—

FALSTAFF. And unbound the rest, and then come in the other.

PRINCE. What, fought you with them all?

FALSTAFF. All! I know not what you call all; but if I fought not with
fifty of them, I am a bunch of radish. If there were not two or three and   150
fifty upon poor old Jack, then am I no two-legg'd creature.

PRINCE. Pray God you have not murdered some of them.

FALSTAFF. Nay, that's past praying for; I have peppered two of them. Two
I am sure I have paid, two rogues in buckram suits. I tell thee what, Hal, if I
tell thee a lie, spit in my face, call me horse. Thou knowest my old ward: here   155
I lay, and thus I bore my point. Four rogues in buckram let drive at me—

PRINCE. What, four? Thou saidst but two even now.

FALSTAFF. Four, Hal; I told thee four.

POINS. Aye, aye, he said four.

FALSTAFF. These four came all a-front, and mainly thrust at me. I made   160
me no more ado but took all their seven points in my target, thus.

PRINCE. Seven? why, there were but four even now.

FALSTAFF. In buckram?

POINS. Ay, four, in buckram suits.

FALSTAFF. Seven, by these hilts, or I am a villain else.   165

PRINCE. Prithee, let him alone; we shall have more anon.

FALSTAFF. Dost thou hear me, Hal?

PRINCE. Ay, and mark thee too, Jack.

FALSTAFF. Do so, for it is worth the listening to. These nine in buckram
that I told thee of—   170

PRINCE. So, two more already.

FALSTAFF. Their points being broken,—

POINS. Down fell their hose.

FALSTAFF. Began to give me ground; but I followed me close, came in
foot and hand, and with a thought seven of the eleven I paid.   175

PRINCE. O monstrous! eleven buckram men grown out of two!

FALSTAFF. But, as the devil would have it, three misbegotten knaves in
Kendal green came at my back and let drive at me; for it was so dark, Hal,
that thou couldst not see thy hand.

PRINCE. These lies are like their father that begets them; gross as a   180

---

154 *paid:* killed; *buckram:* a stiff cotton material.   155 *ward:* a guard position in fencing.
160 *mainly:* violently.   161 *target:* shield.   172 *points:* this word meant both the point
of a sword and the laces that held up the hose.

mountain, open, palpable. Why thou clay-brained guts, thou knotty-pated fool, thou whoreson, obscene, greasy tallow-catch,—

FALSTAFF. What, art thou mad? are thou mad? Is not the truth the truth?

PRINCE. Why, how couldst thou know these men in Kendal green, when it was so dark thou couldst not see thy hand? Come, tell us your reason; what say'st thou to this? 185

POINS. Come, your reason, Jack, your reason.

FALSTAFF. What, upon compulsion? 'Zounds, an I were at the strappado, or all the racks in the world, I would not tell you on compulsion. Give you a reason on compulsion! If reasons were as plenty as blackberries, I would give no man a reason upon compulsion, I. 190

PRINCE. I'll be no longer guilty of this sin. This sanguine coward, this bed-presser, this horseback-breaker, this huge hill of flesh,—

FALSTAFF. 'Sblood, you starveling, you elf-skin, you dried neat's tongue, you bull's pizzle, you stockfish! O for breath to utter what is like thee! you tailor's-yard, you sheath, you bow-case, you vile standing-tuck,— 195

PRINCE. Well, breathe a while, and then to it again; and when thou hast tired thyself in base comparisons, hear me speak but this:—

POINS. Mark, Jack. 200

PRINCE. We two saw you four set on four and bound them, and were masters of their wealth. Mark now, how a plain tale shall put you down. Then did we two set on you four; and, with a word, out-faced you from your prize, and have it, yea, and can show it you here in the house; and, Falstaff, you carried your guts away as nimbly, with as quick dexterity, and roared for mercy, and still run and roared, as ever I heard bull-calf. What a slave art thou, to hack thy sword as thou hast done, and then say it was in fight! What trick, what device, what starting-hole, canst thou now find out to hide thee from this open and apparent shame? 205

POINS. Come, let's hear, Jack; what trick hast thou now? 210

FALSTAFF. By the Lord, I knew ye as well as he that made ye. Why, hear you, my masters: was it for me to kill the heir-apparent? Should I turn upon the true prince? Why, thou knowest I am as valiant as Hercules; but beware instinct; the lion will not touch the true prince. Instinct is a great matter; I was now a coward on instinct. I shall think the better of myself and thee during my life; I for a valiant lion, and thou for a true prince. But, by the Lord, lads, I am glad you have the money. Hostess, clap to the doors! Watch to-night, pray to-morrow. Gallants, lads, boys, heart of gold, all the titles of good fellowship come to you! What, shall we be merry? Shall we have a play extempore? 215

220

---

181 *knotty-pated:* thick-headed.   182 *tallow-catch:* lump of tallow.   189, 190 *strappado, racks:* forms of torture.   191 *reasons:* the word was pronounced like "raisins" and is used here to form a pun in connection with "blackberries."   193 *sanguine:* daring.   196 *stockfish:* dried codfish.   197 *standing-tuck:* rapier standing on end.   203 *out-faced:* frightened.   208 *starting-hole:* a hole used as a refuge by hunted animals.   220 *extempore:* impromptu.

PRINCE. Content; and the argument shall be thy running away.

FALSTAFF. Ah, no more of that, Hal, an thou lovest me!

(*Enter* HOSTESS.)

HOSTESS. O Jesu, my lord the Prince!

PRINCE. How now, my lady the hostess! what say'st thou to me?

HOSTESS. Marry, my lord, there is a nobleman of the court at door 225
would speak with you. He says he comes from your father.

PRINCE. Give him as much as will make him a royal man, and send him
back again to my mother.

FALSTAFF. What manner of man is he?

HOSTESS. An old man. 230

FALSTAFF. What doth Gravity out of his bed at midnight? Shall I give
him his answer?

PRINCE. Prithee, do, Jack.

FALSTAFF. Faith, and I'll send him packing. (*Exit.*)

PRINCE. Now, sirs, by 'r lady, you fought fair; so did you, Peto; so did 235
you, Bardolph. You are lions too, you ran away upon instinct, you will not
touch the true prince; no, fie!

BARDOLPH. Faith, I ran when I saw others run.

PRINCE. Tell me now in earnest, how came Falstaff's sword so hacked?

PETO. Why, he hacked it with his dagger, and said he would swear truth 240
out of England but he would make you believe it was done in fight, and
persuaded us to do the like.

BARDOLPH. Yea, and to tickle our noses with spear-grass to make them
bleed, and then to beslubber our garments with it and swear it was the
blood of true men. I did that I did not this seven year before, I blushed 245
to hear his monstrous devices.

PRINCE. O villain, thou stolest a cup of sack eighteen years ago, and wert
taken with the manner, and ever since thou hast blushed extempore. Thou
hadst fire and sword on thy side, and yet thou ran'st away; what instinct
hadst thou for it? 250

BARDOLPH. My lord, do you see these meteors? Do you behold these
exhalations? [*Pointing to his own face.*]

PRINCE. I do.

BARDOLPH. What think you they portend?

PRINCE. Hot livers and cold purses. 255

BARDOLPH. Choler, my lord, if rightly taken.

(*Re-enter* FALSTAFF.)

PRINCE. No, if rightly taken, halter. Here comes lean Jack, here comes

---

221 *argument:* subject. 227 *a royal man:* give him ten shillings (a royal). 248 *taken
with the manner:* caught in the act; *ever since thou hast blushed extempore:* Bardolph's
red face is a frequent source of wit in the play. 254 *portend:* meteors were supposed
to be omens. 255 *Hot livers and cold purses:* drunkenness and poverty. 256 *Choler:*
anger. 257 *taken:* arrested; *halter:* collar, punning on "choler."

bare-bone. How now, my sweet creature of bombast! How long is 't ago, Jack, since thou sawest thine own knee?

FALSTAFF. My own knee? When I was about thy years, Hal, I was not 260 an eagle's talon in the waist; I could have crept into any alderman's thumb-ring: a plague of sighing and grief! it blows a man up like a bladder. There's villanous news abroad: here was Sir John Bracy from your father; you must to the court in the morning. That same mad fellow of the north, Percy, and he of Wales that gave Amamon the bastinado and 265 made Lucifer cuckold and swore the devil his true liegeman upon the cross of a Welsh hook—what a plague call you him?

POINS. Owen Glendower.

FALSTAFF. Owen, Owen, the same; and his son-in-law Mortimer, and old Northumberland, and that sprightly Scot of Scots, Douglas, that runs 270 a-horseback up a hill perpendicular,—

PRINCE. He that rides at high speed and with his pistol kills a sparrow flying.

FALSTAFF. You have hit it.

PRINCE. So did he never the sparrow. 275

FALSTAFF. Well, that rascal hath good mettle in him; he will not run.

PRINCE. Why, what a rascal art thou then, to praise him so for running!

FALSTAFF. A-horseback, ye cuckoo; but afoot he will not budge a foot.

PRINCE. Yes, Jack, upon instinct.

FALSTAFF. I grant ye, upon instinct. Well, he is there too, and one Mur- 280 doch, and a thousand blue-caps more: Worcester is stolen away to-night: thy father's beard is turn'd white with the news: you may buy land now as cheap as stinking mackerel.

PRINCE. Why, then, it is like, if there come a hot June and this civil buffeting hold, we shall buy maidenheads as they buy hobnails, by the 285 hundreds.

FALSTAFF. By the mass, lad, thou say'st true; it is like we shall have good trading that way. But tell me, Hal, art not thou horrible afeard? Thou being heir-apparent, could the world pick thee out three such enemies again as that fiend Douglas, that spirit Percy, and that devil Glen- 290 dower? Art thou not horribly afraid? Doth not thy blood thrill at it?

PRINCE. Not a whit, i' faith; I lack some of thy instinct.

FALSTAFF. Well, thou wilt be horribly chid to-morrow when thou comest to thy father: if thou love me, practise an answer.

PRINCE. Do thou stand for my father, and examine me upon the par- 295 ticulars of my life.

FALSTAFF. Shall I? Content. This chair shall be my state, this dagger my sceptre, and this cushion my crown.

---

258 *bombast:* padding.   265 *Amamon:* a devil; *bastinado:* a beating.   267 *Welsh hook:* a long-handled weapon.   281 *blue-caps:* Scotsmen.   293 *chid:* scolded.   297 *state:* throne.

PRINCE. Thy state is taken for a joined-stool, thy golden sceptre for a leaden dagger, and thy precious rich crown for a pitiful bald crown!   300

FALSTAFF. Well, an the fire of grace be not quite out of thee, now shalt thou be moved. Give me a cup of sack to make my eyes look red, that it may be thought I have wept; for I must speak in passion, and I will do it in King Cambyses' vein.

PRINCE. Well, here is my leg.   305

FALSTAFF. And here is my speech. Stand aside, nobility.

HOSTESS. O Jesu, this is excellent sport, i' faith!

FALSTAFF. Weep not, sweet queen; for trickling tears are vain.

HOSTESS. O, the father, how he holds his countenance!

FALSTAFF. For God's sake, lords, convey my tristful queen;   310
For tears do stop the flood-gates of her eyes.

HOSTESS. O Jesu, he doth it as like one of these harlotry players as ever I see!

FALSTAFF. Peace, good pint-pot; peace, good tickle-brain. Harry, I do not only marvel where thou spendest thy time, but also how thou art ac-   315
companied; for though the camomile, the more it is trodden on the faster it grows, so youth, the more it is wasted the sooner it wears. That thou art my son, I have partly thy mother's word, partly my own opinion, but chiefly a villanous trick of thine eye and a foolish hanging of thy nether lip, that doth warrant me. If then thou be son to me, here lies the point;   320
why, being son to me, art thou so pointed at? Shall the blessed sun of heaven prove a micher and eat blackberries? a question not to be asked. Shall the son of England prove a thief and take purses? a question to be asked. There is a thing, Harry, which thou hast often heard of and it is known to many in our land by the name of pitch. This pitch, as ancient   325
writers do report, doth defile; so doth the company thou keepest: for, Harry, now I do not speak to thee in drink but in tears; not in pleasure but in passion, not in words only, but in woes also; and yet there is a virtuous man•whom I have often noted in thy company, but I know not his name.   330

PRINCE. What manner of man, an it like your Majesty?

FALSTAFF. A goodly portly man, i' faith, and a corpulent; of a cheerful look, a pleasing eye, and a most noble carriage; and, as I think, his age some fifty, or, by 'r lady, inclining to threescore; and now I remember me, his name is Falstaff. If that man should be lewdly given, he deceiveth   335
me; for, Harry, I see virtue in his looks. If then the tree may be known by the fruit, as the fruit by the tree, then, peremptorily I speak it, there is virtue in that Falstaff; him keep with, the rest banish. And tell me now, thou naughty varlet, tell me, where hast thou been this month?

304 *King Cambyses' vein:* a reference to a contemporary play.   305 *leg:* bow.   309 *holds his countenance:* keeps a straight face.   310 *convey:* lead away; *tristful:* sorrowing. 312 *harlotry:* vagabond.   314 *tickle-brain:* strong liquor.   322 *micher:* truant.

PRINCE. Dost thou speak like a king? Do thou stand for me, and I'll 340
play my father.

FALSTAFF. Depose me? If thou dost it half so gravely, so majestically,
both in word and matter, hang me up by the heels for a rabbit-sucker or
a poulter's hare.

PRINCE. Well, here I am set. 345

FALSTAFF. And here I stand: judge, my masters.

PRINCE. Now, Harry, whence come you?

FALSTAFF. My noble lord, from Eastcheap.

PRINCE. The complaints I hear of thee are grievous.

FALSTAFF. 'Sblood, my lord, they are false.—Nay, I'll tickle ye for a 350
young prince, i' faith.

PRINCE. Swearest thou, ungracious boy? Henceforth ne'er look on me.
Thou art violently carried away from grace: there is a devil haunts thee in
the likeness of an old fat man; a tun of man is thy companion. Why dost
thou converse with that trunk of humours, that bolting-hutch of beastli- 355
ness, that swollen parcel of dropsies, that huge bombard of sack, that
stuffed cloak-bag of guts, that roasted Manningtree ox with the pudding
in his belly, that reverend vice, that grey iniquity, that father ruffian, that
vanity in years? Wherein is he good, but to taste sack and drink it?
wherein neat and cleanly, but to carve a capon and eat it? wherein cun- 360
ning, but in craft? wherein crafty, but in villainy? wherein villanous, but
in all things? wherein worthy, but in nothing?

FALSTAFF. I would your Grace would take me with you: whom means
your Grace?

PRINCE. That villanous abominable misleader of youth, Falstaff, that old 365
white-bearded Satan.

FALSTAFF. My lord, the man I know.

PRINCE. I know thou dost.

FALSTAFF. But to say I know more harm in him than in myself, were to
say more than I know. That he is old, the more the pity, his white hairs 370
do witness it; but that he is, saving your reverence, a whoremaster, that I
utterly deny. If sack and sugar be a fault, God help the wicked! If to be old
and merry be a sin, then many an old host that I know is damned. If to
be fat be to be hated, then Pharaoh's lean kine are to be loved. No, my
good lord; banish Peto, banish Bardolph, banish Poins; but for sweet Jack 375
Falstaff, kind Jack Falstaff, true Jack Falstaff, valiant Jack Falstaff, and
therefore more valiant, being, as he is, old Jack Falstaff, banish not him
thy Harry's company, banish not him thy Harry's company. Banish plump
Jack, and banish all the world.

PRINCE. I do, I will. 380

---

343 *rabbit sucker:* young rabbit.   350 *tickle ye:* amuse you.   355 *bolting-hutch:* a large
flour bin.   356 *bombard:* leather bottle.   363 *take me with you:* make yourself clear
to me.   373 *host:* innkeeper.   374 *Pharaoh's lean kine:* a reference to the story of
Joseph and Pharaoh. See Genesis 41.

[A knocking heard.]   (*Exeunt* HOSTESS, FRANCIS, *and* BARDOLPH.)
                          (*Re-enter* BARDOLPH, *running.*)

BARDOLPH. O, my lord, my lord! the sheriff with a most monstrous watch is at the door.

FALSTAFF. Out, ye rogue! Play out the play; I have much to say in the behalf of that Falstaff.

                          (*Re-enter the* HOSTESS.)

HOSTESS. O Jesu, my lord, my lord!   385

PRINCE. Heigh, heigh! the devil rides upon a fiddlestick: what's the matter?

HOSTESS. The sheriff and all the watch are at the door; they are come to search the house. Shall I let them in?

FALSTAFF. Dost thou hear, Hal? Never call a true piece of gold a coun-   390
terfeit: thou art essentially mad, without seeming so.

PRINCE. And thou a natural coward, without instinct.

FALSTAFF. I deny your major: if you will deny the sheriff, so; if not, let him enter. If I become not a cart as well as another man, a plague on my bringing up! I hope I shall as soon be strangled with a halter as another.   395

PRINCE. Go, hide thee behind the arras; the rest walk up above. Now, my masters, for a true face and good conscience.

FALSTAFF. Both which I have had; but their date is out, and therefore I'll hide me.   [*Hides behind the arras.*]

PRINCE. Call in the sheriff.   (*Exeunt all except the* PRINCE *and* PETO.)   400
                     (*Enter* SHERIFF *and the* CARRIER.)
Now, master sheriff, what is your will with me?

SHERIFF. First, pardon me, my lord. A hue and cry
Hath followed certain men unto this house.

PRINCE. What men?

SHERIFF. One of them is well known, my gracious lord,   405
A gross fat man.

CARRIER.   As fat as butter.

PRINCE. The man, I do assure you, is not here,
For I myself at this time have employ'd him.
And, sheriff, I will engage my word to thee
That I will, by to-morrow dinner-time,   410
Send him to answer thee or any man
For anything he shall be charg'd withal.
And so let me entreat you leave the house.

SHERIFF. I will, my lord. There are two gentlemen
Have in this robbery lost three hundred marks.   415

PRINCE. It may be so: if he have robb'd these men,

---

381 *a most monstrous watch:* a large party of officers.   393 *major:* premise.   394 *If I become not a cart:* if I am not ornamental to the hangman's cart.   396 *arras:* curtains. 409 *engage:* promise.

He shall be answerable; and so farewell.

SHERIFF. Good night, my noble lord.

PRINCE. I think it is good morrow, is it not?

SHERIFF. Indeed, my lord, I think it be two o'clock.   420

(*Exeunt* SHERIFF *and* CARRIER.)

PRINCE. This oily rascal is known as well as Paul's. Go, call him forth.

PETO. Falstaff!—Fast asleep behind the arras, and snorting like a horse.

PRINCE. Hark, how hard he fetches breath. Search his pockets. [*He searches his pockets, and finds certain papers.*] What hast thou found?

PETO. Nothing but papers, my lord.   425

PRINCE. Let's see what they be. Read them.

PETO [*reads*].

Item, A capon .... 2s. 2d.

Item, Sauce .... 4d.

Item, Sack, two gallons .... 5s. 8d.

Item, Anchovies and sack after supper 2s. 6d.   430

Item, Bread .... ob.

PRINCE. O monstrous! but one half-pennyworth of bread to this intolerable deal of sack! What there is else, keep close; we'll read it at more advantage: there let him sleep till day. I'll to the court in the morning. We must all to the wars, and thy place shall be honourable. I'll procure this   435 fat rogue a charge of foot; and I know his death will be a march of twelve-score. The money shall be paid back again with advantage. Be with me betimes in the morning; and so, good morrow, Peto.

PETO. Good morrow, good my lord.   (*Exeunt.*)

ACT III/1   Bangor. The Archdeacon's house.

(*Enter* HOTSPUR, WORCESTER, LORD MORTIMER, *and* OWEN GLENDOWER.)

MORTIMER. These promises are fair, the parties sure,

And our induction full of prosperous hope.

HOTSPUR. Lord Mortimer, and cousin Glendower,

Will you sit down?

And uncle Worcester,—a plague upon it!   5

I have forgot the map.

GLENDOWER.   No, here it is.

Sit, cousin Percy; sit, good cousin Hotspur,

For by that name as oft as Lancaster

---

421 *Paul's:* St. Paul's Cathedral.   431 *ob.:* obolus, a halfpenny.   433 *at more advantage:* when it is more convenient.   436 *charge of foot:* a command in the infantry.   437 *twelve-score:* 240 yards; *advantage:* interest.   438 *betimes:* early.

2 *induction:* beginning.   8 *Lancaster:* the king.

Doth speak of you, his cheek looks pale and with
A rising sigh he wisheth you in heaven.   10
   HOTSPUR. And you in hell, as oft as he hears Owen Glendower spoke of.
   GLENDOWER. I cannot blame him: at my nativity
The front of heaven was full of fiery shapes,
Of burning cressets; and at my birth
The frame and huge foundation of the earth   15
Shak'd like a coward.
   HOTSPUR. Why, so it would have done at the same season, if your
mother's cat had but kittened, though yourself had never been born.
   GLENDOWER. I say the earth did shake when I was born.
   HOTSPUR. And I say the earth was not of my mind,   20
If you suppose as fearing you it shook.
   GLENDOWER. The heavens were all on fire, the earth did tremble.
   HOTSPUR. O, then the earth shook to see the heavens on fire,
And not in fear of your nativity.
Diseased nature oftentimes breaks forth   25
In strange eruptions; oft the teeming earth
Is with a kind of colic pinch'd and vex'd
By the imprisoning of unruly wind
Within her womb; which, for enlargement striving,
Shakes the old beldam earth, and topples down   30
Steeples and moss-grown towers. At your birth
Our grandam earth, having this distemperature,
In passion shook.
   GLENDOWER. Cousin, of many men
I do not bear these crossings. Give me leave
To tell you once again that at my birth   35
The front of heaven was full of fiery shapes,
The goats ran from the mountains, and the herds
Were strangely clamorous to the frighted fields.
These signs have mark'd me extraordinary;
And all the courses of my life do show   40
I am not in the roll of common men.
Where is he living, clipp'd in with the sea
That chides the banks of England, Scotland, Wales,
Which calls me pupil, or hath read to me?
And bring him out that is but woman's son   45
Can trace me in the tedious ways of art
And hold me pace in deep experiments.
   HOTSPUR. I think there's no man speaks better Welsh. I'll to dinner.

---

12 *nativity:* birth.   13 *front:* forehead.   14 *cressets:* lamps consisting of open bowls of
burning oil.   29 *womb:* stomach; *enlargement:* liberation.   30 *beldam:* grandmother.
32 *distemperature:* illness.   34 *crossings:* contradictions.   42 *clipp'd in:* enclosed.   44
read to: taught.   46 *trace:* follow; *art:* magic.   47 *hold me pace:* keep up with me.

MORTIMER. Peace, cousin Percy; you will make him mad.

GLENDOWER. I can call spirits from the vasty deep.   50

HOTSPUR. Why, so can I, or so can any man;
But will they come when you do call for them?

GLENDOWER. Why, I can teach you, cousin, to command
The devil.

HOTSPUR. And I can teach thee, coz, to shame the devil   55
By telling truth. "Tell truth and shame the devil."
If thou have power to raise him, bring him hither,
And I'll be sworn I have power to shame him hence.
O, while you live, tell truth and shame the devil!

MORTIMER. Come, come, no more of this unprofitable chat.   60

GLENDOWER. Three times hath Henry Bolingbroke made head
Against my power; thrice from the banks of Wye
And sandy-bottom'd Severn have I sent him
Bootless home and weather-beaten back.

HOTSPUR. Home without boots, and in foul weather too!   65
How scapes he agues, in the devil's name?

GLENDOWER. Come, here's the map. Shall we divide our right
According to our threefold order ta'en?

MORTIMER. The Archdeacon hath divided it
Into three limits very equally.   70
England, from Trent and Severn hitherto,
By south and east is to my part assign'd;
All westward, Wales beyond the Severn shore,
And all the fertile land within that bound,
To Owen Glendower; and, dear coz, to you   75
The remnant northward, lying off from Trent.
And our indentures tripartite are drawn;
Which being sealed interchangeably,
A business that this night may execute,
To-morrow, cousin Percy, you and I   80
And my good Lord of Worcester will set forth
To meet your father and the Scottish power,
As is appointed us, at Shrewsbury.
My father Glendower is not ready yet,
Nor shall we need his help these fourteen days.   85
Within that space you may have drawn together
Your tenants, friends, and neighbouring gentlemen.

GLENDOWER. A shorter time shall send me to you, lords;
And in my conduct shall your ladies come,
From whom you now must steal and take no leave,   90

---

55 *coz:* cousin. 61 *made head:* raised an army. 64 *Bootless:* unsuccessful. 66 *agues:* malaria. 68 *order:* agreement. 89 *in my conduct:* under my escort.

For there will be a world of water shed
Upon the parting of your wives and you.
   HOTSPUR. Methinks my moiety, north from Burton here,
In quantity equals not one of yours.
See how this river comes me cranking in,   95
And cuts me from the best of all my land
A huge half-moon, a monstrous cantle out.
I'll have the current in this place damm'd up;
And here the smug and silver Trent shall run
In a new channel, fair and evenly.   100
It shall not wind with such a deep indent,
To rob me of so rich a bottom here.
   GLENDOWER. Not wind? It shall, it must; you see it doth.
   MORTIMER. Yea, but
Mark how he bears his course, and runs me up   105
With like advantage on the other side;
Gelding the opposed continent as much
As on the other side it takes from you.
   WORCESTER. Yea, but a little charge will trench him here
And on this north side win this cape of land;   110
And then he runs straight and even.
   HOTSPUR. I'll have it so; a little charge will do it.
   GLENDOWER. I'll not have it alter'd.
   HOTSPUR.   Will not you?
   GLENDOWER. No, nor you shall not.
   HOTSPUR.   Who shall say me nay?
   GLENDOWER. Why, that will I.   115
   HOTSPUR. Let me not understand you, then; speak it in Welsh.
   GLENDOWER. I can speak English, lord, as well as you;
For I was train'd up in the English court;
Where, being but young, I framed to the harp
Many an English ditty lovely well   120
And gave the tongue a helpful ornament,
A virtue that was never seen in you.
   HOTSPUR. Marry,
And I am glad of it with all my heart.
I had rather be a kitten and cry mew   125
Than one of these same metre ballad-mongers;
I had rather hear a brazen canstick turn'd,
Or a dry wheel grate on the axle-tree;
And that would set my teeth nothing on edge,

---

93 *moiety:* portion. 95 *cranking:* bending. 97 *cantle:* piece. 99 *smug:* smooth. 102
bottom: valley. 107 *Gelding:* cutting a part of. 109 *charge:* expense; *trench:* make a
channel. 119 *framed:* composed. 121 *tongue:* language. 127 *canstick:* candlestick.

Nothing so much as mincing poetry.   130
'T is like the forc'd gait of a shuffling nag.
   GLENDOWER. Come, you shall have Trent turn'd.
   HOTSPUR. I do not care. I'll give thrice so much land
To any well-deserving friend;
But in the way of bargain, mark ye me,   135
I'll cavil on the ninth part of a hair.
Are the indentures drawn? Shall we be gone?
   GLENDOWER. The moon shines fair; you may away by night.
I'll haste the writer, and withal
Break with your wives of your departure hence.   140
I am afraid my daughter will run mad,
So much she doteth on her Mortimer.   (*Exit.*)
   MORTIMER. Fie, cousin Percy! how you cross my father!
   HOTSPUR. I cannot choose. Sometime he angers me
With telling me of the moldwarp and the ant,   145
Of the dreamer Merlin and his prophecies,
And of a dragon and a finless fish,
A clip-wing'd griffin and a moulten raven,
A couching lion and a ramping cat,
And such a deal of skimble-skamble stuff   150
As puts me from my faith. I tell you what:
He held me last night at least nine hours
In reckoning up the several devils' names
That were his lackeys. I cried "hum," and "well, go to,"
But mark'd him not a word. O, he is as tedious   155
As a tired horse, a railing wife;
Worse than a smoky house. I had rather live
With cheese and garlic in a windmill, far,
Than feed on cates and have him talk to me
In any summer-house in Christendom.   160
   MORTIMER. In faith, he is a worthy gentleman,
Exceedingly well read, and profited
In strange concealments, valiant as a lion
And wondrous affable, and as bountiful
As mines of India. Shall I tell you, cousin?   165
He holds your temper in a high respect
And curbs himself even of his natural scope
When you come 'cross his humour; faith, he does.
I warrant you, that man is not alive
Might so have tempted him as you have done,   170

---

136 *cavil*: dispute.   140 *Break with*: inform.   145 *moldwarp*: mole.   148 *griffin*: a
mythical beast, half lion, half eagle.   150 *skimble-skamble*: confused.   151 *puts*: sepa-
rates.   154 *go to*: "you don't say."   155 *mark'd*: paid attention to.   159 *cates*: deli-
cacies.   162 *profited*: skilled.   163 *concealments*: secrets.

Without the taste of danger and reproof:
But do not use it oft, let me entreat you.
    WORCESTER. In faith, my lord, you are too wilful-blame;
And since your coming hither have done enough
To put him quite besides his patience.   175
You must needs learn, lord, to amend this fault.
Though sometimes it show greatness, courage, blood,—
And that's the dearest grace it renders you,—
Yet oftentimes it doth present harsh rage,
Defect of manners, want of government,   180
Pride, haughtiness, opinion, and disdain;
The least of which haunting a nobleman
Loseth men's hearts and leaves behind a stain
Upon the beauty of all parts besides,
Beguiling them of commendation.   185
    HOTSPUR. Well, I am school'd: good manners be your speed!
Here come our wives, and let us take our leave.
        (*Re-enter* GLENDOWER *with the Ladies.*)
    MORTIMER. This is the deadly spite that angers me;
My wife can speak no English, I no Welsh.
    GLENDOWER. My daughter weeps; she'll not part with you;   190
She'll be a soldier too, she'll to the wars.
    MORTIMER. Good father, tell her that she and my aunt Percy
Shall follow in your conduct speedily.
        [GLENDOWER *speaks to her in Welsh,*
        and she answers him in the same.]
    GLENDOWER. She is desperate here; a peevish self-willed harlotry, one
that no persuasion can do good upon.   [*The lady speaks in Welsh.*]   195
    MORTIMER. I understand thy looks: that pretty Welsh
Which thou pourest down from these swelling heavens
I am too perfect in; and, but for shame,
In such a parley should I answer thee.
        [*The lady speaks again in Welsh.*]
I understand thy kisses and thou mine,   200
And that's a feeling disputation:
But I will never be a truant, love,
Till I have learn'd thy language; for thy tongue
Makes Welsh as sweet as ditties highly penn'd,
Sung by a fair queen in a summer's bower,   205
With ravishing division, to her lute.

---

173 *wilful-blame:* guilty of being headstrong. 175 *besides:* out of. 178 *dearest grace:*
finest credit. 179 *present:* indicate. 180 *government:* self-discipline. 181 *opinion:*
conceit. 182 *haunting:* associated with. 185 *Beguiling:* cheating. 186 *speed:* good
fortune. 188 *spite:* irritation. 194 *harlotry:* silly girl. 197 *swelling heavens:* her lips.
199 *parley:* speech. 201 *disputation:* discussion. 204 *highly penn'd:* written in a high
style. 206 *division:* song; *lute:* a stringed instrument, generally resembling a guitar.

GLENDOWER. Nay, if you melt, then will she run mad.

[The lady speaks again in Welsh.]

MORTIMER. O, I am ignorance itself in this!

GLENDOWER. She bids you on the wanton rushes lay you down
And rest your gentle head upon her lap, 210
And she will sing the song that pleaseth you
And on your eyelids crown the god of sleep,
Charming your blood with pleasing heaviness,
Making such difference 'twixt wake and sleep
As is the difference betwixt day and night 215
The hour before the heavenly-harness'd team
Begins his golden progress in the east.

MORTIMER. With all my heart I'll sit and hear her sing:
By that time will our book, I think, be drawn.

GLENDOWER. Do so; 220
And those musicians that shall play to you
Hang in the air a thousand leagues from hence,
And straight they shall be here: sit, and attend.

HOTSPUR. Come, Kate, thou are perfect in lying down: come, quick,
quick, that I may lay my head in thy lap. 225

LADY PERCY. Go, ye giddy goose. *[The music plays.]*

HOTSPUR. Now I perceive the devil understands Welsh;
And 't is no marvel he is so humorous.
By 'r lady, he is a good musician.

LADY PERCY. Then should you be nothing but musical, for you are alto- 230
gether governed by humours. Lie still, ye thief, and hear the lady sing in
Welsh.

HOTSPUR. I had rather hear Lady, my brach, howl in Irish.

LADY PERCY. Wouldst thou have thy head broken?

HOTSPUR. No. 235

LADY PERCY. Then be still.

HOTSPUR. Neither; 't is a woman's fault.

LADY PERCY. Now God help thee!

HOTSPUR. To the Welsh lady's bed.

LADY PERCY. What's that? 240

HOTSPUR. Peace! she sings. *[Hear the lady sings a Welsh song.]*

HOTSPUR. Come, Kate, I'll have your song too.

LADY PERCY. Not mine, in good sooth.

HOTSPUR. Not yours, in good sooth! Heart, you swear like a comfit-
maker's wife. "Not you, in good sooth," and "as true as I live," and "as 245
God shall mend me," and "as sure as day;"
And givest such sarcenet surety for thy oaths

---

209 *wanton:* luxurious; *rushes:* used for floor covering. 216 *team:* in Greek mythology,
the horses that draw the chariot of the sun. 219 *book:* the written agreements. 223
straight: promptly. 228 *humorous:* capricious. 231 *humours:* feelings. 233 *brach:*
bitch. 244 *sooth:* truth; *comfit-maker:* confectioner. 247 *sarcenet:* fine silk, hence, flimsy.

As if thou never walk'st further than Finsbury.
Swear me, Kate, like a lady as thou art,
A good mouth-filling oath, and leave "in sooth,"   250
And such protest of pepper-gingerbread,
To velvet-guards and Sunday-citizens.
Come, sing.
    LADY PERCY. I will not sing.
    HOTSPUR. 'T is the next way to turn tailor, or be red-breast teacher. An   255
the indentures be drawn, I'll away within these two hours; and so, come in
when ye will.   (*Exit.*)
    GLENDOWER. Come, come, Lord Mortimer; you are as slow
As hot Lord Percy is on fire to go.
By this our book is drawn; we'll but seal,   260
And then to horse immediately.
    MORTIMER.   With all my heart.   (*Exeunt.*)

ACT III/2   London. The palace.

(*Enter the* KING, PRINCE OF WALES, *and others.*)
    KING. Lords, give us leave; the Prince of Wales and I
Must have some private conference; but be near at hand,
For we shall presently have need of you.   (*Exeunt Lords.*)
I know not whether God will have it so,
For some displeasing service I have done,   5
That, in his secret doom, out of my blood
He'll breed revengement and a scourge for me;
But thou dost in thy passages of life
Make me believe that thou art only mark'd
For the hot vengeance and the rod of heaven   10
To punish my mistreadings. Tell me else,
Could such inordinate and low desires,
Such poor, such bare, such lewd, such mean attempts,
Such barren pleasures, rude society,
As thou art match'd withal and grafted to,   15
Accompany the greatness of thy blood
And hold their level with thy princely heart?
    PRINCE. So please your Majesty, I would I could
Quit all offences with as clear excuse
As well as I am doubtless I can purge   20
Myself of many I am charg'd withal:

---

248 *Finsbury:* a place near London frequented by tradespeople on Sundays.   252 *velvet-guards:* middle-class women, who wore velvet trimmings on their dresses.   255 *next:* easiest; *tailor:* reputed to be good singers; *red-breast teacher:* teach birds to sing.

6 *doom:* judgement.   8 *passages:* actions.   11 *mistreadings:* errors.   13. *attempts:* under-takings.   15 *withal:* with.   17 *hold their level with:* be acceptable to.   19 *Quit:* excuse myself of.   20 *doubtless:* certain.

Yet such extenuation let me beg,
As, in reproof of many tales devis'd,
Which oft the ear of greatness needs must hear,
By smiling pick-thanks and base newsmongers,   25
I may, for some things true, wherein my youth
Hath faulty wander'd and irregular,
Find pardon on my true submission.
    KING. God pardon thee! yet let me wonder, Harry,
At thy affections, which do hold a wing   30
Quite from the flight of all thy ancestors.
Thy place in council thou hast rudely lost,
Which by thy younger brother is supplied,
And art almost an alien to the hearts
Of all the court and princes of my blood: 35
The hope and expectation of thy time
Is ruin'd, and the soul of every man
Prophetically do forethink thy fall.
Had I so lavish of my presence been,
So common-hackney'd in the eyes of men,   40
So stale and cheap to vulgar company,
Opinion, that did help me to the crown,
Had still kept loyal to possession
And left me in reputeless banishment,
A fellow of no mark nor likelihood.   45
By being seldom seen, I could not stir
But like a comet I was wonder'd at;
That men would tell their children, "This is he";
Others would say, "Where, which is Bolingbroke?"
And then I stole all courtesy from heaven,   50
And dress'd myself in such humility
That I did pluck allegiance from men's hearts,
Loud shouts and salutations from their mouths,
Even in the presence of the crowned King.
Thus did I keep my person fresh and new,   55
My presence, like a robe pontifical,
Ne'er seen but wonder'd at; and so my state,
Seldom but sumptuous, show'd like a feast
And won by rareness such solemnity.
The skipping King, he ambled up and down   60
With shallow jesters and rash bavin wits,

---

22 *extenuation*: consideration. 23 *reproof*: disproof. 25 *pick-thanks*: parasites; *news-mongers*: gossips. 30 *hold a wing*: go in a direction. 40 *common-hackney'd*: too familiar. 43 *to possession*: to the king formerly in possession of the crown, Richard II. 57 *state*: appearance in public. 58 *Seldom but sumptuous*: infrequent but handsome. 61 *rash*: quickly burning; *bavin*: light brushwood.

Soon kindled and soon burnt; carded his state,
Mingled his royalty with cap'ring fools,
Had his great name profaned with their scorns,
And gave his countenance, against his name,   65
To laugh at gibing boys and stand the push
Of every beardless vain comparative;
Grew a companion to the common streets,
Enfeoff'd himself to popularity;
That, being daily swallowed by men's eyes,   70
They surfeited with honey and began
To loathe the taste of sweetness, whereof a little
More than a little is by much too much.
So when he had occasion to be seen,
He was but as the cuckoo is in June,   75
Heard, not regarded; seen, but with such eyes
As, sick and blunted with community,
Afford no extraordinary gaze
Such as is bent on sun-like majesty
When it shines seldom in admiring eyes;   80
But rather drows'd and hung their eyelids down,
Slept in his face and render'd such aspéct
As cloudy men use to their adversaries,
Being with his presence glutted, gorg'd and full.
And in that very line, Harry, standest thou;   85
For thou hast lost thy princely privilege
With vile participation. Not an eye
But is a-weary of thy common sight,
Save mine, which hath desir'd to see thee more;
Which now doth that I would not have it do,   90
Make blind itself with foolish tenderness.
    PRINCE. I shall hereafter, my thrice gracious lord,
Be more myself.
    KING.   For all the world
As thou art to this hour was Richard then
When I from France set foot at Ravenspurgh,   95
And even as I was then is Percy now.
Now, by my sceptre and my soul to boot,
He hath more worthy interest to the state
Than thou, the shadow of succession.
For of no right, nor colour like to right,   100

---

62 *carded:* debased.   64 *their scorns:* the scorn they felt.   65 *gave his countenance:* tolerated; *name:* reputation.   66 *stand the push of:* expose himself to.   67 *comparative:*
jokester.   69 *Enfeoff'd:* surrendered; *popularity:* the common people.   77 *community:*
commonness.   83 *cloudy:* frowning.   85 *line:* position.   87 *participation:* company.
98 *interest:* claim.   100 *colour like to right:* anything resembling a right.

He doth fill fields with harness in the realm,
Turns head against the lion's armed jaws,
And, being no more in debt to years than thou,
Leads ancient lords and reverend bishops on
To bloody battles and to bruising arms.   105
What never-dying honour hath he got
Against renowned Douglas! whose high deeds,
Whose hot incursions and great name in arms
Holds from all soldiers chief majority
And military title capital   110
Through all the kingdoms that acknowledge Christ.
Thrice hath this Hotspur, Mars in swathling clothes
This infant warrior, in his enterprises
Discomfited great Douglas, ta'en him once,
Enlarged him and made a friend of him,   115
To fill the mouth of deep defiance up
And shake the peace and safety of our throne.
And what say you to this? Percy, Northumberland,
The Archbishop's grace of York, Douglas, Mortimer,
Capitulate against us and are up.   120
But wherefore do I tell these news to thee?
Why, Harry, do I tell thee of my foes,
Which art my near'st and dearest enemy?
Thou that art like enough, through vassal fear,
Base inclination, and the start of spleen,   125
To fight against me under Percy's pay,
To dog his heels and curtsy at his frowns,
To show how much thou art degenerate.
      PRINCE. Do not think so; you shall not find it so:
And God forgive them that so much have sway'd   130
Your Majesty's good thoughts away from me!
I will redeem all this on Percy's head,
And in the closing of some glorious day
Be bold to tell you that I am your son;
When I will wear a garment all of blood   135
And stain my favours in a bloody mask,
Which, wash'd away, shall scour my shame with it:
And that shall be the day, whene'er it lights,
That this same child of honour and renown,
This gallant Hotspur, this all-praised knight,   140
And your unthought-of Harry chance to meet.
For every honour sitting on his helm,

101 *harness:* men equipped for war.   103 *no more in debt to years:* no older.   109 *ma-jority:* supremacy.   115 *Enlarged:* freed.   120 *Capitulate:* conspire; *up:* ready for com-bat.   125 *spleen:* impulse.   136 *favours:* features.

Would they were multitudes, and on my head
My shames redoubled! For the time will come,
That I shall make this northern youth exchange   145
His glorious deeds for my indignities.
Percy is but my factor, good my lord,
To engross up glorious deeds on my behalf;
And I will call him to so strict account
That he shall render every glory up,   150
Yea, even the slightest worship of his time,
Or I will tear the reckoning from his heart.
This, in the name of God, I promise here;
The which if He be pleas'd I shall perform,
I do beseech your Majesty may salve   155
The long-grown wounds of my intemperance:
If not, the end of life cancels all bands;
And I will die a hundred thousand deaths
Ere break the smallest parcel of this vow.
    KING. A hundred thousand rebels die in this.   160
Thou shalt have charge and sovereign trust herein.
                 (*Enter* BLUNT.)
How now, good Blunt? Thy looks are full of speed.
    BLUNT So hath the business that I come to speak of.
Lord Mortimer of Scotland hath sent word
That Douglas and the English rebels met   165
The eleventh of this month at Shrewsbury.
A mighty and a fearful head they are,
If promises be kept on every hand,
As ever offer'd foul play in a state.
    KING. The Earl of Westmoreland set forth to-day,   170
With him my son, Lord John of Lancaster,
For this advértisement is five days old.
On Wednesday next, Harry, you shall set forward;
On Thursday we ourselves will march. Our meeting
Is Bridgenorth: and, Harry, you shall march   175
Through Gloucestershire; by which account,
Our business valued, some twelve days hence
Our general forces at Bridgenorth shall meet.
Our hands are full of business; let's away.
Advantage feeds him fat, while men delay.   (*Exeunt.*)   180

---

146 *indignities:* unworthy actions.   147 *factor:* agent.   148 *engross:* buy up.   157 *bands:* bonds.   172 *advértisement:* information.   177 *valued:* the time estimated.

ACT III/3   Eastcheap. The Boar's-Head Tavern.

(*Enter* FALSTAFF *and* BARDOLPH.)

FALSTAFF. Bardolph, am I not fallen away vilely since this last action? Do I not bate? Do I not dwindle? Why, my skin hangs about me like an old lady's loose gown: I am withered like an old apple-john. Well, I'll repent, and that suddenly, while I am in some liking: I shall be out of heart shortly, and then I shall have no strength to repent. An I have not 5 forgotten what the inside of a church is made of, I am a peppercorn, a brewer's horse. The inside of a church! Company, villanous company, hath been the spoil of me.

BARDOLPH. Sir John, you are so fretful, you cannot live long.

FALSTAFF. Why, there is it: come sing me a bawdy song; make me 10 merry. I was as virtuously given as a gentleman need to be; virtuous enough, swore little, diced not above seven times a week, went to a bawdy-house not above once in a quarter—of an hour, paid money that I borrowed three or four times, lived well and in good compass; and now I live out of all order, out of all compass. 15

BARDOLPH. Why, you are so fat, Sir John, that you must needs be out of all compass, out of all reasonable compass, Sir John.

FALSTAFF. Do thou amend thy face, and I'll amend my life: thou art our admiral; thou bearest the lantern in the poop, but 't is in the nose of thee: thou art the Knight of the Burning Lamp. 20

BARDOLPH. Why, Sir John, my face does you no harm.

FALSTAFF. No, I'll be sworn; I make as good use of it as many a man doth of a Death's-head or a *memento mori;* I never see thy face but I think upon hell-fire and Dives that lived in purple; for there he is in his robes, burning, burning. If thou wert any way given to virtue, I would swear by 25 thy face; my oath should be, "By this fire, that's God's angel;" but thou are altogether given over, and wert indeed, but for the light in thy face, the son of utter darkness. When thou ran'st up Gadshill in the night to catch my horse, if I did not think thou hadst been an *ignis fatuus* or a ball of wildfire, there's no purchase in money. O, thou art a perpetual triumph, an 30 everlasting bonfire-light! Thou hast saved me a thousand marks in links and torches, walking with thee in the night betwixt tavern and tavern; but the sack that thou has drunk me would have brought me lights as good cheap at the dearest chandler's in Europe. I have maintain'd that sala-

2 *bate:* abate, or decrease.   3 *apple-john:* a shrivelled apple.   4 *in some liking:* in good condition.   4-5 *out of heart:* in poor spirits.   14 *in good compass:* within decent limits. 19 *admiral:* flagship; *the lantern in the poop:* a light at the stern of the flagship for the rest of the fleet to follow.   23 *memento mori:* reminder of death.   24 *Dives:* the rich man in the parable from Luke 16:19–31.   29 *ignis fatuus:* will-o'-the-wisp.   30 *wildfire:* fireworks; *triumph:* celebration with fireworks.   31 *links:* torches.   34 *chandler's:* candle-shop.

mander of yours with fire any time this two and thirty years; God reward 35
me for it.

BARDOLPH. 'Sblood, I would my face were in your belly!

FALSTAFF. God-a-mercy! so should I be sure to be heart-burn'd.

(*Enter* HOSTESS.)

How now, Dame Partlet the hen! have you inquired yet who picked my
pocket? 40

HOSTESS. Why, Sir John, what do you think, Sir John? Do you think
I keep thieves in my house? I have searched, I have inquired, so has my
husband, man by man, boy by boy, servant by servant: the tithe of a hair
was never lost in my house before.

FALSTAFF. Ye lie, hostess: Bardolph was shaved and lost many a hair; 45
and I'll be sworn my pocket was picked. Go to, you are a woman, go.

HOSTESS. Who? I? No; I defy thee. God's light, I was never called so
in mine own house before.

FALSTAFF. Go to, I know you well enough.

HOSTESS. No, Sir John; you do not know me, Sir John; I know you, Sir 50
John; you owe me money, Sir John; and now you pick a quarrel to beguile
me of it: I bought you a dozen of shirts to your back.

FALSTAFF. Dowlas, filthy dowlas. I have given them away to bakers'
wives; they have made bolters of them.

HOSTESS. Now, as I am a true woman, holland of eight shillings an ell. 55
You owe money here besides, Sir John, for your diet, and by-drinkings,
and money lent you, four and twenty pound.

FALSTAFF. He had his part of it; let him pay.

HOSTESS. He? Alas, he is poor; he hath nothing.

FALSTAFF. How! poor? Look upon his face; what call you rich? Let 60
them coin his nose, let them coin his cheeks: I'll not pay a denier. What,
will you make a younker of me? Shall I not take mine ease in mine inn
but I shall have my pocket picked? I have lost a seal-ring of my grandfather's worth forty mark.

HOSTESS. O Jesu, I have heard the Prince tell him, I know not how oft, 65
that that ring was copper!

FALSTAFF. How! the Prince is a Jack, a sneak-cup: 'sblood, an he were
here, I would cudgel him like a dog, if he would say so.

(*Enter the* PRINCE *and* POINS, *marching, and* FALSTAFF *meets them
playing on his truncheon like a fife.*)

How now, lad! is the wind in that door, i' faith? Must we all march?

BARDOLPH. Yea, two and two, Newgate fashion. 70

HOSTESS. My lord, I pray you, hear me.

43 *tithe:* tenth part. 46 *Go to:* go on! 53 *Dowlas:* coarse linen. 54 *bolters:* sieves for
flour. 55 *holland:* fine linen; *ell:* a measure of 45 inches. 56 *by-drinkings:* occasional drinks. 61 *denier:* one-tenth of a penny. 62 *younker:* greenhorn. 67 *Jack:* a
rascal; *sneak-cup:* probably, a secret drinker. 68 (Stage Direction) *truncheon:* short
cane. 70 *Newgate:* a London prison.

PRINCE. What say'st thou, Mistress Quickly? How doth thy husband? I love him well; he is an honest man.

HOSTESS. Good my lord, hear me.

FALSTAFF. Prithee, let her alone, and list to me.   75

PRINCE. What say'st thou, Jack?

FALSTAFF. The other night I fell asleep here behind the arras and had my pocket picked. This house is turned bawdy-house; they pick pockets.

PRINCE. What didst thou lose, Jack?

FALSTAFF. Wilt thou believe me, Hal? Three or four bonds of forty   80
pound a-piece, and a seal-ring of my grandfather's.

PRINCE. A trifle, some eight-penny matter.

HOSTESS. So I told him, my lord, and I said I heard your Grace say so; and, my lord, he speaks most vilely of you, like a foul-mouthed man as he is, and said he would cudgel you.   85

PRINCE. What! he did not?

HOSTESS. There's neither faith, truth, nor womanhood in me else.

FALSTAFF. There's no more faith in thee than in a stewed prune; nor no more truth in thee than in a drawn fox; and for womanhood, Maid Marian may be the deputy's wife of the ward to thee. Go, you thing, go.   90

HOSTESS. Say, what thing? what thing?

FALSTAFF. What thing? Why, a thing to thank God on.

HOSTESS. I am no thing to thank God on, I would thou shouldst know it: I am an honest man's wife; and, setting thy knighthood aside, thou art a knave to call me so.   95

FALSTAFF. Setting thy womanhood aside, thou art a beast to say otherwise.

HOSTESS. Say, what beast, thou knave, thou?

FALSTAFF. What beast? Why, an otter.

PRINCE. An otter, Sir John! Why an otter?   100

FALSTAFF. Why, she's neither fish nor flesh; a man knows not where to have her.

HOSTESS. Thou art an unjust man in saying so: thou or any man knows where to have me, thou knave, thou!

PRINCE. Thou say'st true, hostess; and he slanders thee most grossly.   105

HOSTESS. So he doth you, my lord; and said this other day you ought him a thousand pound.

PRINCE. Sirrah, do I owe you a thousand pound?

FALSTAFF. A thousand pound, Hal! A million. Thy love is worth a million; thou owest me thy love.   110

HOSTESS. Nay, my lord, he called you Jack, and said he would cudgel you.

FALSTAFF. Did I, Bardolph?

---

89 *a drawn fox:* a fox driven into the open, and therefore full of tricks; *Maid Marian:* character of a loose woman in country games.   90 *deputy's wife:* a respectable woman. 93 *on:* for.   106 *ought:* owed.

BARDOLPH. Indeed, Sir John, you said so.

FALSTAFF. Yea, if he said my ring was copper.

PRINCE. I say 't is copper: dar'st thou be as good as thy word now?   115

FALSTAFF. Why, Hal, thou knowest, as thou art but man, I dare; but as thou art Prince, I fear thee as I fear the roaring of the lion's whelp.

PRINCE. And why not as the lion?

FALSTAFF. The King himself is to be feared as the lion: dost thou think I'll fear thee as I fear thy father? Nay, an I do, I pray God my girdle   120 break.

PRINCE. O, if it should, how would thy guts fall about thy knees! But, sirrah, there's no room for faith, truth, nor honesty in this bosom of thine; it is all filled up with guts and midriff. Charge an honest woman with picking thy pocket! Why, thou whoreson, impudent, embossed rascal, if   125 there were anything in thy pocket but tavern-reckonings, memorandums of bawdy-houses, and one poor pennyworth of sugar-candy to make thee long-winded, if thy pocket were enriched with any other injuries but these, I am a villain: and yet you will stand to it; you will not pocket up wrong: art thou not ashamed?   130

FALSTAFF. Dost thou hear, Hal? Thou knowest in the state of inno-cency, Adam fell; and what should poor Jack Falstaff do in the days of villainy? Thou seest I have more flesh than another man, and therefore more frailty. You confess then, you picked my pocket?

PRINCE. It appears so by the story.   135

FALSTAFF. Hostess, I forgive thee: go, make ready breakfast; love thy husband, look to thy servants, cherish thy guests: thou shalt find me tractable to any honest reason; thou seest I am pacified. Still? Nay, prithee, be gone.   (*Exit* HOSTESS.)

Now, Hal, to the news at court: for the robbery, lad, how is that an-   140 swered?

PRINCE. O, my sweet beef, I must still be good angel to thee: the money is paid back again.

FALSTAFF. O, I do not like that paying back; 't is a double labour.

PRINCE. I am good friends with my father and may do anything.   145

FALSTAFF. Rob me the exchequer the first thing thou doest, and do it with unwashed hands too.

BARDOLPH. Do, my lord.

PRINCE. I have procured thee, Jack, a charge of foot.

FALSTAFF. I would it had been of horse. Where shall I find one that   150 can steal well? O for a fine thief, of the age of two and twenty or there-abouts! I am heinously unprovided. Well, God be thanked for these rebels, they offend none but the virtuous. I laud them, I praise them.

PRINCE. Bardolph!

---

125 *embossed:* swollen.   128 *injuries:* things whose loss would be injurious.   140 *an-swered:* accounted for.   147 *with unwashed hands:* without delay.

BARDOLPH. My lord?   155

PRINCE. Go bear this letter to Lord John of Lancaster, to my brother
John; this to my Lord of Westmoreland. [*Exit* BARDOLPH.] Go, Poins, to
horse, to horse; for thou and I have thirty miles to ride yet ere dinner time.
[*Exit* POINS.] Jack, meet me to-morrow in the Temple hall at two o'clock
in the afternoon.   160
There shalt thou know thy charge, and there receive
Money and order for their furniture.
The land is burning; Percy stands on high;
And either we or they must lower lie.   (*Exit.*)

FALSTAFF. Rare words! brave world! Hostess, my breakfast, come!   165
O, I could wish this tavern were my drum!   (*Exit.*)

ACT IV/1   The rebel camp near Shrewsbury.

(*Enter* HOTSPUR, WORCESTER, *and* DOUGLAS.)

HOTSPUR. Well said, my noble Scot! If speaking truth
In this fine age were not thought flattery,
Such attribution should the Douglas have
As not a soldier of this season's stamp
Should go so general current through the world.   5
By God, I cannot flatter; I do defy
The tongues of soothers; but a braver place
In my heart's love hath no man than yourself.
Nay, task me to my word; approve me, lord.

DOUGLAS. Thou art the king of honour.   10
No man so potent breathes upon the ground
But I will beard him.

                 (*Enter a* MESSENGER *with letters.*)

HOTSPUR.   Do so, and 't is well.—
What letters hast thou there?—I can but thank you.

MESSENGER. These letters come from your father.

HOTSPUR. Letters from him! Why comes he not himself?   15

MESSENGER. He cannot come, my lord; he is grievous sick.

HOTSPUR. 'Zounds! how has he the leisure to be sick
In such a justling time? Who leads his power?
Under whose government come they along?

MESSENGER. His letters bear his mind, not I, my lord.   20

WORCESTER. I prithee, tell me, doth he keep his bed?

MESSENGER. He did, my lord, four days ere I set forth;
And at the time of my departure thence

---

162 *furniture*: equipment.

3 *attribution*: praise. 7 *soothers*: flatterers. 9 *approve*: test. 12 *beard*: challenge. 18
justling: busy.

He was much fear'd by his physicians.

WORCESTER. I would the state of time had first been whole　　25
Ere he by sickness had been visited.
His health was never better worth than now.

HOTSPUR. Sick now! droop now! This sickness doth infect
The very life-blood of our enterprise;
'T is catching hither, even to our camp.　　30
He writes me here, that inward sickness—
And that his friends by deputation could not
So soon be drawn, nor did he think it meet
To lay so dangerous and dear a trust
On any soul remov'd but on his own.　　35
Yet doth he give us bold advértisement
That with our small conjunction we should on
To see how fortune is dispos'd to us;
For, as he writes, there is no quailing now,
Because the King is certainly possess'd　　40
Of all purposes. What say you to it?

WORCESTER. Your father's sickness is a maim to us.

HOTSPUR. A perilous gash, a very limb lopp'd off.
And yet, in faith, 't is not; his present want
Seems more than we shall find it: were it good　　45
To set the exact wealth of all our states
All at one cast? to set so rich a main
On the nice hazard of one doubtful hour?
It were not good; for therein should we read
The very bottom and the soul of hope,　　50
The very list, the very utmost bound
Of all our fortunes.

DOUGLAS.　　　　Faith, and so we should;
Where now remains a sweet reversion,
We may boldly spend upon the hope
Of what is to come in.　　55
A comfort of retirement lives in this.

HOTSPUR. A rendezvous, a home to fly unto,
If that the devil and mischance look big
Upon the maidenhead of our affairs.

WORCESTER. But yet I would your father had been here.　　60
The quality and hair of our attempt
Brooks no division: it will be thought

---

24 *He was much fear'd by:* he gave great concern to. 32 *by deputation:* by substitutes.
37 *conjunction:* grouping. 40 *possess'd:* informed. 46 *set:* wager; *states:* estates.
47 *main:* stake. 48 *nice:* delicate. 51 *list:* limit. 53 *reversion:* future wealth. 58
big: imminent. 59 *maidenhead:* beginning. 61 *hair:* nature. 62 *Brooks:* endures.

By some that know not why he is away,
That wisdom, loyalty, and mere dislike
Of our proceedings kept the earl from hence;   65
And think how such an apprehension
May turn the tide of fearful faction
And breed a kind of question in our cause;
For well you know we of the off'ring side
Must keep aloof from strict arbitrement,   70
And stop all sight-holes, every loop from whence
The eye of reason may pry in upon us:
This absence of your father's draws a curtain,
That shows the ignorant a kind of fear
Before not dreamt of.
   HOTSPUR.   You strain too far.   75
I rather of his absence make this use:
It lends a lustre and more great opinion,
A larger dare to our great enterprise,
Than if the earl were here; for men must think,
If we without his help can make a head   80
To push against a kingdom, with his help
We shall o'erturn it topsy-turvy down.
Yet all goes well, yet all our joints are whole.
   DOUGLAS. As heart can think: there is not such a word
Spoke of in Scotland as this term of fear.   85
           (*Enter* SIR RICHARD VERNON.)
   HOTSPUR. My cousin Vernon! welcome, by my soul.
   VERNON. Pray God my news be worth a welcome, lord.
The Earl of Westmoreland, seven thousand strong,
Is marching hitherwards; with him Prince John.
   HOTSPUR. No harm. What more?
   VERNON.   And further, I have learn'd,   90
The King himself in person is set forth,
Or hitherwards intended speedily,
With strong and mighty preparation.
   HOTSPUR. He shall be welcome too. Where is his son,
The nimble-footed madcap Prince of Wales,   95
And his comrades, that daff'd the world aside,
And bid it pass?
   VERNON.   All furnish'd, all in arms;
All plum'd like estridges that with the wind
Bated, like eagles having lately bath'd;

---

67 *faction*: rebellion.   69 *off'ring*: attacking.   70 *arbitrement*: examination.   83 *joints*:
limbs.   96 *daff'd*: put.   98 *estridges*: ostriches.   99 *Bated*: flapped their wings.

Glittering in golden coats, like images;   100
As full of spirit as the month of May,
And gorgeous as the sun at midsummer;
Wanton as youthful goats, wild as young bulls.
I saw young Harry, with his beaver on,
His cuisses on his thighs, gallantly arm'd,   105
Rise from the ground like feathered Mercury,
And vaulted with such ease into his seat,
As if an angel dropp'd down from the clouds
To turn and wind a fiery Pegasus
And witch the world with noble horsemanship.   110
   HOTSPUR. No more, no more! Worse than the sun in March,
This praise doth nourish agues. Let them come!
They come like sacrifices in their trim.
And to the fire-ey'd maid of smoky war
All hot and bleeding will we offer them: 115
The mailed Mars shall on his altar sit
Up to the ears in blood. I am on fire
To hear this rich reprisal is so nigh
And yet not ours. Come, let me taste my horse,
Who is to bear me like a thunderbolt   120
Against the bosom of the Prince of Wales:
Harry to Harry shall, hot horse to horse,
Meet and ne'er part till one drop down a corse.
O that Glendower were come!
   VERNON.   There is more news.
I learn'd in Worcester, as I rode along,   125
He cannot draw his power this fourteen days.
   DOUGLAS. That's the worst tidings that I hear of yet.
   WORCESTER. Ay, by my faith, that bears a frosty sound.
   HOTSPUR. What may the King's whole battle reach unto?
   VERNON. To thirty thousand.
   HOTSPUR.   Forty let it be!   130
My father and Glendower being both away,
The powers of us may serve so great a day.
Come, let us take a muster speedily.
Doomsday is near; die all, die merrily.
   DOUGLAS. Talk not of dying; I am out of fear   135
Of death or death's hand for this one-half year.   (*Exeunt.*)

---

104 *beaver:* helmet.   105 *cuisses:* armor for the thighs.   106 *Mercury:* the messenger of
the gods, portrayed as a handsome young man.   109 *wind:* turn about; *Pegasus:* the
winged horse of Greek mythology.   114 *maid:* Bellona, the war-goddess.   116 *Mars:* the
god of war.   119 *taste:* try.   126 *draw:* muster.   120 *battle:* army.   135 *out of:* free
from.

ACT IV/2   A public road near Coventry.

(*Enter* FALSTAFF *and* BARDOLPH.)

FALSTAFF. Bardolph, get thee before to Coventry; fill me a bottle of sack: our soldiers shall march through; we'll to Sutton Cophill to-night.

BARDOLPH. Will you give me money, captain?

FALSTAFF. Lay out, lay out.

BARDOLPH. This bottle makes an angel.   5

FALSTAFF. An if it do, take it for thy labour; and if it make twenty, take them all; I'll answer the coinage. Bid my lieutenant Peto meet me at town's end.

BARDOLPH. I will, captain; farewell.   (*Exit.*)

FALSTAFF. If I be not ashamed of my soldiers, I am a soused gurnet. I   10
have misused the King's press damnably. I have got, in exchange of a hundred and fifty soldiers, three hundred and odd pounds. I press me none but good householders, yeoman's sons; inquire me out contracted bachelors, such as had been asked twice on the banns; such a commodity of warm slaves, as had as lieve hear the devil as a drum; such as fear the report of   15
a caliver worse than a struck fowl or a hurt wild-duck. I pressed me none but such toasts-and-butter, with hearts in their bellies no bigger than pins' heads; and they have bought out their services; and now my whole charge consists of ancients, corporals, lieutenants, gentlemen of companies, slaves as ragged as Lazarus in the painted cloth, where the glutton's dogs licked   20
his sores; and such as, indeed, were never soldiers, but discarded unjust serving-men, younger sons to younger brothers, revolted tapsters and ostlers trade-fallen, the cankers of a calm world and a long peace, ten times more dishonourable ragged than an old feazed ancient: and such have I, to fill up the rooms of them as have bought out their services, that you would   25
think that I had a hundred and fifty tattered prodigals lately come from swine-keeping, from eating draff and husks. A mad fellow met me on the way and told me I had unloaded all the gibbets and pressed the dead bodies. No eye hath seen such scarecrows. I'll not march through Coventry with them, that's flat: nay, and the villains march wide betwixt the legs,   30
as if they had gyves on; for indeed I had the most of them out of prison. There's not a shirt and a half in all my company; and the half shirt is two napkins tacked together and thrown over the shoulders like an herald's coat without sleeves; and the shirt, to say the truth, stolen from my host at

---

4 *Lay out:* pay the money yourself.   5 *angel:* ten shillings.   10 *soused gurnet:* a pickled fish.   11 *King's press:* the right to conscript soldiers.   14 *asked twice on the banns:* made two announcements that they were about to marry; *commodity:* supply.   16 *caliver:* musket.   18 *bought out their services:* paid a sum of money instead of serving. 19 *ancients:* ensigns.   20 *painted cloth:* tapestry.   23 *trade-fallen:* out of work.   24 *feazed ancient:* patched flag.   27 *draff:* garbage.   28 *pressed:* conscripted.   31 *gyves:* fetters.

Saint Alban's, or the red-nose inn-keeper of Daventry. But that's all one; 35
they'll find linen enough on every hedge.

(*Enter the* PRINCE *and the* LORD OF WESTMORELAND.)

PRINCE. How now, blown Jack! how now, quilt!

FALSTAFF. What, Hal! how now, mad wag! what a devil dost thou in
Warwickshire? My good Lord of Westmoreland, I cry you mercy! I
thought your honour had already been at Shrewsbury. 40

WESTMORELAND. Faith, Sir John, 't is more than time that I were there,
and you too; but my powers are there already. The King, I can tell you,
looks for us all: we must away all night.

FALSTAFF. Tut, never fear me: I am as vigilant as a cat to steal cream.

PRINCE. I think, to steal cream indeed, for thy theft hath already made 45
thee butter. But tell me Jack, whose fellows are these that come after?

FALSTAFF. Mine, Hal, mine.

PRINCE. I did never see such pitiful rascals.

FALSTAFF. Tut, tut; good enough to toss; food for powder, food for
powder; they'll fill a pit as well as better: tush, man, mortal men, mortal 50
men.

WESTMORELAND. Ay, but, Sir John, methinks they are exceeding poor
and bare, too beggarly.

FALSTAFF. Faith, for their poverty, I know not where they had that; and
for their bareness, I am sure they never learned that of me. 55

PRINCE. No, I'll be sworn; unless you call three fingers on the ribs bare.
But, sirrah, make haste. Percy is already in the field.

FALSTAFF. What, is the King encamp'd?

WESTMORELAND. He is, Sir John: I fear we shall stay too long.

FALSTAFF. Well, to the latter end of a fray and the beginning of a 60
feast fits a dull fighter and a keen guest. (*Exeunt.*)

ACT IV/3   The rebel camp near Shrewsbury.

(*Enter* HOTSPUR, WORCESTER, DOUGLAS, *and* VERNON.)

HOTSPUR. We'll fight with him to-night.

WORCESTER.   It may not be.

DOUGLAS. You give him then advantage.

VERNON.   Not a whit.

HOTSPUR. Why say you so? Looks he not for supply?

VERNON. So do we.

HOTSPUR.   His is certain, ours is doubtful.

WORCESTER. Good cousin, be advis'd; stir not to-night. 5

VERNON. Do not, my lord.

37 *blown:* blown up.   43 *must away:* must march.   49 *to toss:* on a spear.
3 *supply:* reinforcements.

DOUGLAS.   You do not counsel well.
You speak it out of fear and cold heart.
   VERNON. Do me no slander, Douglas. By my life,
And I dare well maintain it with my life,
If well-respected honour bid me on,   10
I hold as little counsel with weak fear
As you, my lord, or any Scot that this day lives.
Let it be seen to-morrow in the battle
Which of us fears.
   DOUGLAS.   Yea, or to-night.
   VERNON.   Content.
   HOTSPUR. To-night, say I.   15
   VERNON. Come, come, it may not be. I wonder much,
Being men of such great leading as you are,
That you foresee not what impediments
Drag back our expedition: certain horse
Of my cousin Vernon's are not yet come up;   20
Your uncle Worcester's horse came but to-day;
And now their pride and mettle is asleep,
Their courage with hard labour tame and dull,
That not a horse is half the half of himself.
   HOTSPUR. So are the horses of the enemy   25
In general, journey-bated and brought low.
The better part of ours are full of rest.
   WORCESTER. The number of the King exceedeth ours.
For God's sake, cousin, stay till all come in.
                        [*The trumpet sounds a parley.*]
              (*Enter* SIR WALTER BLUNT.)
   BLUNT. I come with gracious offers from the King,   30
If you vouchsafe me hearing and respect.
   HOTSPUR. Welcome, Sir Walter Blunt; and would to God
You were of our determination!
Some of us love you well; and even those some
Envy your great deservings and good name,   35
Because you are not of our quality,
But stand against us like an enemy.
   BLUNT. And God defend but still I should stand so,
So long as out of limit and true rule
You stand against anointed majesty.   40
But to my charge. The King hath sent to know
The nature of your griefs, and whereupon
You conjure from the breast of civil peace
Such bold hostility, teaching his duteous land

17 *leading*: experience in leadership.   26 *journey-bated*: tired out with travel.   36 *quality*:
party.

Audacious cruelty. If that the King   45
Have any way your good deserts forgot,
Which he confesseth to be manifold,
He bids you name your griefs; and with all speed
You shall have your desires with interest
And pardon absolute for yourself and these   50
Herein misled by your suggestion.
    HOTSPUR. The King is kind; and well we know the King
Knows at what time to promise, when to pay.
My father and my uncle and myself
Did give him that same royalty he wears;   55
And when he was not six and twenty strong,
Sick in the world's regard, wretched and low,
A poor unminded outlaw sneaking home,
My father gave him welcome to the shore;
And when he heard him swear and vow to God   60
He came but to be Duke of Lancaster,
To sue his livery and beg his peace,
With tears of innocence and terms of zeal,
My father, in kind heart and pity mov'd,
Swore him assistance and perform'd it too.   65
Now when the lords and barons of the realm
Perceiv'd Northumberland did lean to him,
The more and less came in with cap and knee;
Met him in boroughs, cities, villages,
Attended him on bridges, stood in lanes,   70
Laid gifts before him, proffer'd him their oaths,
Gave him their heirs as pages, followed him
Even at the heels in golden multitudes.
He presently, as greatness knows itself,
Steps me a little higher than his vow   75
Made to my father, while his blood was poor,
Upon the naked shore at Ravenspurgh;
And now, forsooth, takes on him to reform
Some certain edicts and some strait decrees
That lie too heavy on the commonwealth,   80
Cries out upon abuses, seems to weep
Over his country's wrongs; and by this face,
This seeming brow of justice, did he win
The hearts of all that he did angle for;
Proceeded further; cut me off the heads   85
Of all the favourites that the absent king
In deputation left behind him here,

---

62 *sue his livery:* ask for his inheritance.   68 *more and less:* high and low.   76 *blood:*
   spirit.   79 *strait:* severe.

When he was personal in the Irish war.
 BLUNT. Tut, I came not to hear this.
 HOTSPUR.   Then to the point.
In short time after, he depos'd the King;   90
Soon after that, depriv'd him of his life;
And in the neck of that, task'd the whole state.
To make that worse, suffer'd his kinsman March,
(Who is, if every owner were well plac'd,
Indeed his king) to be engag'd in Wales,   95
There without ransom to lie forfeited;
Disgrac'd me in my happy victories,
Sought to entrap me by intelligence;
Rated mine uncle from the council-board;
In rage dismiss'd my father from the court;   100
Broke oath on oath, committed wrong on wrong,
And in conclusion drove us to seek out
This head of safety; and withal to pry
Into his title, the which we find
Too indirect for long continuance.   105
 BLUNT. Shall I return this answer to the King?
 HOTSPUR. Not so, Sir Walter; we'll withdraw a while.
Go to the King; and let there be impawn'd
Some surety for a safe return again,
And in the morning early shall mine uncle   110
Bring him our purposes: and so farewell.
 BLUNT. I would you would accept of grace and love.
 HOTSPUR. And may be so we shall.
 BLUNT.   Pray God you do. (*Exeunt.*)

ACT IV/4 York. The ARCHBISHOP's palace.

(*Enter the* ARCHBISHOP OF YORK *and* SIR MICHAEL.)
 ARCHBISHOP. Hie, good Sir Michael; bear this sealed brief
With winged haste to the Lord Marshal,
This to my cousin Scroop, and all the rest
To whom they are directed. If you knew
How much they do import, you would make haste.   5
 SIR MICHAEL. My good lord,
I guess their tenour.
 ARCHBISHOP. Like enough you do.
To-morrow, good Sir Michael, is a day

88 *personal*: in personal command. 92 *in the neck of that*: right after that; *task'd*: taxed.
 95 *engag'd*: held as hostage. 98 *intelligence*: spies. 103 *head*: army 108 *impawn'd*:
pledged.

1 *brief*: letter. 7 *tenour*: character.

Wherein the fortune of ten thousand men
Must bide the touch; for, sir, at Shrewsbury, 10
As I am truly given to understand,
The King with mighty and quick-raised power
Meets with Lord Harry; and, I fear, Sir Michael,
What with the sickness of Northumberland,
Whose power was in the first proportion, 15
And what with Owen Glendower's absence thence,
Who with them was a rated sinew too
And comes not in, over-rul'd by prophecies,
I fear the power of Percy is too weak
To wage an instant trial with the King. 20
    SIR MICHAEL. Why, my good lord, you need not fear;
There is Douglas and Lord Mortimer.
    ARCHBISHOP. No, Mortimer is not there.
    SIR MICHAEL. But there is Murdoch, Vernon, Lord Harry Percy,
And there is my Lord of Worcester, and a head 25
Of gallant warriors, noble gentlemen.
    ARCHBISHOP. And so there is; but yet the King hath drawn
The special head of all the land together:
The Prince of Wales, Lord John of Lancaster,
The noble Westmoreland, and warlike Blunt; 30
And many moe corrivals and dear men
Of estimation and command in arms.
    SIR MICHAEL. Doubt not, my lord, they shall be well oppos'd.
    ARCHBISHOP. I hope no less, yet needful 't is to fear;
And, to prevent the worst, Sir Michael, speed; 35
For if Lord Percy thrive not, ere the King
Dismiss his power he means to visit us,
For he hath heard of our confederacy,
And 't is but wisdom to make strong against him:
Therefore make haste. I must go write again 40
To other friends; and so farewell, Sir Michael. (*Exeunt.*)

ACT V/I   The KING's camp near Shrewsbury.

(*Enter the* KING, PRINCE OF WALES, LORD JOHN OF LANCASTER,
SIR WALTER BLUNT, *and* FALSTAFF.)
    KING. How bloodily the sun begins to peer
Above yon busky hill! The day looks pale
At his distemperature.

---

15 *in the first proportion:* the largest.   17 *rated sinew:* force heavily counted on.   20 *wage:* carry on; *instant:* immediate.   31 *moe:* more; *corrivals:* allies.   37 *visit:* attack.

2 *busky:* wooded.   3 *distemperature:* unhealthy appearance.

PRINCE.   The southern wind
Doth play the trumpet to his purposes,
And by his hollow whistling in the leaves   5
Foretells a tempest and a blust'ring day.
   KING. Then with the losers let it sympathize,
For nothing can seem foul to those that win.   [*The trumpet sounds.*]
        (*Enter* WORCESTER *and* VERNON.)
How now, my Lord of Worcester! 't is not well
That you and I should meet upon such terms   10
As now we meet. You have deceiv'd our trust,
And made us doff our easy robes of peace,
To crush our old limbs in ungentle steel:
This is not well, my lord, this is not well.
What say you to it? Will you again unknit   15
This churlish knot of all-abhorred war?
And move in that obedient orb again
Where you did give a fair and natural light,
And be no more an exhal'd meteor,
A prodigy of fear and a portent   20
Of broached mischief to the unborn times?
   WORCESTER. Hear me, my liege.
For mine own part, I could be well content
To entertain the lag-end of my life
With quiet hours; for I do protest,   25
I have not sought the day of this dislike.
   KING. You have not sought it! How comes it, then?
   FALSTAFF. Rebellion lay in his way, and he found it.
   PRINCE. Peace, chewet, peace!
   WORCESTER. It pleas'd your Majesty to turn your looks   30
Of favour from myself and all our house;
And yet I must remember you, my lord,
We were the first and dearest of your friends.
For you my staff of office did I break
In Richard's time; and posted day and night   35
To meet you on the way, and kiss your hand,
When yet you were in place and in account
Nothing so strong and fortunate as I.
It was myself, my brother, and his son,
That brought you home and boldly did outdare   40
The dangers of the time. You swore to us,
And you did swear that oath at Doncaster,
That you did nothing purpose 'gainst the state;

---

17 *move in that obedient orb:* take your proper place, like one of the spheres or orbs of
  the Ptolemaic astronomy. 20 *prodigy:* omen. 21 *broached:* newly begun. 26 *dislike:*
enmity. 29 *chewet:* chatterer. 32 *remember:* remind.

Nor claim no further than your new-fall'n right,
The seat of Gaunt, dukedom of Lancaster.   45
To this we swore our aid. But in short space
It rain'd down fortune show'ring on your head;
And such a flood of greatness fell on you,
What with our help, what with the absent King,
What with the injuries of a wanton time,   50
The seeming sufferances that you had borne,
And the contrarious winds that held the King
So long in his unlucky Irish wars
That all in England did repute him dead;
And from this swarm of fair advantages   55
You took occasion to be quickly woo'd
To gripe the general sway into your hand;
Forgot your oath to us at Doncaster;
And being fed by us you us'd us so
As that ungentle gull, the cuckoo's bird,   60
Useth the sparrow; did oppress our nest;
Grew by our feeding to so great a bulk
That even our love durst not come near your sight
For fear of swallowing; but with nimble wing
We were enforc'd, for safety sake, to fly   65
Out of your sight and raise this present head;
Whereby we stand opposed by such means
As you yourself have forg'd against yourself
By unkind usage, dangerous countenance,
And violation of all faith and troth   70
Sworn to us in your younger enterprise.
    KING. These things indeed you have articulate,
Proclaim'd at market-crosses, read in churches,
To face the garment of rebellion
With some fine colour that may please the eye   75
Of fickle changelings and poor discontents,
Which gape and rub the elbow at the news
Of hurly-burly innovation.
And never yet did insurrection want
Such water-colours to impaint his cause;   80
Nor moody beggars, starving for a time
Of pell-mell havoc and confusion.
    PRINCE. In both your armies there is many a soul
Shall pay full dearly for this encounter,
If once they join in trial. Tell your nephew,   85

---

44 *new-fall'n*: recently inherited. 50 *wanton*: disorderly. 51 *sufferances*: abuses. 57
gripe the general sway: seize control of the government. 60 *gull*: bird. 72 *articulate*:
detailed. 74 *face*: adorn.

The Prince of Wales doth join with all the world
In praise of Henry Percy: by my hopes,
This present enterprise set off his head,
I do not think a braver gentleman,
More active-valiant or more valiant-young,   90
More daring or more bold, is now alive
To grace this latter age with noble deeds.
For my part, I may speak it to my shame,
I have a truant been to chivalry;
And so I hear he doth account me too;   95
Yet this before my father's majesty:
I am content that he shall take the odds
Of his great name and estimation,
And will, to save the blood on either side,
Try fortune with him in a single fight.   100
   KING. And, Prince of Wales, so dare we venture thee,
Albeit considerations infinite
Do make against it. No, good Worcester, no,
We love our people well; even those we love
That are misled upon your cousin's part;   105
And, will they take the offer of our grace,
Both he and they and you, yea, every man
Shall be my friend again and I'll be his:
So tell your cousin, and bring me word
What he will do. But if he will not yield,   110
Rebuke and dread correction wait on us
And they shall do their office. So, be gone;
We will not now be troubled with reply.
We offer fair; take it advisedly.   (*Exeunt* WORCESTER *and* VERNON.)
   PRINCE. It will not be accepted, on my life.   115
The Douglas and the Hotspur both together
Are confident against the world in arms.
   KING. Hence, therefore, every leader to his charge,
For, on their answer, will we set on them;
And God befriend us, as our cause is just!   120
         (*Exeunt all but the* PRINCE OF WALES *and* FALSTAFF.)
   FALSTAFF. Hal, if thou see me down in the battle and bestride me, so;
't is a point of friendship.
   PRINCE. Nothing but a Colossus can do thee that friendship. Say thy
prayers, and farewell.
   FALSTAFF. I would 't were bed-time, Hal, and all well.   125
   PRINCE. Why, thou owest God a death.   (*Exit.*)
   FALSTAFF. 'T is not due yet; I would be loath to pay Him before his

---

88 *set off his head*: excepted.   111 *wait on us*: serve us.   121 *bestride me*: protect me.

day. What need I be so forward with him that calls not on me? Well, 't is no matter; honour pricks me on. Yea, but how if honour prick me off when I come on? How then? Can honour set to a leg? No. Or an arm? No. Or take away the grief of a wound? No. Honour hath no skill in surgery, then? No. What is honour? A word. What is that word honour? Air. A trim reckoning! Who hath it? He that died o' Wednesday. Doth he feel it? No. Doth he hear it? No. 'T is insensible, then? Yea, to the dead. But will it not live with the living? No. Why? Detraction will not suffer it. Therefore I'll none of it. Honour is a mere scutcheon: and so ends my catechism. (*Exit.*)

Act V/2   The rebel camp.

(*Enter* WORCESTER *and* VERNON.)

WORCESTER. O, no, my nephew must not know, Sir Richard,
The liberal and kind offer of the King.

VERNON. 'Twere best he did.

WORCESTER.   Then are we all undone.
It is not possible, it cannot be,
The King should keep his word in loving us.   5
He will suspect us still, and find a time
To punish this offence in other faults:
Suspicion all our lives shall be stuck full of eyes;
For treason is but trusted like the fox,
Who, ne'er so tame, so cherish'd and lock'd up,   10
Will have a wild trick of his ancestors.
Look how we can, or sad or merrily,
Interpretation will misquote our looks,
And we shall feed like oxen at a stall,
The better cherish'd, still the nearer death.   15
My nephew's trespass may be well forgot;
It hath the excuse of youth and heat of blood,
And an adopted name of privilege,
A hare-brain'd Hotspur, govern'd by a spleen.
All his offences live upon my head   20
And on his father's. We did train him on,
And, his corruption being ta'en from us,
We, as the spring of all, shall pay for all.
Therefore, good cousin, let not Harry know,
In any case, the offer of the King.   25

129 *pricks:* spurs, urges; *prick me off:* cancel me. 130 *set to:* graft on. 131 *grief:* pain. 136 *scutcheon:* coat of arms displayed at a funeral.

6 *still:* always. 11 *wild trick:* wildness. 19 *spleen:* temper. 21 *train:* lead.

VERNON. Deliver what you will: I'll say 't is so.
Here comes your cousin.
(Enter HOTSPUR and DOUGLAS.)
HOTSPUR. My uncle is return'd;
Deliver up my Lord of Westmoreland.
Uncle, what news?   30
  WORCESTER. The King will bid you battle presently.
  DOUGLAS. Defy him by the Lord of Westmoreland.
  HOTSPUR. Lord Douglas, go you and tell him so.
  DOUGLAS. Marry, and shall, and very willingly.   (<i>Exit.</i>)
  WORCESTER. There is no seeming mercy in the King.   35
  HOTSPUR. Did you beg any? God forbid!
  WORCESTER. I told him gently of our grievances,
Of his oath-breaking; which he mended thus,
By now forswearing that he is forsworn.
He calls us rebels, traitors; and will scourge   40
With haughty arms this hateful name in us.
(Re-enter DOUGLAS.)
  DOUGLAS. Arm, gentlemen; to arms! for I have thrown
A brave defiance in King Henry's teeth,
And Westmoreland, that was engag'd, did bear it;
Which cannot choose but bring him quickly on.   45
  WORCESTER. The Prince of Wales stepp'd forth before the King,
And, nephew, challeng'd you to single fight.
  HOTSPUR. O, would the quarrel lay upon our heads,
And that no man might draw short breath to-day
But I and Harry Monmouth! Tell me, tell me,   50
How show'd his tasking? Seem'd it in contempt?
  VERNON. No, by my soul; I never in my life
Did hear a challenge urg'd more modestly,
Unless a brother should a brother dare
To gentle exercise and proof of arms.   55
He gave you all the duties of a man,
Trimm'd up your praises with a princely tongue,
Spoke your deservings like a chronicle,
Making you ever better than his praise
By still dispraising praise valued with you;   60
And, which became him like a prince indeed,
He made a blushing cital of himself,
And chid his truant youth with such a grace
As if he master'd there a double spirit
Of teaching and of learning instantly.   65

---

38 *mended:* excused. 39 *forswearing:* denying; *is forsworn:* has broken pledges. 44 *engag'd:* held as hostage. 51 *tasking:* challenge. 60 *valued:* compared. 62 *cital:* mention.

There did he pause; but let me tell the world,
If he outlive the envy of this day,
England did never owe so sweet a hope,
So much misconstrued in his wantonness.
    HOTSPUR. Cousin, I think thou art enamoured   70
On his follies: never did I hear
Of any prince so wild a liberty.
But be he as he will, yet once ere night
I will embrace him with a soldier's arm,
That he shall shrink under my courtesy.   75
Arm, arm with speed! and, fellows, soldiers, friends,
Better consider what you have to do
Than I, that have not well the gift of tongue,
Can lift your blood up with persuasion.
                (*Enter a* MESSENGER.)
    MESSENGER. My lord, here are letters for you.   80
    HOTSPUR. I cannot read them now.
O gentlemen, the time of life is short!
To spend that shortness basely were too long,
If life did ride upon a dial's point,
Still ending at the arrival of an hour.   85
An if we live, we live to tread on kings;
If die, brave death, when princes die with us!
Now, for our consciences, the arms are fair,
When the intent of bearing them is just.
            (*Enter another* MESSENGER.)
    SECOND MESSENGER. My lord, prepare; the King comes on apace.   90
    HOTSPUR. I thank him that he cuts me from my tale,
For I profess not talking; only this—
Let each man do his best; and here draw I
A sword, whose temper I intend to stain
With the best blood that I can meet withal   95
In the adventure of this perilous day.
Now *Esperancé!* Percy! and set on.
Sound all the lofty instruments of war,
And by that music let us all embrace;
For, heaven to earth, some of us never shall   100
A second time do such a courtesy.   [*They embrace and exeunt.*]

---

67 *envy:* malice. 68 *owe:* possess. 69 *wantonness:* irresponsibility. 84 *dial's point:*
hand of a clock.

ACT V/3   Plain between the camps.

(The trumpets sound. The KING *enters with his army and passes over the stage. Noises of battle. Then enter* DOUGLAS *and* SIR WALTER BLUNT.*)*

BLUNT. What is thy name, that in the battle thus
Thou crossest me? What honour dost thou seek
Upon my head?
DOUGLAS.   Know then, my name is Douglas;
And I do haunt thee in the battle thus
Because some tell me that thou art a king.   5
BLUNT. They tell thee true.
DOUGLAS. The Lord of Stafford dear to-day hath bought
Thy likeness, for instead of thee, King Harry,
This sword hath ended him. So shall it thee,
Unless thou yield thee as my prisoner.   10
BLUNT. I was not born a yielder, thou proud Scot;
And thou shalt find a king that will revenge
Lord Stafford's death.   [*They fight,* DOUGLAS *kills* BLUNT.]
                    (*Enter* HOTSPUR.)
HOTSPUR. O Douglas, hadst thou fought at Holmedon thus,
I never had triumph'd upon a Scot.   15
DOUGLAS. All's done, all's won; here breathless lies the King.
HOTSPUR. Where?
DOUGLAS. Here.
HOTSPUR. This, Douglas? No. I know this face full well.
A gallant knight he was, his name was Blunt;   20
Semblably furnish'd like the King himself.
DOUGLAS. A fool go with thy soul, whither it goes!
A borrowed title hast thou bought too dear:
Why didst thou tell me that thou wert a king?
HOTSPUR. The King hath many marching in his coats.   25
DOUGLAS. Now, by my sword, I will kill all his coats;
I'll murder all his wardrobe, piece by piece,
Until I meet the King.
HOTSPUR.   Up, and away!
Our soldiers stand full fairly for the day.   (*Exeunt.*)
                 (*Alarum. Enter* FALSTAFF, *alone.*)
FALSTAFF. Though I could scape shot-free at London, I fear the shot   30
here; here's no scoring but upon the pate. Soft! who are you? Sir Walter
Blunt: there's honour for you! Here's no vanity! I am as hot as molten
lead, and as heavy too: God keep lead out of me! I need no more weight

---

21 *Semblably furnish'd*: equipped to appear.   25 *coats*: coats of arms.   30 *shot-free*: without paying bills.

than mine own bowels. I have led my ragamuffins where they are peppered. There's not three of my hundred and fifty left alive; and they   35
are for the town's end, to beg during life. But who comes here?

(Enter the PRINCE.)

PRINCE. What, stand'st thou idle here? Lend me thy sword.
Many a nobleman lies stark and stiff
Under the hoofs of vaunting enemies,
Whose deaths are yet unreveng'd. I prithee, lend me thy sword.   40

FALSTAFF. O Hal, I prithee, give me leave to breathe a while. Turk
Gregory never did such deeds in arms as I have done this day. I have paid
Percy, I have made him sure.

PRINCE. He is, indeed; and living to kill thee. I prithee, lend me thy
sword.   45

FALSTAFF. Nay, before God, Hal, if Percy be alive, thou gets not my
sword; but take my pistol, if thou wilt.

PRINCE. Give it me. What, is it in the case?

FALSTAFF. Ay, Hal; 't is hot, 't is hot: there's that will sack a city.

[*The* PRINCE *draws it out, and finds it to be a bottle of sack.*]

PRINCE. What, is it a time to jest and dally now?   50

[*He throws the bottle at him. Exit.*]

FALSTAFF. Well, if Percy be alive, I'll pierce him. If he do come in my
way, so; if he do not, if I come in his willingly, let him make a carbonado
of me. I like not such grinning honour as Sir Walter hath: give me life,
which if I can save, so; if not, honour comes unlooked for, and there's
an end.   (*Exit.*)   55

ACT V/4   Another part of the field.

(*Alarum. Excursions. Enter the* KING, *the* PRINCE, LORD JOHN OF
LANCASTER, *and* EARL OF WESTMORELAND.)

KING. I prithee,
Harry, withdraw thyself: thou bleedest too much.
Lord John of Lancaster, go you with him.

LANCASTER. Not I, my lord, unless I did bleed too.

PRINCE. I beseech your Majesty, make up,   5
Lest your retirement do amaze your friends.

KING. I will do so.
My Lord of Westmoreland, lead him to his tent.

WESTMORELAND. Come, my lord, I'll lead you to your tent.

PRINCE. Lead me, my lord? I do not need your help: 10
And God forbid a shallow scratch should drive
The Prince of Wales from such a field as this,

41–42 *Turk Gregory:* a tyrannical Pope.   52 *carbonado:* broiled steak.

5 *make up:* advance.   6 *amaze:* confuse.

Where stain'd nobility lies trodden on,
And rebels' arms triúmph in massacres!
   LANCASTER. We breathe too long. Come, cousin Westmoreland,   15
Our duty this way lies; for God's sake, come.
                (*Exeunt* PRINCE JOHN *and* WESTMORELAND.)
   PRINCE. By God, thou hast deceiv'd me, Lancaster;
I did not think thee lord of such a spirit.
Before, I lov'd thee as a brother, John;
But now, I do respect thee as my soul.   20
   KING. I saw him hold Lord Percy at the point
With lustier maintenance than I did look for
Of such an ungrown warrior.
   PRINCE.   O, this boy
Lends mettle to us all!   (*Exit.*)
               (*Enter* DOUGLAS.)
   DOUGLAS. Another king! they grow like Hydra's heads.   25
I am the Douglas, fatal to all those
That wear those colours on them. What art thou,
That counterfeit'st the person of a king?
   KING. The King himself; who, Douglas, grieves at heart
So many of his shadows thou hast met   30
And not the very King. I have two boys
Seek Percy and thyself about the field;
But, seeing thou fall'st on me so luckily,
I will assay thee; so, defend thyself.
   DOUGLAS. I fear thou art another counterfeit;   35
And yet, in faith, thou bear'st thee like a king.
But mine I am sure thou art, whoe'er thou be,
And thus I win thee.
   [*They fight; the* KING *being in danger, re-enter* PRINCE OF WALES.]
   PRINCE. Hold up thy head, vile Scot, or thou art like
Never to hold it up again! The spirits   40
Of valiant Shirley, Stafford, Blunt, are in my arms.
It is the Prince of Wales that threatens thee,
Who never promiseth but he means to pay.
               [*They fight:* DOUGLAS *flies.*]
Cheerly, my lord, how fares your Grace?
Sir Nicholas Gawsey hath for succour sent,   45
And so hath Clifton: I'll to Clifton straight.
   KING. Stay, and breathe a while.
Thou hast redeem'd thy lost opinion,
And show'd thou mak'st some tender of my life,

---

15 *breathe:* rest.   22 *lustier maintenance:* more vigorous behavior.   25 *Hydra:* in Greek
mythology, a monster who grew two heads whenever one was cut off.   34 *assay:* test.
48 *opinion:* reputation.   49 *mak'st some tender of:* have some concern for.

In this fair rescue thou hast brought to me.   50
  PRINCE. O God! they did me too much injury
That ever said I hearken'd for your death.
If it were so, I might have let alone
The insulting hand of Douglas over you,
Which would have been as speedy in your end   55
As all the poisonous potions in the world,
And sav'd the treacherous labour of your son.
  KING. Make up to Clifton: I'll to Sir Nicholas Gawsey.   (*Exit.*)
                    (*Enter* HOTSPUR.)
  HOTSPUR. If I mistake not, thou art Harry Monmouth.
  PRINCE. Thou speak'st as if I would deny my name.   60
  HOTSPUR. My name is Harry Percy.
  PRINCE.   Why, then I see
A very valiant rebel of the name.
I am the Prince of Wales; and think not, Percy,
To share with me in glory any more:
Two stars keep not their motion in one sphere;   65
Nor can one England brook a double reign
Of Harry Percy and the Prince of Wales.
  HOTSPUR. Nor shall it, Harry; for the hour is come
To end the one of us; and would to God
Thy name in arms were now as great as mine!   70
  PRINCE. I'll make a greater ere I part from thee;
And all the budding honours on thy crest
I'll crop, to make a garland for my head.
  HOTSPUR. I can no longer brook thy vanities.   [*They fight.*]
                    (*Enter* FALSTAFF.)
  FALSTAFF. Well said, Hal! to it, Hal! Nay, you shall find no boy's play   75
here, I can tell you.
(*Re-enter* DOUGLAS; *he fights with* FALSTAFF, *who fall down as if he were
          dead and exit* DOUGLAS. *The* PRINCE *kills* PERCY.)
  HOTSPUR. O, Harry, thou hast robb'd me of my youth!
I better brook the loss of brittle life
Than those proud titles thou hast won of me:
They wound my thoughts worse than thy sword my flesh: 80
But thought's the slave of life, and life time's fool;
And time, that takes survey of all the world,
Must have a stop. O, I could prophesy,
But that the earthy and cold hand of death
Lies on my tongue: no, Percy, thou art dust,   85
And food for—   [*Dies.*]
  PRINCE. For worms, brave Percy: fare thee well, great heart!

58 *Make up:* bring help.   72 *crest:* helmet.   81 *fool:* slave or servant.   82 *takes survey
of:* dominates.

Ill-weav'd ambition, how much art thou shrunk!
When that this body did contain a spirit,
A kingdom for it was too small a bound;   90
But now two paces of the vilest earth
Is room enough: this earth that bears thee dead
Bears not alive so stout a gentleman.
If thou wert sensible of courtesy,
I should not make so dear a show of zeal;   95
But let my favours hide thy mangled face;
And, even in thy behalf, I'll thank myself
For doing these fair rites of tenderness.
Adieu, and take thy praise with thee to heaven!
Thy ignomy sleep with thee in the grave,   100
But not remember'd in thy epitaph!
                    [*He spies* FALSTAFF *on the ground.*]
What, old acquaintance! could not all this flesh
Keep in a little life? Poor Jack, farewell!
I could have better spar'd a better man:
O, I should have a heavy miss of thee,   105
If I were much in love with vanity!
Death hath not struck so fat a deer to-day,
Though many dearer, in this bloody fray.
Embowell'd will I see thee by and by;
Till then in blood by noble Percy lie.   (*Exit.*)   110
    FALSTAFF [*rising up*]. Embowelled; if thou embowel me to-day, I'll give
you leave to powder me and eat me too to-morrow. 'Sblood, 't was time to
counterfeit, or that hot termagant Scot had paid me scot and lot too.
Counterfeit? I lie, I am no counterfeit: to die is to be a counterfeit, for he
is but the counterfeit of a man who hath not the life of a man; but to   115
counterfeit dying, when a man thereby liveth, is to be no counterfeit, but
the true and perfect image of life indeed. The better part of valour is discretion; in the which better part I have saved my life. 'Zounds, I am afraid
of this gunpowder Percy, though he be dead: how, if he should counterfeit
too and rise? By my faith, I am afraid he would prove the better counter-   120
feit. Therefore I'll make him sure; yea, and I'll swear I killed him. Why
may not he rise as well as I? Nothing confutes me but eyes, and nobody
sees me. Therefore, sirrah, [*stabbing him*] with a new wound in your
thigh, come you along with me.   [*Takes up* HOTSPUR *on his back.*]
            (*Re-enter* PRINCE *and* JOHN OF LANCASTER.)
    PRINCE. Come, brother John; full bravely hast thou flesh'd   125
Thy maiden sword.

90 *bound:* limit. 94 *sensible:* able to feel. 95 *dear:* sincere. 96 *favours:* scarf. 100
ignomy: ignominy. 106 *vanity:* frivolity. 109 *Embowell'd:* eviscerated in preparation
for embalming. 112 *powder:* salt. 113 *termagant:* angry; *scot and lot:* fully. 118
part: quality. 125 *flesh'd:* initiated.

LANCASTER.   But, soft! whom have we here?
Did you not tell me this fat man was dead?
     PRINCE. I did; I saw him dead,
Breathless and bleeding on the ground. Art thou alive?
Or is it fantasy that plays upon our eyesight?   130
I prithee, speak; we will not trust our eyes
Without our ears: thou are not what thou seem'st.
     FALSTAFF. No, that's certain; I am not a double man; but if I be not
Jack Falstaff, then am I a Jack. There is Percy [*throwing the body down*].
If your father will do me any honour, so; if not, let him kill the next   135
Percy himself. I look to be either earl or duke, I can assure you.
     PRINCE. Why, Percy I killed myself, and saw thee dead.
     FALSTAFF. Didst thou? Lord, Lord, how this world is given to lying! I
grant you I was down and out of breath, and so was he; but we rose both
at an instant and fought a long hour by Shrewsbury clock. If I may be   140
believed, so; if not, let them that should reward valour bear the sin upon
their own heads. I'll take it upon my death, I gave him this wound in the
thigh: if the man were alive and would deny it, 'zounds, I would make him
eat a piece of my sword.
     LANCASTER. This is the strangest tale that ever I heard.   145
     PRINCE. This is the strangest fellow, brother John.
Come, bring your luggage nobly on your back.
For my part, if a lie may do thee grace,
I'll gild it with the happiest terms I have.   [*A retreat is sounded.*]
The trumpet sounds retreat; the day is ours.   150
Come, brother, let us to the highest of the field,
To see what friends are living, who are dead.
                              (*Exeunt* PRINCE *and* LANCASTER.)
     FALSTAFF. I'll follow, as they say, for reward. He that rewards me, God
reward him! If I do grow great, I'll grow less; for I'll purge, and leave
sack, and live cleanly as a nobleman should do.   (*Exit.*)   155

ACT V/5   Another part of the field.

(*The trumpets sound. Enter the* KING, PRINCE OF WALES, LORD JOHN OF
LANCASTER, EARL OF WESTMORELAND, *with* WORCESTER *and* VERNON
                              prisoners.)
     KING. Thus ever did rebellion find rebuke.
Ill-spirited Worcester! did not we send grace,
Pardon, and terms of love to all of you?
And wouldst thou turn our offers contrary?
Misuse the tenour of thy kinsman's trust?   5
Three knights upon our party slain to-day,

130 *plays upon:* deceives.   133 *double man:* ghost.

A noble earl, and many a creature else
Had been alive this hour,
If like a Christian thou hadst truly borne
Betwixt our armies true intelligence.   10
  WORCESTER. What I have done my safety urg'd me to;
And I embrace this fortune patiently,
Since not to be avoided it falls on me.
  KING. Bear Worcester to the death and Vernon too.
Other offenders we will pause upon.   15
                    (*Exeunt* WORCESTER *and* VERNON *guarded.*)
How goes the field?
  PRINCE. The noble Scot, Lord Douglas, when he saw
The fortune of the day quite turn'd from him,
The noble Percy slain, and all his men
Upon the foot of fear, fled with the rest;   20
And falling from a hill, he was so bruis'd
That the pursuers took him. At my tent
The Douglas is; and I beseech your Grace
I may dispose of him.
  KING.   With all my heart.
  PRINCE. Then, brother John of Lancaster, to you   25
This honourable bounty shall belong.
Go to the Douglas, and deliver him
Up to his pleasure, ransomless and free:
His valours shown upon our crests to-day
Have taught us how to cherish such high deeds   30
Even in the bosom of our adversaries.
  LANCASTER. I thank your Grace for this high courtesy,
Which I shall give away immediately.
  KING. Then this remains, that we divide our power.
You, son John, and my cousin Westmoreland   35
Towards York shall bend you with your dearest speed.
To meet Northumberland and the prelate Scroop,
Who, as we hear, are busily in arms:
Myself and you, son Harry, will towards Wales,
To fight with Glendower and the Earl of March.   40
Rebellion in this land shall lose his sway,
Meeting the check of such another day;
And since this business so fair is done,
Let us not leave till all our own be won.   (*Exeunt.*)

---

15 *pause upon:* consider.   36 *bend you:* turn.   41 *sway:* power.   42 *check:* hindrance.

George Bernard Shaw
Arms and the Man

A pleasant play

ACT I

(*Night: A lady's bedchamber in Bulgaria, in a small town near the Dragoman Pass, late in November in the year 1885. Through an open window with a little balcony a peak of the Balkans, wonderfully white and beautiful in the starlit snow, seems quite close at hand, though it is really miles away. The interior of the room is not like anything to be seen in the west of Europe. It is half rich Bulgarian, half cheap Viennese. Above the head of the bed, which stands against a little wall cutting off the left hand corner of the room, is a painted wooden shrine, blue and gold, with an ivory image of Christ, and a light hanging before it in a pierced metal ball suspended by three chains. The principal seat, placed towards the other side of the room and opposite the window, is a Turkish ottoman. The counterpane and hangings of the bed, the window curtains, the little carpet, and all the ornamental textile fabrics in the room are oriental and gorgeous; the paper on the walls is occidental and paltry. The washstand, against the wall on the side nearest the ottoman and window, consists of an enamelled iron basin with a pail beneath it in a painted metal frame, and a single towel on the rail at the side. The dressing table, between the bed and the window, is a common pine table, covered with a cloth of many colours, with an expensive toilet mirror on it. The door is on the side nearest the bed; and there is a chest of drawers between. This chest of drawers is also covered by a variegated native cloth; and on it there is a pile of paper backed novels, a box of chocolate creams, and a miniature easel with a large photograph of an extremely handsome officer, whose lofty bearing and magnetic glance can be felt even from the portrait. The room is lighted by a candle on the chest of drawers, and another on the dressing table with a box of matches beside it.*

The window is hinged doorwise and stands wide open. Outside, a pair of wooden shutters, opening outwards, also stand open. On the balcony a young lady, intensely conscious of the romantic beauty of the night, and of the fact that her own youth and beauty are part of it, is gazing at the snowy Balkans. She is in her nightgown, well covered by a long mantle of furs, worth, on a moderate estimate, about three times the furniture of the room.

Her reverie is interrupted by her mother, CATHERINE PETKOFF, *a woman over forty, imperiously energetic, with magnificent black hair and eyes, who might be a very splendid specimen of the wife of a mountain farmer, but is determined to be a Viennese lady, and to that end wears a fashionable tea gown on all occasions.*)

CATHERINE (*entering hastily, full of good news*). Raina! (*She pronounces it Rah-eena, with the stress on the ee.*) Raina! (*She goes to the bed, expecting to find* RAINA *there.*) Why, where—? (RAINA *looks into the room.*) Heavens, child! are you out in the night air instead of in your bed? Youll catch your death. Louka told me you were asleep.

RAINA (*dreamily*). I sent her away. I wanted to be alone. The stars are so beautiful! What is the matter?

CATHERINE. Such news! There has been a battle.

RAINA (*her eyes dilating*). Ah! (*She comes eagerly to* CATHERINE.)

CATHERINE. A great battle at Slivnitza! A victory! And it was won by Sergius.

RAINA. (*with a cry of delight*). Ah! (*They embrace rapturously.*) Oh, mother! (*then, with sudden anxiety*) is father safe?

CATHERINE. Of course! he sends me the news. Sergius is the hero of the hour, the idol of the regiment.

RAINA. Tell me, tell me. How was it? (*Ecstatically.*) Oh, mother! mother! mother! (*She pulls her mother down on the ottoman; and they kiss one another frantically.*)

CATHERINE (*with surging enthusiasm*). You cant guess how splendid it is. A cavalry charge! think of that! He defied our Russian commanders—acted without orders—led a charge on his own responsibility—headed it himself—was the first man to sweep through their guns. Cant you see it, Raina: our gallant splendid Bulgarians with their swords and eyes flashing, thundering down like an avalanche and scattering the wretched Serbs and their dandified Austrian officers like chaff. And you! you kept Sergius waiting a year before you would be betrothed to him. Oh, if you have a drop of Bulgarian blood in your veins, you will worship him when he comes back.

RAINA. What will he care for my poor little worship after the acclamations of a whole army of heroes? But no matter: I am so happy! so proud! (*She rises and walks about excitedly.*) It proves that all our ideas were real after all.

CATHERINE (*indignantly*). Our ideas real! What do you mean?

RAINA. Our ideas of what Sergius would do. Our patriotism. Our heroic ideals. I sometimes used to doubt whether they were anything but dreams. Oh, what faithless little creatures girls are! When I buckled on Sergius's sword he looked so noble: it was treason to think of disillusion or humiliation or failure. And yet—and yet— (*She sits down again suddenly.*) Promise me youll never tell him.

CATHERINE. Dont ask me for promises until I know what I'm promising.

RAINA. Well, it came into my head just as he was holding me in his arms and looking into my eyes, that perhaps we only had our heroic ideas because we are so fond of reading Byron and Pushkin, and because we were so delighted with the opera that season at Bucharest. Real life is so seldom like that! indeed never, as far as I knew it then. (*Remorsefully*) Only think, mother: I doubted him: I wondered whether all his heroic qualities and his soldiership might not prove mere imagination when he went into a real battle. I had an uneasy fear that he might cut a poor figure there beside all those clever officers from the Tsar's court.

CATHERINE. A poor figure! Shame on you! The Serbs have Austrian officers who are just as clever as the Russians; but we have beaten them in every battle for all that.

RAINA (*laughing and snuggling against her mother*). Yes: I was only a prosaic little coward. Oh, to think that it was all true! that Sergius is just as splendid and noble as he looks! that the world is really a glorious world for women who can see its glory and men who can act its romance! What happiness! what unspeakable fulfilment!

(*They are interrupted by the entry of* LOUKA, *a handsome proud girl in a pretty Bulgarian peasant's dress with double apron, so defiant that her servility to* RAINA *is almost insolent. She is afraid of* CATHERINE, *but even with her goes as far as she dares.*)

LOUKA. If you please, madam, all the windows are to be closed and the shutters made fast. They say there may be shooting in the streets. (RAINA *and* CATHERINE *rise together, alarmed.*) The Serbs are being chased right back through the pass; and they say they may run into the town. Our cavalry will be after them; and our people will be ready for them, you may be sure, now theyre running away. (*She goes out on the balcony, and pulls the outside shutters to; then steps back into the room.*)

CATHERINE (*businesslike, housekeeping instincts aroused*). I must see that everything is made safe downstairs.

RAINA. I wish our people were not so cruel. What glory is there in killing wretched fugitives?

CATHERINE. Cruel! Do you suppose they would hesitate to kill you—or worse?

RAINA (*to* LOUKA). Leave the shutters so that I can just close them if I hear any noise.

CATHERINE (*authoritatively, turning on her way to the door*). Oh no, dear: you must keep them fastened. You would be sure to drop off to sleep and leave them open. Make them fast, Louka.

LOUKA. Yes, madam. (*She fastens them.*)

RAINA. Dont be anxious about me. The moment I hear a shot, I shall blow out the candles and roll myself up in bed with my ears well covered.

CATHERINE. Quite the wisest thing you can do, my love. Good night.

RAINA. Goodnight. (*Her emotion comes back for a moment.*) Wish me joy. (*They kiss.*) This is the happiest night of my life—if only there are no fugitives.

CATHERINE. Go to bed, dear; and dont think of them. (*She goes out.*)

LOUKA (*secretly to* RAINA). If you would like the shutters open, just give them a push like this. (*She pushes them: they open: she pulls them to again.*) One of them ought to be bolted at the bottom; but the bolt's gone.

RAINA (*with dignity, reproving her*). Thanks, Louka; but we must do what we are told. (LOUKA *makes a grimace.*) Goodnight.

LOUKA (*carelessly*). Goodnight. (*She goes out, swaggering.*)

(RAINA, *left alone, takes off her fur cloak and throws it on the ottoman. Then she goes to the chest of drawers, and adores the portrait there with feelings that are beyond all expression. She does not kiss it or press it to her breast, or shew it any mark of bodily affection; but she takes it in her hands and elevates it, like a priestess.*)

RAINA (*looking up at the picture*). Oh, I shall never be unworthy of you any more, my soul's hero: never, never, never. (*She replaces it reverently. Then she selects a novel from the little pile of books. She turns over the leaves dreamily; finds her page; turns the book inside out at it; and, with a happy sigh, gets into bed and prepares to read herself to sleep. But before abandoning herself to fiction, she raises her eyes once more, thinking of the blessed reality, and murmurs*) My hero! my hero!

(*A distant shot breaks the quiet of the night. She starts, listening; and two more shots, much nearer, follow, startling her so that she scrambles out of bed, and hastily blows out the candle on the chest of drawers. Then, putting her fingers in her ears, she runs to the dressing table, blows out the light there, and hurries back to bed in the dark, nothing being visible but the glimmer of the light in the pierced ball before the image, and the starlight seen through the slits at the top of the shutters. The firing breaks out again: there is a startling fusillade quite close at hand. Whilst it is still echoing, the shutters disappear, pulled open from without; and for an instant the rectangle of snowy starlight flashes out with the figure of a man silhouetted in black upon it. The shutters close immediately; and the room is dark again. But the silence is now broken by the sound of panting. Then there is a scratch; and the flame of a match is seen in the middle of the room.*)

RAINA (*crouching on the bed*). Who's there? (*The match is out instantly.*) Who's there? Who is that?

A MAN'S VOICE (*in the darkness, subduedly, but threateningly*). Sh—sh! Dont call out; or youll be shot. Be good; and no harm will happen to you. (*She is heard leaving her bed, and making for the door.*) Take care: it's no use trying to run away.

RAINA. But who—

THE VOICE (*warning*). Remember: if you raise your voice my revolver will go off. (*Commandingly.*) Strike a light and let me see you. Do you hear? (*Another moment of silence and darkness as she retreats to the chest of drawers. Then she lights a candle; and the mystery is at an end. He is a man of about* 35, *in a deplorable plight, bespattered with mud and blood and snow, his belt and the strap of his revolver case keeping together the torn ruins of the blue tunic of a Serbian artillery officer. All that the candlelight and his unwashed unkempt condition make it possible to discern is that he is of middling stature and undistinguished appearance, with strong neck and shoulders, roundish obstinate looking head covered with short crisp bronze curls, clear quick eyes and good brows and mouth, hopelessly prosaic nose like that of a strong minded baby, trim soldierlike carriage and energetic manner, and with all his wits about him in spite of his desperate predicament: even with a sense of the humor of it, without, however, the least intention of trifling with it or throwing away a chance. Reckoning up what he can guess about* RAINA: *her age, her social position, her character, and the extent to which she is frightened, he continues, more politely but still most determinedly.*) Excuse my disturbing you; but you recognize my uniform? Serb! If I'm caught I shall be killed. (*Menacingly.*) Do you understand that?

RAINA. Yes.

THE MAN. Well, I dont intend to get killed if I can help it. (*Still more formidably.*) Do you understand that? (*He locks the door quickly but quietly.*)

RAINA (*disdainfully*). I suppose not. (*She draws herself up superbly, and looks him straight in the face, adding, with cutting emphasis.*) Some soldiers, I know, are afraid to die.

THE MAN (*with grim goodhumor*). All of them, dear lady, all of them, believe me. It is our duty to live as long as we can. Now, if you raise an alarm—

RAINA (*cutting him short*). You will shoot me. How do you know that *I* am afraid to die?

THE MAN (*cunningly*). Ah; but suppose I dont shoot you, what will happen then? A lot of your cavalry will burst into this pretty room of yours and slaughter me here like a pig; for I'll fight like a demon: they shant get me into the street to amuse themselves with: I know what they are. Are you prepared to receive that sort of company in your present undress? (RAINA, *suddenly conscious of her nightgown, instinctively shrinks and gathers it more closely about her neck. He watches her and adds pitilessly.*) Hardly presentable, eh? (*She turns to the ottoman. He raises his pistol instantly, and cries*) Stop! (*She stops.*) Where are you going?

RAINA (*with dignified patience*). Only to get my cloak.

THE MAN (*passing swiftly to the ottoman and snatching the cloak*). A good idea! I'll keep the cloak; and youll take care that nobody comes in and sees you without it. This is a better weapon than the revolver: eh? (*He throws the pistol down on the ottoman.*)

RAINA (*revolted*). It is not the weapon of a gentleman!

THE MAN. It's good enough for a man with only you to stand between him and death. (*As they look at one another for a moment,* RAINA *hardly able to believe that even a Serbian officer can be so cynically and selfishly unchivalrous, they are startled by a sharp fusillade in the street. The chill of imminent death hushes the man's voice as he adds*) Do you hear? If you are going to bring those blackguards in on me you shall receive them as you are.

(*Clamor and disturbance. The pursuers in the street batter at the house door, shouting*) Open the door! Open the door! Wake up, will you! (*A man servant's voice calls to them angrily from within.*) This is Major Petkoff's house: you cant come in here. (*But a renewal of the clamor, and a torrent of blows on the door, end with his letting a chain down with a clank, followed by a rush of heavy footsteps and a din of triumphant yells, dominated at last by the voice of* CATHERINE, *indignantly addressing an officer with*) What does this mean, sir? Do you know where you are? (*The noise subsides suddenly.*)

LOUKA (*outside, knocking at the bedroom door*). My lady! my lady! get up quick and open the door. If you dont they will break it down.

(*The fugitive throws up his head with the gesture of a man who sees that it is all over with him, and drops the manner he has been assuming to intimidate* RAINA.)

THE MAN (*sincerely and kindly*). No use, dear: I'm done for. (*Flinging the cloak to her.*) Quick! wrap yourself up: they're coming.

RAINA. Oh, thank you. (*She wraps herself up with intense relief.*)

THE MAN (*between his teeth*). Dont mention it.

RAINA (*anxiously*). What will you do?

THE MAN (*grimly*). The first man in will find out. Keep out of the way; and dont look. It wont last long; but it will not be nice. (*He draws his sabre and faces the door, waiting.*)

RAINA. (*impulsively*). I'll help you. I'll save you.

THE MAN. You cant.

RAINA. I can. I'll hide you. (*She drags him towards the window.*) Here! behind the curtains.

THE MAN (*yielding to her*). Theres just half a chance, if you keep your head.

RAINA (*drawing the curtain before him*). S-sh! (*She makes for the ottoman.*)

THE MAN (*putting out his head*). Remember—

RAINA (*running back to him*). Yes?

THE MAN.—nine soldiers out of ten are born fools.

RAINA. Oh! (*She draws the curtain angrily before him.*)

THE MAN (*looking out at the other side*). If they find me, I promise you a fight: a devil of a fight.

(*She stamps at him. He disappears hastily. She takes off her cloak, and throws it across the foot of the bed. Then, with a sleepy, disturbed air, she opens the door.* LOUKA *enters excitedly.*)

LOUKA. One of those beasts of Serbs has been seen climbing up the waterpipe to your balcony. Our men want to search for him; and they are so wild and drunk and furious. (*She makes for the other side of the room to get as far from the door as possible.*) My lady says you are to dress at once and to—(*She sees the revolver lying on the ottoman, and stops, petrified.*)

RAINA (*as if annoyed at being disturbed*). They shall not search here. Why have they been let in?

CATHERINE (*coming in hastily*). Raina, darling, are you safe? Have you seen anyone or heard anything?

RAINA. I heard the shooting. Surely the soldiers will not dare come in here?

CATHERINE. I have found a Russian officer, thank Heaven: he knows Sergius. (*Speaking through the door to someone outside.*) Sir: will you come in now. My daughter will receive you.

(*A young Russian* OFFICER, *in Bulgarian uniform, enters, sword in hand.*)

OFFICER (*with soft feline politeness and stiff military carriage*). Good evening, gracious lady. I am sorry to intrude; but there is a Serb hiding on the balcony. Will you and the gracious lady your mother please to withdraw whilst we search?

RAINA (*petulantly*). Nonsense, sir: you can see that there is no one on the balcony. (*She throws the shutters wide open and stands with her back to the curtain where* THE MAN *is hidden, pointing to the moonlit balcony. A couple of shots are fired right under the window; and a bullet shatters the glass opposite* RAINA, *who winks and gasps, but stands her ground; whilst* CATHERINE *screams, and* THE OFFICER, *with a cry of* Take care! *rushes to the balcony.*)

THE OFFICER (*on the balcony, shouting savagely down to the street*). Cease firing there, you fools: do you hear? Cease firing, damn you! (*He glares down for a moment; then turns to* RAINA, *trying to resume his polite manner.*) Could anyone have got in without your knowledge? Were you asleep?

RAINA. No: I have not been to bed.

THE OFFICER (*impatiently, coming back into the room*). Your neighbors have their heads so full of runaway Serbs that they see them everywhere. (*Politely.*) Gracious lady: a thousand pardons. Goodnight. (*Military bow, which* RAINA *returns coldly. Another to* CATHERINE, *who follows him out.*)

(RAINA *closes the shutters. She turns and sees* LOUKA, *who has been watching the scene curiously.*)

RAINA. Dont leave my mother, Louka, until the soldiers go away.

(LOUKA *glances at* RAINA, *at the ottoman, at the curtain; then purses her lips secretively, laughs insolently, and goes out.* RAINA, *highly offended by this demonstration, follows her to the door, and shuts it behind her with a slam, locking it violently.* THE MAN *immediately steps out from behind the curtain, sheathing his sabre. Then, dismissing the danger from his mind in a business-like way, he comes affably to* RAINA.)

THE MAN. A narrow shave; but a miss is as good as a mile. Dear young lady: your servant to the death. I wish for your sake I had joined the Bulgarian army instead of the other one. I am not a native Serb.

RAINA (*haughtily*). No: you are one of the Austrians who set the Serbs on to rob us of our national liberty, and who officer their army for them. We hate them!

THE MAN. Austrian! not I. Dont hate me, dear young lady. I am a Swiss, fighting merely as a professional soldier. I joined the Serbs because they came first on the road from Switzerland. Be generous: youve beaten us hollow.

RAINA. Have I not been generous?

THE MAN. Noble! Heroic! But I'm not saved yet. This particular rush will soon pass through; but the pursuit will go on all night by fits and starts. I must take my chance to get off in a quiet interval. (*Pleasantly.*) You dont mind my waiting just a minute or two, do you?

RAINA (*putting on her most genteel society manner*). Oh, not at all. Wont you sit down?

THE MAN. Thanks. (*He sits on the foot of the bed.*)

(RAINA *walks with studied elegance to the ottoman and sits down. Unfortu-*

nately she sits on the pistol, and jumps up with a shriek. THE MAN, *all nerves, shies like a frightened horse to the other side of the room.*)

THE MAN (*irritably*). Dont frighten me like that. What is it?

RAINA. Your revolver! It was staring that officer in the face all the time. What an escape!

THE MAN (*vexed at being unnecessarily terrified*). Oh, is that all?

RAINA (*staring at him rather superciliously as she conceives a poorer and poorer opinion of him, and feels proportionately more and more at her ease*). I am sorry I frightened you. (*She takes up the pistol and hands it to him.*) Pray take it to protect yourself against me.

THE MAN (*grinning wearily at the sarcasm as he takes the pistol*). No use, dear young lady: there's nothing in it. It's not loaded. (*He makes a grimace at it, and drops it despairingly into his revolver case.*)

RAINA. Load it by all means.

THE MAN. Ive no ammunition. What use are cartridges in battle? I always carry chocolate instead; and I finished the last cake of that hours ago.

RAINA (*outraged in her most cherished ideals of manhood*). Chocolate! Do you stuff your pockets with sweets—like a schoolboy—even in the field?

THE MAN (*grinning*). Yes: isnt it contemptible? (*Hungrily.*) I wish I had some now.

RAINA. Allow me. (*She sails away scornfully to the chest of drawers, and returns with the box of confectionery in her hand.*) I am sorry I have eaten them all except these. (*She offers him the box.*)

THE MAN (*ravenously*). Youre an angel! (*He gobbles the contents.*) Creams! Delicious! (*He looks anxiously to see whether there are any more. There are none: he can only scrape the box with his fingers and suck them. When that nourishment is exhausted he accepts the inevitable with pathetic goodhumor, and says, with grateful emotion*) Bless you, dear lady! You can always tell an old soldier by the inside of his holsters and cartridge boxes. The young ones carry pistols and cartridges: the old ones, grub. Thank you. (*He hands back the box. She snatches it contemptuously from him and throws it away. He shies again, as if she had meant to strike him.*) Ugh! Dont do things so suddenly, gracious lady. It's mean to revenge yourself because I frightened you just now.

RAINA (*loftily*). Frighten me! Do you know, sir, that though I am only a woman, I think I am at heart as brave as you.

THE MAN. I should think so. You havnt been under fire for three days as I have. I can stand two days without shewing it much; but no man can stand three days: I'm as nervous as a mouse. (*He sits down on the ottoman, and takes his head in his hands.*) Would you like to see me cry?

RAINA (*alarmed*). No.

THE MAN. If you would, all you have to do is to scold me just as if I were a little boy and you my nurse. If I were in camp now, theyd play all sorts of tricks on me.

RAINA (*a little moved*). I'm sorry. I wont scold you. (*Touched by the sympathy in her tone, he raises his head and looks gratefully at her: she immedi-*

ately draws back and stays stiffly) You must excuse me: our soldiers are not like that. (*She moves away from the ottoman.*)

THE MAN. Oh yes they are. There are only two sorts of soldiers: old ones and young ones. I've served fourteen years: half of your fellows never smelt powder before. Why, how is it that youve just beaten us? Sheer ignorance of the art of war, nothing else. (*Indignantly.*) I never saw anything so unprofessional.

RAINA (*ironically*). Oh! was it unprofessional to beat you?

THE MAN. Well, come! is it professional to throw a regiment of cavalry on a battery of machine guns, with the dead certainty that if the guns go off not a horse or man will ever get within fifty yards of the fire? I couldn't believe my eyes when I saw it.

RAINA (*eagerly turning to him, as all her enthusiasm and her dreams of glory rush back on her*). Did you see the great cavalry charge? Oh, tell me about it. Describe it to me.

THE MAN. You never saw a cavalry charge, did you?

RAINA. How could I?

THE MAN. Ah, perhaps not. No: of course not! Well, it's a funny sight. It's like slinging a handful of peas against a window pane: first one comes; then two or three close behind him; and then all the rest in a lump.

RAINA (*her eyes dilating as she raises her clasped hands ecstatically*). Yes, first One! the bravest of the brave!

THE MAN (*prosaically*). Hm! you should see the poor devil pulling at his horse.

RAINA. Why should he pull at his horse?

THE MAN (*impatient of so stupid a question*). It's running away with him, of course: do you suppose the fellow wants to get there before the others and be killed? Then they all come. You can tell the young ones by their wildness and their slashing. The old ones come bunched up under the number one guard: they know that theyre mere projectiles, and that it's no use trying to fight. The wounds are mostly broken knees, from the horses cannoning together.

RAINA. Ugh! But I dont believe the first man is a coward. I know he is a hero!

THE MAN (*goodhumoredly*). Thats what youd have said if youd seen the first man in the charge today.

RAINA (*breathless, forgiving him everything*). Ah, I knew it! Tell me. Tell me about him.

THE MAN. He did it like an operatic tenor. A regular handsome fellow, with flashing eyes and lovely moustache, shouting his war-cry and charging like Don Quixote at the windmills. We did laugh.

RAINA. You dared to laugh!

THE MAN. Yes; but when the sergeant ran up as white as a sheet, and told us theyd sent us the wrong ammunition, and that we couldnt fire a round for the next ten minutes, we laughed at the other side of our mouths. I never felt so sick in my life; though Ive been in one or two very tight places. And I hadnt even a revolver cartridge: only chocolate. We'd no bayonets: nothing. Of course, they just cut us to bits. And there was Don Quixote flourishing like a drum major, thinking he'd done the cleverest thing ever known, whereas he ought to be courtmartialled for it. Of all the fools ever let loose on a field of battle, that man must be the very maddest. He and his regiment simply committed suicide; only the pistol missed fire: thats all.

RAINA (*deeply wounded, but steadfastly loyal to her ideals*). Indeed! Would you know him again if you saw him?

THE MAN. Shall I ever forget him!

(*She again goes to the chest of drawers. He watches her with a vague hope that she may have something more for him to eat. She takes the portrait from its stand and brings it to him.*)

RAINA. That is a photograph of the gentleman—the patriot and hero—to whom I am betrothed.

THE MAN (*recognizing it with a shock*). I'm really very sorry. (*Looking at her.*) Was it fair to lead me on? (*He looks at the portrait again.*) Yes: thats Don Quixote: not a doubt of it. (*He stifles a laugh.*)

RAINA (*quickly*). Why do you laugh?

THE MAN (*apologetic, but still greatly tickled*). I didn't laugh, I assure you. At least I didnt mean to. But when I think of him charging the windmills and imagining he was doing the finest thing—(*He chokes with suppressed laughter.*)

RAINA (*sternly*). Give me back the portrait, sir.

THE MAN (*with sincere remorse*). Of course. Certainly. I'm really very sorry. (*He hands her the picture. She deliberately kisses it and looks him straight in the face before returning to the chest of drawers to replace it. He follows her, apologizing.*) Perhaps I'm quite wrong, you know: no doubt I am. Most likely he had got wind of the cartridge business somehow, and knew it was a safe job.

RAINA. That is to say, he was a pretender and a coward! You did not dare say that before.

THE MAN (*with a comic gesture of despair*). It's no use, dear lady: I cant make you see it from the professional point of view. (*As he turns away to get back to the ottoman, a couple of distant shots threaten renewed trouble.*)

RAINA (*sternly, as she sees him listening to the shots*). So much the better for you!

THE MAN (*turning*). How?

RAINA. You are my enemy; and you are at my mercy. What would I do if I were a professional soldier?

THE MAN. Ah, true, dear young lady: you're always right. I know how good youve been to me: to my last hour I shall remember those three chocolate creams. It was unsoldierly; but it was angelic.

RAINA (*coldly*). Thank you. And now I will do a soldierly thing. You cannot stay here after what you have just said about my future husband; but I will go out on the balcony and see whether it is safe for you to climb down into the street. (*She turns to the window.*)

THE MAN (*changing countenance*). Down that waterpipe! Stop! Wait! I cant! I darent! The very thought of it makes me giddy. I came up it fast enough with death behind me. But to face it now in cold blood—! (*He sinks on the ottoman.*) It's no use: I give up: I'm beaten. Give the alarm. (*He drops his head on his hands in the deepest dejection.*)

RAINA (*disarmed by pity*). Come: dont be disheartened. (*She stoops over him almost maternally: he shakes his head.*) Oh, you are a very poor soldier: a chocolate cream soldier! Come, cheer up! it takes less courage to climb down than to face capture: remember that.

THE MAN (*dreamily, lulled by her voice*). No: capture only means death; and death is sleep: oh, sleep, sleep, sleep, undisturbed sleep! Climbing down the pipe means doing something—exerting myself—thinking! Death ten times over first.

RAINA (*softly and wonderingly, catching the rhythm of his weariness*). Are you as sleepy as that?

THE MAN. Ive not had two hours undisturbed sleep since I joined. I havnt closed my eyes for forty-eight hours.

RAINA (*at her wit's end*). But what am I to do with you?

THE MAN (*staggering up, roused by her desperation*). Of course. I must do something. (*He shakes himself; pulls himself together; and speaks with rallied vigor and courage.*) You see, sleep or no sleep, hunger or no hunger, tired or not tired, you can always do a thing when you know it must be done. Well, that pipe must be got down: (*he hits himself on the chest*) do you hear that, you chocolate cream soldier? (*He turns to the window.*)

RAINA (*anxiously*). But if you fall?

THE MAN. I shall sleep as if the stones were a feather bed. Goodbye. (*He makes boldly for the window; and his hand is on the shutter when there is a terrible burst of firing in the street beneath.*)

RAINA (*rushing to him*). Stop! (*She seizes him recklessly, and pulls him quite round.*) Theyll kill you.

THE MAN (*coolly, but attentively*). Never mind: this sort of thing is all in my day's work. I'm bound to take my chance. (*Decisively.*) Now do what I tell you. Put out the candle; so that they shant see the light when I open the shutters. And keep away from the window, whatever you do. If they see me theyre sure to have a shot at me.

RAINA (*clinging to him*). Theyre sure to see you: it's bright moonlight. I'll save you. Oh, how can you be so indifferent! You want me to save you, dont you?

THE MAN. I really dont want to be troublesome. (*She shakes him in her impatience.*) I am not indifferent, dear young lady, I assure you. But how is it to be done?

RAINA. Come away from the window. (*She takes him firmly back to the middle of the room. The moment she releases him he turns mechanically towards the window again. She seizes him and turns him back, exclaiming*) Please! (*He becomes motionless, like a hypnotized rabbit, his fatigue gaining fast on him. She releases him, and addresses him patronizingly.*) Now listen. You must trust to our hospitality. You do not yet know in whose house you are. I am a Petkoff.

THE MAN. A pet what?

RAINA (*rather indignantly*). I mean that I belong to the family of the Petkoffs, the richest and best known in our country.

THE MAN. Oh yes, of course. I beg your pardon. The Petkoffs, to be sure. How stupid of me!

RAINA. You know you never heard of them until this moment. How can you stoop to pretend!

THE MAN. Forgive me: I'm too tired to think; and the change of subject was too much for me. Dont scold me.

RAINA. I forgot. It might make you cry. (*He nods, quite seriously. She pouts and then resumes her patronizing tone.*) I must tell you that my father holds the highest command of any Bulgarian in our army. He is (*proudly*) a Major.

THE MAN (*pretending to be deeply impressed*). A Major! Bless me! Think of that!

RAINA. You shewed great ignorance in thinking that it was necessary to climb up to the balcony because ours is the only private house that has two rows of windows. There is a flight of stairs inside to get up and down by.

THE MAN. Stairs! How grand! You live in great luxury indeed, dear young lady.

RAINA. Do you know what a library is?

THE MAN. A library? A roomful of books?

RAINA. Yes. We have one, the only one in Bulgaria.

THE MAN. Actually a real library! I should like to see that.

RAINA (*affectedly*). I tell you these things to shew you that you are not in the house of ignorant country folk who would kill you the moment they saw your Serbian uniform, but among civilized people. We go to Bucharest every year for the opera season; and I have spent a whole month in Vienna.

THE MAN. I saw that, dear young lady. I saw at once that you knew the world.

RAINA. Have you ever seen the opera of Ernani?

THE MAN. Is that the one with the devil in it in red velvet, and a soldiers' chorus?

RAINA (*contemptuously*). No!

THE MAN (*stifling a heavy sigh of weariness*). Then I dont know it.

RAINA. I thought you might have remembered the great scene where Ernani, flying from his foes just as you are tonight, takes refuge in the castle of his bitterest enemy, an old Castilian noble. The noble refuses to give him up. His guest is sacred to him.

THE MAN (*quickly, waking up a little*). Have your people got that notion?

RAINA (*with dignity*). My mother and I can understand that notion, as you call it. And if instead of threatening me with your pistol as you did you had simply thrown yourself as a fugitive on our hospitality, you would have been as safe as in your father's house.

THE MAN. Quite sure?

RAINA (*turning her back on him in disgust*). Oh, it is useless to try to make you understand.

THE MAN. Dont be angry: you see how awkward it would be for me if there was any mistake. My father is a very hospitable man: he keeps six hotels; but I couldnt trust him as far as that. What about your father?

RAINA. He is away at Slivnitza fighting for his country. I answer for your safety. There is my hand in pledge of it. Will that reassure you? (*She offers him her hand.*)

THE MAN (*looking dubiously at his own hand*). Better not touch my hand, dear young lady. I must have a wash first.

RAINA (*touched*). That is very nice of you. I see that you are a gentleman.

THE MAN (*puzzled*). Eh?

RAINA. You must not think I am surprised. Bulgarians of really good standing—people in our position—wash their hands nearly every day. So you see I can appreciate your delicacy. You may take my hand. (*She offers it again.*)

THE MAN (*kissing it with his hands behind his back*). Thanks, gracious young lady: I feel safe at last. And now would you mind breaking the news to your mother? I had better not stay here secretly longer than is necessary.

RAINA. If you will be so good as to keep perfectly still whilst I am away.

THE MAN. Certainly. (*He sits down on the ottoman.*)

(RAINA *goes to the bed and wraps herself in the fur cloak. His eyes close. She goes to the door. Turning for a last look at him, she sees that he is dropping off to sleep.*)

RAINA (*at the door*). You are not going asleep, are you? (*He murmurs inarticulately: she runs to him and shakes him.*) Do you hear? Wake up: you are falling asleep.

THE MAN. Eh? Falling aslee—? Oh no: not the least in the world: I was only thinking. It's all right: I'm wide awake.

RAINA (*severely*). Will you please stand up while I am away. (*He rises reluctantly.*) All the time, mind.

THE MAN (*standing unsteadily*). Certainly. Certainly: you may depend on me.

(RAINA *looks doubtfully at him. He smiles weakly. She goes reluctantly, turning again at the door, and almost catching him in the act of yawning. She goes out.*)

THE MAN (*drowsily*). Sleep, sleep, sleep, sleep, slee—(*The words trail off into a murmur. He wakes again with a shock on the point of falling.*) Where am I? Thats what I want to know: where am I? Must keep awake. Nothing keeps me awake except danger: remember that: (*intently*) danger, danger, danger, dan—(*trailing off again: another shock*). Wheres danger? Mus' find it. (*He starts off vaguely round the room in search of it.*) What am I looking for? Sleep—danger—dont know. (*He stumbles against the bed.*) Ah yes: now I know. All right now. I'm to go to bed, but not to sleep. Be sure not to sleep, because of danger. Not to lie down either, only sit down. (*He sits on the bed. A blissful expression comes into his face.*) Ah! (*With a happy sigh he sinks back at full length; lifts his boots into the bed with a final effort; and falls fast asleep instantly.*)

(CATHERINE *comes in, followed by* RAINA.)

RAINA (*looking at the ottoman*). He's gone! I left him here.

CATHERINE. Here! Then he must have climbed down from the—

RAINA (*seeing him*). Oh! (*She points.*)

CATHERINE (*scandalized*). Well! (*She strides to the bed,* RAINA *following until she is opposite her on the other side.*) He's fast asleep. The brute!

RAINA (*anxiously*). Sh!

CATHERINE (*shaking him*). Sir! (*Shaking him again, harder.*) Sir!! (*Vehemently, shaking very hard.*) Sir!!!

RAINA (*catching her arm*). Dont, mamma; the poor darling is worn out. Let him sleep.

CATHERINE (*letting him go, and turning amazed to* RAINA). The poor darling! Raina!!! (*She looks sternly at her daughter.*)

(*The man sleeps profoundly.*)

ACT II

(*The sixth of March, 1886. In the garden of* MAJOR PETKOFF's *house. It is a fine spring morning: the garden looks fresh and pretty. Beyond the paling the tops of a couple of minarets can be seen, shewing that there is a valley there, with the little town in it. A few miles further the Balkan mountains rise and shut in the landscape. Looking towards them from within the garden, the side of the house is seen on the left, with a garden door reached by a little flight of steps. On the right the stable yard, with its gateway, encroaches on the garden. There are fruit bushes along the paling and house, covered with washing spread out to dry. A path runs by the house, and rises by two steps at the corner, where it turns out of sight. In the middle, a small table, with two bent wood chairs at it, is laid for breakfast with Turkish coffee pot, cups, rolls, etc.; but the cups have been used and the bread broken. There is a wooden garden seat against the wall on the right.*

LOUKA, *smoking a cigaret, is standing between the table and the house, turning her back with angry disdain on a man servant who is lecturing her. He is a middle-aged man of cool temperament and low but clear and keen intelligence, with the complacency of the servant who values himself on his rank in servitude, and the imperturbability of the accurate calculator who has no illusions. He wears a white Bulgarian costume: jacket with embroidered border, sash, wide knickerbockers, and decorated gaiters. His head is shaved up to the crown, giving him a high Japanese forehead. His name is* NICOLA.)

NICOLA. Be warned in time, Louka: mend your manners. I know the mistress. She is so grand that she never dreams that any servant could dare be disrespectful to her; but if she once suspects that you are defying her, out you go.

LOUKA. I do defy her. I will defy her. What do I care for her?

NICOLA. If you quarrel with the family, I never can marry you. It's the same as if you quarreled with me!

LOUKA. You take her part against me, do you?

NICOLA (*sedately*). I shall always be dependent on the good will of the family. When I leave their service and start a shop in Sofia, their custom will be half my capital: their bad word would ruin me.

LOUKA. You have no spirit. I should like to catch them saying a word against me!

NICOLA (*pityingly*). I should have expected more sense from you, Louka. But youre young: youre young!

LOUKA. Yes; and you like me the better for it, dont you? But I know some family secrets they wouldnt care to have told, young as I am. Let them quarrel with me if they dare!

NICOLA (*with compassionate superiority*). Do you know what they would do if they heard you talk like that?

LOUKA. What could they do?

NICOLA. Discharge you for untruthfulness. Who would believe any stories you told after that? Who would give you another situation? Who in this house would dare be seen speaking to you ever again? How long would your father be left on his little farm? (*She impatiently throws away the end of her cigaret, and stamps on it.*) Child: you dont know the power such high people have over the like of you and me when we try to rise out of our poverty against them. (*He goes close to her and lowers his voice.*) Look at me, ten years in their service. Do you think I know no secrets? I know things about the mistress that she wouldnt have the master know for a thousand levas. I know things about him that she wouldnt let him hear the last of for six months if I blabbed them to her. I know things about Raina that would break off her match with Sergius if—

LOUKA (*turning on him quickly*). How do you know? I never told you!

NICOLA (*opening his eyes cunningly*). So thats your little secret, is it? I thought it might be something like that. Well, you take my advice and be respectful; and make the mistress feel that no matter what you know or dont know, she can depend on you to hold your tongue and serve the family faithfully. Thats what they like; and thats how youll make most out of them.

LOUKA (*with searching scorn*). You have the soul of a servant, Nicola.

NICOLA (*complacently*). Yes: thats the secret of success in service.

(*A loud knocking with a whip handle on a wooden door is heard from the stable yard.*)

MALE VOICE OUTSIDE. Hollo! Hollo there! Nicola!

LOUKA. Master! back from the war!

NICOLA (*quickly*). My word for it, Louka, the war's over. Off with you and get some fresh coffee. (*He runs out into the stable yard.*)

LOUKA (*as she collects the coffee pot and cups on the tray, and carries it into the house*). Youll never put the soul of a servant into me.

(MAJOR PETKOFF *comes from the stable yard, followed by* NICOLA. *He is a cheerful, excitable, insignificant, unpolished man of about 50, naturally unambitious except as to his income and his importance in local society, but just now greatly pleased with the military rank which the war has thrust on him as a man of consequence in his town. The fever of plucky patriotism which the Serbian attack roused in all the Bulgarians has pulled him through the war; but he is obviously glad to be home again.*)

PETKOFF (*pointing to the table with his whip*). Breakfast out here, eh?

NICOLA. Yes, sir. The mistress and Miss Raina have just gone in.

PETKOFF (*sitting down and taking a roll*). Go in and say Ive come; and get me some fresh coffee.

NICOLA. It's coming, sir. (*He goes to the house door.* LOUKA, *with fresh coffee, a clean cup, and a brandy bottle on her tray, meets him.*) Have you told the mistress?

LOUKA. Yes: she's coming.

(NICOLA *goes into the house.* LOUKA *brings the coffee to the table.*)

PETKOFF. Well: the Serbs havnt run away with you, have they?

LOUKA. No, sir.

PETKOFF. Thats right. Have you brought me some cognac?

LOUKA (*putting the bottle on the table*). Here, sir.

PETKOFF. Thats right. (*He pours some into his coffee.*)

(CATHERINE, *who, having at this early hour made only a very perfunctory toilet, wears a Bulgarian apron over a once brilliant but now half wornout dressing gown, and a colored handkerchief tied over her thick black hair, comes from the house with Turkish slippers on her bare feet, looking astonishingly handsome and stately under all the circumstances.* LOUKA *goes into the house.*)

CATHERINE. My dear Paul: what a surprise for us! (*She stoops over the back of his chair to kiss him.*) Have they brought you fresh coffee?

PETKOFF. Yes: Louka's been looking after me. The war's over. The treaty was signed three days ago at Bucharest; and the decree for our army to demobilize was issued yesterday.

CATHERINE (*springing erect, with flashing eyes*). Paul: have you let the Austrians force you to make peace?

PETKOFF (*submissively*). My dear: they didnt consult me. What could I do? (*She sits down and turns away from him.*) But of course we saw to it that the treaty was an honorable one. It declares peace—

CATHERINE (*outraged*). Peace!

PETKOFF (*appeasing her*)—but not friendly relations: remember that. They wanted to put that in; but I insisted on its being struck out. What more could I do?

CATHERINE. You could have annexed Serbia and made Prince Alexander Emperor of the Balkans. Thats what I would have done.

PETKOFF. I dont doubt it in the least, my dear. But I should have had to subdue the whole Austrian Empire first; and that would have kept me too long away from you. I missed you greatly.

CATHERINE (*relenting*). Ah! (*She stretches her hand affectionately across the table to squeeze his.*)

PETKOFF. And how have you been, my dear?

CATHERINE. Oh, my usual sore throats: thats all.

PETKOFF (*with conviction*). That comes from washing your neck every day. Ive often told you so.

CATHERINE. Nonsense, Paul!

PETKOFF (*over his coffee and cigaret*). I dont believe in going too far with these modern customs. All this washing cant be good for the health: it's not natural. There was an Englishman at Philippopolis who used to wet himself all over with cold water every morning when he got up. Disgusting! It all comes from the English: their climate makes them so dirty that they have to be perpetually washing themselves. Look at my father! he never had a bath in his life; and he lived to be ninety-eight, the healthiest man in Bulgaria. I dont mind a good wash once a week to keep up my position; but once a day is carrying the thing to a ridiculous extreme.

CATHERINE. You are a barbarian at heart still, Paul. I hope you behaved yourself before all those Russian officers.

PETKOFF. I did my best. I took care to let them know that we have a library.

CATHERINE. Ah; but you didnt tell them that we have an electric bell in it? I have had one put up.

PETKOFF. Whats an electric bell?

CATHERINE. You touch a button; something tinkles in the kitchen; and then Nicola comes up.

PETKOFF. Why not shout for him?

CATHERINE. Civilized people never shout for their servants. Ive learnt that while you were away.

PETKOFF. Well, I'll tell you something Ive learnt too. Civilized people dont hang out their washing to dry where visitors can see it; so youd better have all that (*indicating the clothes on the bushes*) put somewhere else.

CATHERINE. Oh, that's absurd, Paul: I dont believe really refined people notice such things.

SERGIUS (*knocking at the stable gates*). Gate, Nicola!

PETKOFF. Theres Sergius. (*Shouting.*) Hollo, Nicola!

CATHERINE. Oh, dont shout, Paul: it really isnt nice.

PETKOFF. Bosh! (*He shouts louder than before.*) Nicola!

NICOLA (*appearing at the house door*). Yes, sir.

PETKOFF. Are you deaf? Dont you hear Major Saranoff knocking? Bring him round this way. (*He pronounces the name with the stress on the second syllable: Sarahnoff.*)

NICOLA. Yes, Major. (*He goes into the stable yard.*)

PETKOFF. You must talk to him, my dear, until Raina takes him off our hands. He bores my life out about our not promoting him. Over my head, if you please.

CATHERINE. He certainly ought to be promoted when he marries Raina. Besides, the country should insist on having at least one native general.

PETKOFF. Yes; so that he could throw away whole brigades instead of regiments. It's no use, my dear: he hasnt the slightest chance of promotion until we're quite sure that the peace will be a lasting one.

NICOLA (*at the gate, announcing*). Major Sergius Saranoff! (*He goes into the house and returns presently with a third chair, which he places at the table. He then withdraws.*)

(MAJOR SERGIUS SARANOFF, *the original of the portrait in* RAINA's *room, is a tall romantically handsome man, with the physical hardihood, the high spirit, and the susceptible imagination of an untamed mountaineer chieftain. But his remarkable personal distinction is of a characteristically civilized type. The ridges of his eyebrows, curving with an interrogative twist round the projections at the outer corners; his jealously observant eye; his nose, thin, keen, and apprehensive in spite of the pugnacious high bridge and large nostril; his assertive chin would not be out of place in a Parisian salon, shewing that the clever imaginative barbarian has an acute critical faculty which has been thrown into intense activity by the arrival of western civilization in the Balkans. The result is precisely what the advent of nineteenth-century thought first produced in England: to wit, Byronism. By his brooding on the perpetual failure, not only of others, but of himself, to live up to his ideals; by his consequent cynical scorn for humanity; by his jejune credulity as to the absolute validity of his concepts and the unworthiness of the world in disregarding them; by his wincings and mockeries under the sting of the petty disillusions which every hour spent among men brings to his sensitive observation, he has acquired the half tragic, half ironic air, the mysterious moodiness, the suggestion of a strange and terrible history that has left nothing but undying remorse, by which Childe Harold fascinated the grandmothers of his English contemporaries. It is clear that here or nowhere is* RAINA's *ideal hero.* CATHERINE *is hardly less enthusiastic about him than her daughter, and much less reserved in shewing her enthusiasm. As he enters from the stable gate, she rises effusively to greet him.* PETKOFF *is distinctly less disposed to make a fuss about him.*)

PETKOFF. Here already, Sergius! Glad to see you.

CATHERINE. My dear Sergius! (*She holds out both her hands.*)

SERGIUS (*kissing them with scrupulous gallantry*). My dear mother, if I may call you so.

PETKOFF (*drily*). Mother-in-law, Sergius: mother-in-law! Sit down; and have some coffee.

SERGIUS. Thank you: none for me. (*He gets away from the table with a certain distaste for* PETKOFF's *enjoyment of it, and posts himself with conscious dignity against the rail of the steps leading to the house.*)

CATHERINE. You look superb. The campaign has improved you, Sergius. Everybody here is mad about you. We were all wild with enthusiasm about that magnificent cavalry charge.

SERGIUS (*with grave irony*). Madam: it was the cradle and the grave of my military reputation.

CATHERINE. How so?

SERGIUS. I won the battle the wrong way when our worthy Russian generals were losing it the right way. In short, I upset their plans, and wounded their self-esteem. Two Cossack colonels had their regiments routed on the most correct principles of scientific warfare. Two major-generals got killed strictly according to military etiquette. The two colonels are now major-generals; and I am still a simple major.

CATHERINE. You shall not remain so, Sergius. The women are on your side; and they will see that justice is done you.

SERGIUS. It is too late. I have only waited for the peace to send in my resignation.

PETKOFF (*dropping his cup in his amazement*). Your resignation!

CATHERINE. Oh, you must withdraw it!

SERGIUS (*with resolute measured emphasis, folding his arms*). I never withdraw.

PETKOFF (*vexed*). Now who could have supposed you were going to do such a thing?

SERGIUS (*with fire*). Everyone that knew me. But enough of myself and my affairs. How is Raina; and where is Raina?

RAINA (*suddenly coming round the corner of the house and standing at the top of the steps in the path*). Raina is here.

(*She makes a charming picture as they turn to look at her. She wears an underdress of pale green silk, draped with an overdress of thin ecru canvas embroidered with gold. She is crowned with a dainty eastern cap of gold tinsel.* SERGIUS *goes impulsively to meet her. Posing regally, she presents her hand: he drops chivalrously on one knee and kisses it.*)

PETKOFF (*aside to* CATHERINE, *beaming with parental pride*). Pretty, isnt it? She always appears at the right moment.

CATHERINE (*impatiently*). Yes; she listens for it. It is an abominable habit.

(SERGIUS *leads* RAINA *forward with splendid gallantry. When they arrive at the table, she turns to him with a bend of the head: he bows; and thus they separate, he coming to his place and she going behind her father's chair.*)

RAINA (*stooping and kissing her father*). Dear father! Welcome home!

PETKOFF (*patting her cheek*). My little pet girl. (*He kisses her. She goes to the chair left by* NICOLA *for* SERGIUS, *and sits down.*)

CATHERINE. And so youre no longer a soldier, Sergius.

SERGIUS. I am no longer a soldier. Soldiering, my dear madam, is the coward's art of attacking mercilessly when you are strong, and keeping out of harm's way when you are weak. That is the whole secret of successful fighting. Get your enemy at a disadvantage; and never, on any account, fight him on equal terms.

PETKOFF. They wouldnt let us make a fair stand-up fight of it. However, I suppose soldiering has to be a trade like any other trade.

SERGIUS. Precisely. But I have no ambition to shine as a tradesman; so I have taken the advice of that bagman of a captain that settled the exchange of prisoners with us at Pirot, and given it up.

PETKOFF. What! that Swiss fellow? Sergius: I've often thought of that exchange since. He over-reached us about those horses.

SERGIUS. Of course he over-reached us. His father was a hotel and livery stable keeper; and he owed his first step to his knowledge of horse-dealing. (*With mock enthusiasm.*) Ah, he was a soldier: every inch a soldier! If only I had bought the horses for my regiment instead of foolishly leading it into danger, I should have been a field-marshal now!

CATHERINE. A Swiss? What was he doing in the Serbian army?

PETKOFF. A volunteer, of course: keen on picking up his profession. (*Chuckling.*) We shouldnt have been able to begin fighting if these foreigners hadn't shewn us how to do it: we knew nothing about it; and neither did the Serbs. Egad, there'd have been no war without them!

RAINA. Are there many Swiss officers in the Serbian Army?

PETKOFF. No. All Austrians, just as our officers were all Russians. This was the only Swiss I came across. I'll never trust a Swiss again. He humbugged us into giving him fifty ablebodied men for two hundred worn out chargers. They werent even eatable!

SERGIUS. We were two children in the hands of that consummate soldier, Major: simply two innocent little children.

RAINA. What was he like?

CATHERINE. Oh, Raina, what a silly question!

SERGIUS. He was like a commercial traveller in uniform. Bourgeois to his boots!

PETKOFF (*grinning*). Sergius: tell Catherine that queer story his friend told us about how he escaped after Slivnitza. You remember. About his being hid by two women.

SERGIUS (*with bitter irony*). Oh yes: quite a romance! He was serving in the very battery I so unprofessionally charged. Being a thorough soldier, he ran away like the rest of them, with our cavalry at his heels. To escape their sabres he climbed a waterpipe and made his way into the bedroom of a young Bulgarian lady. The young lady was enchanted by his persuasive commercial traveller's manners. She very modestly entertained him for an hour or so, and then called in her mother lest her conduct should appear unmaidenly. The old lady was equally fascinated; and the fugitive was sent on his way in the morning, disguised in an old coat belonging to the master of the house, who was away at the war.

RAINA (*rising with marked stateliness*). Your life in the camp has made you coarse, Sergius. I did not think you would have repeated such a story before me. (*She turns away coldly.*)

CATHERINE (*also rising*). She is right, Sergius. If such women exist, we should be spared the knowledge of them.

PETKOFF. Pooh! nonsense! what does it matter?

SERGIUS (*ashamed*). No, Petkoff: I was wrong. (*To* RAINA, *with earnest humility.*) I beg your pardon. I have behaved abominably. Forgive me, Raina. (*She bows reservedly.*) And you too, madam. (CATHERINE *bows graciously and sits down. He proceeds solemnly, again addressing* RAINA.) The glimpses I have had of the seamy side of life during the last few months have made me cynical; but I should not have brought my cynicism here: least of all into your presence, Raina. I— (*Here, turning to the others, he is evidently going to begin a long speech when the* MAJOR *interrupts him.*)

PETKOFF. Stuff and nonsense, Sergius! Thats quite enough fuss about nothing: a soldier's daughter should be able to stand up without flinching to a little strong conversation. (*He rises.*) Come: it's time for us to get to business. We have to get back to Philippopolis: theres no forage for them on the Sofia route. (*He goes towards the house.*) Come along. (SERGIUS *is about to follow him when* CATHERINE *rises and intervenes.*)

CATHERINE. Oh, Paul, cant you spare Sergius for a few moments? Raina has hardly seen him yet. Perhaps I can help you to settle about the regiments.

SERGIUS (*protesting*). My dear madam, impossible: you—

CATHERINE (*stopping him playfully*). You stay here, my dear Sergius: there's no hurry. I have a word or two to say to Paul. (SERGIUS *instantly bows and steps back.*) Now, dear (*taking* PETKOFF's *arm*): come and see the electric bell.

PETKOFF. Oh, very well, very well.

(*They go into the house together affectionately.* SERGIUS, *left alone with* RAINA, *looks anxiously at her, fearing that she is still offended. She smiles, and stretches out her arms to him.*)

SERGIUS (*hastening to her*). Am I forgiven?

RAINA (*placing her hands on his shoulders as she looks up at him with admiration and worship*). My hero! My king!

SERGIUS. My queen! (*He kisses her on the forehead.*)

RAINA. How I have envied you, Sergius! You have been out in the world, on the field of battle, able to prove yourself there worthy of any woman in the world; whilst I have had to sit at home inactive—dreaming—useless—doing nothing that could give me the right to call myself worthy of any man.

SERGIUS. Dearest: all my deeds have been yours. You inspired me. I have gone through the war like a knight in a tournament with his lady looking down at him!

RAINA. And you have never been absent from my thoughts for a moment. (*Very solemnly.*) Sergius: I think we two have found the higher love. When I think of you, I feel that I could never do a base deed, or think an ignoble thought.

SERGIUS. My lady and my saint! (*He clasps her reverently.*)

RAINA (*returning his embrace*). My lord and my—

SERGIUS. Sh—sh! Let me be the worshipper, dear. You little know how unworthy even the best man is of a girl's pure passion!

RAINA. I trust you. I love you. You will never disappoint me, Sergius. (LOUKA *is heard singing within the house. They quickly release each other.*) I cant pretend to talk indifferently before her: my heart is too full. (LOUKA *comes from the house with her tray. She goes to the table, and begins to clear it, with her back turned to them.*) I will get my hat; and then we can go out until lunch time. Wouldnt you like that?

SERGIUS. Be quick. If you are away five minutes, it will seem five hours. (RAINA *runs to the top of the steps, and turns there to exchange looks with him and wave him a kiss with both hands. He looks after her with emotion for a moment; then turns slowly away, his face radiant with the loftiest exaltation. The movement shifts his field of vision, into the corner of which there now comes the tail of* LOUKA's *double apron. His attention is arrested at once. He takes a stealthy look at her, and begins to twirl his moustache mischievously, with his left hand akimbo on his hip. Finally, striking the ground with his heels in something of a cavalry swagger, he strolls over to the other side of the table, opposite her, and says*) Louka: do you know what the higher love is?

LOUKA (*astonished*). No, sir.

SERGIUS. Very fatiguing thing to keep up for any length of time, Louka. One feels the need of some relief after it.

LOUKA (*innocently*). Perhaps you would like some coffee, sir? (*She stretches her hand across the table for the coffee pot.*)

SERGIUS (*taking her hand*). Thank you, Louka.

LOUKA (*pretending to pull*). Oh, sir, you know I didnt mean that. I'm surprised at you!

SERGIUS (*coming clear of the table and drawing her with him*). I am surprised at myself, Louka. What would Sergius, the hero of Slivnitza, say if he saw me now? What would Sergius, the apostle of the higher love, say if he saw me now? What would the half dozen Sergiuses who keep popping in and out of this handsome figure of mine say if they caught us here? (*Letting go her hand and slipping his arm dexterously round her waist.*) Do you consider my figure handsome, Louka?

LOUKA. Let me go, sir. I shall be disgraced. (*She struggles: he holds her inexorably.*) Oh, will you let go?

SERGIUS (*looking straight into her eyes*). No.

LOUKA. Then stand back where we cant be seen. Have you no common sense?

SERGIUS. Ah! thats reasonable. (*He takes her into the stable yard gateway, where they are hidden from the house.*)

LOUKA (*plaintively*). I may have been seen from the windows: Miss Raina is sure to be spying about after you.

SERGIUS (*stung: letting her go*). Take care, Louka. I may be worthless enough to betray the higher love; but do not you insult it.

LOUKA (*demurely*). Not for the world, sir, I'm sure. May I go on with my work, please, now?

SERGIUS (*again putting his arm round her*). You are a provoking little witch, Louka. If you were in love with me, would you spy out of windows on me?

LOUKA. Well, you see, sir, since you say you are half a dozen different gentlemen all at once, I should have a great deal to look after.

SERGIUS (*charmed*). Witty as well as pretty. (*He tries to kiss her.*)

LOUKA (*avoiding him*). No: I don't want your kisses. Gentlefolk are all alike: you making love to me behind Miss Raina's back; and she doing the same behind yours.

SERGIUS (*recoiling a step*). Louka!

LOUKA. It shews how little you really care.

SERGIUS (*dropping his familiarity, and speaking with freezing politeness*). If our conversation is to continue, Louka, you will please remember that a gentleman does not discuss the conduct of the lady he is engaged to with her maid.

LOUKA. It's so hard to know what a gentleman considers right. I thought from your trying to kiss me that you had given up being so particular.

SERGIUS (*turning from her and striking his forehead as he comes back into the garden from the gateway*). Devil! devil!

LOUKA. Ha! ha! I expect one of the six of you is very like me, sir; though I am only Miss Raina's maid. (*She goes back to her work at the table, taking no further notice of him.*)

SERGIUS (*speaking to himself*). Which of the six is the real man? thats the question that torments me. One of them is a hero, another a buffoon, another a humbug, another perhaps a bit of a blackguard. (*He pauses, and looks furtively at* LOUKA *as he adds, with deep bitterness*) And one, at least, is a coward: jealous, like all cowards. (*He goes to the table.*) Louka.

LOUKA. Yes?

SERGIUS. Who is my rival?

LOUKA. You shall never get that out of me, for love or money.

SERGIUS. Why?

LOUKA. Never mind why. Besides, you would tell that I told you; and I should lose my place.

SERGIUS (*holding out his right hand in affirmation*). No! on the honor of a— (*he checks himself; and his hand drops, nerveless, as he concludes sardonically*) —of a man capable of behaving as I have been behaving for the last five minutes. Who is he?

LOUKA. I dont know. I never saw him. I only heard his voice through the door of her room.

SERGIUS. Damnation! How dare you?

LOUKA (*retreating*). Oh, I mean no harm: youve no right to take up my words like that. The mistress knows all about it. And I tell you that if that gentleman ever comes here again, Miss Raina will marry him, whether he likes it or not. I know the difference between the sort of manner you and she put on before one another and the real manner.

(*Sergius shivers as if she had stabbed him. Then, setting his face like iron, he strides grimly to her, and grips her above the elbows with both hands.*)

SERGIUS. Now listen you to me.

LOUKA (*wincing*). Not so tight: youre hurting me.

SERGIUS. That doesnt matter. You have stained my honor by making me a party to your eavesdropping. And you have betrayed your mistress.

LOUKA (*writhing*). Please—

SERGIUS. That shews that you are an abominable little clod of common clay, with the soul of a servant. (*He lets her go as if she were an unclean thing, and turns away, dusting his hands of her, to the bench by the wall, where he sits down with averted head, meditating gloomily.*)

LOUKA (*whimpering angrily with her hands up her sleeves, feeling her bruised arms*). You know how to hurt with your tongue as well as with your hands. But I dont care, now Ive found out that whatever clay I'm made of, youre made of the same. As for her, she's a liar; and her fine airs are a cheat; and I'm worth six of her. (*She shakes the pain off hardily; tosses her head; and sets to work to put the things on the tray.*)

(*He looks doubtfully at her. She finishes packing the tray, and laps the cloth over the edges, so as to carry all out together. As she stoops to lift it, he rises.*)

SERGIUS. Louka! (*She stops and looks defiantly at him.*) A gentleman has no right to hurt a woman under any circumstances. (*With profound humility, uncovering his head.*) I beg your pardon.

LOUKA. That sort of apology may satisfy a lady. Of what use is it to a servant?

SERGIUS (*rudely crossed in his chivalry, throws it off with a bitter laugh, and says slightingly*). Oh! you wish to be paid for the hurt! (*He puts on his shako, and takes some money from his pocket.*)

LOUKA (*her eyes filling with tears in spite of herself*). No: I want my hurt made well.

SERGIUS (*sobered by her tone*). How?

(*She rolls up her left sleeve; clasps her arm with the thumb and fingers of her right hand; and looks down at the bruise. Then she raises her head and looks straight at him. Finally, with a superb gesture, she presents her arm to be kissed. Amazed, he looks at her; at the arm; at her again, hesitates; and then, with shuddering intensity, exclaims*) Never! (*and gets away as far as possible from her.*

Her arm drops. Without a word, and with unaffected dignity, she takes her tray, and is approaching the house when RAINA *returns, wearing a hat and jacket in the height of the Vienna fashion of the previous year, 1885.* LOUKA *makes way proudly for her, and then goes into the house.*)

RAINA. I'm ready. Whats the matter? (*Gaily.*) Have you been flirting with Louka?

SERGIUS (*hastily*). No, no. How can you think such a thing?

RAINA (*ashamed of herself*). Forgive me, dear: it was only a jest. I am so happy today.

(*He goes quickly to her, and kisses her hand remorsefully.* CATHERINE *comes out and calls to them from the top of the steps.*)

CATHERINE (*coming down to them*). I am sorry to disturb you, children; but Paul is distracted over those three regiments. He doesnt know how to send them to Philippopolis; and he objects to every suggestion of mine. You must go and help him, Sergius. He is in the library.

RAINA (*disappointed*). But we are just going out for a walk.

SERGIUS. I shall not be long. Wait for me just five minutes. (*He runs up the steps to the door.*)

RAINA (*following him to the foot of the steps and looking up at him with timid coquetry*). I shall go round and wait in full view of the library windows.

Be sure you draw father's attention to me. If you are a moment longer than five minutes, I shall go in and fetch you, regiments or no regiments.

SERGIUS (*laughing*). Very well. (*He goes in.*)

(RAINA *watches him until he is out of her sight. Then, with a perceptible relaxation of manner, she begins to pace up and down the garden in a brown study.*)

CATHERINE. Imagine their meeting that Swiss and hearing the whole story! The very first thing your father asked for was the old coat we sent him off in. A nice mess you have got us into!

RAINA (*gazing thoughtfully at the gravel as she walks*). The little beast!

CATHERINE. Little beast! What little beast?

RAINA. To go and tell! Oh, if I had him here, I'd cram him with chocolate creams til he couldnt ever speak again!

CATHERINE. Dont talk such stuff. Tell me the truth, Raina. How long was he in your room before you came to me?

RAINA (*whisking round and recommencing her march in the opposite direction*). Oh, I forget.

CATHERINE. You cannot forget! Did he really climb up after the soldiers were gone; or was he there when that officer searched the room?

RAINA. No. Yes: I think he must have been there then.

CATHERINE. You think! Oh, Raina! Raina! Will anything ever make you straightforward? If Sergius finds out, it will be all over between you.

RAINA (*with cool impertinence*). Oh, I know Sergius is your pet. I sometimes wish you could marry him instead of me. You would just suit him. You would pet him, and spoil him, and mother him to perfection.

CATHERINE (*opening her eyes very widely indeed*). Well, upon my word!

RAINA (*capriciously: half to herself*). I always feel a longing to do or say something dreadful to him—to shock his propriety—to scandalize the five senses out of him. (*To* CATHERINE, *perversely.*) I dont care whether he finds out about the chocolate cream soldier or not. I half hope he may. (*She again turns and strolls flippantly away up the path to the corner of the house.*)

CATHERINE. And what should I be able to say to your father, pray?

RAINA (*over her shoulder, from the top of the two steps*). Oh, poor father! As if he could help himself! (*She turns the corner and passes out of sight.*)

CATHERINE (*looking after her, her fingers itching*). Oh, if you were only ten years younger! (LOUKA *comes from the house with a salver, which she carries hanging down by her side.*) Well?

LOUKA. Theres a gentleman just called, madam. A Serbian officer.

CATHERINE (*flaming*). A Serb! And how dare he—(*checking herself bitterly*). Oh, I forgot. We are at peace now. I suppose we shall have them calling every day to pay their compliments. Well: if he is an officer why dont you tell your master? He is in the library with Major Saranoff. Why do you come to me?

LOUKA. But he asks for you, madam. And I dont think he knows who you are: he said the lady of the house. He gave me this little ticket for you. (*She takes a card out of her bosom; puts it on the salver; and offers it to* CATHERINE.)

CATHERINE (*reading*). "Captain Bluntschli"? Thats a German name.

LOUKA. Swiss, madam, I think.

CATHERINE (*with a bound that makes* LOUKA *jump back*). Swiss! What is he like?

LOUKA (*timidly*). He has a big carpet bag, madam.

CATHERINE. Oh Heavens! he's come to return the coat. Send him away: say we're not at home: ask him to leave his address and I'll write to him. Oh stop: that will never do. Wait! (*She throws herself into a chair to think it out.* LOUKA *waits.*) The master and Major Saranoff are busy in the library, arnt they?

LOUKA. Yes, madam.

CATHERINE (*decisively*). Bring the gentleman out here at once. (*Peremptorily.*) And be very polite to him. Dont delay. Here (*impatiently snatching the salver from her*): leave that here; and go straight back to him.

LOUKA. Yes, madam (*going*).

CATHERINE. Louka!

LOUKA (*stopping*). Yes, madam.

CATHERINE. Is the library door shut?

LOUKA. I think so, madam.

CATHERINE. If not, shut it as you pass through.

LOUKA. Yes, madam (*going*).

CATHERINE. Stop. (*Louka stops.*) He will have to go that way (*indicating the gate of the stable yard*). Tell Nicola to bring his bag here after him. Dont forget.

LOUKA (*surprised*). His bag?

CATHERINE. Yes: here: as soon as possible. (*Vehemently.*) Be quick! (LOUKA *runs into the house.* CATHERINE *snatches her apron off and throws it behind a bush. She then takes up the salver and uses it as a mirror, with the result that the handkerchief tied round her head follows the apron. A touch to her hair and a shake to her dressing gown make her presentable.*) Oh, how? how? how can a man be such a fool! Such a moment to select! (LOUKA *appears at the door of the house, announcing* Captain Bluntschli. *She stands aside at the top of the steps to let him pass before she goes in again. He is the man of the midnight adventure in* RAINA's *room, clean, well brushed, smartly uniformed, and out of trouble, but still unmistakably the same man. The moment* LOUKA's *back is turned,* CATHERINE *swoops on him with impetuous, urgent, coaxing appeal.*) Captain Bluntschli: I am very glad to see you; but you must leave this house at once. (*He raises his eyebrows.*) My husband has just returned with my future son-in-law; and they know nothing. If they did, the consequences would be terrible. You are a foreigner: you do not feel our national animosities as we do. We still hate the Serbs: the effect of the peace on my husband has been to make him feel like a lion baulked of his prey. If he discovers our secret, he will never forgive me; and my daughter's life will hardly be safe. Will you, like the chivalrous gentleman and soldier you are, leave at once before he finds you here?

BLUNTSCHLI (*disappointed, but philosophical*). At once, gracious lady. I only came to thank you and return the coat you lent me. If you will allow me to take it out of my bag and leave it with your servant as I pass out, I need detain you no further. (*He turns to go into the house.*)

CATHERINE (*catching him by the sleeve*). Oh, you must not think of going back that way. (*Coaxing him across to the stable gates.*) This is the shortest way out. Many thanks. So glad to have been of service to you. Good-bye.

BLUNTSCHLI. But my bag?

CATHERINE. It shall be sent on. You will leave me your address.

BLUNTSCHLI. True. Allow me. (*He takes out his cardcase, and stops to write his address, keeping* CATHERINE *in an agony of impatience. As he hands her the card,* PETKOFF, *hatless, rushes from the house in a fluster of hospitality, followed by* SERGIUS).

PETKOFF (*as he hurries down the steps*). My dear Captain Bluntschli—

CATHERINE. Oh Heavens! (*She sinks on the seat against the wall.*)

PETKOFF (*too preoccupied to notice her as he shakes* BLUNTSCHLI'S *hand heartily*). Those stupid people of mine thought I was out here, instead of in the —haw!—library (*he cannot mention the library without betraying how proud he is of it*). I saw you through the window. I was wondering why you didn't come in. Saranoff is with me: you remember him, dont you?

SERGIUS (*saluting humorously, and then offering his hand with great charm of manner*). Welcome, our friend the enemy!

PETKOFF. No longer the enemy, happily. (*Rather anxiously.*) I hope youve called as a friend, and not about horses or prisoners.

CATHERINE. Oh, quite as a friend, Paul. I was just asking Captain Bluntschli to stay to lunch; but he declares he must go at once.

SERGIUS (*sardonically*). Impossible, Bluntschli. We want you here badly. We have to send on three cavalry regiments to Philippopolis; and we dont in the least know how to do it.

BLUNTSCHLI (*suddenly attentive and businesslike*). Philippopolis? The forage is the trouble, I suppose. ·

PETKOFF (*eagerly*). Yes: thats it. (*To* SERGIUS.) He sees the whole thing at once.

BLUNTSCHLI. I think I can shew you how to manage that.

SERGIUS. Invaluable man! Come along! (*Towering over* BLUNTSCHLI, *he puts his hand on his shoulder and takes him to the steps,* PETKOFF *following.*)

(RAINA *comes from the house as* BLUNTSCHLI *puts his foot on the first step.*)

RAINA. Oh! The chocolate cream soldier!

(BLUNTSCHLI *stands rigid.* SERGIUS, *amazed, looks at* RAINA, *then at* PETKOFF, *who looks back at him and then at his wife.*)

CATHERINE (*with commanding presence of mind*). My dear Raina, dont you see that we have a guest here? Captain Bluntschli: one of our new Serbian friends.

(RAINA *bows:* BLUNTSCHLI *bows.*)

RAINA. How silly of me! (*She comes down into the centre of the group, between* BLUNTSCHLI *and* PETKOFF.) I made a beautiful ornament this morning for the ice pudding; and that stupid Nicola has just put down a pile of plates on it and spoilt it. (*To* BLUNTSCHLI, *winningly.*) I hope you didn't think that you were the chocolate cream soldier, Captain Bluntschli.

BLUNTSCHLI (*laughing*). I assure you I did. (*Stealing a whimsical glance at her.*) Your explanation was a relief.

PETKOFF (*suspiciously, to* RAINA). And since when, pray, have you taken to cooking?

CATHERINE. Oh, whilst you were away. It is her latest fancy.

PETKOFF (*testily*). And has Nicola taken to drinking? He used to be careful enough. First he shews Captain Bluntschli out here when he knew quite well I was in the library; and then he goes downstairs and breaks Raina's chocolate soldier. He must—(NICOLA *appears at the top of the steps with the bag. He descends; places it respectfully before* BLUNTSCHLI; *and waits for further orders. General amazement.* NICOLA, *unconscious of the effect he is producing, looks perfectly satisfied with himself. When* PETKOFF *recovers his power of speech, he breaks out at him with*) Are you mad, Nicola?

NICOLA (*taken aback*). Sir?

PETKOFF. What have you brought that for?

NICOLA. My lady's orders, major. Louka told me that—

CATHERINE (*interrupting him*). My orders! Why should I order you to bring Captain Bluntschli's luggage out here? What are you thinking of, Nicola?

NICOLA (*after a moment's bewilderment, picking up the bag as he addresses* BLUNTSCHLI *with the very perfection of servile discretion*). I beg your pardon, Captain, I am sure. (*To* CATHERINE.) My fault, madame: I hope youll overlook it. (*He bows, and is going to the steps with the bag, when* PETKOFF *addresses him angrily.*)

PETKOFF. Youd better go and slam that bag, too, down on Miss Raina's ice pudding! (*This is too much for* NICOLA. *The bag drops from his hand almost on his master's toes, eliciting a roar of*) Begone, you butter-fingered donkey.

NICOLA (*snatching up the bag, and escaping into the house*). Yes, Major.

CATHERINE. Oh, never mind. Paul: dont be angry.

PETKOFF (*blustering*). Scoundrel! He's got out of hand while I was away. I'll teach him. Infernal blackguard! The sack next Saturday! I'll clear out the whole establishment—(*he is stifled by the caresses of his wife and daughter, who hang round his neck, petting him*).

CATHERINE ⎫ (*together*) ⎰Now, now, now, it mustnt be
RAINA   ⎭   ⎱Wow, wow, wow: not on your

⎧ angry. He meant no harm. Be good to
⎪ please me, dear. Sh-sh-sh-sh!
⎨ first day at home. I'll make another ice
⎩ pudding. Tch-ch-ch!

PETKOFF (*yielding*). Oh well, never mind. Come Bluntschli: lets have no more nonsense about going away. You know very well youre not going back to Switzerland yet. Until you do go back youll stay with us.

RAINA. Oh, do, Captain Bluntschli.

PETKOFF (*to* CATHERINE). Now, Catherine: it's of you he's afraid. Press him: and he'll stay.

CATHERINE. Of course I shall be only too delighted if (*appealingly*) Captain Bluntschli really wishes to stay. He knows my wishes.

BLUNTSCHLI (*in his driest military manner*). I am at madam's orders.

SERGIUS (*cordially*). That settles it!

PETKOFF (*heartily*). Of course!

RAINA. You see you must stay.

BLUNTSCHLI (*smiling*). Well, if I must, I must.

(*Gesture of despair from* CATHERINE.)

ACT III

(*In the library after lunch. It is not much of a library. Its literary equipment consists of a single fixed shelf stocked with old paper covered novels, broken backed, coffee stained, torn and thumbed; and a couple of little hanging shelves with a few gift books on them: the rest of the wall space being occupied by trophies of war and the chase. But it is a most comfortable sitting room. A row of three large windows shews a mountain panorama, just now seen in one of its friendliest aspects in the mellowing afternoon light. In the corner next the right hand window a square earthenware stove, a perfect tower of glistening pottery, rises nearly to the ceiling and guarantees plenty of warmth. The ottoman is like that in* RAINA's *room, and similarly placed; and the window seats are luxurious with decorated cushions. There is one object, however, hopelessly out of keeping with its surroundings. This is a small kitchen table, much the worse for wear, fitted as a writing table with an old canister full of pens, an eggcup filled with ink, and a deplorable scrap of heavily used pink blotting paper.*

At the side of this table, which stands to the left of anyone facing the window, BLUNTSCHLI *is hard at work with a couple of maps before him, writing orders. At the head of it sits* SERGIUS, *who is supposed to be also at work, but is actually gnawing the feather of a pen, and contemplating* BLUNTSCHLI's *quick, sure, businesslike progress with a mixture of envious irritation at his own incapacity and awestruck wonder at an ability which seems to him almost miraculous, though its prosaic character forbids him to esteem it. The* MAJOR *is comfortably established on the ottoman, with a newspaper in his hand and the tube of his hookah within easy reach.* CATHERINE *sits at the stove, with her back to them, embroidering.* RAINA, *reclining on the divan, is gazing in a daydream out at the Balkan landscape, with a neglected novel in her lap.*

The door is on the same side as the stove, farther from the window. The button of the electric bell is at the opposite side, behind BLUNTSCHLI.)

PETKOFF (*looking up from his paper to watch how they are getting on at the table*). Are you sure I cant help in any way, Bluntschli?

BLUNTSCHLI (*without interrupting his writing or looking up*). Quite sure, thank you. Saranoff and I will manage it.

SERGIUS (*grimly*). Yes: we'll manage it. He finds out what to do; draws up the orders; and I sign em. Division of labor! (BLUNTSCHLI *passes him a paper.*) Another one? Thank you. (*He plants the paper squarely before him; sets his chair carefully parallel to it; and signs with his cheek on his elbow and his protruded tongue following the movements of his pen.*) This hand is more accustomed to the sword than to the pen.

PETKOFF. It's very good of you, Bluntschli: it is indeed, to let yourself be put upon in this way. Now are you quite sure I can do nothing?

CATHERINE (*in a low warning tone*). You can stop interrupting, Paul.

PETKOFF (*starting and looking round at her*). Eh? Oh! Quite right. (*He takes his newspaper up again, but presently lets it drop.*) Ah, you havnt been campaigning, Catherine: you dont know how pleasant it is for us to sit here, after a good lunch, with nothing to do but enjoy ourselves. Theres only one thing I want to make me thoroughly comfortable.

CATHERINE. What is that?

PETKOFF. My old coat. I'm not at home in this one: I feel as if I were on parade.

CATHERINE. My dear Paul, how absurd you are about that old coat! It must be hanging in the blue closet where you left it.

PETKOFF. My dear Catherine, I tell you Ive looked there. Am I to believe my own eyes or not? (CATHERINE *rises and crosses the room to press the button of the electric bell.*) What are you shewing off that bell for? (*She looks at him majestically, and silently resumes her chair and her needlework.*) My dear: if you think the obstinacy of your sex can make a coat out of two old dressing gowns of Raina's, your waterproof, and my mackintosh, youre mistaken. Thats exactly what the blue closet contains at present.

(NICOLA *presents himself.*)

CATHERINE. Nicola: go to the blue closet and bring your master's old coat here: the braided one he wears in the house.

NICOLA. Yes, madame. (*He goes out.*)

PETKOFF. Catherine.

CATHERINE. Yes, Paul.

PETKOFF. I bet you any piece of jewellery you like to order from Sofia against a week's housekeeping money that the coat isnt there.

CATHERINE. Done, Paul!

PETKOFF (*excited by the prospect of a gamble*). Come: heres an opportunity for some sport. Wholl bet on it? Bluntschli: I'll give you six to one.

BLUNTSCHLI (*imperturbably*). It would be robbing you, Major. Madame is sure to be right. (*Without looking up, he passes another batch of papers to* SERGIUS.)

SERGIUS (*also excited*). Bravo, Switzerland! Major: I bet my best charger against an Arab mare for Raina that Nicola finds the coat in the blue closet.

PETKOFF (*eagerly*). Your best char—

CATHERINE (*hastily interrupting him*). Dont be foolish, Paul. An Arabian mare will cost you 50,000 levas.

RAINA (*suddenly coming out of her picturesque revery*). Really, mother, if you are going to take the jewellery, I dont see why you should grudge me my Arab.

(NICOLA *comes back with the coat, and brings it to* PETKOFF, *who can hardly believe his eyes.*)

CATHERINE. Where was it, Nicola?

NICOLA. Hanging in the blue closet, madame.

PETKOFF. Well, I am d—

CATHERINE (*stopping him*). Paul!

PETKOFF. I could have sworn it wasnt there. Age is beginning to tell on me. I'm getting hallucinations. (*To* NICOLA.) Here: help me to change. Excuse me, Bluntschli. (*He begins changing coats,* NICOLA *acting as valet.*) Remember: I didnt take that bet of yours, Sergius. Youd better give Raina that Arab steed yourself, since youve roused her expectations. Eh, Raina? (*He looks round at her; but she is again rapt in the landscape. With a little gush of parental affection and pride, he points her out to them, and says*) She's dreaming, as usual.

SERGIUS. Assuredly she shall not be the loser.

PETKOFF. So much the better for her. *I* shant come off so cheaply, I expect. (*The change is now complete.* NICOLA *goes out with the discarded coat.*) Ah, now I feel at home at last. (*He sits down and takes his newspaper with a grunt of relief.*)

BLUNTSCHLI (*to* SERGIUS, *handing a paper*). Thats the last order.

PETKOFF (*jumping up*). What! Finished?

BLUNTSCHLI. Finished.

PETKOFF (*with childlike envy*). Havnt you anything for me to sign?

BLUNTSCHLI. Not necessary. His signature will do.

PETKOFF (*inflating his chest and thumping it*). Ah well, I think weve done a thundering good day's work. Can I do anything more?

BLUNTSCHLI. You had better both see the fellows that are to take these. (SERGIUS *rises.*) Pack them off at once; and shew them that Ive marked on the orders the time they should hand them in by. Tell them that if they stop to drink or tell stories—if theyre five minutes late, theyll have the skin taken off their backs.

SERGIUS (*stiffening indignantly*). I'll say so. (*He strides to the door.*) And if one of them is man enough to spit in my face for insulting him, I'll buy his discharge and give him a pension. (*He goes out.*)

BLUNTSCHLI (*confidentially*). Just see that he talks to them properly, Major, will you?

PETKOFF (*officiously*). Quite right, Bluntschli, quite right. I'll see to it. (*He goes to the door importantly, but hesitates on the threshold.*) By the bye, Catherine, you may as well come too. Theyll be far more frightened of you than of me.

CATHERINE (*putting down her embroidery*). I daresay I had better. You would only splutter at them. (*She goes out,* PETKOFF *holding the door for her and following her.*)

BLUNTSCHLI. What an army! They make cannons out of cherry trees; and the officers send their wives to keep discipline! (*He begins to fold and docket the papers.*)

(RAINA, *who has risen from the divan, marches slowly down the room with her hands clasped behind her, and looks mischievously at him.*)

RAINA. You look ever so much nicer than when we last met. (*He looks up, surprised.*) What have you done to yourself?

BLUNTSCHLI. Washed; brushed; good night's sleep and breakfast. That's all.

RAINA. Did you get back safely that morning?

BLUNTSCHLI. Quite, thanks.

RAINA. Were they angry with you for running away from Sergius's charge?

BLUNTSCHLI (*grinning*). No: they were glad; because theyd all just run away themselves.

RAINA (*going to the table, and leaning over it towards him*). It must have made a lovely story for them: all that about me and my room.

BLUNTSCHLI. Capital story. But I only told it to one of them: a particular friend.

RAINA. On whose discretion you could absolutely rely?

BLUNTSCHLI. Absolutely.

RAINA. Hm! He told it all to my father and Sergius the day you exchanged the prisoners. (*She turns away and strolls carelessly across to the other side of the room.*)

BLUNTSCHLI (*deeply concerned, and half incredulous*). No! You dont mean that, do you?

RAINA (*turning, with sudden earnestness*). I do indeed. But they dont know that it was in this house you took refuge. If Sergius knew, he would challenge you and kill you in a duel.

BLUNTSCHLI. Bless me! then dont tell him.

RAINA. Please be serious, Captain Bluntschli. Can you not realize what it is to me to deceive him? I want to be quite perfect with Sergius: no meanness, no smallness, no deceit. My relation to him is the one really beautiful and noble part of my life. I hope you can understand that.

BLUNTSCHLI (*sceptically*). You mean that you wouldnt like him to find out that the story about the ice pudding was a—a—a—You know.

RAINA (*wincing*). Ah, dont talk of it in that flippant way. I lied: I know it. But I did it to save your life. He would have killed you. That was the second time I ever uttered a falsehood. (BLUNTSCHLI *rises quickly and looks doubtfully and somewhat severely at her.*) Do you remember the first time?

BLUNTSCHLI. I! No. Was I present?

RAINA. Yes; and I told the officer who was searching for you that you were not present.

BLUNTSCHLI. True. I should have remembered it.

RAINA (*greatly encouraged*). Ah, it is natural that you should forget it first. It cost you nothing: it cost me a lie! A lie!

(*She sits down on the ottoman, looking straight before her with her hands clasped around her knee.* BLUNTSCHLI, *quite touched, goes to the ottoman with a particularly reassuring and considerate air, and sits down beside her.*)

BLUNTSCHLI. My dear young lady, dont let this worry you. Remember: I'm a soldier. Now what are the two things that happen to a soldier so often that he comes to think nothing of them? One is hearing people tell lies (RAINA *recoils*): the other is getting his life saved in all sorts of ways by all sorts of people.

RAINA (*rising in indignant protest*). And so he becomes a creature incapable of faith and of gratitude.

BLUNTSCHLI (*making a wry face*). Do you like gratitude? I dont. If pity is akin to love, gratitude is akin to the other thing.

RAINA. Gratitude! (*Turning on him.*) If you are incapable of gratitude you are incapable of any noble sentiment. Even animals are grateful. Oh, I see now exactly what you think of me! You were not surprised to hear me lie. To you it was something I probably did every day! every hour! That is how men think of women. (*She paces the room tragically.*)

BLUNTSCHLI (*dubiously*). Theres reason in everything. You said youd told only two lies in your whole life. Dear young lady: isnt that rather a short allowance? I'm quite a straightforward man myself; but it wouldnt last me a whole morning.

RAINA (*staring haughtily at him*). Do you know, sir, that you are insulting me?

BLUNTSCHLI. I cant help it. When you strike that noble attitude and speak in that thrilling voice, I admire you; but I find it impossible to believe a single word you say.

RAINA (*superbly*). Captain Bluntschli!

BLUNTSCHLI (*unmoved*). Yes?

RAINA (*standing over him, as if she could not believe her senses*). Do you mean what you said just now? Do you know what you said just now?

BLUNTSCHLI. I do.

RAINA (*gasping*). I! I!!! (*She points to herself incredulously, meaning "I, RAINA PETKOFF tell lies!" He meets her gaze unflinchingly. She suddenly sits down beside him, and adds, with a complete change of manner from the heroic to a babyish familiarity.*) How did you find me out?

BLUNTSCHLI (*promptly*). Instinct, dear young lady. Instinct, and experience of the world.

RAINA (*wonderingly*). Do you know, you are the first man I ever met who did not take me seriously?

BLUNTSCHLI. You mean, dont you, that I am the first man that has ever taken you quite seriously?

RAINA. Yes: I suppose I do mean that. (*Cosily, quite at her ease with him.*) How strange it is to be talked to in such a way! You know, Ive always gone on like that.

BLUNTSCHLI. You mean the—?

RAINA. I mean the noble attitude and the thrilling voice. (*They laugh to-*

gether.) I did it when I was a tiny child to my nurse. She believed in it. I do it before my parents. They believe in it. I do it before Sergius. He believes in it.

BLUNTSCHLI. Yes: he's a little in that line himself, isnt he?

RAINA (*startled*). Oh! Do you think so?

BLUNTSCHLI. You know him better than I do.

RAINA. I wonder—I wonder is he? If I thought that—! (*Discouraged.*) Ah, well; what does it matter? I suppose, now youve found me out, you despise me.

BLUNTSCHLI (*warmly, rising*). No, my dear young lady, no, no, no a thousand times. It's part of your youth: part of your charm. I'm like all the rest of them: the nurse, your parents, Sergius: I'm your infatuated admirer.

RAINA (*pleased*). Really?

BLUNTSCHLI (*slapping his breast smartly with his hand, German fashion*). Hand aufs Herz! Really and truly.

RAINA (*very happy*). But what did you think of me for giving you my portrait?

BLUNTSCHLI (*astonished*). Your portrait! You never gave me your portrait.

RAINA (*quickly*). Do you mean to say you never got it?

BLUNTSCHLI. No. (*He sits down beside her, with renewed interest, and says, with some complacency.*) When did you send it to me?

RAINA (*indignantly*). I did not send it to you. (*She turns her head away, and adds, reluctantly.*) It was in the pocket of that coat.

BLUNTSCHLI (*pursing his lips and rounding his eyes*). Oh-o-oh! I never found it. It must be there still.

RAINA (*springing up*). There still! for my father to find the first time he puts his hand in his pocket! Oh, how could you be so stupid?

BLUNTSCHLI (*rising also*). It doesnt matter: I suppose it's only a photograph: how can he tell who it was intended for? Tell him he put it there himself.

RAINA (*bitterly*). Yes: that is so clever! isn't it? (*Distractedly.*) Oh! what shall I do?

BLUNTSCHLI. Ah, I see. You wrote something on it. That was rash.

RAINA (*vexed almost to tears*). Oh, to have done such a thing for you, who care no more—except to laugh at me—oh! Are you sure nobody has touched it?

BLUNTSCHLI. Well, I cant be quite sure. You see, I couldnt carry it about with me all the time: one cant take much luggage on active service.

RAINA. What did you do with it?

BLUNTSCHLI. When I got through to Pirot I had to put it in safe keeping somehow. I thought of the railway cloak room; but thats the surest place to get looted in modern warfare. So I pawned it.

RAINA. Pawned it!!!

BLUNTSCHLI. I know it doesnt sound nice: but it was much the safest plan. I redeemed it the day before yesterday. Heaven only knows whether the pawnbroker cleared out the pockets or not.

RAINA (*furious: throwing the words right into his face*). You have a low shopkeeping mind. You think of things that would never come into a gentleman's head.

BLUNTSCHLI (*phlegmatically*). Thats the Swiss national character, dear lady. (*He returns to the table.*)

RAINA. Oh, I wish I had never met you. (*She flounces away, and sits at the window fuming.*)

(LOUKA *comes in with a heap of letters and telegrams on her salver, and crosses, with her bold free gait, to the table. Her left sleeve is looped up to the shoulder with a brooch, shewing her naked arm, with a broad gilt bracelet covering the bruise.*)

LOUKA (*to* BLUNTSCHLI). For you. (*She empties the salver with a fling on to the table.*) The messenger is waiting. (*She is determined not to be civil to an enemy, even if she must bring him his letters.*)

BLUNTSCHLI (*to* RAINA). Will you excuse me: the last postal delivery that reached me was three weeks ago. These are the subsequent accumulations. Four telegrams: a week old. (*He opens one.*) Oho! Bad news!

RAINA (*rising and advancing a little remorsefully*). Bad news?

BLUNTSCHLI. My father's dead. (*He looks at the telegram with his lips pursed, musing on the unexpected change in his arrangements.* LOUKA *crosses herself hastily.*)

RAINA. Oh, how very sad!

BLUNTSCHLI. Yes: I shall have to start for home in an hour. He has left a lot of big hotels behind him to be looked after. (*He takes up a fat letter in a long blue envelope.*) Here's a whacking letter from the family solicitor. (*He puts out the enclosures and glances over them.*) Great Heavens! Seventy! Two hundred! (*In a crescendo of dismay.*) Four hundred! Four thousand!! Nine thousand six hundred!!! What on earth am I to do with them all?

RAINA (*timidly*). Nine thousand hotels?

BLUNTSCHLI. Hotels! nonsense. If you only knew! Oh, it's too ridiculous! Excuse me: I must give my fellow orders about starting. (*He leaves the room hastily, with the documents in his hand.*)

LOUKA (*knowing instinctively that she can annoy* RAINA *by disparaging* BLUNTSCHLI). He has not much heart, that Swiss. He has not a word of grief for his poor father.

RAINA (*bitterly*). Grief! A man who has been doing nothing but killing people for years! What does he care? What does any soldier care? (*She goes to the door, restraining her tears with difficulty.*)

LOUKA. Major Saranoff has been fighting too; and he has plenty of heart left. (RAINA, *at the door, draws herself up haughtily and goes out.*) Aha! I thought you wouldnt get much feeling out of your soldier. (*She is following* RAINA *when* NICOLA *enters with an armful of logs for the stove.*)

NICOLA (*grinning amorously at her*). Ive been trying all the afternoon to get a minute alone with you, my girl. (*His countenance changes as he notices her arm.*) Why, what fashion is that of wearing your sleeve, child?

LOUKA (*proudly*). My own fashion.

NICOLA. Indeed! If the mistress catches you, she'll talk to you. (*He puts the logs down, and seats himself comfortably on the ottoman.*)

LOUKA. Is that any reason why you should take it on yourself to talk to me?

NICOLA. Come! dont be so contrary with me. Ive some good news for you. (*She sits down beside him. He takes out some paper money.* LOUKA, *with an eager gleam in her eyes, tries to snatch it; but he shifts it quickly to his left hand, out of her reach.*) See! a twenty leva bill! Sergius gave me that, out of pure swagger. A fool and his money are soon parted. Theres ten levas more. The Swiss gave me that for backing up the mistress' and Raina's lies about him. He's no fool, he isnt. You should have heard old Catherine downstairs as polite as you please to me, telling me not to mind the Major being a little impatient; for they knew what a good servant I was—after making a fool and a liar of me before them all? The twenty will go to our savings; and you shall have the ten to spend if youll only talk to me so as to remind me I'm a human being. I get tired of being a servant occasionally.

LOUKA. Yes: sell your manhood for 30 levas, and buy me for 10! (*Rising scornfully.*) Keep your money. You were born to be a servant. I was not. When you set up your shop you will only be everybody's servant instead of somebody's servant. (*She goes moodily to the table and seats herself regally in* SERGIUS'S *chair.*)

NICOLA (*picking up his logs, and going to the stove*). Ah, wait til you see. We shall have our evenings to ourselves; and I shall be master in my own house, I promise you. (*He throws the logs down and kneels at the stove.*)

LOUKA. You shall never be master in mine.

NICOLA (*turning, still on his knees, and squatting down rather forlornly on his calves, daunted by her implacable disdain*). You have a great ambition in you, Louka. Remember: if any luck comes to you, it was I that made a woman of you.

LOUKA. You!

NICOLA (*scrambling up and going to her*). Yes, me. Who was it made you give up wearing a couple of pounds of false black hair on your head and reddening your lips and cheeks like any other Bulgarian girl! I did. Who taught you to trim your nails, and keep your hands clean, and be dainty about yourself, like a fine Russian lady! Me: do you hear that? me! (*She tosses her head defiantly; and he turns away, adding more coolly*) Ive often thought that if Raina were out of the way, and you just a little less of a fool and Sergius just a little more of one, you might come to be one of my grandest customers, instead of only being my wife and costing me money.

LOUKA. I believe you would rather be my servant than my husband. You would make more out of me. Oh, I know that soul of yours.

NICOLA (*going closer to her for greater emphasis*). Never you mind my soul; but just listen to my advice. If you want to be a lady, your present behaviour to me wont do at all, unless when we're alone. It's too sharp and impudent; and impudence is a sort of familiarity: it shews affection for me. And dont you try being high and mighty with me, either. Youre like all country girls: you think it's genteel to treat a servant the way I treat a stableboy. Thats only your ignorance; and dont forget it. And dont be so ready to defy everybody. Act as if you expected to have your own way, not as if you expected to be ordered about. The way to get on as a lady is the same as the way to get on as a servant: youve got to know your place: thats the secret of it. And you may depend on me to know my place if you get promoted. Think over it, my girl. I'll stand by you: one servant should always stand by another.

LOUKA (*rising impatiently*). Oh, I must behave in my own way. You take all the courage out of me with your cold-blooded wisdom. Go and put those logs in the fire: thats the sort of thing you understand.

(*Before* NICOLA *can retort,* SERGIUS *comes in. He checks himself a moment on seeing* LOUKA; *then goes to the stove.*)

SERGIUS (*to* NICOLA). I am not in the way of your work, I hope.

NICOLA (*in a smooth, elderly manner*). Oh no, sir: thank you kindly. I was only speaking to this foolish girl about her habit of running up here to the library whenever she gets a chance, to look at the books. Thats the worst of her education, sir: it gives her habits above her station. (*To* LOUKA.) Make that table tidy, Louka, for the Major. (*He goes out sedately.*)

(LOUKA, *without looking at* SERGIUS, *pretends to arrange the papers on the table. He crosses slowly to her, and studies the arrangement of her sleeve reflectively.*)

SERGIUS. Let me see: is there a mark there? (*He turns up the bracelet and sees the bruise made by his grasp. She stands motionless, not looking at him: fascinated, but on her guard.*) Ffff! Does it hurt?

LOUKA. Yes.

SERGIUS. Shall I cure it?

LOUKA (*instantly withdrawing herself proudly, but still not looking at him*). No. You cannot cure it now.

SERGIUS (*masterfully*). Quite sure? (*He makes a movement as if to take her in his arms.*)

LOUKA. Dont trifle with me, please. An officer should not trifle with a servant.

SERGIUS (*indicating the bruise with a merciless stroke of his forefinger*). That was no trifle, Louka.

LOUKA (*flinching; then looking at him for the first time*). Are you sorry?

SERGIUS (*with measured emphasis, folding his arms*). I am never sorry.

LOUKA (*wistfully*). I wish I could believe a man could be as unlike a woman as that. I wonder are you really a brave man?

SERGIUS (*unaffectedly, relaxing his attitude*). Yes: I am a brave man. My heart jumped like a woman's at the first shot; but in the charge I found that I was brave. Yes: that at least is real about me.

LOUKA. Did you find in the charge that the men whose fathers are poor like mine were any less brave than the men who are rich like you?

SERGIUS (*with bitter levity*). Not a bit. They all slashed and cursed and yelled like heroes. Psha! the courage to rage and kill is cheap. I have an English bull terrier who has as much of that sort of courage as the whole Bulgarian nation, and the whole Russian nation at its back. But he lets my groom thrash him, all the same. Thats your soldier all over! No, Louka: your poor men can cut throats; but they are afraid of their officers; they put up with insults and blows; they stand by and see one another punished like children: aye, and help to do it when they are ordered. And the officers!!! Well (*with a short harsh laugh*) I am an officer. Oh (*fervently*) give me the man who will defy to the death any power on earth or in heaven that sets itself up against his own will and conscience: he alone is the brave man.

LOUKA. How easy it is to talk! Men never seem to me to grow up: they all have schoolboy's ideas. You dont know what true courage is.

SERGIUS (*ironically*). Indeed! I am willing to be instructed. (*He sits on the ottoman, sprawling magnificently.*)

LOUKA. Look at me! How much am I allowed to have my own will? I have to get your room ready for you: to sweep and dust, to fetch and carry. How could that degrade me if it did not degrade you to have it done for you? But (*with subdued passion*) if I were Empress of Russia, above everyone in the world, then!! Ah then, though according to you I could shew no courage at all, you should see, you should see.

SERGIUS. What would you do, most noble Empress?

LOUKA. I would marry the man I loved, which no other queen in Europe has the courage to do. If I loved you, though you would be as far beneath me as I am beneath you, I would dare to be equal of my inferior. Would you dare as much if you loved me? No: if you felt the beginnings of love for me you would not let it grow. You would not dare: you would marry a rich man's daughter because you would be afraid of what other people would say of you.

SERGIUS (*bounding up*). You lie: it is not so, by all the stars! If I loved you, and I were the Czar himself, I would set you on the throne by my side. You know that I love another woman, a woman as high above you as heaven is above earth. And you are jealous of her.

LOUKA. I have no reason to be. She will never marry you now. The man I told you of has come back. She will marry the Swiss.

SERGIUS (*recoiling*). The Swiss!

LOUKA. A man worth ten of you. Then you can come to me; and I will refuse you. You are not good enough for me. (*She turns to the door.*)

SERGIUS (*springing after her and catching her fiercely in his arms*). I will kill the Swiss; and afterwards I will do as I please with you.

LOUKA (*in his arms, passive and steadfast*). The Swiss will kill you, perhaps. He has beaten you in love. He may beat you in war.

SERGIUS (*tormentedly*). Do you think I believe that she—she! whose worst thoughts are higher than your best ones, is capable of trifling with another man behind my back?

LOUKA. Do you think she would believe the Swiss if he told her now that I am in your arms?

SERGIUS (*releasing her in despair*). Damnation! Oh, damnation! Mockery! mockery everywhere! everything I think is mocked by everything I do. (*He *strikes himself frantically on the breast.*) Coward! liar! fool! Shall I kill myself like a man, or live and pretend to laugh at myself? (*She again turns to go.*) Louka! (*She stops near the door.*) Remember: you belong to me.

LOUKA (*turning*). What does that mean? An insult?

SERGIUS (*commandingly*). It means that you love me, and that I have had you here in my arms, and will perhaps have you there again. Whether that is an insult I neither know nor care: take it as you please. But (*vehemently*) I will not be a coward and a trifler. If I choose to love you, I dare marry you, in spite of all Bulgaria. If these hands ever touch you again, they shall touch my affianced bride.

LOUKA. We shall see whether you dare keep your word. And take care. I will not wait long.

SERGIUS (*again folding his arms and standing motionless in the middle of the room*). Yes: we shall see. And you shall wait my pleasure.

(BLUNTSCHLI, *much preoccupied, with his papers still in his hand, enters, leaving the door open for* LOUKA *to go out. He goes across to the table, glancing at her as he passes.* SERGIUS, *without altering his resolute attitude, watches him steadily.* LOUKA *goes out, leaving the door open.*)

BLUNTSCHLI (*absently, sitting at the table as before, and putting down his papers*). Thats a remarkable looking young woman.

SERGIUS (*gravely, without moving*). Captain Bluntschli.

BLUNTSCHLI. Eh?

SERGIUS. You have deceived me. You are my rival. I brook no rivals. At six o'clock I shall be in the drilling-ground on the Klissoura road, alone, on horseback, with my sabre. Do you understand?

BLUNTSCHLI (*staring, but sitting quite at his ease*). Oh, thank you: thats a cavalry man's proposal. I'm in the artillery; and I have the choice of weapons. If I go, I shall take a machine gun. And there shall be no mistake about the cartridges this time.

SERGIUS (*flushing, but with deadly coldness*). Take care, sir. It is not our custom in Bulgaria to allow invitations of that kind to be trifled with.

BLUNTSCHLI (*warmly*). Pooh! dont talk to me about Bulgaria. You dont know what fighting is. But have it your own way. Bring your sabre along. I'll meet you.

SERGIUS (*fiercely delighted to find his opponent a man of spirit*). Well said, Switzer. Shall I lend you my best horse?

BLUNTSCHLI. No: damn your horse! thank you all the same, my dear fellow. (RAINA *comes in, and hears the next sentence.*) I shall fight you on foot. Horseback's too dangerous; I dont want to kill you if I can help it.

RAINA (*hurrying forward anxiously*). I have heard what Captain Bluntschli said, Sergius. You are going to fight. Why? (SERGIUS *turns away in silence, and goes to the stove, where he stands watching her as she continues, to* BLUNTSCHLI.) What about?

BLUNTSCHLI. I dont know: he hasnt told me. Better not interfere, dear young lady. No harm will be done: Ive often acted as sword instructor. He wont be able to touch me; and I'll not hurt him. It will save explanations. In the morning I shall be off home; and youll never see me or hear of me again. You and he will then make it up and live happily ever after.

RAINA (*turning away deeply hurt, almost with a sob in her voice*). I never said I wanted to see you again.

SERGIUS (*striding forward*). Ha! That is a confession.

RAINA (*haughtily*). What do you mean?

SERGIUS. You love that man!

RAINA (*scandalized*). Sergius!

SERGIUS. You allow him to make love to you behind my back, just as you treat me as your affianced husband behind his. Bluntschli: you knew our relations; and you deceived me. It is for that I call you to account, not for having received favors *I* never enjoyed.

BLUNTSCHLI (*jumping up indignantly*). Stuff! Rubbish! I have received no favors. Why, the young lady doesnt even know whether I'm married or not.

RAINA (*forgetting herself*). Oh! (*Collapsing on the ottoman.*) Are you?

SERGIUS. You see the young lady's concern, Captain Bluntschli. Denial is useless. You have enjoyed the privilege of being received in her own room, late at night—

BLUNTSCHLI (*interrupting him pepperily*). Yes, you blockhead! she received me with a pistol at her head. Your cavalry were at my heels. I'd have blown out her brains if she'd uttered a cry.

SERGIUS (*taken aback*). Bluntschli! Raina: is this true?

RAINA (*rising in wrathful majesty*). Oh, how dare you, how dare you?

BLUNTSCHLI. Apologize, man: apologize. (*He resumes his seat at the table.*)

SERGIUS (*with the old measured emphasis, folding his arms*). I never apologize!

RAINA (*passionately*). This is the doing of that friend of yours, Captain Bluntschli. It is he who is spreading this horrible story about me. (*She walks about excitedly.*)

BLUNTSCHLI. No: he's dead. Burnt alive.

RAINA (*stopping, shocked*). Burnt alive!

BLUNTSCHLI. Shot in the hip in a woodyard. Couldnt drag himself out. Your fellows' shells set the timber on fire and burnt him, with a half a dozen other poor devils in the same predicament.

RAINA. How horrible!

SERGIUS. And how ridiculous! Oh, war! war! the dream of patriots and heroes! A fraud, Bluntschli. A hollow sham, like love.

RAINA (*outraged*). Like love! You say that before me!

BLUNTSCHLI. Come, Saranoff: that matter is explained.

SERGIUS. A hollow sham, I say. Would you have come back here if nothing had passed between you except at the muzzle of your pistol? Raina is mistaken about your friend who was burnt. He was not my informant.

RAINA. Who then? (*Suddenly guessing the truth.*) Ah, Louka! my maid! my servant! You were with her this morning all that time after—after—Oh, what sort of god is this I have been worshipping! (*He meets her gaze with sardonic enjoyment of her disenchantment. Angered all the more, she goes closer to him, and says, in a lower, intenser tone*) Do you know that I looked out of the window as I went upstairs, to have another sight of my hero; and I saw something I did not understand then. I know now that you were making love to her.

SERGIUS (*with grim humor*). You saw that?

RAINA. Only too well. (*She turns away, and throws herself on the divan under the centre window, quite overcome.*)

SERGIUS (*cynically*). Raina: our romance is shattered. Life's a farce.

BLUNTSCHLI (*to* RAINA, *whimsically*). You see: he's found himself out now.

SERGIUS (*going to him*). Bluntschli: I have allowed you to call me a blockhead. You may call me a coward as well. I refuse to fight you. Do you know why?

BLUNTSCHLI. No; but it doesnt matter. I didnt ask the reason when you cried on; and I dont ask the reason now that you cry off. I'm a professional soldier! I fight when I have to, and am very glad to get out of it when I havnt to. Youre only an amateur: you think fighting's an amusement.

SERGIUS (*sitting down at the table, nose to nose with him*). You shall hear the reason all the same, my professional. The reason is that it takes two men— real men—men of heart, blood and honor—to make a genuine combat. I could no more fight with you than I could make love to an ugly woman. Youve no magnetism: youre not a man: youre a machine.

BLUNTSCHLI (*apologetically*). Quite true, quite true. I always was that sort of chap. I'm very sorry.

SERGIUS. Psha!

BLUNTSCHLI. But now that youve found that life isnt a farce, but something quite sensible and serious, what further obstacle is there to your happiness?

RAINA (*rising*). You are very solicitous about my happiness and his. Do you forget his new love—Louka? It is not you that he must fight now, but his rival, Nicola.

SERGIUS. Rival!! (*Bounding half across the room.*)

RAINA. Dont you know that theyre engaged?

SERGIUS. Nicola! Are fresh abysses opening? Nicola!

RAINA (*sarcastically*). A shocking sacrifice, isnt it? Such beauty! such intellect! such modesty! wasted on a middle-aged servant man. Really, Sergius, you cannot stand by and allow such a thing. It would be unworthy of your chivalry.

SERGIUS (*losing all self-control*). Viper! Viper! (*He rushes to and fro, raging.*)

BLUNTSCHLI. Look here, Saranoff: youre getting the worst of this.

RAINA (*getting angrier*). Do you realize what he has done, Captain Bluntschli? He has set this girl as a spy on us; and her reward is that he makes love to her.

SERGIUS. False! Monstrous!

RAINA. Monstrous! (*Confronting him.*) Do you deny that she told you about Captain Bluntschli being in my room?

SERGIUS. No; but—

RAINA (*interrupting*). Do you deny that you were making love to her when she told you?

SERGIUS. No; but I tell you—

RAINA (*cutting him short contemptuously*). It is unnecessary to tell us anything more. That is quite enough for us. (*She turns away from him and sweeps majestically back to the window.*)

BLUNTSCHLI (*quietly, as* SERGIUS, *in an agony of mortification, sinks on the ottoman, clutching his averted head between his fists*). I told you you were getting the worst of it, Saranoff.

SERGIUS. Tiger cat!

RAINA (*running excitedly to* BLUNTSCHLI). You hear this man calling me names, Captain Bluntschli?

BLUNTSCHLI. What else can he do, dear lady? He must defend himself somehow. Come (*very persuasively*): dont quarrel. What good does it do?

(RAINA, *with a gasp, sits down on the ottoman, and after a vain effort to look vexedly at* BLUNTSCHLI, *falls a victim to her sense of humor, and actually leans back babyishly against the writhing shoulder of* SERGIUS.)

SERGIUS. Engaged to Nicola! Ha! ha! Ah well, Bluntschli, you are right to take this huge imposture of a world coolly.

RAINA (*quaintly to* BLUNTSCHLI, *with an intuitive guess at his state of mind*). I daresay you think us a couple of grown-up babies, dont you?

SERGIUS (*grinning savagely*). He does: he does. Swiss civilization nurse-tending Bulgarian barbarism, eh?

BLUNTSCHLI (*blushing*). Not at all, I assure you. I'm only very glad to get you two quieted. There! there! let's be pleasant and talk it over in a friendly way. Where is this other young lady?

RAINA. Listening at the door, probably.

SERGIUS (*shivering as if a bullet had struck him, and speaking with quiet but deep indignation*). I will prove that that, at least, is a calumny. (*He goes with dignity to the door and opens it. A yell of fury bursts from him as he looks out. He darts into the passage, and returns dragging in* LOUKA, *whom he flings violently against the table, exclaiming*) Judge her, Bluntschli. You, the cool impartial man: judge the eavesdropper.

(LOUKA *stands her ground, proud and silent.*)

BLUNTSCHLI (*shaking his head*). I musnt judge her. I once listened myself outside a tent when there was a mutiny brewing. It's all a question of the degree of provocation. My life was at stake.

LOUKA. My love was at stake. I am not ashamed.

RAINA (*contemptuously*). Your love! Your curiosity, you mean.

LOUKA (*facing her and returning her contempt with interest*). My love, stronger than anything you can feel, even for your chocolate cream soldier.

SERGIUS (*with quick suspicion, to* LOUKA). What does that mean?

LOUKA (*fiercely*). I mean—

SERGIUS (*interrupting her slightingly*). Oh, I remember: the ice pudding. A paltry taunt, girl!

(MAJOR PETKOFF *enters, in his shirtsleeves.*)

PETKOFF. Excuse my shirtsleeves, gentlemen. Raina: somebody has been wearing that coat of mine: I'll swear it. Somebody with a differently shaped back. It's all burst open at the sleeve. Your mother is mending it. I wish she'd make haste: I shall catch cold. (*He looks more attentively at them.*) Is anything the matter?

RAINA. No. (*She sits down at the stove, with a tranquil air.*)

SERGIUS. Oh no. (*He sits down at the end of the table, as at first.*)

BLUNTSCHLI (*who is already seated*). Nothing. Nothing.

PETKOFF (*sitting down on the ottoman in his old place*). Thats all right. (*He notices* LOUKA.) Anything the matter, Louka?

LOUKA. No, sir.

PETKOFF (*genially*). Thats all right. (*He sneezes.*) Go and ask your mistress for my coat, like a good girl, will you?

(NICOLA *enters with the coat.* LOUKA *makes a pretence of having business in the room by taking the little table with the hookah away to the wall near the windows.*)

RAINA (*rising quickly as she sees the coat on* NICOLA's *arm*). Here it is papa. Give it to me Nicola; and do you put some more wood on the fire. (*She takes the coat, and brings it to the* MAJOR, *who stands up to put it on.* NICOLA *attends to the fire.*)

PETKOFF (*to* RAINA, *teasing her affectionately*). Aha! Going to be very good to poor old papa just for one day after his return from the wars, eh?

RAINA (*with solemn reproach*). Ah, how can you say that to me, father?

PETKOFF. Well, well, only a joke, little one. Come: give me a kiss. (*She kisses him.*) Now give me the coat.

RAINA. No: I am going to put it on for you. Turn your back. (*He turns his back and feels behind him with his arms for the sleeves. She dexterously takes the photograph from the pocket and throws it on the table before* BLUNTSCHLI, *who covers it with a sheet of paper under the very nose of* SERGIUS, *who looks on amazed, with his suspicions roused in the highest degree. She then helps* PETKOFF *on with his coat.*) There, dear! Now are you comfortable?

PETKOFF. Quite, little love. Thanks. (*He sits down; and* RAINA *returns to her seat near the stove.*) Oh, by the bye, Ive found something funny. Whats the meaning of this? (*He puts his hand into the picked pocket.*) Eh? Hallo! (*He tries the other pocket.*) Well, I could have sworn—! (*Much puzzled, he tries the breast pocket.*) I wonder—(*trying the original pocket*). Where can it—? (*He rises, exclaiming.*) Your mother's taken it!

RAINA (*very red*). Taken what?

PETKOFF. Your photograph, with the inscription: "Raina, to her Chocolate Cream Soldier: a Souvenir." Now you know theres something more in this than meets the eye; and I'm going to find it out. (*Shouting.*) Nicola!

NICOLA (*coming to him*). Sir!

PETKOFF. Did you spoil any pastry of Miss Raina's this morning?

NICOLA. You heard Miss Raina say that I did, sir.

PETKOFF. I know that, you idiot. Was it true?

NICOLA. I am sure Miss Raina is incapable of saying anything that is not true, sir.

PETKOFF. Are you? Then I'm not. (*Turning to the others.*) Come: do you think I dont see it all? (*He goes to* SERGIUS, *and slaps him on the shoulder.*) Sergius: youre the chocolate cream soldier, arnt you?

SERGIUS (*starting up*). I! A chocolate cream soldier! Certainly not.

PETKOFF. Not! (*He looks at them. They are all very serious and very conscious.*) Do you mean to tell me that Raina sends things like that to other men?

SERGIUS (*enigmatically*). The world is not such an innocent place as we used to think, Petkoff.

BLUNTSCHLI (*rising*). It's all right, Major. I'm the chocolate cream soldier. (PETKOFF *and* SERGIUS *are equally astonished.*) The gracious young lady saved my life by giving me chocolate creams when I was starving: shall I ever forget their flavour! My late friend Stolz told you the story of Pirot. I was the fugitive.

PETKOFF. You! (*He gasps.*) Sergius: do you remember how those two women went on this morning when we mentioned it? (SERGIUS *smiles cynically.* PETKOFF *confronts* RAINA *severely.*) Youre a nice young woman, arnt you?

RAINA (*bitterly*). Major Saranoff has changed his mind. And when I wrote that on the photograph, I did not know that Captain Bluntschli was married.

BLUNTSCHLI (*startled into vehement protest*). I'm not married.

RAINA (*with deep reproach*). You said you were.

BLUNTSCHLI. I did not. I positively did not. I never was married in my life.

PETKOFF (*exasperated*). Raina: will you kindly inform me, if I am not asking too much, which of these gentlemen you are engaged to?

RAINA. To neither of them. This young lady (*introducing* LOUKA, *who faces them all proudly*) is the object of Major Saranoff's affections at present.

PETKOFF. Louka! Are you mad, Sergius? Why, this girl's engaged to Nicola.

NICOLA. I beg your pardon, sir. There is a mistake. Louka is not engaged to me.

PETKOFF. Not engaged to you, you scoundrel! Why, you had twenty-five levas from me on the day of your betrothal; and she had that gilt bracelet from Miss Raina.

NICOLA (*with cool unction*). We gave it out so, sir. But it was only to give Louka protection. She had a soul above her station; and I have been no more than her confidential servant. I intend, as you know, sir, to set up a shop later on in Sofia; and I look forward to her custom and recommendation should she marry into the nobility. (*He goes out with impressive discretion, leaving them all staring after him.*)

PETKOFF (*breaking the silence*). Well, I am—hm!

SERGIUS. This is either the finest heroism or the most crawling baseness. Which is it, Bluntschli?

BLUNTSCHLI. Never mind whether it's heroism or baseness. Nicola's the ablest man Ive met in Bulgaria. I'll make him manager of a hotel if he can speak French and German.

LOUKA (*suddenly breaking out at* SERGIUS). I have been insulted by every-one here. You set them the example. You owe me an apology.

(SERGIUS, *like a repeating clock of which the spring has been touched, immediately begins to fold his arms.*)

BLUNTSCHLI (*before he can speak*). It's no use. He never apologizes.

LOUKA. Not to you, his equal and his enemy. To me, his poor servant, he will not refuse to apologize.

SERGIUS (*approvingly*). You are right. (*He bends his knee in his grandest manner.*) Forgive me.

LOUKA. I forgive you. (*She timidly gives him her hand, which he kisses.*) That touch makes me your affianced wife.

SERGIUS (*springing up*). Ah! I forgot that.

LOUKA (*coldly*). You can withdraw if you like.

SERGIUS. Withdraw! Never! You belong to me. (*He puts his arm about her.*)

(CATHERINE *comes in and finds* LOUKA *in* SERGIUS' *arms, with all the rest gazing at them in bewildered astonishment.*)

CATHERINE. What does this mean?

(SERGIUS *releases* LOUKA.)

PETKOFF. Well, my dear, it appears that Sergius is going to marry Louka instead of Raina. (*She is about to break out indignantly at him: he stops her by exclaiming testily*) Dont blame me: Ive nothing to do with it. (*He retreats to the stove.*)

CATHERINE. Marry Louka! Sergius: you are bound by your word to us!

SERGIUS (*folding his arms*). Nothing binds me.

BLUNTSCHLI (*much pleased by this piece of common sense*). Saranoff: your hand. My congratulations. These heroics of yours have their practical side after all. (*To* LOUKA.) Gracious young lady: the best wishes of a good Republican! (*He kisses her hand, to* RAINA's *great disgust, and returns to his seat.*)

CATHERINE. Louka: you have been telling stories.

LOUKA. I have done Raina no harm.

CATHERINE (*haughtily*). Raina!

(RAINA, *equally indignant, almost snorts at the liberty.*)

LOUKA. I have a right to call her Raina: she calls me Louka. I told Major Saranoff she would never marry him if the Swiss gentleman came back.

BLUNTSCHLI (*rising, much surprised*). Hallo!

LOUKA (*turning to* RAINA). I thought you were fonder of him than of Sergius. You know best whether I was right.

BLUNTSCHLI. What nonsense! I assure you, my dear Major, my dear Madame, the gracious young lady simply saved my life, nothing else. She never cared two straws for me. Why, bless my heart and soul, look at the young lady and look at me. She, rich, young, beautiful, with her imagination full of fairy princes and noble natures and cavalry charges and goodness knows what! And I, a common-place Swiss soldier who hardly knows what a decent life is after fifteen years of barracks and battles: a vagabond, a man who has spoiled all his chances in life through an incurably romantic disposition, a man—

SERGIUS (*starting as if a needle had pricked him and interrupting* BLUNTSCHLI *in incredulous amazement*). Excuse me, Bluntschli: what did you say had spoiled your chances in life?

BLUNTSCHLI (*promptly*). An incurably romantic disposition. I ran away from home twice when I was a boy. I went into the army instead of into my father's business. I climbed the balcony of this house when a man of sense would have dived into the nearest cellar. I came sneaking back here to have another look at the young lady when any other man of my age would have sent the coat back—

PETKOFF. My coat!

BLUNTSCHLI.—yes: thats the coat I mean—would have sent it back and gone quietly home. Do you suppose I am the sort of fellow a young girl falls in love with? Why, look at our ages! I'm thirty-four: I dont suppose the young lady is much over seventeen. (*This estimate produces a marked sensation, all the rest turning and staring at one another. He proceeds innocently.*) All that adventure which was life or death to me, was only a schoolgirl's game to her—chocolate creams and hide and seek. Heres the proof! (*He takes the photograph from the table.*) Now, I ask you, would a woman who took the affair seriously have sent me this and written on it "Raina, to her Chocolate Cream Soldier: a Souvenir"? (*He exhibits the photograph triumphantly, as if it settled the matter beyond all possibility of refutation.*)

PETKOFF. Thats what I was looking for. How the deuce did it get there? (*He comes from the stove to look at it, and sits down on the ottoman.*)

BLUNTSCHLI (*to* RAINA, *complacently*). I have put everything right, I hope, gracious young lady.

RAINA (*going to the table to face him*). I quite agree with your account of yourself. You are a romantic idiot. (BLUNTSCHLI *is unspeakably taken aback.*) Next time, I hope you will know the difference between a schoolgirl of seventeen and a woman of twenty-three.

BLUNTSCHLI (*stupefied*). Twenty-three!

(RAINA *snaps the photograph contemptuously from his hand; tears it up; throws the pieces in his face; and sweeps back to her former place.*)

SERGIUS (*with grim enjoyment of his rival's discomfiture*). Bluntschli: my one last belief is gone. Your sagacity is a fraud, like everything else. You have less sense than even I!

BLUNTSCHLI (*overwhelmed*). Twenty-three! Twenty-three!! (*He considers.*) Hm! (*Swiftly making up his mind and coming to his host.*) In that case, Major Petkoff, I beg to propose formally to become a suitor for your daughter's hand, in place of Major Saranoff retired.

RAINA. You dare!

BLUNTSCHLI. If you were twenty-three when you said those things to me this afternoon, I shall take them seriously.

CATHERINE (*loftily polite*). I doubt, sir, whether you quite realize either my daughter's position or that of Major Sergius Saranoff, whose place you propose to take. The Petkoffs and the Saranoffs are known as the richest and most important families in the country. Our position is almost historical: we can go back for twenty years.

PETKOFF. Oh, never mind that, Catherine. (*To* BLUNTSCHLI.) We should be most happy, Bluntschli, if it were only a question of your position; but hang it, you know, Raina is accustomed to a very comfortable establishment. Sergius keeps twenty horses.

BLUNTSCHLI. But who wants twenty horses? We're not going to keep a circus.

CATHERINE (*severely*). My daughter, sir, is accustomed to a first-rate stable.

RAINA. Hush, mother: youre making me ridiculous.

BLUNTSCHLI. Oh well, if it comes to a question of an establishment, here goes! (*He darts impetuously to the table; seizes the papers in the blue envelope; and turns to* SERGIUS.) How many horses did you say?

SERGIUS. Twenty, noble Switzer.

BLUNTSCHLI. I have two hundred horses. (*They are amazed.*) How many carriages?

SERGIUS. Three.

BLUNTSCHLI. I have seventy. Twenty-four of them will hold twelve inside, besides two on the box, without counting the driver and conductor. How many tablecloths have you?

SERGIUS. How the deuce do I know?

BLUNTSCHLI. Have you four thousand?

SERGIUS. No.

BLUNTSCHLI. I have. I have nine thousand six hundred pairs of sheets and blankets, with two thousand four hundred eider-down quilts. I have ten thousand knives and forks, and the same quantity of dessert spoons. I have three hundred servants. I have six palatial establishments, besides two livery stables, a tea garden, and a private house. I have four medals for distinguished services; I have the rank of an officer and the standing of a gentleman; and I have three native languages. Shew me any man in Bulgaria that can offer as much!

PETKOFF (*with childish awe*). Are you Emperor of Switzerland?

BLUNTSCHLI. My rank is the highest known in Switzerland: I am a free citizen.

CATHERINE. Then, Captain Bluntschli, since you are my daughter's choice—

RAINA (*mutinously*). He's not.

CATHERINE (*ignoring her*). —I shall not stand in the way of her happiness. (PETKOFF *is about to speak.*) That is Major Petkoff's feeling also.

PETKOFF. Oh, I shall be only too glad. Two hundred horses! Whew!

SERGIUS. What says the lady?

RAINA (*pretending to sulk*). The lady says that he can keep his tablecloths and his omnibuses. I am not here to be sold to the highest bidder. (*She turns her back on him.*)

BLUNTSCHLI. I wont take that answer. I appealed to you as a fugitive, a beggar, and a starving man. You accepted me. You gave me your hand to kiss, your bed to sleep in, and your roof to shelter me.

RAINA. I did not give them to the Emperor of Switzerland.

BLUNTSCHLI. Thats just what I say. (*He catches her by the shoulders and turns her face-to-face with him.*) Now tell us whom you did give them to.

RAINA (*succumbing with a shy smile*). To my chocolate cream soldier.

BLUNTSCHLI (*with a boyish laugh of delight*). Thatll do. Thank you. (*He looks at his watch and suddenly becomes businesslike.*) Time's up, Major. Youve managed those regiments so well that youre sure to be asked to get rid of some of the infantry of the Timok division. Send them home by way of Lom Palanka. Saranoff: dont get married until I come back: I shall be here punctually at five in the evening on Tuesday fortnight. Gracious ladies (*his heels click*) good evening. (*He makes them a military bow, and goes.*)

SERGIUS. What a man! Is he a man!

William Butler Yeats

Purgatory

PERSONS IN THE PLAY

A BOY, AN OLD MAN

(SCENE: *A ruined house and a bare tree in the background.*)

BOY. Half-door, hall door,
Hither and thither day and night,
Hill or hollow, shouldering this pack,
Hearing you talk.
OLD MAN.   Study that house.
I think about its jokes and stories;   5
I try to remember what the butler
Said to a drunken gamekeeper
In mid-October, but I cannot.
If I cannot, none living can.
Where are the jokes and stories of a house,   10
Its threshold gone to patch a pig-sty?
BOY. So you have come this path before?
OLD MAN. The moonlight falls upon the path,

The shadow of a cloud upon the house,
And that's symbolical; study that tree,   15
What is it like?
    BOY.   A silly old man.
    OLD MAN. It's like—no matter what it's like.
I saw it a year ago stripped bare as now,
So I chose a better trade.
I saw it fifty years ago   20
Before the thunderbolt had riven it,
Green leaves, ripe leaves, leaves thick as butter,
Fat, greasy life. Stand there and look,
Because there is somebody in that house.
                    (*The* BOY *puts down pack and stands in the doorway.*)
    BOY. There's nobody here.
    OLD MAN.   There's somebody there.   25
    BOY. The floor is gone, the window's gone,
And where there should be roof there's sky,
And here's a bit of an egg-shell thrown
Out of a jackdaw's nest.
    OLD MAN.   But there are some
That do not care what's gone, what's left: 30
The souls of Purgatory that come back
To habitations and familiar spots.
    BOY. Your wits are out again.
    OLD MAN.   Re-live
Their transgressions, and that not once
But many times; they know at last   35
The consequence of those transgressions
Whether upon others or upon themselves;
Upon others, others may bring help,
For when the consequence is at an end
The dream must end; if upon themselves,   40
There is no help but in themselves
And in the mercy of God.
    BOY.   I have had enough!
Talk to the jackdaws, if talk you must.
    OLD MAN. Stop! Sit there upon that stone.
That is the house where I was born.   45
    BOY. The big old house that was burnt down?
    OLD MAN. My mother that was your grand-dam owned it,
This scenery and this countryside,
Kennel and stable, horse and hound—
She had a horse at the Curragh, and there met   50
My father, a groom in a training stable,
Looked at him and married him.

Her mother never spoke to her again,
And she did right.
    BOY.   What's right and wrong?
My grand-dad got the girl and the money.   55
    OLD MAN. Looked at him and married him,
And he squandered everything she had.
She never knew the worst, because
She died in giving birth to me,
But now she knows it all, being dead.   60
Great people lived and died in this house;
Magistrates, colonels, members of Parliament,
Captains and Governors, and long ago
Men that had fought at Aughrim and the Boyne.
Some that had gone on Government work   65
To London or to India came home to die,
Or came from London every spring   ,
To look at the may-blossom in the park.
They had loved the trees that he cut down
To pay what he had lost at cards   70
Or spent on horses, drink and women;
Had loved the house, had loved all
The intricate passages of the house,
But he killed the house; to kill a house
Where great men grew up, married, died,   75
I here declare a capital offense.
    BOY. My God, but you had luck! Grand clothes,
And maybe a grand horse to ride.
    OLD MAN. That he might keep me upon his level
He never sent me to school, but some   80
Half-loved me for my half of her:
A gamekeeper's wife taught me to read,
A Catholic curate taught me Latin.
There were old books and books made fine
By eighteenth-century French binding, books   85
Modern and ancient, books by the ton.
    BOY. What education have you given me?
    OLD MAN. I gave the education that befits
A bastard that a pedlar got
Upon a tinker's daughter in a ditch.   90
When I had come to sixteen years old
My father burned down the house when drunk.
    BOY. But that is my age, sixteen years old,
    At the Puck Fair.
    OLD MAN.   And everything was burnt;
Books, library, all were burnt.   95

BOY. Is what I have heard upon the road the truth,
That you killed him in the burning house?
    OLD MAN. There's nobody here but our two selves?
    BOY. Nobody, Father.
    OLD MAN.   I stuck him with a knife,
That knife that cuts my dinner now,   100
And after that I left him in the fire.
They dragged him out, somebody saw
The knife-wound but could not be certain
Because the body was all black and charred.
Then some that were his drunken friends   105
Swore they would put me upon trial,
Spoke of quarrels, a threat I had made.
The gamekeeper gave me some old clothes,
I ran away, worked here and there
Till I became a pedlar on the roads,   110
No good trade, but good enough
Because I am my father's son,
Because of what I did or may do.
Listen to the hoof-beats! Listen, listen!
    BOY. I cannot hear a sound.
    OLD MAN.   Beat! Beat!   115
This night is the anniversary
Of my mother's wedding night,
Or of the night wherein I was begotten.
My father is riding from the public-house,
A whiskey-bottle under his arm.   120
        (*A window is lit showing a young girl.*)
Look at the window; she stands there
Listening, the servants are all in bed,
She is alone, he has stayed late
Bragging and drinking in the public-house.
    BOY. There's nothing but an empty gap in the wall.   125
You have made it up. No, you are mad!
You are getting madder every day.
    OLD MAN. It's louder now because he rides
Upon a graveled avenue
All grass to-day. The hoof-beat stops,   130
He has gone to the other side of the house,
Gone to the stable, put the horse up.
She has gone down to open the door.
This night she is no better than her man
And does not mind that he is half drunk,   135
She is mad about him. They mount the stairs.
She brings him into her own chamber.

And that is the marriage-chamber now.

(The window is dimly lit again.)

Do not let him touch you! It is not true

That drunken men cannot beget   140

And if he touch he must beget

And you must bear his murderer,

Deaf! Both deaf! If I should throw

A stick or a stone they would not hear;

And that's a proof my wits are out.   145

But there's a problem: she must live

Through everything in exact detail,

Driven to it by remorse, and yet

Can she renew the sexual act

And find no pleasure in it, and if not,   150

If pleasure and remorse must both be there,

Which is the greater?

                 I lack schooling.

Go fetch Tertullian; he and I

Will ravel all that problem out

Whilst those two lie upon the mattress   155

Begetting me.

          Come back! Come back!

And so you thought to slip away,

My bag of money between your fingers,

And that I could not talk and see!

You have been rummaging in the pack.   160

(The light in the window has faded out.)

    BOY. You never gave me my right share.

    OLD MAN. And had I given it, young as you are,

You would have spent it upon drink.

    BOY. What if I did? I had a right

To get it and spend it as I chose.   165

    OLD MAN. Give me that bag and no more words.

    BOY. I will not.

    OLD MAN.   I will break your fingers.

(They struggle for the bag. In the struggle it drops, scattering the money.

The OLD MAN *staggers but does not fall. They stand looking at each other.*

    The window is lit up. A man is seen pouring whiskey into a glass.)

    BOY. What if I killed you? You killed my grand-dad,

Because you were young and he was old.

Now I am young and you are old.   170

    OLD MAN *(staring at window)*. Better-looking, those sixteen years—

    BOY. What are you muttering?

    OLD MAN.   Younger—and yet

She should have known he was not her kind.

BOY. What are you saying? Out with it!

OLD MAN (*points to window*).   175

My God! The window is lit up

And somebody stands there, although

The floorboards are all burnt away.

  OLD MAN. The window is lit up because my father

Has come to find a glass for his whiskey.   180

He leans there like some tired beast.

  BOY. A dead, living, murdered man!

  OLD MAN. "Then the bride-sleep fell upon Adam":

Where did I read those words?

                              And yet

There's nothing leaning in the window   185

But the impression upon my mother's mind;

Being dead she is alone in her remorse.

  BOY. A body that was a bundle of old bones

Before I was born. Horrible! Horrible!

                              (*He covers his eyes.*)

  OLD MAN. That beast there would know nothing, being nothing,   190

If I should kill a man under the window

He would not even turn his head.

                              (*He stabs the* BOY.)

My father and my son on the same jack-knife!

That finishes—there—there—there—

                    (*He stabs again and again. The window grows dark.*)

"Hush-a-bye baby, thy father's a knight,   195

Thy mother a lady, lovely and bright."

No, that is something that I read in a book,

And if I sing it must be to my mother,

And I lack rhyme.

     (*The stage has grown dark except where the tree stands in white light.*)

                    Study that tree.

It stands there like a purified soul,   200

All cold, sweet, glistening light.

Dear mother, the window is dark again,

But you are in the light because

I finished all that consequence.

I killed that lad because had he grown up   205

He would have struck a woman's fancy,

Begot, and passed pollution on.

I am a wretched foul old man

And therefore harmless. When I have stuck

This old jack-knife into a sod   210

And pulled it out all bright again,

And picked up all the money that he dropped,

I'll to a distant place, and there
Tell my old jokes among new men.
                    (*He cleans the knife and begins to pick up money.*)
Hoof-beats! Dear God,   215
How quickly it returns—beat—beat—!
Her mind cannot hold up that dream.
Twice a murderer and all for nothing,
And she must animate that dead night
Not once but many times!
                    O God,   220
Release my mother's soul from its dream!
Mankind can do no more. Appease
The misery of the living and the remorse of the dead.

Poetry

A poem with the title of A. E. Housman's "To an Athlete Dying Young" might be expected to express mourning, and it is sometimes a shock for an inexperienced reader to find that Housman is not at all saddened by the young man's death, but is actually congratulating him on it. Housman's reasons for adopting this attitude are, of course, the heart of the poem, but many readers are so puzzled by his uncommon attitude toward death that they do not read the poem carefully enough to see exactly what he is saying. Such a failure to read what the writer says rather than what we expect him to say is common in reading literature, particularly in reading poetry. Casual readers of poetry tend to decide in advance what poetry can say. They expect it to be sentimental, romantic, or preachy, and unless they find their expectations fulfilled, they are likely to be confused or even offended. As a result, they are unwilling to stay with a poem long enough to see to the bottom of it. Such preconceptions by readers who have not had much experience with poetry have had the effect of giving poetry a reputation for difficulty and obscurity. These readers are particularly unfortunate in view of the fact that good poetry's stock in trade is actually novelty and freshness, not familiarity. Like all the arts, poetry is potentially capable of expressing every attitude toward human experiences that has ever been felt, and poems achieve distinction, not because they repeat what has been said before, but because they expand the possibilities of communication into new areas.

A useful way of approaching the problem of understanding an individual poem is to divide the process into two parts, first determining the subject of the poem and then working to grasp as exactly as possible what the poet is saying about his subject. The wise reader, knowing that poetry is a rich and varied art, will realize that it can take almost anything as its subject. The following selection contains poems about a museum, a car, and a rifle, as well as about such traditional subjects as love and the song of the nightingale. But determining the subject involves more than merely identifying what the poem talks about in this general sense. Most good poems have a core of sense, and to understand them we must know what the poet is saying, that is, what he would tell us if he were simply talking about his subject instead of writing a poem about it.

However, this is only the first step. It is well to ask oneself the question, "What is he saying?" or "What does the poem mean?" but it is essential, in analyzing a poem, to go further and to ask, "What feeling or attitude is the poem expressing as it deals with its subject?" The main characteristic of poetry, the quality that distinguishes it from prose, is its greater capacity for expressing emotion. The poem is written, not merely because the poet has a subject, but because he also has a strong feeling about it. In the other forms of literature, the keystone of the structure is likely to be the sort of intellectual formulation we call an idea; much poetry too, of course, is intellectual and presents ideas, but more than any other form of writing, its reason for being is the expression of those essentially incommunicable personal experiences which are called emotions.

Here again, it is important not to prejudge the emotion that the poem will project, not to assume that the poet's feeling about his subject is the one that would be expected. The whole range of feelings, from amused indifference to passionate devotion has appeared in poetry. In Christopher Marlowe's "The Passionate Shepherd to His Love," the shepherd, assuring his sweetheart that they will be happy forever if she will give him her love, expresses a naive and romantic optimism about life as he describes the pleasures they will enjoy. The poem written by Sir Walter Raleigh as a reply to Marlowe's, in which the shepherd's sweetheart answers that love and youth do not last forever, is realistic and cynical. Some of the sonnets of Shakespeare, Andrew Marvell's "To His Coy Mistress," and John Nims' much more recent "Love Poem" communicate still other widely different feelings. These poems, representing several of the possible attitudes toward a single subject, love, illustrate something of the varying moods poetry is capable of capturing.

It is even more important to remember that serious poems often express states of mind that are fairly complicated. A single reading or snap interpretation can never do such poems justice. George Herbert's "The Collar," for example, outlines the emotions involved in a spiritual conflict. The poet, impatient with his life of religious devotion, declares his intention of giving it up and of going out to see the world. Yet he responds to the voice of God that seems to arise within him at the end, which suggests that he has known inwardly all along that his protests were wrong. Thus, the poem presents a mind torn between an ideal of fulfillment and a call to religious duty, which demands self-denial.

Like every art, poetry has methods peculiar to itself. Just as the painter makes use of color, line, and form, so the poet has certain resources which enable him to convey his ideas. The following poems have been chosen partly to illustrate the range of these resources. The three perhaps most basic ones can be described briefly. First, nearly every poem has a clear *rhythm*, a quality which, in poetry, as in music, is associated with the expression of feeling. This rhythm is often augmented by the familiar device of rhyme, and the two together, rhyme and rhythm, are frequently used in certain standard arrangements, to produce such forms as the quatrain, the couplet, and the sonnet. The rhythm of a poem is one of the most important aspects, though by no means the only aspect, of the form of the poem, and much of the special force of a good poem comes from the poet's skill in using it to help him express more exactly his whole meaning rather than as a superficial ornament.

Second, although poetry is written in the familiar medium of language, it exploits this medium in its own way. In informative prose, words are used principally for their denotative value, and their emotional values, though they may be quite important in certain kinds of prose, are secondary. In poetry, this order of importance is characteristically reversed, and the emotional meanings, or *connotations,* of words are brought forward. This does not mean that poetry has a special vocabulary, but that it uses the ordinary vocabulary in a special way. Consider, for example, the effect of the word "twilight" in Shakespeare's lines:

> In me thou see'st the twilight of such day
> As after sunset fadeth in the west . . .

This is one of the ways the poet adopts of saying that he is growing old. The dictionary meaning of "twilight" is simply a particular time of day, but Shakespeare uses it here in preference to some such matter-of-fact expression as "evening" or "six P.M." because it suggests the fading of something vital and beautiful, an idea directly related to the thought of the poem.

Finally, among the most interesting resources of poetry are poetic comparisons, often called *figures of speech,* which can be divided into *similes* and *metaphors.* These enable the poet to express himself with special force and vividness and present him with opportunities for imaginative insights. Frost resorts to a comparison of this kind in "Two Tramps in Mud Time" as a way of explaining his doctrine that work should also be a pleasure, a combination of a job and a hobby:

> My object in living is to unite
> My avocation and my vocation
> As my two eyes make one in sight.

Few poetic comparisons, however, are as clearly stated as this one. Most of them are subtly implied by the language of the poem, and the reader must be alert to grasp these suggested comparisons, for they are one of the most important special resources of poetry.

None of these resources is unique to poetry. To some degree they exist in all uses of language except that informative scientific writing that strives to exclude as far as possible all expression of emotion and attitude and is perhaps at its purest in the formula. But poetry stands at the opposite pole of communication and uses these and other similar resources to a greater degree than any other form of writing. As a reader's skill in understanding these uses of language increases, his understanding and enjoyment of poetry grows.

Ballads

Sir Patrick Spens

    The king sits in Dunfermline toune
      Drinking the blude-reid wine:
    "O whar will I get guid sailor,
      To sail this schip of mine?"

    Up and spak an eldern knicht,   5
      Sat at the kings richt kne:
    "Sir Patrick Spens is the best sailor
      That sails upon the se."

    The king has written a braid letter,
      And signed it wi' his hand,   10
    And sent it to Sir Patrick Spens,
      Was walking on the sand.

    The first line that Sir Patrick red,
      A loud lauch lauched he;
    The next line that Sir Patrick red,   15
      The teir blinded his ee.

    "O wha is this has don this deid,
      This ill deid don to me,
    To send me out this time o' the yeir,
      To sail upon the se!   20

    "Mak hast, mak hast, my mirry men all,
      Our guid schip sails the morne":
    "O say na sae, my master deir,
      For I feir a deadlie storme.

    "Late late yestreen I saw the new moone,   25
      Wi the auld moone in hir arme,
    And I feir, I feir, my deir master,
      That we will cum to harme."

    O our Scots nobles wer richt laith
      To weet their cork-heild schoone;   30
    Bot lang owre a' the play wer playd,
      Thair hats they swam aboone.

    O lang, lang may their ladies sit,
      Wi thair fans into their hand,
    Or eir they se Sir Patrick Spens   35
      Cum sailing to the land.

6 *richt:* right. 9 *braid:* broad. 16 *ee:* eye. 25 *yestreen:* yesterday evening. 29 *richt laith:* "right loath," i.e., unwilling. 30 *weet:* wet. 31 *lang owre:* long before. 32 *aboone:* above. 35 *Or eir:* before.

O lang, lang may the ladies stand,
  Wi thair gold kems in their hair,
Waiting for thair ain deir lords,
  For they'll se thame na mair.   40

Haf owre, haf owre to Aberdour,
  It's fiftie fadom deip,
And thair lies guid Sir Patrick Spens,
  Wi the Scots lords at his feit.

Lord Randal

"O where hae ye been, Lord Randal, my son?
O where hae ye been, my handsome young man?"
  "I hae been to the wild wood; mother, make my bed soon,
  For I'm weary wi hunting, and fain wald lie down."

"Where gat ye your dinner, Lord Randal, my son?   5
Where gat ye your dinner, my handsome young man?"
  "I dined wi my true love; mother, make my bed soon,
  For I'm weary wi hunting, and fain wald lie down."

"What gat ye to your dinner, Lord Randal, my son?
What gat ye to your dinner, my handsome young man?"   10
  "I gat eels boiled in broo; mother, make my bed soon,
  For I'm weary wi hunting, and fain wald lie down."

"What became of your bloodhounds, Lord Randal, my son?
What became of your bloodhounds, my handsome young man?"
  "O they swelld and they died; mother, make my bed soon,   15
  For I'm weary wi hunting, and fain wald lie down."

"O I fear ye are poisond, Lord Randal, my son!
O I fear ye are poisond, my handsome young man!"
  "O yes! I am poisond; mother, make my bed soon,
  For I'm sick at the heart, and I fain wald lie down."   20

Edward

"Why dois your brand sae drap wi bluid,
    Edward, Edward,
Why dois your brand sae drap wi bluid,

---

38 *kems:* combs.

---

4 *wald:* would.   11 *broo:* broth or juice.

---

1 *brand:* sword.

And why sae sad gang yee O?"
"O I hae killed my hauke sae guid,   5
   Mither, mither,
O I hae killed my hauke sae guid,
   And I had nae mair bot hee O."

"Your haukis bluid was nevir sae reid,
   Edward, Edward,   10
Your haukis bluid was nevir sae reid,
   My deir son I tell thee O."
"O I hae killed my reid-roan steid,
   Mither, mither,
O I hae killed my reid-roan steid,   15
   That erst was sae fair and frie O."

"Your steid was auld, and ye hae gat mair,
   Edward, Edward,
Your steid was auld, and ye hae gat mair,
   Sum other dule ye drie O."   20
"O I hae killed my fadir deir,
   Mither, mither,
O I hae killed my fadir deir,
   Alas, and wae is mee O!"

"And whatten penance wul ye drie for that,   25
   Edward, Edward?
And whatten penance will ye drie for that?
   My deir son, now tell me O."
"Ile set my feit in yonder boat,
   Mither, mither,   30
Ile set my feit in yonder boat,
   And Ile fare ovir the sea O."

"And what wul ye doe wi your towirs and your ha,
   Edward, Edward?
And what wul ye doe wi your towirs and your ha,   35
   That were sae fair to see O?"
"Ile let thame stand tul they doun fa,
   Mither, mither,
Ile let thame stand tul they doun fa,
   For here nevir mair maun I bee O."   40

"And what wul ye leive to your bairns and your wife,
   Edward, Edward?
And what wul ye leive to your bairns and your wife,
   Whan ye gang ovir the sea O?"

---

4 *why sae sad gang ye:* why are you so sad. 16 *erst:* once. 20 *Sum other dule ye drie:* you are suffering from some other sorrow. 21 *fadir:* father. 25 *whatten penance wul ye drie:* what penance will you suffer. 41 *bairns:* children.

"The warldis room, late them beg thrae life,   45
   Mither, mither,
The warldis room, late them beg thrae life,
   For thame nevir mair wul I see O."

"And what wul ye leive to your ain mither deir,
   Edward, Edward?   50
And what wul ye leive to your ain mither deir?
   My deir son, now tell me O."
"The curse of hell frae me sall ye beir,
   Mither, mither,
The curse of hell frae me sall ye beir,   55
   Sic counseils ye gave to me O."

The Lyke-Wake Dirge

This ae nighte, this ae nighte,
   —Every nighte and alle,
Fire and sleet and candle-lighte,
   And Christe receive thy saule.

When thou from hence away art past,   5
   —Every nighte and alle,
To Whinny-muir thou com'st at last;
   And Christe receive thy saule.

If ever thou gavest hosen and shoon,
   —Every nighte and alle,   10
Sit thee down and put them on;
   And Christe receive thy saule.

If hosen and shoon thou ne'er gav'st nane
   —Every nighte and alle,
The whinnes sall prick thee to the bare bane;   15
   And Christe receive thy saule.

From Whinny-muir when thou may'st pass,
   —Every nighte and alle,
To Brig o' Dread thou com'st at last;
   And Christe receive thy saule.   20

From Brig o' Dread when thou may'st pass,
   —Every nighte and alle,

45 *The warldis room:* the world's room.   56 *Sic counseils:* such advice.

Lyke-wake: a vigil kept over a corpse before burial.   1 *ae:* one.   7 *Whinny-muir:* "thorn-
moor."   9 *hosen and shoon:* stockings and shoes.   15 *whinnes:* prickles or thorns; *bane:*
bone.   19 *Brig:* bridge.

To Purgatory fire thou com'st at last;
And Christe receive thy saule.

If ever thou gavest meat or drink,   25
—Every nighte and alle,
The fire sall never make thee shrink;
And Christe receive thy saule.

If meat or drink thou ne'er gav'st nane,
—Every nighte and alle,   30
The fire will burn thee to the bare bane;
And Christe receive thy saule.

This ae nighte, this ae nighte,
—Every nighte and alle,
Fire and sleet and candle-lighte,   35
And Christe receive thy saule.

Geoffrey Chaucer (ca. 1343-1400)

Truth: Balade de Bon Conseyl

Flee fro the prees, and dwelle with sothfastnesse,
Suffyce unto thy good, though it be smal;
For hord hath hate, and climbing tikelnesse,
Prees hath envye, and wele blent overal;
Savour no more than thee bihove shal;   5
Reule wel thyself, that other folk canst rede;
And trouthe thee shal delivere, it is no drede.

Tempest thee noght al croked to redresse,
In trust of hir that turneth as a bal:
Gret reste stant in litel besinesse;   10
Be war also to sporne ayeyns an al;
Stryve not, as doth the crokke with the wal.
Daunte thyself, that dauntest otheres dede;
And trouthe thee shal delivere, it is no drede.

That thee is sent, receyve in buxumnesse,   15
The wrastling for this world axeth a fal.
Her is non hoom, her nis but wildernesse:

Title: Ballad of Good Counsel.   1 *prees:* crowd; *sothfastnesse:* truth.   2 *Suffyce unto:*
be content with.   3 *hord:* wealth; *climbing:* ambition; *tikelnesse:* danger.   4 *wele:* good
fortune; *blent:* blinds; *overal:* everywhere.   5 *Savour:* taste; *thee bihove shal:* you will
need.   6 *Reule:* discipline; *that:* so that; *rede:* advise.   7 *delivere:* free; *it is no drede:*
there is no fear.   8 *Tempest:* trouble; *croked:* crooked; *redresse:* correct.   9 *hire that*
turneth as a bal: Dame Fortune.   10 *stant:* stands; *besinesse:* business.   11 *sporne ayeyns*
an al: kick against the sharp point of an awl.   12 *Stryve:* struggle; *crokke:* jar.   13
Daunte: control; *dede:* deeds.   15 *That:* whatever; *buxumnesse:* an obedient spirit.
16 *axeth:* asks.   17 *Her is non boom:* here is no home; *nis:* is not.

Forth, pilgrim, forth! Forth, beste, out of thy stal!
Know thy contree, look up, thank God of al;
Hold the heye wey, and lat thy gost thee lede;   20
And trouthe thee shal delivere, it is no drede.

ENVOY

Therfore, thou Vache, leve thyn old wrecchednesse
Unto the world; leve now to be thral;
Crye him mercy, that of his hy goodnesse
Made thee of noght, and in especial   25
Draw unto him, and pray in general
For thee, and eek for other, hevenlich mede;
And trouthe thee shal delivere, it is no drede.

    Explicit Le bon counseill de G. Chaucer.

Sir Thomas Wyatt (1503-1542)
They Flee from Me

They flee from me, that sometime did me seek
With naked foot, stalking in my chamber.
I have seen them gentle, tame, and meek
That now are wild, and do not remember
That sometime they put themselves in danger   5
To take bread at my hand; and now they range
Busily seeking with a continual change.

Thanked be fortune it hath been otherwise
Twenty times better; but once, in special,
In thin array, after a pleasant guise,   10
When her loose gown from her shoulders did fall,
And she me caught in her arms long and small,
Therewith all sweetly did me kiss
And softly said, "Dear heart, how like you this?"

It was no dream: I lay broad waking.   15
But all is turned, through my gentleness,
Into a strange fashion of forsaking;
And I have leave to go of her goodness,
And she also to use newfangleness.
But since that I so kindly am served,   20
I would fain know what she hath deserved.

---

18 *beste:* beast.   20 *the heye way:* the main road; *gost:* spirit.   22 *Vache:* the poem was probably addressed to a contemporary of Chaucer's, Sir Philip la Vache.   23 *leve:* cease; *thral:* slave.   26 *mede:* reward.

---

1 *sometime:* formerly.   7 *change:* capriciousness.   10 *after:* according to; *guise:* way of speaking.   19 *to use newfangleness:* to seek something new.

George Peele (1552-1598)

A Farewell to Arms

His golden locks Time hath to silver turn'd;
　O Time too swift, O swiftness never ceasing!
His youth 'gainst Time and Age hath ever spurn'd,
　But spurn'd in vain; youth waneth by increasing:
Beauty, strength, youth, are flowers but fading seen;　5
Duty, faith, love, are roots, and ever green.

His helmet now shall make a hive for bees,
　And, lovers' sonnets turn'd to holy psalms,
A man-at-arms must now serve on his knees,
　And feed on prayers, which are Age his alms:　10
But though from court to cottage he depart,
His saint is sure of his unspotted heart.

And when he saddest sits in homely cell,
　He'll teach his swains this carol for a song,—
'Blest be the hearts that wish my sovereign well,　15
　Curst be the souls that think her any wrong.'
Goddess, allow this aged man his right,
To be your beadsman now that was your knight.

Sir Edward Dyer (d. 1607)

The Lowest Trees Have Tops, the Ant Her Gall

The lowest trees have tops, the ant her gall,
　The fly her spleen, the little sparks their heat;
The slender hairs cast shadows, though but small,
　And bees have stings, although they be not great;
Seas have their source, and so have shallow springs;　5
And love is love, in beggars as in kings.

Where rivers smoothest run, deep are the fords;
　The dial stirs, yet none perceives it move;
The firmest faith is in the fewest words;
　The turtles cannot sing, and yet they love:　10
True hearts have eyes and ears, no tongues to speak;
They hear and see, and sigh, and then they break.

---

18 *beadsman:* one who says prayers for another.

---

10 *The turtles:* turtledoves.

Sir Philip Sidney (1554-1586)

from *Astrophel and Stella*

XXXI

With how sad steps, O Moon, thou climb'st the skies!
How silently, and with how wan a face!
What, may it be that even in heavenly place
That busy archer his sharp arrows tries?
Sure, if that long-with-love-acquainted eyes   5
Can judge of love, thou feel'st a lover's case.
I read it in thy looks; thy languished grace,
To me that feel the like, thy state descries.
Then, even of fellowship, O Moon, tell me,
Is constant love deemed there but want of wit?   10
Are beauties there as proud as here they be?
Do they above love to be loved, and yet
Those lovers scorn whom that love doth possess?
Do they call virtue there ungratefulness?

XXXIX

Come, Sleep! O Sleep, the certain knot of peace,
The baiting-place of wit, the balm of woe,
The poor man's wealth, the prisoner's release,
The indifferent judge between the high and low;
With shield of proof shield me from out the prease   5
Of those fierce darts Despair at me doth throw;
Oh make in me those civil wars to cease.
I will good tribute pay, if thou do so.
Take thou of me smooth pillows, sweetest bed,
A chamber deaf to noise and blind to light,   10
A rosy garland and a weary head;
And if these things, as being thine by right,
Move not thy heavy grace, thou shalt in me,
Livelier than elsewhere, Stella's image see.

---

2 *baiting-place:* scene of entertainment; a term derived from the sport of bear-baiting.
5 *proof:* good quality; *prease:* pressure.

Christopher Marlowe (1564-1593)

The Passionate Shepherd to His Love

Come live with me and be my love,
And we will all the pleasures prove
That hills and valleys, dales and fields,
And all the craggy mountains yields.

There will we sit upon the rocks   5
And see the shepherds feed their flocks,
By shallow rivers, to whose falls
Melodious birds sing madrigals.

There will I make thee beds of roses
And a thousand fragrant posies,   10
A cap of flowers, and a kirtle
Embroider'd all with leaves of myrtle.

A gown made of the finest wool,
Which from our pretty lambs we pull,
Fair linèd slippers for the cold,   15
With buckles of the purest gold.

A belt of straw and ivy buds
With coral clasps and amber studs:
And if these pleasures may thee move,
Come live with me and be my love.   20

The shepherd swains shall dance and sing
For thy delight each May-morning:
If these delights thy mind may move,
Then live with me and be my love.

Sir Walter Raleigh (1552-1618)

The Nymph's Reply to the Shepherd

If all the world and love were young,
And truth in every shepherd's tongue,
These pretty pleasures might me move
To live with thee and be thy Love.

2 *prove:* test.   11 *kirtle:* tunic or coat.

Time drives the flocks from field to fold, 5
When rivers rage and rocks grow cold;
And Philomel becometh dumb;
The rest complains of cares to come.

The flowers do fade, and wanton fields
To wayward winter reckoning yields: 10
A honey tongue, a heart of gall,
Is fancy's spring, but sorrow's fall.

Thy gowns, thy shoes, thy beds of roses,
Thy cap, thy kirtle, and thy posies
Soon break, soon wither, soon forgotten, 15
In folly ripe, in reason rotten.

Thy belt of straw and ivy buds,
Thy coral clasps and amber studs,
All these in me no means can move
To come to thee and be thy Love. 20

But could youth last, and love still breed,
Had joys no date, nor age no need,
Then these delights my mind might move
To live with thee and be thy Love.

His Pilgrimage

Give me my scallop-shell of quiet,
My staff of faith to walk upon,
My scrip of joy, immortal diet,
My bottle of salvation,
My gown of glory, hope's true gage; 5
And thus I'll take my pilgrimage.

Blood must be my body's balmer;
No other balm will there be given;
Whilst my soul, like a quiet palmer,
Traveleth toward the land of heaven, 10
Over the silver mountains,
Where spring the nectar fountains.
There will I kiss
The bowl of bliss,
And drink mine everlasting fill 15
On every milken hill.

7 *Philomel:* the nightingale.

---

1 *scallop-shell:* an insignia often worn by pilgrims. 3 *scrip:* a pilgrim's wallet or bag.
5 *gage:* pledge. 7 *Blood:* the blood of Christ.

My soul will be a-dry before;
But, after, it will thirst no more.

Then by that happy, blissful day
   More peaceful pilgrims I shall see,   20
That have cast off their rags of clay,
   And walk appareled fresh like me.
         I'll take them first,
         To quench their thirst
And taste of nectar suckets,   25
         At those clear wells
         Where sweetness dwells,
Drawn up by saints in crystal buckets.

   And when our bottles and all we
Are filled with immortality,   30
Then the blessed paths we'll travel,
Strowed with rubies thick as gravel;
Ceilings of diamonds, sapphire floors,
High walls of coral, and pearly bowers.

   From thence to heaven's bribeless hall,   35
Where no corrupted voices brawl;
No conscience molten into gold;
No forged accuser bought or sold;
No cause deferred, no vain-spent journey,
For there Christ is the king's attorney,   40
Who pleads for all, without degrees,
And he hath angels but no fees.
   And when the grand twelve million jury
Of our sins, with direful fury,
Against our souls black verdicts give,   45
Christ pleads his death; and then we live.

   Be Thou my speaker, taintless pleader!
Unblotted lawyer! true proceeder!
Thou giv'st salvation, even for alms,
Not with a bribèd lawyer's palms.   50
   And this is mine eternal plea
To Him that made heaven and earth and sea:
That since my flesh must die so soon,
And want a head to dine next noon,
Just at the stroke, when my veins start and spread,   55
Set on my soul an everlasting head!
Then am I ready, like a palmer fit,
To tread those blest paths, which before I writ.

Of death and judgment, heaven and hell,
Who oft doth think, must needs die well.   60

---

25 *suckets:* candied fruits or vegetables.   38 *forged:* bribed.   42 *angel:* the name for a gold coin.   57 *palmer:* pilgrim.

Samuel Daniel (1562-1619)

To Delia

SONNET XLV

Care-charmer Sleep, son of the sable Night,
Brother to Death, in silent darkness born:
Relieve my languish, and restore the light,
With dark forgetting of my care return.
And let the day be time enough to mourn   5
The shipwreck of my ill-adventured youth:
Let waking eyes suffice to wail their scorn,
Without the torment of the night's untruth.
Cease, dreams, the images of day-desires,
To model forth the passions of the morrow: 10
Never let rising sun approve you liars,
To add more grief to aggravate my sorrow.
Still let me sleep, embracing clouds in vain.
And never wake to feel the day's disdain.

Michael Drayton (1563-1631)

Since There's No Help, Come, Let Us Kiss and Part

Since there's no help, come, let us kiss and part.
    Nay, I have done; you get no more of me,
And I am glad, yea, glad with all my heart,
    That thus so cleanly I myself can free;
Shake hands for ever, cancel all our vows,   5
    And when we meet at any time again,
Be it not seen in either of our brows
    That we one jot of former love retain,
Now at the last gasp of Love's latest breath,
    When, his pulse failing, Passion speechless lies,   10
When Faith is kneeling by his bed of death,
    And Innocence is closing up his eyes,
      Now if thou wouldst, when all have given him over,
      From death to life thou mightst him yet recover.

11 *approve:* prove.

---

7 *brows:* faces.   13 *given him over:* given him up.

Thomas Nashe (1567-1601)

Adieu, Farewell Earth's Bliss

Adieu, farewell earth's bliss,
This world uncertain is;
Fond are life's lustful joys,
Death proves them all but toys,
None from his darts can fly.   5
I am sick, I must die.
   Lord, have mercy on us!

Rich men, trust not in wealth,
Gold cannot buy you health;
Physic himself must fade,   10
All things to end are made,
The plague full swift goes by;
I am sick, I must die.
   Lord, have mercy on us!

Beauty is but a flower   15
Which wrinkles will devour:
Brightness falls from the air,
Queens have died young and fair,
Dust hath closed Helen's eye.
I am sick, I must die.   20
   Lord, have mercy on us!

Strength stoops unto the grave,
Worms feed on Hector brave,
Swords may not fight with fate.
Earth still holds ope her gate;   25
Come! come! the bells do cry.
I am sick, I must die.
   Lord, have mercy on us!

Wit with his wantonness
Tasteth death's bitterness;   30
Hell's executioner
Hath no ears for to hear
What vain art can reply.
I am sick, I must die.
   Lord, have mercy on us!   35

Haste, therefore, each degree,
To welcome destiny.
Heaven is our heritage,

---

3 *Fond:* foolish.   10 *Physic:* the science of medicine.   23 *Hector:* a hero of the Trojan war.   36 *degree:* social class.

Earth but a player's stage;
Mount we unto the sky.   40
I am sick, I must die.
    Lord, have mercy on us!

William Shakespeare (1564-1616)

Songs

Blow, blow, thou winter wind,
Thou art not so unkind
    As man's ingratitude;
Thy tooth is not so keen,
Because thou art not seen,   5
    Although thy breath be rude.
Heigh-ho! sing, heigh-ho! unto the green holly.
Most friendship is feigning, most loving mere folly.
    Then, heigh-ho! the holly!
    This life is most jolly.   10

Freeze, freeze, thou bitter sky,
That dost not bite so nigh
    As benefits forgot;
Though thou the waters warp,
Thy sting is not so sharp   15
    As friend remember'd not.
Heigh-ho! sing, heigh-ho! unto the green holly.
Most friendship is feigning, most loving mere folly.
    Then, heigh-ho! the holly!
    This life is most jolly.   20

Fear no more the heat o' the sun,
    Nor the furious winter's rages;
Thou thy worldly task hast done,
    Home art gone, and ta'en thy wages.
Golden lads and girls all must,   5
As chimney-sweepers, come to dust.

Fear no more the frown o' the great;
    Thou art past the tyrant's stroke;
Care no more to clothe and eat;
    To thee the reed is as the oak.   10

14 *warp*: beat or strike.

The scepter, learning, physic, must
All follow this, and come to dust.

Fear no more the lightning-flash,
    Nor the all-dreaded thunder-stone;
Fear not slander, censure rash;   15
    Thou hast finished joy and moan.
All lovers young, all lovers must
Consign to thee, and come to dust.

No exorciser harm thee!
    Nor no witchcraft charm thee!   20
Ghost unlaid forbear thee!
    Nothing ill come near thee!
Quiet consummation have;
    And renownéd be thy grave!

—

Full fathom five thy father lies:
    Of his bones are coral made;
Those are pearls that were his eyes;
    Nothing of him that doth fade
But doth suffer a sea-change   5
Into something rich and strange.
Sea-nymphs hourly ring his knell:
                                    Ding-dong!
Hark! now I hear them—Ding-dong, bell!

Sonnets

XV

When I consider everything that grows
Holds in perfection but a little moment,
That this huge stage presenteth nought but shows
Whereon the stars in secret influence comment;
When I perceive that men as plants increase,   5
Cheeréd and checked even by the self-same sky,
Vaunt in their youthful sap, at height decrease,
And wear their brave state out of memory—
Then the conceit of this inconstant stay
Sets you most rich in youth before my sight,   10
Where wasteful Time debateth with Decay,

---

11 *physic:* the science of medicine.   14 *thunder-stone:* thunderbolt.

---

7 *Vaunt:* display themselves vaingloriously.   9 *conceit:* thought; *stay:* residence in a particular place, sojourn.

To change your day of youth to sullied night;
And all in war with Time for love of you,
As he takes from you, I engraft you new.

XXIX

When, in disgrace with fortune and men's eyes,
I all alone beweep my outcast state,
And trouble deaf heaven with my bootless cries,
And look upon myself, and curse my fate,
Wishing me like to one more rich in hope,   5
Featured like him, like him with friends possessed,
Desiring this man's art and that man's scope,
With what I most enjoy contented least;
Yet in these thoughts myself almost despising,
Haply I think on thee—and then my state,   10
Like to the lark at break of day arising
From sullen earth, sings hymns at heaven's gate;
    For thy sweet love remembered such wealth brings
    That then I scorn to change my state with kings.

XXX

When to the sessions of sweet silent thought
I summon up remembrance of things past,
I sigh the lack of many a thing I sought,
And with old woes new wail my dear time's waste.
Then can I drown an eye, unused to flow,   5
For precious friends hid in death's dateless night,
And weep afresh love's long since canceled woe,
And moan the expense of many a vanished sight.
Then can I grieve at grievances foregone,
And heavily from woe to woe tell o'er   10
The sad account of fore-bemoanéd moan,
Which I new pay as if not paid before.
    But if the while I think on thee, dear friend,
    All losses are restored and sorrows end.

XXXIII

Full many a glorious morning have I seen
Flatter the mountain-tops with sovereign eye,
Kissing with golden face the meadows green,
Gilding pale streams with heavenly alchemy;

14 *engraft:* restore what you have lost.

---

2 *beweep:* lament.   3 *bootless:* useless.   6 *Featured like him:* having a face like his.

---

4 *dear:* precious.   6 *dateless:* timeless.   8 *expense:* loss.   9 *foregone:* preceding.   10 *tell o'er:* count up.

Anon permit the basest clouds to ride   5
With ugly rack on his celestial face,
And from the forlorn world his visage hide,
Stealing unseen to west with this disgrace:
Even so my sun one early morn did shine
With all-triumphant splendour on my brow;   10
But out, alack! he was but one hour mine;
The region cloud hath mask'd him from me now.
    Yet him for this my love no whit disdaineth;
    Suns of the world may stain when heaven's sun staineth.

LXXIII

That time of year thou mayst in me behold
When yellow leaves, or none, or few, do hang
Upon those boughs which shake against the cold,
Bare ruined choirs, where late the sweet birds sang.
In me thou see'st the twilight of such day   5
As after sunset fadeth in the west,
Which by and by black night doth take away,
Death's second self, that seals up all in rest.
In me thou see'st the glowing of such fire
That on the ashes of his youth doth lie,   10
As the death-bed whereon it must expire,
Consumed with that which it was nourished by.
    This thou perceivest, which makes thy love more strong,
    To love that well which thou must leave ere long.

CXLVI

Poor soul, the center of my sinful earth,
Thrall to these rebel powers that thee array,
Why dost thou pine within and suffer dearth,
Painting thy outward walls so costly gay?
Why so large cost, having so short a lease,   5
Dost thou upon thy fading mansion spend?
Shall worms, inheritors of this excess,
Eat up thy charge? Is this thy body's end?
Then, soul, live thou upon thy servant's loss,
And let that pine to aggravate thy store;   10
Buy terms divine in selling hours of dross;
Within be fed, without be rich no more:
    So shalt thou feed on Death, that feeds on men,
    And Death once dead, there's no more dying then.

---

6 *rack:* mist.   12 *region cloud:* a small local cloud.

---

4 *late:* recently.

---

2 *array:* clothe.   10 *aggravate:* increase.   11 *dross:* waste.

John Donne (1572-1631)

A Valediction: Forbidding Mourning

As virtuous men pass mildly away,
  And whisper to their souls to go,
Whilst some of their sad friends do say,
  The breath goes now, and some say, No;

So let us melt, and make no noise,   5
  No tear-floods, nor sigh-tempests move;
'Twere profanation of our joys
  To tell the laity our love.

Moving of th' earth brings harms and fears,
  Men reckon what it did and meant;   10
But trepidation of the spheres,
  Though greater far, is innocent.

Dull sublunary lovers' love,
  Whose soul is sense, cannot admit
Absence, because it doth remove   15
  Those things which elemented it.

But we by a love so much refined
  That ourselves know not what it is,
Inter-assurèd of the mind,
  Care less eyes, lips, hands to miss.   20

Our two souls therefore, which are one,
  Though I must go, endure not yet
A breach, but an expansion,
  Like gold to airy thinness beat.

If they be two, they are two so   25
  As stiff twin compasses are two;
Thy soul, the fixed foot, makes no show
  To move, but doth if th' other do.

And though it in the center sit,
  Yet when the other far doth roam,   30
It leans, and hearkens after it,
  And grows erect as that comes home.

---

9 *Moving of th' earth:* earthquakes. 11 *trepidation of the spheres:* in the Ptolemaic astronomy, it was believed that the sky was formed of a series of concentric spheres which sometimes underwent vibrations. 13 *sublunary:* belonging to this world. 16 *elemented it:* made it up, comprised it. 26 *compasses:* the familiar instrument for drawing circles.

Such wilt thou be to me who must,
   Like th' other foot, obliquely run,
Thy firmness makes my circle just,   35
   And makes me end where I begun.

A Lecture Upon the Shadow

Stand still, and I will read to thee
A lecture, love, in love's philosophy.
   These three hours that we have spent
   Walking here, two shadows went
Along with us, which we ourselves produced;   5
   But, now the sun is just above our head,
   We do those shadows tread,
And to brave clearness all things are reduced.
   So whilst our infant loves did grow,
   Disguises did, and shadows, flow   10
From us and our cares, but now 'tis not so.

That love hath not attained the high'st degree,
Which is still diligent lest others see.

Except our loves at this noon stay,
We shall new shadows make the other way.   15
   As the first were made to blind
   Others, these which come behind
Will work upon ourselves, and blind our eyes.
   If our loves faint, and westwardly decline,
   To me thou falsely thine,   20
And I to thee, mine actions shall disguise.
   The morning shadows wear away,
   But these grow longer all the day;
   But oh, love's day is short, if love decay.

Love is a growing, or full constant light;   25
And his first minute, after noon, is night.

The Anniversary

All kings, and all their favorites,
   All glory of honors, beauties, wits,
The sun itself, which makes times, as they pass,
Is elder by a year, now, than it was

35 *just:* correct.

14 *Except:* unless.

When thou and I first one another saw: 5
All other things to their destruction draw,
   Only our love hath no decay;
This, no tomorrow hath, nor yesterday,
Running it never runs from us away,
But truly keeps his first, last, everlasting day.   10

   Two graves must hide thine and my corse,
    If one might, death were no divorce.
Alas, as well as other princes, we
(Who prince enough in one another be)
Must leave at last in death, these eyes, and ears,   15
Oft fed with true oaths, and with sweet salt tears;
   But souls where nothing dwells but love
(All other thoughts being inmates) then shall prove
This, or a love increaséd there above,
When bodies to their graves, souls from their graves remove.   20

   And then we shall be throughly blest,
    But we no more than all the rest;
Here upon earth, we are kings, and none but we
Can be such kings, nor of such subjects be.
Who is so safe as we? where none can do   25
Treason to us, except one of us two.
   True and false fears let us refrain,
Let us love nobly, and live, and add again
Years and years unto years, till we attain
To write threescore: this is the second of our reign.   30

Holy Sonnets

VII

At the round earth's imagined corners, blow
Your trumpets, angels, and arise, arise
From death, you numberless infinities
Of souls, and to your scattered bodies go;
All whom the flood did, and fire shall o'erthrow;   5
All whom war, dearth, age, agues, tyrannies,
Despair, law, chance, hath slain, and you whose eyes
Shall behold God, and never taste death's woe.
But let them sleep, Lord, and me mourn a space,
For, if above all these, my sins abound,   10
'Tis late to ask abundance of Thy grace,

---

11 *corse:* corpse.   18 *inmates:* temporary lodgers; *prove:* experience.   20 *remove:* move.
27 *refrain:* abstain from.

---

6 *dearth:* famine; *agues:* illnesses.

When we are there; here on this lowly ground,
Teach me how to repent; for that's as good
As if Thou hadst sealed my pardon, with Thy blood.

IX

If poisonous minerals, and if that tree
Whose fruit threw death on else immortal us,
If lecherous goats, if serpents envious
Cannot be damned, Alas! why should I be?
Why should intent or reason, born in me,   5
Make sins, else equal, in me more heinous?
And mercy being easy, and glorious
To God, in his stern wrath why threatens he?
But who am I, that dare dispute with thee,
O God? O! of thine only worthy blood,   10
And my tears, make a heavenly Lethean flood,
And drown in it my sin's black memory;
That thou remember them, some claim as debt,
I think it mercy, if thou wilt forget.

X

Death, be not proud, though some have callèd thee
Mighty and dreadful, for thou art not so;
For, those whom thou think'st thou dost overthrow,
Die not, poor Death, nor yet canst thou kill me.
From rest and sleep, which but thy pictures be,   5
Much pleasure; then from thee much more must flow;
And soonest our best men with thee do go,
Rest of their bones, and soul's delivery.
Thou art slave to Fate, Chance, kings, and desperate men,
And dost with poison, war, and sickness dwell,   10
And poppy or charms can make us sleep as well
And better than thy stroke. Why swell'st thou then?
One short sleep past, we wake eternally,
And death shall be no more. Death, thou shalt die!

XIV

Batter my heart, three personed God; for you
As yet but knock, breathe, shine, and seek to mend;
That I may rise and stand, o'erthrow me and bend

---

1 *that tree:* the Tree of Knowledge in the Book of Genesis.   2 *on else immortal us:* on us,
who would have been immortal if this had not happened.   5 *intent:* understanding.
11 *Lethean:* relating to Lethe, a river of the underworld in Greek mythology, whose
waters brought forgetfulness.

---

6 *Much pleasure,* etc.: some verb like "comes" is to be understood here.   12 *swell'st,* etc.:
why do you swell with pride?

Your force to break, blow, burn and make me new.
I, like an usurped town, to another due,   5
Labour to admit you, but Oh, to no end;
Reason, your viceroy in me, me should defend,
But is captived and proves weak or untrue.
Yet dearly I love you and would be loved fain,
But am betrothed unto your enemy: 10
Divorce me, untie or break that knot again,
Take me to you, imprison me, for I
Except you enthrall me, never shall be free,
Nor ever chaste, except you ravish me.

Robert Herrick (1591-1674)

To the Virgins to Make Much of Time

Gather ye rosebuds while ye may,
    Old Time is still a-flying;
And this same flower that smiles today,
    Tomorrow will be dying.

The glorious lamp of heaven, the sun,   5
    The higher he's a-getting,
The sooner will his race be run,
    And nearer he's to setting.

That age is best which is the first,
    When youth and blood are warmer;   10
But being spent, the worse and worst
    Times still succeed the former.

Then be not coy, but use your time,
    And while ye may, go marry;
For, having lost but once your prime,   15
    You may forever tarry.

11 *being spent:* when youth and blood are used up.

Thomas Carew (1594?-1639?)

Ask Me No More Where Jove Bestows

Ask me no more where Jove bestows,
When June is past, the fading rose;
For in your beauty's orient deep
These flowers, as in their causes, sleep.

Ask me no more whither doth stray 5
The golden atoms of the day;
For in pure love heaven did prepare
Those powders to enrich your hair.

Ask me no more whither doth haste
The nightingale when May is past; 10
For in your sweet dividing throat
She winters, and keeps warm her note.

Ask me no more where those stars light
That downwards fall in dead of night;
For in your eyes they sit, and there 15
Fixèd become as in their sphere.

Ask me no more if east or west
The phoenix builds her spicy nest;
For unto you at last she flies,
And in your fragrant bosom dies. 20

George Herbert (1593-1633)

The Collar

I struck the board, and cried, "No more;
I will abroad."
What, shall I ever sigh and pine?
My lines and life are free; free as the road,
Loose as the wind, as large as store. 5
Shall I be still in suit?
Have I no harvest but a thorn

---

3 *orient:* shining, resplendent.   4 *causes:* origins (?).   *atoms:* sunbeams.   11 *dividing:* warbling.   16 *sphere:* a reference to the belief that the stars were attached to invisible revolving "spheres" that enclosed the earth.   18 *phoenix:* a mythical bird.

---

6 *in suit:* at prayer.

To let me blood, and not restore
What I have lost with cordial fruit?
  Sure there was wine   10
 Before my sighs did dry it; there was corn
  Before my tears did drown it;
 Is the year only lost to me?
 Have I no bays to crown it,
No flowers, no garlands gay? all blasted,   15
  All wasted?
 Not so, my heart; but there is fruit,
  And thou hast hands.
 Recover all thy sigh-blown age
On double pleasures; leave thy cold dispute 20
Of what is fit and not; forsake thy cage,
  Thy rope of sands
Which petty thoughts have made, and made to thee
 Good cable, to enforce and draw,
  And be thy law,   25
While thou didst wink and wouldst not see.
  Away! take heed;
  I will abroad.
Call in thy death's-head there, tie up thy fears;
  He that forbears   30
  To suit and serve his need
  Deserves his load.
But as I raved and grew more fierce and wild
  At every word,
 Methought I heard one calling, "Child";   35
 And I replied, "My Lord."

Virtue

Sweet day, so cool, so calm, so bright,
The bridal of the earth and sky;
The dew shall weep thy fall tonight,
  For thou must die.

Sweet rose, whose hue angry and brave   5
Bids the rash gazer wipe his eye;
Thy root is ever in its grave,
  And thou must die.

---

8 *To let me blood:* to bleed me. 9 *cordial fruit:* fruit supposedly stimulating to the heart.
14 *bays:* laurels, symbols of fame. 29 *death's-head:* skull.

---

2 *bridal:* wedding.

Sweet spring, full of sweet days and roses,
A box where sweets compacted lie; 10
My music shows ye have your closes,
       And all must die.

Only a sweet and virtuous soul,
Like seasoned timber, never gives;
But though the whole world turn to coal, 15
       Then chiefly lives.

Henry Vaughan (1622-1695)

The Retreat

Happy those early days, when I
Shined in my angel-infancy!
Before I understood this place
Appointed for my second race,
Or taught my soul to fancy aught 5
But a white, celestial thought;
When yet I had not walked above
A mile or two from my first love,
And looking back at that short space,
Could see a glimpse of his bright face; 10
When on some gilded cloud or flower
My gazing soul would dwell an hour,
And in those weaker glories spy
Some shadows of eternity;
Before I taught my tongue to wound 15
My conscience with a sinful sound,
Or had the black art to dispense,
A several sin to every sense,
But felt through all this fleshly dress
Bright shoots of everlastingness. 20
   O, how I long to travel back,
And tread again that ancient track,
That I might once more reach that plain,
Where first I left my glorious train;
From whence the enlightened spirit sees 25
That shady city of palm trees.

10 *compacted:* set closely together. 11 *closes:* endings.

18 *several:* individual.

But ah! my soul with too much stay
Is drunk, and staggers in the way!
Some men a forward motion love,
But I by backward steps would move;   30
And when this dust falls to the urn,
In that state I came, return.

Andrew Marvell (1621-1678)

Bermudas

Where the remote Bermudas ride
In th' ocean's bosom unespy'd,
From a small boat that rowed along,
The list'ning winds receiv'd this song:

"What should we do but sing His praise,   5
That led us through the watery maze,
Unto an isle so long unknown,
And yet far kinder than our own?
Where He the huge sea-monsters wracks,
That lift the deep upon their backs.   10
He lands us on a grassy stage,
Safe from the storms, and prelate's rage.
He gave us this eternal spring,
Which here enamels everything,
And sends the fowls to us in care,   15
On daily visits through the air.
He hangs in shades the orange bright,
Like golden lamps in a green night,
And does in the pomegranates close
Jewels more rich than Ormus shows.   20
He makes the figs our mouths to meet,
And throws the melons at our feet.
But apples plants of such a price,
No tree could ever bear them twice.
With cedars, chosen by His hand,   25
From Lebanon, he stores the land,
And makes the hollow seas, that roar

31 *urn:* a vessel for containing the remains of the dead.

---

9 *wracks:* oppresses.   12 *prelate's rage:* Marvell's friend, John Oxenbridge, is thought to
have been driven to Bermuda by the persecutions of Archbishop Laud.   20 *Ormus:* or
Hormuz, an island and town off the south coast of Iran.   23 *apples:* pineapples.

Proclaim the ambergris on shore.
He cast (of which we rather boast)
The Gospel's pearl upon our coast   30
And in these rocks for us did frame
A temple, where to sound His name.
Oh let our voice His praise exalt,
Till it arrive at Heaven's vault,
Which thence (perhaps) rebounding, may   35
Echo beyond the Mexique Bay."

   Thus sung they, in the English boat,
An holy and a cheerful note;
And all the way, to guide their chime,
With falling oars they kept the time.   40

To His Coy Mistress

Had we but world enough, and time,
This coyness, lady, were no crime.
We would sit down, and think which way
To walk, and pass our long love's day.
Thou by the Indian Ganges' side   5
Should'st rubies find: I by the tide
Of Humber would complain. I would
Love you ten years before the Flood,
And you should, if you please, refuse
Till the conversion of the Jews.   10
My vegetable love should grow
Vaster than empires, and more slow.
An hundred years should go to praise
Thine eyes, and on thy forehead gaze:
Two hundred to adore each breast: 15
But thirty thousand to the rest;
An age at least to every part,
And the last age should show your heart.
For, lady, you deserve this state,
Nor would I love at lower rate.   20
   But at my back I always hear
Time's wingèd chariot hurrying near;
And yonder all before us lie
Deserts of vast eternity.

28 *ambergris:* a precious source of perfume originating in the intestines of whales.

---

5 *Ganges:* the sacred river of India. 7 *Humber:* a river in the north of England. 8 *the Flood:* the deluge associated with Noah.

Thy beauty shall no more be found, 25
Nor in thy marble vault shall sound
My echoing song; then worms shall try
That long preserved virginity,
And your quaint honor turn to dust,
And into ashes all my lust. 30
The grave's a fine and private place,
But none, I think, do there embrace.
   Now therefore, while the youthful hue
Sits on thy skin like morning dew,
And while thy willing soul transpires 35
At every pore with instant fires,
Now let us sport us while we may;
And now, like am'rous birds of prey,
Rather at once our time devour,
Than languish in his slow-chapped power. 40
Let us roll all our strength, and all
Our sweetness, up into one ball;
And tear our pleasures with rough strife
Thorough the iron gates of life.
Thus, though we cannot make our sun 45
Stand still, yet we will make him run.

The Mower to the Glow-worms

Ye living lamps, by whose dear light
The nightingale does sit so late,
And studying all the summer night,
Her matchless songs does meditate:

Ye country comets, that portend 5
No war nor prince's funerall,
Shining unto no higher end
Than to presage the grass's fall:

Ye glow-worms, whose officious flame
To wandering mowers shows the way, 10
That in the night have lost their aim,
And after foolish fires do stray:

Your courteous lights in vain you waste,
Since Juliana here is come,
For she my mind hath so displaced 15
That I shall never find my home.

---

27 *try*: test.   40 *slow-chapped power*: the power of his slow jaws.

Abraham Cowley (1618-1667)

Underneath This Myrtle Shade

Underneath this myrtle shade,
On flowery beds supinely laid,
With odorous oils my head o'erflowing,
And around it roses growing,
What should I do but drink away   5
The heat and troubles of the day?
In this more than kingly state
Love himself on me shall wait.
Fill to me, Love! nay, fill it up!
And mingled cast into the cup   10
Wit and mirth and noble fires,
Vigorous health and gay desires.
The wheel of life no less will stay
In a smooth than rugged way:
Since it equally doth flee,   15
Let the motion pleasant be.
Why do we precious ointments shower?—
Nobler wines why do we pour?—
Beauteous flowers why do we spread
Upon the monuments of the dead?   20
Nothing they but dust can show,
Or bones that hasten to be so.
Crown me with roses while I live,
Now your wines and ointments give:
After death I nothing crave,   25
Let me alive my pleasures have:
All are Stoics in the grave.

John Milton (1608-1674)

How Soon Hath Time

How soon hath Time the subtle thief of youth,
Stol'n on his wing my three and twentieth year!
My hasting days fly on with full career,
But my late spring no bud or blossom shew'th.
Perhaps my semblance might deceive the truth,   5
That I to manhood am arriv'd so near,

27 *Stoics:* philosophers who believed in resisting feelings, particularly pleasure and pain.

And inward ripeness doth much less appear,
That some more timely-happy spirits indu'th.
Yet be it less or more, or soon or slow,
It shall be still in strictest measure ev'n,   10
To that same lot, however mean, or high,
Toward which Time leads me, and the will of Heav'n;
All is, if I have grace to use it so,
As ever in my great task Master's eye.

On the Late Massacre in Piedmont

Avenge O Lord thy slaughter'd Saints, whose bones
Lie scatter'd on the Alpine mountains cold,
Ev'n them who kept thy truth so pure of old
When all our Fathers worship't Stocks and Stones,
Forget not: in thy book record their groans   5
Who were thy Sheep and in their ancient Fold
Slain by the bloody *Piedmontese* that roll'd
Mother with Infant down the Rocks. Their moans
The Vales redoubl'd to the Hills, and they
To Heav'n. Their martyr'd blood and ashes sow   10
O'er all th' *Italian* fields where still doth sway
The triple Tyrant: that from these may grow
A hundred-fold, who having learnt thy way
Early may fly the *Babylonian* woe.

On His Blindness

When I consider how my light is spent
Ere half my days in this dark world and wide,
And that one talent which is death to hide
Lodged with me useless, though my soul more bent
To serve therewith my Maker, and present   5
My true account, lest he returning chide,
"Doth God exact day-labor, light denied?"
I fondly ask. But Patience, to prevent
That murmur, soon replies, "God doth not need
Either man's work or his own gifts. Who best   10
Bear his mild yoke, they serve him best. His state
Is kingly: thousands at his bidding speed,
And post o'er land and ocean without rest;
They also serve who only stand and wait."

---

8 *indu'th:* clothes or invests.

"On the Late Massacre in Piedmont" was written to protest the persecution of a Protestant
sect by the Duke of Savoy in 1655.   14 *the Babylonian woe:* the Roman Catholic Church.

Jonathan Swift (1667-1744)

A Description of the Morning

Now hardly here and there an hackney-coach
Appearing, showed the ruddy morn's approach.
Now Betty from her master's bed had flown,
And softly stole to discompose her own;
The slip-shod 'prentice from his master's door   5
Had pared the dirt, and sprinkled round the floor.
Now Moll had whirled her mop with dexterous airs,
Prepared to scrub the entry and the stairs.
The youth with broomy stumps began to trace
The kennel-edge, where wheels had worn the place.   10
The small-coal man was heard with cadence deep,
Till drowned in shriller notes of chimney-sweep:
Duns at his lordship's gate began to meet;
And brickdust Moll had screamed through half the street.
The turnkey now his flock returning sees,   15
Duly let out a-nights to steal for fees:
The watchful bailiffs take their silent stands,
And schoolboys lag with satchels in their hands.

Alexander Pope (1688-1745)

from Essay on Man

EPISTLE II

Know then thyself, presume not God to scan,
The proper study of mankind is man.
Placed on this isthmus of a middle state,
A being darkly wise and rudely great:
With too much knowledge for the skeptic side,   5
With too much weakness for the stoic's pride,
He hangs between; in doubt to act, or rest;
In doubt to deem himself a god, or beast;
In doubt his mind or body to prefer;
Born but to die, and reasoning but to err;   10
Alike in ignorance, his reason such,
Whether he thinks too little, or too much:

6 *pared:* reduced or diminished.   10 *kennel:* gutter.   13 *Duns:* creditors pestering their debtors for payment.   15 *turnkey:* a prison keeper.   17 *bailiffs:* officers of the law.

Chaos of thought and passion, all confused;
Still by himself abused, or disabused;
Created half to rise, and half to fall;   15
Great lord of all things, yet a prey to all;
Sole judge of truth, in endless error hurled:
The glory, jest, and riddle of the world!
   Go, wondrous creature; mount where science guides,
Go, measure earth, weigh air, and state the tides;   20
Instruct the planets in what orbs to run,
Correct old Time, and regulate the sun;
Go, soar with Plato to th' empyreal sphere,
To the first good, first perfect, and first fair;
Or tread the mazy round his followers trod,   25
And quitting sense call imitating God;
As eastern priests in giddy circles run,
And turn their heads to imitate the sun.
Go, teach Eternal Wisdom how to rule—
Then drop into thyself, and be a fool!   30
   Superior beings, when of late they saw
A mortal man unfold all nature's law,
Admired such wisdom in an earthly shape,
And showed a Newton, as we show an ape.
   Could he, whose rules the rapid comet bind,   35
Describe or fix one movement of his mind?
Who saw its fires here rise, and there descend,
Explain his own beginning or his end?
Alas! what wonder! Man's superior part
Unchecked may rise, and climb from art to art;   40
But when his own great work is but begun,
What reason weaves, by passion is undone.
   Trace science, then, with modesty thy guide;
First strip off all her equipage of pride;
Deduct but what is vanity or dress;   45
Or learning's luxury, or idleness,
Or tricks to show the stretch of human brain,
Mere curious pleasure, or ingenious pain;
Expunge the whole, or lop th' excrescent parts
Of all our vices have created arts;   50
Then see how little the remaining sum,
Which served the past, and must the times to come!

   II. Two principles in human nature reign;
Self-love to urge, and reason to restrain;
Nor this a good, nor that a bad we call,   55
Each works its end to move or govern all:
And to their proper operation still

---

14 *Still:* always.   23 *empyreal:* in the Ptolemaic astronomy, pertaining to the outermost
sphere.   45 *Deduct:* subtract.

Ascribe all good; to their improper, ill.
　　Self-love, the spring of motion, acts the soul;
Reason's comparing balance rules the whole.　　　　　　60
Man, but for that, no action could attend,
And, but for this, were active to no end:
Fixed like a plant on his peculiar spot,
To draw nutrition, propagate, and rot;
Or, meteor-like, flame lawless thro' the void,　　　　　65
Destroying others, by himself destroyed.
　　Most strength the moving principle requires;
Active its task, it prompts, impels, inspires:
Sedate and quiet, the comparing lies,
Formed but to check, deliberate, and advise.　　　　　70
Self-love still stronger, as its objects nigh;
Reason's at distance and in prospect lie:
That sees immediate good by present sense;
Reason, the future and the consequence.
Thicker than arguments, temptations throng,　　　　　75
At best more watchful this, but that more strong.
The action of the stronger to suspend,
Reason still use, to reason still attend.
Attention, habit, and experience gains;
Each strengthens reasons, and self-love restrains.　　　80
　　Let subtle schoolmen teach these friends to fight,
More studious to divide than to unite;
And grace and virtue, sense and reason split,
With all the rash dexterity of wit.
Wits, just like fools, at war about a name,　　　　　85
Have full as oft no meaning, or the same.
Self-love and reason to one end aspire,
Pain their aversion, pleasure their desire;
But greedy that, its object would devour,
This taste the honey, and not wound the flower:　　　　90
Pleasure, or wrong or rightly understood,
Our greatest evil, or our greatest good.

Ode on Solitude

Happy the man whose wish and care
　　A few paternal acres bound,
Content to breathe his native air,
　　　　In his own ground.

Whose herds with milk, whose fields with bread,　　　5
　　Whose flocks supply him with attire,

---

59 *acts*: activates.　69 A word like "power" should be understood after *comparing*.
71 *nigh*: come near.　92 "is" should be understood before *our*.

Whose trees in summer yield him shade,
    In winter fire.

Blest, who can unconcern'dly find
    Hours, days, and years slide soft away,   10
In health of body, peace of mind,
    Quiet by day,

Sound sleep by night; study and ease,
Together mixt; sweet recreation;
And Innocence, which most does please   15
    With meditation.

Thus let me live, unseen, unknown,
    Thus unlamented let me die,
Steal from the world, and not a stone
    Tell where I lie.   20

Samuel Johnson (1709-1784)

On the Death of Dr. Robert Levet

Condemn'd to hope's delusive mine,
    As on we toil from day to day,
By sudden blasts, or slow decline,
    Our social comforts drop away.

Well tried through many a varying year,   5
    See LEVET to the grave descend;
Officious, innocent, sincere,
    Of ev'ry friendless name the friend.

Yet still he fills affection's eye,
    Obscurely wise, and coarsely kind;   10
Nor, letter'd arrogance, deny
    Thy praise to merit unrefin'd.

When fainting nature call'd for aid,
    And hov'ring death prepar'd the blow,
His vig'rous remedy display'd   15
    The power of art without the show.

In misery's darkest caverns known,
    His useful care was ever nigh,
Where hopeless anguish pour'd his groan,
    And lonely want retir'd to die.   20

1 *mine:* in antiquity, prisoners were often condemned to work in mines.

No summons mock'd by chill delay,
   No petty gain disdain'd by pride,
The modest wants of ev'ry day
   The toil of ev'ry day supplied.

His virtues walk'd their narrow round,   25
   Nor made a pause, nor left a void;
And sure th' Eternal Master found
   The single talent well employ'd.

The busy day, the peaceful night,
   Unfelt, uncounted, glided by;   30
His frame was firm, his powers were bright,
   Tho' now his eightieth year was nigh.

Then with no throbbing fiery pain,
   No cold gradations of decay,
Death broke at once the vital chain,   35
   And free'd his soul the nearest way.

William Collins (1721-1759)

Ode

Written in the beginning of the year 1746

How sleep the brave who sink to rest
By all their country's wishes blest!
When Spring, with dewy fingers cold,
Returns to deck their hallowed mold,
She there shall dress a sweeter sod   5
Than Fancy's feet have ever trod.

By fairy hands their knell is rung,
By forms unseen their dirge is sung;
There Honor comes, a pilgrim gray,
To bless the turf that wraps their clay;   10
And Freedom shall awhile repair,
To dwell a weeping hermit there!

4 *mold:* grave.

Oliver Goldsmith (1728-1774)

from *The Deserted Village*

Sweet Auburn! loveliest village of the plain;
Where health and plenty cheered the labouring swain,
Where smiling spring its earliest visit paid,
And parting summer's lingering blooms delayed:
Dear lovely bowers of innocence and ease,   5
Seats of my youth, when every sport could please,
How often have I loitered o'er thy green,
Where humble happiness endeared each scene!
How often have I paused on every charm,
The sheltered cot, the cultivated farm,   10
The never-failing brook, the busy mill,
The decent church that topped the neighbouring hill.
The hawthorn bush, with seats beneath the shade,
For talking age and whispering lovers made!
How often have I blest the coming day,   15
When toil remitting lent its turn to play,
And all the village train, from labour free,
Led up their sports beneath the spreading tree,
While many a pastime circled in the shade,
The young contending as the old surveyed;   20
And many a gambol frolicked o'er the ground,
And sleights of art and feats of strength went round.
And still, as each repeated pleasure tired,
Succeeding sports the mirthful band inspired;
The dancing pair that simply sought renown,   25
By holding out to tire each other down;
The swain mistrustless of his smutted face,
While secret laughter tittered round the place;
The bashful virgin's side-long looks of love,
The matron's glance that would those looks reprove: 30
These were thy charms, sweet village! sports like these,
With sweet succession, taught even toil to please:
These round thy bowers their cheerful influence shed;
These were thy charms—but all these charms are fled.

2 *swain:* peasant. 4 *delayed:* lingered. 6 *Seats:* abodes. 10 *cot:* cottage. 12 *decent:*
well-formed, attractive. 27 *mistrustless:* unsuspecting.

William Cowper (1731-1800)

The Poplar Field

The poplars are felled; farewell to the shade
And the whispering sound of the cool colonnade;
The winds play no longer and sing in the leaves,
Nor Ouse on his bosom their image receives.

Twelve years have elapsed since I first took a view   5
Of my favourite field, and the bank where they grew;
And now in the grass behold they are laid,
And the tree is my seat that once lent me a shade.

The blackbird has fled to another retreat
Where the hazels afford him a screen from the heat,   10
And the scene where his melody charmed me before
Resounds with his sweet-flowing ditty no more.

My fugitive years are all hasting away,
And I must ere long lie as lowly as they
With a turf on my breast, and a stone at my head,   15
Ere another such grove shall arise in its stead.

'Tis a sight to engage me, if anything can,
To muse on the perishing pleasures of man;
Though his life be a dream, his enjoyments, I see,
Have a being less durable even than he.

Robert Burns (1759-1796)

To a Mouse

On turning up her nest with the plow, November, 1785

Wee, sleekit, cowrin, tim'rous beastie,
O, what a panic's in thy breastie!
Thou need na start awa sae hasty
    Wi' bickering brattle!
I wad be laith to rin an' chase thee,   5
    Wi' murdering pattle!

I'm truly sorry man's dominion
Has broken Nature's social union,

---

1 *sleekit:* sleek; *cowrin:* cowering.   4 *bickering brattle:* rushing noise.   5 *wad be laith:* would be unwilling.   6 *pattle:* a small, long-handled shovel.

An' justifies that ill opinion
  Which makes thee startle   10
At me, thy poor, earth-born companion
  An' fellow-mortal!

I doubt na, whyles, but thou may thieve;
What then? poor beastie, thou maun live:
A daimen icker in a thrave   15
  'S a sma' request;
I'll get a blessin wi' the lave,
  An' never miss 't!

Thy wee-bit housie, too, in ruin!
Its silly wa's the win's are strewin!   20
An' naething, now, to big a new ane,
  O' foggage green!
An' bleak December's win's ensuin,
  Baith snell an' keen!

Thou saw the fields laid bare an' waste, 25
An' weary winter comin' fast,
An' cozie here, beneath the blast,
  Thou thought to dwell,
Till, crash! the cruel coulter passed
  Out through thy cell.   30

That wee bit heap o' leaves an' stibble,
Has cost thee monie a weary nibble!
Now thou's turned out, for a' thy trouble,
  But house or hald,
To thole the winter's sleety dribble,   35
  An' cranreuch cauld!

But Mousie, thou art no thy lane,
In proving foresight may be vain:
The best-laid schemes o' mice an' men
  Gang aft agley,   40
An' lea'e us naught but grief an' pain,
  For promised joy!

Still thou art blest, compared wi' me!
The present only toucheth thee:
But och! I backward cast my e'e,   45
  On prospects drear!
An' forward, though I canna see,
  I guess an' fear!

---

10 *startle:* run aimlessly about. 13 *whyles:* sometimes. 14 *maun:* must. 15 *A daimen icker in a thrave:* an occasional ear of grain out of twenty-four sheaves. 17 *lave:* remainder. 20 *silly wa's:* pitiful walls. 21 *big:* build. 22 *foggage:* grass. 24 *Baith:* both; *snell:* sharp. 29 *coulter:* the blade of a plow. 31 *stibble:* stubble. 34 *hald:* dwelling-place. 35 *thole:* endure. 36 *cranreuch:* hoar-frost. 37 *no thy lane:* not alone. 40 *Gang aft agley:* go often awry.

William Blake (1757-1827)

The Tiger

Tiger! Tiger! burning bright
In the forests of the night,
What immortal hand or eye
Could frame thy fearful symmetry?

In what distant deeps or skies   5
Burnt the fire of thine eyes?
On what wings dare he aspire?
What the hand dare seize the fire?

And what shoulder, and what art,
Could twist the sinews of thy heart?   10
And when thy heart began to beat,
What dread hand? and what dread feet?

What the hammer? what the chain?
In what furnace was thy brain?
What the anvil? what dread grasp   15
Dare its deadly terrors clasp?

When the stars threw down their spears,
And watered heaven with their tears,
Did he smile his work to see?
Did he who made the Lamb make thee?   20

Tiger! Tiger! burning bright
In the forests of the night,
What immortal hand or eye
Dare frame thy fearful symmetry?

The Clod and the Pebble

"Love seeketh not itself to please,
Nor for itself hath any care,
But for another gives its ease,
And builds a Heaven in Hell's despair."

So sung a little Clod of Clay,   5
Trodden with the cattle's feet,
But a Pebble of the brook
Warbled out these meters meet:

"Love seeketh only Self to please,
To bind another to its delight,   10
Joys in another's loss of ease,
And builds a Hell in Heaven's despite."

Ah! Sun-flower

Ah, Sun-flower! weary of time,
Who countest the steps of the Sun,
Seeking after that sweet golden clime
Where the traveller's journey is done:

Where the Youth pined away with desire   5
And the pale Virgin shrouded in snow
Arise from their graves and aspire
Where my Sun-flower wishes to go.

A Poison Tree

I was angry with my friend:
I told my wrath, my wrath did end.
I was angry with my foe:
I told it not, my wrath did grow.

And I watered it in fears   5
Night and morning with my tears,
And I sunnéd it with smiles
And with soft deceitful wiles.

And it grew both day and night,
Till it bore an apple bright,   10
And my foe beheld it shine,
And he knew that it was mine—

And into my garden stole
When the night had veiled the pole;
In the morning, glad, I see   15
My foe outstretched beneath the tree.

London

I wander through each chartered street,
Near where the chartered Thames does flow,
And mark in every face I meet
Marks of weakness, marks of woe.

In every cry of every man,   5
In every infant's cry of fear,
In every voice, in every ban,
The mind-forged manacles I hear:

1 *chartered:* sold into private ownership.

How the chimney-sweeper's cry
Every blackening church appalls,   10
And the hapless soldier's sigh
Runs in blood down palace walls.

But most, through midnight streets I hear
How the youthful harlot's curse
Blasts the new-born infant's tear,   15
And blights with plagues the marriage hearse.

Stanzas from Milton

And did those feet in ancient time
    Walk upon England's mountain green?
And was the holy Lamb of God
    On England's pleasant pastures seen?

And did the Countenance Divine   5
    Shine forth upon our clouded hills?
And was Jerusalem builded here
    Among these dark Satanic mills?

Bring me my bow of burning gold!
    Bring me my arrows of desire!
Bring me my spear! O clouds, unfold!   10
    Bring me my chariot of fire!

I will not cease from mental fight,
    Nor shall my sword sleep in my hand,
Till we have built Jerusalem   15
    In England's green and pleasant land.

William Wordsworth (1770-1850)

Lines Written in Early Spring

I heard a thousand blended notes,
While in a grove I sate reclined,
In that sweet mood when pleasant thoughts
Bring sad thoughts to the mind.

To her fair works did Nature link   5
The human soul that through me ran;
And much it grieved my heart to think
What man has made of man.

Through primrose tufts, in that green bower,
The periwinkle trailed its wreaths;   10
And 'tis my faith that every flower
Enjoys the air it breathes.

The birds around me hopped and played,
Their thoughts I cannot measure—
But the least motion which they made,   15
It seemed a thrill of pleasure.

The budding twigs spread out their fan,
To catch the breezy air;
And I must think, do all I can,
That there was pleasure there.   20

If this belief from heaven be sent,
If such be Nature's holy plan,
Have I not reason to lament
What man has made of man?

A Slumber Did My Spirit Seal

A slumber did my spirit seal;
    I had no human fears:
She seemed a thing that could not feel
    The touch of earthly years.

No motion has she now, no force;   5
    She neither hears nor sees;
Rolled round in earth's diurnal course,
    With rocks, and stones, and trees.

My Heart Leaps Up When I Behold

My heart leaps up when I behold
    A rainbow in the sky:
So was it when my life began;
So is it now I am a man:
So be it when I shall grow old,   5
    Or let me die!
The Child is father of the Man;
And I could wish my days to be
Bound each to each by natural piety.

7 *diurnal:* daily.

Composed Upon Westminster Bridge

Earth has not anything to show more fair:
Dull would he be of soul who could pass by
A sight so touching in its majesty:
This City now doth like a garment wear
The beauty of the morning; silent, bare,   5
Ships, towers, domes, theaters, and temples lie
Open unto the fields, and to the sky;
All bright and glittering in the smokeless air.
Never did sun more beautifully steep
In his first splendor valley, rock, or hill;   10
Ne'er saw I, never felt, a calm so deep!
The river glideth at his own sweet will:
Dear God! the very houses seem asleep;
And all that mighty heart is lying still!

The Solitary Reaper

Behold her, single in the field,
Yon solitary Highland lass!
Reaping and singing by herself;
Stop here, or gently pass!
Alone she cuts and binds the grain,   5
And sings a melancholy strain;
O listen! for the vale profound
Is overflowing with the sound.

No nightingale did ever chaunt
More welcome notes to weary bands   10
Of travelers in some shady haunt,
Among Arabian sands:
A voice so thrilling ne'er was heard
In springtime from the cuckoo-bird,
Breaking the silence of the seas   15
Among the farthest Hebrides.

Will no one tell me what she sings?—
Perhaps the plaintive numbers flow
For old, unhappy, far-off things,
And battles long ago: 20
Or is it some more humble lay,
Familiar matter of today?

9 *steep:* bathe or soak.

---

16 *Hebrides:* isolated islands off the northwest coast of Scotland.   18 *numbers:* metrical verses.

Some natural sorrow, loss, or pain,
That has been, and may be again?

Whate'er the theme, the maiden sang   25
As if her song could have no ending;
I saw her singing at her work,
And o'er the sickle bending;—
I listened, motionless and still;
And, as I mounted up the hill,   30
The music in my heart I bore,
Long after it was heard no more.

She Was a Phantom of Delight

She was a phantom of delight
When first she gleamed upon my sight;
A lovely apparition, sent
To be a moment's ornament;
Her eyes as stars of twilight fair;   5
Like twilight's too, her dusky hair;
But all things else about her drawn
From May-time and the cheerful dawn;
A dancing shape, an Image gay,
To haunt, to startle, and waylay.   10

I saw her upon nearer view,
A spirit, yet a woman too!
Her household motions light and free,
And steps of virgin liberty;
A countenance in which did meet   15
Sweet records, promises as sweet;
A creature not too bright or good
For human nature's daily food:
For transient sorrows, simple wiles,
Praise, blame, love, kisses, tears, and smiles.   20

And now I see with eye serene
The very pulse of the machine;
A being breathing thoughtful breath,
A Traveler between life and death;
The reason firm, the temperate will,   25
Endurance, foresight, strength, and skill,
A perfect woman, nobly planned,
To warn, to comfort, and command;
And yet a spirit still, and bright
With something of angelic light.   30

The World Is Too Much with Us

The world is too much with us; late and soon,
Getting and spending, we lay waste our powers:
Little we see in Nature that is ours;
We have given our hearts away, a sordid boon!
The sea that bares her bosom to the moon;   5
The winds that will be howling at all hours,
And are up-gathered now like sleeping flowers;
For this, for everything, we are out of tune;
It moves us not.—Great God! I'd rather be
A Pagan suckled in a creed outworn;   10
So might I, standing on this pleasant lea,
Have glimpses that would make me less forlorn;
Have sight of Proteus rising from the sea;
Or hear old Triton blow his wreathéd horn.

Samuel Taylor Coleridge (1772-1834)

Kubla Khan; or, A Vision in a Dream

In Xanadu did Kubla Khan
A stately pleasure-dome decree:
Where Alph, the sacred river, ran
Through caverns measureless to man
　　Down to a sunless sea.   5
So twice five miles of fertile ground
With walls and towers were girdled round:
And here were gardens bright with sinuous rills,
Where blossomed many an incense-bearing tree;
And here were forests ancient as the hills,   10
Enfolding sunny spots of greenery.

But oh! that deep romantic chasm which slanted
Down the green hill athwart a cedarn cover!
A savage place! as holy and enchanted
As e'er beneath a waning moon was haunted   15
By woman wailing for her demon-lover!

2 *Getting:* acquiring. 11 *lea:* meadow. 13, 14 *Proteus, Triton:* sea-gods of Greek mythology.

1 *Xanadu:* a name drawn by Coleridge from a book of travels; *Kubla Khan:* a Chinese emperor of the thirteenth century. 3 *Alph:* a name invented by Coleridge. 8 *sinuous:* winding.

And from this chasm, with ceaseless turmoil seething,
As if this earth in fast thick pants were breathing
A mighty fountain momently was forced;
Amid whose swift half-intermitted burst   20
Huge fragments vaulted like rebounding hail,
Or chaffy grain beneath the thresher's flail:
And 'mid these dancing rocks at once and ever
It flung up momently the sacred river.
Five miles meandering with a mazy motion   25
Through wood and dale the sacred river ran,
Then reached the caverns measureless to man,
And sank in tumult to a lifeless ocean:
And 'mid this tumult Kubla heard from far
Ancestral voices prophesying war!   30

    The shadow of the dome of pleasure
    Floated midway on the waves;
    Where was heard the mingled measure
    From the fountain and the caves.
It was a miracle of rare device,   35
A sunny pleasure-dome with caves of ice!
    A damsel with a dulcimer
    In a vision once I saw:
    It was an Abyssinian maid,
    And on her dulcimer she played,   40
    Singing of Mount Abora.
    Could I revive within me,
    Her symphony and song,
    To such a deep delight 'twould win me,
That with music loud and long,   45
I would build that dome in air,
That sunny dome! those caves of ice!
And all who heard should see them there,
And all should cry, Beware! Beware!
His flashing eyes, his floating hair!   50
Weave a circle round him thrice,
And close your eyes with holy dread,
For he on honey-dew hath fed,
And drunk the milk of Paradise.

---

19 *momently*: at every moment.   20 *half-intermitted*: half-interrupted.   37 *dulcimer*: a musical instrument with strings struck by hammers.   41 *Mount Abora*: a name invented by Coleridge.   53 *honey-dew*: a sweet substance.

Percy Bysshe Shelley (1792-1822)

Ode to the West Wind

I

O wild West Wind, thou breath of Autumn's being,
Thou, from whose unseen presence the leaves dead
Are driven, like ghosts from an enchanter fleeing,

Yellow, and black, and pale, and hectic red,
Pestilence-stricken multitudes: O thou,   5
Who chariotest to their dark wintry bed

The wingèd seeds, where they lie cold and low,
Each like a corpse within its grave, until
Thine azure sister of the Spring shall blow

Her clarion o'er the dreaming earth, and fill   10
(Driving sweet buds like flocks to feed in air)
With living hues and odors plain and hill:

Wild Spirit, which art moving everywhere;
Destroyer and preserver; hear! oh, hear!

II

Thou on whose stream, mid the steep sky's commotion,   15
Loose clouds like earth's decaying leaves are shed,
Shook from the tangled boughs of Heaven and Ocean,

Angels of rain and lightning: there are spread
On the blue surface of thine airy surge,
Like the bright hair uplifted from the head   20

Of some fierce Mænad, even from the dim verge
Of the horizon to the zenith's height,
The locks of the approaching storm. Thou dirge

Of the dying year, to which this closing night
Will be the dome of a vast sepulcher,   25
Vaulted with all thy congregated might

Of vapors, from whose solid atmosphere
Black rain, and fire, and hail will burst: oh, hear!

III

Thou who didst waken from his summer dreams
The blue Mediterranean, where he lay,   30
Lulled by the coil of his crystàlline streams,

21 *Mænad*: in Greek and Roman religion, a woman who took part in the frenzied worship of the god of wine.

Beside a pumice isle in Baiæ's bay,
And saw in sleep old palaces and towers
Quivering within the wave's intenser day,

All overgrown with azure moss and flowers   35
So sweet, the sense faints picturing them! thou
For whose path the Atlantic's level powers

Cleave themselves into chasms, while far below
The sea-blooms and the oozy woods which wear
The sapless foliage of the ocean, know   40

Thy voice, and suddenly grow gray with fear,
And tremble and despoil themselves: oh, hear!

IV

If I were a dead leaf thou mightest bear;
If I were a swift cloud to fly with thee;
A wave to pant beneath thy power, and share   45

The impulse of thy strength, only less free
Than thou, O uncontrollable! If even
I were as in my boyhood, and could be

The comrade of thy wanderings over heaven,
As then, when to outstrip thy skiey speed   50
Scarce seemed a vision; I would ne'er have striven

As thus with thee in prayer in my sore need.
Oh lift me as a wave, a leaf, a cloud!
I fall upon the thorns of life! I bleed!

A heavy weight of hours has chained and bowed   55
One too like thee: tameless, and swift, and proud.

V

Make me thy lyre, even as the forest is:
What if my leaves are falling like its own!
The tumult of thy mighty harmonies

Will take from both a deep, autumnal tone,   60
Sweet though in sadness. Be thou, spirit fierce,
My spirit! Be thou me, impetuous one!

Drive my dead thoughts over the universe
Like withered leaves to quicken a new birth!
And, by the incantation of this verse,   65

---

32 *Baiæ's bay:* the bay of Naples.   42 *despoil themselves:* drop parts of their foliage.

Scatter, as from an unextinguished hearth
Ashes and sparks, my words among mankind!
Be through my lips to unawakened earth

The trumpet of a prophecy! Oh, wind,
If Winter comes, can Spring be far behind?   70

Mutability

We are as clouds that veil the midnight moon;
   How restlessly they speed, and gleam, and quiver,
Streaking the darkness radiantly!—yet soon
   Night closes round, and they are lost for ever:

Or like forgotten lyres, whose dissonant strings   5
   Give various response to each varying blast,
To whose frail frame no second motion brings
   One mood or modulation like the last.

We rest.—A dream has power to poison sleep;
   We rise.—One wandering thought pollutes the day;   10
We feel, conceive or reason, laugh or weep;
   Embrace fond woe, or cast our cares away:

It is the same!—For, be it joy or sorrow,
   The path of its departure still is free:
Man's yesterday may ne'er be like his morrow;   15
Naught may endure but Mutability.

John Keats (1795-1821)

On First Looking Into Chapman's Homer

Much have I traveled in the realms of gold,
And many goodly states and kingdoms seen;
Round many western islands have I been
Which bards in fealty to Apollo hold.
Oft of one wide expanse had I been told   5
That deep-browed Homer ruled as his demesne;
Yet did I never breathe its pure serene
Till I heard Chapman speak out loud and bold:
Then felt I like some watcher of the skies

1 *the realms of gold:* classical literature.   4 *in fealty to:* under the authority of; *Apollo:* the god of song.   6 *demesne:* domain.   8 *Chapman:* the author of a translation of Homer which Keats had just read.

When a new planet swims into his ken;   10
  Or like stout Cortez when with eagle eyes
He stared at the Pacific—and all his men
  Looked at each other with a wild surmise—
Silent, upon a peak in Darien.

La Belle Dame Sans Merci

O what can ail thee, Knight at arms,
  Alone and palely loitering?
The sedge has withered from the Lake
  And no birds sing!

O what can ail thee, Knight at arms,   5
  So haggard, and so woe begone?
The Squirrel's granary is full
  And the harvest's done.

I see a lily on thy brow
  With anguish moist and fever dew,   10
And on thy cheeks a fading rose
  Fast withereth too—

I met a Lady in the Meads,
  Full beautiful, a faery's child
Her hair was long, her foot was light   15
  And her eyes were wild—

I made a Garland for her head,
  And bracelets too, and fragrant Zone
She look'd at me as she did love
  And made sweet moan—   20

I set her on my pacing steed
  And nothing else saw all day long
For sidelong would she bend and sing
  A faery's song—

She found me roots of relish sweet   25
  And honey wild and manna dew
And sure in language strange she said
  I love thee true—

She took me to her elfin grot
  And there she wept and sigh'd full sore,   30

---

11 *Cortez:* Keats' error; the Pacific was discovered by Balboa.

Title: "The beautiful lady without pity."   3 *sedge:* grassy plants characteristic of marshes.
13 *Meads:* meadows.

And there I shut her wild wild eyes
   With kisses four.

And there she lulled me asleep
   And there I dream'd, Ah Woe betide!
The latest dream I ever dreamt   35
   On the cold hill side.

I saw pale Kings, and Princes too
   Pale warriors, death pale were they all;
They cried, La belle dame sans merci
   Thee hath in thrall.   40

I saw their starv'd lips in the gloam
   With horrid warning gaped wide,
And I awoke, and found me here
   On the cold hill's side.

And this is why I sojourn here   45
   Alone and palely loitering;
Though the sedge is withered from the Lake
   And no birds sing—

Ode to a Nightingale

My heart aches, and a drowsy numbness pains
   My sense, as though of hemlock I had drunk,
Or emptied some dull opiate to the drains
   One minute past, and Lethe-wards had sunk:
'Tis not through envy of thy happy lot,   5
   But being too happy in thine happiness—
     That thou, light-wingèd Dryad of the trees,
      In some melodious plot
   Of beechen green, and shadows numberless,
     Singest of summer in full-throated ease.   10

O, for a draught of vintage! that hath been
   Cooled a long age in the deep-delvèd earth,
Tasting of Flora and the country green,
   Dance, and Provençal song, and sunburnt mirth!
O for a beaker full of the warm South,   15
   Full of the true, the blushful Hippocrene,

---

4 *Lethe:* the river of forgetfulness in Greek mythology. 7 *Dryad:* a wood-nymph. 9
beechen: formed of beech trees. 11 *vintage:* wine. 12 *deep-delvèd:* deeply dug. 13
Flora: Roman goddess of flowers. 14 *Provençal:* characteristic of Provence, in southern
France. 16 *Hippocrene:* a fountain supposed to give poetic inspiration.

With beaded bubbles winking at the brim,
  And purple-stainèd mouth;
That I might drink, and leave the world unseen,
  And with thee fade away into the forest dim: 20

Fade far away, dissolve, and quite forget
  What thou among the leaves hast never known,
The weariness, the fever, and the fret
  Here, where men sit and hear each other groan;
Where palsy shakes a few, sad, last gray hairs,   25
  Where youth grows pale, and specter-thin, and dies;
    Where but to think is to be full of sorrow
      And leaden-eyed despairs,
  Where Beauty cannot keep her lustrous eyes,
    Or new Love pine at them beyond tomorrow.   30

Away! away! for I will fly to thee,
  Not charioted by Bacchus and his pards,
But on the viewless wings of Poesy,
  Though the dull brain perplexes and retards:
Already with thee! tender is the night,   35
  And haply the Queen-Moon is on her throne,
    Clustered around by all her starry Fays;
      But here there is no light,
  Save what from heaven is with the breezes blown
    Through verdurous glooms and winding mossy ways.   40

I cannot see what flowers are at my feet,
  Nor what soft incense hangs upon the boughs,
But, in embalmèd darkness, guess each sweet
  Wherewith the seasonable month endows
The grass, the thicket, and the fruit-tree wild;   45
  White hawthorn, and the pastoral eglantine;
    Fast fading violets covered up in leaves;
      And mid-May's eldest child.
  The coming musk-rose, full of dewy wine,
    The murmurous haunt of flies on summer eves.   50

Darkling I listen: and, for many a time,
  I have been half in love with easeful Death,
Called him soft names in many a musèd rime,
  To take into the air my quiet breath;
Now more than ever seems it rich to die,   55
  To cease upon the midnight with no pain,
    While thou art pouring forth thy soul abroad
      In such an ecstasy!

32 *Bacchus and his pards:* the Roman god of wine is sometimes portrayed in a cart drawn by leopards.   33 *viewless:* invisible.   37 *Fays:* fairies.   40 *verdurous:* leafy.   51 *Darkling:* in the dark.

Still wouldst thou sing, and I have ears in vain—
  To thy high requiem become a sod. 60

Thou wast not born for death, immortal Bird!
  No hungry generations tread thee down;
The voice I hear this passing night was heard
  In ancient days by emperor and clown:
Perhaps the self-same song that found a path 65
    Through the sad heart of Ruth, when, sick for home,
    She stood in tears amid the alien corn;
        The same that oft-times hath
    Charmed magic casements, opening on the foam
      Of perilous seas, in faery lands forlorn. 70

Forlorn! the very word is like a bell
  To toll me back from thee to my sole self,
Adieu! the fancy cannot cheat so well
  As she is famed to do, deceiving elf.
Adieu! adieu! thy plaintive anthem fades 75
    Past the near meadows, over the still stream,
      Up the hillside; and now 'tis buried deep
        In the next valley glades:
    Was it a vision, or a waking dream?
      Fled is that music—Do I wake or sleep? 80

Ode on a Grecian Urn

I

Thou still unravish'd bride of quietness,
  Thou foster-child of silence and slow time,
Sylvan historian, who canst thus express
  A flowery tale more sweetly than our rhyme:
What leaf-fring'd legend haunts about thy shape 5
    Of deities or mortals, or of both,
      In Tempe or the dales of Arcady?
    What men or gods are these? What maidens loth?
What mad pursuit? What struggle to escape?
      What pipes and timbrels? What wild esctasy? 10

---

66 *Ruth:* the young widow of the Bible who accompanied her mother-in-law to a foreign land.   69 *casements:* windows that open on hinges.

---

3 *Sylvan:* pertaining to forests.   7 *Tempe:* a valley in Greece sacred to Apollo, the god of song; *Arcady:* a secluded area of ancient Greece.   10 *timbrels:* tambourines.

II

Heard melodies are sweet, but those unheard
   Are sweeter; therefore, ye soft pipes, play on;
Not to the sensual ear, but, more endear'd,
   Pipe to the spirit ditties of no tone:
Fair youth, beneath the trees, thou canst not leave   15
   Thy song, nor ever can those trees be bare;
      Bold Lover, never, never canst thou kiss,
Though winning near the goal—yet, do not grieve;
   She cannot fade, though thou hast not thy bliss,
      For ever wilt thou love, and she be fair!   20

III

Ah, happy, happy boughs! that cannot shed
   Your leaves, nor ever bid the Spring adieu;
And, happy melodist, unwearièd,
   For ever piping songs for ever new;
More happy love! more happy, happy love!   25
   For ever warm and still to be enjoy'd,
      For ever panting, and for ever young;
All breathing human passion far above,
   That leaves a heart high-sorrowful and cloy'd,
      A burning forehead, and a parching tongue.   30

IV

Who are these coming to the sacrifice?
   To what green altar, O mysterious priest,
Lead'st thou that heifer lowing at the skies,
   And all her silken flanks with garlands drest?
What little town by river or sea shore,   35
   Or mountain-built with peaceful citadel,
      Is emptied of this folk, this pious morn?
And, little town, thy streets for evermore
   Will silent be; and not a soul to tell
      Why thou art desolate, can e'er return.   40

V

O Attic shape! Fair attitude! with brede
   Of marble men and maidens overwrought,
With forest branches and the trodden weed;
   Thou, silent form, dost tease us out of thought
As doth eternity: Cold Pastoral!   45
   When old age shall this generation waste,

---

29 *cloy'd*: disgusted through over-indulgence.   41 *Attic*: characteristic of Attica, the region of Athens; *brede*: braided pattern.

Thou shalt remain, in midst of other woe
Than ours, a friend to man, to whom thou say'st,
"Beauty is truth, truth beauty,"—that is all
Ye know on earth, and all ye need to know.   50

Edgar Allan Poe (1809-1849)

To Helen

Helen, thy beauty is to me
    Like those Nicèan barks of yore,
That gently, o'er a perfumed sea,
    The weary, way-worn wanderer bore
To his own native shore.   5

On desperate seas long wont to roam,
    Thy hyacinth hair, thy classic face,
Thy Naiad airs have brought me home
    To the glory that was Greece,
And the grandeur that was Rome.   10

Lo! in yon brilliant window-niche
    How statue-like I see thee stand,
The agate lamp within thy hand!
Ah! Psyche, from the regions which
    Are Holy-Land!   15

Alfred, Lord Tennyson (1809-1892)

The Splendor Falls on Castle Walls

The splendor falls on castle walls
    And snowy summits old in story;
The long light shakes across the lakes,
    And the wild cataract leaps in glory.
Blow, bugle, blow, set the wild echoes flying,   5
Blow, bugle; answer, echoes, dying, dying, dying.

2 *Nicèan:* pertaining to the ancient city of Nicaea, located in what is now northwestern
Turkey. 8 *Naiad:* a goddess of lakes and streams. 14 *Psyche:* in Greek mythology, a
maiden loved by Eros, the god of love.

Oh hark, O hear! how thin and clear,
   And thinner, clearer, farther going!
O sweet and far from cliff and scar
   The horns of Elfland faintly blowing!   10
Blow, let us hear the purple glens replying,
Blow, bugle; answer, echoes, dying, dying, dying.

O love, they die in yon rich sky,
   They faint on hill or field or river;
Our echoes roll from soul to soul,   15
   And grow forever and forever.
Blow, bugle, blow, set the wild echoes flying.
And answer, echoes, answer, dying, dying, dying.

Now Sleeps the Crimson Petal

Now sleeps the crimson petal, now the white;
Nor waves the cypress in the palace walk;
Nor winks the gold fin in the porphyry font.
The firefly wakens; waken thou with me.

Now droops the milk-white peacock like a ghost,   5
And like a ghost she glimmers on to me.

Now lies the Earth all Danaë to the stars,
And all thy heart lies open unto me.

Now slides the silent meteor on, and leaves
A shining furrow, as thy thoughts in me.   10

Now folds the lily all her sweetness up,
And slips into the bosom of the lake.
So fold thyself, my dearest, thou, and slip
Into my bosom and be lost in me.

Ulysses

It little profits that an idle king,
By this still hearth, among these barren crags,
Matched with an aged wife, I mete and dole
Unequal laws unto a savage race,

---

3 *porphyry font:* a fountain made of a valuable purple stone.   7 *Danaë:* a maiden in
Greek mythology who bore a son to the god Zeus.

Ulysses: the hero of Homer's epic is speaking as an old man, long after he has returned
to his home island of Ithaca.

That hoard, and sleep, and feed, and know not me.   5
I cannot rest from travel; I will drink
Life to the lees. All times I have enjoyed
Greatly, have suffered greatly, both with those
That loved me, and alone; on shore, and when
Through scudding drifts the rainy Hyades   10
Vexed the dim sea. I am become a name;
For always roaming with a hungry heart
Much have I seen and known—cities of men
And manners, climates, councils, governments,
Myself not least, but honored of them all—   15
And drunk delight of battle with my peers,
Far on the ringing plain of windy Troy.
I am a part of all that I have met;
Yet all experience is an arch wherethrough
Gleams that untraveled world whose margin fades   20
Forever and forever when I move.
How dull it is to pause, to make an end,
To rust unburnished, not to shine in use!
As though to breathe were life! Life piled on life
Were all too little, and of one to me   25
Little remains; but every hour is saved
From that eternal silence, something more,
A bringer of new things; and vile it were
For some three suns to store and hoard myself,
And this gray spirit yearning in desire   30
To follow knowledge like a sinking star,
Beyond the utmost bound of human thought.
    This is my son, mine own Telemachus,
To whom I leave the scepter and the isle—
Well-loved of me, discerning to fulfill   35
This labor, by slow prudence to make mild
A rugged people, and through soft degrees
Subdue them to the useful and the good.
Most blameless is he, centered in the sphere
Of common duties, decent not to fail   40
In offices of tenderness, and pay
Meet adoration to my household gods,
When I am gone. He works his work, I mine.
    There lies the port; the vessel puffs her sail;
There gloom the dark, broad seas. My mariners,   45
Souls that have toiled, and wrought, and thought with me—
That ever with a frolic welcome took
The thunder and the sunshine, and opposed
Free hearts, free foreheads—you and I are old;
Old age hath yet his honor and his toil.   50

10 *Hyades*: a group of stars that were said to foretell rain. 40 *decent*: well-behaved.
42 *Meet*: appropriate.

Death closes all; but something ere the end,
Some work of noble note, may yet be done,
Not unbecoming men that strove with gods.
The lights begin to twinkle from the rocks;
The long day wanes; the slow moon climbs; the deep 55
Moans round with many voices. Come, my friends.
'Tis not too late to seek a newer world.
Push off, and sitting well in order smite
The sounding furrows; for my purpose holds
To sail beyond the sunset, and the baths 60
Of all the western stars, until I die.
It may be that the gulfs will wash us down;
It may be we shall touch the Happy Isles,
And see the great Achilles, whom we knew.
Though much is taken, much abides; and though 65
We are not now that strength which in old days
Moved earth and heaven; that which we are, we are—
One equal temper of heroic hearts,
Made weak by time and fate, but strong in will
To strive, to seek, to find, and not to yield. 70

Robert Browning (1812-1889)

My Last Duchess

Ferrara

That's my last Duchess painted on the wall,
Looking as if she were alive. I call
That piece a wonder, now: Frà Pandolf's hands
Worked busily a day, and there she stands.
Will't please you sit and look at her? I said 5
"Frà Pandolf" by design, for never read
Strangers like you that pictured countenance,
The depth and passion of its earnest glance
But to myself they turned (since none puts by
The curtain I have drawn for you, but I) 10
And seemed as they would ask me, if they durst,
How such a glance came there; so, not the first
Are you to turn and ask thus. Sir, 'twas not
Her husband's presence only, called that spot
Of joy into the Duchess' cheek: perhaps 15
Frà Pandolf chanced to say, "Her mantle laps

---

63 *Happy Isles:* the Greek Paradise. 64 *Achilles:* a greek hero of the Trojan war.

Over my lady's wrist too much," or "Paint
Must never hope to reproduce the faint
Half-flush that dies along her throat": such stuff
Was courtesy, she thought, and cause enough   20
For calling up that spot of joy. She had
A heart—how shall I say?—too soon made glad,
Too easily impressed: she liked whate'er
She looked on, and her looks went everywhere.
Sir, 'twas all one! My favor at her breast,   25
The dropping of the daylight in the West,
The bough of cherries some officious fool
Broke in the orchard for her, the white mule
She rode with round the terrace—all and each
Would draw from her alike the approving speech,   30
Or blush, at least. She thanked men—good! but thanked
Somehow—I know not how—as if she ranked
My gift of a nine-hundred-years-old name
With anybody's gift. Who'd stoop to blame
This sort of trifling? Even had you skill   35
In speech—which I have not—to make your will
Quite clear to such an one, and say, "Just this
Or that in you disgusts me; here you miss,
Or there exceed the mark"—and if she let
Herself be lessoned so, nor plainly set   40
Her wits to yours, forsooth, and made excuse—
E'en then would be some stooping; and I choose
Never to stoop. Oh, sir, she smiled, no doubt,
Whene'er I passed her; but who passed without
Much the same smile? This grew; I gave commands;   45
Then all smiles stopped together. There she stands
As if alive. Will 't please you rise? We'll meet
The company below, then. I repeat,
The Count your master's known munificence
Is ample warrant that no just pretense   50
Of mine for dowry will be disallowed;
Though his fair daughter's self, as I avowed
At starting, is my object. Nay, we'll go
Together down, sir. Notice Neptune, though,
Taming a sea-horse, thought a rarity,   55
Which Claus of Innsbruck cast in bronze for me!

54 *Neptune:* god of the sea.   56 *Claus of Innsbruck:* a sculptor invented by Browning.

Soliloquy of the Spanish Cloister

Gr-r-r—there go, my heart's abhorrence!
   Water your damned flower-pots, do!
If hate killed men, Brother Lawrence,
   God's blood, would not mine kill you!
What? your myrtle-bush wants trimming?   5
   Oh, that rose has prior claims—
Needs its leaden vase filled brimming?
   Hell dry you up with its flames!

At the meal we sit together;
   Salve tibi! I must hear   10
Wise talk of the kind of weather,
   Sort of season, time of year:
Not a plenteous cork-crop: scarcely
   Dare we hope oak-galls, I doubt;
What's the Latin name for "parsley"?   15
   What's the Greek name for Swine's Snout?

Whew! We'll have our platter burnished,
   Laid with care on our own shelf!
With a fire-new spoon we're furnished,
   And a goblet for ourself,   20
Rinsed like something sacrificial
   Ere 'tis fit to touch our chaps—
Marked with L. for our initial!
   (He-he! There his lily snaps!)

Saint, forsooth! While brown Dolores   25
   Squats outside the Convent bank
With Sanchicha, telling stories,
   Steeping tresses in the tank,
Blue-black, lustrous, thick like horsehairs,
   —Can't I see his dead eye glow,   30
Bright as 'twere a Barbary corsair's?
   (That is, if he'd let it show!)

When he finishes refection,
   Knife and fork he never lays
Cross-wise, to my recollection,   35
   As do I, in Jesu's praise.
I the Trinity illustrate,
   Drinking watered orange-pulp—
In three sips the Arian frustrate;
   While he drains his at one gulp.   40

10 *Salve tibi!:* greetings to you (Latin).   31 *Barbary:* the north coast of Africa, famous for
its pirates.   39 *Arian:* a believer in a heresy which rejected the doctrine of the Trinity.

Oh, those melons? If he's able
    We're to have a feast! so nice!
One goes to the Abbot's table,
    All of us get each a slice.
How go on your flowers? None double?   45
    Not one fruit-sort can you spy?
Strange!—And I, too, at such trouble,
    Keep them close-nipped on the sly!

There's a great text in Galatians,   50
    Once you trip on it, entails
Twenty-nine distinct damnations,
    One sure, if another fails:
If I trip him just a-dying,
    Sure of heaven as sure as can be,   55
Spin him round and send him flying
    Off to hell, a Manichee?

Or, my scrofulous French novel
    On grey paper with blunt type!
Simply glance at it, you grovel   60
    Hand and foot in Belial's gripe:
If I double down its pages
    At the woeful sixteenth print,
When he gathers his greengages,
    Ope a sieve and slip it in 't?   65

Or, there's Satan!—one might venture
    Pledge one's soul to him, yet leave
Such a flaw in the indenture
    As he'd miss till, past retrieve,
Blasted lay that rose-acacia   70
    We're so proud of! *Hy, Zy, Hine* . . .
'St, there's Vespers! *Plena gratiâ*
    Ave, Virgo! Gr-r-r—you swine!

The Bishop Orders His Tomb at Saint Praxed's Church

Rome, 15—

Vanity, saith the preacher, vanity!
Draw round my bed; is Anselm keeping back?

50 *Galatians:* the Epistle to the Galatians, the ninth book of the New Testament. 57
Manichee: an adherent of the non-Christian religion called Manichaeism. 61 *Belial:*
the devil. 71 *Hy, Zy, Hine:* these words have never been satisfactorily explained.
72-3: *Plena gratiâ, Ave, Virgo!:* "Hail Virgin, full of grace," the beginning of the evening prayer.

Nephews—sons mine . . . ah, God, I know not! Well—
She, men would have to be your mother once,
Old Gandolf envied me, so fair she was!   5
What's done is done, and she is dead beside,
Dead long ago, and I am Bishop since,
And as she died so must we die ourselves,
And thence ye may perceive the world's a dream.
Life, how and what is it? As here I lie   10
In this state-chamber, dying by degrees,
Hours and long hours in the dead night, I ask,
"Do I live, am I dead?" Peace, peace seems all.
Saint Praxed's ever was the church for peace;
And so, about this tomb of mine. I fought   15
With tooth and nail to save my niche, ye know—
Old Gandolf cozened me, despite my care;
Shrewd was that snatch from out the corner South
He graced his carrion with, God curse the same!
Yet still my niche is not so cramped but thence   20
One sees the pulpit o' the epistle-side,
And somewhat of the choir, those silent seats,
And up into the aëry dome where live
The angels, and a sunbeam's sure to lurk;
And I shall fill my slab of basalt there,   25
And 'neath my tabernacle take my rest,
With those nine columns round me, two and two,
The odd one at my feet where Anselm stands:
Peach-blossom marble all, the rare, the ripe
As fresh-poured red wine of a mighty pulse.   30
—Old Gandolf with his paltry onion-stone,
Put me where I may look at him! True peach,
Rosy and flawless; how I earned the prize!
Draw close; that conflagration of my church—
What then? So much was saved if aught were missed!   35
My sons, ye would not be my death? Go dig
The white-grape vineyard where the oil-press stood,
Drop water gently till the surface sink,
And if ye find . . . Ah, God, I know not, I! . . .
Bedded in store of rotten fig-leaves soft,   40
And corded up in a tight olive-frail,
Some lump, ah, God, of *lapis lazuli,*
Big as a Jew's head cut off at the nape,
Blue as a vein o'er the Madonna's breast . . .
Sons, all have I bequeathed you, villas, all,   45
That brave Frascati villa with its bath,

5 *Gandolf:* the former bishop.   17 *cozened:* cheated.   21 *the epistle-side:* to the right of
the church, as one faces the altar.   25 *basalt:* a hard black rock.   26 *tabernacle:* a protective canopy.   31 *onion-stone:* inferior marble, whose layers peeled like an onion's.
41 *frail:* basket.   42 *lapis luzuli:* a semi-precious bluish stone.

So, let the blue lump poise between my knees,
Like God the Father's globe on both his hands
Ye worship in the Jesu Church so gay,
For Gandolf shall not choose but see and burst!   50
Swift as a weaver's shuttle fleet our years;
Man goeth to the grave, and where is he?
Did I say basalt for my slab, sons? Black—
'Twas ever antique-black I meant! How else
Shall ye contrast my frieze to come beneath?   55
The bas-relief in bronze ye promised me,
Those Pans and Nymphs ye wot of, and perchance
Some tripod, thyrsus, with a vase or so,
The Savior at his sermon on the mount,
Saint Praxed in a glory, and one Pan   60
Ready to twitch the Nymph's last garment off,
And Moses with the tables . . . but I know
Ye mark me not! What do they whisper thee,
Child of my bowels, Anselm? Ah, ye hope
To revel down my villas while I gasp   65
Bricked o'er with beggar's moldy travertine
Which Gandolf from his tomb-top chuckles at!
Nay, boys, ye love me—all of jasper, then!
'Tis jasper ye stand pledged to, lest I grieve
My bath must needs be left behind, alas!   70
One block, pure green as a pistachio-nut,
There's plenty jasper somewhere in the world—
And have I not Saint Praxed's ear to pray
Horses for ye, and brown Greek manuscripts,
And mistresses with great smooth marbly limbs?   75
—That's if ye carve my epitaph aright
Choice Latin, picked phrase, Tully's every word,
No gaudy ware like Gandolf's second line—
Tully, my masters? Ulpian serves his need!
And then how I shall lie through centuries,   80
And hear the blessed mutter of the Mass,
And see God made and eaten all day long,
And feel the steady candle-flame, and taste
Good strong thick stupefying incense-smoke!
For as I lie here, hours of the dead night,   85
Dying in state and by such slow degrees,
I fold my arms as if they clasped a crook,
And stretch my feet forth straight as stone can point,
And let the bedclothes, for a mortcloth, drop

---

57 *Pans and Nymphs:* pagan deities.   58 *thyrsus:* a staff used in the worship of Bacchus,
god of wine.   66 *travertine:* a cheap soft stone.   68 *jasper:* a handsome, hard green
stone.   77 *Tully:* Marcus Tullius Cicero, the great Latin stylist.   79 *Ulpian:* an inferior
Latin writer.   82 *God made and eaten:* the sacrament of the mass.   87 *crook:* the
Bishop's staff of office.   89 *mortcloth:* a shroud.

Into great laps and folds of sculptor's work;   90
And as yon tapers dwindle, and strange thoughts
Grow, with a certain humming in my ears
About the life before I lived this life,
And this life too, popes, cardinals, and priests,
Saint Praxed at his sermon on the mount,   95
Your tall pale mother with her talking eyes,
And new-found agate urns as fresh as day,
And marble's language, Latin pure, discreet—
Aha, ELUCESCEBAT quoth our friend?
No Tully, said I, Ulpian at the best!   100
Evil and brief hath been my pilgrimage.
All *lapis*, all sons! Else I give the Pope
My villas! Will ye ever eat my heart?
Ever your eyes were as a lizard's quick,
They glitter like your mother's for my soul,   105
Or ye would heighten my impoverished frieze,
Piece out its starved design, and fill my vase
With grapes, and add a visor and a term,
And to the tripod ye would tie a lynx
That in his struggle throws the thyrsus down,   110
To comfort me on my entablature
Whereon I am to lie till I must ask
"Do I live, am I dead?" There, leave me, there!
For ye have stabbed me with ingratitude
To death—ye wish it—God, ye wish it! Stone—   115
Gritstone, a-crumble! Clammy squares which sweat
As if the corpse they keep were oozing through—
And no more *lapis* to delight the world!
Well, go! I bless ye. Fewer tapers there,
But in a row: and, going, turn your backs   120
—Ay, like departing altar-ministrants,
And leave me in my church, the church for peace,
That I may watch at leisure if he leers—
Old Gandolf—at me, from his onion-stone,
As still he envied me, so fair she was!   125

90 *laps:* loose folds.   99 *Elucescebat:* apparently a word from the inscription on Gandolf's
tomb. It means "he was famous." The Bishop considers it stylistically inferior.   108
term: a pillar topped with a statue.   111 *entablature:* the part of a wall resting on a
column.   116 *Gritstone:* coarse sandstone.

Matthew Arnold (1822-1888)

Dover Beach

The sea is calm tonight,
The tide is full, the moon lies fair
Upon the straits;—on the French coast the light
Gleams and is gone; the cliffs of England stand,
Glimmering and vast, out in the tranquil bay.   5
Come to the window, sweet is the night-air!

Only, from the long line of spray
Where the sea meets the moon-blanched land,
Listen! you hear the grating roar
Of pebbles which the waves draw back, and fling,   10
At their return, up the high strand,
Begin, and cease, and then again begin,
With tremulous cadence slow, and bring
The eternal note of sadness in.

Sophocles long ago   15
Heard it on the Aegean, and it brought
Into his mind the turbid ebb and flow
Of human misery; we
Find also in the sound a thought,
Hearing it by this distant northern sea.   20

The Sea of Faith
Was once, too, at the full, and round earth's shore
Lay like the folds of a bright girdle furled.
But now I only hear
Its melancholy, long, withdrawing roar,   25
Retreating, to the breath
Of the night-wind, down the vast edges drear
And naked shingles of the world.

Ah, love, let us be true
To one another! for the world, which seems   30
To lie before us like a land of dreams,
So various, so beautiful, so new,
Hath really neither joy, nor love, nor light,
Nor certitude, nor peace, nor help for pain;
And we are here as on a darkling plain   35
Swept with confused alarms of struggle and flight,
Where ignorant armies clash by night.

---

15 *Sophocles:* the Greek dramatist. Arnold is referring to a passage from his *Antigone*.
16 *Aegean:* the sea east of Greece.   28 *shingles:* rocky beaches.

Henry David Thoreau (1817-1862)

Terminus

It is time to be old,
To take in sail:—
The god of bounds,
Who sets to seas a shore,
Came to me in his fatal rounds,   5
And said: "No more!
No farther shoot
Thy broad ambitious branches, and thy root.
Fancy departs: no more invent;
Contract thy firmament   10
To compass of a tent.
There's not enough for this and that,
Make thy option which of two;
Economize the failing river,
Not the less revere the Giver,   15
Leave the many and hold the few.
Timely wise accept the terms,
Soften the fall with wary foot;
A little while
Still plan and smile,   20
And,—fault of novel germs,—
Mature the unfallen fruit.
Curse, if thou wilt, thy sires,
Bad husbands of their fires,
Who, when they gave thee breath,   25
Failed to bequeath
The needful sinew stark as once,
The Baresark marrow to thy bones,
But left a legacy of ebbing veins,
Inconstant heat and nerveless reins,—   30
Amid the Muses, left thee deaf and dumb,
Amid the gladiators, halt and numb."
    As the bird trims her to the gale,
I trim myself to the storm of time,
I man the rudder, reef the sail,   35
Obey the voice at eve obeyed at prime:
"Lowly faithful, banish fear,
Right onward drive unharmed;
The port, well worth the cruise, is near,
And every wave is charmed."   40

Title: this is the name of the Roman "god of bounds" mentioned in line 3 of the poem.
28 *Baresark:* name applied to Norse warriors who fought without armor. It means
"bare shirt."

The Moon Now Rises to Her Absolute Rule

The moon now rises to her absolute rule,
And the husbandman and hunter
Acknowledge her for their mistress.
Asters and golden reign in the fields
And the life everlasting withers not.   5
The fields are reaped and shorn of their pride
But an inward verdure still crowns them;
The thistle scatters its down on the pool
And yellow leaves clothe the river—
And nought disturbs the serious life of men.   10
But behind the sheaves and under the sod
There lurks a ripe fruit which the reapers have not gathered,
The true harvest of the year—the boreal fruit
Which it bears forever,
With fondness annually watering and maturing it.   15
But man never severs the stalk
Which bears this palatable fruit.

Walt Whitman (1819-1892)

A Noiseless Patient Spider

A noiseless patient spider,
I mark'd where on a little promontory it stood isolated,
Mark'd how to explore the vacant vast surrounding,
It launched forth filament, filament, filament, out of itself.
Ever unreeling them ever tirelessly speeding them.   5

And you O my soul where you stand,
Surrounded, detached, in measureless oceans of space,
Ceaselessly musing, venturing, throwing, seeking the spheres to connect
    them.
Till the bridge you will need be formed, till the ductile anchor hold,
Till the gossamer thread you fling catch somewhere, O my soul.   10

---

13 *boreal:* pertaining to Boreas, the north wind.

George Meredith (1828-1909)

Lucifer in Starlight

On a starred night Prince Lucifer uprose.
Tired of his dark dominion swung the fiend
Above the rolling ball in cloud part screened,
Where sinners hugged their spectre of repose.
Poor prey to his hot fit of pride were those.   5
And now upon his western wing he leaned,
Now his huge bulk o'er Afric's sands careened,
Now the black planet shadowed Arctic snows.
Soaring through wider zones that pricked his scars
With memory of the old revolt from Awe,   10
He reached a middle height, and at the stars,
Which are the brain of heaven, he looked, and sank.
Around the ancient track marched, rank on rank,
The army of unalterable law.

Emily Dickinson (1830-1886)

Success Is Counted Sweetest

Success is counted sweetest
By those who ne'er succeed.
To comprehend a nectar
Requires sorest need.

Not one of all the purple host   5
Who took the flag today
Can tell the definition,
So clear, of victory,

As he, defeated, dying,
On whose forbidden ear   10
The distant strains of triumph
Break, agonized and clear.

The Heart Asks Pleasure First

The heart asks pleasure first,
And then, excuse from pain;
And then, those little anodynes
That deaden suffering;

And then, to go to sleep; 5
And then, if it should be
The will of its Inquisitor,
The liberty to die.

The Soul Selects Her Own Society

The soul selects her own society,
Then shuts the door;
On her divine majority
Obtrude no more.

Unmoved, she notes the chariot's pausing 5
At her low gate;
Unmoved, an emperor is kneeling
Upon her mat.

I've known her from an ample nation
Choose one; 10
Then close the valves of her attention
Like stone.

After Great Pain a Formal Feeling Comes

After great pain a formal feeling comes—
The nerves sit ceremonious like tombs;
The stiff heart questions—was it He that bore?
And yesterday—or centuries before?

The feet mechanical go round 5
A wooden way,
Of ground or air or Ought,
Regardless grown;
A quartz contentment like a stone.

This is the hour of lead 10
Remembered if outlived
As freezing persons recollect
The snow—
First chill, then stupor, then
The letting go. 15

3 *He:* Christ.   7 *Ought:* zero.

I Heard a Fly Buzz When I Died

I heard a fly buzz when I died;
The stillness in the room
Was like the stillness in the air
Between the heaves of storm.

The eyes around had wrung them dry,   5
And breaths were gathering firm
For that last onset when the king
Be witnessed in the room.

I willed my keepsakes, signed away
What portion of me be   10
Assignable—and then it was
There interposed a fly,

With blue, uncertain, stumbling buzz
Between the light and me;
And then the windows failed, and then   15
I could not see to see.

Ample Make This Bed

Ample make this bed.
Make this bed with awe;
In it wait till judgment break
Excellent and fair.

Be its mattress straight,   5
Be its pillow round;
Let no sunrise' yellow noise
Interrupt this ground.

Gerard Manley Hopkins (1844-1889)

The Habit of Perfection

Elected silence sing to me
And beat upon my whorlèd ear,
Pipe me to pastures still and be
The music that I care to hear.
Shape nothing lips; be lovely-dumb: 5
It is the shut, the curfew sent

1 *Elected:* specially chosen by God. 6 *the shut:* the closing.
From *Poems of Gerard Manley Hopkins,* third edition. Edited by W. H. Gardner. Copyright 1948 by Oxford University Press, Inc. Reprinted by permission.

From there where all surrenders come
Which only makes you eloquent.

Be shellèd, eyes, with double dark
And find the uncreated light: 10
This ruck and reel which you remark
Coils, keeps, and teases simple sight.

Palate, the hutch of tasty lust,
Desire not to be rinsed with wine:
The can must be so sweet, the crust   15
So fresh that come in fasts divine!

Nostrils, your careless breath that spend
Upon the stir and the keep of pride,
What relish shall the censers send
Along the sanctuary side!   20

O feel-of-primrose hands, O feet
That want the yield of plushy sward,
But you shall walk the golden street
And you unhouse and house the Lord.

And, Poverty, be thou the bride   25
And now the marriage feast begun,
And lily-coloured clothes provide
Your spouse not laboured-at nor spun.

God's Grandeur

The world is charged with the grandeur of God.
   It will flame out, like shining from shook foil;
   It gathers to a greatness, like the ooze of oil
Crushed. Why do men then now not reck his rod?
Generations have trod, have trod, have trod;   5
   And all is seared with trade; bleared, smeared with toil;
   And wears man's smudge and shares man's smell: the soil
Is bare now, nor can foot feel, being shod.
   And for all this, nature is never spent;
     There lives the dearest freshness deep down things;   10
   And though the last lights off the black West went
     Oh, morning, at the brown brink eastward, springs—
   Because the Holy Ghost over the bent
     World broods with warm breast and with ah! bright wings.

11 *ruck:* crowd. 12 *Coils:* stirs, disturbs. 13 *hutch:* a small box or house. 15 *can:* drinking-cup. 18 *keep:* an innermost enclosure. 20 *sanctuary side:* the part of a church where the altar is located.

The Windhover

(*To Christ our Lord*)

I caught this morning morning's minion, kingdom
    of daylight's dauphin, dapple-dawn-drawn Falcon,
        in his riding
Of the rolling level underneath him steady air, and striding
High there, how he rung upon the rein of a wimpling wing
In his ecstasy! then off, off forth on swing,   5
    As a skate's heel sweeps smooth on a bow-bend: the hurl and gliding
    Rebuffed the big wind. My heart in hiding
Stirred for a bird,—the achieve of, the mastery of the thing!

Brute beauty and valour and act, oh, air, pride, plume, here
    Buckle! AND the fire that breaks from thee then, a billion   10
Times told lovelier, more dangerous, O my chevalier!

  No wonder of it: shéer plód makes plough down sillion
Shine, and blue-bleak embers, ah my dear,
    Fall, gall themselves, and gash gold-vermilion.

No Worst, There Is None

No worst, there is none. Pitched past pitch of grief,
More pangs will, schooled at forepangs, wilder wring.
Comforter, where, where is your comforting?
Mary, mother of us, where is your relief?
My cries heave, herds-long; huddle in a main, a chief   5
Woe, world-sorrow; on an age-old anvil wince and sing—
Then lull, then leave off. Fury had shrieked "No lingering!
Let me be fell: force I must be brief."
    O the mind, mind has mountains; cliffs of fall
Frightful, sheer, no-man-fathomed. Hold them cheap   10
May who ne'er hung there. Nor does long our small
Durance deal with that steep or deep. Here! creep,
Wretch, under a comfort serves in a whirlwind: all
Life death does end and each day dies with sleep.

---

1 *minion:* servant.   2 *dauphin:* prince.   4 *wimpling:* falling in folds.   6 *skate:* the ray-fish.   12 *sillion:* a strip of cultivated land.

---

2 *schooled at:* taught by.   8 *fell:* cruel.   12 *Durance:* endurance.

Carrion Comfort

Not, I'll not, carrion comfort, Despair, not feast on thee;
Not untwist—slack they may be—these last strands of man
In me ór, most weary, cry *I can no more*. I can;
Can something, hope, wish day come, not choose not to be.
But ah, but O thou terrible, why wouldst thou rude on me   5
Thy wring-world right foot rock? lay a lionlimb against me? scan
With darksome devouring eyes my bruisèd bones? and fan,
O in turns of tempest, me heaped there; me frantic to avoid thee
      and flee?
  Why? That my chaff might fly; my grain lie, sheer and clear.
Nay in all that toil, that coil, since (seems) I kissed the rod,   10
Hand rather, my heart lo! lapped strength, stole joy, would
      laugh, chéer.
Cheer whom though? the hero whose heaven-handling flung me,
      fóot tród.
Me? or me that fought him? O which one? is it each one?
  That night, that year
Of now done darkness I wretch lay wrestling with (my God!)
      my God.   15

Thomas Hardy (1840-1928)

The Darkling Thrush

I leant upon a coppice gate
  When Frost was specter-gray,
And Winter's dregs made desolate
  The weakening eye of day.
The tangled bine-stems scored the sky   5
  Like strings of broken lyres,
And all mankind that haunted nigh
  Had sought their household fires.

The land's sharp features seemed to be
  The Century's corpse outleant,   10
His crypt the cloudy canopy,
  The wind his death-lament.

---

1 *coppice:* grove.   5 *bine-stems:* plants with twining stems; *scored:* cut or marked.   10 *The Century's corpse:* the poem was written on the last day of the nineteenth century.

The ancient pulse of germ and birth
　　Was shrunken hard and dry,
And every spirit upon earth   15
　　Seemed fervorless as I.

At once a voice arose among
　　The bleak twigs overhead
In a full-hearted evensong
　　Of joy illimited;   20
An aged thrush, frail, gaunt, and small,
　　In blast-beruffled plume,
Had chosen thus to fling his soul
　　Upon the growing gloom.

So little cause for carolings   25
　　Of such ecstatic sound
Was written on terrestrial things
　　Afar or nigh around,
That I could think there trembled through
　　His happy good-night air   30
Some blessed Hope, whereof he knew
　　And I was unaware.

The Convergence of the Twain

Lines on the loss of the "Titanic"

I

In a solitude of the sea
　　Deep from human vanity,
And the Pride of Life that planned her, stilly couches she.

II

Steel chambers, late the pyres
　　Of her salamandrine fires,   5
Cold currents thrid, and turn to rhythmic tidal lyres.

III

Over the mirrors meant
　　To glass the opulent
The sea-worm crawls—grotesque, slimed, dumb, indifferent.

3 *couches:* rests.   5 *salamandrine:* according to legend, the salamander can pass through
　fire unharmed.   6 *thrid:* to thread, penetrate.

IV

Jewels in joy designed   10
To ravish the sensuous mind
Lie lightless, all their sparkles bleared and black and blind.

V

Dim moon-eyed fishes near
Gaze at the gilded gear
And query: "What does this vaingloriousness down here?"   15

VI

Well: while was fashioning
This creature of cleaving wing,
The Immanent Will that stirs and urges everything

VII

Prepared a sinister mate
For her—so gaily great   20
A Shape of Ice, for the time far and dissociate.

VIII

And as the smart ship grew
In stature, grace, and hue,
In shadowy silent distance grew the Iceberg too.

IX

Alien they seemed to be;   25
No mortal eye could see
The intimate welding of their later history,

X

Or sign that they were bent
By paths coincident
On being anon twin halves of one august event,   30

XI

Till the Spinner of the Years
Said "Now!" And each one hears,
And consummation comes, and jars two hemispheres.

18 *Immanent Will:* Hardy's name for the supreme power.

The Oxen

Christmas Eve, and twelve of the clock.
　　"Now they are all on their knees,"
An elder said as we sat in a flock
　　By the embers in hearthside ease.

We pictured the meek mild creatures where　　　　5
　　They dwelt in their strawy pen,
Nor did it occur to one of us there
　　To doubt they were kneeling then.

So fair a fancy few would weave
　　In these years! Yet, I feel,　　　　10
If someone said on Christmas Eve,
　　"Come; see the oxen kneel,

"In the lonely barton by yonder coomb
　　Our childhood used to know,"
I should go with him in the gloom,　　　　15
　　Hoping it might be so.

The Walk

You did not walk with me
Of late to the hill-top tree
　　By the gated ways,
　　As in earlier days;
　　You were weak and lame,　　　　5
　　So you never came,
And I went alone, and I did not mind,
Not thinking of you as left behind.

I walked up there to-day
Just in the former way;　　　　10
　　Surveyed around
　　The familiar ground
　　By myself again:
　　What difference, then?
Only that underlying sense　　　　15
Of the look of a room on returning thence.

Reprinted with permission of The Macmillan Company, The Estate of Thomas Hardy, Macmillan & Co., Ltd., London, and The Macmillan Company of Canada Limited from *Collected Poems* by Thomas Hardy. Copyright The Macmillan Company 1925.

The Death of Regret

I opened my shutter at sunrise,
    And looked at the hill hard by,
And I heartily grieved for the comrade
    Who wandered up there to die.

I let in the morn on the morrow,   5
    And failed not to think of him then,
As he trod up that rise in the twilight,
    And never came down again.

I undid the shutter a week thence,
    But not until after I'd turned   10
Did I call back his last departure
    By the upland there discerned.

Uncovering the casement long later,
    I bent to my toil till the gray,
When I said to myself, "Ah—what ails me,   15
    To forget him all the day!"

As daily I flung back the shutter
    In the same blank bald routine,
He scarcely once rose to remembrance
    Through a month of my facing the scene.   20

And ah, seldom now do I ponder
    At the window as heretofore
On the long valued one who died yonder,
    And wastes by the sycamore.

Nature's Questioning

When I look forth at dawning, pool,
    Field, flock, and lonely tree,
    All seem to gaze at me
Like chastened children sitting silent in a school;

    Their faces dulled, constrained, and worn,   5
        As though the master's ways
        Through the long teaching days
Had cowed them till their early zest was overborne.

Reprinted with permission of The Macmillan Company, The Estate of Thomas Hardy, Macmillan & Co., Ltd., London, and The Macmillan Company of Canada Limited from *Collected Poems* by Thomas Hardy. Copyright The Macmillan Company 1925.

Upon them stirs in lippings mere
 (As if once clear in call,   10
 But now scarce breathed at all)—
"We wonder, ever wonder, why we find us here!

"Has some Vast Imbecility,
 Mighty to build and blend,
 But impotent to tend,   15
Framed us in jest, and left us now to hazardry?

"Or come we of an Automaton
 Unconscious of our pains? . . .
 Or are we live remains
Of Godhead dying downwards, brain and eye now gone?   20

"Or is it that some high Plan betides,
 As yet not understood,
 Of Evil stormed by Good,
We the Forlorn Hope over which Achievement strides?"

Thus things around. No answerer I . . .   25
 Meanwhile the winds, and rains,
 And Earth's old glooms and pains
Are still the same, and Life and Death are neighbours nigh.

The Fallow Deer at the Lonely House

One without looks in to-night
 Through the curtain-chink
From the sheet of glistening white;
One without looks in to-night
 As we sit and think   5
 By the fender-brink.

We do not discern those eyes
 Watching in the snow;
Lit by lamps of rosy dyes
We do not discern those eyes   10
 Wondering, aglow,
 Fourfooted, tiptoe.

In a Wood

from *The Woodlanders*

Pale beech and pine so blue,
 Set in one clay,
Bough to bough cannot you
 Live out your day?
When the rains skim and skip,   5
Why mar sweet comradeship,
Blighting with poison-drip
 Neighbourly spray?

Heart-halt and spirit-lame,
 City-opprest,   10
Unto this wood I came
 As to a nest;
Dreaming that sylvan peace
Offered the harrowed ease—
Nature a soft release   15
 From men's unrest.

But, having entered in,
 Great growths and small
Show them to men akin—
 Combatants all: 20
Sycamore shoulders oak,
Bines the slim sapling yoke,
Ivy-spun halters choke
 Elms stout and tall.

Touches from ash, O wych,   25
 Sting you like scorn!
You, too, brave hollies, twitch
 Sidelong from thorn.
Even the rank poplars bear
Lothly a rival's air,   30
Cankering in black despair
 If overborne.

Since, then, no grace I find
 Taught me of trees,
Turn I back to my kind,   35
 Worthy as these.
There at least smiles abound,
There discourse trills around,
There, now and then, are found
 Life-loyalties.   40

A. E. Housman (1859-1936)

To an Athlete Dying Young

The time you won your town the race
We chaired you through the market-place;
Man and boy stood cheering by,
And home we brought you shoulder-high.

To-day, the road all runners come,   5
Shoulder-high we bring you home,
And set you at your threshold down,
Townsman of a stiller town.

Smart lad, to slip betimes away
From fields where glory does not stay,   10
And early though the laurel grows
It withers quicker than the rose.

Eyes the shady night has shut
Cannot see the record cut,
And silence sounds no worse than cheers   15
After earth has stopped the ears.

Now you will not swell the rout
Of lads that wore their honors out,
Runners whom renown outran
And the name died before the man.   20

So set, before its echoes fade,
The fleet foot on the sill of shade,
And hold to the low lintel up
The still-defended challenge-cup.

And round that early-laurelled head   25
Will flock to gaze the strengthless dead,
And find unwithered on its curls
The garland briefer than a girl's.

2 *chaired:* carried him seated on the shoulders of a crowd. 9 *betimes:* early. 11 *laurel:* the traditional symbol of fame. 14 *the record cut:* the American idiom is "the record broken." 23 *lintel:* the beam across the top of a door or window.

Bredon Hill

In summertime on Bredon
  The bells they sound so clear;
Round both the shires they ring them
  In steeples far and near,
  A happy noise to hear.   5

Here of a Sunday morning
  My love and I would lie,
And see the colored counties,
  And hear the larks so high
  About us in the sky.   10

The bells would ring to call her
  In valleys miles away:
"Come all to church, good people;
  Good people, come and pray."
  But here my love would stay.   15

And I would turn and answer
  Among the springing thyme,
"Oh, peal upon our wedding,
  And we will hear the chime,
  And come to church in time."   20

But when the snows at Christmas
  On Bredon top were strown,
My love rose up so early
  And stole out unbeknown
  And went to church alone.   25

They tolled the one bell only,
  Groom there was none to see,
The mourners followed after,
  And so to church went she,
  And would not wait for me.   30

The bells they sound on Bredon,
  And still the steeples hum.
"Come all to church, good people,—"
  Oh, noisy bells, be dumb;
  I hear you, I will come.   35

From *Complete Poems* by A. E. Housman. Copyright, 1940 © 1959, by Henry Holt and Company, Inc. By permission of Holt, Rinehart and Winston, Inc., The Society of Authors, and Jonathan Cape, Ltd.

On Wenlock Edge

On Wenlock Edge the wood's in trouble;
   His forest fleece the Wrekin heaves;
The gale, it plies the saplings double,
   And thick on Severn snow the leaves.

'Twould blow like this through holt and hanger   5
   When Uricon the city stood:
'Tis the old wind in the old anger,
   But then it threshed another wood.

Then, 'twas before my time, the Roman
   At yonder heaving hill would stare: 10
The blood that warms an English yeoman,
   The thoughts that hurt him, they were there.

There, like the wind through woods in riot,
   Through him the gale of life blew high;
The tree of man was never quiet: 15
   Then 'twas the Roman, now 'tis I.

The gale, it plies the saplings double,
   It blows so hard, 'twill soon be gone:
To-day the Roman and his trouble
   Are ashes under Uricon.   20

Into My Heart an Air That Kills

Into my heart an air that kills
   From yon far country blows:
What are those blue remembered hills,
   What spires, what farms are those?

That is the land of lost content,   5
   I see it shining plain,
The happy highways where I went
   And cannot come again.

1 *Wenlock:* a town in Shropshire.   2 *Wrekin:* a volcanic hill in Shropshire.   3 *Severn:* a Shropshire river.   5 *holt and hanger:* wooded hills.   6 *Uricon:* Roman name of Wenlock.

Edwin Arlington Robinson (1869-1935)

Mr. Flood's Party

Old Eben Flood, climbing alone one night
Over the hill between the town below
And the forsaken upland hermitage
That held as much as he should ever know
On earth again of home, paused warily.   5
The road was his with not a native near;
And Eben, having leisure, said aloud,
For no man else in Tilbury Town to hear:

"Well, Mr. Flood, we have the harvest moon
Again, and we may not have many more;   10
The bird is on the wing, the poet says,
And you and I have said it here before.
Drink to the bird." He raised up to the light
The jug that he had gone so far to fill,
And answered huskily: "Well, Mr. Flood,   15
Since you propose it, I believe I will."

Alone, as if enduring to the end
A valiant armor of scarred hopes outworn,
He stood there in the middle of the road
Like Roland's ghost winding a silent horn.   20
Below him, in the town among the trees,
Where friends of other days had honored him,
A phantom salutation of the dead
Rang thinly till old Eben's eyes were dim.

Then, as a mother lays her sleeping child   25
Down tenderly, fearing it may awake,
He set the jug down slowly at his feet
With trembling care, knowing that most things break;
And only when assured that on firm earth
It stood, as the uncertain lives of men   30
Assuredly did not, he paced away,
And with his hand extended paused again:

"Well, Mr. Flood, we have not met like this
In a long time; and many a change has come
To both of us, I fear, since last it was   35
We had a drop together. Welcome home!"
Convivially returning with himself,

20 *Roland*: the hero of the *Song of Roland*, who called for help by sounding his horn.

Again he raised the jug up to the light;
And with an acquiescent quaver said:
"Well, Mr. Flood, if you insist, I might.   40

"Only a very little, Mr. Flood—
For auld lang syne. No more, sir; that will do."
So, for the time, apparently it did,
And Eben evidently thought so too;
For soon amid the silver loneliness   45
Of night he lifted up his voice and sang,
Secure, with only two moons listening,
Until the whole harmonious landscape rang—

"For auld lang syne." The weary throat gave out,
The last word wavered; and the song being done,   50
He raised again the jug regretfully
And shook his head, and was again alone.
There was not much that was ahead of him,
And there was nothing in the town below—
Where strangers would have shut the many doors   55
That many friends had opened long ago.

For a Dead Lady

No more with overflowing light
Shall fill the eyes that now are faded,
Nor shall another's fringe with night
Their woman-hidden world as they did.
No more shall quiver down the days   5
The flowing wonder of her ways,
Whereof no language may requite
The shifting and the many-shaded.

The grace, divine, definitive,
Clings only as a faint forestalling;   10
The laugh that love could not forgive
Is hushed, and answers to no calling;
The forehead and the little ears
Have gone where Saturn keeps the years;
The breast where roses could not live   15
Has done with rising and with falling.

The beauty, shattered by the laws
That have creation in their keeping,
No longer trembles at applause,
Or over children that are sleeping;   20
And we who delve in beauty's lore
Know all that we have known before
Of what inexorable cause
Makes Time so vicious in his reaping.

Walter de la Mare (1873-1956)

The Listeners

"Is there anybody there?" said the Traveller,
    Knocking on the moonlit door;
And his horse in the silence champed the grasses
    Of the forest's ferny floor:
And a bird flew up out of the turret,   5
    Above the Traveller's head:
And he smote upon the door again a second time;
    "Is there anybody there?" he said.
But no one descended to the Traveller;
    No head from the leaf-fringed sill   10
Leaned over and looked into his grey eyes,
    Where he stood perplexed and still.
But only a host of phantom listeners
    That dwelt in the lone house then
Stood listening in the quiet of the moonlight   15
    To that voice from the world of men:
Stood thronging the faint moonbeams on the dark stair,
    That goes down to the empty hall,
Hearkening in an air stirred and shaken
    By the lonely Traveller's call.   20
And he felt in his heart their strangeness,
    Their stillness answering his cry,
While his horse moved, cropping the dark turf,
    'Neath the starred and leafy sky;

For he suddenly smote on the door, even   25
  Louder, and lifted his head:—
"Tell them I came, and no one answered,
  "That I kept my word," he said.
Never the least stir made the listeners,
  Though every word he spake   30
Fell echoing through the shadowiness of the still house
  From the one man left awake:
Ay, they heard his foot upon the stirrup,
  And the sound of iron on stone,
And how the silence surged softly backward,   35
  When the plunging hoofs were gone.

William Carlos Williams (1883-1963)

The Yachts

contend in a sea which the land partly encloses
shielding them from the too-heavy blows
of an ungoverned ocean which when it chooses

tortures the biggest hulls, the best man knows
to pit against its beatings, and sinks them pitilessly.   5
Mothlike in mists, scintillant in the minute

brilliance of cloudless days, with broad bellying sails
they glide to the wind tossing green water
from their sharp prows while over them the crew crawls

ant-like, solicitously grooming them, releasing,   10
making fast as they turn, lean far over and having
caught the wind again, side by side, head for the mark.

In a well-guarded arena of open water surrounded by
lesser and greater craft which, sycophant, lumbering
and flittering follow them, they appear youthful, rare   15

as the light of a happy eye, live with the grace
of all that in the mind is feckless, free and
naturally to be desired. Now the sea which holds them

is moody, lapping their glossy sides, as if feeling
for some slightest flaw but fails completely. 20
Today no race. Then the wind comes again. The yachts

move, jockeying for a start, the signal is set and they
are off. Now the waves strike at them but they are too
well made, they slip through, though they take in canvas.

Arms with hands grasping seek to clutch at the prows. 25
Bodies thrown recklessly in the way are cut aside.
It is a sea of faces about them in agony, in despair

until the horror of the race dawns staggering the mind,
the whole sea become an entanglement of watery bodies
lost to the world bearing what they cannot hold. Broken, 30

beaten, desolate, reaching from the dead to be taken up
they cry out, failing, failing! their cries rising
in waves still as the skillful yachts pass over.

D. H. Lawrence (1885-1930)

Piano

Softly, in the dusk, a woman is singing to me;
Taking me back down the vista of years, till I see
A child sitting under the piano, in the boom of the tingling strings
And pressing the small, poised feet of a mother who smiles as
    she sings.

In spite of myself, the insidious mastery of song 5
Betrays me back, till the heart of me weeps to belong
To the old Sunday evenings at home, with winter outside
And hymns in the cozy parlor, the tinkling piano our guide.

So now it is vain for the singer to burst into clamor
With the great black piano appassionato. The glamour 10
Of childish days is upon me, my manhood is cast
Down in the flood of remembrance, I weep like a child for the past.

10 *appassionato:* deeply emotional.

William Butler Yeats (1865-1939)

To a Friend Whose Work Has Come to Nothing

Now all the truth is out,
Be secret and take defeat
From any brazen throat,
For how can you compete,
Being honour bred, with one   5
Who, were it proved he lies,
Were neither shamed in his own
Nor in his neighbours' eyes?
Bred to a harder thing
Than Triumph, turn away   10
And like a laughing string
Whereon mad fingers play
Amid a place of stone,
Be secret and exult,
Because of all things known   15
That is most difficult.

The Wild Swans at Coole

The trees are in their autumn beauty,
The woodland paths are dry,
Under the October twilight the water
Mirrors a still sky;
Upon the brimming water among the stones   5
Are nine-and-fifty swans.

The nineteenth autumn has come upon me
Since I first made my count;
I saw, before I had well finished,
All suddenly mount   10
And scatter wheeling in great broken rings
Upon their clamorous wings.

I have looked upon those brilliant creatures,
And now my heart is sore.
All's changed since I, hearing at twilight,   15
The first time on this shore,
The bell-beat of their wings above my head,
Trod with a lighter tread.

Unwearied still, lover by lover,
They paddle in the cold   20
Companionable streams or climb the air;
Their hearts have not grown old;
Passion or conquest, wander where they will,
Attend upon them still.

But now they drift on the still water,   25
Mysterious, beautiful;
Among what rushes will they build,
By what lake's edge or pool
Delight men's eyes when I awake some day
To find they have flown away?   30

The Second Coming

Turning and turning in the widening gyre
The falcon cannot hear the falconer;
Things fall apart; the centre cannot hold;
Mere anarchy is loosed upon the world,
The blood-dimmed tide is loosed, and everywhere   5
The ceremony of innocence is drowned;
The best lack all conviction, while the worst
Are full of passionate intensity.

Surely some revelation is at hand;
Surely the Second Coming is at hand.   10
The Second Coming! Hardly are those words out
When a vast image out of *Spiritus Mundi*
Troubles my sight: somewhere in sands of the desert
A shape with lion body and the head of a man,
A gaze blank and pitiless as the sun,   15
Is moving its slow thighs, while all about it
Reel shadows of the indignant desert birds.

Title: refers to the return of Christ to earth. 1 *gyre:* a circling movement. 12 *Spiritus Mundi:* the spirit of the world, or essence of life.

The darkness drops again; but now I know
That twenty centuries of stony sleep
Were vexed to nightmare by a rocking cradle,   20
And what rough beast, its hour come round at last,
Slouches towards Bethlehem to be born?

Sailing to Byzantium

I

That is no country for old men. The young
In one another's arms, birds in the trees,
—Those dying generations—at their song,
The salmon-falls, the mackerel-crowded seas,
Fish, flesh, or fowl, commend all summer long   5
Whatever is begotten, born, and dies.
Caught in that sensual music all neglect
Monuments of unageing intellect.

II

An aged man is but a paltry thing,
A tattered coat upon a stick, unless   10
Soul clap its hands and sing, and louder sing
For every tatter in its mortal dress,
Nor is there singing school but studying
Monuments of its own magnificence;
And therefore I have sailed the seas and come   15
To the holy city of Byzantium.

III

O sages standing in God's holy fire
As in the gold mosaic of a wall,
Come from the holy fire, perne in a gyre,
And be the singing-masters of my soul.   20
Consume my heart away; sick with desire
And fastened to a dying animal
It knows not what it is; and gather me
Into the artifice of eternity.

IV

Once out of nature I shall never take   25
My bodily form from any natural thing,

19 *perne in a gyre:* whirl in a circle.

But such a form as Grecian goldsmiths make
Of hammered gold and gold enamelling
To keep a drowsy Emperor awake;
Or set upon a golden bough to sing   30
To lords and ladies of Byzantium
Of what is past, or passing, or to come.

from *The Tower*

III

It is time that I wrote my will;
I choose upstanding men
That climb the streams until
The fountain leap, and at dawn
Drop their cast at the side   5
Of dripping stone; I declare
They shall inherit my pride,
The pride of people that were
Bound neither to Cause nor to State,
Neither to slaves that were spat on,   10
Nor to the tyrants that spat,
The people of Burke and of Grattan
That gave, though free to refuse—
Pride, like that of the morn,
When the headlong light is loose,   15
Or that of the fabulous horn,
Or that of the sudden shower
When all streams are dry,
Or that of the hour
When the swan must fix his eye   20
Upon a fading gleam,
Float out upon a long
Last reach of glittering stream
And there sing his last song.
And I declare my faith: 25
I mock Plotinus' thought
And cry in Plato's teeth,
Death and life were not
Till man made up the whole,
Made lock, stock and barrel   30
Out of his bitter soul,

12 *Burke, Grattan:* famous Irish statesmen.   26, 27: *Plotinus, Plato:* great philosophers of
antiquity.

Aye, sun and moon and star, all,
And further add to that
That, being dead, we rise,
Dream and so create   35
Translunar Paradise.
I have prepared my peace
With learned Italian things
And the proud stones of Greece,
Poet's imaginings   40
And memories of love,
Memories of the words of women,
All those things whereof
Man makes a superhuman
Mirror-resembling dream.   45

As at the loophole there
The daws chatter and scream,
And drop twigs layer upon layer.
When they have mounted up,
The mother bird will rest   50
On their hollow top,
And so warm her wild nest.
I leave both faith and pride
To young upstanding men
Climbing the mountain side,   55
That under bursting dawn
They may drop a fly;
Being of that metal made
Till it was broken by
This sedentary trade.   60

Now shall I make my soul,
Compelling it to study
In a learned school
Till the wreck of body,
Slow decay of blood,   65
Testy delirium
Or dull decrepitude,
Or what worse evil come—
The death of friends, or death
Of every brilliant eye   70
That made a catch in the breath—
Seem but the clouds of the sky
When the horizon fades;
Or a bird's sleepy cry
Among the deepening shades.   75

47 *daws:* jackdaws.

Swift's Epitaph

Swift has sailed into his rest;
Savage indignation there
Cannot lacerate his breast.
Imitate him if you dare,
World-besotted traveller; he   5
Served human liberty.

Robert Frost (1875-1963)

Fire and Ice

Some say the world will end in fire;
Some say in ice.
From what I've tasted of desire
I hold with those who favor fire.
But if it had to perish twice,   5
I think I know enough of hate
To know that for destruction ice
Is also great
And would suffice.

Stopping by Woods on a Snowy Evening

Whose woods these are I think I know.
His house is in the village though;
He will not see me stopping here
To watch his woods fill up with snow.

My little horse must think it queer   5
To stop without a farmhouse near
Between the woods and frozen lake
The darkest evening of the year.

He gives his harness bells a shake
To ask if there is some mistake.   10
The only other sound's the sweep
Of easy wind and downy flake.

The woods are lovely, dark and deep.
But I have promises to keep,
And miles to go before I sleep,   15
And miles to go before I sleep.

After Apple-Picking

My long two-pointed ladder's sticking through a tree
Toward heaven still,
And there's a barrel that I didn't fill
Beside it, and there may be two or three
Apples I didn't pick upon some bough.   5
But I am done with apple-picking now.
Essence of winter sleep is on the night,
The scent of apples: I am drowsing off.
I cannot rub the strangeness from my sight
I got from looking through a pane of glass   10
I skimmed this morning from the drinking trough
And held against the world of hoary grass.
It melted, and I let it fall and break.
But I was well
Upon my way to sleep before it fell,   15
And I could tell
What form my dreaming was about to take.
Magnified apples appear and disappear,
Stem-end and blossom-end,
And every fleck of russet showing clear.   20
My instep arch not only keeps the ache,
It keeps the pressure of a ladder-round.
I feel the ladder sway as the boughs bend.
And I keep hearing from the cellar bin
The rumbling sound   25
Of load on load of apples coming in.
For I have had too much
Of apple-picking: I am overtired
Of the great harvest I myself desired.
There were ten thousand fruit to touch,   30
Cherish in hand, lift down, and not let fall.
For all
That struck the earth,

No matter if not bruised or spiked with stubble,
Went surely to the cider-apple heap   35
As of no worth.
One can see what will trouble
This sleep of mine, whatever sleep it is.
Were he not gone,
The woodchuck could say whether it's like his   40
Long sleep, as I describe its coming on,
Or just some human sleep.

Once by the Pacific

The shattered water made a misty din.
Great waves looked over others coming in,
And thought of doing something to the shore
That water never did to land before.
The clouds were low and hairy in the skies,   5
Like locks blown forward in the gleam of eyes.
You could not tell, and yet it looked as if
The shore was lucky in being backed by cliff,
The cliff in being backed by continent;
It looked as if a night of dark intent   10
Was coming, and not only a night, an age.
Someone had better be prepared for rage.
There would be more than ocean-water broken
Before God's last *Put out the Light* was spoken.

Two Tramps in Mud-Time

Out of the mud two strangers came
And caught me splitting wood in the yard.
And one of them put me off my aim
By hailing cheerily "Hit them hard!"
I knew pretty well why he dropped behind   5
And let the other go on a way.
I knew pretty well what he had in mind:
He wanted to take my job for pay.

Good blocks of beech it was I split,
As large around as the chopping-block;   10
And every piece I squarely hit
Fell splinterless as a cloven rock.
The blows that a life of self-control

Spares to strike for the common good
That day, giving a loose to my soul,   15
I spent on the unimportant wood.

The sun was warm but the wind was chill.
You know how it is with an April day:
When the sun is out and the wind is still,
You're one month on in the middle of May.   20
But if you so much as dare to speak,
A cloud comes over the sunlit arch,
A wind comes off a frozen peak,
And you're two months back in the middle of March.

A bluebird comes tenderly up to alight   25
And fronts the wind to unruffle a plume,
His song so pitched as not to excite
A single flower as yet to bloom.
It is snowing a flake: and he half knew
Winter was only playing possum.   30
Except in color he isn't blue,
But he wouldn't advise a thing to blossom.

The water for which we may have to look
In summertime with a witching-wand,
In every wheelrut's now a brook,   35
In every print of a hoof a pond.
Be glad of water, but don't forget
The lurking frost in the earth beneath
That will steal forth after the sun is set
And show on the water its crystal teeth.   40

The time when most I loved my task
These two must make me love it more
By coming with what they came to ask.
You'd think I never had felt before
The weight of an ax head poised aloft,   45
The grip on earth of outspread feet,
The life of muscles rocking soft
And smooth and moist in vernal heat.

Out of the woods two hulking tramps
(From sleeping God knows where last night   50
But not long since in the lumber camps).
They thought all chopping was theirs of right.
Men of the woods and lumber-jacks,
They judged me by their appropriate tool.
Except as a fellow handled an ax,   55
They had no way of knowing a fool.

Nothing on either side was said.
They knew they had but to stay their stay

And all their logic would fill my head:
As that I had no right to play   60
With what was another man's work for gain.
My right might be love but theirs was need.
And where the two exist in twain
Theirs was the better right—agreed.

But yield who will to their separation,   65
My object in life is to unite
My avocation and my vocation
As my two eyes make one in sight.
Only where love and need are one,
And the work is play for mortal stakes,   70
Is the deed ever really done
For Heaven and the future's sakes.

Desert Places

Snow falling and night falling fast oh fast
In a field I looked into going past,
And the ground almost covered smooth in snow,
But a few weeds and stubble showing last.

The woods around it have it—it is theirs.   5
All animals are smothered in their lairs.
I am too absent-spirited to count;
The loneliness includes me unawares.

And lonely as it is, that loneliness
Will be more lonely ere it will be less—   10
A blanker whiteness of benighted snow
With no expression, nothing to express.

They cannot scare me with their empty spaces
Between stars—on stars where no human race is.
I have it in me so much nearer home   15
To scare myself with my own desert places.

Design

I found a dimpled spider, fat and white,
On a white heal-all, holding up a moth
Like a white piece of rigid satin cloth—
Assorted characters of death and blight
Mixed ready to begin the morning right,   5

Like the ingredients of a witches' broth—
A snow-drop spider, a flower like a froth,
And dead wings carried like a paper kite.

What had that flower to do with being white,
The wayside blue and innocent heal-all?   10
What brought the kindred spider to that height,
Then steered the white moth thither in the night?
What but design of darkness to appall?—
If design govern in a thing so small.

A Considerable Speck

(*Microscopic*)

A speck that would have been beneath my sight
On any but a paper sheet so white
Set off across what I had written there.
And I had idly poised my pen in air
To stop it with a period of ink   5
When something strange about it made me think.
This was no dust speck by my breathing blown,
But unmistakably a living mite
With inclinations it could call its own.
It paused as with suspicion of my pen,   10
And then came racing wildly on again
To where my manuscript was not yet dry;
Then paused again and either drank or smelt—
With loathing, for again it turned to fly.
Plainly with an intelligence I dealt.   15
It seemed too tiny to have room for feet,
Yet must have had a set of them complete
To express how much it didn't want to die.
It ran with terror and with cunning crept.
It faltered: I could see it hesitate;   20
Then in the middle of the open sheet
Cower down in desperation to accept
Whatever I accorded it of fate.
I have none of the tenderer-than-thou
Collectivistic regimenting love   25
With which the modern world is being swept.
But this poor microscopic item now!
Since it was nothing I knew evil of
I let it lie there till I hope it slept.

I have a mind myself and recognize   30
Mind when I meet with it in any guise.
No one can know how glad I am to find
On any sheet the least display of mind.

T. S. Eliot (1888-1965)

The Love Song of J. Alfred Prufrock

> *S'io credesse che mia risposta fosse*
> *A persona che mai tornasse al mondo,*
> *Questa fiamma staria senza piu scosse.*
> *Ma perciocche giammai di questo fondo*
> *Non torno vivo alcun, s'i' odo il vero,*
> *Senza tema d'infamia ti rispondo.*

Let us go then, you and I,
When the evening is spread out against the sky
Like a patient etherized upon a table;
Let us go, through certain half-deserted streets,
The muttering retreats   5
Of restless nights in one-night cheap hotels
And sawdust restaurants with oyster-shells:
Streets that follow like a tedious argument
Of insidious intent
To lead you to an overwhelming question. . . .   10
Oh, do not ask, "What is it?"
Let us go and make our visit.

In the room the women come and go
Talking of Michelangelo.

The yellow fog that rubs its back upon the window-panes,   15
The yellow smoke that rubs its muzzle on the window-panes
Licked its tongue into the corners of the evening,
Lingered upon the pools that stand in drains,
Let fall upon its back the soot that falls from chimneys,
Slipped by the terrace, made a sudden leap,   20

The epigraph, *S'io credesse,* etc. is a quotation from Dante's *Divine Comedy.* It has been translated as follows: "If I thought my answer were to one who ever could return to the world, this flame should shake no more; but since none ever did return alive from this depth, if what I hear be true, without fear of infamy I answer thee."

And seeing that it was a soft October night,
Curled once about the house, and fell asleep.

And indeed there will be time
For the yellow smoke that slides along the street,
Rubbing its back upon the window-panes;   25
There will be time, there will be time
To prepare a face to meet the faces that you meet;
There will be time to murder and create,
And time for all the works and days of hands
That lift and drop a question on your plate;   30
Time for you and time for me,
And time yet for a hundred indecisions,
And for a hundred visions and revisions,
Before the taking of a toast and tea.

In the room the women come and go   35
Talking of Michelangelo.

And indeed there will be time
To wonder, "Do I dare?" and, "Do I dare?"
Time to turn back and descend the stair,
With a bald spot in the middle of my hair—   40
(They will say: "How his hair is growing thin!")
My morning coat, my collar mounting firmly to the chin,
My necktie rich and modest, but asserted by a simple pin—
(They will say: "But how his arms and legs are thin!")
Do I dare   45
Disturb the universe?
In a minute there is time
For decisions and revisions which a minute will reverse.

For I have known them all already, known them all:
Have known the evenings, mornings, afternoons,   50
I have measured out my life with coffee spoons;
I know the voices dying with a dying fall
Beneath the music from a farther room.
    So how should I presume?

And I have known the eyes already, known them all—   55
The eyes that fix you in a formulated phrase,
And when I am formulated, sprawling on a pin,
When I am pinned and wriggling on the wall,
Then how should I begin
To spit out all the butt-ends of my days and ways?   60
    And how should I presume?

And I have known the arms already, known them all—
Arms that are braceleted and white and bare
(But in the lamplight, downed with light brown hair!)
Is it perfume from a dress   65
That makes me so disgress?

Arms that lie along a table, or wrap about a shawl,
   And should I then presume?
   And how should I begin?

Shall I say, I have gone at dusk through narrow streets   70
And watched the smoke that rises from the pipes
Of lonely men in shirt-sleeves, leaning out of windows? . . .

I should have been a pair of ragged claws
Scuttling across the floors of silent seas.

And the afternoon, the evening, sleeps so peacefully!   75
Smoothed by long fingers,
Asleep . . . tired . . . or it malingers,
Stretched on the floor, here beside you and me.
Should I, after tea and cakes and ices,
Have the strength to force the moment to its crisis?   80
But though I have wept and fasted, wept and prayed,
Though I have seen my head (grown slightly bald) brought in
    upon a platter,
I am no prophet—and here's no great matter;
I have seen the moment of my greatness flicker,
And I have seen the eternal Footman hold my coat, and snicker,   85
And in short, I was afraid.

And would it have been worth it, after all,
After the cups, the marmalade, the tea,
Among the porcelain, among some talk of you and me,
Would it have been worth while,   90
To have bitten off the matter with a smile,
To have squeezed the universe into a ball
To roll it toward some overwhelming question,
To say: "I am Lazarus, come from the dead,
Come back to tell you all, I shall tell you all"—   95
If one, settling a pillow by her head,
   Should say: "That is not what I meant at all;
   That is not it, at all."

And would it have been worth it, after all,
Would it have been worth while,   100
After the sunsets and the dooryards and the sprinkled streets,
After the novels, after the teacups, after the skirts that trail along the
    floor—
And this, and so much more?—
It is impossible to say just what I mean!
But as if a magic lantern threw the nerves in patterns on a screen: 105
Would it have been worth while
If one, settling a pillow or throwing off a shawl,

---

82 *brought in upon a platter:* a reference to the death of the "prophet," John the Baptist.
  94 *Lazarus:* the man who returned from the dead in John 11.

And turning toward the window, should say:
  "That is not it at all,
  That is not what I meant, at all."   110

No! I am not Prince Hamlet, nor was meant to be;
Am an attendant lord, one that will do
To swell a progress, start a scene or two,
Advise the prince; no doubt, an easy tool,
Deferential, glad to be of use,   115
Politic, cautious, and meticulous;
Full of high sentence, but a bit obtuse;
At times, indeed, almost ridiculous—
Almost, at times, the Fool.

I grow old. . . . I grow old. . . .   120
I shall wear the bottoms of my trousers rolled.

Shall I part my hair behind? Do I dare to eat a peach?
I shall wear white flannel trousers, and walk upon the beach.
I have heard the mermaids singing, each to each.

I do not think that they will sing to me.   125

I have seen them riding seaward on the waves
Combing the white hair of the waves blown back
When the wind blows the water white and black.

We have lingered in the chambers of the sea
By sea-girls wreathed with seaweed red and brown   130
Till human voices wake us, and we drown.

Preludes

(1)

The winter evening settles down
With smell of steaks in passageways.
Six o'clock.
The burnt-out ends of smoky days.
And now a gusty shower wraps   5
The grimy scraps
Of withered leaves about your feet
And newspapers from vacant lots;
The showers beat

---

113 *swell a progress:* increase the size of a royal procession.

On broken blinds and chimney-pots,
And at the corner of the street
A lonely cab-horse steams and stamps.
And then the lighting of the lamps.

(II)

The morning comes to consciousness
Of faint stale smells of beer
From the sawdust-trampled street
With all its muddy feet that press
To early coffee-stands.
With the other masquerades
That time resumes,
One thinks of all the hands
That are raising dingy shades
In a thousand furnished rooms.

(III)

You tossed a blanket from the bed,
You lay upon your back, and waited;
You dozed, and watched the night revealing
The thousand sordid images
Of which your soul was constituted;
They flickered against the ceiling.
And when all the world came back
And the light crept up between the shutters,
And you heard the sparrows in the gutters,
You had such a vision of the street
As the street hardly understands;
Sitting along the bed's edge, where
You curled the papers from your hair,
Or clasped the yellow soles of feet
In the palms of both soiled hands.

(IV)

His soul stretched tight across the skies
That fade behind a city block,
Or trampled by insistent feet
At four and five and six o'clock;
And short square fingers stuffing pipes,
And evening newspapers, and eyes
Assured of certain certainties,
The conscience of a blackened street
Impatient to assume the world.
I am moved by fancies that are curled
Around these images, and cling:
The notion of some infinitely gentle
Infinitely suffering thing.

Wipe your hand across your mouth, and laugh;
The worlds revolve like ancient women
Gathering fuel in vacant lots.

Gerontion

Thou hast nor youth nor age
But as it were an after dinner sleep
Dreaming of both.

Here I am, an old man in a dry month,
Being read to by a boy, waiting for rain.
I was neither at the hot gates
Nor fought in the warm rain
Nor knee deep in the salt marsh, heaving a cutlass,   5
Bitten by flies, fought.
My house is a decayed house,
And the jew squats on the window sill, the owner,
Spawned in some estaminet of Antwerp,
Blistered in Brussels, patched and peeled in London.   10
The goat coughs at night in the field overhead;
Rocks, moss, stonecrop, iron, merds.
The woman keeps the kitchen, makes tea,
Sneezes at evening, poking the peevish gutter.
                    I an old man,   15
A dull head among windy spaces.

Signs are taken for wonders. "We would see a sign!"
The word within a word, unable to speak a word,
Swaddled with darkness. In the juvescence of the year
Came Christ the tiger   20

In depraved May, dogwood and chestnut, flowering judas,
To be eaten, to be divided, to be drunk
Among whispers; by Mr. Silvero
With caressing hands, at Limoges
Who walked all night in the next room;   25
By Hakagawa, bowing among the Titians;
By Madame de Tornquist, in the dark room

The epigraph, *Thou hast nor youth nor age,* etc. is from Act III of Shakespeare's *Measure for Measure.* 3 *the hot gates:* a reference to the heroic resistance of the Greeks at the battle of Thermopylae. 9 *estaminet:* café. 12 *merds:* excrement. 23, 26 etc.: *Mr. Silvero, Hakagawa,* etc.: names of characters invented by Eliot.

Shifting the candles; Fräulein von Kulp
Who turned in the hall, one hand on the door.
    Vacant shuttles   30
Weave the wind. I have no ghosts,
An old man in a draughty house
Under a windy knob.

After such knowledge, what forgiveness? Think now
History has many cunning passages, contrived corridors   35
And issues, deceives with whispering ambitions,
Guides us by vanities. Think now
She gives when our attention is distracted
And what she gives, gives with such supple confusions
That the giving famishes the craving. Gives too late   40
What's not believed in, or if still believed,
In memory only, reconsidered passion. Gives too soon
Into weak hands, what's thought can be dispensed with
Till the refusal propagates a fear. Think
Neither fear nor courage saves us. Unnatural vices   45
Are fathered by our heroism. Virtues
Are forced upon us by our impudent crimes.
These tears are shaken from the wrath-bearing tree.

The tiger springs in the new year. Us he devours. Think at last
We have not reached conclusion, when I   50
Stiffen in a rented house. Think at last
I have not made this show purposelessly
And it is not by any concitation
Of the backward devils
I would meet you upon this honestly.   55
I that was near your heart was removed therefrom
To lose beauty in terror, terror in inquisition.
I have lost my passion: why should I need to keep it
Since what is kept must be adulterated?
I have lost my sight, smell, hearing, taste and touch: 60
How should I use them for your closer contact?

These with a thousand small deliberations
Protract the profit of their chilled delirium,
Excite the membrane, when the sense has cooled,
With pungent sauces, multiply variety   65
In a wilderness of mirrors. What will the spider do,
Suspend its operations, will the weevil
Delay? De Bailhache, Fresca, Mrs. Cammell, whirled
Beyond the circuit of the shuddering Bear
In fractured atoms. Gull against the wind, in the windy straits 70
Of Belle Isle, or running on the Horn,

---

48 *tree:* the tree of the knowledge of good and evil in the Book of Genesis. 53 *concitation:* arousing. 69 *Bear:* the constellation of Ursa Major.

White feathers in the snow, the Gulf claims,
And an old man driven by the Trades
To a sleepy corner.

               Tenants of the house,   75
Thoughts of a dry brain in a dry season.

Journey of the Magi

"A cold coming we had of it,
Just the worst time of the year
For a journey, and such a long journey:
The ways deep and the weather sharp,
The very dead of winter."   5
And the camels galled, sore-footed, refractory,
Lying down in the melting snow.
There were times we regretted
The summer palaces on slopes, the terraces,
And the silken girls bringing sherbet.   10
Then the camel men cursing and grumbling
And running away, and wanting their liquor and women,
And the night-fires going out, and the lack of shelters,
And the cities hostile and the towns unfriendly
And the villages dirty and charging high prices: 15
A hard time we had of it.
At the end we preferred to travel all night,
Sleeping in snatches,
With the voices singing in our ears, saying
That this was all folly.   20

Then at dawn we came down to a temperate valley,
Wet, below the snow line, smelling of vegetation;
With a running stream and a water-mill beating the darkness,
And three trees on the low sky,
And an old white horse galloped away in the meadow.   25
Then we came to a tavern with vine-leaves over the lintel,
Six hands at an open door dicing for pieces of silver,
And feet kicking the empty wine-skins.
But there was no information, and so we continued
And arrived at evening, not a moment too soon   30
Finding the place; it was (you may say) satisfactory.

All this was a long time ago, I remember,
And I would do it again, but set down

---

73 *the Trades:* the Trade Winds.

This set down
This: were we led all that way for   35
Birth or Death? There was a Birth, certainly,
We had evidence and no doubt. I had seen birth and death,
But had thought they were different; this Birth was
Hard and bitter agony for us, like Death, our death.
We returned to our places, these Kingdoms,   40
But no longer at ease here, in the old dispensation,
With an alien people clutching their gods.
I should be glad of another death.

John Crowe Ransom (1888-   )

Blue Girls

Twirling your blue skirts, travelling the sward
Under the towers of your seminary,
Go listen to your teachers old and contrary
Without believing a word.

Tie the white fillets then about your lustrous hair   5
And think no more of what will come to pass
Than bluebirds that go walking on the grass
And chattering on the air.

Practice your beauty, blue girls, before it fail;
And I will cry with my loud lips and publish   10
Beauty which all our power shall never establish,
It is so frail.

For I could tell you a story which is true:
I know a lady with a terrible tongue,
Blear eyes fallen from blue,   15
All her perfections tarnished—and yet it is not long
Since she was lovelier than any of you.

From *Selected Poems*, by John Crowe Ransom. Copyright 1927, 1945 by Alfred A. Knopf, Inc. Reprinted by permission of Alfred A. Knopf, Inc.

Archibald MacLeish (1892-   )

You, Andrew Marvell

And here face down beneath the sun
And here upon earth's noonward height
To feel the always coming on
The always rising of the night

To feel creep up the curving east   5
The earthy chill of dusk and slow
Upon those under lands the vast
And ever climbing shadow grow

And strange at Ecbatan the trees
Take leaf by leaf the evening strange   10
The flooding dark about their knees
The mountains over Persia change

And now at Kermanshah the gate
Dark empty and the withered grass
And through the twilight now the late   15
Few travelers in the westward pass

And Baghdad darken and the bridge
Across the silent river gone
And through Arabia the edge
Of evening widen and steal on   20

And deepen on Palmyra's street
The wheel rut in the ruined stone
And Lebanon fade out and Crete
High through the clouds and overblown

And over Sicily the air   25
Still flashing with the landward gulls
And loom and slowly disappear
The sails above the shadowy hulls

And Spain go under and the shore
Of Africa the gilded sand   30
And evening vanish and no more
The low pale light across that land

Nor now the long light on the sea:

And here face downward in the sun
To feel how swift how secretly   35
The shadow of the night comes on . . .

From *Collected Poems, 1917–1952*, by Archibald MacLeish. Reprinted by permission of and arrangement with Houghton Mifflin Company, the authorized publishers.

Wallace Stevens (1879-1955)

Anecdote of the Jar

I placed a jar in Tennessee,
And round it was, upon a hill.
It made the slovenly wilderness
Surround that hill.

The wilderness rose up to it,   5
And sprawled around, no longer wild.
The jar was round upon the ground
And tall and of a port in air.

It took dominion everywhere.
The jar was gray and bare.   10
It did not give of bird or bush,
Like nothing else in Tennessee.

Of Modern Poetry

The poem of the mind in the act of finding
What will suffice. It has not always had
To find: the scene was set; it repeated what
Was in the script.
        Then the theatre was changed   5
To something else. Its past was a souvenir.
It has to be living, to learn the speech of the place.
It has to face the men of the time and to meet
The women of the time. It has to think about war
And it has to find what will suffice. It has   10
To construct a new stage. It has to be on that stage
And, like an insatiable actor, slowly and
With meditation, speak words that in the ear,
In the delicatest ear of the mind, repeat,
Exactly, that which it wants to hear, at the sound   15
Of which, an invisible audience listens,
Not to the play, but to itself, expressed
In an emotion as of two people, as of two
Emotions becoming one. The actor is
A metaphysician in the dark, twanging   20
An instrument, twanging a wiry string that gives
Sounds passing through sudden rightnesses, wholly

Containing the mind, below which it cannot descend,
Beyond which it has no will to rise.
                                    It must   25
Be the finding of a satisfaction, and may
Be of a man skating, a woman dancing, a woman
Combing. The poem of the act of the mind.

Richard Eberhart (1904-   )

If I Could Only Live at the Pitch That Is Near Madness

If I could only live at the pitch that is near madness
When everything is as it was in my childhood
Violent, vivid, and of infinite possibility:
That the sun and the moon broke over my head.

Then I cast time out of the trees and fields,   5
Then I stood immaculate in the Ego;
Then I eyed the world with all delight,
Reality was the perfection of my sight.

And time has big handles on the hands,
Fields and trees a way of being themselves.   10
I saw battalions of the race of mankind
Standing stolid, demanding a moral answer.

I gave the moral answer and I died
And into a realm of complexity came
Where nothing is possible but necessity   15
And the truth wailing there like a red babe.

The Groundhog

In June, amid the golden fields,
I saw a groundhog lying dead.
Dead lay he; my senses shook,
And mind outshot our naked frailty.
There lowly in the vigorous summer   5
His form began its senseless change,
And made my senses waver dim

From *Collected Poems 1930–1960*, by Richard Eberhart. © by Richard Eberhart. Reprinted by permission of Oxford University Press, Inc., and Chatto and Windus, Ltd.

Seeing nature ferocious in him.
Inspecting close his maggots' might
And seething cauldron of his being,   10
Half with loathing, half with a strange love,
I poked him with an angry stick.
The fever arose, became a flame
And Vigour circumscribed the skies,
Immense energy in the sun,   15
And through my frame a sunless trembling.
My stick had done nor good nor harm.
Then stood I silent in the day
Watching the object, as before;
And kept my reverence for knowledge   20
Trying for control, to be still,
To quell the passion of the blood;
Until I had bent down on my knees
Praying for joy in the sight of decay.
And so I left; and I returned   25
In Autumn strict of eye, to see
The sap gone out of the groundhog,
But the bony sodden hulk remained.
But the year had lost its meaning,
And in intellectual chains   30
I lost both love and loathing,
Mured up in the wall of wisdom.
Another summer took the fields again
Massive and burning, full of life,
But when I chanced upon the spot   35
There was only a little hair left,
And bones bleaching in the sunlight
Beautiful as architecture;
I watched them like a geometer,
And cut a walking stick from a birch.   40
It has been three years, now.
There is no sign of the groundhog.
I stood there in the whirling summer,
My hand capped a withered heart,
And thought of China and of Greece,   45
Of Alexander in his tent;
Of Montaigne in his tower,
Of Saint Theresa in her wild lament.

The Fury of Aerial Bombardment

You would think the fury of aerial bombardment
Would rouse God to relent; the infinite spaces
Are still silent. He looks on shock-pried faces.
History, even, does not know what is meant.

You would feel that after so many centuries   5
God would give man to repent; yet he can kill
As Cain could, but with multitudinous will,
No farther advanced than in his ancient furies.

Was man made stupid to see his own stupidity?
Is God by definition indifferent, beyond us all?   10
Is the eternal truth man's fighting soul
Wherein the Beast ravens in its own avidity?

Of Van Wettering I speak, and Averill,
Names on a list, whose faces I do not recall
But they are gone to early death, who late in school   15
Distinguished the belt feed lever from the belt holding pawl.

The Horse Chestnut Tree

Boys in sporadic but tenacious droves
Come with sticks, as certainly as Autumn,
To assault the great horse chestnut tree.

There is a law governs their lawlessness,
Desire is in them for a shining amulet   5
And the best are those that are highest up.

They will not pick them easily from the ground.
With shrill arms they fling to the higher branches,
To hurry the work of nature for their pleasure.

I have seen them trooping down the street   10
Their pockets stuffed with chestnuts shucked, unshucked.
It is only evening keeps them from their wish.

Sometimes I run out in a kind of rage
To chase the boys away; I catch an arm,
Maybe, and laugh to think of being the lawgiver.   15

From *Collected Poems 1930–1960* by Richard Eberhart. © 1960 by Richard Eberhart. Reprinted by permission of Oxford University Press, Inc., and Chatto & Windus, Ltd.

I was once such a young sprout myself
And fingered in my pocket the prize and trophy.
But still I moralize upon the day

And see that we, outlaws on God's property,
Fling out imagination beyond the skies   20
Wishing a tangible good from the unknown.

And likewise death will drive us from the scene
With the great flowering world unbroken yet,
Which we held in idea, a little handful.

Robert Penn Warren (1905-   )

Original Sin: A Short Story

Nodding, its great head rattling like a gourd,
And locks like seaweed strung on the stinking stone,
The nightmare stumbles past, and you have heard
It fumble your door before it whimpers and is gone:
It acts like the old hound that used to snuffle your door and moan.   5

You thought you had lost it when you left Omaha,
For it seemed connected then with your grandpa, who
Had a wen on his forehead and sat on the veranda
To finger the precious protuberance, as was his habit to do,
Which glinted in sun like rough garnet or the rich old brain bulging
        through.   10

But you met it in Harvard Yard as the historic steeple
Was confirming the midnight with its hideous racket,
And you wondered how it had come, for it stood so imbecile,
With empty hands, humble, and surely nothing in pocket:
Riding the rods, perhaps—or Grandpa's will paid the ticket.   15

You were almost kindly then, in your first homesickness,
As it tortured its stiff face to speak, but scarcely mewed.
Since then you have outlived all your homesickness,
But have met it in many another distempered latitude:
Oh, nothing is lost, ever lost! at last you understood.   20

But it never came in the quantum glare of sun
To shame you before your friends, and had nothing to do
With your public experience or private reformation:

But it thought no bed too narrow—it stood with lips askew
And shook its great head sadly like the abstract Jew.   25

Never met you in the lyric arsenical meadows
When children call and your heart goes stone in the bosom—
At the orchard anguish never, nor ovoid horror,
Which is furred like a peach or avid like the delicious plum.
It takes no part in your classic prudence or fondled axiom.   30

Not there when you exclaimed: "Hope is betrayed by
Disastrous glory of sea-capes, sun-torment of whitecaps
—There must be a new innocence for us to be stayed by."
But there it stood, after all the timetables, all the maps,
In the crepuscular clutter of *always, always,* or *perhaps.*   35

You have moved often and rarely left an address,
And hear of the deaths of friends with a sly pleasure,
A sense of cleansing and hope, which blooms from distress;
But it has not died, it comes, its hand childish, unsure,
Clutching the bribe of chocolate or a toy you used to treasure.   40

It tries the lock; you hear, but simply drowse:
There is nothing remarkable in that sound at the door.
Later you may hear it wander the dark house
Like a mother who rises at night to seek a childhood picture;
Or it goes to the backyard and stands like an old horse cold in the
     pasture.   45

Louis MacNeice (1907-   )

Museums

Museums offer us, running from among the 'buses,
A centrally heated refuge, parquet floors and sarcophaguses,
Into whose tall fake porches we hurry without a sound
Like a beetle under a brick that lies, useless on the ground.
Warmed and cajoled by the silence, the cowed cipher revives,   5
Mirrors himself in the cases of pots, paces himself by marble lives,
Makes believe it was he that was the glory that was Rome,
Soft on his cheek the nimbus of other people's martyrdom,
And then returns to the street, his mind an arena where sprawls
Any number of consumptive Keatses and dying Gauls.   10

5 *cowed cipher:* frightened zero; hence, a nonentity.   8 *nimbus:* halo.

From *Eighty-Five Poems,* by Louis MacNeice. © Louis MacNeice, 1959. Used by permission of Oxford University Press, Inc., and Faber & Faber, Ltd.

Theodore Roethke (1908-1963)

Dolor

I have known the inexorable sadness of pencils,
Neat in their boxes, dolor of pad and paper-weight,
All the misery of manila folders and mucilage,
Desolation in immaculate public places,
Lonely reception room, lavatory, switchboard,   5
The unalterable pathos of basin and pitcher,
Ritual of multigraph, paper-clip, comma,
Endless duplication of lives and objects.
And I have seen dust from the walls of institutions,
Finer than flour, alive, more dangerous than silica,   10
Sift, almost invisible, through long afternoons of tedium,
Dropping a fine film on nails and delicate eyebrows,
Glazing the pale hair, the duplicate gray standard faces.

The Adamant

Thought does not crush to stone.
The great sledge drops in vain.
Truth never is undone;
Its shafts remain.

The teeth of knitted gears   5
Turn slowly through the night,
But the true substance bears
The hammer's weight.

Compression cannot break
A center so congealed;   10
The tool can chip no flake:
The core lies sealed.

Root Cellar

Nothing would sleep in that cellar, dank as a ditch,
Bulbs broke out of boxes hunting for chinks in the dark,
Shoots dangled and drooped,
Lolling obscenely from mildewed crates,
Hung down long yellow evil necks, like tropical snakes.   5
And what a congress of stinks!—
Roots ripe as old bait,
Pulpy stems, rank, silo-rich,
Leaf-mold, manure, lime, piled against slippery planks.
Nothing would give up life: 10
Even the dirt kept breathing a small breath.

The Waking

I wake to sleep, and take my waking slow.
I feel my fate in what I cannot fear.
I learn by going where I have to go.

We think by feeling. What is there to know?
I hear my being dance from ear to ear.   5
I wake to sleep, and take my waking slow.

Of those so close beside me, which are you?
God bless the Ground! I shall walk softly there,
And learn by going where I have to go.

Light takes the Tree; but who can tell us how?   10
The lowly worm climbs up a winding stair;
I wake to sleep, and take my waking slow.

Great Nature has another thing to do
To you and me; so take the lively air,
And, lovely, learn by going where to go.   15

This shaking keeps me steady. I should know.
What falls away is always. And is near.
I wake to sleep, and take my waking slow.
I learn by going where I have to go.

A Walk in Late Summer

I

A gull rides on the ripples of a dream,
White upon white, slow-settling on a stone;
Across my lawn the soft-backed creatures come;
In the weak light they wander, each alone.
Bring me the meek, for I would know their ways;   5
I am a connoisseur of midnight eyes.
The small! The small! I hear them singing clear
On the long banks, in the soft summer air.

II

What is there for the soul to understand?
The slack face of the dismal pure inane?   10
The wind dies down; my will dies with the wind,
God's in that stone, or I am not a man!
Body and soul transcend appearances
Before the caving-in of all that is;
I'm dying piecemeal, fervent in decay;   15
My moments linger—that's eternity.

III

A late rose ravages the casual eye,
A blaze of being on a central stem.
It lies upon us to undo the lie
Of living merely in the realm of time.   20
Existence moves toward a certain end—
A thing all earthly lovers understand.
That dove's elaborate way of coming near
Reminds me I am dying with the year.

Elegy for Jane

My student, thrown by a horse

I remember the neckcurls, limp and damp as tendrils;
And her quick look, a sidelong pickerel smile;
And how, once startled into talk, the light syllables leaped for her,
And she balanced in the delight of her thought,

A wren, happy, tail into the wind,   5
Her song trembling the twigs and small branches.
The shade sang with her;
The leaves, their whispers turned to kissing;
And the mold sang in the bleached valleys under the rose.

Oh, when she was sad, she cast herelf down into such a pure depth,   10
Even a father could not find her:
Scraping her cheek against straw;
Stirring the clearest water.

My sparrow, you are not here,
Waiting like a fern, making a spiny shadow.   15
The sides of wet stones cannot console me,
Nor the moss, wound with the last light.

If only I could nudge you from this sleep,
My maimed darling, my skittery pigeon.
Over this damp grave I speak the words of my love: 20
I, with no rights in this matter,
Neither father nor lover.

Stephen Spender (1909-   )

I Think Continually of Those Who Were Truly Great

I think continually of those who were truly great.
Who, from the womb, remembered the soul's history
Through corridors of light where the hours are suns,
Endless and singing. Whose lovely ambition
Was that their lips, still touched with fire,   5
Should tell of the spirit clothed from head to foot in song.
And who hoarded from the spring branches
The desires falling across their bodies like blossoms.

What is precious is never to forget
The delight of the blood drawn from ageless springs   10
Breaking through rocks in worlds before our earth;

Never to deny its pleasure in the simple morning light,
Nor its grave evening demand for love;
Never to allow gradually the traffic to smother
With noise and fog the flowering of the spirit.   15

Near the snow, near the sun, in the highest fields
See how these names are fêted by the wavering grass,
And by the streamers of white cloud,
And whispers of wind in the listening sky;
The names of those who in their lives fought for life,   20
Who wore at their hearts the fire's center.
Born of the sun they traveled a short while towards the sun,
And left the vivid air signed with their honor.

An Elementary School Classroom in a Slum

Far far from gusty waves, these children's faces.
Like rootless weeds, the torn hair round their pallor.
The tall girl with her weighed-down head. The paper-
seeming boy with rat's eyes. The stunted unlucky heir
Of twisted bones, reciting a father's gnarled disease,   5
His lesson from his desk. At back of the dim class
One unnoted, sweet and young: his eyes live in a dream
Of squirrels' game, in tree room, other than this.

On sour cream walls, donations. Shakespeare's head
Cloudless at dawn, civilized dome riding all cities.   10
Belled, flowery, Tyrolese valley. Open-handed map
Awarding the world its world. And yet, for these
Children, these windows, not this world, are world,
Where all their future's painted with a fog,
A narrow street sealed in with a lead sky,   15
Far far from rivers, capes, and stars of words.

Surely, Shakespeare is wicked, the map a bad example
With ships and sun and love tempting them to steal—
For lives that slyly turn in their cramped holes
From fog to endless night? On their slag heap, these children   20
Wear skins peeped through by bones, and spectacles of steel
With mended glass, like bottle bits on stone.
All of their time and space are foggy slum,
So blot their maps with slums as big as doom.

Unless, governor, teacher, inspector, visitor,   25
This map becomes their window and these windows
That shut upon their lives like catacombs,
Break O break open till they break the town
And show the children to green fields, and make their world
Run azure on gold sands, and let their tongues   30
Run naked into books, the white and green leaves open
History theirs whose language is the sun.

W. H. Auden (1907-   )

Musée des Beaux Arts

About suffering they were never wrong,
The Old Masters: how well they understood
Its human position; how it takes place
While someone else is eating or opening a window or just walking
    dully along;
How, when the aged are reverently, passionately waiting   5
For the miraculous birth, there always must be
Children who did not specially want it to happen, skating
On a pond at the edge of the wood:
They never forgot
That even the dreadful martyrdom must run its course   10
Anyhow in a corner, some untidy spot
Where the dogs go on with their doggy life and the torturer's horse
Scratches its innocent behind on a tree.

In Brueghel's *Icarus,* for instance: how everything turns away
Quite leisurely from the disaster; the ploughman may   15
Have heard the splash, the forsaken cry,
But for him it was not an important failure; the sun shone
As it had to on the white legs disappearing into the green
Water; and the expensive delicate ship that must have seen
Something amazing, a boy falling out of the sky,   20
Had somewhere to get to and sailed calmly on.

14 *Brueghel's Icarus:* a painting by the Dutch artist, Pieter Brueghel (1564?–1638).

The Unknown Citizen

*(To JS/07/M/378
This marble monument is erected by the state)*

He was found by the Bureau of Statistics to be
One against whom there was no official complaint,
And all the reports on his conduct agree
That, in the modern sense of an old-fashioned word, he was a saint,
For in everything he did he served the Greater Community.   5
Except for the War till the day he retired
He worked in a factory and never got fired,
But satisfied his employers, Fudge Motors Inc.
Yet he wasn't a scab or odd in his views,
For his Union reports that he paid his dues,   10
(Our report on his Union shows it was sound)
And our Social Psychology workers found
That he was popular with his mates and liked a drink.
The Press are convinced that he bought a paper every day
And that his reactions to advertisements were normal in every way.   15
Policies taken out in his name prove that he was fully insured,
And his Health-card shows he was once in hospital but left it cured.
Both Producers Research and High-Grade Living declare
He was fully sensible to the advantages of the Instalment Plan
And had everything necessary to the Modern Man,   20
A phonograph, a radio, a car and a frigidaire.
Our researchers into Public Opinion are content
That he held the proper opinions for the time of year;
When there was peace, he was for peace; when there was war, he
    went.
He was married and added five children to the population,   25
Which our Eugenist says was the right number for a parent of
    his generation,
And our teachers report that he never interfered with their education.
Was he free? Was he happy? The question is absurd:
Had anything been wrong, we should certainly have heard.

Lay Your Sleeping Head, My Love

Lay your sleeping head, my love,
Human on my faithless arm;
Time and fevers burn away
Individual beauty from
Thoughtful children, and the grave   5

Proves the child ephemeral:
But in my arms till break of day
Let the living creature lie,
Mortal, guilty, but to me
The entirely beautiful.   10

Soul and body have no bounds:
To lovers as they lie upon
Her tolerant enchanted slope
In their ordinary swoon,
Grave the vision Venus sends   15
Of supernatural sympathy,
Universal love and hope;
While an abstract insight wakes
Among the glaciers and the rocks
The hermit's sensual ecstasy.   20

Certainty, fidelity
On the stroke of midnight pass
Like vibrations of a bell,
And fashionable madmen raise
Their pedantic boring cry: 25
Every farthing of the cost,
All the dreaded cards foretell,
Shall be paid, but from this night
Not a whisper, not a thought,
Not a kiss nor look be lost.   30

Beauty, midnight, vision dies:
Let the winds of dawn that blow
Softly round your dreaming head
Such a day of sweetness show
Eye and knocking heart may bless,   35
Find the mortal world enough;
Noons of dryness see you fed
By the involuntary powers,
Nights of insult let you pass
Watched by every human love.   40

Fish in the Unruffled Lakes

Fish in the unruffled lakes
The swarming colours wear,
Swans in the winter air
A white perfection have,
And the great lion walks   5

Through his innocent grove;
Lion, fish, and swan
Act, and are gone
Upon Time's toppling wave.

We till shadowed days are done,   10
We must weep and sing
Duty's conscious wrong,
The Devil in the clock,
The Goodness carefully worn
For atonement or for luck;   15
We must lose our loves,
On each beast and bird that moves
Turn an envious look.

Sighs for folly said and done
Twist our narrow days;   20
But I must bless, I must praise
That you, my swan, who have
All gifts that to the swan
Impulsive Nature gave,
The majesty and pride,   25
Last night should add
Your voluntary love.

Nothing Is Given: We Must Find Our Law

Nothing is given: we must find our law.
Great buildings jostle in the sun for domination;
Behind them stretch like sorry vegetation
The low recessive houses of the poor.

We have no destiny assigned us: 5
Nothing is certain but the body; we plan
To better ourselves; the hospitals alone remind us
Of the equality of man.

Children are really loved here, even by police:
They speak of years before the big were lonely,   10
And will be lost.

        And only
The brass bands throbbing in the parks foretell
Some future reign of happiness and peace.

We learn to pity and rebel.

The Quarry

O what is that sound which so thrills the ear
  Down in the valley drumming, drumming?
Only the scarlet soldiers, dear,
  The soldiers coming.

O what is that light I see flashing so clear   5
  Over the distance brightly, brightly?
Only the sun on their weapons, dear,
  As they step lightly.

O what are they doing with all that gear,
  What are they doing this morning, this morning?   10
Only their usual maneuvers, dear,
  Or perhaps a warning.

O why have they left the road down there,
  Why are they suddenly wheeling, wheeling?
Perhaps a change in their orders, dear.   15
  Why are you kneeling?

O haven't they stopped for the doctor's care,
  Haven't they reined their horses, their horses?
Why, they are none of them wounded, dear,
  None of these forces.   20

O is it the parson they want, with white hair,
  Is it the parson, is it, is it?
No, they are passing his gateway, dear,
  Without a visit.

O it must be the farmer who lives so near.   25
  It must be the farmer so cunning, so cunning?
They have passed the farmyard already, dear,
  And now they are running.

O where are you going? Stay with me here!
  Were the vows you swore, deceiving, deceiving?   30
No, I promised to love you, dear,
  But I must be leaving.

O it's broken the lock and splintered the door,
  O it's the gate where they're turning, turning;
Their boots are heavy on the floor   35
  And their eyes are burning.

Dylan Thomas (1914-1953)

The Force That Through the Green Fuse Drives the Flower

The force that through the green fuse drives the flower
Drives my green age; that blasts the roots of trees
Is my destroyer.
And I am dumb to tell the crooked rose
My youth is bent by the same wintry fever.   5

The force that drives the water through the rocks
Drives my red blood; that dries the mouthing streams
Turns mine to wax.
And I am dumb to mouth unto my veins
How at the mountain spring the same mouth sucks.   10

The hand that whirls the water in the pool
Stirs the quicksand; that ropes the blowing wind
Hauls my shroud sail.
And I am dumb to tell the hanging man
How of my clay is made the hangman's lime.   15

The lips of time leech to the fountain head;
Love drips and gathers, but the fallen blood
Shall calm her sores.
And I am dumb to tell a weather's wind
How time has ticked a heaven round the stars.   20

And I am dumb to tell the lover's tomb
How at my sheet goes the same crooked worm.

Especially When the October Wind

Especially when the October wind
With frosty fingers punishes my hair,
Caught by the crabbing sun I walk on fire
And cast a shadow crab upon the land,
By the sea's side, hearing the noise of birds,   5
Hearing the raven cough in winter sticks,
My busy heart who shudders as she talks
Sheds the syllabic blood and drains her words.

Shut, too, in a tower of words, I mark
On the horizon walking like the trees   10
The wordy shapes of women, and the rows
Of the star-gestured children in the park.
Some let me make you of the vowelled beeches,
Some of the oaken voices, from the roots
Of many a thorny shire tell you notes,   15
Some let me make you of the water's speeches.

Behind a pot of ferns the wagging clock
Tells me the hour's word, the neural meaning
Flies on the shafted disk, declaims the morning
And tells the windy weather in the cock.   20
Some let me make you of the meadow's signs;
The signal grass that tells me all I know
Breaks with the wormy winter through the eye.
Some let me tell you of the raven's sins.

Especially when the October wind   25
(Some let me make you of autumnal spells,
The spider-tongued, and the loud hill of Wales)
With fists of turnips punishes the land,
Some let me make you of the heartless words.
The heart is drained that, spelling in the scurry   30
Of chemic blood, warned of the coming fury.
By the sea's side hear the dark-vowelled birds.

A Refusal to Mourn the Death, by Fire, of a Child in London

Never until the mankind making
Bird beast and flower
Fathering and all humbling darkness
Tells with silence the last light breaking
And the still hour   5
Is come of the sea tumbling in harness

And I must enter again the round
Zion of the water bead
And the synagogue of the ear of corn
Shall I let pray the shadow of a sound   10
Or sow my salt seed
In the least valley of sackcloth to mourn

---

13 *Some let me make you, etc.:* Let me compose some poems for you, etc.   19 *the shafted disk:* the face of a clock.

The majesty and burning of the child's death.
I shall not murder
The mankind of her going with a grave truth 15
Nor blaspheme down the stations of the breath
With any further
Elegy of innocence and youth.

Deep with the first dead lies London's daughter,
Robed in the long friends, 20
The grains beyond age, the dark veins of her mother
Secret by the unmourning water
Of the riding Thames.
After the first death, there is no other.

Poem in October

It was my thirtieth year to heaven
Woke to my hearing from harbour and neighbour wood
And the mussel pooled and the heron
Priested shore
The morning beckon 5
With water praying and call of seagull and rook
And the knock of sailing boats on the net-webbed wall
Myself to set foot
That second
In the still sleeping town and set forth. 10

My birthday began with the water-
Birds and the birds of the winged trees flying my name
Above the farms and the white horses
And I rose
In rainy autumn 15
And walked abroad in a shower of all my days.
High tide and the heron dived when I took the road
Over the border
And the gates
Of the town closed at the town awoke. 20

A springful of larks in a rolling
Cloud and the roadside bushes brimming with whistling
Blackbirds and the sun of October
Summery
On the hill's shoulder, 25

Here were fond climates and sweet singers suddenly
Come in the morning where I wandered and listened
To the rain wringing
Wind blow cold
In the wood faraway under me.   30

Pale rain over the dwindling harbour
And over the sea-wet church the size of a snail
With its horns through mist and the castle
Brown as owls,
But all the gardens   35
Of spring and summer were blooming in the tall tales
Beyond the border and under the lark-full cloud.
There could I marvel
My birthday
Away but the weather turned around.   40

It turned away from the blithe country,
And down the other air and the blue altered sky
Streamed again a wonder of summer
With apples
Pears and red currants,   45
And I saw in the turning so clearly a child's
Forgotten mornings when he walked with his mother
Through the parables
Of sunlight
And the legends of the green chapels   50

And the twice told fields of infancy
That his tears burned my cheeks and his heart moved in mine
These were the woods the river and sea
Where a boy
In the listening   55
Summertime of the dead whispered the truth of his joy
To the trees and the stones and the fish in the tide.
And the mystery
Sang alive
Still in the water and singing birds.   60

And there could I marvel my birthday
Away but the weather turned around. And the true
Joy of the long-dead child sang burning
In the sun.
It was my thirtieth   65
Year to heaven stood there then in the summer noon
Though the town below lay leaved with October blood.
O may my heart's truth
Still be sung
On this high hill in a year's turning.   70

Do Not Go Gentle Into That Good Night

Do not go gentle into that good night,
Old age should burn and rave at close of day;
Rage, rage against the dying of the light.

Though wise men at their end know dark is right,
Because their words had forked no lightning they   5
Do not go gentle into that good night.

Good men, the last wave by, crying how bright
Their frail deeds might have danced in a green bay,
Rage, rage against the dying of the light.

Wild men who caught and sang the sun in flight,   10
And learn, too late, they grieved it on its way,
Do not go gentle into that good night.

Grave men, near death, who see with blinding sight
Blind eyes could blaze like meteors and be gay,
Rage, rage against the dying of the light.   15

And you, my father, there on the sad height,
Curse, bless, me now with your fierce tears, I pray.
Do not go gentle into that good night.
Rage, rage against the dying of the light.

In My Craft or Sullen Art

In my craft or sullen art
Exercised in the still night
When only the moon rages
And the lovers lie abed
With all their griefs in their arms,   5
I labour by singing light
Not for ambition or bread
Or the strut and trade of charms
On the ivory stages
But for the common wages   10
Of their most secret heart.

Not for the proud man apart
From the raging moon I write
On these spindrift pages
Not for the towering dead   15
With their nightingales and psalms

But for the lovers, their arms
Round the griefs of the ages,
Who pay no praise or wages
Nor heed my craft or art.   20

John Frederick Nims (1913-   )

Love Poem

My clumsiest dear, whose hands shipwreck vases,
At whose quick touch all glasses chip and ring,
Whose palms are bulls in china, burs in linen,
And have no cunning with any soft thing

Except all ill-at-ease fidgeting people: 5
The refugee uncertain at the door
You make at home; deftly you steady
The drunk clambering on his undulant floor.

Unpredictable dear, the taxi drivers' terror,
Shrinking from far headlights pale as a dime   10
Yet leaping before red apoplectic streetcars—
Misfit in any space. And never on time.

A wrench in clocks and the solar system. Only
With words and people and love you move at ease.
In traffic of wit expertly manoeuvre   15
And keep us, all devotion, at your knees.

Forgetting your coffee spreading on our flannel,
Your lipstick grinning on our coat,
So gayly in love's unbreakable heaven
Our souls on glory of spilt bourbon float.   20

Be with me, darling, early and late. Smash glasses—
I will study wry music for your sake.
For should your hands drop white and empty
All the toys of the world would break.

From *The Iron Pastoral*, by John Frederick Nims. Copyright © 1947 by John Frederick Nims. Reprinted by permission of William Sloane Associates.

Karl Shapiro (1913-   )

Drug Store

I do remember an apothecary,
And hereabouts 'a dwells—

It baffles the foreigner like an idiom,
And he is right to adopt it as a form
Less serious than the living-room or bar;
   For it disestablishes the café,
Is a collective, and on basic country.   5

Not that it praises hygiene and corrupts
The ice-cream parlor and the tobacconist's
Is it a center; but that the attractive symbols
   Watch over puberty and leer
Like rubber bottles waiting for sick-use.   10

Youth comes to jingle nickels and crack wise;
The baseball scores are his, the magazines
Devoted to lust, the jazz, the Coca-Cola,
   The lending-library of love's latest.
He is the customer; he is heroized.   15

And every nook and cranny of the flesh
Is spoken to by packages with wiles.
"Buy me, buy me," they whimper and cajole;
   The hectic range of lipstick pouts,
Revealing the wicked and the simple mouth.   20

With scarcely any evasion in their eye
They smoke, undress their girls, exact a stance;
But only for a moment. The clock goes round;
   Crude fellowships are made and lost;
They slump in booths like rags, not even drunk.   25

Buick

As a sloop with a sweep of immaculate wing on her delicate spine
And a keel as steel as a root that holds in the sea as she leans,
Leaning and laughing, my warm-hearted beauty, you ride, you ride,
You tack on the curves with parabola speed and a kiss of good bye,
Like a thoroughbred sloop, my new high-spirited spirit, my kiss.   5

As my foot suggests that you leap in the air with your hips of a girl,
My finger that praises your wheel and announces your voices of song,
Flouncing your skirts, you blueness of joy, you flirt of politeness,
You leap, you intelligence, essence of wheelness with silvery nose,
And your platinum clocks of excitement stir like the hairs of a fern.   10

But how alien you are from the booming belt of your birth and
      the smoke
Where you turned on the stinging lathes of Detroit and Lansing at
      night
And shrieked at the torch in your secret parts and the amorous tests,
But now with your eyes that enter the future of roads you forget;
You are all instinct with your phosphorous glow and your streak-
      ing hair.   15

And now when we stop it is not as the bird from the shell that I leave
Or the leathery pilot who steps from his bird with a sneer of delight,
And not as the ignorant beast do you squat and watch me depart,
But with exquisite breathing you smile, with satisfaction of love,
And I touch you again as you tick in the silence and settle in sleep.   20

Henry Reed (1914-   )

Lessons of the War: Naming of Parts

(*to Alan Michell*)

Vixi duellis nuper idoneus
Et militavi non sine gloria

Today we have naming of parts. Yesterday,
We had daily cleaning. And tomorrow morning,
We shall have what to do after firing. But today,
Today we have naming of parts. Japonica
Glistens like coral in all of the neighbouring gardens,   5
      And today we have naming of parts.

The epigraph is a witty variant of the first two lines of Horace's Ode XXVI, Book III,
which read:

> *Vixi puellis nuper idoneus,*
> *Et militavi non sine gloria.*

These lines mean, "Formerly I lived in a way suited for the girls, and made love not
without fame." By changing the first letter of the word "puellis,"—girls—Reed has
changed the meaning to: "Formerly I lived in a way suited for a soldier, and waged
war not without fame."

This is the lower sling swivel. And this
Is the upper sling swivel, whose use you will see,
When you are given your slings. And this is the piling swivel
Which in your case you have not got. The branches   10
Hold in the gardens their silent, eloquent gestures,
    Which in our case we have not got.

This is the safety-catch, which is always released
With an easy flick of the thumb. And please do not let me
See anyone using his finger. You can do it quite easy   15
If you have any strength in your thumb. The blossoms
Are fragile and motionless, never letting anyone see
    Any of them using their finger.

And this you can see is the bolt. The purpose of this
Is to open the breech, as you see. We can slide it   20
Rapidly backwards and forwards: we call this
Easing the spring. And rapidly backwards and forwards
The early bees are assaulting and fumbling the flowers:
    They call it easing the Spring.

They call it easing the Spring: it is perfectly easy   25
If you have any strength in your thumb; like the bolt,
And the breech, and the cocking-piece, and the point of balance,
Which in our case we have not got; and the almond-blossom
Silent in all of the gardens and the bees going backwards and
        forwards,
    For today we have naming of parts.   30

John Berryman (1914-   )

Life, Friends, Is Boring

Life, friends, is boring. We must not say so.
After all, the sky flashes, the great sea yearns,
we ourselves flash and yearn,
and moreover my mother told me as a boy
(repeatingly) "Ever to confess you're bored   5
means you have no

Inner Resources." I conclude now I have no
inner resources, because I am heavy bored.
Peoples bore me,
literature bores me, especially great literature,   10
Henry bores me, with his plights & gripes
as bad as achilles,

who loves people and valiant art, which bores me.
And the tranquil hills, & gin, look like a drag
and somehow a dog   15
has taken itself & its tail considerably away
into mountains or sea or sky, leaving
behind: me, wag.

Howard Nemerov (1920-   )

Santa Claus

Somewhere on his travels the strange Child
Picked up with this overstuffed confidence man,
Affection's inverted thief, who climbs at night
Down chimneys, into dreams, with this world's goods.
Bringing all the benevolence of money,   5
He teaches the innocent to want, thus keeps
Our fat world rolling. His prescribed costume,
White flannel beard, red belly of cotton waste,
Conceals the thinness of essential hunger,
An appetite that feeds on satisfaction;   10
Or, pregnant with possessions, he brings forth
Vanity and the void. His name itself
Is corrupted, and even Saint Nicholas, in his turn,
Gives off a faint and reminiscent stench,
The merest soupçon, of brimstone and the pit.   15

Now, at the season when the Child is born
To suffer for the world, suffer the world,
His bloated Other, jovial satellite
And sycophant, makes his appearance also
In a glitter of goodies, in a rock candy glare.   20
Played at the better stores by bums, for money,
This annual savior of the economy
Speaks in the parables of the dollar sign:
Suffer the little children to come to Him.

At Easter, he's anonymous again,   25
Just one of the crowd lunching on Calvary.

Reprinted from *The Next Room of the Dream: Poems and Two Plays.* © 1962 by Howard
Nemerov. Reprinted by permission of the author's agent, the Margot Johnson Agency.

To David, About His Education

The world is full of mostly invisible things,
And there is no way but putting the mind's eye,
Or its nose, in a book, to find them out,
Things like the square root of Everest
Or how many times Byron goes into Texas,   5
Or whether the law of the excluded middle
Applies west of the Rockies. For these
And the like reasons, you have to go to school
And study books and listen to what you are told.

And sometimes try to remember. Though I don't know   10
What you will do with the mean annual rainfall
On Plato's Republic, or the calorie content
Of the Diet of Worms, such things are said to be
Good for you, and you will have to learn them
In order to become one of the grown-ups   15
Who sees invisible things neither steadily nor whole,
But keeps gravely the grand confusion of the world
Under his hat, which is where it belongs,
And teaches small children to do this in their turn.

Richard Wilbur (1921-   )

Mind

Mind in its purest play is like some bat
That beats about in caverns all alone,
Contriving by a kind of senseless wit
Not to conclude against a wall of stone.

It has no need to falter or explore;   5
Darkly it knows what obstacles are there,
And so may weave and flitter, dip and soar
In perfect courses through the blackest air.

And has this simile a like perfection?
The mind is like a bat. Precisely. Save   10
That in the very happiest intellection
A graceful error may correct the cave.

Reprinted from *The Next Room of the Dream: Poems and Two Plays*. © 1962 by Howard
   Nemerov. Reprinted by permission of the author's agent, the Margot Johnson Agency.

Reprinted from *Things of This World*, © 1956 by Richard Wilbur. Reprinted by permission of Harcourt, Brace & World, Inc.

Years-End

Now winter downs the dying of the year,
And night is all a settlement of snow;
From the soft street the rooms of houses show
A gathered light, a shapen atmosphere,
Like frozen-over lakes whose ice is thin   5
And still allows some stirring down wtihin.

I've known the wind by water banks to shake
The late leaves down, which frozen where they fell
And held in ice as dancers in a spell
Fluttered all winter long into a lake;   10
Graved on the dark in gestures of descent,
They seemed their own most perfect monument.

There was perfection in the death of ferns
Which laid their fragile cheeks against the stone
A million years. Great mammoths overthrown   15
Composedly have made their long sojourns,
Like palaces of patience, in the gray
And changeless lands of ice. And at Pompeii

The little dog lay curled and did not rise
But slept the deeper as the ashes rose   20
And found the people incomplete, and froze
The random hands, the loose unready eyes
Of men expecting yet another sun
To do the shapely thing they had not done.

These sudden ends of time must give us pause.   25
We fray into the future, rarely wrought
Save in the tapestries of afterthought.
More time, more time. Barrages of applause
Come muffled from a buried radio.
The New-year bells are wrangling with the snow.   30

Reprinted from *Ceremony and Other Poems* by permission of Harcourt, Brace & World, Inc. Copyright 1949 by Richard Wilbur. First published in *The New Yorker.*

Donald Hall (1928-   )

My Son, My Executioner

My son, my executioner,
   I take you in my arms,
Quiet and small and just astir,
   And whom my body warms.

Sweet death, small son, our instrument   5
   Of immortality,
Your cries and hungers document
   Our bodily decay.

We twenty-five and twenty-two,
   Who seemed to live forever,   10
Observe enduring life in you
   And start to die together.

I take into my arms the death
   Maturity exacts,
And name with my imperfect breath   15
   The mortal paradox.

The Body Politic

I shot my friend to save my country's life,
And when the happy bullet struck him dead,
I was saluted by the drum and fife
Corps of a high school, while the traitor bled.

I never thought until I pulled the trigger   5
But that I did the difficult and good.
I thought republics stood for something bigger,
For the mind of man, as Plato said they stood.

So when I heard the duty they assigned,
Shooting my friend seemed only sanity;   10
To keep disorder from the state of mind
Was mental rectitude, it seemed to me.

Reprinted by permission of Curtis Brown, Ltd. Copyright 1954 by The New Yorker Magazine, Inc.

Reprinted by permission of Curtis Brown, Ltd. Copyright 1955 by Donald Hall.

The audience dispersed. I felt depressed.
I went to where my orders issued from,
But the right number on the street was just   15
A vacant lot. Oh, boy, had I been dumb!

I tried to find the true address, but where?
Nobody told me what I had to know,
And secretaries sent me here and there
To other secretaries, just for show.   20

Poor Fred. His presence will be greatly missed
By children and by cronies by the score.
The State (I learn too late) does not exist;
Man lives by love, and not by metaphor.

Anne Halley (1928-   )

Dear God, the Day Is Grey

Dear God, the day is grey. My house
is not in order. Lord, the dust
sifts through my rooms and with my fear,
I sweep mortality, outwear
my brooms, but not this leaning floor   5
which lasts and groans. I, walking here,
still loathe the labors I would love
and hate the self I cannot move.

And God, I know the unshined boards,
the flaking ceiling, various stains   10
that mottle these distempered goods,
the greasy cloths, the jagged tins,
the dog that paws the garbage cans.
I know what laborings, love, and pains,
my blood would will, yet will not give: 15
the knot of hair that clogs the drains
clots in my throat. My dyings thrive.

The refuse, Lord, that I put out
burns in vast pits incessantly.
All piecemeal deaths, trash, undevout   20
and sullen sacrifice, to thee.

Reprinted by permission of the University of Massachusetts Press.

Index of Titles and Authors